Language *Arts*

Language *Arts*

Integrating Skills for Classroom Teaching

Mildred R. Donoghue
California State University, Fullerton

Los Angeles • London • New Delhi • Singapore

For information:

SAGE Publications, Inc.
2455 Teller Road
Thousand Oaks, California 91320
E-mail: order@sagepub.com

SAGE Publications Ltd.
1 Oliver's Yard
55 City Road
London EC1Y 1SP
United Kingdom

SAGE Publications India Pvt. Ltd.
B 1/I 1 Mohan Cooperative Industrial Area
Mathura Road, New Delhi 110 044
India

SAGE Publications Asia-Pacific Pte. Ltd.
33 Pekin Street #02-01
Far East Square
Singapore 048763

Printed in the United States of America

Library of Congress Cataloging-in-Publication Data

Donoghue, Mildred R.
Language arts: Integrating skills for classroom teaching/Mildred R. Donoghue.
    p. cm.
Includes bibliographical references and index.
ISBN 978-1-4129-4049-8 (pbk.)
  1. Language arts (Elementary) 2. Curriculum planning—United States. I. Title.

LB1576.D59 2009
372.6'044—dc22   2008006235

Printed on acid-free paper

08 09 10 11 12 10 9 8 7 6 5 4 3 2 1

Acquiring Editor:	Diane McDaniel
Editorial Assistant:	Leah Mori
Production Editor:	Sarah K. Quesenberry
Copy Editor:	Gail Naron Chalew
Proofreader:	Theresa Kay
Indexer:	Wendy Allex
Typesetter:	C&M Digitals (P) Ltd.
Cover Designer:	Candice Harman
Marketing Manager:	Christy Guilbault

To my daughter Kathleen who, as an elementary school librarian, thoughtfully and effectively helps children daily to discover the joys of reading and sharing books.

Brief Contents

Detailed Contents

Part III Writing as a Language Art

Part IV Oral Language Arts

Preface

Language Arts: Integrating Skills for Classroom Teaching incorporates new approaches tailored to the needs of an increasingly diverse student teacher population. This text offers current content such as keyboarding, creative drama, working with English Language Learners, and motivational strategies needed to promote writing among primary and intermediate students. It provides an in-depth analysis of both formal and authentic assessment measures and lists more than 500 excellent books for children that promote reading and writing activities.

Critically important national literacy standards, as defined by the National Council of Teachers of English and the International Reading Association, prevail throughout the book, and the standards relevant to each chapter are listed specifically at its beginning. Each chapter also emphasizes activities to involve parents as educational partners, a detailed lesson plan, and techniques to integrate the language arts across all the subjects in the elementary curriculum. The text further includes extensive professional reading lists and technology-based resources to bring returning teachers up to date, and to educate student teachers about the rapidly changing field they are preparing to enter.

The English language arts are the most potent discipline in the entire elementary curriculum; they are the foundation for all other subjects commonly taught to children. My aim, then, in writing this textbook has been to combine the best of traditional language arts training with new concepts to deepen the teaching repertoire of student teachers and returning instructors.

Organization of the Text

The book is divided into four parts.

Part I: Foundations of the Language Arts

Chapter 1: Language and the English Language Arts includes an outline of the six arts as defined by the National Council of Teachers of English and the International Reading Association, as well as a discussion of the functions, characteristics, and structure of language itself. **Chapter 2: Children as Language Learners and Thinkers** is concerned with both first- and second-language acquisition as well as linguistically diverse learners. **Chapter 3: Formal and Authentic Assessment** addresses the issue of assessment, which is of increasing importance in today's high-stakes testing society. **Chapter 4: Integrating Language Arts Across the Curriculum** promotes the subtitle of the book. Both Chapters 3 and 4 are overviews of their subjects, as the topics reappear at the end of every chapter throughout the book to emphasize their importance.

Part II: Reading as a Language Art

The second part covers reading as a language art and properly occupies the predominant part of the book. **Chapter 5: Word Recognition Skills and Vocabulary Development** includes an examination of word recognition elements such as phonemic awareness, phonic analysis, and sight words, as well as a detailed discussion of the principles and importance of vocabulary development. **Chapter 6: Reading Principles, Approaches, Comprehension, and Fluency** describes reading principles and four major instructional approaches, followed by a lengthy discussion of the crucial area of comprehension categories and strategies. Finally, **Chapter 7: Reading and Children's Literature** discusses the elements and genres of children's literature, including multicultural books; it describes both motivational and interpretive instructional activities, especially literature circles, which promote reading comprehension and a love of facts. The chapter also lists more than 250 quality books for children.

Part III: Writing as a Language Art

Chapter 8: Writing: Process, Genres, and Motivational Strategies defines the process and genres of writing, as well as motivational strategies and writing development throughout the grades. Samples of children's work complete the chapter. **Chapter 9: Writing Tools: Handwriting, Keyboarding, Spelling, and Grammar** describes tools involved in all writing efforts. **Chapter 10: The Writers' Workshop** depicts the essentials, implementation, and major components of the writers' workshop.

Part IV: Oral Language Arts

Chapter 11: Listening and Speaking involves two aspects of the oral language arts. The first outlines the types of listening and strategies for teaching this often-neglected language art. The second focuses on the primary types of elementary speech, such as readers theater, storytelling, and choral speaking. **Chapter 12: Creative Drama** is concerned with the values, components, and major types of this important language art.

The book concludes with an **Appendix** of technology connections linked to each chapter as well as a brief **Glossary**.

Features of the Text

In this book both novice and experienced teachers will find the following special features to be particularly useful:

Applicable IRA/NCTE Standards

Each chapter includes applicable IRA/NCTE Standards to help connect chapter content to practice. A full listing of the IRA/NCTE Standards appears at the end of the Preface.

Graphic Organizers

Readily understood diagrams introduce each chapter, providing both a preview—and later a review—of its contents.

Vignettes

Two scenarios per chapter, placed strategically near the techniques they describe, cover Grades K–6 and bring the material to life.

Working With English Language Learners

This rapidly growing group of elementary students receives special attention at the end of every chapter regardless of their proficiency: beginning ELLs, early intermediate and intermediate ELLs, and early advanced and advanced ELLs. Special help for these children is also offered, wherever appropriate, throughout the book.

Practical Instructional Activities and Ideas

Located at the end of every chapter and varying in number from 6 to 12, these activities can be incorporated as needed by the classroom teacher into the day's planning. Because of their variety they meet the needs of various age groups and ability levels.

Lesson Plans

The end of each chapter has a lesson plan, which stresses one or two of the six language arts. The formats for these plans vary so teachers may choose a style they like. All include the minimum standard components: objectives, materials, content standards, vocabulary, procedures, and assessment. An additional component, which some districts have adopted recently to conclude the lesson plan, is reflection; whereas assessment concerns student efforts, reflection relates to teacher performance. All elementary grades are represented, beginning with kindergarten.

Parents as Partners

Parental involvement in the education of their children is an integral part of elementary education, and while parents are eager to participate, they usually do not know exactly how to do so. Therefore, at the end of each chapter, there are specific suggestions that parents can follow to support their children's learning.

Bibliography of Children's Literature

Literature must permeate the literacy area. Consequently, titles of quality children's books can be found throughout the book, and a bibliography of those titles can be found at the end of every chapter. In all, more than 500 titles are included.

Integration Across the Curriculum

The end of each chapter shows how the contents of that chapter can be incorporated into different content areas under the following subject headings: science, social studies, math, literature, visual and performing arts, health, physical education, and music. *Briefly, this represents the theme of the book.*

When taken together, these pedagogical features should enhance the utility and effectiveness of the text.

Supplemental Material

Additional ancillary materials further support and enhance the learning goals of *Language Arts: Integrating Skills for Classroom Teaching.* These ancillary materials include the following:

Instructor's Resources CD

This CD offers the instructor a variety of resources that supplement the book material, including PowerPoint® lecture slides, test questions, and video clips (also found on the Student Resources CD). Additional resources include teaching tips, sample syllabi, and Web resources.

Student Resources CD

This CD is bound into students' textbooks and contains video clips that correlate with key concepts found in the text. Each clip includes a pre-video and post-video question to stimulate class discussion.

Web-Based Student Study Site

www.sagepub.com/donoghuestudy

This Web-based student study site provides a variety of additional resources to enhance students' understanding of the book content and to take their learning one step further. The site includes comprehensive study materials such as chapter summaries, practice tests, and flashcards. The site also includes the following special features: Web resources, standards resources, and "Learning From SAGE Research Articles."

IRA/NCTE Standards for the English Language Arts

1. Students read a wide range of print and nonprint texts to build an understanding of texts, of themselves, and of the cultures of the United States and the world; to acquire new information; to respond to the needs and demands of society and the workplace; and for personal fulfillment. Among these texts are fiction and non-fiction, classic and contemporary works.

2. Students read a wide range of literature from many periods in many genres to build an understanding of the many dimensions (e.g., philosophical, ethical, aesthetic) of human experience.

3. Students apply a wide range of strategies to comprehend, interpret, evaluate, and appreciate texts. They draw on their prior experience, their interactions with other readers and writers, their knowledge of word meaning and of other texts, their word identification strategies, and their understanding of textual features (e.g., sound-letter correspondence, sentence structure, context, graphics).

4. Students adjust their use of spoken, written, and visual language (e.g., conventions, style, vocabulary) to communicate effectively with a variety of audiences and for different purposes.

5. Students employ a wide range of strategies as they write and use different writing process elements appropriately to communicate with different audiences for a variety of purposes.

6. Students apply knowledge of language structure, language conventions (e.g., spelling and punctuation), media techniques, figurative language, and genre to create, critique, and discuss print and nonprint texts.

7. Students conduct research on issues and interests by generating ideas and questions, and by posing problems. They gather, evaluate, and synthesize data from a variety of sources (e.g., print and nonprint texts, artifacts, people) to communicate their discoveries in ways that suit their purpose and audience.

8. Students use a variety of technological and information resources (e.g., libraries, databases, computer networks, video) to gather and synthesize information and to create and communicate knowledge.

9. Students develop an understanding of and respect for diversity in language use, patterns, and dialects across cultures, ethnic groups, geographic regions, and social roles.

10. Students whose first language is not English make use of their first language to develop competency in the English language arts and to develop understanding of content across the curriculum.

11. Students participate as knowledgeable, reflective, creative, and critical members of a variety of literacy communities.

12. Students use spoken, written, and visual language to accomplish their own purposes (e.g., for learning, enjoyment, persuasion, and the exchange of information).

SOURCE: *Standards for the English Language Arts,* by the International Reading Association and the National Council of Teachers of English, Copyright 1996 by the International Reading Association and the National Council of Teachers of English. Reprinted with permission.

Acknowledgments

I would like to thank my colleagues who were involved in reviewing each stage of the manuscript and made numerous helpful suggestions:

- Tami Craft Al-Hazza, Old Dominion University
- Kim P. Baker, The Sage Colleges
- Vikki K. Collins, Columbus State University
- Richard C. Ingram, Winthrop University
- Taida Kelly, Governors State University
- DeAnna M. Laverick, Indiana University of Pennsylvania
- D. John McIntyre, Southern Illinois University Carbondale
- Scott Popplewell, Ball State University
- Sara Runge-Pulte, Northern Kentucky University
- Paul J. Schafer, St. Bonaventure University
- Sandra Fox Sudduth, Jacksonville State University
- Denise Dole Tallakson, University of Northern Iowa
- Christina D. Walton, Morehead State University
- Jeff L. Whittingham, University of Central Arkansas.

I would also like to acknowledge the professional support of:

- Christine Jones of Coto de Caza, CA
- Jordan Fabish of Long Beach, CA
- Laurie Hansen of Placentia, CA
- Rebekah Hendershot of Fullerton, CA
- Teeanna Rizkallah of Pasadena, CA
- Jennifer Taylor of Nashville, TN
- Mona Wolfe of Fullerton, CA

Although many persons helped during the preparation of this book, I particularly wish to express my appreciation to Diane McDaniel, acquisitions editor; Sarah K. Quesenberry, production editor; and Ashley Plummer and Leah Mori, editorial assistants, all of whom encouraged and supported my writing.

—Mildred R. Donoghue
California State University, Fullerton

PART I
Foundations of the Language Arts

Language and the English Language Arts

Literacy is critical to success in a democracy. Without the ability to read and write competently and confidently, children have only limited opportunities for academic and career success. Proficient reading and writing abilities represent the key that students need to become independent learners in all the subject areas in the elementary school. They are the foundation of the English language arts, which also include listening, speaking, and visual literacy (i.e., viewing and visual representation) and are therefore involved in standards mandated by either or both government and professional agencies.

Anticipation Statements

Complete this exercise before reading Chapter 1.

Do you agree or disagree with the following statements? Circle your answer. Be prepared to discuss questions in blue.

1.	There are two kinds of standards: content standards and performance standards.	Agree	Disagree
2.	The IRA/NCTE have broadened the definition of *text* "to refer not only to printed texts but also to spoken language, graphics, and technological communications."	Agree	Disagree
3.	State standards do not supersede national standards, and these vary from state to state.	Agree	Disagree
4.	The six language arts cannot and should not receive equal time and attention in the classroom because literacy (reading and writing) is one of the two most crucial subjects in the elementary curriculum.	Agree	Disagree
5.	More time is spent in reading than in any other language art.	Agree	Disagree
6.	It is the responsibility of parents and teachers to give children gentle guidance in the area of pragmatics.	Agree	Disagree
7.	Teachers must implement more hands-on experiences and individual and group projects allowing students to "probe deeply in a small number of topics."	Agree	Disagree
8.	Even though each language mode is often studied separately, each is rarely used alone.	Agree	Disagree
9.	Some consider thinking the seventh language art.	Agree	Disagree
10.	Language development does not affect children's thinking or intellectual development.	Agree	Disagree

Standards for the English Language Arts

Considerable discussion exists in the schools regarding **standards**. These have been defined as "specific definitions of what students should know or demonstrate," according to Spafford, Pesce, and Grosser (1998, p. 271). Standards include both *content* standards, which relate to the knowledge that is to be taught in the various academic subjects, and *performance* standards, which specify how students will demonstrate their mastery of that knowledge. Briefly, standards represent expectations of what students should know to become functional members of society (Hammer, 1998). Teachers are asked to adhere to standards in their instructional planning, regardless of grade level, while still incorporating students' strengths and needs in that planning. Nevertheless, the

Young children start school eagerly, looking forward to learning to read and write.

Applicable IRA/NCTE Standards

Standard 4   Students adjust their use of spoken, written, and visual language (e.g., conventions, style, vocabulary) to communicate effectively with a variety of audiences and for different purposes.

Standard 11   Students participate as knowledgeable, reflective, creative, and critical members of a variety of literacy communities.

Standard 12   Students use spoken, written, and visual language to accomplish their own purposes (e.g., for learning, enjoyment, persuasion, and the exchange of information).

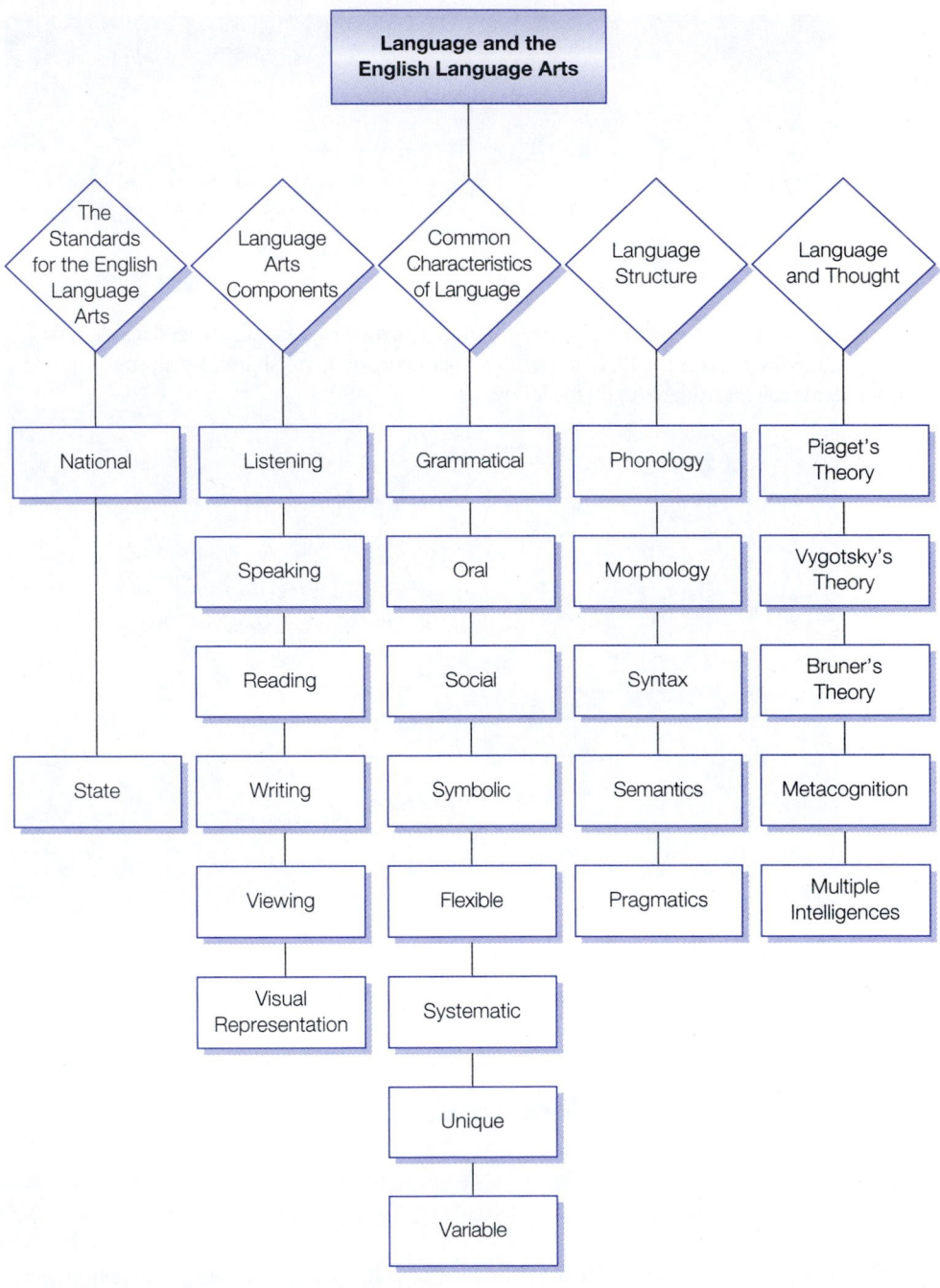

A Graphic Summary of the Contents of This Chapter

content of these standards has remained a controversial area among educators for nearly two decades, especially since some federal legislation (e.g., No Child Left Behind Act) and most state departments of education and school districts have mandated their implementation.

Both state departments of education and national professional organizations have issued standards in specific subject areas. In the field of language arts, for example, the International

Reading Association and the National Council of Teachers of English (IRA/NCTE) have issued a joint document titled *Standards for the English Language Arts* (IRA/NCTE, 1996). The two organizations had three motivations for defining standards in language arts: (1) to "prepare students for the literacy demands of today and tomorrow," (2) to "present a shared vision of literacy education," and (3) to "promote equity and excellence for all" (pp. 4–6). The last objective involves areas such as adequate staffing, equal access to resources, safe and well-equipped schools, and teaching students how to learn (i.e., develop specific competencies; acquire knowledge; and be able to both reflect upon, and monitor, their own learning). The IRA/NCTE standards also broaden the definition of *text* "to refer not only to printed texts but also to spoken language, graphics, and technological communications" (p. 2).

Although state standards supersede national standards, they vary from state to state; therefore, in this book, the focus is on the IRA/NCTE (1996) standards that are shared by all states. These twelve standards call for students to do the following:

1. Read a range of print and nonprint texts to develop an understanding of those texts, of themselves, and of the culture of the United States and the world.

2. Read a range of literature from many genres to develop an understanding of the many dimensions of the human experience.

3. Apply a range of strategies to comprehend, evaluate, and appreciate texts.

4. Adjust their use of spoken, written, and visual language to communicate effectively for different purposes with different audiences.

5. Employ a range of strategies as they write, using different process elements properly to communicate with different audiences.

6. Apply knowledge of language structure and conventions, media techniques, figurative language, and genre to create and discuss print and nonprint texts.

7. Conduct research on issues and interests by posing problems and generating ideas and questions.

8. Use a variety of technological and informational resources to gather and synthesize information and to create and communicate knowledge.

9. Develop an understanding of, and respect for, diversity in language use and dialects across cultures, geographic regions, and social roles.

10. For English Language Learners (ELLs), make use of their first language to develop competency in the English language arts and also to develop understanding of content across the curriculum.

11. Participate as knowledgeable, critical, and creative members of a variety of literacy groups.

12. Use spoken, written, and visual language to accomplish their own purposes (e.g., learning, enjoyment, persuasion, and an exchange of information).

Language Arts: Components and Integration

Language arts represent that part of the elementary school curriculum that concerns activities involving listening, speaking, reading, writing, viewing, and visual representation. These six components are essential to all areas of the curriculum and, by their very nature, are integrated and connected to each other.

Language arts can be categorized by processes and by dimensions. Processes include *oral* (i.e., listening and speaking), *written* (i.e., reading and writing), and *visual* (i.e., viewing and visual representation). In *receptive processes*, which include listening, reading, and viewing, the individual is receiving information. In *productive processes*, which include speaking, writing, and visual representation, the individual is producing information.

Another means of grouping the language arts, according to the major professional organizations (IRA/NCTE, 1996), is by dimensions: the content dimension, the purpose dimension, and the development dimension. The first describes *what* students should learn in the English language arts: how to work with a broad range of texts (including literature as well as informational/academic texts); how to use strategies and processes for comprehending texts and producing them; and finally, how to use language systems and structures such as spelling, grammar, and punctuation. The second dimension articulates *why* students should learn the English language arts: to obtain and communicate a myriad of information, to evoke aesthetically literary responses and expressions, to seek solutions to problems, and to learn and reflect through discussion and journaling. The third dimension defines *how* the students should learn the English language arts. It involves two separate issues: how students gain knowledge and, over time, become competent through practice, and how they learn to use the language clearly, creatively, and critically.

Regardless of the categorization used, note that these six language arts cannot and should not receive equal time and attention in the classroom because literacy (i.e., reading and writing) is one of the two most crucial subjects in the elementary curriculum, the other being mathematics. Reading and writing far outrank the other four language arts or modes.

Literacy is a crucial component of the elementary curriculum, so teachers may need to take extra time to help some students master reading and writing.

Even though each language mode is often studied separately, each is rarely used alone. Instead, nearly every language arts activity demands more than one language mode; sometimes as many as three or four may be involved. For example, ELLs need the support of viewing and visual representation to aid development of their oral and written language processes.

Even beginning teachers soon realize the interrelatedness of the language arts. They see, for example, how creative drama sessions are more engaging when they follow the telling or reading aloud of a piece of quality literature, how handwriting lessons are considerably more effective when they contain words the children can read by themselves, and how spelling scores improve when the words come from the students' own writing or from vocabulary introduced during reading assignments.

Integrating the language arts demands a careful selection of materials, curriculum, and teaching techniques. Materials should be authentic and brought in from the real world. Language modes should be combined because separations that seem logical to adults do not make sense to children and do not help them learn the skills they must eventually master. Furthermore, teaching strategies should encourage imitation of written and spoken models and should provide opportunities for oral communication that is a purposeful exchange of ideas and represents genuine oral interaction. Finally, according to Pappas, Kiefer, and Levstik (1999), effective integration requires careful organization, motivation, and engagement to succeed.

Teachers should be aware of three principles that guide integration. First, if the goal of elementary language arts is broad communication effectiveness, students need significant and applicable language attitudes, processes, skills, and knowledge as they go on learning for a lifetime. Second, language learning is optimal when it occurs in meaningful situations; children learn language best when they use it in cognitive contexts, social contexts, and expressive contexts. And third, the intrinsic interrelationship among the various language arts is maximized when language is integrated throughout the curriculum but diminished when it is not.

Listening

Although its development starts before birth, **listening** is the first language art that children acquire. From the beginning, their listening vocabulary exceeds their speaking vocabulary, and this continues into adulthood. However, because some teachers believe that students already know how to listen before they start school, they devote little instructional time to teaching listening; studies, however, have repeatedly shown that listening skills affect speaking, reading, and writing abilities. Students listen differently in different situations, depending on the amount of concentration needed. Marginal listening (or background listening) is required to distinguish sounds, appreciative or aesthetic listening promotes enjoyment, attentive or efferent listening aids children in acquiring information, and critical listening helps them evaluate that information. More time is spent in listening than in any other language art. (Listening is discussed at length in Chapter 11.)

Speaking

Since effective oral communication is not innate, most of what students know about language when they enter kindergarten has been learned accidentally. They have used their listening skills to develop their speaking abilities, by hearing and innately mastering the sounds of their first language. Speech habits formed in the preschool years vary greatly among children, and elementary teachers must both recognize these variations and modify their programs to meet student needs. Oral language is the mode in which students feel most secure and is also the one that is most commonly used among adults and children alike. Furthermore, students' experience with spoken language is fundamental to their learning to read and affects their ability to write. (Speaking is discussed at length in Chapter 11.)

Reading

This highly debated language art concerns comprehension of written language, which is facilitated by word recognition as its prerequisite. Reading processes meaning from the printed page; therefore, students with broad experiential backgrounds are more likely to be familiar with many reading themes and so better able to relate to them, thereby becoming good readers. These same readers also need a supportive literacy environment (with caring and informed persons) to progress in their reading skills. Those persons should be knowledgeable about the balanced, comprehensive reading program as defined by the National Reading Panel Report (2000): It involves instruction in five areas—comprehension strategies, phonemic awareness, phonics, fluency, and vocabulary development. (Reading is discussed at length in Chapters 5 to 7.)

Writing

While writing is the most complex language art to master, young children attempt it even before reading, although their early scribbles are only meaningful to them and cannot be deciphered by adults. When they reach kindergarten, however, they begin to use invented or temporary spelling to help them express their thoughts and ideas since they lack spelling proficiency—a developmental process. Elementary school students learn to write using the five stages of the process approach: prewriting (or brainstorming), drafting, revising, editing, and publishing (or sharing their work with others). They use the writing process to prepare narrative, persuasive, expository, and poetic work. Tools that they need to accomplish the job are spelling, grammar, handwriting, keyboarding, and punctuation. (Writing is discussed at length in Chapters 8 to 10.)

Viewing and Visual Representation

Viewing is a receptive language art that allows the learner to gain knowledge. **Visual representation** is the flip side of viewing because it is a productive process that allows learners to convey information. Both have permeated the other four language arts for decades; for example, students have drawn (or *visually represented*) their reactions as they listened to Dvorak's *New World Symphony;* children have examined (or *viewed*) wordless books such as Wiesner's *Flotsam* (Clarion, 2006) in an effort to determine the plot through discussion or writing.

In response to the incredible growth of the information age and the mass media since the mid-1990s, the IRA/NCTE has deemed it wise to place special emphasis on teaching children to understand and critically analyze the types of technological advances that exist and will continue to be developed during the 21st century. These professional organizations (IRA/NCTE, 1996) therefore jointly created *viewing* and *visual representation* as two separate and additional language arts, raising the long-established total of four arts to six. This change reflects recent brain research indicating, according to Sousa (2006), that children learn best when provided with a variety of learning modalities and modes.

Viewing: This receptive language art allows learners to gain knowledge. It is a communication process during which students view and interpret a broad variety of visual materials including (but not restricted to) videos, films, CD-ROMs, advertising, television programs, magazines, newspapers, photographs, charts, tables, maps, and computer games. According to Flood, Lapp, and Wood (1998), viewing involves these abilities: listening, thinking, perceiving, connecting, responding, and evaluating these materials in a variety of formats.

Thousands of picture books (both fiction and nonfiction) for preschool and primary children (as well as some for older children) make increased use of viewing possibilities integrated with text. Books for older students now contain more graphics than ever before. Consequently, elementary school children must be taught viewing skills along with the skills of comprehending printed materials. Their teachers must be knowledgeable about both students' interests and abilities when choosing texts to be certain that they are culturally relevant. The use of such texts increases children's ability to view other media critically. Obviously, this criterion is especially important in schools with large numbers of ELLs.

Picture books provide an effective introduction to teaching viewing skills. In classrooms with overhead projectors, teachers can project an illustration from a picture book on a screen where everyone can see it; in this way children become acquainted with the work of writer-illustrators (such as Tomie dePaola, Steven Kellogg, Kevin Henkes, and Patricia Polacco) and with major artistic styles as reflected in illustrations, for example, realism as in Say's *Emma's Rug* (1996), surrealism as in Wiesner's *June 29, 1999* (1992), impressionism as in McCully's *Mirette on the High Wire* (1992), expressionism as in Ringgold's *Tar Beach* (1991), and cartoon art as in Rothman's *Officer Buckle and Gloria* (1995)—all of these were illustrated by their authors.

The most common type of picture book is the *picture storybook,* defined as a book in which the illustrations and text work together (i.e., part of the story is told through the pictures and part is told through the text), according to Temple and his colleagues (2002). Such books offer readers "the opportunity to deepen their understanding of visual communication" (p. 190).

Some teachers of beginning readers use a *picture walk* to introduce a picture book. They first show the book cover to the students, asking questions to determine their prior knowledge and also to activate predictions about the illustrations and storyline. The questioning continues as the children advance through the picture book, as part of the guided reading approach (Clay, 1991).

Viewing skills are often taught indirectly by teachers who use them to help students "walk through" chapters in social studies and science textbooks. This effort previews the new content in the form of photographs, maps, diagrams, charts, and other graphics.

Teaching viewing skills directly is of great importance today in connection to using the Internet. Described by Heide and Stilborne (1999) as having a broad range of resources available for "electronic field trips," the Internet offers pictures, sound, and text and is considered a learning tool by many students. Since it was created originally for adult use, however, teachers must regularly discuss classroom rules and safety guidelines for using the Internet. Adult supervision is the key to making certain that students access appropriate resources on the Internet.

Visual Representation: Said to be the flip side of viewing in which the students *receive information,* visual representing is a productive process that allows learners to *convey information* or express themselves to others through such means as artwork, photography, or physical performance. For instance, they can create murals, collages, maps, diagrams, graphs, posters, timelines, and charts; they can dance, do mime, or participate in story dramatization; and depending on the school's resources, they can prepare technology productions such as digital photographs, PowerPoint presentations, or Web pages. Since visual representation stimulates knowledge and interest in several subject areas and advances the development of multiple intelligences, teachers should plan to include specific activities targeting this language art much like Miss Perez does in Vignette 1.1 with her third graders.

For material related to this concept, go to Video Clip 1.1 on the Student Resource CD bound into the back of your textbook.

VIGNETTE 1.1   Using Visual Representation

"Stir-crazy" is the word, thought Miss Perez. *Or maybe "cabin fever."* Although it was only 10 a.m., she'd already reprimanded three different students for talking and laughing during the class's independent work time. And it wasn't just today—her normally well-behaved third graders had been more talkative and less focused all week.

At this point in the school year, between the fun of spring break and the promise of summer vacation, students always had trouble concentrating. Miss Perez had planned a new activity to incorporate visuals and self-expression into the language arts unit, and she decided to introduce it this morning. *These kids are already expressing themselves*, she thought wryly. *Let's channel it toward learning*.

Since many of the students took short trips over spring break or were looking forward to a vacation in the summer, Miss Perez knew they would enjoy *Three Days on a River in a Red Canoe* by Vera B. Williams. The book not only told the story of two children camping and canoeing with their mothers but also included easy recipes for campground cooking, maps of the trip, and step-by-step instructions for pitching a tent and tying a knot. Charming colored-pencil illustrations filled the pages of this kid-friendly "travel guide."

"Class, we're going to have Reading Circle at a different time today," Miss Perez announced. "Please gather on the Reading Rug to hear the story. After I share the book, I'll explain a new project."

Glad to be free of their desks and long-division homework papers, the students hurried to the special multicolored rug where they enjoyed story time each day. Once they were seated, Miss Perez introduced the new book and read it aloud. The students liked the descriptions of camping supplies, the pictures of the river route, and the illustrations of the catfish, trout, and perch that the characters catch for dinner.

After finishing the book, Miss Perez introduced the new assignment. "This book includes a lot of information. Some of it comes from the words, but much of it is communicated through the illustrations. What do the pictures teach us?"

"How to make fruit stew!" said Alicia.

"And the directions to the river," added Jose. "She drew a map to the part where they started the trip."

"Exactly right," said Miss Perez. "The author also illustrated how to carry a canoe down into the water, and different types of ducks, and many other things. When an author uses drawings or maps or charts to share information, she's communicating visually. Today, we're also going to be authors who use visual information to tell stories."

Miss Perez outlined the assignment to her interested audience. "Some of you went on a trip over spring break. Some will take a vacation this summer. Or maybe you haven't traveled like the characters in today's book, but you've visited your grandparents or moved to a new house or hiked on a new trail in your neighborhood. There are all kinds of adventures! I want each of you to think of a journey in your own life and write a story to tell the rest of the class about that experience."

"Can we put maps in our story?" Seth asked.

"Absolutely! In fact, that's what this assignment is all about. I want you to write a good story, but I want you to also use pictures to help us understand. You might draw a map, or show the steps involved in a new skill, or illustrate the before and after of something that happened, or anything else that will share information. Tomorrow we'll take turns reading our stories to the class and showing the pictures. Take a few minutes to decide what you want to write about, and then we'll get started."

The students returned to their desks, talking again, but this time about the new assignment. Miss Perez knew the energy level would remain high for the rest of the semester, but this project would funnel some of the excitement into a productive activity. Even more important, the exercise would broaden the children's understanding of literature and sharpen their ability to communicate. At the same time, the students would develop stronger viewing skills as they enjoyed each other's stories. She looked forward to seeing the finished creations—and to the quiet while the class created them.

In their weekly agenda, elementary teachers can readily include the following activities after hearing or reading these picture books:

For Younger Children

- Martin, Jr. and Archambault's *The Ghost-Eye Tree* (1988): Children in small groups create a mural showing the house, the path, the tree, and Mr. Cowlander's barn. Then they retell the story using puppets.

- Ahlberg and Ahlberg's *The Jolly Postman: Or Other People's Letters* (2006): Children individually design picture postcards of their own city or of places they have visited or studied in class.

- Ehlert's *Red Leaf, Yellow Leaf* (1991): Children individually prepare an illustrated definition of one of the important nouns in the book (e.g., *staking, roots, nursery*). The pictures are then collected and placed in a book for the library table.

- Rosen's *We're Going on a Bear Hunt* (1997): Children imitate the sounds heard and act out the situations described in the book, using hand motions or pantomime.

- Hoffman's *Amazing Grace* (1991): Children create acronyms (an easy beginning free verse form) around Grace's name. Each word chosen to describe her might indicate how she is amazing. For enrichment, students could also create "amazing" acronyms for their own names.

- Aliki's *My Visit to the Zoo* (1999): Children are each given one square of red, yellow, brown, or black construction paper. Those with yellow paper (for healthy animals, as described in the book) come to the front. This process is repeated with red paper (for vulnerable or threatened animals), brown paper (for endangered animals), and black paper (for extinct ones). The class discusses what is happening to each group of animals as each group comes up to the front.

- Parker and Wright's *Bugs* (1988): Children are assigned to groups that each get a ball of self-hardening clay to make a model of an imaginary insect complete with body parts, wings, and legs. Each insect receives a name and is displayed before the class.

- Leedy's *The Edible Pyramid: Good Eating Every Day* (1996): Children in pairs design a collage of nutritious foods by cutting colored pictures out of discarded magazines and gluing them onto poster board. Then they label each item according to the food group to which it belongs. Collages should be checked for accuracy.

For Intermediate Students

- Lobel's *The Book of Pigericks* (1983): Children work individually or in small groups to create and illustrate their own book of limerick variations, possibly a book of "catericks" or "fishericks." They may wish to place their animals in different U.S. cities, just as Lobel did, and draw the background location of each animal after using the Internet.

- Van Allsburg's *The Mysteries of Harris Burdick* (1984): Children make small drawings using the same materials as the author: pencil illustrations on Strathmore paper. Then they discuss why these materials are effective and why they believe that Van Allsburg chose them to his advantage.

- Smith's *Return to Bitter Creek* (1988): Children reread the pages that describe the symbols on the quilt that Grandmom had made. Then they design a symbol to introduce each new chapter, following the introduction to symbolism on p. 124.

- MacLachlan's *Sarah, Plain and Tall* (2004): Children draw scenes of the prairie and the Maine coast, based on the author's descriptions of these locations and using blue, green, gray, and black colored pencils or crayons—the colors that Sarah brought with her. Some may wish to investigate informational books that describe the two landscapes.

- Wiesner's *Tuesday* (1997): Since the book is nearly wordless and yet filled with characters and actions, the children first write a script for dramatizing the story and then present the final production to other classes.

- Paulsen's *Woodsong* (2002): Children map the course of the annual 17-day run of the Iditarod in Alaska.

- Siebert's *Heartland* (1989): Children in small groups each select their favorite part of this book-length poem. Then, they organize a readers theatre presentation under careful supervision so the production moves along smoothly.

- Coerr's *Mieko and the Fifth Treasure* (2003): Children each create an origami, a paper craft popular in Japan.

Functions and Characteristics of Language

Many students in the kindergarten–primary grades acquire language naturally to fulfill basic needs within their environment. Language, however, is also a social tool, allowing children to interact with others and to express their own individuality. Halliday (1976) describes language development as a process by which all children progressively "learn how to mean" because they learn to convey meaning through speech through their relationships and dealings with others. They use oral language for many purposes, particularly the seven universal language *functions* that Halliday has delineated:

1. Instrumental language used to satisfy needs and get things done (e.g., "I want that cookie"; "I need a pencil"; "I would like a drink")

2. Regulatory language used to control the behavior of others (e.g., "Move here"; "Go away"; "Do this next")

3. Interactional language used during social activities for the purpose of getting along with others and building cooperative relationships (e.g., "Let's play together"; "Take me with you"; "You and I can keep score")

4. Personal language used to express private opinions or to allow a child to tell about him- or herself (e.g., "I want to be a pilot"; "I like this one best"; "I think I want to pitch this year")

5. Heuristic language used to seek information and ask questions (e.g., "How does it work?"; "Why is it snowing?"; "Do all dogs bark?")

6. Imaginative language used to create a fantasy or to engage in make-believe (e.g., "Once upon a time"; "Let's pretend you're Harry Potter"; "Let's pretend that we're shipwrecked")

7. Informative or representational language used to inform others and to receive new knowledge (e.g., "The birthday party will be on Saturday afternoon"; "Will you give your report on Australia this week, Kim?"; "Mom, our class had the best attendance this month!")

Here is presented a brief *summary* of the developmental functions listed above—the role that language plays in the everyday life of children and adults—to promote a better understanding of the characteristics of language: Language alters and controls behavior, pinpoints needs and wants, allows persons to establish and maintain fuller interaction with others, promotes cognitive growth by allowing persons to add to their knowledge through experiences and new information, and, last, permits people to establish their own individuality by sharing personal feelings and opinions.

The English language and all other languages throughout the world possess several *characteristics* in common:

- *Every language has a grammar:* Although the grammar of each language is different, some closely related languages (such as English and Spanish) share many features that denote meaning or the relationships of elements in sentences. Children who speak two languages often have problems with the differences in the grammar of these languages. Because word order (or syntax) is a crucial part of grammar, ELLs who speak Japanese, for example, will be asking ungrammatical questions should they persist in using the Japanese order when asking questions in English.

- *Every language is oral:* Scholars have counted nearly 7,000 living languages (Gordon, 2005), although less than half of them have ever been represented in writing. Spoken language is older and more widespread and communicates ideas better than written language. Most children learn to talk with little or no formal assistance, whereas they ordinarily learn to write only with the help of others, and then that writing is a representation of their earlier speech.

- *Every language is social:* The form of each language reflects the social needs of the group that uses it. Children may possess the biological capacity for language, but they cannot develop that potential without interaction with others in their society. Some evidence indicates that language learning is inhibited when social interaction becomes blocked.

- *Every language is symbolic and arbitrary:* Words (the symbols of language) permit children to discuss, for example, a ride on the space shuttle even though they have not yet experienced it directly. Language is a type of code that allows abstract ideas and experiences to be encoded by the speaker, transmitted by speech, and decoded by the hearer. Although words symbolize real objects or events, they themselves are arbitrary. English speakers, for example, call a four-legged animal that gives milk a *cow,* but there is no inherent trait in the animal that demands that it be called *cow.* Even onomatopoeic words are arbitrary symbols and do not, therefore, have meaning in themselves. Consequently, the dog that says *bow-wow* in the English community barks *wang-wang* in the Chinese community. Every language has different words to symbolize the numbers 1 to 10. The English language is alphabetic with 26 letters, but the Chinese language with no alphabet has about 50,000 characters, with each character representing a word or part of a word.

- *Every language is flexible and changes:* Because it is spoken by living people, language too is alive and therefore changing. New ideas, products, and institutions make the need for such change necessary. Thousands of words related to science and technology have increased the English vocabulary in the recent past. Too, since English and the other languages exist in the oral expression of the persons who use them, some of their colloquial expressions and slang are a constantly changing part of language.

- *Every language is systematic and describable:* All languages in the world can be described using identical techniques, according to the science of descriptive linguistics. Each is consistent in its structure and not a haphazard collection of symbols and sounds. Most sentences therefore, although they are created spontaneously, still follow a system of rules of which even its users are often not totally aware. Children learn the system as they learn the language.

- *Each language is unique and diverse:* To comprehend how unique each language is, it is important to recall that the most popular definition of a language is that it is the form understood by members of one speech community (such as France) but not by those of another speech community (such as Italy). Among Native Americans, for example, there are nearly 30 different language families. When groups of persons are socially or geographically separated from one another, their speech reflects changes in grammar, vocabulary, and pronunciation. Such language diversity is generally a cumulative process.

- *Each language is variable:* Languages contain various dialects or different versions of the same language being spoken by different groups. In India, for example, more than 20 languages and 80 dialects are spoken. In the United States dialect differences appear in the vocabulary, pronunciation, or syntax of different geographic communities or even among different social groups in one community.

Language Structure

For the most part, students acquire their understanding of the underlying structure of the English language in an informal manner. However, there are portions of that knowledge that can be and are formally studied in school, for example, learning about affixes in the intermediate grades.

The English language is a structure of arbitrary systems relating sounds and meanings. A child or adult is described as having a command of the language when he or she understands the sounds used (phonology), the basic units of meaning (morphology), the grammatical rule system (syntax), the construction of meaning from spoken or written language (semantics), and the language choices people make in cultural and social interactions and contexts (pragmatics).

Phonology: Phonology refers to the sounds of language. These are called **phonemes** and are represented by symbols called **graphemes**. In the English language the number of phonemes ranges between 41 and 46, depending on the dialect of the geographic area of the United States in which one lives. Since the English alphabet has only 26 letters, there is some irregularity in letter-sound relationships. Because there are more sounds than letters, certain letters plainly represent more than one sound in the written language system (e.g., vowels often represent several sounds and thus are more irregular than consonants). This has created the misconception that English is a very difficult language to spell. However, Venezky (1999) recently found that English is not as irregular as was believed earlier.

Phonological development begins, according to Shore (1997), when speech sounds activate neural networks in the fetal brain. Scientists around the world are discovering that recognition of early speech actually starts in the womb at about six months (Jusczyk, 1997). After birth, interactions with caregivers offer babies the chance to specialize in the sounds of their native language(s). The critical period for mastering sound discrimination occurs within the first six months of the baby's life. Infants who consistently hear more than one language during this period may become native bilingual or trilingual speakers since they retain the ability to distinguish among the subtle and discrete sounds.

An important aspect of English phonology is **intonation** (i.e., pitch or highness or lowness of the voice), **juncture** (i.e., pauses or interruptions or suspensions in the flow of sound), and **stress** (i.e., the amount of emphasis given to a syllable or word).

Morphology: Morphology concerns the forms or structures of a language. The smallest unit of meaning in a language is a **morpheme**: It cannot be broken down into any smaller parts and is not necessarily identical with words or syllables. The major morpheme classes in English are bases or roots and affixes. Most bases stand alone as words and are therefore described as free morphemes. Affixes never stand alone; they are always attached to bases, either before them as prefixes or after them as suffixes, and so are called bound morphemes.

When students speak, they utter a sequence of individually meaningless phonemes as well as a sequence of meaningful morphemes; for example, the sentence *The cat chased the birds* consists of vowels and consonants spoken at varied pitches with different degrees of stress. It is simultaneously a string of the following morphemes: {the}, {cat}, {chase}, {d}, {the}, {bird}, {z}.

Syntax: Morphemes cannot be arranged one after another in any elective order. Instead, for each language there are orderly combinations or constructions in which morphemes can be put together in an utterance. **Syntax** deals with word order and how words or groups of words are arranged to convey meaning. For example, the words *the* and *cat* can be grouped together in the construction *the cat* but not *cat the*. The largest English construction is the sentence.

By about the age of six years, the child has mastered a major part of the syntax of his or her first language; more complex syntactic or grammatical structures used by adults develop in the student after the age of six (Chomsky, 1974). However, semantics, which is another aspect of language structure, becomes increasingly complex throughout a person's entire life.

Semantics: The most important aspect of language is meaning, and **semantics** is the study of word meanings or the role of language in human life. Such meanings usually reflect the concerns and values of the particular culture.

Because semantics deals with word meanings, children must learn about concrete concepts (such as the difference between *horse* and *dog*) as well as about the more difficult abstract concepts (such as *color*). They must become familiar with spatial relationships (*behind* and *here*) and with opposites (*hot* and *cold*).

However, semantics also deals with the attitudes that people have toward particular words and expressions. It thus covers both the *denotation* (or literal, objective meaning) of a word and the *connotation* (or personal, subjective meaning) of a word. When words are so often learned in different settings, it is little wonder that the identical word may have a variety of associations for various children or adults.

Students today must understand certain concepts about language content primarily because they are constantly exposed to the pervasive effects of the media. They must learn to comprehend propaganda and persuasion techniques. They must learn to distinguish between what is actually reported, what is inferred from the report, and what judgment has been formed. They must be taught the importance of context and how words or sentences lifted out of context can distort meaning. They must learn to realize that the attitudes of writers and speakers can often be discerned by studying the words they use. Magazine, newspaper, and television ads are readily accessible sources that students can use for examining and analyzing how language can be manipulated.

Pragmatics: Pragmatics concerns the choices that people make in cultural and social interactions and settings. It deals with the conventions of becoming a competent language user (e.g., how to begin and end a conversation with others).

There are rules for proper language use in a variety of social situations; for example, what is discussed at a funeral may not be appropriate at a wedding. Gleason (1989) describes successful conversations as those marked by appropriateness in relevance, quality, quantity, and manner of speaking. As children mature, they become better able to adapt their speech and mannerisms to accommodate different social situations.

It is the responsibility of parents and teachers to give children gentle guidance in the area of pragmatics.

Language and Thought

Some consider thinking to be the seventh language art; others realize that thinking truly infuses all of the language arts and has both a critical component and a creative component. While there are some distinctions between these components, they are not mutually exclusive mental operations.

Growth in the language arts is promoted when teachers give students numerous opportunities to engage in both critical and creative thinking (Foster, Sawicki, Schaeffer, & Zelinski, 2002).

Language development deeply affects children's thinking or intellectual development. As they acquire language, they also acquire learning strategies and thought structures that can be used in learning to read and write (Cramer, 2001). Ranked among the 20th century's leading developmental psychologists are Jean Piaget of Switzerland, Lev Vygotsky of Russia, and Jerome Bruner of the United States: Each proposed related but slightly different theories of language and cognition.

Piaget (1962) believed that thinking promotes language acquisition, which in turn depends on sensorimotor schemata: models in the brain that store information necessary for higher-level thinking. The thinking that children do develops from their actions upon the concrete world. Therefore, long before they have the language to describe or name certain objects, they can see, hear, touch, smell, or taste them and so come to understand their properties and functions. Language transmits thinking. While it does not organize it, what it does do is refine and elaborate it. Language and thinking influence one another and are interactive.

There are three terms associated with Piaget's view on language and thought; all concern continuous processes. *Assimilation* takes place any time that new data are fitted into already present knowledge systems or schemata. *Accommodation* occurs when those schemata must be changed to accommodate new experiences or information since that input cannot be structured into existing ones. Finally, *equilibrium* involves the intricate and congruous balance between assimilation and accommodation.

Vygotsky (1986) believed that thought development was partially determined by language development because language plays a major role in the child's experiences with the world. In his opinion, the key to the growth of complex thought processes is the child's ability to think out loud. One aspect of this development is *egocentric speech*, which is talk not directed to another person or object. That type of speech represents the major transition leading toward true thought as characterized by inner speech. Then as speech is internalized, it is used to control thinking.

It is the influence of adults on children that shapes both their language patterns and their thought patterns. Verbal and cognitive developments are promoted through meaningful social interactions between children and adults. Without the proper adult modeling, the thought process of children is limited.

Bruner (1986) believed as Vygotsky did that children learn to think abstractly only through the use of language and that adult modeling is critical to language growth in children. By conversing with adults, boys and girls learn to examine and reflect on their own experiences, thereby scaffolding or building on the structure offered by supportive adults. Strategies acquired during such language learning are useful for other types of thought maturation, including concept development. That development involves the creation of schemata in which language plays an ever-increasing role as the child matures. Bruner's theories on the formation of schemata are applied in elementary classrooms in which semantic mapping/webbing is used to help students better comprehend text material they have read or are about to read: Students first discuss the material, then help produce a visual representation, and, finally, obtain a mental image that can be stored for later problem solving (Tierney & Readence, 2000).

Metacognition: Thinking critically about thinking defines the word **metacognition**, which has been further delineated by Weaver (1994) as the conscious knowledge that individuals have about how they learn. It occurs before, during, and after reading, viewing, speaking, listening, writing, and visual representation.

During the preschool years most of the knowledge that children possess is at a subconscious or "tacit" level (Tirosh, 1992). As they grow and develop, however, children begin to think about their own thinking on a conscious or explicit level; they are then able to move beyond the present and their own perspective. They must know about knowing: how and when to know and the reasons for knowing (Verhoeven & Snow, 2001). Active learners who use metacognitive strategies first think about the assignment; next, establish goals for themselves; and finally, monitor their progress. Then at some point, if it becomes apparent that their efforts are not helping them meet their goals, they promptly determine why not and change strategies.

Both *self-knowledge* (becoming aware of what one needs or wants to know) and *procedural knowledge* (becoming aware of how one can acquire that information) are dependent on metacognition. According to Derry and Murphy (1986), teaching children to use metacognition demands that teaching be indirect, thereby making students accountable for their own learning.

For material related to this concept, go to Video Clip 1.2 on the Student Resource CD bound into the back of your textbook.

Multiple Intelligences: It is critical that teachers accept the fact that every child is different, not just physically and culturally but mentally as well. This concept was reinforced when the traditional theory about intelligence as comprising mostly linguistic and logical abilities was deemed too narrow (Armstrong, 1994; Gardner, 1983). Instead, human beings possess several separate intelligences in varying degrees that work together, not in isolation (Gardner, 2000). These **multiple intelligences** are linguistic, musical, logical-mathematical, spatial, bodily-kinesthetic, intrapersonal, interpersonal, naturalist, existentialist, and spiritualistic intelligences.

Gardner (1983) believes that schools must therefore broaden their definition of intelligence to include more than the traditional reasoning and verbal abilities. Instead, all of the intelligences he describes should be included when weekly lesson plans are made because any subject matter—even language arts—can be taught in more than one way. In his opinion, the fundamental goal of education should be "genuine understanding—going beyond repetitive learning and short answers" (p. 27). To meet that goal, Gardner (2003) proposes that teachers implement more hands-on experiences and individual and group projects that allow students to "probe deeply in a small number of topics" (p. 9). Mrs. Weber's astute planning for her fifth graders in Vignette 1.2 illustrates how Gardner's proposal can be implemented in the elementary classroom.

A sample lesson plan incorporating the concepts introduced in this chapter appears on p. 24.

VIGNETTE 1.2   Book Projects for Multiple Intelligences

As she pulled out her calendar to begin drafting lesson plans, Mrs. Weber thought back to her own elementary school years. She remembered "living" for recess and gym class; the opportunity to kick a soccer ball or run across the playground for a game of tag released her pent-up energy and made her feel alive. She had also enjoyed math, especially as she moved into the higher grades and the work moved from the basics of arithmetic to higher-level reasoning and analysis.

But neither gym nor geometry could help her with the reading, writing, and listening skills required so often throughout the rest of the curriculum. Although the other students seemed to excel, she disliked writing reports and creating stories. She often felt out of place and wondered if she was as smart as the other students.

After she took an introductory educational psychology class during her freshman year at the university, Mrs. Weber discovered the reason behind her childhood struggles: Although she was extremely gifted in mathematics and had above-average motor skills, her language arts class work tapped into other kinds of intelligence. Mrs. Weber felt relieved to learn that her intelligence was just as real, and as valuable, as that of her classmates who loved to read and write. At the end of "Ed Psych," she decided to become a teacher and to create a classroom environment that encouraged many forms of giftedness. Today she loved every minute of teaching fifth grade.

She smiled as she allowed herself one more moment of nostalgia. *But this won't get my lessons planned*, she thought to herself. *I'd better get to work*. Not surprisingly, she had already planned the week's math lesson, as well as most of the other subjects. This afternoon she would plan language arts.

The class had been reading Raskin's Newbery Award–winning young adult novel, *The Westing Game* (1997). On Wednesday they would finish the "puzzle mystery" and begin work on individual projects based on the story. Instead of one paper or assignment, she wanted to offer a variety of options for different learning styles and give each student the opportunity to choose one.

Although developing projects for her linguistically gifted students was the most straightforward option, she wanted to guard against simply assigning another book report. After several moments of thought, she decided that some of her students would enjoy authoring a chapter themselves. *The Westing Game* concluded with an interesting epilogue that revisited each character some 20 years after the main story. Imagining what might happen next would require students to build on their knowledge of the book's many characters and consider its themes from a fresh angle. In many ways it would help the students master the material as well as a book report, with the additional bonus of challenging their creative writing skills.

However, the children gifted with logical and mathematical skills would find that assignment frustrating, and she'd already brainstormed a project this group could complete. Because the entire novel contained clues to help the reader solve its big mystery, this assignment would ask students to review the story and complete a large chart analyzing when the author included each clue, why she may have chosen that point in the story, what it led the reader to believe, and what the clue ultimately meant. Like all good mysteries, the book intentionally included lots of possible suspects and potential motives, and students choosing this assignment would need to review each page to do a good job.

When first thinking about an option for the children with spatial intelligence, Mrs. Weber considered asking the students to create a diorama or "shadow box" of a scene. However, this project, like the others, needed to encompass the entire story and not only one moment or chapter. Since many of the novel's crucial scenes took place in the Westing mansion, and because it served as a key symbol throughout the story, she decided these students would draw a floorplan or blueprint of the mansion and mark the location of integral moments. Then, after pinpointing the "where" of the action, students would also be asked the "why": Mrs. Weber would require a one-page paper explaining the significance of each moment in relation to the rest of the story. She quickly developed a list of plot points for the children to use as a checklist. The assignment would allow students to "see" in three dimensions—and would definitely require a thorough knowledge of the book.

Some of the kinesthetically gifted students would enjoy this assignment as well, but she decided to provide another option for those with a knack for acting. Several other teachers in the school experimented with readers theatre (RT); with its emphasis on dramatic interpretation of written works, minimal use of sets and costumes, and acceptance of reading scripts rather than memorizing lines, an RT project could be a great success.

Mrs. Weber realized this option would require students to form groups of three or four and work together to review narrative passages, assign dialogue, and practice. She identified six scenes that her beginning actors could script and perform and created a sign-up sheet for interested students. She would ask each group to choose three of the six scenes, perform them for the class, and briefly explain the significance of each scene and its relation to the book's themes. Mrs. Weber decided to allow groups to choose a few of the same scenes; the overlap would reinforce the material to the students watching the performances and might even lead to an interesting classroom discussion after the groups completed the assignment.

She glanced at her watch and was relieved to see she had just enough time to plan one more project. Although she wanted to provide options for every learning style, several didn't lend themselves to this material. She'd finish with a project idea for interpersonal intelligence and create musical and intrapersonal opportunities at other points.

For the interpersonal assignment, she would offer interested students the chance to play "armchair psychologist." *The Westing Game* featured 16 fascinating characters, including an attention-seeking secretary, a guilt-driven judge, and a rebellious daughter. In addition to propelling the action forward, these characters and their secrets made the book a spellbinding read. So for this project, Mrs. Weber would ask the children to write a two- or three-paragraph analysis of each character's motivations, character flaws, strengths, and behavior. Why did Mr. Hoo ignore his wife? Why did Grace Wexler care so much about her reputation? Completing this assignment would, again, encourage a complete understanding of the book, and in a way her interpersonally gifted students would love.

It was getting late, and Mrs. Weber needed to get home and start dinner. She stacked her weekly planner, the list of plot points and characters, and her worn paperback copy of the novel on her desk and thought once more about her own fifth-grade experience. She might have learned more of the material—and enjoyed the process more—if only her teachers had appreciated her unique gifts. She couldn't change the past, but what a delight to make a difference for her own students.

Assessment

Most state departments of education and school districts mandate the implementation of English language arts standards, which include what is to be taught at each grade level and how students will demonstrate mastery of that information. Teachers need to begin with those standards to guide their instructional planning. However, it is extremely important, especially for ELLs, that each student's strengths and needs be included in that planning.

For several reasons a variety of assessments should accompany the standardized testing used to measure success in meeting the standards. First, to avoid placing students in an inappropriate program, their test results should be confirmed and clarified with interviews, work samples, demonstrations, and anecdotal records. Their language skills may cloud the results of a standardized assessment. Second, to avoid making instructional decisions by comparing the scores of ELL students to those of a very different normed group, other results should be considered along with the standardized results. Finally, a variety of assessments should accompany the standardized testing to take advantage of the interrelatedness of the language arts. Finding out what students already know, what they need or want to know, and how they can learn it not only helps clarify the results of the standardized testing but also assists the teacher in guiding the students to success on the standards for the English language arts.

Working With English Language Learners

Beginning ELLs: The IRA/NCTE standards, which are shared by all states, include concepts that will help make the beginning ELL student successful. According to this document, students will make use of their first language to develop competency in the English language arts and also to develop understanding across the curriculum.

Early intermediate and intermediate ELLs: Students at this level need academic support, which is addressed in the standards. They employ a range of strategies, use a variety of technological and informational resources, and use spoken, written, and visual language to accomplish their own purposes.

Early advanced and advanced ELLs: Early advanced and advanced ELLs continue to be successful as they adjust their use of spoken, written, and visual language to communicate effectively for different purposes with different audiences.

Practical Instructional Activities and Ideas

- *Listening center:* To develop listening skills, the teacher should set up a listening center for the students that may be used for a variety of purposes: to listen to books for enjoyment, to listen to sections of textbooks, and to record and listen to their own reading for fluency practice.

- *Microphone:* To develop speaking skills, the teacher should have a microphone available for the students to use when they share their ideas, present information, and read aloud.

- *Timed reading for fluency:* To develop reading fluency skills, the teacher pairs up the students and has them time each other when reading an appropriate passage (one that is at their instructional level) to see how many words each student can read in one minute. This is the cold read, and they graph the score on their chart in one color. The students then practice reading the entire passage together. After practicing, the students time each other again and chart the new, improved score in a different color.

- *Book clubs:* To develop reading comprehension skills, students meet in book clubs or literature circles to read and discuss a book at their instructional level. The teacher offers minilessons teaching comprehension strategies before each session. During the session, the teacher acts as the facilitator to lift the level of conversation and participation.

- *Writers' workshop:* To develop writing skills, students may participate in a daily writing workshop. The block of time begins with a five- to ten-minute minilesson by the teacher directly instructing writing skills and applications. This is followed by 30 minutes of independent writing time in which the students engage in the writing process, including peer and teacher response. The session ends with a five- to ten-minute group sharing session for celebration and clarification.

- *Direct drawing:* To develop viewing and visual representation skills, the teacher selects any social studies or science standard to use as the basis for a direct drawing. For instance, to help the students understand the path of electricity from the power plant to the home, the teacher draws and tells the story sequentially, one part at a time, on chart paper in front of the class as the students listen and draw on their own piece of 12″ × 18″ drawing paper. The students later use their own drawings to tell the story.

LESSON PLAN 1.1   Visual Representation

Language Art Components: Viewing and Visual Representation

Grades: 3–5

Topic: Literature

Time Frame: one week

Objective

Students improve viewing and visual representation skills by working collaboratively.

Materials

- *The Mysteries of Harris Burdick* by Chris Van Allsburg
- Narrative story maps
- Writing paper
- 12" × 18" drawing paper
- Charcoal pencils

Content Standards

English Language Development (ELD): Viewing and Visual Representation

- Students use spoken, written, and visual language to accomplish their own purposes (e.g., for learning, enjoyment, persuasion, and the exchange of information).

Vocabulary

- Vignette
- Story map
- Graphic organizer

Procedures

Day 1

- The teacher shows the class one of the pages from *The Mysteries of Harris Burdick*. As a group the class verbally describes the illustration and begins orally constructing a short story to solve the mystery of the page. As they talk the teacher fills in a narrative story map using their ideas.

- The teacher divides the class into groups of four. Two of the four students in each group receive one of the other pages from *The Mysteries of Harris Burdick,* and the other two receive a third page. The students do not let anyone see the page except their partners.
- Together the two students examine the illustration and then speculate and discuss what might be happening. As they discuss, the students fill in the story map that will help them draft their vignette to explain their interpretation of the page.

Day 2

- The teacher reviews the previous lesson. Using the story map from the first day discussed by the class as a whole, the class and the teacher draft a short narrative to describe the scene and offer a solution to the mystery.
- The students each go back to the same partner, and using their story map, the pair writes a short narrative describing and explaining the illustration and the solution to their mystery page.
- Students continue drafting, revising, and editing.

Day 3

- Without showing the illustrations from the book, the pairs in the group switch stories.
- The students read the story the other pair has written and using charcoal pencils sketch a drawing on the 12" × 18" paper to depict their interpretation of the story.

Day 4

- Students meet in their groups of four and share the visual representations they have made of each other's stories. All four compare their creations with the book illustrations and discuss the work. The teacher leads the students in a discussion of revisions that might be made to the writing to help clarify it for the artists. This discussion highlights the importance of using accurate words and descriptions.
- Each group glues the student writing, student illustrations, and book illustrations onto a piece of poster board to display.

Assessment

Day 5

- Each group of four stands in front of a different poster to observe and discuss it.
- After three minutes, the teacher rings a bell and the students rotate to the next poster.
- The class continues in this manner until the students return to their starting place.
- The class meets as a group to reflect on their learning.

Integration Across the Curriculum

Science and Social Studies

- Students watch a *Bill Nye the Science Guy* video one time to listen and enjoy it. The second time they view it, they take notes on a graphic organizer; these notes include at least one key idea and two or three details about that idea. Students write a paragraph to tell what was learned through viewing the video and then illustrate the completed paragraph. They share and display the work.
- Students draw a map displaying the route taken by an explorer as it is described in the text.

Literature

- The teacher chooses a passage from a piece of children's literature with particularly descriptive language, for example, *Amos and Boris* by William Steig (1992), *Cherries and Cherry Pits* by Vera B. Williams (1991), or *Charlotte's Web* by E. B. White (2004). The teacher gives each student a copy of the passage on the bottom of a 12″ × 18″ piece of drawing paper. The students draw an illustration to represent their interpretation of the text.

Visual and Performing Arts

- Students create a travel brochure after reading a story from another country.
- Students create a collage or PowerPoint presentation about a historical event.
- Students pantomime the actions in a wordless picture book.]

Health

- Teams of students create a presentation in the medium of their choice (poem, song, poster, choral reading, etc.) to express how to maintain a healthy body and/or mind.

Physical Education

- Students play a "Follow the Directions" relay game. The teacher divides the class into several teams, which line up next to each other. The first person in each line runs for the team bucket, which is placed directly across the field from each team's line. The student reaches in and takes out one of the cards. He or she reads the directions out loud and does what it tells him or her to do. For example, the card might say, "Put your hands on your shoulders, jump up and down, and recite the alphabet." The student follows the directions, runs back to the line, tags the next person so he or she can run to the bucket, and, finally, sits at the end of the line. The first team to have everyone back to the line and sitting wins.

Music

- Students listen to CDs of sounds from different biomes such as the rainforest or the desert. They make a sketch of an image or scene they visualized as they listen.
- Students learn and perform songs to help them remember the different parts of speech.

Parents as Partners

- *Visits to the classroom:* Parents may come to the classroom to view or to help videotape student performances.
- *Homework reading log:* Parents listen to their child read daily and record the number of minutes in a reading log.
- *Exploring on the Web:* Parents visit educational Web sites with their children either on a home computer or at the local library.
- *Taking picture walks:* Parents participate in picture walks with their child before they read textbooks and/or a piece of fiction.
- *Sending in pictures from home:* Parents select and send in photographs and magazine pictures for the students to use as subjects for discussion and writing.

Student Study Site

The Companion Web site for *Language Arts: Integrating Skills for Classroom Teaching*
www.sagepub.com/donoghuestudy
Visit the Web-based study site to enhance your understanding of the chapter content. The study materials include chapter summaries, practice tests, flashcards, and Web resources.

Additional Professional Readings

Berghoff, B., Egawa, K., Harste, J., & Hoonan, B. (2000). *Beyond reading and writing: Inquiry, curriculum, and multiple ways of knowing.* Urbana, IL: National Council of Teachers of English.

Bomer, K. (2005). Missing the children: When politics and programs impede our teaching. *Language Arts, 83,* 168–176.

Glasgow, J. (1999). Recognizing students' multiple intelligences in cross-age buddy journals. *English Journal, 88,* 88–96.

Goodman, Y. (2003). *Valuing language: Inquiry into language for elementary and middle school.* Urbana, IL: National Council of Teachers of English.

Johnston, P. (2004). *Choice of words: How our language affects children's learning.* Portland, ME: Stenhouse.

Lightbown, P., & Spada, N. (1999). *How languages are learned.* Oxford: Oxford University Press.

Marquez-Zenkow, K. (2003). The "public art" of language arts: A new lens on educational standards. *Language Arts, 80,* 384–391.

Ohanian, S. (1999). *One size fits few: The folly of educational standards.* Portsmouth, NH: Heinemann.

Seefeldt, C. (2005). *How to work with standards in the early childhood curriculum.* New York: Teachers College Press.

Van Sluys, K., & Laman, T. (2006). Learning about language: Written conversations and elementary language learners. *The Reading Teacher, 60,* 222–233.

Children's Literature Cited in the Text

Ahlberg, J., & Ahlberg, A. (2006). *The jolly postman: Or other people's letters.* New York: Little, Brown.

Aliki. (1999). *My visit to the zoo.* New York: Harper Trophy.

Coerr, E. (2003). *Mieko and the fifth treasure.* New York: Puffin.

Ehlert, L. (1991). *Red leaf, yellow leaf.* San Diego, CA: Harcourt.

Hoffman, M. (1991). *Amazing Grace.* New York: Dial.

Leedy, L. (1996). *The edible pyramid: Good eating every day.* New York: Holiday House.

Lobel, A. (1983). *The book of pigericks*. New York: HarperCollins.

MacLachlan, P. (2004). *Sarah, plain and tall*. New York: Joanna Cotler.

Martin, B., Jr., & Archambault, J. (1988). *The ghost-eye tree*. New York: Henry Holt.

McCully, E. A. (1992). *Mirette on the high wire*. New York: Putnam.

Parker, N. W., & Wright, J. R. (1988). *Bugs*. New York: HarperCollins.

Paulsen, G. (2002). *Woodsong*. New York: Aladdin.

Raskin, E. (1997). *The Westing game*. New York: Puffin.

Rathmann, P. (1995). *Officer Buckle and Gloria*. New York: Putnam.

Ringgold, F. (1991). *Tar Beach*. New York: Crown.

Rosen, M. (1997). *We're going on a bear hunt*. New York: Little Simon.

Say, A. (1996). *Emma's rug*. New York: Houghton.

Siebert, D. (1989). *Heartland*. New York: HarperCollins.

Smith, D. B. (1988). *Return to Bitter Creek*. New York: Puffin.

Steig, W. (1992). *Amos and Boris*. New York: Farrar, Straus and Giroux.

Van Allsburg, C. (1984). *The mysteries of Harris Burdick*. New York: Houghton.

White, E. B. (2004). *Charlotte's web*. New York: Harper Trophy.

Wiesner, D. (1992). *June 29, 1999*. New York: Clarion.

Wiesner, D. (1997). *Tuesday*. New York: Clarion.

Wiesner, D. (2006). *Flotsam*. New York: Clarion.

Williams, V. B. (1984). *Three days on a river in a red canoe*. New York: Harper Trophy.

Williams, V. B. (1991). *Cherries and cherry pits*. New York: Harper Trophy.

References

Armstrong, T. (1994). *Multiple intelligence in the classroom*. Arlington, VA: Association for Supervision and Curriculum Development.

Bruner, J. (1986). *Actual minds, possible worlds*. Cambridge, MA: Harvard University Press.

Chomsky, N. (1974). *Aspects of the theory of syntax*. Cambridge, MA: Harvard University Press.

Clay, M. (1991). Introducing a new storybook to young readers. *The Reading Teacher, 43,* 264–273.

Cramer, R. (2001). *Creative power: The nature and nurture of children's writing*. New York: Longman.

Derry, S., & Murphy, D. (1986). Designing systems that train learning ability: From theory to practice. *Review of Educational Research, 56,* 1–39.

Flood, J., Lapp, D., & Wood, K. (1998). Viewing: The neglected communication process or "when what you see isn't what you get." *The Reading Teacher, 52,* 300–304.

Foster, G., Sawicki, E., Schaeffer, H., & Zelinski, V. (2002). *I think, therefore I learn*. Portland, ME: Stenhouse.

Gardner, H. (1983). *Frames of mind: The theories of multiple intelligences*. New York: Basic Books.

Gardner, H. (2000). *Intelligence reframed: Multiple intelligences for the 21st century*. New York: Basic Books.

Gardner, H. (2003, April). *Multiple intelligences after twenty years*. Paper presented at the American Educational Association, Chicago.

Gleason, J. (Ed.). (1989). *The development of language* (2nd ed.). Columbus, OH: Merrill.

Gordon, R. (Ed.). (2005). *Ethnologue: Languages of the world* (15th ed.). Dallas: SIL International.

Halliday, M. (1976). *System and function in language*. London: Oxford University Press.

Hammer, D. (1998). *The standards teacher*. Washington, DC: Council for Basic Education.

Heide, A., & Stilborne, L. (1999). *The teacher's complete and easy guide to the Internet*. New York: Teachers College Press.

International Association of Teachers of Reading and National Council of Teachers of English. (1996). *Standards for the English language arts*. Newark, DE, & Urbana, IL: Author

Jusczyk, P. (1997). *The discovery of spoken language*. Cambridge: MIT Press.

National Reading Panel. (2000). *Report of the National Reading Panel*. Washington, DC: National Institute of Child Health and Human Development Clearinghouse.

Pappas, C., Kiefer, B., & Levstik, I. (1999). *Integrated language perspective in the elementary school* (3rd ed.). Boston: Allyn & Bacon.

Piaget, J. (1962). *The language and thought of the child*. New York: Humanities Press.

Shore, R. (1997). *Rethinking the brain: New insights into early development*. New York: Families and Work Institute.

Sousa, D. (2006). *How the brain learns*. Thousand Oaks, CA: Corwin Press.

Spafford, C., Pesce, A., & Grosser, G. (1998). *The cyclopedic education dictionary*. Albany, NY: Delmar.

Temple, C., Martinez, M., Yokota, J., & Naylor, A. (2002). *Children's books in children's hands* (2nd ed.). Boston: Allyn & Bacon.

Tierney, R., & Readence, J. (2000). *Reading strategies and practices*. Boston: Allyn & Bacon.

Tirosh, D. (1992). *Implicit and explicit knowledge: An educational approach*. Norwood, NJ: Ablex.

Venezky, R. (1999). *The American way of spelling: The structure and origins of American English orthography*. New York: Guilford.

Verhoeven, L., & Snow, C. (2001). *Literacy and motivation: Reading engagement in individuals and groups*. Mahwah, NJ: Lawrence Erlbaum.

Vygotsky, L. (1986). *Thought and language*. Cambridge: MIT Press.

Weaver, C. (1994). *Reading process and practice: From sociopsycholinguists to whole language*. Portsmouth, NH: Heinemann.

Anticipation Statement Answers

1. Agree

2. Agree

3. Disagree

4. Agree

5. Disagree

6. Agree

7. Agree

8. Agree

9. Agree; thinking is a brain function that infuses all of the language arts—it is not one of them. However, growth in the language arts occurs when students are given opportunities to think.

10. Disagree; language development deeply affects children's thinking. As students acquire language, they also acquire learning strategies and thought structures that can be used to read and write. Thinking and intellectual development may be enhanced by language development, but children who have problems with language development still develop intellectually.

Children as Language Learners and Thinkers

Small children are not taught a language but learn it by themselves without conscious effort and application. Because they seem to possess an inborn faculty for language generally, the language they learn depends wholly on the language—or languages—to which they are exposed until nearly the age of puberty.

By the time children are ready for kindergarten, they already have marvelous control over the syntax (word order), phonology (pronunciation), and semantics (meaning) of their native language as they have learned it from their families and playmates. The school then begins to share with the home and community the responsibility for children's language development. Both inside and outside the school environment, children continually increase their command of the language through such informal means as conversing; listening to adult dialogue; watching videos and television; reading signs, magazines, and books; and writing shopping lists and notes. Consequently, and to a greater extent than in any other discipline, the language arts program is built on a knowledge of each student's cultural and family background as well as his or her social, emotional, and intellectual development.

Due to the variety of student experiences at any level and in any grade, an effective program in language learning must focus on students as individuals. Girls and boys must be involved actively and positively in genuine learning situations that have meaning for them.

Anticipation Statements

Complete this exercise before reading Chapter 2.

Do you agree or disagree with the following statements? Circle your answer. Be prepared to discuss questions in blue.

1.	Small children are not taught a language, but learn it by themselves without conscious effort and application.	Agree	Disagree
2.	Models of natural language learning infer that, by interacting with others and using language for genuine reasons in natural settings, children learn language.	Agree	Disagree
3.	Cambourne's conditions of natural language learning are not applicable to natural literacy learning in the primary classroom.	Agree	Disagree
4.	The *behaviorists* believe that children learn their first language through imitation of adult models and environmental conditioning.	Agree	Disagree
5.	The *nativists* maintain that boys and girls learn their language from within themselves because language is innate.	Agree	Disagree
6.	The *cognitivists* believe that language development is dependent on cognition or thought structures.	Agree	Disagree
7.	There are not many factors that can alter the rate of normal language production.	Agree	Disagree
8.	Research has shown that second-language acquisition is different from first-language acquisition.	Agree	Disagree
9.	To better appraise the English Language Learners in their classroom, teachers should be aware of the stages through which second-language learners progress.	Agree	Disagree
10.	One guideline for enriching the language environment in the classroom is to promote active learning.	Agree	Disagree

Models of Natural Language Learning

Most children learn to talk without specific instruction in sounds, grammar, or meanings. They become proficient in language use rather effortlessly. Possible explanations for this ease of learning lie in the models of natural language learning that have been developed, separately, by researchers Holdaway (1979) and Cambourne (1988). Both models infer that, by interacting with others and using language for genuine reasons in natural settings, children learn language.

Holdaway's Model

Natural learning proceeds according to four steps: (1) observation of demonstration (e.g., Ana watches Mother set the table); (2) guided participation (Ana places the plates, cups, and silverware on the table as Mother watches); (3) unsupervised practice reenactment (Ana tries to set the table by herself, knowing that she can get assistance from Mother if necessary); and (4) performance: a celebration of accomplishment (e.g., Ana sets the table successfully as her family applauds).

In much the same way as Ana learned to set the table, children learn to talk (and later, to read and write): They watch others talking, they are encouraged to talk with the help of others, they talk on their own (often going between guided language use and independent efforts), and finally they master certain words or sentences. The last event is positively and happily reinforced by others.

Cambourne's Model

Believing that to learn to talk a person must both be a human being (not another species) *and* encounter certain operating conditions that allow language learning to occur, Cambourne specified seven conditions necessary for language learning. These seem to apply to all kinds of language learning, including learning to read and write *and* learning a second language.

1. *Immersion:* Children are surrounded by successful users of the language that they will eventually learn, and so they absorb the rhythms, sounds, and meanings of that language. Furthermore, the language they learn is not nonsense or fragmented language but purposeful and whole. *In school,* the teacher arranges for immersion.

2. *Demonstration:* Language users in the children's environment model hundreds of meaningful uses of spoken language (e.g., during mealtime, at the market, in the park, at bedtime). Both the vast number of these demonstrations and their frequent repetition help children incorporate the conventions used for meaningful language production. *In school,* the teacher arranges for demonstration.

Applicable IRA/NCTE Standards

Standard 4	Students adjust their use of spoken, written, and visual language (e.g., conventions, style, vocabulary) to communicate effectively with a variety of audiences and for different purposes.
Standard 9	Students develop an understanding of and respect for diversity in language use, patterns, and dialects across cultures, ethnic groups, geographic regions, and social roles.
Standard 10	Students whose first language is not English make use of their first language to develop competency in the English language arts and to develop understanding of content across the curriculum.

SOURCE: *Standards for the English Language Arts*, by the International Reading Association and the National Council of Teachers of English, Copyright 1996 by the International Reading Association and the National Council of Teachers of English. Reprinted with permission. http://www.ncte.org/about/over/standards/110846.htm

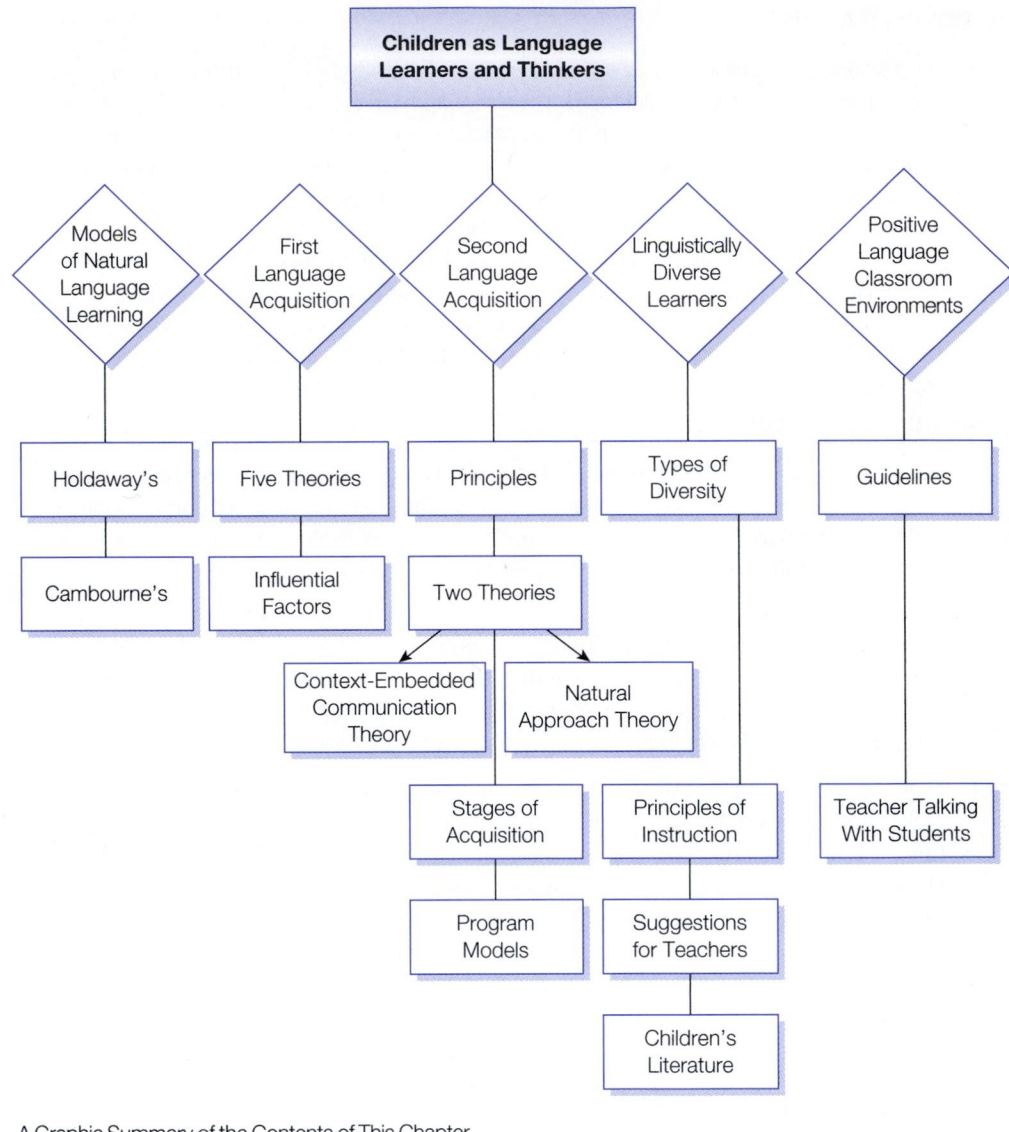

A Graphic Summary of the Contents of This Chapter

---

3. *Expectation:* A subtle form of communication that children acquire from parents and family, expectation helps them learn language and master it. Thus, when learning language, they do not experience the type of pressure or anxiety that may come with learning, for example, to play the piano. *In school,* the teacher sets standards that are realistically demanding, and so children can be expected to attain them successfully.

4. *Responsibility*: Children bear the complete responsibility for the order and pace of their language learning. They master certain grammatical constructions in different combinations and at different ages. By the time they start kindergarten, however, they have all reached approximately the same state of first-language use. Nevertheless, they have attained that goal through different paths since they bear the power to make decisions about their own involvement in the learning. *In school,* therefore, responsibility is a condition that the students bring to the learning process.

5. *Approximation:* Closely tied to the expectation condition that children will talk, approximation involves adult acceptance and celebration of their children's efforts to speak. Were the caregiver prone to constantly correcting early pronunciation and grammatical constructions, children would talk less. However, through encouragement by the caregiver, children's approximations gradually become closer to adult speech. *In school,* approximation is a condition that the students bring to the learning process.

6. *Use or employment:* Children talk all day long in many settings during virtually every activity. By so doing, they have endless opportunities to practice the conventions of oral language whenever they wish to communicate. Were this speech to be restricted, however, it would reduce the amount of practice the children receive, and more important, it would be an unnatural situation. *In school,* use is a condition that the students bring to the learning process.

7. *Response:* In response to considerable and specialized feedback from parents or caregivers, children progress from using single words (e.g., "Milk") to phrases (e.g., "Chocolate milk"), to complete sentences (e.g., "I want some chocolate milk"). Concerned parents or caregivers will often (a) repeat a child's message but expand on it, thereby modeling adult use of conventions, and (b) react to the child's intended meaning. Feedback must be given again and again, always focused on the meaning of the language, so the child will continue efforts to become language proficient. *In school,* the teacher arranges response.

Note that, while based on language development, Cambourne's conditions of natural language learning are also applicable to natural literacy learning in the primary classroom.

First-Language Acquisition

Young children in all cultures appear to master the complex task of acquiring an understanding of the phonology (sound units), morphology (meaning units), syntax (rules of grammar), and semantics (variations in meaning) of their native language. This competence enables them to produce an infinite variety of sentences, to understand and make judgments about sentences, and to develop an unconscious awareness of both the limitations and creative capacity of language. Most of this knowledge is acquired early in life (primarily between the ages of two and five) without direct instruction. Psycholinguists are still investigating how children attain this knowledge; thus far, they have not been able to generate any explanation that is acceptable to everyone.

The best-known theories or perspectives of how language is acquired and how it works once it is acquired are the behaviorist, the nativist, the cognitivist, and the social-interactionist. The most recently developed theory—a neurobiological perspective—supports elements of the others.

The *behaviorists* believe that children learn their first language through imitation of adult models and environmental conditioning. Children who produce desired language patterns receive social and material reinforcements as rewards. Critics of this theory contend, however, that (1) children utter certain expressions that they have never heard anyone say (so their language is hardly a faithful imitation), (2) children's speech is highly resistant to alteration by adult intervention, and (3) the practical task of memorizing all of the possible language structures is virtually impossible.

The *nativists* maintain that boys and girls learn their language from within themselves because language is innate: Children are preprogrammed (or "hard-wired") genetically to acquire it. Chomsky (1965) has termed this innate capacity an LAD (language acquisition device). Supporters of this theory contend that (1) the onset and accomplishment of minimal language development seem unaffected by linguistic or cultural variations; (2) language cannot be taught to nonhuman forms of life, whereas the suppression of language acquisition among humans is almost impossible; and (3) only humans possess the necessary physiological and anatomical features to engage in sustained language. Opponents argue that language learning cannot be separated from cognitive development.

The *cognitivists* believe that language development is dependent on cognition or thought structures. According to Piaget (1962), thinking is a prerequisite of language that develops as a result of reasoning and experiencing. Children develop knowledge of the world generally (nonlinguistic knowledge) and then "map" this knowledge onto language relations and categories. Any teaching aimed at developing the intellect will simultaneously promote language, and students can learn to impose prior knowledge of language systems to give meaning to new information. Opponents of this theory contend, however, that, because new knowledge can be generated through talking and writing, language itself affects cognition.

The *social-interactionists* acknowledge the influence of both the behaviorists and the nativists. In addition, however, they also emphasize the child's personal participation in language learning and the construction of meaning. Their view of language development is based on the work of Vygotsky (1986), who believed that language develops amid social interaction and language use. Children internalize the way that their society uses language to represent meaning, but they need adult support to help their language growth within their zone of proximal development (or the distance between their independent level and their potential level).

While the theories of language acquisition already discussed were developed by linguists, psychologists, and anthropologists who had to infer language origins and brain activity from observations of *external* behavior, since the 1980s neuroscientists have been able to use noninvasive brain-imaging techniques to record and display *internal* three-dimensional images of a living brain as it processes information (Sochurek, 1987). According to the *neurobiologists,* the ability to learn language starts with brain cells called neurons that emerge during the early stages of fetal development and grow at a rate of 250,000 per minute (Swerdlow, 1995). As neurons multiply, they proceed along a complex genetic path; brain imaging has allowed scientists to pinpoint specific areas in the brain devoted to hearing, speaking, and interpreting language. Infant brains are born capable of speaking any of the more than 3,000 human languages (Kuhl, 1993). However, Sylvester (1995) believes that the language a child actually learns depends on the language that he or she hears spoken in the home. Furthermore, parents and caregivers who converse with infants and young children help them develop neural networks that lead to language proficiency and fluency (Kotulak, 1997; Oates & Grayson, 2004; Sprenger, 1999).

Factors Influencing Language Acquisition

Several factors, in addition to medical problems such as hearing loss, can alter the rate of normal language production. The first of these is *gender differences*, with the majority of girls talking earlier and more than the majority of boys (Kalb & Namuth, 1997). However, although research supports the dominant role of nature in language acquisition, the matter of nurture cannot be overlooked: Adults engage in longer conversations with girls than they do with boys. Huttenlocher (1991) suggests that girls talk earlier and talk more because they receive language stimulation that boys do not.

The second factor is *socioeconomic differences,* with children from professional families having more than three times the linguistic input by age four than children from welfare families (Hart & Risley, 1995). Furthermore, while both middle-income and lower-income mothers spent considerable time nurturing their infants, it was only the middle-income women who interacted verbally with the children and so fostered both receptive and expressive language.

The third factor is *cultural differences*. Attention must be given to the needs that verbal language meets in a particular culture because spoken language is a reflection of that culture. Babies who are carried around much of the time, for example, learn to send messages nonverbally (Bhavnagri & Gonzales-Mena, 1997), whereas babies who are physically apart from their caregivers learn verbal communication. Furthermore, in some cultures receptive language is emphasized and children are taught to listen as their adults speak.

Second-Language Acquisition

Research has shown that second-language acquisition is similar to first-language acquisition (Spangenberg-Urbschat & Pritchard, 1994). From that research can be abstracted three principles: (1) The age of the learner does not matter because learning strategies are similar, whether the students are young children, older boys and girls, or adults; (2) just as they did when learning their first language, second-language learners move through developmental stages; and (3) second-language learners must have the opportunity to use the new language for genuine purposes in meaningful situations—just as they did when acquiring their first language.

Two linguists offering theories in the area of second-language acquisition are James Cummins of Canada and Stephen Krashen of the United States. The first proposes the context-embedded communication theory. The second advocates the natural approach.

Cummins (1980) believes that *context-embedded communication* (i.e., the amount of contextual support available when a person is learning a second language) determines his or her proficiency in two critical dimensions of language: (1) basic interpersonal communication skills (BICS) that are used routinely in social situations and take two years of practice for the average second-language learner to acquire and (2) cognitive academic language proficiency (CALP), which is concerned with school tasks that demand five to seven years of practice for the average second-language learner to acquire. CALP is further broken down into two categories: (1) context-embedded communication occurring between speakers and often supported by contextual clues and (2) context-reduced communication in which there are few clues to meaning. There are also cognitively hard, demanding tasks such as writing a report and cognitively easy, undemanding tasks such as standing in the lunch line.

A major goal of schooling, according to Cummins (1980), is to teach the child to manipulate and understand cognitively demanding context-reduced text. The more that literacy instruction can be related to the child's experience, the more successful it will be. This same concept holds for second-language instruction.

The major goal of the natural approach that Krashen (1982) advocates is the development of communication skills. He distinguishes between language learning and language acquisition, believing that the first is associated with school and involves learning grammar rules and new vocabulary as well as the ability to translate from one language to another; the second is a nearly subconscious process that permits the learner to function in a given setting. Such production of language must emerge in stages and teaching must encompass language acquisition activities that lower children's anxiety and promote self-confidence. This theory has five hypotheses:

1. Acquisition learning hypothesis, which differentiates natural acquisition through daily use in genuine communication from the formal learning of language rules

2. Natural order hypothesis, which infers that language rules are learned in a sequential order

3. Monitor hypothesis, which implies that learning the rules only facilitates self-correction but not the acquisition of language

4. Input hypothesis, which stresses that language acquisition (not language learning) develops from understanding messages somewhat beyond the learner's present level of proficiency

5. Affective filter hypothesis, which states that language acquisition will increase when students have low levels of anxiety but are highly motivated and confident, but will decrease when they have high levels of anxiety, lack confidence, and are unmotivated to speak the new language.

One of the keys to second-language acquisition, according to Krashen (1982), is being exposed to comprehensible input or meaningful communication comprised of the following: topics related to the student's prior knowledge, paralinguistic clues (e.g., gestures), contextual clues (e.g., common objects in familiar settings), language already known to the student plus some new vocabulary, and linguistic modifications (e.g., clear pronunciation, slower speech). Comprehensible input has been described succinctly as the type of speech used to communicate with young children.

To better appraise English Language Learners (ELLs) in their classroom, teachers should be aware of the stages through which second-language learners progress. According to Krashen and Terrell (1987), those stages are as follows:

- *Preproduction:* Silent stage, active listening and comprehension. This period lasts from a few hours to several weeks or even months. In this stage it is the teacher who talks most of the time, often using visual aids, with the students responding to simple directions (e.g., "Touch your nose").
- *Early production:* Single words and short phrases. This period lasts from a few months to a year or longer as students begin to speak. The teacher asks questions that demand one-word answers or a mere "yes" or "no" (e.g., "What is your brother's name?" and "Do you have a pet?").
- *Extending production:* Use of sentences, longer narratives, and English conventions. This period occurs slowly, taking up to three years, and includes open-ended dialogues and open-ended sentences. It is further broken down into three levels: intermediate fluency, advanced fluency, and speech emergence.

A simple lesson using the natural approach, as suggested by Hadaway, Vardell, and Young (2002), uses picture books or poems about families. The teacher shares pictures of different kinds of families, using new vocabulary while pointing to the family members, and then hands out books to the students. After key vocabulary has been introduced through a series of visual examples distributed to the class, the teacher starts to ask questions of the students (e.g., "Who has a picture with a baby?"). Next, the teacher draws a picture of his or her own family and labels the members, encouraging the children to each do the same with their own family. Finally, the teacher writes a sentence about his or her family. Beginning ELLs may draw a family picture and choose either to label the members or write a short sentence about their family.

Program Models

Following the work of Krashen and Cummins, as well as that of other linguists in the field of *second-language* acquisition, three different program models have emerged in schools (Peregoy & Boyle, 1997). These models are in accordance with educational theories used to explain *first-language* acquisition discussed earlier in this chapter:

1. *Pull-out programs:* Second-language students leave their homeroom or regular classroom for daily lessons in another classroom where a specialist works with them until they are proficient in English and can thereby function in all subjects in the regular classroom. These programs have become less common, due both to their costs and the research findings that students learn English more quickly by simply interacting with native English speakers in their homeroom (Goodman & Freeman, 1993).

2. *Total immersion programs:* Second-language students spend the day in the regular classroom where they learn English alongside others their own age (Freeman & Freeman, 2001).

3. *Nature and nurture programs (which have different names):* These emphasize both Vygotsky's social interaction and Krashen's comprehensible input theories. When only one language besides English is being used in the classroom (e.g., Korean), a bilingual teacher or paraprofessional first explains a concept in English, then checks for understanding in English, and finally repeats the concept in the other language. The bonus feature of these programs is that native English speakers benefit because they can learn a second language.

Linguistically Diverse Learners

Although **diversity** exists in every elementary classroom in matters of race, gender, ethnicity, and special education needs, three broad types of diversity must receive particular recognition: academic diversity (i.e., learning style and pace), cultural diversity (i.e., the students' background experiences, family, and socioeconomic status), and linguistic diversity. Many teachers must concentrate on students in the last group while keeping in mind the other two types of diversity that may affect second-language learning and learners.

Students exhibiting linguistic diversity fall into several groups:(a) those who speak dialects representative of the regional location in the United States where they previously lived, (b) those who were born in the United States of parents who had come from another country and speak only that language in the home, and (c) children who were not born in the United States but came from another country and are divided between long-term residents and recent arrivals. Except for those African American students who speak a distinct dialect known as Black English, the vast majority of linguistically diverse students in the elementary classroom are ELLs.

Before they start kindergarten, native English speakers have had five or more years of oral language and cultural background. Most English second-language learners have had a similar experience in oral language except that theirs was in a different cultural background and a different language—which cannot be discounted or termed deficient.

Teachers should acknowledge and value diversity as they implement certain principles in their instruction with these ELLs (Delpit, 1995; Fitzgerald, 1993; Freeman & Freeman, 2001), just as Miss Wiseman does with her kindergarten class in Vignette 2.1.

For material related to this concept, go to Video Clip 2.1 on the Student Resource CD bound into the back of your textbook.

Linguistically diverse learners exist in many elementary classrooms.

VIGNETTE 2.1   Teaching Cultural Diversity

Miss Wiseman completely agreed with the state mandate that the kindergarten language arts experience should help students understand their culture and the cultures of others. For years she'd created bulletin boards, read picture books, and shown photographs to help her young students develop an awareness of the larger world. She had organized holiday observances and even invited guest speakers.

But as she began her fifth year of teaching, Miss Wiseman wanted to try something new. She'd completed two graduate courses over the summer and came away from the classes convinced that students—especially her five- and six-year-olds—developed literacy as much from speaking and listening as they did from reading and writing. Her previous attempts at building cultural awareness had primarily used rather didactic methods; creating opportunities for more personal involvement with the concepts would both improve the students' language skills and enhance their multicultural appreciation.

Miss Wiseman decided to link portions of classroom work to the real cultures, ethnic backgrounds, and daily lives of her young students. For several weeks she shared books about Native Americans, African Americans, and other groups during the daily read-aloud story time. In addition to highlighting these North American cultural experiences, she also included nonfiction books full of interesting pictures and facts about Asian, South American, and European countries. After each story time she led the class in a conversation about connections between the story or information and their own experiences.

Toward the end of January, Miss Wiseman read *Lanterns and Firecrackers: A Chinese New Year Story* (Zucker, 2003). The children enjoyed learning about the special foods, parades, and other traditions associated with this ancient holiday.

"The Chinese New Year will happen in just a few weeks," Miss Wiseman said. She planned to segue from the story into the explanation of a new activity—but Henry beat her to it.

"Audrey, will you have firecrackers and go to parades?" Henry asked. Although Audrey was born in America, her parents, grandparents, and most other relatives were Chinese. Miss Wiseman waited to see how Audrey would receive the question.

"Yes, and this year I get to help make some of the big dinner," she said with a smile.

"Henry, I liked your question," said Miss Wiseman. "And Audrey, thank you for your answer. It's fun to tell each other about our families and our culture, isn't it?" The children nodded.

"I want to try something new in our story times," she said, continuing with her explanation. "Each one of you has a family story. For some of you, like Audrey, it's because your moms and dads or your grandmas and grandpas came from another country. Others of you might be like me—my family has lived in America a very long time. But my family of many years ago, my ancestors, also came here from another place."

She paused to let the idea sink in. "So here's what I want you to do. You can work on this tonight or this weekend, whenever your mommy or daddy has time. I want you to ask one of your parents or grand-parents to tell you your family story—what country your ancestors came from and how long ago. Maybe they can tell you a story about growing up in another place or show you pictures. Work on this and we'll take turns telling our family stories during story time."

In addition to this introduction, Miss Wiseman made sure to include a fuller description of the project and its purpose in her weekly newsletter to the parents. She also encouraged parents to help their child draw a picture or bring an item that would help tell the family story.

On Monday after story time, Miss Wiseman asked for a volunteer to share his or her story. She was pleased to see several hands shoot into the air and selected Jasmine, an African American student, to begin.

Softly at first, then with growing confidence, Jasmine told the class about her "great and great and great grandparents" who came from Africa. She spoke about the different climate of Africa and commented, "My an . . . anc . . . Miss Wiseman, what was that word?"

"Ancestors," Miss Wiseman answered.

"Yeah, ancestors. They didn't want to come here but they had to come over on a boat."

"Why?" asked Tyler.

"They had to be slaves. They didn't get a choice. So they came over but now me and my family—we're not slaves."

Miss Wiseman listened carefully, ready to guide the potentially difficult conversation. "Many of our African American friends have ancestors who came from Africa—that's why we use that name for their culture," she explained. "Next month is Black History Month and we're going to talk more about this. For now, who has another question for Jasmine?"

"Me," said Andrew. "What did you bring in to show us?"

Jasmine grinned. "This is our kinara. We use it to hold candles during Kwanzaa."

"What's Kwanzaa?" Andrew asked.

Jasmine explained the holiday and her family's celebration each December.

"You mean you get more presents after Christmas?" Andrew exclaimed. "I want to do Kwanzaa."

Miss Wiseman smiled and ended the sharing time with a promise that another student could tell his or her story tomorrow. She felt energized from the teaching moment and thrilled that for a change it involved one student teaching another. The class had gained age-appropriate, easily understandable information about a cultural background from another peer. Just as important, while the class practiced active listening Jasmine had expanded her speaking skills and connected schoolwork to life outside of school. Eventually every student would have the same experience, and Miss Wiseman looked forward to the conversations.

For material related
to this concept, go
to Video Clip 2.2
on the Student
Resource CD bound
into the back of
your textbook.

- *Build the self-worth and dignity* of the second-language learners so they can participate fully in the classroom context.
- *Provide the children with a sense of family and caring,* showing them that classrooms can be a place where they are accepted and belong and where they have both privileges and responsibilities.
- *Facilitate authentic dialogue by encouraging talk* and allowing, respectfully, for cultural variations; language exercises do not promote genuine conversations.
- *Demand critical thinking* because second-language learners do not know less; they can only express less in the new language.
- *Assess children's needs* and then meet them with different learning styles that build on identified strengths.
- *Respect the children's home culture* and use the students' understanding of that culture to support their movement into a new culture.
- *Recognize linguistic variety* as it leads to greater appreciation for the strengths the children bring to school.
- *Teach language in the context of functional and meaningful reading and writing* because literacy skills represent the foundations of the school curriculum.
- *Use familiar experiences derived from home and community* and extend the language from these into the new language and experiences.
- *Immerse the students in literacy across the curriculum* as content areas such as social studies and science promote purposeful literacy learning.
- *Create classroom communities* in which relationships are established through social interaction between English speakers and English learners.
- *Understand the role of cultural and social contexts* in second-language learning as the emphasis on schooling (especially for girls) varies among cultures and families; therefore, communication with parents is critical and may involve home visits.

What Teachers Need to Understand

Numerous interviews with immigrant students led Igoa (1995) to offer several suggestions for facilitating second-language acquisition. First, teachers need to understand other cultures' attitudes toward teachers as well as the cultural backgrounds of immigrant students. Second, teachers need also to understand the education that the older students had received in their home countries and how the educational system in this country may discriminate on the basis of language alone. Third, immigrant children need to feel valued and accepted by teachers who are models and "educational parents" worthy of trust.

To help students appreciate the difficulties involved in learning a second language, teachers can share quality books such as the following picture books and chapter books:

Picture Books

- Levine's *I Hate English!* (1995): When her Chinese family from Hong Kong moves to New York, Mei Mei is angry until she learns that she can have the best of two worlds by learning to communicate in two languages.
- Pryor's *The Dream Jar* (1996): When her Russian family moves to America, Valentina learns English so she can teach it to other immigrants.
- Recorvits' *My Name Is Yoon* (2003): After her Korean family moves to America, Yoon must learn to write her name in the English language (where all the circles and lines stand alone).

Chapter Books

- Creech's *Bloomability* (1998): A preteen from the United States is enrolled in the American School in Lugano, Switzerland, where she learns to speak Italian (and to ski).
- Shaw's *Kirsten Learns a Lesson* (1986): In 1854 when her Swedish family moves to Midwest America, Kirsten has difficulty learning English in school until she makes friends with a Native American girl eager to learn the language.

Positive Language Classroom Environments

Teachers should create an enriching language environment in the classroom that meets the needs of both native speakers and ELLs.

Students need environments that promote active learning. Girls and boys are not passive receptors of information who, having once been presented with proper language forms, will promptly and continuously use those forms well. Instead, language learning is an interactive process, and students must be regarded as active participants in it. They need to practice and to do so without having their efforts constantly corrected by teachers or other adults.

Students need environments that are accepting of their attempts to communicate. Continued scrutiny of student speech, for example, reduces confidence. Therefore, teachers should focus on the meaning of communicative efforts, rather than their form. They should be attentive listeners and show an interest in what the child is saying. In such an atmosphere, teachers accept whatever type of verbal communication the child offers. The student then finds talking to be more rewarding because teachers truly attend to what he or she is saying.

Students need print-rich environments with numerous materials of varying difficulties but that all promote basic concepts. A **print-rich environment** is an area, such as a classroom, that has numerous materials of multiple difficulties that promote basic concepts and affect both written and spoken language development. Well-organized and easily accessible materials facilitate both written and spoken language development, helping children learn about language and literacy (Neuman & Roskos, 1993).

Students need teachers who read to them daily and engage in discussions about the books. Read-aloud sessions are important, but studies have shown that it is the talking about the books before, during, and after the reading that helps students make connections between the text and their own experiences (Heath, 1983). Clay (1991) terms these discussions "grand conversations."

Students need opportunities to use literacy for real purposes. They are more likely to be motivated when asked to read and write in ways that are linked to their lives outside of school. Such motivation, according to Gambrell and Mazzoni (1999), is deep and internalized. Authentic language arts tasks extend into the home and community.

Students need to hear and read children's literature as it provides a foundation for language learning. Morrow and Gambrell (2000) affirm the many benefits of children's literature: increasing vocabulary, providing a writing model, and inspiring inquiry within and across disciplines.

Students need an integrated program involving listening, speaking, reading, writing, viewing, and visual representation since experience in one modality will promote growth throughout the language system. Although differences exist among the language arts, similarities among them are more prevalent than the distinctions.

Students need to be assessed in a variety of ways. Both standardized instruments and informal ongoing assessments should be used since multiple sources of data increase the likelihood of an accurate appraisal of children's literacy learning and knowledge (IRA/NCTE, 1994). Teachers must continue to respect the individual progress of each child despite the pressure to meet national and state standards.

Linguistically diverse learners should have informal, ongoing assessments.

Finally, students *need to have their developmental, cultural, and linguistic diversity respected*. They cannot be asked to enter a "hybrid culture" when they enter school (Au & Kawakami, 1991). Instead, the instruction the children receive at school must fit with their language and culture in addition to meeting the developmental status of other students at that grade level. This is why Mr. Struyk goes out of his way to learn Spanish to help the students in his tutoring group in Vignette 2.2.

VIGNETTE 2.2   Teacher and Students Learning From Each Other

To supplement his student teaching experience, Mr. Struyk volunteered to tutor in a weekly after-school program organized by a local learning center. Although he looked forward to furthering his development as a teacher, he knew that most children attending the tutoring sessions came from households that spoke only Spanish, and he worried about his ability to communicate effectively with them. His three years of high school Spanish classes had hardly left him fluent in the language!

When he arrived for the first Wednesday afternoon session, he felt relieved to hear the children chatting in English and to see a large sign on one wall with the words "English Only Please!" written in large block letters.

"As you know, most of these kids speak only Spanish at home, and many prefer to talk in Spanish to each other at school also," said Mrs. Enzo, the learning center's director. "The 'English only' rule is not intended to de-value these students' background, but to help them—we want each child to become truly bilingual, which means competence in English as well as their first language."

Mr. Struyk understood and agreed with the philosophy. To be most successful as American citizens, the students would need proficiency in speaking and writing English. He looked forward to being part of helping them.

For the first few weeks, Mr. Struyk spent the tutoring sessions getting to know each of the five students assigned to his group and helping them with arithmetic, book reports, science projects, and social studies reading. Because the group included children from two different schools and three different grades, he knew the experience was a valuable supplement to his student teaching work.

After several Wednesday sessions, however, Mr. Struyk noticed a troubling habit among his students. Although they tried to follow the rules and speak only English, at times they had trouble remembering the English words for phrases they knew in Spanish. As a result, his group members often resorted to a mix of the two languages and sometimes lapsed into Spanish entirely.

Mr. Struyk knew he wasn't equipped to handle every complexity of this problem, but he did want to help the children develop more competency in everyday speaking, writing, and listening. After conferring with Mrs. Enzo, he developed a simple game to help the students master more English vocabulary and syntax.

He began with Leslie. The week before, while working on a book summary, she'd asked for the English spelling of three different words. He'd noted the words for today's review, and, after making sure the other four students were busy working on their own assignments, asked Leslie to try his new game.

"Leslie, pick anything in the room and let's see if I know the word for it in Spanish," he said. She smiled; Leslie liked to tease Mr. Struyk about his inability to speak Spanish and he knew she'd enjoy this challenge.

"Ummm . . . chair," she said.

"Oh, that's easy," he quickly replied. "*Silla*. You're going to have to try harder than that!"

"Okay, okay," she laughed. "Workbook."

"Well, I know book is *libro*," he answered. "But I don't think I know workbook."

"*Libra de trabajo!*" she announced.

"Of course, that makes sense. 'Book of work.'" Mr. Struyk then made a transition in the game. "Now it's my turn. I'll ask a word in Spanish and you say it in English."

"Really?" she said dubiously, unsure that he knew enough Spanish for this part of the game to be fun.

"Really. Okay, *agudo*," he said, and watched as her eyes gazed off into the distance, trying to remember the word she learned the week before. After a few seconds she said triumphantly, "Sharp!"

"Right!" he said. "Good job! Now—can you use it in a sentence?"

"Only if you use *silla* in a sentence," she answered mischievously.

"Fair enough," he laughed. "Let's both write a sentence."

For the next 15 minutes Leslie and Mr. Struyk took turns suggesting words and translating them back and forth between languages. By the end of the tutoring session Leslie had successfully remembered and used the three words that puzzled her the week before, and she enjoyed the game so much she learned three new words, too.

As they played, Mr. Struyk realized his lack of fluency in Spanish had become an advantage. Instead of a dreary, one-sided vocabulary lesson, the game was an opportunity for Leslie to teach as well as to learn. The give-and-take of the dialogue validated the importance of both languages, and Mr. Struyk even learned a few new words. While he might not have occasion to use them outside the learning center, he would remember them—no doubt Leslie would quiz him again.

"Okay, we have five more minutes. One more for me," Mr. Struyk said.

Leslie thought for a minute. "Here we say things are 'cool.' How do you say that in Venezuela where my parents used to live?"

Mr. Struyk knew when he was beat. "No idea."

"*Chévere*," she said. She giggled as he clumsily repeated the word. "Can we play again next week?" she asked.

"Next week is someone else's turn," Mr. Struyk said. "Everyone will have a chance to play."

"Good!" said Cristian, another student in the group. "Now I have all week to think of tricky words. I'll be ready for you, Mr. Struyk."

"Cool," Mr. Struyk said. "*Chévere*."

Students need child-centered speech from adults. Rather than reflecting the child's concerns, adult speech often reflects the adult's concerns. The wise teacher, however, uses child-centered speech when addressing the child's topic. In this way, he or she conveys respect for the student and also makes it easier for that student to recall what has been discussed because it is personally meaningful.

When talking with children, especially those who are ELLs or young students, teachers should use these five techniques (Dumtschin, 1988):

The first is *modeling,* in which adults use grammatically correct speech to allow the student to hear and, it is hoped, internalize grammatical rules.

The second is *expatiation* whereby the teacher continues discussing the child's topic but also adds other important information so that new concepts are introduced meaningfully (e.g., Child: "It's hot." Teacher: "It's always hot in the summer.").

Open-ended questioning is a third approach. It stimulates thinking and allows the student to respond without the threat of being wrong (e.g., Teacher, on seeing the young child put a "pie" into a toy oven, asks, "How did you make your pie?").

A fourth technique is **expansion** or corrective feedback, which restates (partly or wholly) the student's incomplete statement and thereby makes it a logical and complete thought (e.g., Child: "Rope." Teacher: "Yes, today we have a new jump rope."). All of this occurs without any negative response or any demand that the student repeat the first statement in a new or better way.

The fifth approach is *recasting*, a form of expansion in which the statement's content is maintained, but its grammatical structure is changed (e.g., Child: "I like oranges." Teacher: "Oranges taste good, don't they?").

A sample lesson plan incorporating the concepts introduced in this chapter appears on p. 48.

Assessment

An effective program in language learning must focus on students as individuals. Therefore, it is important to gather information on each student's current level of English language proficiency. Since the language arts program is built on a knowledge of each student's cultural and family background as well as his or her social, emotional, and intellectual development, it is important to assess students in a variety of ways. Interviews, work samples, demonstrations, and anecdotal records as well as standardized assessments are important.

Assessment is critical for several reasons. The results can be used to place students in the most effective program. They may also be used to monitor the student's progress and plan for future instruction. Assessment data are often used to judge the effectiveness of the program being used. Therefore, when assessing children as language learners and thinkers all of the principles of instruction and suggestions for teachers should be considered.

Working With English Language Learners

Beginning ELLs: Beginning ELLs need social, emotional, and academic support. Assigning another student in the class to be the friend who partners with the child throughout the day helps the beginner feel more secure. The teacher and the other students can provide the assistance necessary to enable the new student to participate in lessons.

Early intermediate and intermediate ELLs: Students at this level need academic support. By providing a positive language classroom environment and employing the techniques for teachers when talking with children, the teacher will be promoting language development.

Early advanced and advanced ELLs: Early advanced and advanced ELLs continue to be successful when visuals and concrete experiences are used to enhance verbal lessons and instructions.

Practical Instructional Activities and Ideas

- *Buddy system:* The teacher should assign a buddy to the new student to help the child feel secure and to give the child a sense of belonging.
- *Proper seating:* The new student should be seated in the front of the classroom for easy observation and inclusion.
- *Grouping:* The teacher can use collaborative grouping to provide social learning experiences and to develop habits of positive interaction.
- *Sharing ancestry:* Building a classroom community can be promoted by sharing family stories and mapping ancestry to acknowledge and celebrate diversity.
- *Wall work:* All charts and graphic organizers presented in the lessons should be kept on the wall to be read, reread, and added to regularly.

LESSON PLAN 2.1 Creating a Class Book

Language Arts Component: Writing and Visual Representation

Grades: 1–2

Topic: Class Book

Time Frame: 1 week

Objective

Students get to know one another by each creating a personal page for the class book.

Materials

- *The Important Book* by Margaret Wise Brown
- Chart paper
- Graphic organizer of a cluster
- Highlighters (two different colors)
- Writing paper
- 12" × 18" drawing paper
- Watercolors
- Fine-line black markers

Content Standards

- Students learn to write a narrative about an experience in the first grade and write a narrative for a different audience and purpose in the second grade.

Day 1

- Teacher reads *The Important Book* to the class as the children listen and look at the illustrations. The teacher reads it a second time, and the students may join in with the repeating pattern portion of the text.
- Teacher models making a cluster of all the things that are important to know about oneself.
- In pairs for support, the students create their own clusters about themselves using words, pictures, or both.

Day 2

- Teacher rereads *The Important Book* as the students join in on the repeating portion of the text.
- Teacher reviews his or her cluster with the class, highlighting the most important point in one color and two more important points in another color.
- With their partners, the students go off to discuss and highlight their own clusters.
- The class comes back together and the teacher models drafting his or her paragraph by following the pattern of the book. Sentence strips or a poster of the text is placed where all students can see it as they go off to work with partners to draft their own paragraphs.

Day 3

- Teacher models peer conferencing by reading his or her paragraph to a student for feedback. They discuss and make any of the changes in front of the class.
- Students continue to work together to finish the draft of their paragraph.
- Students edit their draft.

Day 4

- Teacher models illustrating the paragraph on the top half of a 12" × 18" piece of drawing paper.
- Some students begin their illustrations as others take turns word processing the paragraph for the class book.
- Students watercolor their drawings.

Day 5

- Students each use a fine-line black marker to outline their painting. They each print out a copy of their paragraph to glue to the bottom of the illustration and they move about the room sharing their work.
- When everyone is finished, the teacher makes a class book. The students take turns taking it home to introduce their classmates to their families.

Integration Across the Curriculum

Science and Social Studies

- When providing direct instruction in science and social studies the teacher uses visuals, realia, multimedia, graphics, experiments, charts, observations, and field trips to actively engage the learners.
- All charts and graphic organizers presented in the lessons should be kept on the wall to be read, reread, and added to regularly.

Literature

- The teacher chooses a piece of children's literature listed in this chapter and reads it aloud once for the story. During the second reading, the teacher models making text-to-self connections in a double-entry journal. In the first column the student writes the page number and a quote from the text that evoked the connection. In the second column, the student writes the event from his or her life that the text brought to mind. Share and discuss as a class.

Visual and Performing Arts

- The students create "All About Me" posters to share with the class and to display in the classroom.
- The students create a collage or PowerPoint presentation about themselves to share with the class.
- The students take turns standing in front of the class and talking about family holidays.

Health

- Teams of students create a presentation of their choice (e.g., poem, song, poster, choral reading) to express why it is healthy for the class to create a safe, stress-free classroom environment together.

Physical Education

- Students play team-building collaborative games during physical education. One example would be letter building. The teacher calls out a letter of the alphabet and each team uses their bodies together to form the letter.

Music

- Students listen to the music of composers from a variety of native countries represented by the student population. Students make a sketch of an image or setting they visualized as they listened.
- Students learn and perform songs that represent the heritage of each student in the class.

Parents as Partners

- Parents may come into the classroom to share their careers or expertise in a particular area.
- Parents may present heirlooms and/or family history to the class as a part of unit studies.
- Parents may visit the classroom to help host a holiday celebration unique to their home culture.
- Parents may come into the classroom to teach the students how to prepare foods from their ancestry. Students share in a multicultural feast.

Student Study Site

The Companion Web site for *Language Arts: Integrating Skills for Classroom Teaching*
www.sagepub.com/donoghuestudy
Visit the Web-based study site to enhance your understanding of the chapter content. The study materials include chapter summaries, practice tests, flashcards, and Web resources.

Additional Professional Readings

Buhrow, B., & Garcia, A. (2006). *Ladybugs, tornadoes, and swirling galaxies: English language learners discover their world through inquiry.* Portland, ME: Stenhouse.

Dutro, E., Kazemi, E., & Balf, R. (2005). The aftermath of "You're only half": Multiracial identities in the literacy classroom. *Language Arts, 83,* 96–106.

Fain, J. (2006). Family talk about language diversity and culture. *Language Arts, 83,* 310–320.

Freeman, Y., Freeman, D., & Ramirez, R. (Eds.) (2008). *Diverse learners in the mainstream classroom: Strategies for supporting ALL students across content areas.* Portsmouth, NH: Heinemann.

Gaitan, C. (2006). *Building culturally responsive classrooms.* Thousand Oaks, CA: Corwin Press.

Glasgow, N., McNary, S., & Hicks, C. (2006). *What successful teachers do in diverse classrooms.* Thousand Oaks, CA: Corwin Press.

Kottler, E., Kottler, J., & Street, C. (2008). *English language learners in your classroom: Strategies that work* (3rd ed.). Thousand Oaks, CA: Corwin Press.

Lenski, S., Ehlers-Zavala, F., Daniel, M., & Sun-Irminger, K. (2006). Assessing English language learners in mainstream classrooms. *The Reading Teacher, 30,* 24–34.

Mokhtari, K., & Sheorey, R. (2008). *Reading strategies of first- and second-language learners: See how they read.* Norwood, MA: Christopher-Gordon.

Zuniga-Dunlap, C., & Weisman, E. (2006). *Helping English language learners succeed.* Huntington Beach, CA: Shell.

Children's Literature Cited in the Text

Brown, M. W. (1990). *The important book.* New York: Harper Trophy.

Creech, S. (1998). *Bloomability.* New York: HarperCollins.

Levine, E. (1995). *I hate English!* New York: Scholastic.

Pryor, B. (1996). *The dream jar.* New York: HarperCollins.

Recorvits, H. (2003). *My name is Yoon.* New York: Farrar, Straus and Giroux.

Shaw, J. B. (1986). *Kirsten learns a lesson.* Middleton, WI: Pleasant Company.

Zucker, J. (2003). *Lanterns and firecrackers: A Chinese New Year story.* New York: Barron's Educational Series.

References

Au, K., & Kawakami, J. (1991). Culture and ownership: Schooling of minority students. *Childhood Education, 67,* 280–284.

Bhavnagri, N., & Gonzales-Mena, J. (1997). The cultural context of infant caregiving. *Childhood Education, 74,* 2–8.

Cambourne, B. (1988). *The whole story: Natural learning and the acquisition of literacy.* Jefferson City, MO: Scholastic.

Chomsky, N. (1965). *Aspects of the theory of syntax.* Cambridge: MIT Press.

Clay, M. (1991). *Becoming literate.* Portsmouth, NH: Heinemann.

Cummins, J. (1980). The cross-lingual dimensions of language proficiency: Implications for bilingual education and the optimal age issue. *TESOL Quarterly, 14,* 175–187.

Delpit, L. (November 1995). *Other people's children.* Paper presented at the National Reading Conference, New Orleans.

Dumtschin, J. (1988). Recognize language development and delay in early childhood. *Young Children, 43,* 21–23.

Fitzgerald, J. (1993). Literacy and students who are learning English as a second language. *The Reading Teacher, 46,* 638–647.

Freeman, D., & Freeman, Y. (2001). *Between worlds: Access to second language acquisition.* Portsmouth, NH: Heinemann.

Gambrell, L., & Mazzoni, S. (1999). Principles of best practice: Finding the common ground. In L. Gambrell, L. Morrow, S. Neuman, & M. Pressley (Eds.), *Best practices in literacy instruction* (pp. 11–21). New York: Guilford.

Goodman, K., & Freeman, D. (1993). What's simple in simplified language. In M. Tickoo (Ed.), *Simplification: Theory and application.* Anthology Series 31 (ERIC Document Reproduction Service No. ED 371–5781).

Hadaway, N., Vardell, S., & Young, T. (2002). *Literature-based teaching with English language learners.* Boston: Allyn & Bacon.

Hart, B., & Risley, T. (1995). *Meaningful differences in the everyday experiences of young American children.* Baltimore: Brookes.

Heath, S. (1983). What no bedtime story means: Narrative skills at home and school. *Language in Society, 11,* 49–76.

Holdaway, D. (1979). *The foundations of literacy.* New York: Scholastic.

Huttenlocher, P. (1991). Early vocabulary growth: Relations to language input and gender. *Developmental Psychology, 27,* 236–248.

Igoa, C. (1995). *The inner world of the immigrant child.* New York: St. Martin's Press.

International Reading Association and National Council of Teachers of English. (1994). *Standards for the assessment of reading and writing.* Newark, DE, & Urbana, IL: Author.

Kalb, C., & Namuth, T. (1997, Spring/Summer). When a child's silence isn't golden. *Newsweek: Your Child* [Special edition].

Kotulak, R. (1997). *Inside the brain: Revolutionary discoveries of how the mind works.* Kansas City, MO: A. McMeel.

Krashen, S. (1982). *Principles and practice in second language acquisition.* Oxford: Pergamon.

Krashen, S., & Terrell, J. (1987). *The natural approach: Language acquisition in the classroom.* Englewood Cliffs, NJ: Prentice Hall.

Kuhl, P. K. (1993). Early linguistic experience and phonetic perception: Implications for theories of developmental speech perception. *Journal of Phonetics, 21,* 125–139.

Morrow, I., & Gambrell, L. (2000). Literature-based reading instruction. In M. Kamil, P. Mosenthal, M. Pearson, & M. Barr (Eds.), *Handbook of reading research* (Vol. 3, pp. 563–580). Mahwah, NJ: Lawrence Erlbaum.

National Council of Teachers of English. (1996). Exploring language arts standards within a cycle of learning. *Language Arts, 73,* 10–13.

Neuman, S., & Roskos, K. (1993). *Language and literacy learning in the early years.* Fort Worth, TX: Harcourt.

Oates, J., & Grayson, A. (2004). *Cognitive and language development in children.* Malden, MA: Wiley-Blackwell.

Peregoy, S., & Boyle, O. (1997). *Reading, writing, and learning in ESL: A resource book for K-12 teachers.* New York: Longman.

Piaget, J. (1962). *The language and thought of the child.* New York: Humanities Press.

Sochurek, H. (1987). Medicine's new vision. *National Geographic, 171*(1), 2–41.

Spangenberg-Urbschat, K., & Pritchard, R. (1994). *Kids come in all languages: Reading instruction for ESL students.* Newark, DE: International Reading Association.

Sprenger, M. (1999). *Learning and memory: The brain in action.* Alexandria, VA: Association for Supervision and Curriculum Development.

Swerdlow, J. (1995). Quiet miracles of the brain. *National Geographic, 187*(6).

Sylvester, R. (1995). *A celebration of neutrons.* Alexandria, VA: Association for Supervision and Curriculum Development.

Vygotsky, L. (1986). *Thought and language.* Cambridge: MIT Press.

Anticipation Statement Answers

1. Agree
2. Agree
3. Disagree
4. Agree
5. Agree
6. Agree
7. Disagree
8. Disagree
9. Agree: Knowing the stages prior to assessment improves the teacher's ability to gather information about the student. However, knowing the stages prior to assessment will not affect the assessment process.
10. Agree: ELL students will be more engaged, and language learning is an interactive process. However, ELL students may feel more comfortable listening and watching as opposed to participating, especially if they are in the pre-production or early production stage.

Formal and Authentic Assessment

Defined simply as the process of gathering data to better understand student learning, assessment has a primary component: Teachers must begin the assessment process by deciding what they value about children's development as readers, writers, speakers, listeners, and viewers. Only after making that determination can teachers choose the appropriate tools for gathering information.

Principles and Purposes for the Assessment of the Language Arts

With the continuing emphasis on assessing the language arts, the International Reading Association and the National Council of Teachers of English (1994) issued a position statement that can be summarized as comprising the following *principles:* Teachers' assessment should become more authentic, reflecting students' production of in-depth knowledge; provide for collaborative reflection between themselves and their students and, in some instances, with the parents; and reveal where students are in their own educational development and not where they are in a constantly changing peer population. Teachers should measure language and thinking skills simultaneously as these work interactively to create a measurable product and should recognize that the most effective and lasting form of feedback to students is to give them detailed guidance immediately after their class performance. Teachers should make both planned and unplanned assessments, the unplanned type occurring *during* instruction to reveal impromptu insight and understanding of new skills while the planned type takes place generally *after* a lesson. Finally, while teachers must include statewide and national standardized tests as one component in the language arts program, their own teacher-made tests should assess a wider range of talents and abilities than in the past.

Teachers, professionally concerned with assessing their language arts programs, do so for the *purposes* of evaluating their own planning and implementation of classroom instruction, monitoring children's learning, and reflecting about their own teaching processes. There are four other groups who also want to know about students' performance in this subject area. Their *purposes* vary:

Administrators at every level are interested in being able to describe the growth of large numbers of students in terms of test scores, percentages, and comparisons to local and state standards and, in some instances, to national standards as well.

Parents are most concerned about their children's growth and achievement in the school setting, especially in their ability to read and write. They may need help in interpreting test scores (often weighted heavily in the area of literacy) when these are reported in the local papers. Conferences, report cards, and portfolios are always helpful.

Community members believe that they have the right to know about the effectiveness of school programs since it is tax money that supports these and their teachers. Community members and legislators often examine test scores without any contextual information about factors affecting those scores including socioeconomic issues, class size, and the number of English Language Learners.

Students need feedback daily about their progress in oral language work and in literacy. Some teachers even send home weekly written reports with the children; others use email.

Applicable IRA/NCTE Standards

Standard 4   Students adjust their use of spoken, written, and visual language (e.g., conventions, style, vocabulary) to communicate effectively with a variety of audiences and for different purposes.

Standard 5   Students employ a wide range of strategies as they write and use different writing process elements appropriately to communicate with different audiences for a variety of purposes.

Standard 7   Students conduct research on issues and interests by generating ideas and questions, and by posing problems. They gather, evaluate, and synthesize data from a variety of sources (e.g., print and nonprint texts, artifacts, people) to communicate their discoveries in ways that suit their purpose and audience.

Standard 10   Students whose first language is not English make use of their first language to develop competency in the English language arts and to develop understanding of content across the curriculum.

Standard 12   Students use spoken, written, and visual language to accomplish their own purposes (e.g., for learning, enjoyment, persuasion, and the exchange of information).

SOURCE: *Standards for the English Language Arts*, by the International Reading Association and the National Council of Teachers of English, Copyright 1996 by the International Reading Association and the National Council of Teachers of English. Reprinted with permission. http://www .ncte.org/about/over/standards/110846.htm

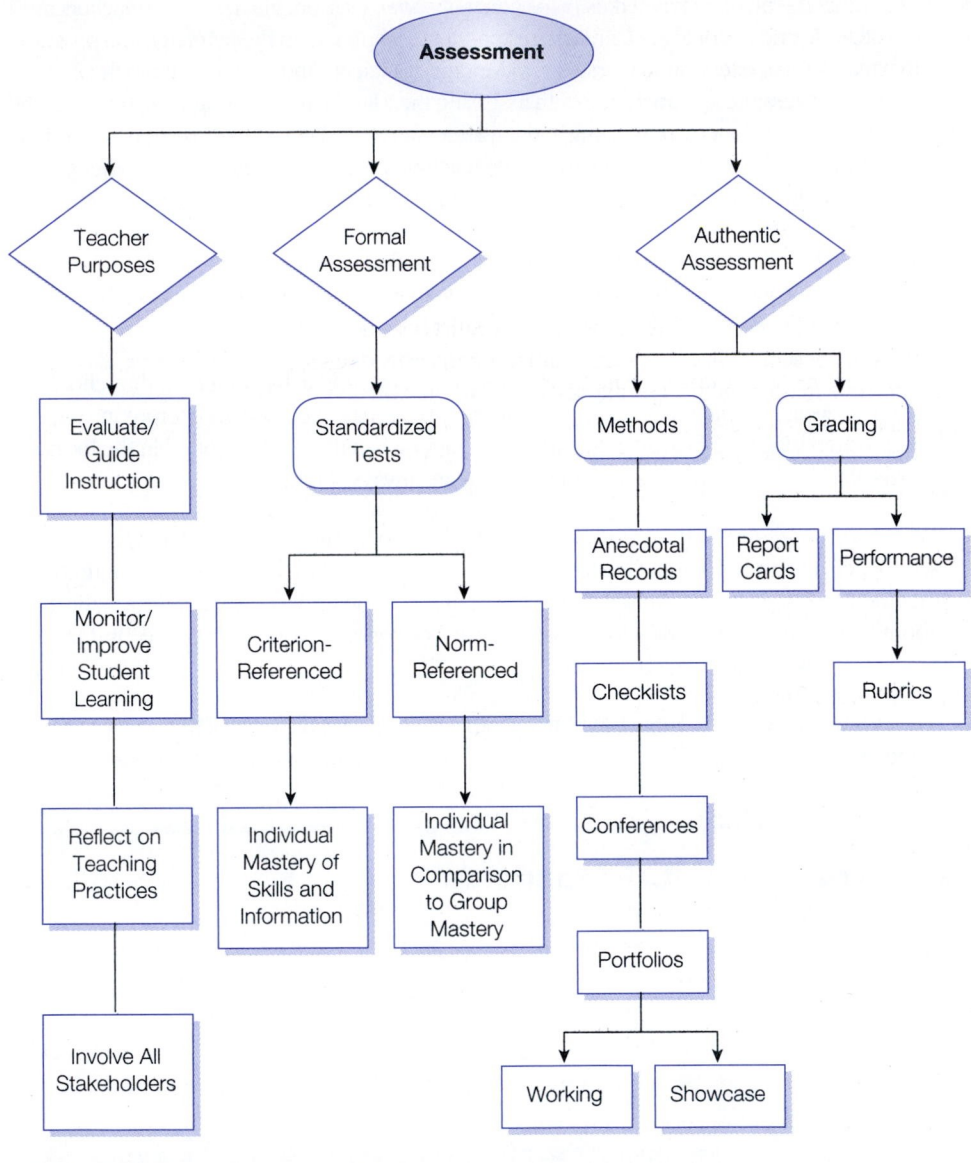

A Graphic Summary of the Contents of This Chapter

Feedback is crucial and motivating if students are to continue to improve and maintain a positive concept as learners of the language arts (Farr, 1992).

Formal Assessment: Standardized Tests

There are two broad types of assessment: **formal or traditional assessment**, which has been defined in *The Literacy Dictionary* (Harris & Hodges, 1995) as "the collection of data using standardized tests or procedures under controlled conditions" (p. 86), and **authentic assessment**, which has been described as the direct examination of student performance on useful intellectual tasks.

Standardized tests are mandated by local school boards, state departments of education, and, in some cases, at the federal level because it is believed that they can produce data that tell how well students have acquired basic facts and how they compare to others of the same age or grade level (Herman, Aschbacher, & Winters, 1992). These tests have had a strong impact on language arts instruction, and their results have been reported to parents, school boards, legislators, and the general public who like the fact that these tests are relatively inexpensive and easy to administer.

Although there are several test formats, all are administered, scored, and interpreted in the same prescribed manner. They are paper-and-pencil tests, given only periodically, mostly in the form of multiple-choice and short-answer questions/passages, although there are also some true/false and matching questions. Teachers have no voice in determining which tests will be used in their school; that decision is made by the state or district boards.

Two types of standardized tests are **criterion-referenced tests**, whose goal is for all students to demonstrate mastery of the specific skills and information they have been taught according to district and state learning standards (e.g., to capitalize all proper nouns, words at the beginning of sentences, months and days of the week, and titles and initials of people); and **norm-referenced tests**, which compare the accomplishments of one grade-level classroom to all of the same grade-level classrooms in the district, state, or even across the country to determine if that school's curriculum reflects the state or national expectations of what students should know at a specific grade level. Briefly, on an individual student basis, a criterion-referenced test tells what a student is able to do while the norm-referenced test tells how she or he compares with others.

High-Stakes Testing

In recent years with the implementation of the No Child Left Behind (NCLB) Act and other regulations, standardized tests at both the national and state levels list specific tasks and procedures so that comparisons may be made across various schools and communities. Such testing is termed **high-stakes testing** since, according to Heubert and Huser (1999), failing or passing has enormous consequences on students, teachers, and other *stakeholders* (i.e., parents, legislators, minorities, and the public in general). These tests now determine retention, tracking, and even graduation.

Since every state and federal standard stresses the importance of oral language development and the interrelationships among the language arts, elementary teachers must help students prepare for high-stakes testing. An analysis of the literature yields the following strategies for teachers to implement in an effort to reduce test anxiety among children in Grades 3 to 6 or even Grades 2 to 6 in some states (Guthrie, 2002; McCabe, 2005; Santman, 2002):

- Practice activities that mimic the format and administration of the test the students will take (e.g., teach students to use their time efficiently, check their answers, and use deductive reasoning on multiple-choice items to determine the best possible answers). Model test-taking strategies that involve careful reading, reflection, and response.
- Immerse the students, wherever possible, in materials exactly like the format of the test they will take. Some states provide item samplers for teachers to use, but many teachers design their own practice tests with the same kinds of items that students will have to answer.
- Place long-term emphasis on using effective reading comprehension strategies since this component accounts for about 40% of the difference among students' performance on high-stakes tests. The second most important component of reading test performance is content knowledge, which is estimated to account for 20% of the difference among their performance.
- Plan on months of independent reading (both in and out of class) before the test date because both the volume and the frequency of such reading have an impact on vocabulary development and on general comprehension.
- Include both unrelated narrative and expository passages on the practice tests.
- Schedule practice sessions for students on a regular basis.

- Begin with untimed tests and then move to timed tests as students become more experienced in test taking.
- Simulate testing conditions in the classroom to better prepare the class and reduce student stress.

In Vignette 3.1, experienced teacher Miss Alvarez wisely incorporates some of these strategies in her efforts to promote the reading comprehension skills that weigh heavily in high-stakes testing.

Online tools provide an engaging way for students to sharpen their reading comprehension skills in preparation for formal high-stakes testing.

VIGNETTE 3.1 Comprehension and Standardized Testing

After teaching for more than 20 years, Miss Alvarez knew standardized tests were here to stay. The state department of education regularly updated and published "standards of learning" (SOLs) for each grade and subject area, and each winter the school board mandated another year of formal tests to assess progress toward the SOLs.

Miss Alvarez had mixed feelings about the process; while she appreciated the need for standards and accountability, she also knew some children showed potential but scored poorly on paper-and-pencil tests.

Since comprehension strategies were not only a key to high test scores but also a foundation of language arts instruction, Miss Alvarez regularly devoted time to developing this skill with her fourth-grade students.

She used a variety of strategies to help students remember their reading: identifying main sentences, summarizing information, and connecting stories and nonfiction studies to their own experiences. And of course she encouraged use of these techniques across many subject areas, often asking the students to share the major points of a current newspaper story or to visualize a historical event during social studies reading.

Each of these exercises promoted comprehension, but she found questioning to be one of the most effective skills for students to practice. This year's round of formal tests was just two weeks away, and today Miss Alvarez would review this skill during independent reading.

As the class found their books and prepared for the half-hour of silent reading, Miss Alvarez asked the students to open their question logs as well. She incorporated the logs into classwork at least once each week and the students were familiar with the assignment. They retrieved their notebooks from their desks and backpacks.

On the front chalkboard she wrote "I wonder . . . ." in large letters.

"Take a minute and write what you wonder about in your reading," she instructed. The students bent over their papers; as Miss Alvarez walked among the rows of desks she noted Julia's questions about the next plot twist in her scary ghost story and Sun Yi's notes about the model cars in his magazine.

Eddie raised his hand. "I'm starting a new book today, so I don't know how to ask questions about it," he said.

"With a new book you should have more questions than anyone else!" Miss Alvarez replied. "Let's see." She picked up his copy of Cleary's *Dear Mr. Henshaw* (2000) and inspected the back cover.

"Who is Mr. Henshaw? Why is Leigh writing to him? Is Mr. Henshaw a real person?" She modeled the technique and then returned the novel to Eddie with a smile. "You don't know very much about the book, so all questions are good questions right now."

Eddie nodded as Miss Alvarez continued prepping the students.

"Okay, if you have any predictions about your reading, be sure to include those in your question log as well, and remember to write down the answers you discover. After reading we'll have time to talk about anything new we learned."

After another minute of finding comfortable positions, chewing on pencils, and writing questions in their logs, the students settled down to read. Miss Alvarez had to smile as she walked past Tim's desk and read the question scrawled across the top of his notebook: *I wonder. . . . if I will ever finish this book for my book report.*

"You will," she promised, briefly laying an encouraging hand on his shoulder. "Just keep at it."

She returned to her desk while the students read quietly. In a half-hour she would conclude the exercise by inviting each of the students to share insights from their reading, questions still unanswered, and predictions about upcoming chapters. Although the students read a variety of materials and the questions didn't always make sense to their classmates, the process of sharing them aloud improved each child's ability to ask good questions and encouraged interest in new genres for future reading.

Miss Alvarez still did not look forward to the upcoming test week, but she felt confident the students were prepared to read the test material thoroughly and answer the exam questions. By consistently learning to make predictions and then find answers, the students developed comprehension skills that would be effective no matter what the subject—or the test.

Finally, classroom teachers should be cognizant of the strong opposition that the International Reading Association (1999) has to high-stakes testing. It believes that "assessment should be used to improve instruction and benefit students rather than compare and pigeonhole them" (p. 3).

A more professional assessment therefore would be an authentic or performance assessment, which is discussed in the next section.

Authentic Assessment: What, Why, and How

For material related to this concept, go to Video Clip 3.1 on the Student Resource CD bound into the back of your textbook.

Authentic assessment, also known as performance assessment or alternative assessment, refers to all types of assessment other than formal standardized tests. It is the most valid type of assessment because it measures real-life literacy behaviors and how students perform in daily activities (Johnson, 1997; Leslie & Jett-Simpson, 1997). It was both concern about standardized tests and the need to examine students' work more carefully that caused educators to consider alternative measures.

Authentic assessment differs from standardized testing in the following ways:

- Decisions on materials to be assessed are made by the teachers and students themselves, not by outsiders.
- Information is compiled on an ongoing basis, not just periodically.
- Multiple sources of information are considered, not just results on paper-and-pencil tests.
- Information is gathered routinely as part of each day's planning and therefore does not interrupt the classroom schedule for days or even weeks.

Authentic assessment allows a teacher to judge a student's work based on its own merits rather than having students compete against each other.

Other principles of authentic assessment are that its primary purpose is improvement of student learning; it is equitable and fair for all students; and it involves everyone in the educational community, including parents and students as well as the general public and the administration (Roe, Smith, & Burns, 2005).

An integral part of teaching and learning, authentic assessment is more than testing. It helps teachers determine whether or not their instructional goals are being met. It allows students to compete against themselves and not have their work compared to that of others. Finally, it reveals individual student growth by the collection of multiple and dated work samples over a long period of time.

In an effort to determine what students really know, teachers should use assessment practices that have the following qualities:

- Student-centered, focusing on what students do during their daily use of language, thereby helping teachers plan lessons that address and challenge their children's needs and interests (Rhodes & Dudley-Marling, 1996).
- Collaborative, involving learners and teachers and allowing students to take an active role in their own assessment in an effort to help them understand their weaknesses and strengths; parents may be involved as well, and their insights can include family and cultural interpretations of student responses to language arts lessons (Tierney, Crumpler, Bertelson, & Bond, 2003).
- *Extensive*, using a variety of sources and methods to help teachers consider how the child functions within particular contexts and assignments; only then can teachers identify learner strengths and learner needs (Valencia, Hiebert, & Afflerbach, 1994).
- *Continuous*, involving a long-term and ongoing process; documentation must be collected over a period of time to properly determine language development and growth, and students are also assessed daily during the course of instruction.

Through daily monitoring of student learning, teachers can use those results to help them plan further instruction and better understand both their children and themselves. This section describes four ways to monitor student progress.

Anecdotal Record

As defined in *The Literacy Dictionary* (Harris & Hodges, 1995), an **anecdotal record** is "a description of behavior; a reporting of observed behavioral incidents" (p. 10). It is a clear and objective written account of a specific incident in the classroom that the teacher has observed (Rhodes & Nathenson-Majia, 1992; see Figure 3.1). The record describes the event in sufficient detail so that, when the teacher reviews it, he or she can mentally reconstruct the incident. It is especially helpful when tracking the progress of children who are English Language Learners or are at-risk students as teachers who regularly keep anecdotal records of these children become more sensitive to their interests and needs (Baskwill & Whitman, 1988). A good time for teachers to write anecdotal records is when the entire class is writing (e.g., during journal time). Such records document student growth and gradually spotlight problem areas. *Anecdotal entries must be dated to be an effective means of assessment.*

Anecdotal records can be maintained in several ways, and each teacher should determine which procedure is most comfortable for him or her. One possible way is using index cards that are placed in a small file on the teacher's desk. A second way is to keep anecdotal notes on a sticky note pad kept in the teacher's pocket and then transfer these notes to a spiral-bound notebook with dividers for each child. A third way is to write anecdotes on anecdotal record forms and place these in the student assessment folders. A sample form is shown in Figure 3.1. Teachers may choose to develop other means for keeping anecdotal records that are useful at times for sharing with parents and administrators. A recently introduced form is an interactive anecdotal record in which students respond to their teacher's notes. The dialogue then becomes a collaborative ongoing assessment.

Figure 3.1 Sample Anecdotal Record Form

Child's Name: Meredith M.

Date: 5/20/08

Activity: SSR

Details: Self-selects book. Grins as she reads *Amelia Bedelia*. Pokes Maria (her neighbor) to share a picture from the book.

Summary: Has begun to self-select books and enjoy them. Attention span is longer and she is less restless during any reading activity. Asking to take books home to read to her parents, more confident.

Source: Adapted from *The Child and the English Language Arts* by Mildred Donoghue, 1990, Dubuque, IA: Wm. C. Brown Publishers.

Checklist

Defined in *The Literacy Dictionary* (Harris & Hodges, 1995) as "a list of specific skills or behaviors to be marked off by an observer as a student performs them" (p. 28), a **checklist** is useful for recording information about student accomplishments and seeing quickly what has been achieved and what further work is needed. Teachers have learned that sometimes a student will behave one day in a particular way and then not repeat that behavior again for several weeks; therefore, it is wise to use a checklist several times over the year in an effort to gain an accurate picture of the child's ability.

Consequently, when teachers complete several checklists for each child and keep them in a folder, they have a written record of each student's progress over time. The types of checklists available to describe students' development seem nearly endless. A sample checklist is shown in Figure 3.2.

Conference

As defined in *The Literacy Dictionary* (Harris & Hodges, 1995), a conference is "a discussion about student work between a teacher and student or a teacher and parent" (p. 41). Whether they are brief or long, conferences have to be conducted in a secure place because anxious, insecure students are fearful of taking risks when they share their ideas. Comfort occurs if the student does most of the talking and if the teacher appears supportive of the student's efforts and asks only a few open-ended questions. Conferences usually run five to ten minutes and should be purposeful, seeking information regarding the student's learning, attitudes, and interests. Teachers should make written records of each conference in any form they wish and include the purpose, the student's thoughts, and any decisions reached.

In addition to planned assessment conferences, there are also impromptu, "on the spot" conferences that run less than a minute and occur at the student's desk. During such conferences, the teacher is eager to check on the progress of a particular assignment by answering any brief questions the student may have. These conferences are not recorded and may even be termed conversations.

Portfolio

As defined in *The Literacy Dictionary* (Harris & Hodges, 1995), a **portfolio** is a "selected, usually chronological, collection of a student's work that may be used to evaluate learning progress" (p. 190). It should be an integral part of authentic assessment in all language arts classrooms, according to Tierney and colleagues (2003), as it is child-centered, collaborative, and extensive while focusing on the literacy behaviors of individual children. Furthermore, it has been determined that it is not the portfolio itself but the process of its implementation that actually promotes a classroom environment in which both students and teachers recognize the importance of learning.

Figure 3.2 Classroom Teacher's Evaluation of Student Speech

Student's Name: _____   Date: _____

(The teacher should check the vocal difficulties below each speech technique that is rated *average* or *unsatisfactory*.)

Tempo   Very Good _____   Average _____   Unsatisfactory _____

_____ Too fast

_____ Too slow

_____ Unvarying, monotonous

_____ Poor phrasing; irregular rhythm of speaking

_____ Hesitations

Loudness   Very Good _____   Average _____   Unsatisfactory _____

_____ Too loud

_____ Too weak

_____ Lack of variety

_____ Force overused as a form of emphasis

Pitch   Very Good _____   Average _____   Unsatisfactory _____

_____ General level too high

_____ General level too low

_____ Lack of variety

_____ Fixed pattern monotonously repeated

_____ Lack of relationships between pitch changes and meaning

_____ Exaggerated pitch changes

Quality   Very Good _____   Average _____   Unsatisfactory _____

_____ Nasal

_____ Hoarse

_____ Breathy

_____ Throaty and guttural

_____ Strained and harsh

_____ Flat

SOURCE: Adapted from *The Child and the English Language Arts* by Mildred Donoghue, 1990, Dubuque, IA: Wm. C. Brown Publishers.

The following principles guide the use of portfolios in the classroom:

- Reliable assessment must be based on authentic tasks that can be translated into the real world.
- Assessment should be a continuous process, and student work must be included regularly so that growth (or its lack) can be identified.
- Literacy assessments should be multidimensional and include a wide range of reading and writing performances and behaviors.
- Evaluation tools must facilitate cooperative reflection between the student and the teacher, which should occur periodically.
- Portfolios should be aligned with curriculum and instruction (Valencia & Place, 1994).

For material related to this concept, go to Video Clip 3.2 on the Student Resource CD bound into the back of your textbook.

The benefits of implementing portfolios in the classroom are numerous, the most important one being that *students become more involved in the evaluation of their work and therefore more reflective about its quality* (Tompkins, 2006). Students also feel ownership of their work and become more responsible for it. They set goals and are motivated to work toward meeting them, recognizing the connection between learning and assessing. Finally, their self-esteem is enhanced as they reflect upon all that they have accomplished.

There are two kinds of portfolios: *working portfolios* and *showcase portfolios*. The first provides a description of how a student is developing, since the work samples are not representations of the child's best work but simply examples of everyday assignments. From them the student, usually with the help of the teacher, chooses pieces to be placed in the second or showcase portfolio, which exhibits the finest work that the student has produced. Still, everything the student does is not saved for the portfolio; some products are sent home.

The work samples in the working portfolio display performance related to specific content standards that the district or state has mandated. From those samples are chosen pieces for the showcase portfolio that relate to those standards. Mrs. Murphy in Vignette 3.2 asks her students to choose ten pieces for the showcase portfolio, which she will share with parents during the upcoming parent conference week.

VIGNETTE 3.2 Showcase Portfolios and Parent Conferences

It was hard to believe the first semester was more than half over. In the last few weeks October's warm Indian summer had given way to the raw, blustery days of November, and soon the holiday season would begin.

But even without the weather and the decorated department stores to remind her, Mrs. Murphy knew November had come; each fall the school organized parent-teacher conferences at this point in the term, and she could count on spending extra time preparing for them.

Although many teachers dreaded the experience, she always enjoyed meeting the parents of her sixth-grade students and updating them on class activities. The process became especially effective two years ago when she added an ongoing portfolio assignment to both the language arts and social studies curricula. Instead of bulletin boards showing just a small sampling, Mrs. Murphy could now share a variety of projects and papers with each parent. The moms and dads usually left the conferences with a much broader understanding of the curriculum, and the tangible examples of each child's work made it easier for her to address problem areas and concerns.

In preparation for the upcoming conferences, Mrs. Murphy had asked each student to choose ten pieces for a showcase portfolio. She knew the children would enjoy the opportunity to "show off" special projects or good grades, and realizing their parents would periodically view portions of their work often served as a motivating factor during the school year. Mrs. Murphy usually added her own evaluations and notes, resulting in a comprehensive overview for each parent.

Today Mrs. Murphy would begin meeting individually with the students to finalize their choices. In addition, the short meetings would provide another valuable opportunity for the students to evaluate their own progress.

"Class, it's time for our conferences about your portfolios," she reminded the students, many of whom were still digging through the large file folders storing their work. "If you have finished choosing your ten pieces, please read quietly until I call your name. Mark, let's start with you."

She settled at a table in the back of the room, far enough from the other students to afford some privacy for the meetings. Mark followed her, dropping papers as he walked.

"Mark, remember you only need to choose ten things," Mrs. Murphy said, smiling as he bent over to retrieve a report on John Adams and dropped his haiku collection in the process.

"I know, but I can't decide," he answered.

"It's great you have so much work you feel proud of," she congratulated him. "Why don't we make two piles? The 'definitely' ones and the 'maybe' ones."

"Okay. These are my definitely ones," he said, laying a stack of papers to his right. "There are only eight," he added quickly. Mark loved to write and almost always chose reports, papers, and other writing assignments when offered the opportunity. His portfolio contained quite a bit of paper.

"Great. How many others did you bring?" Mrs. Murphy asked.

"Five. So I need to get rid of three."

"Well, not get rid of them," she said wryly and examined the eight already chosen. "These are mostly reports and other written projects," she said. "And they're really good. But maybe your mom would enjoy seeing some of the other things you can do."

He pondered his remaining choices and selected photographs from the class dramatization of *The Lion, the Witch and the Wardrobe*. The "production" had primarily served as a comprehension exercise for the students and, like many informal classroom dramas, included little in the way of costumes or props. Still, Mrs. Murphy allowed the children to invite their families to the play and even provided parents with discussion questions for the drive home. Mark's single mom worked two jobs and couldn't attend that evening; Mrs. Murphy remembered Mark's disappointment.

"That is a great choice," she affirmed as Mark dropped the photos onto the "definitely" pile. "Your mom will love seeing those pictures. Did you tell her about the play?"

"Yeah, I told her about being one of the frozen statues and being unfrozen at the end," he said.

"Being in the play was new for you. Did you like it?" she asked.

"Well . . . yeah. I was nervous about getting up in front of people but since I was frozen I didn't have any lines to forget," he grinned.

"Then it was a good first step," she said. "If we do another play, would you like a part with a couple of lines?"

He considered the offer, then nodded. "I'd try it."

She smiled again and jotted a note about his progress in this area.

"Okay, last choice," she said.

After a moment's thought, he selected a large map of the Oregon Trail. Mark had labored over the map for weeks as part of a group project on the pioneers. Although he wrote far above his grade level, he struggled with work involving spatial measurements and precise details. She knew the map had not been easy.

"I'm a little surprised to see you pick the map," she said. "Tell me why you chose it."

"I wanted to be in the group that wrote the stories about the pioneers," he said. "But I worked a long time on the map and even asked my big brother for help. My mom knew it was a big deal so I want her to see it all finished."

Mrs. Murphy smiled gently. "Mark, I'm really proud of you. You're right—you worked very hard on this project and created a good map. Your mom will be proud of you too."

Mark blushed and gathered up his remaining work to return to his desk. Mrs. Murphy would assemble the ten chosen pieces into a new folder and return the showcase work to the students after the conferences.

Still smiling a little, Mrs. Murphy called Avery to the back table. Avery had strong opinions and a strong will; Mrs. Murphy looked forward to seeing her selections and doubted Avery would arrive asking her advice as Mark had.

As expected, Avery arrived full of thoughts and with ten selections in hand. For several minutes she enthusiastically shared her rationale for choosing each piece, then stopped with a question.

"Mrs. Murphy, what are you going to tell my parents about my portfolio?" she asked.

"What do you think I should tell them?" Mrs. Murphy countered. She would answer Avery's question, but only after encouraging Avery to share her own perspective.

"Well, I'm super good at book reports," Avery said. "And when we did the class newspaper I worked really hard, even during recess one day."

Mrs. Murphy nodded at both self-evaluations.

"You are a good speaker and a hard worker," she said. "I will absolutely share that with your mom and dad, and I'm glad you know these things about yourself. Is there anything that's harder for you?"

Avery nodded. "I'm not very good at spelling," she said. "Words don't look the way I see them in my head."

Mrs. Murphy was impressed with Avery's awareness and her candor. "The good thing is you can improve at spelling if you work at it. Would you be willing to do a little more practice each week?"

Avery hesitantly nodded yes. "Okay. But tell my mom and dad!"

Like Mark, Avery left her ten prized assignments and returned to her seat as Mrs. Murphy noted the new commitment in her notes. She was already looking forward to the conferences with Mark and Avery's parents and to her individual meetings with the rest of the students. The semester might only be half over, but the children were making real progress.

The New Standards Project (1994) recommends that the selection of items for inclusion in showcase portfolios occur at least three times a year. The key to deciding on the frequency of selection, however, is the number of products or artifacts that the students have created and stored.

Samples of work to be included in portfolios are numerous and varied, ranging from writing in different modes, biographies and autobiographies, and drawings/diagrams/charts to journals, checklists, literature circle activities, self-evaluations, inventories, multimedia programs, projects from thematic units, letters, and poems, to name just a few.

A popular work sample form for including in the portfolios—and one with which most parents can identify—is a type of book report called a *book critique*. Unlike the traditional book report (once described as having done more to kill the love of reading in Americans ages 9 to 18 than any other idea to come from the schools), a book critique allows the writer to criticize the book while discussing both its merits and demerits. Recently published books that should easily elicit written reactions include the following:

Upper Primary

- Cazet's *The Shrunken Head* (2007)
- Cook & Charlton's *Hey Batta Batta Swing! The Wild Old Days of Baseball* (2007)
- Mills' *Being Teddy Roosevelt* (2007)
- Seuling's *Robert and the Happy Endings* (2007)

Intermediate

- McKissack's *A Friendship for Today* (2007)
- Parkinson's *Second Fiddle: Or How to Tell a Blackbird From a Sausage* (2007)
- Tarshis's *Emma-Jean Lazarus Fell out of a Tree* (2007)
- Woodson's *Feathers* (2007)

The practical starting point for portfolio assessment is determining the right storage space. Portfolios can come in different shapes and sizes. Least expensive and most readily available for storing children's work are manila folders or envelopes. File folders are also useful. Expandable or accordion files permit students to categorize their artifacts and add written feedback. These can all be stored in plastic crates or large cardboard boxes. Students label dated items as they place them in their portfolios. Some schools require that every item in the portfolio, regardless of where it is stored, have an attached index card explaining what it is and why it was selected for the portfolio.

Since portfolio assessment involves considerable time and effort on the part of teachers and children, many teachers advocate that showcase portfolios be shared with peers, parents, school administrators, and community members. They believe that this sharing helps students accept responsibility for their own learning. Some even organize "Portfolio Share Days" at the end of the school year to celebrate student accomplishments (Porter & Cleland, 1995).

Authentic Assessment: Grading

While assigning grades is challenging for all teachers, they should always remember that grades must be used to encourage children's achievement and not to defeat it. Grade reports can help every student continue to progress by enabling the child and parents to understand his or her successes and challenges with the language arts.

Grade reports or report cards can take various forms, including those with the traditional or numerical grades and/or narrative summaries. Some school districts have recently redesigned their report cards to correspond to state standards.

Happily, authentic assessment involves a positive way of grading since its procedures document what children do during the course of language arts assignments. Although making evaluations about complex literacy growth is admittedly difficult, it is possible to be fair when the grading criteria are explicit (e.g., through *rubrics*). A **rubric** describes student performance at different levels of proficiency in different content areas. Students and teachers use rubrics to analyze the information collected in portfolios, projects, daily work, or other learning activities. Used correctly, rubrics are effective assessment and instructional tools. An *analytic* rubric has specific guidelines while a *holistic* rubric is a general rubric for student writing. See Figure 3.3 for a holistic rubric for student writing adapted from Wiseman, Elish-Piper, and Wiseman (2005).

In this performance-based assessment, the literacy behaviors that a teacher expects to see as a result of literacy learning and teaching are listed along a continuum, reflecting different levels of achievement (Valencia et al., 1994). While formats for rubrics vary, most share two features: (1) standards (or levels at which children perform tasks) and (2) criteria (or what is being evaluated).

Teachers should follow these guidelines when constructing rubrics:

- Base levels on samples of student work that represent each stage of proficiency.
- Use specific wording that clearly describes behaviors in terms that children in that classroom can understand.
- Construct rubrics with a 3-, 4-, or 5-point scale, with the highest number representing the highest level.
- Limit criteria to a reasonable number.
- Avoid negative statements (e.g., "Has difficulty with punctuation"; Garcia & Verville, 1994).

When constructing rubrics, teachers may invite children as young as second and third graders to suggest criteria for inclusion (Skillings & Ferrell, 2000). When this process is done gradually and with careful guidance, it helps students develop critical thinking and metacognitive skills.

A sample lesson plan incorporating the concepts introduced in this chapter appears on p. 72.

Figure 3.3 Sample Holistic Rubric for Student Writing

Score of 3

_____ Writing samples demonstrate strong skill in organization and mechanics.

_____ Writing samples demonstrate well-developed ideas.

_____ Writing samples demonstrate original and mature use of language.

Score of 2

_____ Writing samples demonstrate some skill in organization and mechanics.

_____ Writing samples demonstrate fairly well-developed ideas.

_____ Writing samples demonstrate competent use of language.

Score of 1

_____ Writing samples show little skill in organization and mechanics.

_____ Writing samples show little or no sign of original ideas.

_____ Writing samples partially suggest competent use of language.

Working With English Language Learners

When assessing English Language Learners (ELLs), teachers need to be aware of language and cultural differences that may inaccurately represent or adversely affect measured levels of performance. For example, beginning ELLs often exhibit a reluctance to speak, even in one-on-one situations, and therefore evaluations may not be indicative of a student's English-language proficiency or knowledge of the subject matter. As do all students, ELLs require frequent opportunities to demonstrate understanding, and teachers should observe students routinely and systematically in a variety of situations. ELLs in Grades 3 through 8 are required by the No Child Left Behind Act (2001) to participate in national testing in English language arts, math, and science just like their peers. However, testing accommodations such as more time, flexible scheduling, small group or individual testing, and tests administered in the student's primary language may be implemented if determined to be necessary and appropriate.

In addition to meeting English language arts standards, federal law mandates that states test ELLs according to English language development guidelines. ELLs in kindergarten through Grade 12 are assessed annually for English-language proficiency on tests such as the CELDT (California English Language Development Test) that measure reading, writing, speaking, and listening skills. Wait time for test results, however, is often lengthy, and data can become quickly outdated. Although the information is valuable in tracking long-term growth, it lacks usefulness in planning individual instruction based on current needs.

The following assessment strategies can assist teachers in more accurately determining current levels of performance and knowledge of ELLs. At all language proficiency levels, students should be provided opportunities for higher-level thinking, demonstrating breadth of knowledge, self-evaluation, and reflection. The language arts portfolio described earlier in the chapter is one meaningful and appropriate assessment tool for ELLs at all levels of proficiency.

Beginning ELLs: Teachers should first determine beginning ELLs' proficiency and educational background in their primary language. School specialists can provide detailed diagnostic testing information, but classroom teachers can immediately assess students through informal reading activities. For example, teachers can provide students with books in their primary language to determine fluency in their primary language. Even if teachers are unfamiliar with the student's language, they can observe and listen to the student's interaction with the text. Does the student struggle or hesitate when reading? Does the student follow the text and read with inflection?

To determine listening comprehension, teachers can have nonreaders perform simple, nonverbal tasks such as matching activities and pointing to objects such as a book or a chair. Teachers can display pictures and ask the student to point to "the boy in the blue shirt" or "the yellow flower." Checklists are helpful in charting and documenting student responses. Teachers can ask students to "open the book" or write the numbers 1–10. Writing journals are another way to determine writing proficiency and the amount of instruction received in the student's primary language. Pre-emergent readers can draw pictures; copy letters, words, and sentences; and tell stories aloud.

Teachers should also be cognizant of non-Roman alphabets such as Chinese that do not connect symbols to sounds—ELLs with these language backgrounds will require intensive phonemic awareness instruction. Beginning ELLs should be given multiple opportunities in a variety of settings to demonstrate their skills and knowledge, especially new students who may have a heightened sense of self-consciousness. Students may feel uncomfortable in either large or small groups or even in one-on-one situations with the teacher. Evaluations at the beginning level should focus on listening and speaking rather than reading and writing.

Early intermediate and intermediate ELLs: At the intermediate level, ELLs can be assessed with methods similar to those used to evaluate English-speaking students. Informal reading inventories (IRIs), running records, quizzes, and student writing samples can offer ongoing documentation of students' current performance levels. Direct observation, however, remains a critical component in the evaluation process. Teachers can record observational notes about students engaged in a variety of learning tasks: classroom discussions, cooperative learning groups, writers' workshops, literature circles, and independent reading. Through the use of checklists and streamlined assessment tools, teachers can routinely and quickly take notes on word-attack skills, oral language, comprehension, participation, attitudes, and effort.

Early advanced and advanced ELLs: Students at the advanced level may demonstrate conversational competence, but mastery of *academic* language skills generally develops more slowly than *social* language; ELLs often fall behind their English-speaking peers. Teachers, therefore, need to give special attention to ELLs when assessing understanding of more complex concepts and vocabulary terms as learners advance through the grade levels. It is imperative that teachers systematically evaluate ELLs' knowledge of English grammar structures, figurative language, and vocabulary development. Teachers can create a matrix for learning tasks that differentiate language skills from academic content. For example, if students are learning about algebraic formulas, a math journal is evaluated separately for written conventions and clarity, while mathematical procedures and calculations are examined for accuracy and problem-solving skills.

As previously stated, all learners should be given multiple and ongoing opportunities in a variety of situations to demonstrate mastery of skills and understanding. Even for advanced ELLs, it may be more pragmatic for students to verbally or visually express their depth of learning when involved with cognitively demanding concepts. Rubrics and/or guidelines should be distributed and reviewed in advance so all learners have clear expectations and goals for assignments.

Practical Instructional Activities and Ideas

- *Multimedia presentations:* Teachers can assess student learning through PowerPoint, Keynote, and iMovie presentations and other forms of digital technology that require students to synthesize knowledge in new and creative ways. Multimedia activities encourage the multimodal expression of literacy skills and promote higher-level thinking. Additionally, multidimensional presentations can integrate material from other content areas. For example, students may develop a newscast in a unit on Lewis and Clark that covers standards in science, social studies, language arts, technology, fine arts, and math. Rubrics and teacher/peer evaluations are appropriate methods of assessment.
- *Big books:* Oversized books with enlarged print and colorful pictures provide informal opportunities to observe students' knowledge of concepts of print, rhyme, sight word recognition, and other emerging reading skills. Teachers can ask students to point to capital letters, periods, and other punctuation marks; locate sight words such as "and" or "the"; count the number of sentences; or find pairs of rhyming words. Checklists can be helpful in tracking participation and the number of correct responses and thus assist teachers in planning future instruction. Teachers can encourage shy students to volunteer responses and provide "safe" situations for reticent students to demonstrate literacy skills.

- *Choral reading:* While students read aloud together in small groups or the whole class, teachers can check for understanding by observing and listening. Teachers can circulate around the classroom and listen to individual students or small groups to check for proficiency in fluency, inflection, and pacing. Do students follow along with the text and turn pages at appropriate times? Do students try to sound out words and break them into manageable chunks or syllables to decode unfamiliar words? Teachers can utilize index cards or other individual record keeping systems to quickly record observations. Teachers can elect to focus on selected students during each session to make the task of assessment more manageable.

- *Whiteboards:* Individual whiteboards provide teachers with a quick and informal means of assessment. On them students can write math problems and spelling words, divide words into syllables, or indicate simple agree/disagree responses. Students hold up the individual whiteboards when finished for the teacher to visually assess. Every student has an opportunity to respond individually and receive immediate feedback. Teachers can immediately determine which students are having difficulty and adjust instruction accordingly for the whole group or for individual students.

- *Popsicle stick indicators:* Teachers can have students cut out and color two pictures from a template and then glue them on opposites sides of a popsicle stick or tongue depressor. For example, when learning short vowel sounds, students can cut out pictures of an *igloo* and an *alligator* that represent the short *i* and the short *a* vowel sounds. As the teacher recites words such as *apple* or *itch*, students hold up the picture of the short vowel sound they hear. As with the use of individual whiteboards discussed earlier, teachers can instantly evaluate student responses and provide feedback to students.

- *Audio books:* Teachers can provide a listening center with books on tape for students. Follow-up activities such as retelling the beginning, middle, and end of the story in pictorial, verbal, dramatic, or written form depending on the student's ability level or interest can help teachers evaluate listening comprehension. A written summary or storyboard format would be an alternative for more advanced students.

- *Student-recorded audio books:* Students read and record their own books-on-tape at their independent reading level. This activity can be repeated several times throughout the school year. Teachers, parents, and students can "hear" students' progress from the beginning to the end of the school year. The tapes may be included in the student's language arts portfolio.

- *Bookmaking:* Students can create handmade books on a variety of subjects. Teachers can have students write important details from informational texts in these books. For example, when learning about the topic "bats," students can write and illustrate ten important facts (e.g., bats are nocturnal, bats are mammals, bats use echolocation). Teachers can evaluate books based on a rubric or rating scale. Artistic skill, creativity, and knowledge in other content areas can be assessed separately.

- *Poetry T-shirts:* After a lesson on writing haikus, cinquains, or free verse poetry, students can write and illustrate their own poems on inexpensive T-shirts to wear or to give as a special gift. Instead of being a walking advertisement for a popular clothing brand or rock-and-roll band, students can proudly wear their own original work on their chest.

- *Self-evaluation:* Teachers can provide students with regular opportunities to self-evaluate their performance. Rating scales that use numbers or smiley faces are simple for students to use for quick self-assessment on a variety of literacy tasks. Teachers can have students rate themselves not only on quality and effort but also on such items as group cooperation, providing assistance to classmates, time management, problem solving, and creativity. Thus, students can gain experience not only in self-evaluating both the quality and completeness of a finished product but also in reflecting on the learning process itself. Teachers need to explicitly instruct students in effective self-evaluation skills and provide frequent opportunities to practice new skills. Students can become competent critics of their own strengths and weaknesses and set goals for personal improvement.

LESSON PLAN 3.1   Introduction to the Portfolio Process

The following lesson plan is designed to familiarize students, teachers, and parents with the preparation of the language arts portfolio. The lesson is most effective when introduced at the beginning of a new school year to encourage all stakeholders to think about the purpose and selection process of student work. Additionally, the lesson can be an excellent "icebreaker" or introductory lesson to acquaint teachers, students, and their families with each other. This language arts portfolio project is integrated with a second-grade history/social studies unit (e.g., All About Me) that investigates the concept of the individual or "self" within the larger group of family, neighborhood, community, and world culture. The focus of the lesson, however, can easily be modified to correlate with other themes and grade-level content standards.

Language Art Components: Listening, Speaking, and Writing

Grade: 2

ELL Level: Early Intermediate to Advanced

Topic: Social Studies

Time Frame: 2 to 3 weeks

Objectives

Students identify different types of portfolios (digital, paper, electronic) and different purposes of portfolios.

- Students create a "Self-Portrait" portfolio.
- Students cite and justify reasons for portfolio choices.

Materials

- Portfolio samples and "nonexamples" (photo albums, scrapbooks, etc.)
- Chart paper
- Brainstorming worksheet
- Parent letters
- Student-selected materials
- Art materials: assortment of paper, markers, glue, pattern scissors, bookbinding materials, and the like
- Computer/scanner
- Storage containers and devices—digital (CDs, flash drives), accordion files, manila folders, plastic containers

Content Standards

English Language Development (ELD): Listening, Speaking, Writing

- Students orally identify main ideas of discussions and conversations.
- Students create simple sentences with some assistance.
- Students use standard word order and grammatical forms.
- Students revise writing to reflect basic language conventions of punctuation and capitalization.

History/Social Studies

- Students describe the roles of individuals in the family and within the school community.
- Students explain and compare the different ways that families document their history.
- Students demonstrate an understanding that individuals and families have different customs, beliefs, and traditions.
- Students distinguish among past, present, and future events.

Language Arts: Writing

- Students write for a purpose and audience.
- Students write in complete and coherent sentences.
- Students use and apply basic rules of punctuation and capitalization.

Vocabulary

- Portfolio
- Personal reflection

Open

Engage

- Teacher provides examples and nonexamples of portfolios in different areas of the classroom. If computer access is available, students can examine digital examples online of student and professional portfolios created for different purposes (artist, architect, teaching, modeling, financial, writing, etc.).
- In small groups, students examine various portfolios and "nonexamples," which are collections of items such as scrapbooks, photo albums, baseball card collections, and recipe files.
- Teacher asks students to write comments on chart paper posted at each "center" visited about what they liked/disliked, whether they thought it was/was not a portfolio, and did it help them understand more about the person who created it?

Body

Explore

- Teacher regroups students after they have had an opportunity to visit each center.
- Students discuss reactions/responses to portfolios.

- Teacher clarifies which samples were actual portfolios and which samples were "collections."
- Teacher explains that they will be creating a portfolio about their life, accomplishments, meaningful people in their lives, hobbies, interests, and goals to give others an idea of who they are and what they are working toward.
- Teacher explains and passes out "Brainstorming" worksheet. Students are prompted to create lists, answer questions, and/or fill-in-the-blanks. Here are some examples of questions on the worksheet:
  - What is your biggest accomplishment?
  - What is your favorite activity/sport/hobby?
  - What was the most difficult problem you ever had to solve?
  - What is your dream job?
  - What makes you a good friend?
  - What people have helped you most?
  - What will your goals be when you are age 25?
- Be sure to include a "blank" section for students to be creative and generate any new ideas not included in the set of questions.
- Students work alone, with a partner, or in small groups to answer questions and generate lists about "self."

Expand

- When most students are finished with the worksheet, Teacher calls the whole group back and asks volunteers to share some responses. Discuss relevance of the answers—why are they important or significant?
- Teacher explains to students that they will use these lists to help them gather and create samples to include in their "Self-Portrait" portfolios. Teacher clarifies that students will be required to explain *why* they selected the items because each entry will have a short, written reflection.
- Teacher explains that students can select their preferred style of portfolio—either digital or written.
- Teacher sends worksheet home with two copies of the letter to parents (one to keep for reference and one to sign and return) describing the activity and the importance of their assistance in collecting and deciding what items to include. Examples could include photos, work from previous grades, awards, current work, or anything that helps demonstrate the strengths and personality of their child. Original samples can be scanned, photocopied, or photographed (if three-dimensional) by the parent or the teacher and returned. The letter to parents will also explain the purpose of this assignment: It is an introductory assignment to build beginning skills in selecting relevant samples because they will be creating language arts (and possibly other) portfolios throughout the year to show their growth as readers and writers.
- Teacher provides students and parents with a rubric or checklist for the assignment.

Close

Apply

- After providing sufficient time for sample creation/selection, students begin assembling and creating their "Self-Portrait" portfolios.

- Students write a short reflection or explanation for each entry.
- Students share portfolios with class at Portfolio Share Day. Invite parents if possible.
- Students discuss/evaluate peers' portfolios by stating one strength and one recommendation for improvement for each portfolio. This evaluation can be conducted in small peer-evaluation groups or as a whole class discussion.
- Teacher discusses with students how they will be creating a language arts portfolio and how this assignment might help them make selections for reading and writing and speaking samples.

Assessment

- Students complete self-evaluations.
- Teacher has individual conferences with students and provides feedback based on rubric.

Integration Across the Curriculum

Because this chapter focuses on assessment, the integration section is organized according to an intermediate thematic unit titled Our Earth. Thematic units provide multiple opportunities to assess students across subject areas and observe them in a wide variety of authentic learning tasks.

Science

- After learning about the water cycle, students demonstrate understanding through an assignment they choose: create a visual representation (e.g., poster, book, PowerPoint) and label stages, write and dramatize a script in a small group, compose a written explanation that includes graphics, or write a chant or song describing the cycle: transpiration, evaporation, collection, percolation, and precipitation. Students are assessed according to a rubric or rating scale passed out in advance.
- During a unit on erosion and the catastrophic effects of the Dust Bowl, students can engage in a debate about its key causes: Was the Dust Bowl caused by poor land management practices or was it an unfortunate natural occurrence? Groups can be assessed according to a rubric that includes such criteria as using a clear viewpoint, supporting fact and statements, and a clear speaking voice and the relevance of arguments. After debates, individuals can write a letter to the Bureau of Land Management or other government agency to plead their stance on current land issues; such letters may question the use of recreational vehicles, dam construction, animal grazing, mining, and other factors that have an impact on our environment.

Social Studies

- Before a unit on the earth's resources, teachers and students can brainstorm a list of ways to protect our earth such as planting trees, recycling, walking or riding a bike instead of driving, and conserving water. Teachers can use a K-W-L (What I Know, What I Want to Know, What I Learned) chart or similar format and add information and questions during the course of the lesson. As a culminating activity and assessment, students can propose and write about a way to solve a current environmental issue.

- Students can create brochures about a national park. Teachers evaluate students on predetermined criteria including writing conventions, legibility, descriptive language, writing to an audience, visual appeal, and research skills.

Math

- Students and teachers can go out and "clean the green," picking up litter from the school campus or a nearby park. They can sort and classify postconsumer waste items according to paper, plastic, aluminum, glass, and nonrecyclables. Students can also save containers from lunch to recycle. After the above items are sorted, students can graph their "trash" and analyze and ask questions about the data. Teachers can observe students during group activities to assess learning.

Literature

- Teachers can use a variety of informational, historical, and fictional books to assess student levels of reading comprehension, comparing and contrasting skills, fluency, and vocabulary. To support the Our Earth theme, students can read books such as Collard's *Butterfly Count* (2002), Showers' *Where Does the Garbage Go?* (1994), Silverstein's *The Giving Tree* (2004), and Seuss's *The Lorax* (1971).

Visual and Performing Arts

- Teachers can introduce students to folk and "outsider" artists who create artwork from trash, junk, or recycled items. Books such as Greenblat's *Aunt Ippy's Museum of Junk* (1991), Slaymaker's *Bottle Houses: The Creative World of Grandma Prisbey* (2004) and Zelver's *The Wonderful Towers of Watts* (1994) show students that they can "make something out of nothing" with a little imagination and resourcefulness.
- After studying a unit on folk art, teachers can have students create multimedia art pieces constructed from recycled, found, and trash items. Students can write a personal reflection or "artist's statement" explaining the meaning of the piece and the process. The students are graded on visual arts, writing, creativity, and problem-solving skills.
- Students write and perform a play about recycling at home and use "found" or recycled materials to create props and costumes.

Health

- The spread of germs and infectious diseases is a good lesson to present and discuss with students for the Our Earth unit. Teachers can support good hygienic practices by providing rubber gloves for "trash picking" during recycling activities and promoting regular handwashing. Books such as Berger's *Germs Make Me Sick!* (1995) help reinforce the concept of microbes and germs. Teachers can evaluate student understanding of germs by observing their use of hand sanitizer, gloves, tissues, and handwashing when appropriate.
- In connection with a science lesson about the water cycle, students can research how the water supply becomes contaminated through illegal dumping of waste and surface water runoff of pesticides and chemicals. Students can locate local watersheds on maps and identify potential sources of water supply contamination. Teachers can have students investigate and respond to the question "which is better—bottled or tap water?" based on new information. Teachers can evaluate students on research and map reading skills and also competency in composing a persuasive essay.

Physical Education

- If time and space permit, a class garden is the perfect choice for the Earth theme and to provide healthy exercise. Students can weed, water, cultivate, and reap the rewards of good food. Students can also grow plants that are indigenous to the area or drought-tolerant varieties to emphasize the delicate balance of ecosystems. Teachers have the opportunity to observe students in a variety of activities.

Music

- Students can save boxes, coffee cans, toilet paper rolls, bottle caps, and other clean recyclables to create homemade musical instruments. They can experiment with tone and pitch to make a variety of sounds. Teachers can evaluate student performance by having students work in small groups or "bands" to write lyrics and musical scores to perform for class or parents.

Parents as Partners

Parents often do not participate in the assessment process, but the following six suggestions provide ways in which family members can take an active role in student evaluations.

1. *Parent-friendly report cards:* Teachers can work with school districts to improve the readability of student report cards. School staff and teachers can create a FAQ (frequently asked questions) sheet to assist parents and families in the interpretation of confusing items or areas of common misunderstanding.

2. *Regular feedback:* Teachers should not limit parent-teacher interactions to one or two parent-teacher conferences during the school year. Teachers can update parents frequently about their child's progress and maintain the lines of communication. Parents can provide teachers with an alternative perspective on their child's strengths, capabilities, and personality. For example, a student who is quiet in the classroom is often much more outgoing in the home environment and more willing to take risks. Teachers can use parent insights to adjust and plan learning activities.

3. *Project proposal sheets:* When teachers assign long-term projects such as informational reports, teachers can send home information sheets with rubrics and/or guidelines. Parents sign and return the confirmation slip indicating they are aware of the requirements, due dates, and extra support they may need to provide to ensure their child's success. Any questions are thus answered at the beginning of the assignment, which helps eliminate unexpected "surprises."

4. *Portfolio selection:* Typically, students and teachers jointly decide which pieces should be included in student portfolios. However, teachers can schedule short meetings with parents to review their child's work and provide input about what they think would best represent their child's growth, creativity, and mastery of skills.

5. *Parent groups:* Teachers, schools, and districts can assist parents in forming parent advisory groups that encourage families to assume an important role in all aspects of their child's education including assessment. Parents can offer an alternate and valuable perspective on a variety of educational issues including textbook adoptions, dress codes, discipline policies, home-school connections, and literacy programs.

6. *Translators:* Whenever possible, translation services should be available for non-English-speaking families. Written notes and letters, report cards, telephone conversations, and parent-teacher conferences will only be effective if both families and teachers can clearly communicate information.

Student Study Site

The Companion Web site for *Language Arts: Integrating Skills for Classroom Teaching*
www.sagepub.com/donoghuestudy
Visit the Web-based study site to enhance your understanding of the chapter content. The study materials include chapter summaries, practice tests, flashcards, and Web resources.

Additional Professional Readings

Burke, K. (2006). *From standards to rubrics in six steps: Tools for assessing learning, K–8*. Thousand Oaks, CA: Corwin Press.

Cizek, G., & Burg, S. (2006). *Addressing test anxiety in a high-stakes environment*. Thousand Oaks, CA: Corwin Press.

Clarke, S. (2008). *Formative assessment in action*. New York: Richard C. Owen.

Gallagher, C. (2007). *Reclaiming assessment: A better alternative to the accountability agenda*. Portsmouth, NH: Heinemann.

Gentry, R. (2007). *Assessing early literacy with Richard Gentry*. Portsmouth, NH: Heinemann.

Gottlieb, M. (2008). *Assessing English language learners: Bridges from language proficiency to academic achievement*. Thousand Oaks, CA: Corwin Press.

Groeber, J. (2007). *Designing and using rubrics for reading and language arts, K–6*. (2nd ed.). Thousand Oaks, CA: Corwin Press.

Jones, P., Ataya, R., & Carr, J. (2006). *A pig don't get fatter the more you weigh it: Classroom assessments that work*. New York: Teachers College Press.

Paratore, J., & McCormack, R. (Eds.). (2007). *Classroom literacy assessment*. New York: Guilford.

Shea, M., Murray, R., & Harlin, R. (2005). *Drowning in data: How to collect, organize, and document, student performance*. Portsmouth, NH: Heinemann.

Children's Literature Cited in the Text

Berger, M. (1995). *Germs make me sick!* New York: Harper Trophy.

Cazet, D. (2007). *Grandpa Spanielson's chicken pox stories: Story #3: The shrunken head*. New York: Harper Collins.

Cleary, B. (2000). *Dear Mr. Henshaw*. New York: Harper Trophy.

Collard, S. (2002). *Butterfly count*. New York: Holiday House.

Cook, S., & Charlton, J. (2007). *Hey batta batta swing! The wild old days of baseball*. New York: Margaret K. McElderry.

Grenblat, R. A. (1991). *Aunt Ippy's museum of junk*. New York: HarperCollins.

McKissack, P. (2007). *A friendship for today*. New York: Scholastic.

Mills, C. (2007). *Being Teddy Roosevelt*. New York: Farrar.

Parkinson, S. (2007). *Second fiddle: Or how to tell a blackbird from a sausage*. New York: Roaring Brook Press.

Seuling, B. (2007). *Robert and the happy endings*. Peru, IL: Carus.

Seuss, Dr. (1971). *The lorax*. New York: Random House.

Showers, P. (1994). *Where does the garbage go?* New York: HarperCollins.

Silverstein, S. (1964). *The giving tree*. New York: HarperCollins.

Slaymaker, M. E. (2004). *Bottle houses: The creative world of Grandma Prisbey*. New York: Holt.

Tarshis, L. (2007). *Emma-Jean Lazarus fell out of a tree*. New York: Dial.

Woodson, J. (2007). *Feathers*. New York: Putnam.

Zelver, P. (1996). *The wonderful towers of Watts*. New York: Harper Trophy.

References

Baskwill, J., & Whitman, P. (1988). *Evaluation: Whole language, whole child*. Toronto: Scholastic.

Farr, R. (1992). Putting it all together: Solving the reading assessment puzzle. *The Reading Teacher, 46,* 26–37.

Garcia, M., & Verville, K. (1994). Redesigning teaching and learning: The Arizona student assessment program. In S. Valencia, E. Hiebert, &

P. Afflerbach (Eds.), *Authentic reading assessment: Practices and possibilities*. Newark, DE: International Reading Association.

Guthrie, J. (2002). Preparing students for high stakes testing in reading. In A. Farstrup & S. Samuels (Eds.), *What research has to say about reading instruction* (3rd ed). Newark, DE: International Reading Association.

Harris, T., & Hodges, R. (Eds.). (1995). *The literacy dictionary.* Newark, DE: International Reading Association.

Herman, J., Aschbacher, P., & Winters, I. (1992). *A practical guide to alternative assessment.* Alexandria, VA: Association for Supervision and Curriculum Development

Heubert, J., & Huser, R. (Eds.). (1999). *High stakes: Testing for tracking, promotion and graduation.* Washington, DC: National Academy Press.

International Reading Association. (1999). *High stakes assessment in reading: A position statement of the International Reading Association.* Newark, DE: Author.

International Reading Association & National Council of Teachers of English. (1994). *Standards for the assessment of reading and writing.* Newark, DE, & Urbana, IL: Authors.

Johnson, P. (1997). *Knowing literacy: Constructive literacy assessment.* York, ME: Stenhouse.

Leslie, L., & Jett-Simpson, M. (1997). *Authentic literacy assessment: An ecological approach.* New York: Longman.

McCabe, P. (2005). Enhancing self-efficacy for high stakes reading tests. *The Reading Teacher, 57,* 12–20.

New Standards Project. (1994). *Elementary English language arts teacher portfolio handbook: Field trial version.* Urbana, IL: Author.

Porter, C., & Cleland, J. (1995). *The portfolio as a learning strategy.* Portsmouth, NH: Heinemann.

Rhodes, L., & Dudley-Marling, C. (1996). *Readers and writers with a difference: A holistic approach to teaching struggling readers and writers.* Portsmouth, NH: Heinemann.

Rhodes, L., & Nathenson-Majia, S. (1992). Anecdotal records: A powerful tool for ongoing literacy assessment. *The Reading Teacher, 45,* 502–509.

Roe, B., Smith, S., & Burns, P. (2005). *Teaching reading in today's elementary schools* (9th ed.). Boston: Houghton Mifflin.

Santman, D. (2002). Teaching to the test: Test preparation in the reading workshop. *Language Arts, 79,* 203–211.

Skillings, M., & Ferrell, R. (2000). Student-generated rubrics: Bringing students into the assessment process. *The Reading Teacher, 53,* 452–455.

Tierney, R., Crumpler, T., Bertelson, C., & Bond, E. (2003). *Interactive assessment: Teachers, parents, and students.* Norwood, MA: Christopher-Gordon.

Tompkins, G. (2006). *Literacy for the 21st century* (4th ed.). Columbus, OH: Merrill/Prentice Hall.

Valencia, S., Hiebert, E., & Afflerbach, P. (1994). *Authentic reading assessment: Practices and possibilities.* Newark, DE: International Reading Association.

Valencia, S., & Place, N. (1994). Portfolios: A process for enhancing teaching and learning. *The Reading Teacher, 47,* 666–669.

Wiseman, D., Elish-Piper, L., & Wiseman, A. (2005). *Learning to teach language arts in a field-based setting.* Scottsdale, AZ: Holcomb Hathaway.

Anticipation Statement Answers

1. Agree

2. Disagree

3. Agree

4. Disagree

5. Agree

6. Agree

7. Disagree

8. Disagree

9. Disagree: Although teachers should be cognizant of desired learning outcomes, questions should be open-ended and encourage individual interpretation. However, beginning teachers might feel more comfortable with predetermined answers.

10. Disagree: Teachers should routinely take notes as a means of tracking student behavior and performance. Anecdotal records and other written observations can provide insightful documentation that may go unnoticed when only using formal assessment methods. However, large classes may prevent teachers from compiling extensive notes on each child.

Integrating Language Arts Across the Curriculum

CHAPTER 4

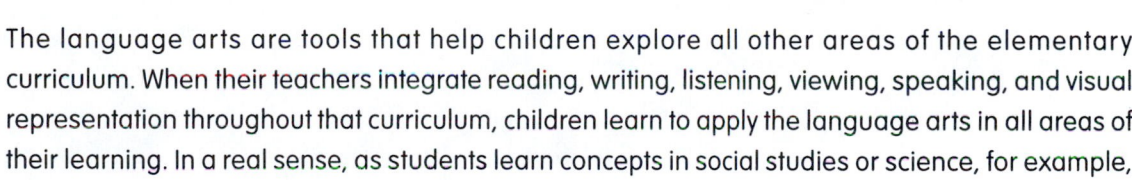

The language arts are tools that help children explore all other areas of the elementary curriculum. When their teachers integrate reading, writing, listening, viewing, speaking, and visual representation throughout that curriculum, children learn to apply the language arts in all areas of their learning. In a real sense, as students learn concepts in social studies or science, for example, they are also practicing one or more of their language skills.

Anticipation Statements

Complete this exercise before reading Chapter 4.

Do you agree or disagree with the following statements? Circle your answer. Be prepared to discuss questions in blue.

1.	Integration of the language arts throughout the subject areas promotes higher-level thinking skills and personal connections.	Agree	Disagree
2.	*Literature-based* units are broader in focus than *integrated* units of study.	Agree	Disagree
3.	Teachers need not completely examine all children's books/print resources before their use in integrated units.	Agree	Disagree
4.	Social studies and science are the most common subjects used as a unifying element in a thematic unit.	Agree	Disagree
5.	Primary sources are a valuable tool in making learning more interesting and accessible to students.	Agree	Disagree
6.	Community resources help students connect their lives to other people and the world.	Agree	Disagree
7.	Students should have limited input to theme topics and activities because integrated units require careful correlation with standards and curriculum guidelines.	Agree	Disagree
8.	An initiating activity in an integrated unit stimulates student interest and piques curiosity in inquiry topics.	Agree	Disagree
9.	Thematic units are carefully preplanned by teacher well in advance of implementation.	Agree	Disagree
10.	Culminating activities for integrated units should include pencil-and-paper tests, essays, and formal research projects.	Agree	Disagree

Integration: Definition, Principles, and Benefits

Integration of language arts means teaching listening, speaking, reading, writing, viewing, and visual representation while teaching in the content areas of social studies, mathematics, science, music, and the arts.

Promoting language across the curriculum is based on three principles, according to Bullock (1975): The means to learn is one function of language, all genuine learning is based on discovery, and the best way to learn is using language arts for that discovery.

There are several benefits that occur when language arts are included in content area instruction. First, students are enabled through their language abilities to discuss and write about concepts and ideas discovered in content areas (Shanahan, 1996). Teachers encourage such discovery together with the application of new knowledge to present-day situations. Second, integration encourages content area lessons to be more student-centered, departing from the usual teacher- and test-centered classroom. Britton (1970) synthesized the theories of both Vygotsky and Bruner (discussed earlier in this book) and urged schools to promote learners' inclination to use reading, writing, and oral language skills for real-life purposes.

Third, an integrated school day in which students participate more intensely and therefore develop deeper background knowledge about topics enables them to incorporate content information into their own lives. Textbooks cannot generally serve that purpose because their subject range is necessarily broad and does not allow for in-depth coverage of most topics. Furthermore, allowing English Language Learners (ELLs) and less able students to read children's literature and trade books (defined as any nontextbook books, including teaching materials devoted to particular topics) for content area instruction helps raise their self-esteem because the readability levels are often lower and the books more captivating and understandable (Caswell & Duke, 1998). Students consider trade books to be more informative, relevant, and enjoyable than textbooks.

Applicable IRA/NCTE Standards

Standard 1   Students read a wide range of print and nonprint texts to build an understanding of texts, of themselves, and of the cultures of the United States and the world; to acquire new information; to respond to the needs and demands of society and the workplace; and for personal fulfillment. Among these texts are fiction and nonfiction, classic and contemporary works.

Standard 2   Students read a wide range of literature from many periods in many genres to build an understanding of the many dimensions (e.g., philosophical, ethical, aesthetic) of human experience.

Standard 7   Students conduct research on issues and interests by generating ideas and questions, and by posing problems. They gather, evaluate, and synthesize data from a variety of sources (e.g., print and non-print texts, artifacts, people) to communicate their discoveries in ways that suit their purpose and audience.

Standard 8   Students use a variety of technological and information resources (e.g., libraries, databases, computer networks, video) to gather and synthesize information and to create and communicate knowledge.

Standard 11   Students participate as knowledgeable, reflective, creative, and critical members of a variety of literacy communities.

Standard 12   Students use spoken, written, and visual language to accomplish their own purposes (e.g., for learning, enjoyment, persuasion, and the exchange of information).

SOURCE: *Standards for the English Language Arts*, by the International Reading Association and the National Council of Teachers of English, Copyright 1996 by the International Reading Association and the National Council of Teachers of English. Reprinted with permission. http://www.ncte.org/about/over/standards/110846.htm

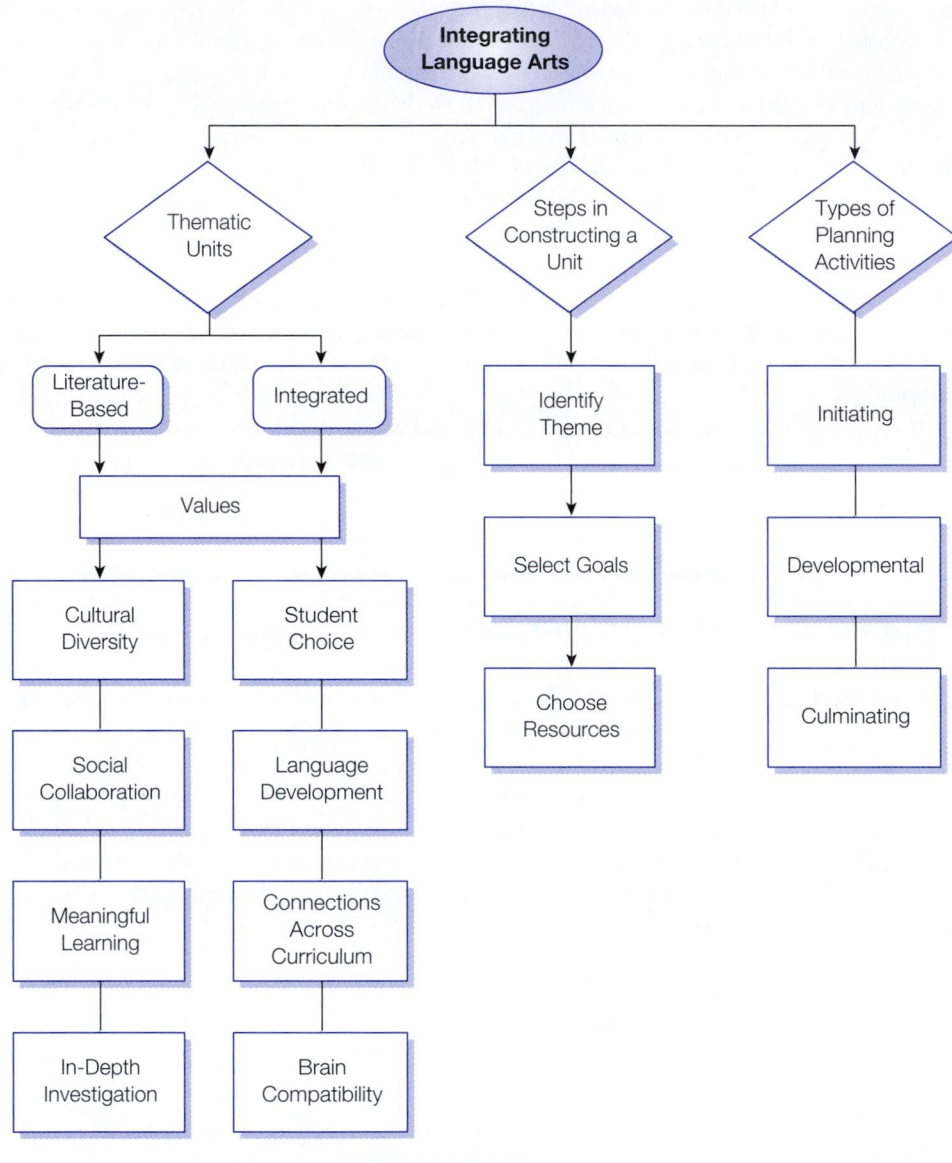

A Graphic Summary of the Contents of This Chapter

Finally, allowing children, especially boys, to read and write in areas of special interest as found in nonfiction content books enhances language arts skills and increases their knowledge of the subject matter.

Fourth, integration of content area topics and language arts instruction enables a focus on major ideas about our "human condition" (Bruner, 1998). This focus reduces teachers' frustration over attempts to cover too many topics in too short a period of time. Intense concentration on a single topic can truly affect literacy skills of students and increase their higher-level thinking, as one hopes will occur in Miss O'Connell's first grade when she introduces a unit on space in Vignette 4.1.

VIGNETTE 4.1   Language Arts in Space

Each year Miss O'Connell anticipated introducing her first-grade students to the wonders of the universe. The children already possessed a natural curiosity about the sun, moon, and stars and always enjoyed the science unit on the solar system.

And she noticed that the students' enthusiasm for the material extended beyond the lessons she prepared. Many of the children also wrote in their journals about walking on the moon, drew pictures of themselves in space suits, or selected books on related subjects during free reading at the library. This year, Miss O'Connell planned to capitalize on their interest and intentionally incorporate language arts activities into the science curriculum.

In previous years she began by listing the planets in order and teaching a mnemonic device to help the children remember the lineup. Although she still wanted the students to absorb this information, she decided to emphasize the attributes of the various planets—instead of just their distance from the sun—at the beginning of this new unit. Friday afternoon she stayed late to finish final preparations for the first activity.

As the children arrived Monday morning, they were delighted to find the desks rearranged into 10 small groups around the room. Large color posters of the sun, the moon, and each of the eight planets perched near each cluster of desks, and for several minutes Miss O'Connell allowed the children to examine each picture. The students especially enjoyed the photographs of Saturn's rings, Jupiter's Great Red Spot, and the large canyon cracking the surface of Mars.

As the children found their seats, Miss O'Connell introduced the new unit.

"Today we're starting a study of space," she said. "To start, look at the poster by your desk and sound out the big word at the bottom."

The children again inspected the large images and she heard little voices reading the names of the planets. James raised his hand.

"Our poster is the moon, but the moon isn't a planet. I know because my big brother told me all the planets," he said proudly.

"You're right, James," Miss O'Connell answered. "We will study the planets, but space holds a lot more than that! We'll also talk about the moon, the sun, and stars."

"And black holes?" asked Clay. "They're awesome."

Miss O'Connell smiled—Clay must have an older sibling sharing advanced information as well.

"Clay, there's a book about black holes on our bookshelves—maybe you can check it out during silent reading." He nodded and she continued.

"Next to the big photographs near your desks, you should also see another poster listing three facts. I'd like you to read these sentences to the class. James, let's start with your group—please share some information about the moon."

To ensure a positive read-aloud experience and to maximize comprehension, Miss O'Connell had intentionally written each group of sentences at a first-grade level; she planned to introduce new vocabulary in later lessons. James and the other members of his group slowly took turns reading aloud the three facts from their poster.

"Great job!" she said when they finished. She quickly reviewed the information. "Our moon group taught us it doesn't rain on the moon, the moon is smaller than Earth, and the moon is shaped like what?"

"An egg!" said Sanjeev.

"Right," she said. "Okay sun group, your turn."

One at a time she led each group in reading the new information to the class. The simple exercise not only provided excellent practice for the beginning readers but also reinforced good listening skills.

"We've learned so many interesting things today," Miss O'Connell said after all the groups finished. "And we're just getting started! Tomorrow we'll find out more."

"Can we still have the pictures?" Rachael asked.

"Yes, we'll keep the posters in the room and I'll give you more time to look at them," Miss O'Connell replied, pleased at their interest in the images. "Right now I want you to write about your group's planet—or sun, or moon," she added, catching James's eye. "You may write a poem, or a story, or your favorite thing you learned. Take a few minutes to think and then work quietly."

As the students bent over their desks, Miss O'Connell evaluated her progress so far. Combining science content with language arts skills was new for her, but she had worked hard to incorporate reading, writing, viewing, listening, and speaking into the first day. In the coming week she would continue to include various techniques while emphasizing several of the skills in more depth.

For now, she looked forward to reading the finished products from this writing assignment and gauging the children's comprehension. Like previous years' classes, they already demonstrated a high level of interest in the subject matter—new opportunities for self-expression with language would only help them learn more.

Fifth, integration is a process that occurs within the learners themselves and is not something that teachers can plan and implement (Block, 2001). When curriculum units begin with children's interests and are instigated by their concern about real-world problems, students can recognize the connections between themselves, the world, and reading and writing.

Sixth and last, with integration comes students' increased understanding of themselves and their place in the world. As students gain the skills needed to be successful learners, their abilities in the language arts develop simultaneously with their gains in content areas. As a result, they become able to function as contributing members of society, according to Harvey (1998), with decision-making skills and social attributes that benefit not only themselves but also the classroom community and society in general.

Thematic Units: Overview

A useful method for integrating the language arts is through thematic units. While authorities differ as to the names and/or number of such units, this book identifies two of them: **literature-based units** (or intradisciplinary units) and **integrated units** (or interdisciplinary units). The first has a

An integrated unit on physical science can include reading biographies of Benjamin Franklin and Thomas Edison and applying the principles they discovered to students' own experiments.

narrower focus than the second as it integrates the language arts during a study of one author (e.g., William Steig or Patricia MacLachlan) or a particular literary genre (e.g., historical fiction or modern fantasy), but it does not directly include other curricular areas. An integrated unit, on the other hand, does include most or all of the curricular areas centered about a unifying theme (e.g., The Ocean or Ancient Egypt) and integrates more than just the language arts.

There are numerous values to using thematic units, as they encourage the following:

- *An understanding of cultural diversity:* Students from different backgrounds learn to appreciate each other's traits as they join together on projects and activities.
- *Social collaboration:* Students and teacher work together to develop and implement the units, accepting differences of opinion.

For material related to this concept, go to Video Clip 4.1 on the Student Resource CD bound into the back of your textbook.

- *Meaningful learning of issues and skills:* Issues of personal and social significance are more useful and relevant than practicing skills in isolation.
- *In-depth investigation:* Students are given both time and opportunity to pursue subject areas of special interest.
- *Choice:* Instead of whole-class assignments, students may opt to investigate projects that interest them personally and to do so in ways and with others who have similar outlooks.
- *Language development:* Students use all language forms purposefully in their investigations as language is integrated in the content areas.
- *Connections across the curriculum:* Students become aware of the need to move across curricular boundaries to solve problems.
- *Brain compatibility:* The more that knowledge is unified, the better the brain functions as it processes information effectively through patterns and connections (Roe & Ross, 2006).

Children's literature is the core component in the development of any thematic unit. By becoming knowledgeable about both the grade-level curriculum and quality children's books, teachers can learn to match literature to the content areas. They can do so by (a) making certain that books with a wide variety of reading levels are available as resources for all children; (b) matching books with individual student inquiries and interests; (c) connecting literature to reading, writing, listening, speaking, viewing, and visual representation activities in the content areas; (d) choosing related read-alouds that describe a common experience and focus on the language of a particular unit; and (e) introducing new genres for reading in the content areas.

As mentioned earlier, content area teaching and learning demand the use of children's literature and trade books primarily because textbooks treat many topics in a superficial manner (Temple, Martinez, Yokota, & Naylor, 2002). Quality books, on the other hand, including trade books, engage child readers and open up new perspectives to keep them learning as well.

Finally, the most important characteristic of thematic teaching is that it helps children make sense of their world (Mitchell & David, 1992). It demands that teachers become fully aware of their students' needs and interests. Teachers can list possible themes that children would enjoy exploring, as suggested from the following sources: age-appropriate knowledge, themes defined by state or district standards, and community or culturally related themes. Furthermore, thematic teaching also demands that teachers know themselves—their own interests and experiences and their knowledge about the subject matter. Such information will assist them in developing activities based on their strengths. It will also alert them to the need to learn more about a theme before teaching it.

Constructing a Thematic Unit

Whether it is a literature-based unit or an integrated unit, there are general steps involved in constructing a thematic unit. Although there is some overlap among these steps and some back-and-forth actions among them, it is wise to consider each step carefully, as third-grade teacher Mrs. Reid does in Vignette 4.2, before finally embarking on a unit that may take a month or longer to teach.

VIGNETTE 4.2   Healthy Eating Across the Curriculum

Mrs. Reid sighed as she stared at the blank sheet of notebook paper. Already today she'd cleaned out two closets and washed a sink full of dishes. Her house looked wonderful, but it was time to stop procrastinating and start planning the next unit for her third-grade class.

She knew her students retained more of the material when a theme integrated the main ideas across several subject areas. But even after ten years as an elementary school teacher, she still found the planning process a little overwhelming.

Fortunately, she'd already completed the first task—selecting a theme. Last week as she walked through the cafeteria at lunch time, she'd been appalled to see many of the students eating nothing but French fries, candy bars, and other snacks.

"Shouldn't you eat some fruits and vegetables with your lunch?" she asked one of the children.

"I have ketchup on my hot dog," he replied, then resumed munching.

Mrs. Reid shook her head ruefully at the memory. She knew the importance of eating for health and worried that her young students were establishing bad habits. When she realized the third-grade health curriculum called for an emphasis on nutrition, it seemed the perfect time to launch a new unit.

It's still a good idea, she thought to herself. Just get to work!

After considering a few titles, Mrs. Reid settled on "Healthy Eating Choices" and began brainstorming goals for the unit. She liked to involve the students in determining some of these goals, but she retained responsibility for ensuring that the unit covered a variety of subjects and explored the theme comprehensively.

The curriculum required that students learn about vitamins, the food pyramid, and the connection between nutrition and health. Mrs. Reid jotted down these broad goals. Connecting food choices to personal health is a good start, she thought. But I'd like to include some science experiments, and I want to reference the cultural and ethnic backgrounds represented in the class. She noted these thoughts as well, beginning to feel excited about the possibilities.

Next, resource selection, she thought, turning to a fresh notebook page. She planned to research new materials at the library, but several books already on her shelves would be perfect for the unit. *Bread and Jam for Frances* (1993), about a little badger who discovers the wonderful variety of foods after limiting herself to only bread and jam, was a classic favorite. Mrs. Reid also liked *Little Pea* (2005), a charming picture book about a small pea who must eat his dinner of candy so he can have spinach for dessert. Her struggling students would enjoy the easy-to-read story during independent reading. *Gregory, the Terrible Eater* (1989) would be another great addition on the fiction side, and fun informational books like *The Monster Health Book* (2006) would teach the food groups, the importance of exercise, and more.

As the students read about food choices, she could also offer homework choices across the spectrum of language arts. Some children would enjoy creating collages of healthy foods, while the more analytical might be drawn to "pro and con" menu reviews. And of course she would ask the students to write—perhaps requiring the children to write essays describing the changes they planned to make in their own eating habits would be a positive culminating activity.

As she reviewed her resource list, Mrs. Reid also began building connections to other subjects. What a great opportunity to explore different cultures, she thought. Perhaps the students can bring homemade food—a favorite regional specialty or family recipe—to share with the class. She knew many of her students' families came from Mexico, and she looked forward to made-from-scratch guacamole and tortillas.

Mrs. Reid also remembered *Hungry Planet: What the World Eats* (2005), a wonderful photographic essay detailing the eating habits of families around the globe. Although some of the text might challenge her young students, the better readers would enjoy the book as an extended or supplementary selection, and every child would benefit from examining the pictures.

And we could cook in class! she thought, pencil flying over the page as she captured each new thought. *I know of so many wonderful cookbooks for kids, and some lessons teach valuable science principles as well. Even a simple study of why popcorn pops or why gelatin congeals would be interesting—and delicious.*

It was coming together. She could also explore the possibility of a short field trip to a local organic farm, and her good friend Greg worked as a chef in a downtown hotel. He'd love to visit the class.

She stretched her neck and set down her pencil, pleased at the progress she'd made in just over an hour. *That wasn't so bad,* she thought. *It feels great to have so many ideas. And if even one student stops thinking of ketchup as a vegetable, it will all be worth it.*

Identifying a Theme

Several factors must be considered when selecting a theme: students' areas of expressed interest, curriculum requirements, compatibility with state and district standards, and students' developmental needs. Kindergarten–primary children can understand concrete themes readily (e.g., a "hands-on" theme such as Growing Plants) or those that involve an abstract theme such as Friendship brought to a concrete level. Intermediate students can work well with more abstract concepts such as Water Quality in Our Community and State. At both primary and intermediate levels, it has been recommended that there be a "tension" to the theme, which encourages students to stretch their thinking and develop a deeper understanding of an abstract topic. Here are sample themes that can be explored to some degree at all elementary grade levels:

Authors and/or Illustrators

Family or Family Roots

Journeys

Growing Things

Courage

Stories in Which the Heroine Is the Problem Solver

Changes in Seasons

The Importance of Being Different

The Fun of Eating

Fantasy Versus Reality

Typically, the unifying framework is provided by social studies or science. When planning thematic units, the teacher should consider both language arts standards and content area standards. He or she should also wisely consider a theme that is broad enough to incorporate a varied group of books, resources, and activities but not so broad that the children miss the connections that exist among areas to be studied. The theme may even be selected with the help of the students themselves to give them a sense of ownership. Finally, it should challenge them to go beyond their present knowledge levels (Roe & Ross, 2006).

Selecting Unit Goals

Once again, the standards mandated by the state board of education, the local school district, and (in some cases) federal legislation—both language arts standards and content area standards— must play a determining role in the choice of goals for a thematic unit. Teachers must be aware of the major concepts and generalizations that students at a particular grade level should acquire. They must also consider their knowledge of the students (in this particular classroom) and their own knowledge of language arts skills and concepts and of the skills and concepts in other subject matter areas required in the district curriculum.

Once a theme has been selected, some teachers shrewdly assess their students' prior knowledge by using the K-W-L procedure (What I Know, What I Want to Know, What I Have Learned) and helping the class complete the first two columns. It becomes easier to plan the unit when teachers are familiar with the levels of understanding that a class already has (or is interested in acquiring) in a subject.

Choosing Resources

One of the objectives of thematic learning is to provide students with experiences with a broad range of learning resources (Pappas, Kiefer, & Levstik, 2006). Such a broad range is particularly significant for exploring varied cultural perspectives, which are represented in books readily available today.

Therefore, a critical aspect of constructing a thematic unit is selecting and locating resources needed for that unit. That responsibility lies with the teacher and must be completed before he or she develops instructional activities and lessons from one of several major types of resources.

Printed resources rank first, especially children's literature, and guidelines for selecting such literature include (1) the use of a variety of genres (e.g., picture books, nonfiction informational books, nonfiction biographies, historical fiction, realistic fiction); (2) the inclusion of books at different levels of difficulty or readability; (3) the representation of students' interests in the topics within the overall theme or the writings of favorite authors or illustrators; and (4) the avoidance of stereotyping in illustrations and texts to promote cultural authenticity.

Next, the teacher must actually read the selected books (or, in the case of books for intermediate grades, skim them) and carefully consider whether they match the theme and unit goals. The teacher should also separate them, according to Templeton (1997), into the following three categories:

1. Core selections for the entire class, usually in a read-aloud format; for example, Speare's *The Sign of the Beaver* (1983), which students can discuss intensively in a unit about Colonial America

2. Extended selections for some children; for a unit on the theme of the Civil War, students can discuss in small groups Cosner's *The Underground Railroad* (1991)

3. Recreational or motivational selections for individual readers during sustained silent reading; for example, Lee's *Landed* (2006), which concerns immigration in the early 20th century

Children's literature that promotes student knowledge of the content areas of mathematics, science, and social studies is shown in Figures 4.1, 4.2, and 4.3, respectively. Children's literature that adds to student appreciation of the fine arts is listed in Figure 4.4.

All titles appear in one or more of the following reference books: Barr and Gillespie's *Best Books for Children* (2006), McClure and Kristo's *Adventuring With Books* (2002), and *Notable Social Studies Trade Books for Young People: 2007* (2007). Experienced teachers try to include both fiction and nonfiction books in a thematic unit, and therefore both kinds are included in Figures 4.1 through 4.4.

Another consideration when collecting books for a thematic unit is the *purpose* for which certain materials will be used. Teachers should ask themselves the following questions when selecting materials:

- Are they materials suitable for read-alouds? These include books that students would not read for themselves (e.g., poetry) that apply to all grade levels as well as books that are developmentally appropriate for only certain grade levels. Read-alouds may provoke questions about writing styles or stimulate discussions about sensitive and important issues; such queries and deliberation will affect the unit under study, making it more meaningful to this particular group of students.
- Are they materials suitable for group activities? Such books not only have literary qualities but are appropriate for literature circle groups or other small group work that does not demand direct instruction. Books like O'Dell's *Island of the Blue Dolphins* (1990) or Paterson's *Bridge to Terabithia* (2004) encourage reading that allows students to reflect beyond the book narrative itself and thereby develop their critical thinking skills.
- Are they materials suitable for personal exploration? As teachers become familiar with the special interests of individual students, they should include books that some children will enjoy reading simply for personal pleasure. They may read these during sustained silent reading time or other times when they have completed their regular assignments satisfactorily and are waiting for their peers to finish as well (Pappas et al., 2006).

Figure 4.1 Recent Children's Literature That Promotes Student Knowledge of Mathematics

Counting and Number Operations

Anderson, L. (2000). *Tea for Ten*. R&S Books.

Capucilli, A. (2001). *Mrs. McTats and Her Houseful of Cats*. McElderry.

Cuyler, M. (2000). *100th Day Worries*. Simon & Schuster.

Guettier, B. (1999). *The Father Who Had 10 Children*. Dial.

Hoban, T. (1999). *Let's Count*. Greenwillow.

MacDonald, S. (2000). *Look Whoooo's Counting*. Scholastic.

Tang, G. (2001). *The Grapes of Math: Mind-Stretching Math Riddles*. Scholastic.

Wells, R. (2000). *Emily's First 100 Days of School*. Hyperion.

Geometry and Algebra

Demi. (1997). *One Grain of Rice: A Mathematical Folktale*. Scholastic.

Fleischman, P. (2000). *Lost! A Story in String*. Henry Holt.

Franco, B. (1999). *Grandpa's Quilt*. Children's Press.

Grover, M. (1996). *Circles and Squares Everywhere*. Harcourt.

Harris, T. (2000). *Pattern Fish.* Millbrook.

Hoban, T. (2000). *Cubes, Cones, Cylinders & Spheres.* Greenwillow.

Murphy, S. (1996). *Too Many Kangaroo Things to Do.* HarperCollins.

Measurement

Axelrod, A. (1997). *Pigs in the Pantry: Fun With Math and Cooking.* Simon & Schuster.

Maestro, B. (1999). *The Story of Clocks and Calendars: Making a Millennium.* HarperCollins.

McMillan, B. (1996). *Jelly Beans for Sale.* Scholastic.

Mollel, T. (1999). *My Rows and Piles of Coins.* Clarion.

Murphy, S. J. (1996). *The Best Bug Parade.* Harper Trophy.

Nagda, A., & Bickel, C. (2000). *Tiger Math: Learning to Graph From a Baby Tiger.* Henry Holt.

Figure 4.2   Recent Children's Literature That Promotes Student Knowledge of Science

Earth Sciences

Bortz, A. & Bortz, F. (2001). *Collision Course!* Millbrook.

Gans, R. (1997). *Let's Go Rock Collecting.* HarperCollins.

Lauber, P. (1996). *You're Aboard Spaceship Earth.* HarperCollins.

Ross, M. (2001). *Earth Cycles.* Millbrook.

Steele, P. (1998). *Rocking and Rolling.* Candlewick.

Sutherland, L. (2000). *Earthquakes and Volcanoes.* Reader's Digest.

Vogel, C. (2000). *Nature's Fury.* Scholastic.

Life Sciences

Batten, M. (2000). *The Winking Blinking Sea.* Millbrook.

Cerullo, M. (2000). *The Truth About Great White Sharks.* Chronicle.

George, J. C. (2000). *How to Talk to Your Cat.* HarperCollins.

George, T. (2000). *Jellies: The Life of Jellyfish.* Millbrook.

Goodall, J. (2001). *The Chimpanzees I Love.* Scholastic.

Markle, S. (2001). *Growing Up Wild: Wolves.* Atheneum.

Swinbourne, S. (2001). *Bobcat: America's Cat.* Boyds Mills.

Webb, S. (2000). *My Season With Penguins: An Antarctic Journal.* Houghton Mifflin.

Physical Sciences

Branley, L. (1996). *Day Light, Night Light: Where Light Comes From.* HarperCollins.

Challoner, J. (1997). *Floating and Sinking.* Steck-Vaughn.

Fowler, A. (1997). *Energy From the Sun.* Children's Press.

Health Sciences

Darling, K. (2000). *There's a Zoo on You.* Millbrook.

Ganeri, A. (1997). *Funny Bones and Other Body Parts.* Scholastic.

Simon, S. (1997). *The Brain: Our Nervous System.* Morrow.

Figure 4.3   Recent Children's Literature That Promotes Student Knowledge of Social Studies

U.S. Biography

Calenza, A. (2006). *Gershwin's Rhapsody in Blue.* Charlesbridge.

Giblin, J. (2006). *The Amazing Life of Benjamin Franklin.* Tandem Library.

Laskey, K. (2006). *John Muir: America's First Environmentalist.* Candlewick.

Parr, A. (2006). *Gordon Parks: No Excuses.* Pelican Publish.

Rodriguez, R. (2006). *Through Georgia's Eyes.* Henry Holt.

Wong, L. (2006). *Good Fortune: My Journey to Gold Mountain.* Peachtree.

U.S. History and Culture

Avi. (2001). *Prairie School.* HarperCollins.

Curlee, L. (2000). *Liberty.* Atheneum.

Freedman, R. (2000). *Give Me Liberty! The Story of the Declaration of Independence.* Holiday House.

Haskins, J., & Benson, K. (1999). *Bound for America: The Forced Migration of Africans to the New World.* Harper.

U. S. Historical Fiction

Borden, L. (2006). *Across the Blue Pacific: A World War II Story.* Houghton Mifflin.

Cotton, C. (2006). *Abbie in Stitches.* Farrar, Straus and Giroux.

Murphy, J. (2006). *Desperate Journey.* Scholastic.

Spooner, M. (2001). *Daniel's Walk.* Henry Holt.

World History and Culture

Ancona, G. (1999). *Carnaval.* Harcourt.

Kurlansky, M. (2001). *The Cod's Tale.* Putnam.

Levine, E. (2000). *Darkness Over Denmark: The Danish Resistance and the Rescue of the Jews.* Holiday House.

McMahon, P. (1999). *One Belfast Boy.* Houghton Mifflin.

Figure 4.4   Recent Children's Literature That Promotes Student Knowledge of the Fine Arts

Music and Musicians

Austin, P. (2001). *The Cat Who Loved Mozart.* Holiday House.

Cutler, J. (1999). *The Cello of Mr. O.* Dutton.

George-Warner, H. (2001). *Shake, Rattle, and Roll: The Founders of Rock and Roll.* Houghton Mifflin.

Koscielniak, B. (2000). *The Story of the Incredible Orchestra: An Introduction to Musical Instruments and the Symphony Orchestra.* Houghton Mifflin.

Weatherford, C. (2000). *The Sound That Jazz Makes.* Walker.

Art and Artists

Brenner, B. (1999). *The Boy Who Loved to Draw: Benjamin West.* Houghton Mifflin.

Browne, A. (2000). *Willy's Pictures.* Candlewick.

Christelow, E. (1999). *What Do Illustrators Do?* Clarion.

Elleman, B. (1999). *Tomie dePaola: His Art and His Stories.* Putnam.

Emberley, E. (2000). *Ed Emberley's Fingerprint Drawing Book.* Little, Brown.

Gherman. B. (2000). *Norman Rockwell: Storyteller With a Brush.* Atheneum.

Greenberg, J., & Jordan, S. (2001). *Vincent van Gogh: Portrait of an Artist.* Delacorte.

Marciano, J. (1999). *Bemelmans: The Life and Art of Madeline's Creator.* Viking.

Dance and Dancers

Glover, S., & Weber, B. (2000). *Savion! My Life in Tap.* HarperCollins.

Marshall, J. (1999). *Swine Lake.* HarperCollins.

McMahon, P. (2000). *Dancing Wheels.* Houghton Mifflin.

Tallchief, M., & Wells, R. (1999). *Tallchief: America's Prima Ballerina.* Viking.

Drama and Dramatists

Coville, B. (1997). *William Shakespeare's Macbeth.* Dial.

Ganeri, A. (1999). *Young Person's Guide to Shakespeare.* Dial.

- Are there primary source materials suitable for supplementing other printed resources? Newspapers, magazines, maps, ledgers, and other materials that offer firsthand information about the community (e.g., aerial photographs) or about real persons who lived in other times (e.g., journals they kept) are not always easy to obtain. However, such primary sources help make the thematic unit come to life, especially for children who may not otherwise be interested in the core subject matter.

Technological resources such as the Internet are now accessible in most elementary schools. They help students gather information and also provide opportunities for them to collaborate with other students both locally and in other parts of the country/world. For students in preK through Grade 12, the International Society for Technology in Education (ISTE) has developed basic standards of technology literacy that cover (a) the use of basic operations and concepts; (b) the use of tools for productivity, communication, research, and problem solving; and (c) the understanding of social issues relating to the use of technology. Appendix A lists software titles that present elementary students with concepts and information relevant to thematic units.

Hands-on resources consist of both natural objects and objects such as tools and machinery that are products of human culture. Human-made artifacts vary from Indian arrowheads and ceremonial masks to old watches and household items. They are valuable for use in certain units because they help students speculate and hypothesize about how different peoples live today and how they lived in the past.

Community resources are readily available to connect the classroom to people, places, and events in the community. There are museums of various types as well as farms, zoos, aquariums, and even cemeteries that are resources for thematic units and can be reached by short walking trips or longer field trips, depending on district resources. Teachers should also realize that the children themselves are a good resource, offering firsthand information on such topics as national parks or the desert to which they have traveled during school breaks. Some parents too may be willing to share their expertise on cultural traditions while others may be willing to discuss their business or professional careers.

The arts as resources can and should be incorporated into thematic teaching. These include the fine arts as listed in Figure 4.4 as well as architecture, crafts, television, and film, among others. They provide sources of information about the past and the present in American culture and cultures around the world. The arts are an especially valuable resource for at-risk students and English Language Learners as they embody all six of the language arts in an engaging and exciting manner.

Planning Instructional Activities

Depending on the maturity of the class and the students' prior knowledge, the teacher should involve the children in each step of the thematic unit from selecting the theme to implementing it. In any case, the teacher should especially ask them to brainstorm possible activities and then add these to his or her own list to provide a well-rounded unit (Brazee & Capelluti, 1995). They may be whole-class, small-group, or individual activities.

Wiseman and colleagues (2005) warn, however, that thematic instruction must be more than a series of activities; instead it must make connections between the language arts and other subjects. Unless activities are centered around critical concepts/beliefs and connected by standards, they are "nothing more than a loosely connected series of ideas" (p. 48).

Three different types of activities are contained in the typical thematic unit:

1. *Initiating* activities at the start of the unit that promote interest in the theme and set goals for the unit. Here are two examples:
    a. Thematic unit on insects and spiders for grade levels preK–3 could be initiated as follows: The teacher brings in several clear jars (with small holes in the lids) that each contain an insect or a nonpoisonous spider for the students to observe. Each jar is placed on a table with a magnifying glass. Children observe the insect or spider and write or tell everything they can find out about the creature.
    b. Thematic unit on humpback whales for Grades 2–5 could be initiated as follows: The teacher reads aloud Tokuda and Hall's *Humphrey, the Lost Whale: A True Story* (Heian, 1992) or shows the video with the same title. Then she or he arouses curiosity by asking such questions as "How would a whale get stranded?" and "Can you find out on a map where Humphrey was stranded?" Finally, the children are told that they will be learning much more about humpback whales (Roe & Ross, 2006).

2. *Developmental* activities running throughout the unit, which involve the bulk of the lessons that provide the actual instruction concerned with the theme. Some examples from a thematic unit on American pioneers for Grades 4–8 are as follows:
    a. The teacher provides individual maps of the United States so that students can mark the routes of early pioneers (e.g., Oregon Trail), identifying natural hazards for each route and computing the mileage.
    b. The children learn folksongs and ballads sung during the pioneer period such as "Sweet Betsy From Pike," and the teacher makes an audio recording of their musical efforts.
    c. The students identify problems of frontier life (e.g., preserving food) and determine solutions.
    d. The teacher helps form literature circles that will read different Wilder's *Little House* books; later, members of each circle will choose a scene to dramatize in front of their classmates.
    e. The students create art projects such as models of covered wagons and murals of pioneer villages.

A volunteer aide can help young children in an integrated unit on growing plants by helping them draw or visually represent the plants they are studying.

    f. The teacher helps the children plan a menu and prepare the food for a typical pioneer lunch (e.g., baked beans, dried apples, soup, and other foods whose ingredients can be purchased at a local market today) and then enjoys the meal with the class (Roe & Ross, 2006).

3. *Culminating* activities that occur near the conclusion of the unit as students review their new-found knowledge and put that learning into action. Two examples from the thematic unit on insects and spiders for Grades preK–3 (discussed under initiating activities) are as follows:

    a. Children each create an imaginary insect or spider, naming it, describing it, and labeling its parts. All are encouraged to write stories about their creatures that will be published and placed in a class book.

    b. The teacher helps each child write and illustrate one page in a class dictionary of Insects and Spiders, alphabetizing the pages and publishing it as a reference book (Roe & Ross, 2006).

In all grades, field trips often are the culminating activity in a unit. In the intermediate grades, however, teachers may also assign action projects on aspects of the unit that allow students to apply their learning to real-life situations (e.g., writing letters to the editor of the school or local newspaper expressing their concern about the growing problem of litter in the public parks and how it could be resolved).

Teachers contemplating the construction of a thematic unit, especially the interdisciplinary kind, may wish to review the outline of a sample unit shown in Figure 4.5. They should recall, however, that units come with varied outlines and headings; *no two units are ever alike* even if they are prepared for the same grade level and the same theme. The major difference among them is always the intended audience of learners.

Figure 4.5 Outline of a Sample Thematic Unit

Theme

Grade Levels

Duration

Goals

> Standards: State-mandated, etc.
> Standards: Language arts
> Standards: Content areas
> Concepts in content areas

Resources and Materials

> Printed resources: Trade books
> Printed resources: Children's literature
> Technological resources: Internet, etc.
> Hands-on resources: Artifacts, etc.
> The arts: Graphic, decorative, etc.
> Community resources

Cross-Curriculum Connections

> Science
> Social studies
> Math
> Literature
> Music
> Visual and performing arts
> Health
> Physical education

Instructional Activities

> Initiating
> Developmental
> Teacher-directed
> Student-directed
> Culminating

Evaluation

Implementing a Thematic Unit

For material related to this concept, go to Video Clip 4.2 on the Student Resource CD bound into the back of your textbook.

The teacher may present the children with a carefully preplanned unit or else choose to involve them from the beginning in preparing that unit. That decision will depend mainly both on the maturity of the class and the expected length of the unit. In either instance, since a thematic unit has a flexible framework, each child should have the opportunity to offer ideas and make choices regarding his or her role in the evolution of the unit. The teacher, however, must never lose sight of the fact that the integration of content material from across the curriculum takes exceptional and continuous planning since *thematic units do not match textbook chapters from subject areas.*

One useful approach to involving students from Pappas and colleagues (2006) concerns agreements made between the teacher and each student, whereby both are able to track the child's progress in meeting the responsibilities involved in completing certain tasks. While initial expectations may be general, soon specific assignments with dates must be clearly outlined. Only in that way will the children be able to participate in a wide variety of activities that use language across the curriculum. At that point, agreements may have to be renegotiated.

At the start of the unit, the teacher must decide on several activities that represent primary ways to introduce and promote the theme. Students then each decide which activity interests them and whether they wish to work independently or with a small group. Once that point has been negotiated (as the teacher recognizes the strengths and potential weaknesses of each child), he or she must furnish sufficient materials for each group so that members can explore the various activities and individually decide their top choices. Then the teacher must again renegotiate group membership to accommodate student interests and abilities (rather than reading levels) so that during the days to come children will each work productively with different classmates. Final agreements are then signed with due dates for varied assignments to promote self-monitoring by the students.

It is the teacher, however, who must still decide the pace at which the unit moves and how much time can be spent on each segment by any group. This timing will depend to a great extent on the duration of the unit (usually from one to two months), the grade level, the enthusiasm of the students, and the length of each day's lesson.

For the teacher who has developed much of the unit personally or has purchased a commercial unit, another approach is to incorporate the children's abilities and interests into each day's lesson plans while still overseeing the progress of the unit. Day-to-day lesson planning, together with weekly planning, is critically important under either approach but especially so for a commercial unit for which the class has not had much opportunity to offer input or make choices in its construction.

Some teachers prefer to immerse the class in a unit with substantial time spent every day on its implementation while others prefer a slower pace of shorter sessions three times a week. Any unit, however, should end before the children's interest dissipates, and it is a wise teacher who senses when it is time for a culminating activity for the unit finale.

A sample lesson plan incorporating the concepts introduced in this chapter appears on p. 102.

Assessment

Integrated units provide frequent opportunities for ongoing assessment of student learning in the language arts and throughout the subject areas. Formative assessments supply teachers with important diagnostic information at the outset and during the course of a unit. Regular evaluations help teachers determine both students' background knowledge and what students have learned and assist in planning future instruction. Teachers can assess students as they engage in a variety of activities that a well-planned thematic unit contains. Students can be observed in both cooperative and individual learning tasks, permitting teachers not only to evaluate their level of understanding but also to learn about areas that may require reteaching and the strengths and weakness of the unit itself. Was the unit successful in achieving the expected learning outcomes? What modifications are needed to improve the unit and increase student learning of stated objectives?

Culminating activities such as cooperative and individual projects offer teachers a means of summative, or end-of-unit, authentic assessment. Through challenging activities, students can synthesize and demonstrate learning according to individual learning styles and interests. Teachers should provide students and parents with a clearly written rubric and/or guidelines, and all stakeholders should be notified well in advance of due dates and deadlines. However, criteria for language arts skills and standards need to remain distinct from other content area requirements. For example, in grading a science research report, distinctions should be made among oral presentation, writing, research skills, use of visual aids, and subject matter knowledge. If the culminating activity is a collaborative project, then group work performance is assessed under separate criteria.

Additionally, activities that require students to present projects to the whole class not only serve as a type of summative assessment but also provide additional learning opportunities for students. When students share with the class, they receive practice in oral language skills, experience alternate viewpoints, obtain new information, and reinforce newly acquired vocabulary and concepts. End-of-unit assessments should include a self-evaluation component that allows students to reflect on what they have learned, what questions they may still have, and areas of weakness they can improve upon in the future.

Working With English Language Learners

Well-organized, standards-based thematic units provide all learners with comprehensive and rich learning experiences, but English Language Learners (ELLs) in particular benefit from the extra support of integrated learning. When units are carefully designed to align with the existing curriculum and include a wide variety of challenging tasks, ELLs receive increased comprehensible input across the domains and frequent practice in listening, speaking, reading, writing, viewing, and visual representation. Interdisciplinary learning gives students the opportunity to develop background knowledge, make meaningful connections, and pursue personal interests. Within the structure of a interdisciplinary unit, ELLs are better prepared to grasp difficult concepts and vocabulary, most notably in social studies and science. Through in-depth exposure and multiple experiences, ELLs build concepts and develop literacy and higher-level thinking skills throughout the content areas.

Beginning ELLs: Through collaborative learning and the support of peers, beginning ELLs can experience accelerated progress in oral language acquisition and concept development. While working in positive and nonthreatening group situations, ELLs have increased opportunities to use both social and academic language. Like their English-speaking counterparts, ELLs are more likely to be motivated when learning is based on personal interests and connects to real-life situations. Basal readers, beginning-level readers, and trade books related to the topic can help students practice phonics skills in a meaningful context while enriching content area knowledge. Frequent read-alouds of quality children's literature based on the theme scaffold ELLs' retention of new concepts and terms. The inclusion of concrete materials, word banks, teacher modeling, and brainstorming activities helps ELLs process and understand new information.

Early intermediate and intermediate ELLs: Intermediate ELLs continue to benefit from collaborative and cooperative learning situations. When activities and group members are carefully selected, teachers maximize learning and foster the interdependency of individuals within the group. Teachers should continue to brainstorm, model, and use visual aids and concrete materials as integral resources. Demonstrations and hands-on activities are an excellent way to introduce ELLs to new vocabulary and concepts. For example, rather than reading about the process of erosion in a textbook, students can build mountains of sand, clay, and topsoil and pour water down the slope; students thus concretely and tangibly experience how the water alters the landscape. Additionally, when students perform the experiment with a partner or small group, ELLs receive social and academic oral language development in a meaningful context. Intermediate ELLs can draw, label, record, and begin to read simpler texts with support. In the upper grade levels, if students are required to take notes, teachers can provide ELLs with outlines or a "fill-in" template to facilitate writing and a focus on understanding of key concepts.

Early advanced and advanced ELLs: At the advanced levels, ELLs begin to engage in more complex tasks. Teachers can continue to provide quality and culturally relevant literature for independent reading periods. Because content areas become more rigorous and abstract at the higher grade levels, teachers can supplement ELLs' instruction with prereading and preteaching activities in small, sheltered groups that scaffold comprehension and retention. Teachers support students in their evolving awareness of reading and writing for a purpose and enable them to practice comprehension skills with different types of texts. Although advanced ELLs are capable of completing many reading and writing tasks independently, teachers should not abandon the use of concrete examples, hands-on activities, and read-alouds because these instructional strategies motivate and benefit ALL learners in forming new concepts, meeting the linguistic demands of complicated informational texts, and making real-life connections.

Practical Instructional Activities and Ideas

- *Adopt-a-tree:* Teachers can have students adopt a tree on campus or at a local park. Students can sketch, measure, research, compare/contrast, and describe their palm tree, alder, or oak. Students can make leaf rubbings and compose poems.

- *Interactive bulletin boards:* For the theme under study, teachers can create a bulletin board that invites exploration and critical thinking. On it teachers can display student work; ask trivia questions; and provide challenge activities, maps, games, books, and music. The bulletin board can be part of a learning center or a place for "early finishers" to visit and investigate.

- *Magazines:* For a small investment, a teacher can subscribe to children's magazines such as *Zoobooks, Ranger Rick, National Geographic Kids, Calliope,* and *Cricket* that pique student interest and provide exposure to both fictional and informational articles. Their colorful pictures, photographs, and illustrations heighten their popular appeal. Many publications are written at different "levels" to accommodate a range of reading abilities.

- *Internet Web sites:* Although teachers need to carefully review Web sites for appropriateness and educational value, many quality sites exist that will enhance learning during the course of a thematic unit. Students can watch volcanoes erupt, view an orchard of cherry blossoms in Japan, or operate a lemonade stand. Teachers can bookmark links for quick and easy access. For example, if learning about ocean life, teachers can preview and provide access to kid-friendly Web sites that contain information on topics ranging from jellyfish to the Mariana Trench.

- *Own backyard:* Field trips offer great opportunities for discovery, but unfortunately, organized excursions are not always practical or possible. Teachers can encourage students to explore their own immediate environments (e.g., backyard, school grounds, or neighborhood) for sources of scientific inquiry. Teachers can start the "I wonder . . . ?" wheels spinning by bringing in their own items or questions. For example, an odd-looking seed pod might inspire "where did this come from?" questions. Or, an everyday item such as a Red Delicious apple can be looked at through new eyes and examined for symmetry, internal structure, smell, and taste. Thus, the ordinary assumes an extraordinary status when examined through the eyes of a careful observer. Students can write descriptive paragraphs, record ideas in a science log, or complete compare/contrast activities. If space permits, teachers can provide a center for students to display their discoveries or a special "I wonder..." box in which to submit thoughts.

- *Beyond their own backyard:* Teachers can help students brainstorm and carry out a plan based on new learning to benefit the neighborhood or community. Ideas can be as simple as picking up litter at a local park after a lesson on ecology, or singing songs at a retirement community after a unit on Sharing or Family. Older students can begin a buddy-tutoring program with a primary class. Teachers supervise and facilitate, but project ideas should be student-centered so learners can take ownership and pride in their accomplishments that travel beyond the boundaries of their "own backyard."

- *Music centers:* Teachers can set up a listening station with songs about the current theme. Many tapes and CDs are commercially available on a wide variety of topics from seasons to animals to the solar system, or teachers can easily create their own custom versions. Environmental music that re-creates sounds heard in nature (e.g., under the sea, in a forest) can also be a selection in the listening center or played for the whole class during quiet, independent work periods.

- *Simulations:* Teachers can have students participate in "make-believe" but realistic activities that re-create historical time periods, events, or situations. Activities might focus on stock market speculation, how a bill becomes a law, or assuming the role of an immigrant to Ellis Island or Angel Island. Similar to thematic units, simulations can range from short to long term in length and require the same extensive research and planning as an integrated unit to provide students with a successful and rich learning experience.

- *Fictional country:* Students can work individually or in groups to create a "country." Each group/student must outline the climate, population, topography, and natural resources of a fictional country. Based on these parameters, students use critical thinking skills to address such issues as supply/demand, food production, manufacturing, tourism, and any other factors that influence the prosperity and quality of life of a country and its people.

- *Explicit instruction in the use of trade books:* Teachers can familiarize students with the unique format of informational trade books by providing instructional activities that help students locate specific features such as the table of contents, chapter headings, glossary, charts, graphs, and bold print words. Often students are not aware that the graphic features are there to assist them in finding information or, in the case of illustrations and photos, to help in understanding and visualizing key points.

LESSON PLAN 4.1   Artifact Box: Clues From the Past

This lesson plan is the anticipatory lesson plan in a thematic unit titled The Great Depression. The unit investigates the causes and effects of the Great Depression such as the Dust Bowl, migration, and the impact on economics and the people through the start of World War II while incorporating Hesse's work of children's literature, *Out of the Dust* (1999).

Language Arts Components: Viewing, Reading, Speaking, and Writing

Grade: 5

ELL Level: Beginning to Advanced

Topic: The Great Depression

Time Frame: 1 week

Objectives

- Students examine a variety of objects from the Depression era (1929–1939) and make predictions about life during this time period.
- Students generate questions on what they want to find out about life and culture during the Depression.

Materials

- Decorated box or container with pictures, maps, postcards, recipes, copies of letters/newspaper articles from the Depression era or another suitable container that will pique student interest
- Suggested objects for artifact box:

- Photographs (e.g., Dorothea Lange, Walker Evans) of Dust Bowl, migrant workers, hoboes, stock market crash; produce (fresh or play food) such as oranges, lemons, and ears of corn; war ration booklets; cookbooks; postcards from "Sunny California"; maps; copies of WPA posters or newspaper articles or sections (advertisements, want ads, cartoons); toys or reproductions; period dress (a doll or teacher can dress up); household items such as eggbeater, clothespins, food tins, and any items that reflect life during the Depression to World War II period
  - *Optional:* Audiotapes or CDs (recorded accounts, both songs and interviews, are available from the Library of Congress; *American Memory Collection* as a good primary source) or a song selected from a Woody Guthrie CD such as *Dust Bowl Ballads*
- Chart paper
- Felt-tip markers

Content Standards

English Language Development (ELD): Listening, Speaking, Writing

- Students listen attentively to information and identify main ideas of discussions and conversation.
- Students use standard word order and grammatical forms.
- Students use drawings and write words and sentences to respond to information.

History/Social Studies

- Students use critical thinking skills to make predictions about life in the Great Depression based on visual and written information.
- Students distinguish among past, present, and future events.
- Students work cooperatively in groups to achieve common goals.

Language Arts: Viewing, Writing, Reading

- Students write to communicate ideas to an audience.
- Students read written text to draw conclusions/make predictions.
- Students examine artifacts and draw conclusions.

Vocabulary

- Archaeologist
- Artifact
- Great Depression

◇◇◇◇◇◇◇◇◇◇◇◇◇◇◇◇◇◇◇◇◇◇◇◇◇◇◇◇◇

Open

Engage

- Teacher (dressed in period clothing if desired) introduces and displays artifact box to whole group.

- Teacher explains to class about the artifact box while it is passed around the room for each student to examine outside only (no peeking!). Teacher asks students to define the word *artifact.* Teacher invites discussion about how *artifacts* are "clues" to people's daily lives or a specific period of time in history. (Optional: Teacher may elect to introduce the term *primary source*).
- Teacher elicits examples from students of how a person may glean information based on simply examining object(s). Examples: items in a shopping cart, a curbside garbage can, how a student decorates a notebook or bedroom, or a fossil.

Body

Explore

- After the box has circulated around the classroom, teacher pulls each item out individually. Teacher asks students to first describe each object without disclosing predictions yet. This process will give all students time to form thoughtful responses and help clarify any confusion about items with which students may not be familiar, such as an old-fashioned potato masher or a photograph of people in line at a soup kitchen.
- When all of the artifacts have been unearthed and examined (or "listened to" if using audio), Teacher explains to students that now that they have observed the items, they will use these "clues" as *archaeologists* to develop hypotheses in small groups.
- Teacher assigns students to heterogeneous groups of no more than five students and instructs students that each group will record and/or illustrate its ideas on chart paper. Teacher suggests categories such as work, home, children, or school. Teacher can hold up a picture of a migrant family and ask, "What clues or story does this photograph tell you about this family?" Teacher elicits responses and discusses with students to model thoughtful and relevant responses.

Expand

- Teacher distributes several items to each group to ensure a good variety of print, visual, and audio materials.
- Teacher circulates around the room, mediating and offering guidance as needed. However, students should be allowed freedom to explore and form hypotheses with minimal input from Teacher. Teacher's main role during this portion is to monitor behavior and ensure that students are on task and participating.
- When students have finished recording at least one hypothesis for each item, Teacher will bring class back together to share and discuss response in whole group.

Close

Apply

- Teacher asks students to continue in groups and generate questions about artifacts and add it to their group's chart paper.
- Teacher records information on a KWL (or similar) chart.
- Teacher displays charts for future reference and adds additional information later during course of unit.

- Teacher defines "depression" and explains that this is the topic of their next theme of study. Teacher adds any additional questions to K-W-L chart as needed.

Assessment

- Teacher observes students during class discussions and group activities.
- Teacher evaluates group charts for completeness.

Extension

- Students can create a personal artifact box.
- Students can bring in one personal artifact to share/discuss with class.

Parents as Partners

- *Questionnaires:* At the beginning of the school year, teachers can distribute surveys and/or questionnaires asking parents (or anyone they know who is willing!) about skills, hobbies, jobs, and interests that they would be willing to share with the class. If Miguel's aunt is a veterinary assistant or Jordan's great-grandfather painted murals for the Works Progress Administration (WPA) during the Depression, find a way to incorporate their skills, talents, and personal histories. Resend "pleas" for speakers, presenters, and "guest" teachers throughout the year as needed for special themes and projects. Teachers can encourage parents to participate and share their backgrounds and knowledge with the class.
- *Resources on loan:* In conjunction with the guest teachers described above, teachers can also request family members, friends, and community members to loan resources. Guest teachers can be encouraged to bring supporting concrete materials. However, since these items are most likely prized possessions, teachers need to review with students clear expectations about treatment of and respect for personal property. Items to share might include photographs, newspaper articles, cookbooks, clothing, toys, books, fossils, paintings, and any other realia that will help students visualize and connect with the topic. For example, a geologist might bring in a variety of rock samples of quartz, mica, obsidian, granite, and shale. These types of objects are tangible and sturdy, permitting curious students not just to look but also touch.
- *"Engraved" invitations:* Because thematic units stretch over longer periods of time, culminating activities give students opportunities to showcase their hard work in creative ways. Teachers can have students write invitations to family, friends, and community members to visit, view, and participate in these activities—the invitations certainly need not be "engraved," but a personal touch encourages families to attend and directly involves students in the planning process.

- *Enrichment activity suggestions:* Teachers can provide parents at the onset of each thematic unit with a list of suggested activities that they can do together with their children, thus strengthening the "big ideas" of the unit. Activities can include going on short excursions, cooking, interviewing family members, and reading books. For example, for a unit titled The Food Pyramid and Healthy Living, teachers can prompt parents and children to read nutritional labels on favorite snack foods or cereal boxes. Teachers can challenge students to see if they can go a day (or maybe even a week!) without eating any junk food.
- *Think tank:* Teachers can provide opportunities for parents to help brainstorm ideas for thematic units. Just as students should be involved in the creative planning stages of the unit, parents can also be valuable contributors. Teachers can hold "think tank" sessions and get parent input. Teachers should make sure, however, that the units maintain a central focus and remain student centered.

Student Study Site

The Companion Web site for *Language Arts: Integrating Skills for Classroom Teaching* www.sagepub.com/donoghuestudy

Visit the Web-based study site to enhance your understanding of the chapter content. The study materials include chapter summaries, practice tests, flashcards, and Web resources.

Additional Professional Readings

Beane, J. (1997). *Curriculum integration: Designing the core of democratic education.* New York: Teachers College Press.

Helm, J., & Beneke, S. (Eds.). (2003). *The power of projects: Meeting contemporary challenges in early childhood classrooms—Strategies and solutions.* New York: Teachers College Press.

Hinchman, K. (1999). Working together separately: A research collaborative reflects on the meaning of collaboration for children. *Language Arts, 77,* 143–147.

Katz, L., & Chard, S. (2000). *Engaging children's minds: The project approach* (2nd ed.). Norwood, NJ: Ablex.

Krogh, S. (1995). *The integrated early childhood curriculum* (2nd ed.). New York: McGraw-Hill.

Levstik, L., & Barton, K. (2001). *Doing history: Investigating with children in elementary and middle schools.* Mahwah, NJ: Lawrence Erlbaum.

Lipson, M., Valencia S., Wisson, K., & Peters, C. (1993). Integration and thematic teaching: Integration to improve teaching and learning. *Language Arts, 70,* 251–263.

Morris, R. (2003). A guide to curricular integration. *Kappa Delta Pi Record, 39,* 164–167.

Roberts, P., & Kellough, R. (1996). *A guide for developing an interdisciplinary thematic unit.* New York: Prentice Hall.

Seely, A. (1996). *Integrated thematic units.* Westminster, CA: Teacher Created Materials.

Children's Literature Cited in the Text

Ancona, G. (1999). *Carnaval.* San Diego, CA: Harcourt.

Anderson, L. (2000). *Tea for ten* (E. K. Dyssegaard, Trans.). Stockholm: R&S Books.

Austin, P. (2001). *The cat who loved Mozart.* New York: Holiday House.

Avi. (2001). *Prairie school.* New York: HarperCollins.

Axelrod, A. (1997). *Pigs in the pantry: Fun with math and cooking.* New York: Simon & Schuster.

Batten, M. (2000). *The winking blinking sea.* Brookfield, CT: Millbrook.

Borden, L. (2006). *Across the blue Pacific: A World War II story.* New York: Houghton Mifflin.

Bortz, A. B., & Bortz, F. (2001). *Collision course! Cosmic impacts and life on earth*. Brookfield, CT: Millbrook.

Branley, F. M. (1998). *Day light, night light: Where light comes from*. New York: HarperCollins.

Brenner, B. (1999). *The boy who loved to draw: Benjamin West*. New York: Houghton Mifflin.

Browne, A. (1999). *Willy's pictures*. Cambridge, MA: Candlewick.

Capucilli A. S. (2001). *Mrs. McTats and her houseful of cats*. New York: Margaret K. McElderry.

Celenza, A. H. (2006). *Gershwin's Rhapsody in Blue*. Watertown, MA: Charlesbridge.

Cerullo, M. M. (2000). *The truth about great white sharks*. San Francisco: Chronicle.

Challoner, J. (1997). *Floating and sinking*. Orlando, FL: Steck-Vaughn.

Christelow, E. (1999). *What do illustrators do?* New York: Clarion.

Cosner, S. (1991). *The underground railroad*. London: Franklin Watts.

Cotton, C. (2006). *Abbie in stitches*. New York: Farrar, Straus and Giroux.

Coville, B. (1997). *William Shakespeare's Macbeth*. New York: Dial.

Curlee, L. (2000). *Liberty*. New York: Atheneum.

Cutler, J. (1999). *The cello of Mr. O*. New York: Dutton.

Cuyler, M. (2000). *100th day worries*. New York: Simon & Schuster.

Darling, K. (2000). *There's a zoo on you*. Brookfield, CT: Millbrook.

Demi. (1997). *One grain of rice: A mathematical folktale*. New York: Scholastic.

Elleman, B. (1999). *Tomie dePaola: His art and his stories*. New York: Putnam.

Emberley, E. (2001). *Ed Emberley's fingerprint drawing book*. New York: Little, Brown.

Fleischman, P. (2000). *Lost! A story in string*. New York: Henry Holt.

Fowler, A. (1997). *Energy from the sun*. New York: Children's Press.

Franco, B. (1999). *Grandpa's quilt*. New York: Children's Press.

Freedman, R. (2000). *Give me liberty! The story of the Declaration of Independence*. New York: Holiday House.

Ganeri, A. (1997). *Funny bones and other body parts*. New York: Simon & Schuster.

Ganeri, A. (1999). *The young person's guide to Shakespeare*. San Diego, CA: Harcourt.

Gans, R. (1997). *Let's go rock collecting*. New York: HarperCollins.

George, J. C. (2000). *How to talk to your cat*. New York: HarperCollins.

George, T. (2000). *Jellies: The life of jellyfish*. Brookfield, CT: Millbrook.

George-Warren, H. (2001). *Shake, rattle, and roll: The founders of rock and roll*. New York: Houghton Mifflin.

Gherman, B. (2000). *Norman Rockwell: Storyteller with a brush*. New York: Atheneum.

Giblin, J. C. (2006). *The amazing life of Benjamin Franklin*. Minneapolis, MN: Tandem Library.

Glover, S., & Weber, B. (2000). *Savion! My life in tap*. New York: HarperCollins.

Goodall, J. (2001). *The chimpanzees I love: Saving their world and ours*. New York: Scholastic.

Greenberg, J., & Jordan, S. (2001). *Vincent van Gogh: Portrait of an artist*. New York: Delacorte.

Grover, M. (1996). *Circles and squares everywhere*. New York: Harcourt.

Harris, T. (2000). *Pattern fish*. Brookfield, CT: Millbrook.

Haskins, J., & Benson, K. (1999). *Bound for America: The forced migration of Africans to the New World*. New York: HarperCollins.

Hesse, K. (1999). *Out of the dust*. New York: Scholastic.

Hoban, R. (1993). *Bread and jam for Frances*. New York: Harper Trophy.

Hoban, T. (1999). *Let's count*. New York: Greenwillow.

Hoban, T. (2000). *Cubes, cones, cylinders & spheres*. New York: Greenwillow.

Koscielniak, B. (2000). *The story of the incredible orchestra: An introduction to musical instruments and the symphony orchestra*. New York: Houghton Mifflin.

Kurlansky, M. (2001). *The cod's tale*. New York: Putnam.

Lasky, K. (2006). *John Muir: America's first environmentalist*. Cambridge, MA: Candlewick.

Lauber, P. (1996). *You're aboard spaceship Earth*. New York: HarperCollins.

Lee, M. (2006). *Landed*. New York: Farrar, Straus and Giroux.

Levine, E. (2000). *Darkness over Denmark: The Danish Resistance and the rescue of the Jews*. New York: Holiday House.

Macdonald, S. (2000). *Look whoooo's counting*. New York: Scholastic.

Maestro, B. (1999). *The story of clocks and calendars: Marking a millennium*. New York: HarperCollins.

Marciano, J. B. (1999). *Bemelmans: The life and art of Madeline's creator*. New York: Viking.

Markle, S. (2001). *Growing up wild: Wolves*. New York: Athenum.

Marshall, J. (1999). *Swine lake*. New York: HarperCollins.

McMahon, P. (1999). *One Belfast boy*. New York: Houghton Mifflin.

McMahon, P. (2000). *Dancing wheels*. New York: Houghton Mifflin.

McMillan, B. (1996). *Jelly beans for sale*. New York: Scholastic.

Menzel, P. (2005). *Hungry planet: What the world eats*. Berkeley, CA: Ten Speed Press.

Miller, E. (2006). *The monster health book: A guide to eating healthy, being active, & feeling great for monsters & kids!* New York: Holiday House.

Mollel, T. (1999). *My rows and piles of coins*. New York: Clarion.

Murphy, J. (2006). *Desperate journey*. New York: Scholastic.

Murphy, S. J. (1996a). *The best bug parade*. New York: HarperTrophy.

Murphy, S. J. (1996b). *Too many kangaroo things to do!* New York: HarperCollins.

Nagda, A. W., & Bickel, C. (2000). *Tiger math: Learning to graph from a baby tiger*. New York: Henry Holt.

O'Dell, S. (1990). *Island of the blue dolphins*. New York: Houghton Mifflin.

Parr, A. (2006). *Gordon Parks: No excuses.* Gretna, LA: Pelican.

Paterson, K. (2004). *Bridge to Terabithia.* New York: HarperCollins.

Rodriguez, R. V. (2006). *Through Georgia's eyes.* New York: Henry Holt.

Rosenthal, A. K. (2005). *Little pea.* San Francisco: Chronicle.

Ross, M. (2001). *Earth cycles.* Brookfield, CT: Millbrook.

Sharmat, M. (1989). *Gregory the terrible eater.* New York: Scholastic.

Simon, S. (1997). *The brain: Our nervous system.* New York: HarperCollins.

Speare, E. G. (1983). *The sign of the beaver.* Boston: Houghton Mifflin.

Spooner, M. (2001). *Daniel's walk.* New York: Henry Holt.

Steele, P. (1998). *Rocking and rolling.* Cambridge, MA: Candlewick.

Sutherland, L. (2000). *Earthquakes and volcanoes.* Pleasantville, NY: Reader's Digest.

Swinburne, S. R. (2001). *Bobcat: North America's cat.* Honesdale, PA: Boyds Mills.

Tallchief, M., & Wells, R. (1999). *Tallchief: America's prima ballerina.* New York: Viking.

Tang, G. (2001). *The grapes of math: Mind-stretching math riddles.* New York: Scholastic.

Tokuda, W., & Hall, R. (1992). *Humphrey, the lost whale: A true story.* Berkeley, CA: Heian.

Vogel, C. G. (2000). *Nature's fury: Eyewitness reports of natural disasters.* New York: Scholastic.

Weatherford, C. B. (2000). *The sound that jazz makes.* New York: Walker.

Webb, S. (2000). *My season with penguins: An Antarctic journal.* New York: Houghton Mifflin.

Wells, R. (2000). *Emily's first 100 days of school.* New York: Hyperion.

Wong, L. K. (2006). *Good fortune: My journey to Gold Mountain.* Atlanta: Peachtree.

References

Barr, C., & Gillespie, J. (Eds.). (2006). *Best books for children* (8th ed.). Westport, CT: Libraries Unlimited.

Block, C. (2001). *Teaching the language arts* (3rd ed.). Boston: Allyn & Bacon.

Brazee, E., & Capelluti, J. (1995). *Dissolving boundaries: Toward an integrated curriculum.* Columbus, OH: National Middle School Association.

Britton, J. (1970). *Language and learning.* Harmondsworth, UK: Penguin.

Bruner, J. (1998). *The human condition.* Paper presented at the annual meeting of the American Psychological Association, Boston.

Bullock, A. (1975). *A language for life.* London: Her Majesty's Stationery Office.

Caswell, L., & Duke, N. (1998). Non-narrative as a catalyst for literacy development. *Language Arts, 75,* 108–117.

Harvey, S. (1998). *Nonfiction matters.* York, ME: Stenhouse.

McClure, A., & Kristo, J. (Eds.). (2002). *Adventuring with books* (13th ed.). Urbana, IL: National Council of Teachers of English.

Mitchell, A., & David, J. (Eds.). (1992). *Explorations with young children: A curriculum guide from the Bank Street College of Education.* Beltsville, MD: Gryphon House.

National Council for the Social Studies. (2007). *Notable social studies trade books for young people: 2007.* Silver Spring, MD: Author.

Pappas, C., Kiefer, B., & Levstik, L. (2006). *An integrated language perspective in the elementary school* (4th ed.). Boston: Allyn & Bacon.

Roe, B., & Ross, E. (2006). *Integrating language arts through literature and thematic units.* Boston: Allyn & Bacon.

Shanahan, T. (1996). Reading-writing relationships, thematic units, inquiry learning. . . . In Pursuit of effective literacy instruction. *The Reading Teacher, 51,* 12–19.

Temple, C., Martinez, M., Yokota, J., & Naylor, A. (2002). *Children's books in children's hands.* Boston: Allyn & Bacon.

Templeton, S. (1997). *Teaching the integrated language arts* (2nd ed.). Boston: Houghton Mifflin.

Walmsley, T., & Wolf, T. (1990). Integrating literature and composing into the language arts curriculum: Philosophy and practice. *Elementary School Journal, 90,* 251–274.

Wiseman, D., Elish-Piper, L., & Wiseman, A. (2005). *Learning to teach language arts in a field-based setting.* Scottsdale, AZ: Holcomb Hathaway.

Anticipation Statement Answers

1. Agree
2. Disagree
3. Disagree

4. Agree

5. Agree

6. Agree

7. Disagree

8. Agree

9. Disagree: Organization and preplanning by the teacher are essential for a successful unit. However, student interests and student questions should help shape and direct the unit.

10. Disagree: Teachers should include some formal or standardized assessments. However, activities such as multimedia presentations and those that require students to synthesize new learning are more authentic and meaningful.

PART II
Reading as a Language Art

CHAPTER 5   Word Recognition Skills and Vocabulary Development

CHAPTER 6   Reading: Principles, Approaches, Comprehension, and Fluency

CHAPTER 7   Reading and Children's Literature

Word Recognition Skills and Vocabulary Development

CHAPTER
5

The report of the National Reading Panel (NRP, 2000) lists five major components that it believes are important aspects of a complete and comprehensive reading program. One of them—vocabulary—is discussed in the second part of this chapter. Two others—comprehension and fluency—are described in Chapter 8. The first two components—phonemic awareness and phonics—are explored in this section. It must be understood, however, that no single component alone can teach students to read. Instead, all of the five are important together with those additional components that experienced elementary teachers, especially those in the early grades or those working with English Language Learners (ELLs) at any grade, have found to be significant in producing successful readers.

The NRP's findings also indicate that systematic and sequential instruction in the components should be taught directly so that students progress from simple to more complex skills in word recognition under the close supervision of their teacher. That instruction should always be tied to meaningful reading experiences.

Anticipation Statements

Complete this exercise before reading Chapter 5.

Do you agree or disagree with the following statements? Circle your answer. Be prepared to discuss questions in blue.

1.	The terms "phonemic awareness" and "phonological awareness" can be used interchangeably.	Agree	Disagree
2.	Teachers should postpone literacy instruction until students master phonological awareness skills.	Agree	Disagree
3.	Phonemic awareness is a good predictor of reading proficiency.	Agree	Disagree
4.	Phonics analysis instruction helps learners break apart and decode new words.	Agree	Disagree
5.	Structural analysis or "chunking" is an appropriate word recognition skill for students beginning in the upper primary grades.	Agree	Disagree
6.	The most effective method of teaching sight word recognition is through daily review such as practice with flashcards.	Agree	Disagree
7.	When selecting books for classroom read-alouds, teachers should choose books at the students' grade level.	Agree	Disagree
8.	Vocabulary improvement requires the teacher to provide students with adequate opportunities to use and practice new words in meaningful contexts.	Agree	Disagree
9.	Picture clues or picture walks to develop concepts and vocabulary should be used sparingly in the upper grade levels.	Agree	Disagree
10.	The most important factor that affects vocabulary growth is socioeconomic status (SES).	Agree	Disagree

Word Recognition Skills

Phonemic Awareness

Phonemic awareness is simply the ability to manipulate the sounds or phonemes in words. As mentioned earlier, phonemes are the smallest units of speech. An estimated 40 to 44 phonemes in the English language represent the basic building blocks of spoken words (Wolfe & Nevills,

2004). Reading experts believe that a lack of phonemic awareness is a major cause of reading difficulties in children and in adults who are poor readers (Adams, Foorman, Lundberg, & Beeler, 1998). Without direct instruction, about 25% of middle-class first graders and an even greater percent of those from less "literacy-rich backgrounds" will lack phonemic awareness. Its importance is impressive since, by the end of first grade, such awareness has been shown to account for 50% of the variance in students' reading proficiency.

Infants are born with the capacity to pronounce all the phonemes in the English language as well as the phonemes of all other languages. However, it is the sounds they hear repeated again and again that strengthen certain neural connections while the connections to the phonemes they do not hear begin to disappear (Kuhl, Williams, Lacerda, Stevens, & Lindblom, 1992). Thus, infants begin to produce the sounds of their native language because those are the phonemes whose production satisfies their varied needs.

Teachers sometimes confuse phonemic awareness and phonological awareness. The first is actually a subset of the second. **Phonological awareness** is the umbrella term that includes not only phonemic awareness but also an awareness of the words, rhymes, syllables, and sounds in language together with the ability to blend individual phonemes into meaningful spoken words.

Confusion also exists sometimes about the connection between phonemic awareness and *phonics*. The first relates to spoken language, the second to written language. Phonemic awareness is *not* phonics although they develop reciprocally as children learn to read, and improvement in one area generally results in a corresponding improvement in the other. Young students would find it difficult to figure out how the alphabet works if they did not understand the connections between the sounds of spoken language and the letter combinations used to represent those sounds. This basic understanding results from phonemic awareness, which allows children to benefit fully from phonics instruction (Snow, Burns, & Griffin, 1998).

Since phonemic awareness helps students make connections between speech and written text, they should participate in reading and writing activities that promote their emerging literacy

Applicable IRA/NCTE Standards

Standard 3 Students apply a wide range of strategies to comprehend, interpret, evaluate, and appreciate texts. They draw on their prior experience, their interactions with other readers and writers, their knowledge of word meaning and of other texts, their word identification strategies, and their understanding of textual features (e.g., sound–letter correspondence, sentence structure, context, graphics).

Standard 6 Students apply knowledge of language structure, language conventions (e.g., spelling and punctuation), media techniques, figurative language, and genre to create, critique, and discuss print and nonprint texts.

Standard 10 Students whose first language is not English make use of their first language to develop competency in the English language arts and to develop understanding of content across the curriculum.

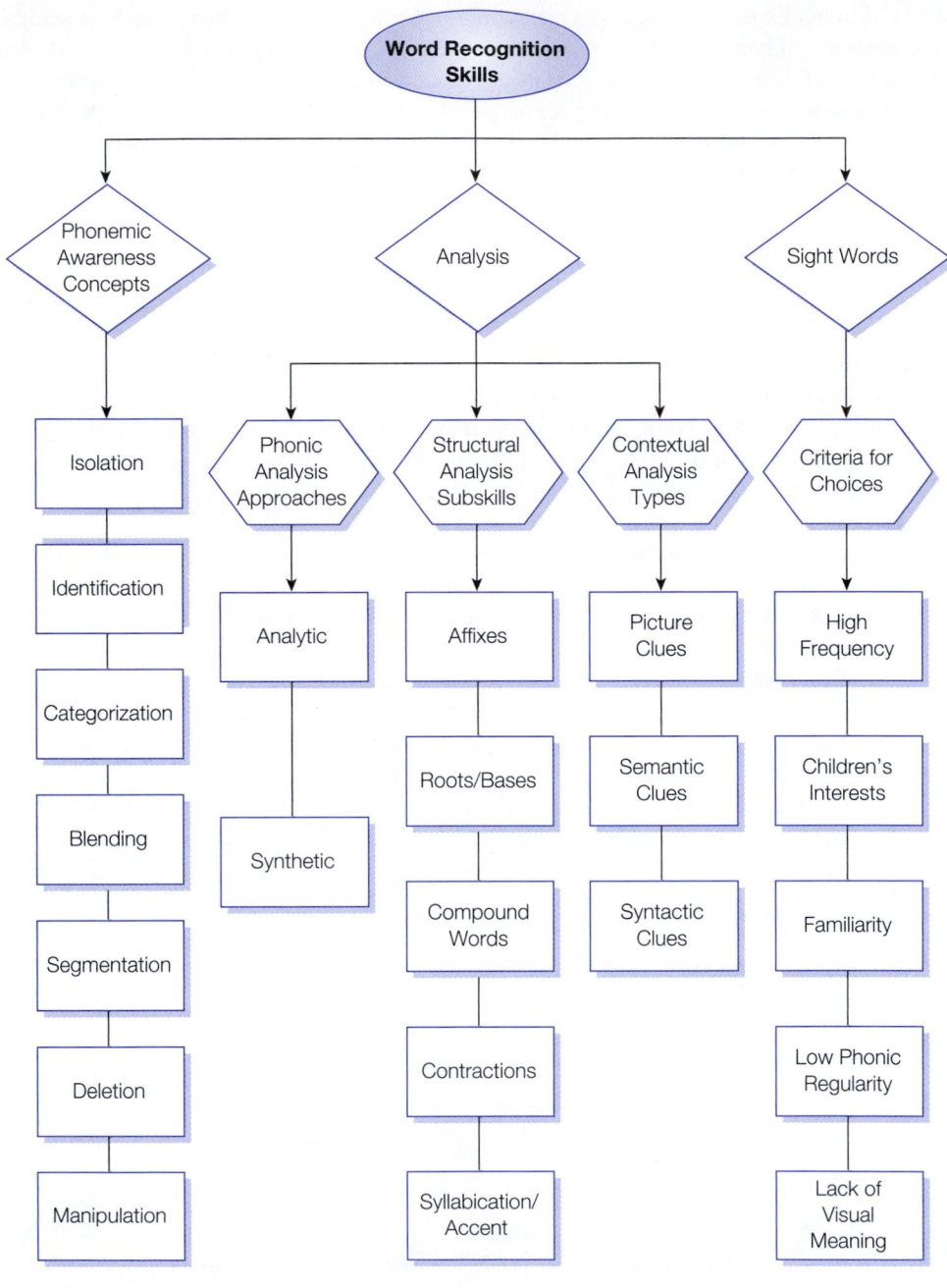

A Graphic Summary of the Contents of This Section

(Barone, Hardman, & Taylor, 2006). Such experiences include listening to read-alouds, engaging in *pretend reading* by handling books and telling stories from the pictures, and engaging in *pretend writing* by scribbling and drawing using letter-like forms. However, although some students will benefit from such activities, many others will not because they lack the necessary background experience in oral language and literacy. To them, the teacher must present systematically and directly the following phonemic awareness concepts:

- Phoneme isolation: Recognition of individual sounds in words (e.g., the sound of /f/ in the word *fan*)
- Phoneme identification: Selection of common sounds in different words (e.g., the sound of /p/ in the words *pan, put, pull*)
- Phoneme categorization: Grouping of words with similar sounds (e.g., the sound of /g/ in *tug, hug, dog*)
- Phoneme blending: Grouping of a sequential series of sounds into a word (e.g., the sounds of /k/, /a/, /r/ in the word *car*)
- Phoneme segmentation: Saying, counting, or clapping out the individual sounds in a word (e.g., sounds of /t/, /a/, /k/ in the word *tack*)
- Phoneme deletion: Identification of the word remaining after a phoneme is deleted (e.g., the word *lap* is the word *flap* without the /f/)
- Phoneme manipulation: Substitution of the sounds in a word to create a new word (e.g., dropping the sound /d/ in the word *dig* and replacing it with the sound /f/ to make the word *fig*); addition of a phoneme to an existing word to make a new word (e.g., adding the sound /c/ to the beginning of the word *lap* to make the word *clap*) (Armbruster, Lehr, & Osborn, 2003).

Teachers concerned about when to begin phonemic awareness instruction and to whom it should be directed are advised to begin instruction in mid-kindergarten and continue it throughout the early primary grades if needed. They should discontinue formal instruction once students have demonstrated phonemic awareness through decoding abilities and invented spellings. However, they should continue to plan instruction for older students who are poor readers or nonreaders and frequently involve these same older students in intensive practice lessons with a focus on blending exercises that link sounds with spelling (Honig, Diamond, & Gutlohn, 2000).

Teachers concerned about the phonemic awareness ability of any student may wish to administer a phonemic awareness screening test such as the Yopp-Singer Test of Phoneme Segmentation (Figure 5.1).

Instructional Practices

To ensure that phonemic awareness instruction is effective and proportionate to student needs, teachers should include the following practices in their effort to promote greater sensitivity to word sounds:

- Set aside a maximum of 20 hours to teach phonemic awareness, with the most time assigned to students with low sound awareness; those with a high level of such awareness may need as few as 5 hours. Differentiate instruction so that more time is given to helping children with low awareness while those with high awareness can move on to other literacy activities.
- Teach phonemic awareness early, in kindergarten and first grade, to help students understand the alphabetic principle.
- Teach phonemic awareness to small groups so that each child has numerous opportunities to respond.
- Teach only one or two skills at a time as this promotes mastery of those skills.
- Teach awareness first of beginning sounds, then of ending sounds, and finally, of middle sounds since this is the correct sequence developmentally.

Figure 5.1 The Yopp-Singer Test of Phoneme Segmentation

Student's Name: _____   Date: _____

Score (number correct) _____

Directions: Today we're going to play a word game. I'm going to say a word and I want you to break the word apart. You are going to tell me each sound in the word in order. For example, if I say "old," you should say /o/-/l/-/d/." (*Administrator: Be sure to say the sounds, not the letters, in the word.*) Let's try a few together.

Practice items: (*Assist the child in segmenting these items as necessary.*) ride, go, man

Test items: (*Circle those items that the student correctly segments; incorrect responses may be recorded on the blank line following the item.*)

1. dog _____	12. lay _____
2. keep _____	13. race _____
3. fine _____	14. zoo _____
4. no _____	15. three _____
5. she _____	16. job _____
6. wave _____	17. in _____
7. grew _____	18. ice _____
8. that _____	19. at _____
9. red _____	20. top _____
10. me _____	21. by _____
11. sat _____	22. do _____

The author, Hallie Kay Yopp, California State University, Fullerton, grants permission for this test to be reproduced. The author acknowledges the contribution of the late Harry Singer to the development of this test.

SOURCE: From "A test for assessing phonemic awareness in young children" by H. K. Yopp, 2005, *The Reading Teacher*, *49*(1), 20–29. Copyright International Reading Association. Reprinted with permission.

- Start with short two-sound words that begin with a vowel (e.g., *eat*).
- Differentiate plainly between speech sounds and letter names, pronouncing either the sounds to be emphasized *or* the alphabetic letter.
- Encourage children to finger-point read since this strategy helps them become aware of words in speech, of the beginning sounds in words, and of letter–sound knowledge.
- Teach phonemic awareness along with letter sounds and letter names since when phonics and phonemic awareness are taught together they reinforce one another (Ehri et al., 2001; Juel & Minden-Cupp, 2000; National Reading Panel, 2000; Stuart, 1999; Uhry, 2002).
- Model how to use phonemic awareness when reading and spelling new words, and then give children many chances to practice such skills under supervision.

Mrs. Brody in Vignette 5.1 uses many of these practices in her work with kindergartners.

VIGNETTE 5.1   Promoting Phonics

Mrs. Brody's kindergarten class was working hard. In addition to painting and drawing, learning to write, and feeding the classroom fish (Gus), the children were also absorbing the English language through story times and learning centers. Mrs. Brody considered phonics and phonemics practice a high priority and planned her daily classroom time accordingly; although many of the children already recognized individual sight words, she knew these prereaders would only become proficient with a solid foundation in phonics.

But like all young children, Mrs. Brody's students often struggled with "the squirmies" and sometimes found it difficult to stay seated and quiet. After a particularly trying morning, Mrs. Brody decided to harness the students' natural energy into a more interactive phonics lesson.

When the students returned from music time that afternoon, they discovered large posterboard letters, in order from A to Z, propped against the chalkboard and around the walls of the room. As the children settled into their seats, Mrs. Brody introduced the new activity.

"Today we're going to keep learning about letters and how they fit together to make words. But I need some help," she said. "I'm going to choose three people, and if I don't choose you now, don't worry—everyone will have the chance to participate."

First she asked Katie to come to the front of the room and grab the "A" poster. Next she asked Carlos to find the "T," and chose Anthony to pick out the "E." After all three students selected the correct letter and stood in front of the class, Mrs. Brody continued.

"Our three helpers are spelling a word, and it's a tricky one," she said. "So let's sound it out together." The students often sounded out new words as part of the phonics lessons, and eagerly followed along as Mrs. Brody coached them in saying the individual letters and blending the sounds.

When the children reached the "e," many of them included the long e sound in their pronunciation. Mrs. Brody expected this.

"'Aye-tee' isn't really a word, is it?" she said, smiling as several students giggled and shook their heads.

"Sometimes words have a letter at the end that we don't say when we sound out the word. This is one of those times. What does the word sound like when we don't say the last letter?"

This time, the students successfully sounded out "ate."

"We can change words by adding and taking away letters," she said. "Let's change this word by putting new letters in front. Carmen, can you find the D poster?"

Carmen shyly picked up the large piece of posterboard and, at Mrs. Brody's urging, stood to the right of the other three students in front of the class.

"Now we have a new word," Mrs. Brody said. "Let's sound it out together—and remember, we don't say the 'e.'"

As the class finished saying "date," Daniel grinned mischievously and piped up, "My sister has dates!"

"Remember to raise your hand, Daniel," Mrs. Brody said, suppressing a smile. "But good job reading the new word. Let's make another one."

One at a time, Mrs. Brody asked the children to select letters from around the room and join Katie, Carlos, and Anthony to form new words. In just a few minutes the class had successfully "spelled" and pronounced *gate*, *late*, and *rate*. Mrs. Brody wrote each new word in large letters on the chalkboard.

"Now let's try something different," she said. "Anthony and Leesha, please put your letters back in place and return to your seat." As Anthony returned the "E" and Leesha replaced the "R," Mrs. Brody began part two of the lesson.

"Because we took away our 'e,' we don't have the same word," she said. "And even though we didn't say the e at the end, when we take it away it changes how we say the rest of the letters. Sometimes it's hard to understand, so we're going to practice it. Let's start by trying out our new word."

Katie and Carlos remained up front, proudly holding the "A" and "T," and Mrs. Brody coached the class in reading the new word.

"That's right!" she said. "When we take away the *e*, the *a* sounds different. Try it again."

Once the class felt comfortable with the new letter combination, Mrs. Brody invited Leesha to return and step back in place with the "R."

"Now let's sound it out again," she said. With a little practice, the class successfully read "rat." Mrs. Brody started a new list on the board and began the exercise again, this time inviting a new group of students to add consonant letters to the beginning. In quick succession the class spelled and said *bat*, *cat*, *hat*, *mat*, and *sat*.

The entire lesson had taken only 20 minutes—long enough to provide plenty of practice with the new idea, and short enough for the little ones' wavering attention spans. Mrs. Brody wanted to finish the phonics session while the students were still engaged and enjoying the work.

"I'd like all our volunteers to return to their seats," she said. "Now look at our list of new words on the board and get out some clean paper. Please pick just one of the words we learned today, and write that word at the bottom of your paper."

"I'm going to write *cat* because I have a cat," Daniel said.

Mrs. Brody made a mental note to continue working with Daniel on asking permission to speak in class, but she appreciated his enthusiasm.

"After you pick your word, draw a story picture about that word," she said. "Work quietly for a little while, and later we'll share our pictures with each other in the Reader's Circle."

The students assembled large boxes of crayons and began drawing, glancing up to the chalkboard for reference. As Mrs. Brody walked through the class, she felt pleased at the activity's success. In addition to providing a more active learning experience, the lesson also taught individual sounds within words and the grouping of similar sounds.

Mrs. Brody knew the students would need more practice, especially with the silent *e*, and she would provide other opportunities to learn the new concept. She knew the students would continue to work hard—even Daniel.

Instructional Activities

Teachers must accept the fact that phonemic awareness instruction is only one aspect of a comprehensive literacy program. Other factors that teachers must keep in mind when planning phonemic awareness activities include teaching explicitly and intentionally those (seven) concepts listed earlier in this chapter and presenting activities that are developmentally appropriate such as songs, nursery rhymes, chants, and word games that are playful and engaging to students emerging into literacy (Yopp & Yopp, 2000).

Other useful activities include encouraging children to use invented spelling; sharing alphabet books such as Arnosky's *Mouse Letters: A Very First Alphabet Book* (1999) and Hobbie's *Toot and Puddle: Puddle's ABC* (2000); and experimenting with sounds and nonsense words after hearing such books as Most's *Cock-a-Doodle-Moo!* (1996) and Degen's *Jamberry* (1983).

Activities that are *not* productive are using workbook pages, flashcard drills, or "trace-the-alphabet" dittos because they are nonauthentic literacy activities (Barone et al., 2006).

Phonic Analysis

The English language is based on the alphabetic principle of using letters (graphemes) to represent sounds (phonemes). **Phonic analysis**, known popularly as phonics, consists of the relationships between those letters and sounds, and of approaches for teaching those

For material related to this concept, go to Video Clip 5.1 on the Student Resource CD bound into the back of your textbook.

Phonic analysis, the study of the relationships between letters and sounds, offers a shortcut to word learning and a large student vocabulary.

relationships. It is included as part of word recognition skills in almost all classroom reading programs because it is a shortcut to word learning and helps children develop a large *fluent reading vocabulary*. Instruction in phonic analysis should begin early, in kindergarten or first grade, as teachers explain and demonstrate phonics knowledge and how to use it during daily reading and writing experiences (Armbruster et al., 2001). Once children have developed a strong understanding of phonics, they can recognize familiar words readily and also decode or break apart new words to figure them out.

However, children who have difficulty discriminating among phonemes (i.e., lack auditory discrimination) or among letter forms (i.e., lack visual discrimination) may encounter problems in learning phonics. Beginning readers must be able to distinguish among the sounds of spoken English and among the varied sequences of those sounds. This ability may often be affected by speech impairments, dialect variations, and differences in native language backgrounds. Children must also be capable of visually perceiving and distinguishing among the letters of the English alphabet and the sequences of those letters. They must also understand the distinction between letter names and the sounds the letters represent.

Teachers should be familiar with terms commonly used in phonic analysis, as shown in Figure 5.2.

Major Approaches

The two major approaches to phonics instruction are *analytic* and *synthetic*. Briefly, **analytic phonics** is a whole-to-part-to-whole approach that begins with whole words, whereas **synthetic phonics** is a part-to-whole approach, starting with letter sounds.

The analytic approach involves first teaching some sight words and then teaching the individual sounds of the letters within those words. **Sight words** are words that are instantly recognized on seeing them either in isolation or in context (and are discussed later in this section). This approach often identifies unknown words by word families. Two problems associated with it are the stress it places on phonemic segmentation (or the ability to identify separate speech sounds in spoken words) and the emphasis it puts on previous knowledge of sounds associated with the separate letters. According to the National Reading Panel (2000) the *analytic or embedded approach* tends to leave certain aspects of the sound–grapheme relationships untaught, thereby resulting in incomplete phonics knowledge.

Figure 5.2   Terms Commonly Used in Phonic Analysis

Terms	Definition and/or Examples
Vowels	Letters *a, e, i, o,* and *u.* Letters *y* (often in the middle or final position in a word or syllable) and *w* (when in the final position in a word or syllable).
Consonants	Letters other than *a, e, i, o,* and *u.* Letters *w* and *y* in the initial position in a word or syllable.
Consonant blends	Two or three adjacent consonant sounds that are combined although each retains its separate identity (e.g., *smell, twig*).
Consonant digraphs	Two adjacent consonant letters that are combined into a single speech sound (e.g., *ship, phone, this, what, ring, neck*).
Vowel digraphs	Two adjacent vowel letters that are combined into a single speech sound (e.g., *day, each, foot, road, fair, meet*).
Diphthongs	Two vowel sounds combined, beginning with the first and gliding smoothly into the second (e.g., *oy* as in *toy; oi* as in *oil*).
Rimes	The vowel and the following consonants in a syllable (e.g., *ake in cake, ick in pick*). Also called word families or phonograms.

The synthetic method is concerned with instructing students in the phonemes that are associated with individual letters, and it is generally accompanied by repeated drills on sound–grapheme relationships. Children blend the separate sounds of a word to form the complete word, such as *cuh-a-tuh* to enunciate the word *cat*. Blending is the critical stage. A *synthetic or explicit approach* is more effective for students' growth and development in reading and spelling because it is concerned with all aspects of the sound–grapheme correspondences in the English language and teaches them systematically.

In addition to the two major approaches, there are others that are less well known (Fox, 2004). Among them are a linguistic approach and an analogy-based approach, both of which are concerned with words that belong to the same word family. *Most experienced teachers draw from varied approaches to meet the phonic needs of a particular class of students.*

To summarize, while there are several ways to teach phonics, the National Reading Panel (2000) found that phonics instruction is more effective than nonphonics approaches for younger students who are at risk of developing future reading problems and for older struggling readers. Furthermore, explicit phonics instruction is most effective when introduced in kindergarten or first grade or before students have learned to read independently. That instruction should last about two to three years and have an impact on comprehension, decoding, word reading, and spelling.

Instructional Principles and Strategies

After a lengthy research review on phonics instruction, Stahl, Duffy-Hester, and Stahl (1998) suggest that good phonics instruction achieves the following aims: It develops phonological awareness, which includes phonemic awareness and other factors; develops the alphabetic principle that letters represent sounds and so provides a thorough familiarity with the letters; provides enough practice in reading words—in isolation, in stories, and in writing—to lead to automatic word recognition; and represents one part of reading instruction.

The sequence in which sounds should be introduced to students has not been firmly determined. However, most teachers find it sensible to begin with the sounds and letters that are used most often in the words the children encounter in the text they read and write. One suggestion is to begin instruction with the *consonants s, m, d, p, t, n, g, b, r, f,* and *l* and the *short vowels a, o, i, u,* and *e* (Adams, Foorman, Lundberg, & Beeler, 1998). When children begin with a few consonants and a short vowel, they can learn to spell and decode a number of words immediately; by continuing to work with these letters, they can master simple spelling patterns known as *phonograms* or *rimes* (e.g., *an, at*). Word families are words that share the same spelling pattern (e.g., *fan, man; bat, mat*).

Teachers new to presenting a lesson in phonic elements to beginning readers according to the synthetic approach may wish to review these five steps (Johns, Lenski, & Elish-Piper, 2002):

1. Choose a phonic element to be taught and write on the board, chart, or transparency the letter (or letters) that represent it (e.g., "d").

2. Tell the children, "The letter 'd' makes the /d/ sound," and ask them to pronounce the /d/ sound while pointing to the letter.

3. Ask the children to write the letter "d" on their papers and then pronounce the sound as they point to the letter.

4. Present the children with several words that use the "d," preferably sharing a picture with each word to help them understand the meaning. Then ask the class to pronounce the target sound in such words as *dog, door, drum*.

5. Engage in a lesson extension depending on the maturity of the students. Ask the children to each write sentences about the pictured words or, as a class, brainstorm other words with the same phonic element.

Phonics Generalizations

Many phonics rules or generalizations are not very useful since there are more exceptions to those rules than words that apply. Still there are some that teachers may choose to present to broaden the classroom phonics program, provided that they are taught as "guides to best guesses," according to Roe, Smith, and Burns (2005). Several authorities cite the following dozen as among the most useful generalizations:

1. When two like consonants are adjacent to each other, only one is sounded (e.g., *lass*).
2. When a word has only one vowel and it is at the end of the word, the vowel generally represents its long sound (e.g., *me*).
3. When a word has only one vowel and it is not at the end of the word, the vowel generally represents its short sound (e.g., *man*).
4. When a word has two vowels and one is a final *e,* the first vowel is usually long and the final *e* is not sounded (e.g., *kite*).
5. When *kn* are the first two letters in a word, the *k* is not sounded (e.g., *know*).
6. When *wr* are the first two letters in a word, the *w* is not sounded (e.g., *wrong*).
7. When *ck* are the last two letters in a word, the sound of *k* is given (e.g., *brick*).
8. The sound of a vowel preceding *r* is neither long nor short (e.g., *car*).
9. In the vowel combinations *oa, ee,* and *ay,* the first vowel is usually long and the second is not sounded (e.g., *coat. beet, ray*). This rule may also apply to other double vowel combinations.
10. The digraph *ch* usually has the sound heard in *church,* but it also sometimes sounds like *k* (e.g., *chord*) or *sh* (e.g., *chef*).
11. The double vowels *oi, oy,* and *ou* usually form diphthongs (e.g., *boil, boy, out,* respectively). Although the *ow* combination often represents the long *o* sound, it may also form a diphthong (e.g., *now*).
12. When the letters *c* and *g* are followed by *o, a,* or *u,* they generally have hard sounds: *c* has the sound of *k* (e.g., *cat*), and *g* has its own special sound (e.g., *gut*). When the letters *c* and *g* are followed by *e, i,* or *y,* they generally have soft sounds: *c* has the sound of *s* (e.g., *city*), and *g* has the sound of *j* (e.g., *gym*).

Phonics generalizations should be presented inductively and one at a time. They must be carefully chosen so that each is learned thoroughly before another is introduced. It has been found that while children may not recite a particular generalization word-for-word, they are still able to analyze unfamiliar words incorporating it. This supports Piaget's theory regarding children in the concrete operations stage of development: They can perform actions physically that they have difficulty describing verbally.

Decodable Books

Another area of debate besides the teaching of phonics generalization is the use of **decodable books**. These are defined as texts that are written with a high percentage of words that use letter–sound relationships that the students already know. They also have simple sentence structure, controlled spelling patterns, and controlled use of high-frequency sight words. Each book concentrates on one phonic element (e.g., the short *a*), and the difficulty of the texts increases gradually as the grade level increases.

Proponents argue that such texts are an integral part of the K–3 reading program, as they reinforce the connection between phonics instruction and reading. They are helpful to struggling

readers because they offer them confidence and remind them that all letters in a word are important. They are also helpful to ELLs who need support and scaffolding to learn a new language,
as decodable texts give them success in learning a limited number of words and word patterns
(Jenkins, Vadasy, Peyton, & Sanders, 2003). Two popular series of phonetically controlled text (in
numerous storybooks) are *Bob Books for Young Readers/Set 1* and *More Bob Books for Young
Readers/Set 2* (2006) and *Primary Phonics* and *More Primary Phonics* (1995).

Opponents, however, argue that many decodable texts use tightly controlled language patterns
that do not always follow the linguistic patterns that children hear in oral language or the patterns
children's authors use in books shared during read-alouds. This feature makes decodable texts
often nonsensical (Barone et al., 2006).

A middle road in this debate notes that although the exact contributions that decodable texts
make to learning have yet to be found, they can supplement the texts that students read in the
classroom (Hiebert, 1999). Teachers should include decodable texts as part of phonics instruction,
choosing them as an infrequently used supplement to high-quality reading materials and selecting
only those that are highly interesting to beginning readers and comprehensible to them.

Instructional Activities

Although there are many commercial materials available for promoting phonics skills, the following is a sample of teacher-developed activities that offer group or individual practice in those skills:

- *Playing "I Spy":* Each child in a small group takes a turn locating an object in the classroom
  that begins with a particular sound. (e.g., "I spy something that begins like *cheese*"). The
  player who names the correct object (*chair*) then has a turn. The teacher may direct the
  choice of a beginning or final sound that the class has been studying.
- *Mounting pictures:* Students find in discarded magazines pictures of objects that begin
  with certain consonant blends or consonant digraphs. They mount the pictures on separate
  sheets of paper and label each one correctly.
- *Planning a meal:* Children pretend to be meal planners as each in turn names something
  to eat that begins with the letter *a*. When a student cannot add to the list, she or he begins
  naming foods starting with the letter *b*. This activity may be an ongoing one, taking place
  as children wait to be dismissed each day, or as a culmination to a group reading session
  every day for one week.
- *Working with a puppet:* The teacher brings in a favorite puppet that has a very large mouth
  that opens and closes. The puppet says two or more words and the group then decides if
  the words begin alike or if they rhyme (e.g., *jug/jig* or *man/pan*). Children indicate their
  decision in a thumbs-up or thumbs-down fashion. Sometimes the puppet "asks" the group
  to suggest other combinations of words that begin alike or rhyme.
- *Sharing riddles:* The teacher develops a list of five to ten riddles and asks for volunteers to
  help solve them (e.g., "I am thinking of a word that rhymes with *top*. We use it to clean the
  floor. What is it?" [*Mop*]).
- *Follow that letter:* The teacher gives each child a sheet of lined paper that is blank except
  for a large consonant letter at the top. Students must then write as many words as they can
  that begin with the same sound as the consonant letter on their sheet. (This activity may be
  timed for additional motivation with groups that do *not* include ELLs or at-risk students.)

Structural Analysis

Structural analysis is most often used in conjunction with phonic analysis. **Structural analysis**
is a word recognition skill that uses word parts to determine the meaning and pronunciation of
unfamiliar words. Knowledge of such word parts helps students isolate the root of a word, after
which they apply phonic analysis. When the word parts are familiar ones, they can be blended

together to determine the pronunciation of the word. Structural analysis is particularly useful in figuring out the pronunciation of a unfamiliar word that is composed of familiar word parts such as *affixes* (prefixes and suffixes) and *roots* or base words. Recently, the term *chunking* has become popular as a synonym for structural analysis as it simplifies the instructional vocabulary that students understand and use.

The *components* of structural analysis include not only affixes and roots but also compound words, contractions, and syllabication and accent. Structural analysis becomes a worthwhile technique in the upper primary and intermediate grades because, for example, knowing the meanings of affixes, in particular, can help readers add many more words to their vocabulary. As early as second grade, for instance, children can be introduced to several structural generalizations for changing base words before adding a suffix (e.g., if a one-syllable word ends in an "e," drop the "e" when adding the suffix "ing" as in *chase* and *chasing*). Structural analysis rather than phonic analysis should be used by readers when attacking unknown words because it deals with units larger than single graphemes.

Practices for Teaching Affixes

Children in Grades 3 through 5 who understand how affixes affect word meaning are better at comprehending text than students who do not understand that property (Carlisle, 2000). Successful practices for teaching students about affixes show them how to reveal familiar base words by peeling away affixes, especially from long words. In the first and second grade, teach inflectional suffixes (e.g., *-sles, -ed, -ing, -er, -est, -ly*) since the first three in particular appear in books for young readers and the others are important for understanding comparisons. In the third grade and above, teach derivational suffixes (e.g., *-able, -ous, -ment*) since these change the grammatical function of words and older students can appreciate and use them in their writing.

Teachers should provide students with opportunities to practice reading and writing many different words with the same affixes because these are significant features of syntax and reinforce syntactic cues. For children who do not know the meaning of base words or else cannot already read them, postpone the teaching of affixes until after the base words have been learned (Fox, 2004).

Activities for Teaching Roots or Base Words

The following activities can be used with small groups or even individual students:

- Given lists of unfamiliar words, the students must separate the suffix from each word that contains a suffix and then correctly pronounce both the suffix and the root word.
- Given lists of words containing suffixes, the students must use each root word in a sentence.
- Given lists of words containing common suffixes, the students must identify the root or base in each word by underlining it.
- Given lists of words containing common prefixes, the students must identify the root or base in each word by underlining it.
- Given drawings of several different "trees" with "roots" (or base words) like *play* or *fair*, the students add "branches" to the trees by writing in appropriate prefixes or suffixes such as *player* or *unfair*. This is especially helpful in Grades 3 and above in which students can use dictionaries to add several branches to each tree.

Compound Words

Compound words are made up of two (or sometimes three) words that have been joined together to form a new word (e.g., *snowman*). The new word may be one (a) whose meaning is the sum of its parts such as *houseboat,* (b) whose meaning is related to but not totally represented by the sum of its parts such as *shipyard,* (c) whose meaning is not literally related to the sum of its parts such as *moonstruck,* or (d) whose parts result in multiple meanings such as *doghouse.* Knowing the individual words that make up the compound word, however, does not guarantee that the students will know its meaning, even though each part of a compound word retains its original spelling.

As early as first grade, children can be introduced to compound words and learn to divide such words into the smaller words that compose them. They can even discuss the reasons for combining certain small words, such as *cow* and *boy, fire* and *man, play* and *house,* and *police* and *woman.* When the words that make up the compound are already in the students' fluent reading vocabularies, pronouncing the compound word should offer no difficulty.

Contractions

Also introduced in the first grade are *contractions.* Students encounter them in everyday reading material and so should be taught to recognize them. Contractions should be presented by sight at first because beginning readers are generally unable to determine which part of the word has been left out when the contraction is formed. Some teachers introduce contractions in related groups (e.g., those in which *have* is the reduced part).

Later, students can be taught that a contraction is formed when one or more letters (and sounds) are omitted from words and replaced by an apostrophe. The apostrophe is a visual clue informing readers that a word has been abbreviated (e.g., *he's, let's*). Children must realize that the words have exactly the same meaning whether written individually or as abbreviations.

Syllabication/Accent

Syllabication and accent are also often introduced in the primary grades with syllabication being presented in second grade and stress or accenting in the third grade. The teaching of accent is actually built on the skills of syllabication because accent has much to do with the vowel sound heard in a syllable.

A letter or group of letters that forms a pronunciation unit is called a *syllable,* and every syllable contains a vowel sound. It is important not to confuse sounds and letters because some words (e.g., *weave*) have several vowel letters but only one vowel sound and therefore only one syllable.

There are both **open syllables** (which end in vowel sounds that are usually long) and **closed syllables** (which end in consonants with the vowels typically representing short sounds). There are also accented syllables (which are given greater stress) and unaccented ones (which are given little stress).

Here are some useful generalizations about syllabication and accent: Prefixes and suffixes generally form separate syllables; words contain as many syllables as they have vowel sounds (e.g., *se/vere*); the first syllable of a two-syllable word is usually accented; and all one-syllable words are accented syllables. When two consonants are located between two vowels, the word is divided between the two consonants (e.g., *mon/key*); a compound word is divided between the two words that form the compound as well as between syllables within the component parts (e.g., *thun/der/ storm*); and words are divided between the affix and the root word (e.g., *re/gain, help/ful*). The primary accent usually falls on the first word of compounds (e.g., *base'-ball*); affixes are usually not accented; and when there are two of the same consonant letters within a word, the syllable before the double consonant is generally accented (e.g., *but/ter*).

Contextual Analysis

Defined in *The Literacy Dictionary* (Harris & Hodges, 1995) as the search for the meaning of an unknown word through an examination of its context, **contextual analysis** is based on meaning clues or context clues contained in the passage that surrounds the unfamiliar word. These clues may appear in the same sentence or in preceding or following sentences. Common types of context clues found in the same sentence are as follows:

- *Definition* (e.g., Lava, which is melted rock, flowed down the mountainside.)
- *Restatement* (e.g., The hardware store sold some rope made from jute—a tropical plant.)
- *Example* (e.g., The stage manager rented properties such as tables, chairs, and dishes for the play.)

The earliest context clues that children use are *picture clues*. Therefore, before introducing a story to help develop concepts and vocabulary, the teacher may use a "picture walk" by going through the selection and having the students analyze the pictures for information. The teacher should promote the use of picture clues together with, but not separate from, the clues in the printed text. Picture clues should not be overemphasized as they are most useful in the initial stages of instruction before students advance to more difficult material with fewer illustrations. However, for ELLs and at-risk students, picture clues continue to aid their reading even in the intermediate grades.

Other types of context clues are *semantic and syntactic clues*. The former are clues derived from the meanings of the words, phrases, and sentences that surround the unfamiliar word. Syntactic clues, on the other hand, are provided by the syntax (or word order) of our language, which demands that certain types of words appear in certain positions in spoken English sentences (e.g., adjectives usually precede the noun they are modifying). Native English students who have been speaking English since they were in preschool or earlier have a sensitivity to the syntax of the language. This sensitivity translates into recognition of syntactic clues. Roe and colleagues (2005) warn, however, that syntactic clues must be used together with semantic clues to unlock unfamiliar words.

Teachers must also realize that the *reading material offered to the students must be at an independent or instructional level* before students can employ context effectively.

Developing a Sight Vocabulary

Throughout elementary school instruction in word recognition skills, it must be stressed that the ultimate goal is to have each student learn to identify instantly as many words as possible as wholes. Once the child recognizes such words as **sight words**, he or she no longer needs to analyze them by using one or more of the skills already discussed. Consequently, *developing sight vocabulary* is crucial and basic, both for native English speakers and ELLs.

Because they have small sight vocabularies, beginning readers rely on contextual, structural, or phonetic analysis more than experienced readers do. However, the English language has too many words in too many specialized areas—with thousands more added every year—for anyone to recognize every word by sight. Consequently, word recognition skills are needed throughout any reader's lifetime, but happily, mature readers use them only when they encounter an unfamiliar word. No wonder that one goal of reading instruction, according to Roe et al. (2005), is to turn into sight words all the words that students continuously need to recognize in print.

A large sight vocabulary is important for several reasons. First, it allows the reader to attend to the meaning of the written passage, and comprehension is of critical importance. Second, it permits the use of the valuable word attack skill involving context clues since many unknown words can be identified by close consideration of the words around them (provided of course that the surrounding words can all be smoothly read). Third, it encourages the development of another important word recognition skill—phonic analysis—because children who know several sight words that begin with the same letter, for example, can then use those words as a basis for learning a generalization about sound-letter correspondences. Fourth, many of the most frequently used words in the English language are phonetically irregular even though they appear in many beginning reading programs and must therefore be recognized on sight as whole configurations. Finally, acquiring at least a beginning sight vocabulary at the very start of reading instruction gives students greater success and consequently a more positive attitude toward the entire reading program.

The choice of words for a beginning sight vocabulary should be based on five criteria: high frequency (e.g., *to, and*); children's interests (e.g., *Megan, homerun*), familiarity (e.g., *house, jump*); low phonic regularity (e.g., *where, said*), and lack of visual meaning (e.g., *because, could*). Word length is *not* a criterion, however, as short words are not always easier for students to learn than longer ones.

Sight words should be introduced gradually, reviewed often, and always presented in a meaningful context. Although some authorities (Veatch, 1996) support the so-called key vocabulary approach in which students themselves choose the words they wish to learn that have an intense meaning for them, a more sensible solution is to combine that idea with teacher selection of high-frequency words from varied lists. One of these compilations of high-frequency sight words is Fry's New Instant Word List (Fry, 1980) of 300 words that make up about 65% of all written material (Figure 5.3). The first 10 words make up about 24% of all written material and the first 100 words (and their common variants) about 50%.

Instructional Activities

The most natural approach to teaching sight words is reading to children as they follow along. This can be done when the teacher uses big books with groups so that every child can see the words. When multiple copies of books are available, each student or pair of students follows along as the teacher reads aloud. Books with accompanying tapes can promote sight vocabulary in a similar fashion. Predictable books, those in which students can use patterns or background knowledge to anticipate upcoming text, have also been found helpful in developing sight vocabulary (McGill-Franzen, 1993; Saccardi, 1996).

Using flashcards is a popular method for teaching sight words, but does not provide an opportunity to connect words with meaning. It is therefore better to use them *after* the words have been learned because flashcards foster automaticity in word recognition (Nicholson, 1998).

Games, whether passive or physically active, are more effective in increasing sight vocabularies than worksheets. Building a "word wall" display on a bulletin board or chalkboard helps children gradually acquire sight words needed for reading and writing (Figure 5.4).

While no one method for teaching sight words is best for every student, it has been recommended that words should always be presented in context rather than in isolation because reading is a language process for obtaining meaning.

Figure 5.3 Fry's New Instant Word List

The Instant Words First Hundred

First 25 Group 1a	Second 25 Group 1b	Third 25 Group 1c	Fourth 25 Group 1d
the	or	will	number
of	one	up	no
and	had	other	way
a	by	about	could
to	word	out	people
in	but	many	my
is	not	then	than
you	what	them	first
that	all	these	water
it	were	so	been
he	we	some	call
was	when	her	who
for	your	would	oil
on	can	make	now
are	said	like	find
as	there	him	long
with	use	into	down
his	an	time	day
they	each	has	did
I	which	look	get
at	she	two	come
be	do	more	made
this	how	write	may
have	their	go	part
from	if	see	over

Common suffixes: *s, ing, ed*

The Instant Words Second Hundred

First 25 Group 2a	Second 25 Group 2b	Third 25 Group 2c	Fourth 25 Group 2d
new	great	put	kind
sound	where	end	hand
take	help	does	picture
only	through	another	again
little	much	well	change
work	before	large	off
know	line	must	play
place	right	big	spell
year	too	even	air
live	mean	such	away
me	old	because	animal
back	any	turn	house
give	same	here	point
most	tell	why	page
very	boy	ask	letter

The Instant Words Second Hundred (Cont.)

First 25 Group 2a	Second 25 Group 2b	Third 25 Group 2c	Fourth 25 Group 2d
after	follow	went	mother
thing	came	men	answer
our	want	read	found
just	show	need	study
name	also	land	still
good	around	different	learn
sentence	form	home	should
man	three	us	America
think	small	move	world
say	set	try	high

Common suffixes: *s, ing, ed, er, ly, est*

The Instant Words Third Hundred

First 25 Group 3a	Second 25 Group 3b	Third 25 Group 3c	Fourth 25 Group 3d
every	left	until	idea
near	don't	children	enough
add	few	side	eat
food	while	feet	face
between	along	car	watch
own	might	mile	far
below	close	night	Indian
country	something	walk	real
plant	seem	white	almost
last	next	sea	let
school	hard	began	above
father	open	grow	girl
keep	example	took	sometimes
tree	begin	river	mountain
never	life	four	cut
start	always	carry	young
city	those	state	talk
earth	both	once	soon
eye	paper	book	list
light	together	hear	song
thought	got	stop	leave
head	group	without	family
under	often	second	body
story	run	late	music
saw	important	miss	color

Common suffixes: *s, ing, ed, er, ly, est*

SOURCE: Adapted from *The Child and the English Language Arts* by Mildred Donoghue, 1990, Dubuque, IA: Wm. C. Brown Publishers.

Figure 5.4 Sample Word Wall for Mid-Year First Grade: 50–70 words

Word Wall	Aa an ask any also	Bb by been believe	Cc call came carry could	Dd do did does	Ee eat ever	Ff for from fall
Gg go goes give	Hh he him has have her	Ii I it if	Jj jump just jolly	Kk keep key	Ll like look	Mm my more most
Nn no night now	Oo once out one	Pp put play please	Qq quit quick	Rr ride room	Ss some soon	Tt this then try
Uu use uncle	Vv very	Ww with went where	Xx	Yy yes you	Zz zoo	

SOURCE: Adapted from "Mastering words: Making the most of a word wall," by K. McNeal, 2004, in G. Tompkins & C. Blanchfield, (Eds.), *Teaching vocabulary.* Columbus, OH: Merrill/ Prentice Hall.

Vocabulary Development

Types of Vocabularies

According to *The Literacy Dictionary* (Harris & Hodges, 1995), there are nearly a dozen different types of vocabularies. However, the elementary teacher is only concerned with developing four of them: listening or hearing, speaking or oral, reading, and writing. These vocabularies are accessed both separately and together in the brain (Wolfe & Nevills, 2004). Two of these—listening and reading—are receptive and emphasize understanding and decoding. Speaking and writing vocabularies, on the other hand, are expressive and can be viewed as encoding in its broadest definition. All four overlap and develop continuously into adulthood, although at different rates. Of course, it is initially the listening and speaking vocabularies that contribute to reading and writing skills.

The hearing or *listening vocabulary* includes all the words that children recognize and understand when they hear them. It is the first vocabulary to develop during the language acquisition stage and is also the one that continues to grow most rapidly during the elementary school years. It remains substantially larger than a student's visual vocabulary until the seventh or eighth grade (Biemiller, 2003).

The teacher must realize that the listening child may comprehend one meaning of a word or one shade of meaning and yet be wholly ignorant of the other denotations. In addition, the teacher

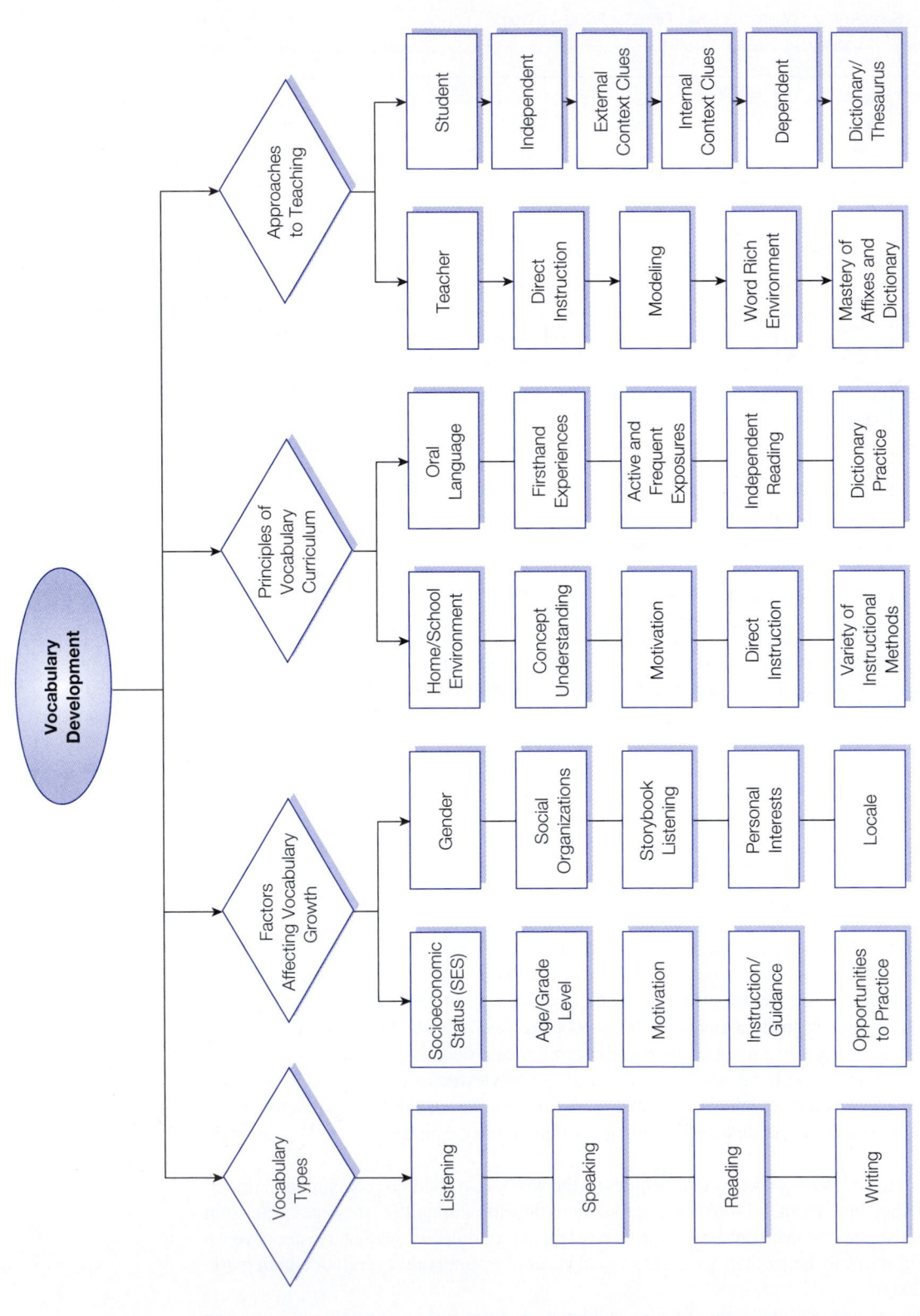

A Graphic Summary of the Contents of This Section

must recognize that the size of a primary child's listening vocabulary ordinarily will not affect his or her reading progress until the third grade.

The *speaking vocabulary* includes all the words that children use in everyday speech. It forms the basis for the development of the reading and writing vocabularies, and it is at the oral/aural level that vocabulary development generally takes place in the classroom. The recommendation has been made that children possess sizable speaking vocabularies in a language before they begin reading lessons in that language, whether it is their native or second tongue. Fortunately, their active vocabularies for both speaking and listening expand as children progress in school.

The *reading vocabulary* consists of all the words that children recognize and understand in print or in writing. When they enter school their reading vocabularies are generally limited, and according to Barone and colleagues (2006), typical everyday oral language experiences do not provide a sufficient number of new words to promote substantial vocabulary development. Therefore, students require exposure to print through "wide reading" to develop a solid basis of word knowledge. Wide reading includes both a large volume of reading (number of words) and different types or genres of reading. Incidentally, the kind of books that young children can read for themselves do not effectively expand their vocabularies, according to Beck and McKeon (2001).

It is thus crucial that the teacher chooses materials for read-alouds that are several levels above the children's own reading levels. In fact, Walsh (2003) recommends that selections be as much as two years ahead of the grade level to promote vocabulary growth. Books introduce students to more new words than television or conversation (Snow et al., 1998). "Book language" consists of a more advanced or sophisticated vocabulary than children hear every day, opening their minds to a variety of authors and genres.

The *writing vocabulary* is reported to lag perpetually behind the other three. It is the last to develop and includes only the words that children use in their written work. Moreover, writing vocabularies are generally nonexistent when children start school and are primarily learned during the school years. They are closely tied to spelling instruction, beginning with invented or temporary spelling in kindergarten–first grade. As students move into the intermediate grades, their writing vocabularies advance as well, together with their abilities in spelling and grammar. Students' writing vocabularies reportedly overlap strongly with their speaking vocabularies.

Factors Affecting Vocabulary Growth

There are numerous factors that influence the development of vocabulary in children. While some are beyond the domain of the teacher, classroom instruction can have an impact on other factors.

The first factor is the *socioeconomic status (SES) of the child's family*. Recent research concerning children entering kindergarten and first grade has shown that those from high-SES homes know twice as many words as those from low-SES homes (Beck, McKeown, & Kucan, 2002). The vocabulary of students from high-SES homes is enhanced in the following ways: Students have more background knowledge, as these children participate with their families in a wider range of activities that promote vocabulary; they have more book experience, as they visit the library regularly, are read to daily, and may have their own book collection; and their parents have a higher vocabulary level, using a more complex vocabulary when talking to their children.

Furthermore, high-SES children learn more words and learn them faster than low-SES students. The vocabularies of high-SES students develop at a surprising rate of 3,000 to 4,000 words a year, whereas low-SES students acquire words at a much slower rate. In fact, by the time they graduate from high school, high-SES students have vocabularies ranging from 25,000 to 40,000 words or more.

An earlier but classic study of word knowledge of children from middle-SES families stressed the need to develop vocabulary as early as preschool. Hart and Risley (1995) designated those children as the "fortunate group" since by age three they had heard 30 million more words than their peers from low-SES families. (The latter were labeled the "unfortunate group.") Students in the fortunate group started school with a beginning vocabulary of 6,000 more words than their peers in the unfortunate group. Furthermore, by the end of high school, despite all the instruction the unfortunate group had received in vocabulary development and reading, it was four times behind the fortunate group in word knowledge and its parents had a lower vocabulary than the three-year-olds in the fortunate group.

Another important factor is the *age or grade level of the child*. The older the child, the more words he or she knows. Even second graders have been known to outperform first graders in vocabulary surveys. The factor of *motivation* is always crucial. Motivated individuals can increase their working vocabularies in part by bringing into sharper focus those words or parts of words and those expressions whose meanings are presently fuzzy. The teacher can help motivate students into moving some of those troubling words or phrases into their working vocabularies.

Instruction and guidance in the use of words are vital. In addition to teachers, the children's parent(s), grandparents, and other interested adults—at home or in the community—can and should take the time to explain unfamiliar vocabulary to girls and boys. Conversing briefly but routinely with the mail carrier, for instance, can help children enrich their use of words.

Furthermore, students must have *repeated opportunities to practice a new word* so that it can be assimilated into their individual word banks. According to Kuhn and Stahl (1998, 2003) a new word has to be encountered eight to twelve times to be learned. Consequently, teachers expecting children to acquire new vocabulary through their reading alone without specific instruction have unrealistic expectations, especially of struggling or even average readers. When more than 2% of the words in a text are unfamiliar to the reader, his or her comprehension is blocked (Carver, 1994). ELLs have even greater difficulty in the acquisition of vocabulary since they lack full control of English grammar and so may encounter a larger proportion of words they do not recognize (Carlo et al., 2004).

Continued and regular listening to storybooks is also a critical factor in vocabulary development. Words appear to be learned best by young children in a context of emotional as well as intellectual meaning. ELLs and at-risk students find it particularly difficult to deal with words in isolation. Listening to read-alouds, however, has resulted in increasing both the size and quality of the listeners' vocabularies. Furthermore, when teachers find storybooks that are examples of quality children's literature *and* cover content area material, ELLs and at-risk students are able to make even better use of the read-aloud sessions. Here are examples of such books, which can be used occasionally (Donoghue, 2001):

In earth science: Peters' *The Sun, the Wind, and the Rain* (1988) discusses Elizabeth and her experiences at the beach.

In health science: Sharmat's *Gregory, the Terrible Eater* (1988) describes a goat who likes people food.

In physical science: Adams' *The Great Valentine's Day Balloon Race* (1986) concerns Orson Abbot who builds a hot air balloon with the help of his friend Bonnie.

In algebra: Ernst's *Sam Johnson and the Blue-Ribbon Quilt* (1983) tells about a farmer who learns to quilt.

In measurement: Hutchins' *Clocks and More Clocks* (1994) involves Mr. Higgins, who finds a clock in his attic one day.

In data analysis: Munsch's *Moira's Birthday* (1987) talks about Moira, who invites 200 children to her birthday party.

In social studies: Cooney's *Miss Rumphius* (1985) discusses Miss Rumphius who wants to leave the world a more beautiful place.

In social studies: Friedman's *How My Parents Learned to Eat* (1987) explores the meeting between Aiko, a Japanese girl, and John, an American sailor stationed in Japan.

In social studies: Monjo's *The Drinking Gourd* (1983) explains how Tommy Fuller becomes involved in the Underground Railroad before the Civil War.

Still another contributing factor to vocabulary growth relates to the *child's personal interests*. Students involved in sports or music readily acquire the specialized vocabulary that their avocation demands.

Sex differences have also been noted in all types of vocabulary development. Girls develop larger speaking vocabularies before they start kindergarten, and they soon exceed elementary boys in reading vocabularies. These differences level off, however, as students enter adolescence.

The *social organizations* to which girls and boys belong make a difference in the range and depth of their vocabularies. If they regularly attend a synagogue or church, for example, they are more likely to be acquainted with biblical terms than if they do not attend.

The last factor influencing vocabulary growth is *locale,* which is becoming less significant under the influence of the mass media. Nevertheless, for example, there are words dealing with coal mining or condominiums that are not familiar to everyone in the nation.

Principles of Vocabulary Development

Based on research studies and classroom experiences, a curriculum that promotes vocabulary growth in children should incorporate the following principles.

The vocabulary of the home and community greatly affects the school program in vocabulary development. Not only have children learned to listen and speak long before they enter kindergarten, but even after they enroll in school, they continue to spend many hours listening and talking at home and in their neighborhoods. In this delicate area of home-school relations, it is critical that students do not develop feelings of inadequacy about their families or communities due to matters of vocabulary.

Vocabulary development is closely related not only to general maturation but also to varied interactions in a stimulating out-of-school environment. At-risk students growing up in an out-of-school environment favorable to language growth are more likely to have a better vocabulary than students who are not at-risk but living in a relatively sterile environment.

Developing a vocabulary requires understanding of the meanings and concepts that underlie words. Concepts can be expanded both by generalization and by differentiation. For example, children learn to group lemons and limes under *fruit*. They also learn to separate *cats* into manx, angora, and Persian. However, ELLs or at-risk students find it hard to recognize the various meanings of a single word such as *big* because they find such multiple meanings confusing.

Motivation is the major quality of any school environment that promotes word study. It is as important as any other aspect of vocabulary instruction, and no classroom teacher genuinely concerned about teaching vocabulary will overlook it.

Children need direct instruction in vocabulary. Whether in reading or in content areas such as social studies or science, direct instruction is important. Since word boundaries are difficult to identify during conversations, especially for ELLs, it is more helpful to have the students' own words shown in print, as during language–experience activities (which are discussed further in Chapter 6).

Direct instruction by a teacher promoting specialized vocabulary, as in a science unit, is critical.

Using a variety of instructional methods appears to be more effective than using any single method. Useful strategies for fostering vocabulary development may be categorized as the teacher's direct instructional approach, the learner's independent approach, and the learner's dependent approach. Each is described later in this chapter.

In the lower grades, growth in a student's meaning vocabulary is obtained chiefly through oral language, which allows for interaction and feedback. Furthermore, oral language also typically contains a smaller proportion of low-frequency or difficult words than written language. This makes it easier to learn the new words that do occur.

Vocabulary development must grow out of experiences that are real to the learner. A teacher cannot overlook the need for carefully structured events and settings. For primary children particularly, firsthand experiences are the best and often the only source of conceptual development. The teacher must recognize that students at any grade who lag behind their peers in vocabulary growth do not need additional written work. Instead, they will profit from nonprint media and direct experiences.

Children's work with words should be as active and as frequent as the teacher can arrange because vocabulary improvement requires periodic use of the new words by the teacher and the students. For students to be able to classify and reinforce word meanings, they must have adequate opportunities to use the new vocabulary. Four exposures, regardless of whether through reading, writing, or conversation, are not enough for children—or most adults—to recall a new word or attach meaning to it (Stahl, 2003). Teachers have found that 12 exposures are enough for most readers but some children must use a word as many as 20 or more times to recall it automatically.

The major determinant of vocabulary growth, beginning in about the third grade, is the amount of free reading done individually.

The dictionary is a valuable tool for extending vocabularies. The teacher should informally evaluate the dictionary competencies of the class and periodically schedule group lessons in its use. Each child should have access to a dictionary appropriate to his or her reading and maturity level. (This guideline is discussed later in this chapter.)

Students learn concepts and vocabulary in four ways: relating known words to concepts (e.g., a child learning *cat* relates it to a pet as well as a family of wild animals); relating new words to existing concepts (e.g., a child learning *gigantic* relates it to the familiar concept or word of *size*); relating existing words to new concepts (e.g., a child who knows what a *column* represents in math learns that *column* also refers to a kind of newspaper article); and learning both new concepts and new words (e.g., a child who learns in science about the *condensation* process also learns a corresponding new word) (Templeton & Pikulski, 2000). Mr. Wan in Vignette 5.2 is able to connect new vocabulary with his third-grade health/science unit.

VIGNETTE 5.2 **Developing Specialized Vocabulary**

"Who's afraid of going to the dentist?" Mr. Wan asked his class of third graders. A few students immediately raised their hands, while several boys smirked and acted brave.

"Well, sometimes I get scared too," he continued, amused to see looks of amazement replace the boys' proud smiles. Mr. Wan, a recent college graduate and an excellent surfer, was also the only male teacher in this small southern California elementary school. The boys idolized him.

The class was finishing its health unit on personal care, focusing specifically on the teeth and gums. Mr. Wan routinely incorporated elements of one discipline into another, and last week he linked their studies to the science curriculum by conducting an experiment to determine the effects of juice and soda on the teeth. This week he'd make the connection to vocabulary.

"Tomorrow will be our last day to study this topic, and my friend Dr. Krueger will speak to our class," Mr. Wan said. "Dr. Krueger is a dentist. Who can tell me why the doctors who take care of our teeth are called 'dentists'?"

No one raised a hand. Mr. Wan walked to the side of the class and tried again.

"Okay, I'll give you a clue. Who can think of another word that has d-e-n-t as part of it?" he asked, writing the four letters on the white board spanning the side wall.

"Dentures," Angela volunteered. The class giggled.

"You're right!" he said. "Replacement teeth are called dentures. Who can think of another 'dent' word?"

"Dental floss," said Mia.

"Right again," he answered. "We also learned a new word yesterday that includes 'dent.' Who remembers?"

"Dentin," said Sam after a moment.

"Great job," said Mr. Wan. "Can you tell me what dentin is?"

"It's . . . the stuff between your outer teeth and the insides," Sam answered.

"Good," Mr. Wan said. "Between your tooth enamel and the tooth pulp is dentin. So *dentist, dentures, dental*, and *dentin* all have something in common—the root word 'dent.'" Quickly he listed the four words on the whiteboard and underlined the common letters in each one.

"Like root canals," Jake laughed. Mr. Wan caught the pun and smiled.

"And root canals happen in your...." He trailed off and waited for his students to make the connection.

"Teeth!" several of them said.

"Right," said Mr. Wan. "'Dent' comes from the Latin word for *tooth*, and many words related to our teeth have the root word 'dent' or 'dont.'"

"Like orthodontist," Melanie said. Melanie hated her braces.

"Like orthodontist," he agreed. "When Dr. Krueger speaks tomorrow, he'll probably use these words, and others like them, to describe his work." To ensure the lesson's effectiveness, he had asked Dr. Krueger to intentionally include several such words.

"I want you to listen well and learn more information about taking care of your teeth," Mr. Wan continued. "You are always a good audience for our guests, but this time I want you to listen extra carefully. Each time Dr. Krueger uses a word with 'dent' or 'dont' as a root word, I want you to write it down. At the end of his time with us, you can ask him questions about any words you don't know—and of course you can also ask him about being a dentist."

Satisfied that the students understood, Mr. Wan ended the vocabulary lesson and prepared the children for silent reading. He would review the assignment again before Dr. Krueger spoke the next morning.

Mr. Wan looked forward to observing the class during the special presentation and hearing their questions for his friend. He also planned to debrief the class after the experience and allow them to share their word lists. If the students absorbed the information—and enjoyed the process—as much as he anticipated, he would create other experiences to reinforce vocabulary concepts.

In the meantime, even today's short discussion helped the children understand a common base word and formed a practical connection to their health studies; tomorrow's talk might even make a few of them less scared of their next visit to the dentist.

Writers of vocabulary development curriculum should also recall some *misconceptions* about words generally and about the nature of vocabulary learning in particular: (a) All words are equally learnable (in reality, nouns and verbs, for example, are easier to learn than prepositions and pronouns); (b) all words have only one meaning (in reality, common words such as *back* or *go* often have several uses); (c) pronunciation is the goal of vocabulary instruction (in reality, emphasizing detailed phonic analysis at the expense of concept development makes vocabulary instruction a form of applied phonics with a corresponding loss in text comprehension); and (d) older readers need little or no direct vocabulary instruction (in reality, a good program continues in the intermediate grades with an emphasis on in-depth development of key concept words, with opportunities to practice independent word recognition skills, and always with the understanding of the differing needs of older students).

Finally, curriculum writers of vocabulary development should be familiar with the history of the English language.

History of the English Language

The earliest source of the English language was a prehistoric language that modern scholars term Proto-Indo-European (PIE), which was probably spoken some 5,000 years ago by people living in southeastern Europe in an area north of the Black Sea. These people migrated through the centuries and gradually developed new languages. One group of these people who spoke PIE migrated west and divided into groups that spoke languages that were the ancestors of the Germanic, Greek, and Latin languages. The Germanic languages developed into Dutch, German, Scandinavian—and English. The ancient Greek language became modern Greek, and the ancient Latin developed into French, Italian, and Spanish.

The earliest known language in what is presently Britain was spoken by a people called the Celts who were under Roman control until early 400 C.E. During the mid-fifth century Germanic people belonging to three main tribes—the Angles, the Jutes, and the Saxons—invaded Britain. Their language became known as English, and its history can be divided into three main periods: Old English (450–1100), Middle English (1100–1500), and Modern English (1500 to the present).

Old English Period (450–1100)

Old English resembles modern German more than it does modern English. Its word order and pronunciation were similar to those of modern German, as were its many inflections (i.e., the addition of affixes to the root word). Latin words had been brought over by the Germanic people when they arrived in Britain, and later as Christianity spread to England during the sixth and seventh centuries more Latin words were added. During the late ninth century when Viking invaders settled in northeast England, words from the Scandinavian languages also became part of Old English.

This process of adopting words from one language into another is called *borrowing* and often results from external contacts through war, trade, and tourism; pronunciation and spelling changes may then occur.

Middle English Period (1100–1500)

The Norman Conquest of 1066 by the French caused "tremendous" changes, according to West (1975), in the word order, grammar, as well as vocabulary of the English language. In fact, the changes were so great that Middle English is a different language completely from Old English, as shown in the following (West, 1975, p. 77):

Old English: Daeghwamlice man unriht raerde calles to wide gynd calle pas peode.

Translation: Every day they have committed injustice all too widely in all this nation.

Middle English: This carpenter hadde wedded newe wyf, which that he lovede moore than his lyf. (No translation needed.)

During this Middle English period, the English people borrowed thousands of French words and made them part of their language. However, as the Normans intermarried with the English and began to speak English in daily life, the French influence declined. By the end of the 1300s English was used again in business, the government, and the courts.

Modern English Period (1500 to the Present)

The beginning of the Modern English period was marked by the introduction in 1476 of the printing press, which helped standardize spelling in written communication and also provided more people with more books. By about 1485 English had lost most of the Old English inflections, and its word order and pronunciations closely resembled those of today. Over the next few centuries the English vocabulary expanded through borrowing as the English explored and colonized Australia, India, Africa, and North America. In these areas, different dialects of the English language grew.

In addition to the expansion of vocabulary during the Modern English period, there were also some changes in pronunciation. While the pronunciation of short vowels has remained stable, there has been a marked change in the pronunciation of long vowels. Known as the Great Vowel Shift, it occurred during the 1500s and is considered by some (Alexander, 1962) to be the most important sound change in the history of the English language. It should be stressed that when a word is borrowed from another language, a sound change usually and gradually occurs because the phonetics of the culture borrowing the word rarely resembles that of the culture from which it is borrowed.

Today the English language includes words from immigrant groups from around the world as well as words from Native American peoples. Here are a sample dozen of the thousands of borrowed words that have entered the English language from another culture:

dollar from the German

freight from the Dutch

jungle from the Hindi

lasso from the Spanish

moose from the Native American Algonquian

restaurant from the French

robot from the Czech

tattoo from the Polynesian

tycoon from the Chinese

umbrella from the Italian

yogurt from the Turkish

zero from the Arabic

Teaching English Vocabulary: Approaches

For material related to this concept, go to Video Clip 5.2 on the Student Resource CD bound into the back of your textbook.

As mentioned earlier in this chapter, the major method for promoting vocabulary development is the teacher's direct instructional approach. However, students also benefit individually if they learn to use context clues wisely and become familiar with the dictionary and thesaurus.

Teacher's Direct Instructional Approach

After reviewing research conducted on teaching vocabulary directly, Blachowicz and Fisher (2006) identified guidelines that teachers should follow in this area: *Model for students* word learning strategies while teaching vocabulary in reading and other subjects; *immerse students* in vocabulary by building a word-rich environment in the classroom (e.g., word walls); *prepare students to become independent* vocabulary learners by teaching them skills such as mastery of affixes and proper use of the dictionary; and *assess students* on the growth of their vocabulary knowledge to determine to what extent instructional goals have been reached.

In addition to the guidelines listed above, teachers should be careful to *select words that students encounter during reading* so that they are exposed to them more frequently; this exposure will not occur if the chosen words are obscure or unusual. They should also *teach words in relation to other words* or within the context of concept development and *help students relate words to their background knowledge.* They should *teach words every day, moving beyond a simple definition,* so students will learn new vocabulary efficiently and independently. Finally, teachers should *introduce words with enthusiasm,* thereby promoting a contagious interest for vocabulary work in the classroom (Vacca, Vacca, & Gove, 1991).

Before children begin a reading lesson, teachers must read through the material themselves and preteach new vocabulary that might be unfamiliar, choosing, however, only those words that may be challenging to the students in that classroom (Beck & McKeown, 2001). They can use the following criteria to help them choose which vocabulary words to preteach: Is the word critical to comprehending the text? Will students encounter the word repeatedly in this or other texts? Will understanding the word help in other subject areas?

After the reading lesson, teachers should use class discussion to reinforce concepts and vocabulary the children have learned. This will help students link the vocabulary they are learning to their own experiential background.

Teachers must also recognize the importance of read-alouds. Students often learn as many words while listening to a text being read to them as they do by reading it themselves. Such read-alouds of texts introduce the children to the more formal *book language* in contrast to the language they encounter in daily experiences. Since ELLs and at-risk students are often reluctant to read by themselves, read-alouds provide a strong medium for increasing their exposure to the more complex language found in books.

Finally, teachers will find it useful to follow this five-step strategy for presenting new words, especially those that have unusual or infrequent letter combinations:

> Step 1. *Seeing the word:* The new word is first written on the chalkboard, a flashcard, a wall chart, or worksheet. It is then pronounced. Then, with some nouns (e.g., *clock, squash*), three-dimensional objects can be displayed and labeled. With many other words (e.g., *astronomer, cloud*), flat pictures can be used to promote understanding of the new terms.

> Step 2. *Discussing the word:* After Step 1, the new word (e.g., *cavity*) is reviewed orally and tied to earlier or ongoing experiences or interests of the children.

> Step 3. *Using the word:* After Steps 1 and 2, students recite or write a sentence that uses the new word. Sometimes they may offer synonyms or synonymous phrases. In every case, the teacher writes the sentence on the chalkboard in an attempt to clarify any misunderstandings (as in homographs, such as *lead/lead* or *conduct/conduct*).

> Step 4. *Defining the word:* After Steps 1, 2, and 3, the children tell in their own words what the new term means. They should not need to use the dictionary or basal glossary to define a common word like *manufacture.*

> Step 5. *Writing the word:* After Steps 1 through 4, students practice writing the new word in their vocabulary journals. They can also write the word during some of the instructional activities outlined later in this chapter because it takes repeated exposures in a variety of contexts to provide the needed overlearning of an unfamiliar word to make it part of the children's vocabulary.

Students' Independent Approaches

Independent approaches gradually enable students to unlock the meanings of many unknown words by using knowledge of familiar words. The approaches use internal context clues (i.e., mastery of affixes and mastery of roots) and external context clues.

By using *external context clues,* a child can often determine the meaning of an unfamiliar word without using a dictionary. Teachers may demonstrate the various kinds of context clues by constructing several sentences to illustrate a certain kind of clue, pointing out random context clues in paragraphs the child is reading, or presenting sentences that typify three or four kinds of clues and letting the student explain which kind each sentence represents. External clues include the following:

Definition by *contrast* (e.g., A papaya is not a vegetable.)

Definition by *synonym* (e.g., Fortitude is courage.)

Definition by *antonym* (e.g., He was pugnacious, but his wife was peaceful.)

Definition by *apposition* (e.g., Mango, a fruit, grows in the tropics.)

Most context clues demand some degree of inferential thinking. The reader should gradually learn to use the meaning of the sentence or the surrounding sentences as an aid in identifying the probable meaning of a difficult word.

Although most students accept the importance of context, some of them do not understand morphology or how words also derive meaning from their component parts. To introduce the valuable aid of using internal context clues, the teacher must start with a familiar word, break it into its meaningful parts, and then transfer the meaning of these parts of new words. He or she should move stepwise from known words (such as *triangle* or *good*) to unknown words (such as *tricolor* or *goodness*). Children will then be able to infer the meaning of a difficult word if they know the meaning of the prefix or suffix used to form the word and if they realize that meanings of mastered *prefixes* and *suffixes* (known collectively as *affixes*) can be transferred from one word to another.

Common *prefixes* include *ab* (away from), *ad* (toward, to), *be* (overly, on all sides), *com, con, co* (together, with), *de* (downward, reversal, from), *dis* (apart from, not, opposite), *en* (in, into, to cover), *ex* (former, out of), *in* (not, into), *pre* (before), *pro* (for, before, in favor of), *re* (again, restore), *sub* (under, beneath), and *un* (not, the opposite of).

Suffixes may be either inflectional or derivational. The latter generally do not change the part of speech to which a word belongs, whereas *inflectional suffixes* do. Inflectional suffixes that students can easily learn include verb tenses (*helps, helping, helped*), plurals (*dogs, plates, babies*), possessives (*Wendy's, girls'*), and comparisons (*smaller, smallest*).

Common *derivational suffixes* include *able, ble, ible* (can be done, inclined to), *al, ial* (relating to), *fy* (make, form into), *ic, ical* (in the nature of), *ism* (system, state of), *ist* (person who), *less* (without), *let* (small), *ment* (concrete result, process, state of), *ness* (quality, condition of), *ory* (place where), and *ward* (course, direction).

Primary teachers should recall that the relationship between children's reading abilities in Grades 1 and 2 and their abilities to apply inflections is closer than the relationship between their reading ability and either visual or auditory perception. Young children in a classic study (Brittain, 1970) were able to change pseudowords (such as *wog*) to plurals, past and progressive verb tenses, possessives, and comparatives or superlatives with ease.

Unlike affixes, which are bound morphemes, most *root words* are free morphemes. Nevertheless, mastery of roots or base words will also help students attack new words that may come up while reading outside the classroom. With a knowledge of base words, children will be able to unlock dozens of words by transferring the meaning of a single root to other words.

During a beginning lesson, for instance, the students could be asked to underline the common element in the following words: *telephone, microphone, saxophone, phonics*. They could discuss the meaning of *phon* (sound) and then write other words they know that contain the same root. Finally, some students might even make up new words.

Common roots the children can learn include *cap* (head), *cav* (hollow), *circ* (ring), *dent* (tooth), *form* (shape), *geo* (earth), *gram* (letter), *mari* (sea), *min* (small), *mov* (move), *scrib* or *script* (write), and *vis* (see).

Students' Dependent Approach: The Dictionary or Thesaurus

A dependent approach to vocabulary development, such as that involved in learning more about the use of the dictionary/thesaurus, does not teach for transfer of word knowledge. Instead, the child studies one word at a time and learns it only under the supervision of the teacher (or interested parent). Still the approach is organized, and any systematic strategy to vocabulary growth is preferable to incidental or unorganized learning. The major technique is *dictionary/thesaurus study*.

Teaching English Vocabulary: Instructional Activities

Vocabulary building requires attention. Every day at least a few minutes should be taken for discussion of words that are used for the communication of ideas. This is the best way that precise meanings can be learned. If words are introduced too quickly or too casually, students receive only vague impressions of their definitions. Therefore, multiple exposures to unfamiliar words are needed to improve comprehension and vocabulary.

Some of the following instructional activities appeal especially to ELLs, to at-risk children, or to younger students. Others will interest intermediate students or advanced readers at all levels. Finally there are activities suggested for both primary and intermediate classes that can be completed individually, with partners, or even in groups.

- Listing things needed to (a) go camping, (b) build a tree house, (c) bake cookies, (d) set the table, or (e) go to school on a rainy day
- Giving more than one meaning to words such as *run, pipe, can, shell, ice, bark, sheet, park, slip, call, date, yarn, strike, spring, roll, light, fall, cut, check,* and *charge*
- Illustrating mathematical and geographical terms such as *perpendicular* and *diagonal,* and *plateau* and *delta,* respectively
- Making a sound train by painting and lettering shoeboxes and then filling them with small objects (or their paper pictures) whose names begin or end with the letters shown
- Keeping a list of unfamiliar words that appear in the headlines of one issue of the *Weekly Reader*
- Describing one food item according to the five senses (e.g., *pickles* are *green, crunchy, sour, slippery, briny*)
- Developing an alphabet of words originating from famous names (e.g., *pasteurization* from Louis Pasteur); the list might begin with *America* (Amerigo Vespucci), *Braille* printing (Louis Braille*), Celsius* thermometer (Anders Celsius), and *diesel* engine (Rudolph Diesel)
- Drawing five UGH (!) terms such as *fish guts*
- Listing some one-word palindromes or words that can be read backward and forward with the same result (e.g., *rotor, nun, Otto*)
- Drawing some amusing and confusing figures of speech such as *fork in the road* and *foot in his mouth*

- Listing some of the specialized vocabulary used by sportscasters or found on the sports pages of local newspapers
- Expressing one action word (e.g., *catapult*) graphically through an art medium
- Listing items composed wholly or partly of synthetics (e.g., *vinyl, nylon*)
- Miming *outrage, delight, horror,* and other emotional reactions
- Writing words to reveal their meaning (e.g., *fat* would be drawn or written with thick letters *f, a,* and *t* , whereas *flag* could have a flag drawn in place of the *f*)
- Collecting job words about anthropologists, pediatricians, or other specialized workers
- Discovering how three acronyms (e.g., *radar*) have developed
- Collecting "loaded" words or propaganda devices (as discussed later in Chapter 11) gleaned from speeches made by politicians at election times
- Preparing menus based on a single food category such as sandwiches or desserts
- Writing some riddles about homophones or words that sound the same but are spelled differently and have different meanings (e.g., Why are Saturday and Sunday the strongest days of the *week*? Because all the others are *weak* days.)

A sample lesson plan incorporating the concepts introduced in this chapter appears on p. 148.

Assessment

The ongoing process of assessment in phonological awareness serves two main purposes: (1) to determine the current ability level of the student and (2) to guide future instruction. By using carefully designed assessment tools such as the Yopp-Singer Phonemic Segmentation Test and other instruments that check student levels of skill in rhyme, sound segmentation and blending, sound manipulation, and sound–letter recognition, teachers can evaluate and target students' areas of strengths and weaknesses. Formal assessments, however, need to be supplemented by observational measures. Teachers can record student participation and efforts in individual and group literacy activities. Does the student use word attack skills to decode and sound out words, or does the student skip over unknown words or quickly ask for help? Does the student demonstrate knowledge of common word patterns and generalizations? Does the student participate and express interest in group phonemic awareness activities? In addition, teachers should recognize, especially in younger children, factors such as attention span, lack of concentration, shyness, and hearing and/or vision difficulties that may influence evaluation results, thus further emphasizing the need for multiple means of assessment. Tests that include nonverbal responses, such as pointing to colorful pictures and playing matching games, and shorter evaluation sessions can be beneficial in decreasing some of these influences.

Vocabulary assessment follows similar guidelines as those for phonological awareness assessment. Instruments such as Fry's New Instant Word List can establish a quick, baseline evaluation of sight vocabulary words, but should be used in conjunction with more comprehensive assessments. Informal teacher observations, student writing samples, and individual reading inventories provide a more complete picture of vocabulary skills because students use and analyze new vocabulary in context rather than in isolation. Teachers can observe students in authentic reading activities such as literature circles and independent reading. Do students use contextual clues, both graphic and semantic, to determine the meaning of unfamiliar words? Do older students use knowledge of affixes and/or base/root words to help derive meaning? Does the student make use of reference tools such as a dictionary and thesaurus? Teachers should be aware that listening and speaking vocabularies can be quite different from reading vocabulary and should therefore provide students with opportunities to develop an academic vocabulary. Teachers can assemble student portfolios of writing samples, vocabulary quizzes, and other relevant "word work" to provide authentic examples of student progress over time.

Working With English Language Learners

At all levels of English language development, factors that influence assessment and instruction include age, grade level, and literacy proficiency in the student's primary language. If students have received literacy instruction in their primary language, they will be more likely to make rapid progress in English. In addition, if their primary language is closely related to English (Spanish, Italian, French), they will be more likely to make associations through "cognates" or similar sounding words such as *office (oficina* in Spanish) and *blue (blau* in German). Grammatical and syntactic patterns, idioms, and words with multiple meanings will prove difficult and confusing at all levels as will concrete vs. abstract nouns. Read-alouds continue to be important for gleaning meaning of new vocabulary and terms at all ELL levels. Integrated thematic units (e.g., The Farm, The Human Body) that give students multiple opportunities to revisit vocabulary and concepts in a variety of situations and content areas are helpful to all learners. Audio books or tapes in English and the student's primary language and computer software programs that highlight spoken text assist ELLs in identifying oral language with written text.

Beginning ELLs: At the beginning ELL levels, instruction in phonological awareness and vocabulary should focus on listening and speaking skills used in a meaningful context. All students benefit from poems, chants, games, and songs that stress rhyme, alliteration, and play with sounds. However, teachers should recognize differences in speech/letter sounds between English and the student's native language. For example, the letter "v" in Spanish makes the /b/ sound, and many Asian languages use the "r" sound and the "l" sounds interchangeably. Depending on the student's age and instruction in his or her primary language, teachers can begin systematic instruction in phonemic awareness by introducing sound–letter recognition, blending/segmenting activities, and common sight words such as "is" and "my."

Vocabulary development at the beginning level should include hands-on activities, teacher created-drawings and charts, realia, and pictures to assist students in grasping the meaning of new words. Labeling of objects in the classroom will also help students recall names of concrete nouns. Abstract words such as "stubborn" and "beautiful" will require more time and effort to convey their meaning and will need the aid of meaningful context. Teachers can preteach new vocabulary to ELLs before giving whole-group lessons to allow students to have additional interaction with new vocabulary. Beginning ELL students can vary in age and grade level, and older ELL students face the challenge of learning more complex academic language, most notably in content areas of social studies and science; therefore, the above-mentioned techniques are even more important in classroom instruction. Other strategies that teachers can use with beginning ELL students are speaking slowly and clearly, using gestures and facial expressions, and providing quality computer software designed for building phonemic awareness and vocabulary skills.

Early intermediate and intermediate ELLs: As ELL students develop listening and speaking skills, they need less explicit instruction in phonological awareness. However, teachers need to continue to evaluate individual students for any gaps or areas of weakness and then target specific skills for instruction. Intermediate ELL students continue to build their sight word vocabularies. Teachers can provide decodable books and continue to provide quality literature for read-alouds, taking care to include a wide variety of fictional and informational texts, and books for silent reading at the student's independent reading level. Teachers should continue to preteach vocabulary words to ELLs and present information in a variety of ways. Students can begin to analyze words through affixes, base, and root words and rely less heavily on picture clues to derive meaning. Students make expanded use of structural clues such as syllabication and accents to pronounce new words. Cooperative learning and group settings scaffold intermediate ELL students in developing conversational and academic vocabulary through social and meaningful interactions with peers.

Early advanced and advanced ELLs: ELLs at the advanced level are developing more fluent reading skills and possess a variety of word attack strategies to sound out and decode words. However, even though learners at the advanced level are less dependent on teacher and/or peer support, regular assessment of their phonological awareness and sight word knowledge remains important in planning literacy instruction according to individual needs. Teachers should continue to provide a wide variety of comprehensible input that includes pictorials, preteaching, realia, videos, and concrete learning experiences. In addition, students should make use of visual tools such as graphic organizers and concept maps to assist in comprehension of complex concepts. Teachers continue to read aloud to older students, but students are also encouraged to read independently. Students benefit from carefully planned and modeled cooperative learning that help ELL learners build skills with peer assistance and project- or theme-based learning. Students build dictionary skills and make use of reference tools. Teachers provide advanced ELL students with comprehensive instruction in figurative language, idiomatic expressions, and words with multiple meanings. Such students become more proficient in the use of Latin and Greek roots and affixes to discern word meanings. Ideally, by this stage, students will be "reading to learn" instead of "learning to read."

Practical Instructional Activities and Ideas

- *Alliteration:* Teacher can select books for read-alouds such as Bayer's *A, My Name is Alice* (1987) and Grover's *The Accidental Zucchini: An Unexpected Alphabet* (1997) that emphasize the alphabet and alliteration. Students can sit in a circle after listening to the book and compose their own imaginative alliterations while clapping out the rhythm. Finally, students can illustrate and write "My Name Is..." poems for individual display or a class book.
- *Tactile letters:* Teacher can provide students with modeling clay, bread or cookie dough, marzipan, or any other suitable medium to form letters of the alphabet. Students can also etch or trace letters in wet sand, rolled clay or dough, or fingerpaint.
- *"Sticky" notes:* While reading text as a class or individually, students can jot down unfamiliar words on "sticky" notes. Teacher can give students the opportunity to discuss words as

a whole group activity or practice dictionary skills. Students then can either write or illustrate the definition of the new vocabulary word or words.

- *Highlighter pens:* Using printable or reproducible books that focus on a phonics or a structural analysis skill (such as the diphthong "ow" or the affix "-ed"), students search for, and highlight with colorful markers, those words that fit the pattern or rule.

- *Toss around:* Students toss around a beach ball or bean bag outside or in the classroom. Teacher starts the "toss," modeling proper underhand technique, and says a word such as "dog." The student who catches the object must come up with a word that begins with the ending sound of "dog" such as "gum." The student then tosses the object for the next student to catch. The next student may say "map" and play continues.

- *Pictorial input charts:* Teacher faintly outlines image(s) on large piece of chart paper to be filled in later with colored markers. Examples may include layers of the rainforest, the solar system, parts of the human body, and the water cycle. During a whole-group lesson/discussion, teacher traces over the predrawn image, labels important vocabulary, and provides verbal input. The chart remains on display for students and teachers to refer to during the course of the unit. Teachers can provide students with outlined diagram or blank paper for students to sketch, color, and label independently.

- *Word wizards:* Students give examples of vocabulary words learned in class that they discover outside of class. Did they read the word *communication* on a billboard advertising cell phones or hear the term *savory* on a commercial for barbeque sauce? Teachers can decide whether to reward students with points or prizes for their keen word recognition skills or simply revel in the satisfaction of a job well done.

- *Relay races:* Teacher assigns students to relay race teams. Students must run to the far end and pick an item from a bag or box that begins with a specific letter of the alphabet before they can run back and "tag" the next member of the team. For example, the box may contain for the letter "b" a ball, a bone, a book, and a balloon, but also "nonexamples" such as a spoon, a cup, and a pillow. Teacher can have students run with partners to accommodate different ability levels.

- *Graphic organizers:* Semantic maps and word webs assist students in visually and conceptually organizing new vocabulary and ideas. For example, students can brainstorm synonyms and related words for "fun," thus eliminating a "dead" word and offering a variety of more creative word choices. A class map or chart can be created as a whole-group project and added to as students think of new ideas or encounter unknown vocabulary during reading. This is an especially helpful tool when reading informational texts that introduce a high number of new academic terms and concepts.

- *Whiteboards:* Students can practice adding and deleting beginning, middle, and ending sounds using individual whiteboards and markers. Additionally, students can sort words into categories by making a "T" chart and placing words under the correct heading. For example:

oy	*oi*
boy	soil
Roy	coin
toy	join

LESSON PLAN 5.1   Word Families Workout

Linking Phonemic Awareness and Physical Education

Language Arts Components: Listening, Reading, and Writing

Grade: 1

ELL Level: Early Intermediate to Advanced

Topic: Sound–letter recognition, consonant-vowel-consonant pattern words

Time Frame: 1 hour

Objectives

- Students sort words into word families by identifying CVC (consonant-vowel-consonant) word patterns.
- Students spell and read words in the word family sort accurately.
- Students follow directions to complete various physical movements.

Materials

- *The Cat in the Hat* by Dr. Seuss
- Master set of letter cards (*a*, and selected consonants: *b, c, f, h, 1, m, n, p, r, s, t, v*) to represent members of the word family "-at"
- Individual sets of letter cards for word sorts
- Chart with letter "codes"
- Open space

Content Standards

English Language Development (ELD): Listening, Speaking, Reading

- Understand and follow simple directions by using physical actions and other means of nonverbal communication.
- Listen attentively to stories and information and identify important details and concepts.
- Recognize and reproduce English phonemes.
- Recognize and apply sound/symbol relationships and basic word formation rules.

Language Arts: Reading

- Students read a wide variety of texts.
- Students use strategies to comprehend and understand textual features.
- Students apply knowledge of language conventions to discuss texts.

Physical Education

- Students perform various balancing and movement activities including jumping, hopping, clapping, bending, twisting, and tossing an object.

Vocabulary

- Word family
- Rhyme

Open

Engage

- Teacher reads Seuss's *The Cat in the Hat* (or similar book or poem such as Seuss's *Hop on Pop)* that targets a particular "word family" or phonogram. Teacher, before reading, asks students to listen for rhyming words. Teacher asks students to give examples of rhyming words.
- Teacher discusses book with students, eliciting the correct rhyming patterns, and introduces a new vocabulary "word family" while explaining how rhyming words are "related" much like mothers, fathers, sisters, and brothers in student families.

Body

Explore

- Teacher reviews target sounds of short vowel sound "*a*" and consonants *b, c, f, h, m, n, p, r, s, t,* and *v* using large letter cards and/or picture cards if available.
- Teacher displays individual letter sheets, with same letters as above, and explains to students that they will be cutting the letters out along the dotted lines and building words from the "-at" word family.
- Teacher models cutting and word building with student input. For example, a student may suggest "cat," and teacher segments word sounds and places corresponding letter to form word.
- Teacher then tells students that, after they have constructed a word, they will need to consult the chart to exercise their "brains" and their "bodies."
- Teacher displays chart. (Chart optimally should include illustrations or icons so students do not need to recall/read directions.)

> a = hop on right foot 10 times
>
> b = leap like a frog 5 times
>
> c = clap 12 times
>
> d = do 7 jumping jacks
>
> e = take 15 steps like an elephant
>
> f = run in place and count to 20
>
> g = sing "Happy Birthday" and stomp your feet
>
> h = "skate" around while saying the ABC's
>
> i = hop on left foot 10 times
>
> j = recite "The Itsy Bitsy Spider"
>
> k = jump up and down 8 times
>
> l = "swim" like a fish for 16 strokes
>
> m = march 10 times in place

- Teacher explains and models word such as *cat* with student volunteer. Student acts out by clapping, hopping, and swimming like a fish the appropriate number of times.
- Teacher checks for understanding by asking students to repeat directions and/or ask questions. If needed, Teacher gives another example.
- Teacher reviews classroom rules of safety and behavior.
- Students independently complete activity while Teacher circulates classroom, providing guidance as needed.

Expand

- After students have successfully completed several word sorts, receiving a sufficient workout for brain and body, Teacher brings whole group back together.

Close

Apply

- Teacher asks students what members of the "word families" they created and lists on whiteboard or chart paper.
- Teacher brainstorms with students other "exercises" they could do (wiggle, dance, touch your toes, gallop, etc.).
- Teacher asks students if they can think of more word families that they could create.

Assessment

- Teacher observes students during word family sorts to see if students correctly form CVC words with "-at" rime. Is each student able to form one or more words?
- Teacher observes students performing physical activity for appropriate movements.
- During whole-group discussions, do students participate and ably think of other rhyming words?

Integration Across the Curriculum

Science

- Students can draw and label diagrams in science learning logs. For example, after a unit on earth science, teachers can have students sketch the layers of the earth or illustrate the concept of earthquake faults or plate tectonics. Younger students can label parts of a flower or map out the life cycle of a butterfly.

- Thematic units on topics such as weather and animal habitats offer opportunities to incorporate all content areas. Teachers can implement research, writing, reading, technology, songs, poems, art, social studies, and math. A fourth grade unit on The Westward Expansion can include folk music, square dancing, conservation of the earth's resources, graphing activities, Internet research, descriptive writing, Native American culture, and inclusion of biographies and primary sources. Through multiple exposures in different contexts to vocabulary terms, students will be more likely to retain the meaning of words.

Social Studies

- Teachers can link word origins and histories with social studies. Students studying Greek and Roman mythology can learn the meanings of root or base words. Additional ways to activate students' interest in history and to enable them to think more deeply about the English language are activities that study *eponyms* and *idioms*. The *Amelia Bedelia* book series by Peggy Parish portrays the comical outcomes of literal interpretations of common idioms like "dressing a turkey" for dinner and "drawing the curtains." Examples of eponyms include "sandwich" and "boycott."

- Students can create ABC books about their communities or other units of study. Younger children can illustrate and write "A" is for Astronaut, "B" is for Baker, "C" is for Carpenter, and continue through the letter "Z." The book would most likely be a year-long project that students can display during an open house in the spring. Alternatively, class books can be created over a shorter period of time by assigning each student a letter or vocabulary term to describe and illustrate, such as key words from a lesson on Vocations and Occupations.

Math

- Teachers can help students create bar graphs of student names according to their beginning letters to practice beginning sounds. Graphs provide a visual opportunity to introduce math vocabulary such as *data, total, more than,* and *less than*. Teachers can reinforce key terms by creating a math word wall.

- Phonemic awareness activities can reinforce math concepts. By breaking apart words into beginning, middle, and end sounds, students practice sequencing skills. Clapping out syllables reinforces counting. Segmenting and blending word activities emphasize concepts such as "part" and "whole."

- In addition, the above math activities can be supplemented with concept books that reinforce math vocabulary such as Murphy's *The Best Bug Parade* (1996) that emphasizes concepts of size (small/smaller/smallest) and Leedy's *The Great Graph Contest* (2005) that introduces children to the many different types of graphs and data collection procedures.

Literature

- Teachers can provide a wide assortment of alphabet books, nursery rhymes, and books that play with word sounds such as Slepian's *The Hungry Thing Goes to a Restaurant* (1992).

- Quality children's literature can be a motivating means of learning vocabulary terms needed to discuss literature intelligently. Teachers can explicitly teach terms related to story elements such as plot, character, and setting and genres such as historical fiction, fantasy, and fables. When books are introduced thematically such as in units on Ancient China or Transportation, students experience multiple opportunities to revisit and practice new vocabulary and concepts.

Visual and Performing Arts

- Teachers can target specific art vocabulary words. For example, teachers can have students create artworks with "warm" or "cool" colors and discuss how they help the artist evoke a mood or feeling. The different meanings of "warm" and "cool" can be further explored in a science unit on weather or energy. Teachers can help students make connections between written and visual forms of communication that convey mood.
- Students can create their own alphabet flashcards similar to illuminated manuscripts that focus on a particular theme. A lesson on plants could depict A is for Aster, B is for Bonsai, C is for Cactus, and so on. Self-created vocabulary cards can serve a similar artistic and pragmatic purpose.
- Intermediate students can dramatize the meanings of words associated with the American Revolution (e.g., minuteman).

Health

- Health- and fitness-related vocabulary can be explored through a variety of visual and print sources and hands-on food preparation. Teachers can read aloud "silly" books such as Wescott's *Never Take a Pig to Lunch* (1994) and Palatini's *Zak's Lunch* (1998). Teacher can display and discuss the new Food Pyramid guidelines. Students can examine fast-food menus and propose healthier choices that represent the various food groups. They can construct "You Are What You Eat" collages from magazines, supermarket flyers, and recycled food packaging. Students can examine nutritional labels for fat, sugar, and salt content. Older students can calculate percentages of vitamins and minerals, using math and critical thinking skills to determine if a product is "healthy" or if advertisers are misrepresenting the product.

Physical Education

- Jump rope songs such as "Teddy Bear, Teddy Bear" offer a traditional way to incorporate elements of rhyme, rhythm, and alliteration. Teachers can encourage students to compose new and original jump rope songs.

Music

- Rhythm sticks can be used to tap out the beat of children's songs that rhyme and/or practice vocabulary. A class set can be inexpensively constructed out of dowel rods.
- Many children's CDs are available that teach specific vocabulary such as "Head and Shoulders, Knees and Toes" for younger students and help older students memorize information such as the names of states and capitals through "catchy" tunes.
- As previously suggested for visual arts activities, abstract vocabulary terms such as "mood" can be explored through listening to music. Students can express mood by drawing, dancing, sculpting, or writing during or after listening to a piece of music.

Parents as Partners

The following suggestions offer ideas to foster active parent participation in their child's learning.

- *Mystery bags:* Teachers can send home paper bags with the "Letter of the Week" written on the outside. Parents help students select one or two items that represent that letter to share with the class. For example, a student may bring in a pretzel and a postcard to show the beginning sound "p."
- *Magnetic letters:* Teachers can print the letters of the alphabet on magnetic sheets for students to take home to build words. They write a letter to parents explaining activities they can work on with their children at home such as changing initial letter of CVC words (e.g., take away the beginning sound of /p/ in "pot" and change it to the /d/ sound and make "dot"). Children can use the refrigerator in the kitchen or a cookie sheet while riding in the car on errands.
- *Computers:* If families are fortunate enough to have home computers, teachers can provide a list of Web sites that are appropriate and/or educational for students such as www.starfall .com and www.brainpopjr.com for primary grades.
- *Handouts:* At the beginning of the school year, teachers can assemble a list of "tips" for parents that give simple ideas to help their child succeed in the upcoming months. Parents of younger children can be encouraged to play rhyming games, recite nursery rhymes, and practice tongue twisters. Parents of older students can help stir up interest in learning new vocabulary words. At all grade levels, parents can read aloud to children and engage them in conversation. The list can be revised and redistributed at other times of the year, perhaps during the holidays, asking parents and children to discuss a special family tradition or reading a favorite childhood book together.
- *Word of the day:* Teachers can enlist parents' help in stimulating children's interest in new words. Students can try and "stump" classmates, and better yet, the teacher with a new word brought from home discovered while reading, watching television, or listening to the radio.
- *Word games:* Teachers can provide parents with word games they can play at home with their children. Many matching games, bingo, and other printable and reproducible games that focus on various topics from compound words to science-based themes are available for free download via the Internet. The games can replace a portion of the traditional homework packet or worksheets.

Student Study Site

The Companion Web site for *Language Arts: Integrating Skills for Classroom Teaching* www.sagepub.com/donoghuestudy

Visit the Web-based study site to enhance your understanding of the chapter content. The study materials include chapter summaries, practice tests, flashcards, and Web resources.

Additional Professional Readings

Bear, D., Invernizzi, M., Templeton, S., & Johnston, F. (2008). *Words their way* (4th ed.). Columbus, OH: Merrill Prentice Hall.

Blachman, B., Ball, E., Black, R., & Tangle, D. (2000). *Read to the code: A phonological awareness program for young children.* Baltimore: Brookes.

Brand, M. (2004). *Word savvy.* Portland, ME: Stenhouse.

Cunningham, P. (2003). *Big words for big kids.* Greensboro, NC: Carson-Dellosa.

DeBruin-Parecki, A., & Hohmann, M. (2003). *Letter links: Alphabet learning with children's names.* Clifton Park, NY: Thomson Delmar Learning.

Graves, M. (2006). *The vocabulary book: Learning and instruction.* Newark, DE: International Reading Association.

Hendricks, C. (2007). *Teaching word recognition skills* (7th ed.). Columbus, OH: Merrill Prentice Hall.

Irvin, J. (2001). Assisting struggling readers in building vocabulary and background knowledge. *Voices From the Middle, 8,* 37–43.

O'Connor, R. (2007). *Teaching word recognition: Effective strategies for students with learning difficulties.* New York: Guilford.

Sinatra, R. (2003). *Word recognition and vocabulary development.* Norwood, ME: Christopher-Gordon.

Children's Literature Cited in the Text

Adams, A. (1986). *The great Valentine's Day balloon race.* New York: Macmillan.

Arnosky, J. (1999). *Mouse letters: A very first alphabet book.* New York: Clarion.

Bayer, J. E. (1987) *A, my name is Alice.* New York: Dial.

Cooney, B. (1985). *Miss Rumphius.* New York: Puffin.

Degen, B. (1985). *Jamberry.* New York: HarperCollins.

Ernst, L. (1983). *Sam Johnson and the blue-ribbon quilt.* New York: Lothrop.

Friedman, I. (1987). *How my parents learned to eat.* Boston: Houghton.

Grover, M. (1997). *The accidental zucchini: An unexpected alphabet.* New York: Voyager.

Hobbie, H. (2000). *Toot and Puddle: Puddle's ABC.* Boston: Little, Brown.

Hutchins, P. (1994). *Clocks and more clocks.* New York: Macmillan.

Leedy, L. (2005). *The great graph contest.* New York: Holiday House.

Maslen, B. L., & Maslen, J. R. (2006) *Bob Books* (Sets 1–6). New York: Scholastic.

Monjo, F. (1983). *The drinking gourd.* New York: HarperCollins.

Most, B. (1996). *Cock-a-doodle-moo!* San Diego: Harcourt.

Munsch, R. (1987). *Moira's birthday.* Toronto: Annick Press.

Murphy, S. J. (1996). *The best bug parade.* New York: Harper Trophy.

Palatini, M. (1998). *Zak's lunch.* New York: Clarion.

Peters, L. (1988). *The sun, the wind and the rain.* New York: Henry Holt.

Sharmat, M. (1988). *Gregory, the terrible eater.* New York: Macmillan.

Slepian, J. (1992). *The hungry thing goes to a restaurant.* New York: Scholastic.

Wescott, N. B. (1994). *Never take a pig to lunch.* New York: Orchard.

References

Adams, M., Foorman, B., Lundberg, I., & Beeler, T. (1998). *Phonemic awareness in young children.* Baltimore, MD: Paul H. Brookes.

Alexander, H. (1962). *The story of our language.* Garden City, NY: Doubleday.

Armbruster, B., Lehr, F., & Osborn, J. (2003). *Put reading first: The research building blocks for teaching children to read* (2nd ed.). Washington, DC: National Institute for Literacy.

Barone, D., Hardman, D., & Taylor, J. (2006). *Reading First in the classroom.* Boston: Allyn & Bacon.

Beck, I., & McKeown, M. (2001). Text talk: Capturing the benefits of read-aloud experiences of young children. *The Reading Teacher, 55,* 10–21.

Beck, I., McKeown, M., & Kucan, I. (2002). *Bringing words to life: Robust vocabulary instruction.* New York: Guilford.

Biemiller, A. (2003). Oral comprehension sets the ceiling on reading comprehension. *American Educator, 27,* 23.

Blachowicz, C., & Fisher, P. (2006). *Teaching vocabulary in all classrooms* (3rd ed.). Columbus, OH: Merrill Prentice Hall.

Brittain, M. (1970). Inflectional performance and early reading achievement. *Reading Research Quarterly, 6,* 34–50.

Carlisle, J. (2000). Awareness of the structure and meaning of morphologically complex words: Impact on reading. *Reading and Writing: An Interdisciplinary Journal, 12,* 169–190.

Carlo, M., August, D., McLaughlin, B., Snow, D., Dressler, D., & Lippman, D., et al. (2004). Closing the gap: Addressing the vocabulary needs of English language learners in bilingual and mainstream classrooms. *Reading Research Quarterly, 39,* 188–215.

Carver, R. (1994). Percentage of unknown vocabulary words in text as a function of the relative difficulty of the text: Implications for instruction. *Journal of Reading Behavior, 26,* 413–437.

Donoghue, M. (2001). *Using literature activities to teach content areas to emergent readers.* Boston: Allyn & Bacon.

Ehri, L., Nunes, S., Willows, D., Schuster, B., Yaghoub-Zadeh, Z., & Shanahan, T. (2001). Phonemic awareness instruction helps children learn to read: Evidence from the National Reading Panel's meta-analysis. *Reading Research Quarterly, 36,* 250–287.

Fox, B. (2004). *Word identification strategies* (3rd ed.). Columbus, OH: Merrill Prentice Hall.

Fry, E. (1980). The New Instant Word List. *The Reading Teacher, 34,* 289–294.

Harris, T., & Hodges, R. (Eds.). (1995). *The literacy dictionary.* Newark, DE: International Reading Association.

Hart, B., & Risley, T. (1995). *Meaningful differences in the everyday experiences of young American children.* Baltimore: Paul H. Brookes.

Hiebert, E. (1999). Text matters in learning to read. *The Reading Teacher, 52,* 552–566.

Honig, B., Diamond, L., & Gutlohn, L. (2000). *Teaching reading sourcebook for kindergarten through eighth grade.* Novato: CA: Arena Press.

Jenkins, J., Vadasy, P., Peyton, J., & Sanders, F. (2003). Decodable text—where to find it. *The Reading Teacher, 57,* 185–189.

Johns, J., Lenski, S., & Elish-Piper, L. (2002). *Teaching beginning readers: Linking assessment and instruction* (2nd ed.). Dubuque, IA: Kendall Hunt.

Juel, C., & Minden-Cupp, C. (2000). Learning to read words: Linguistic units and instructional strategies. *Reading Research Quarterly, 35,* 458–492

Kuhl, P., Williams, K., Lacerda, F., Stevens, K., & Lindblom, B. (1992). Linguistic experience alters phonetic perception in infants by 6 months of age. *Science, 255,* 606–608.

Kuhn, M., & Stahl, S. (1998). Teaching children to learn word meanings from context: A synthesis and some questions. *Journal of Literacy Research, 30,* 19–38.

McGill-Franzen, A. (1993). "I could read the words!" Selecting good books for inexperienced readers. *The Reading Teacher, 46,* 424–426.

National Reading Panel. (2000). *Teaching children to read: An evidence-based assessment of the scientific research literature on reading and its implications for reading instruction.* Washington, DC: National Institute of Child Health and Human Development.

Nicholson, T. (1998). The flashcard strikes back. *The Reading Teacher, 52,* 188–192.

Roe, B., Smith, S., & Burns, P. (2005). *Teaching reading in today's elementary schools* (9th ed.). Boston: Houghton Mifflin.

Saccardi, M. (1996). Predictable books: Gateways to a lifetime of reading. *The Reading Teacher, 49,* 632–642.

Snow, C., Burns, M., & Griffin, P. (1998). *Preventing reading difficulties in young children.* Washington, D.C.: National Academy Press.

Stahl, S. (2003, Spring). How words are learned incrementally over multiple exposures. *American Educator, 27,* 18–19.

Stahl, S., Duffy-Hester, A., & Stahl, K. (1998). Everything you wanted to know about phonics (but were afraid to ask). *Reading Research Quarterly, 33,* 338–355.

Stuart, M. (1999). Getting ready for reading: Early phonemic awareness and phonics teaching improve reading and spelling in inner-city second language learners. *British Journal of Educational Psychology, 69,* 587–605.

Templeton, S., & Pikulski, J. (2000). *Building the foundation of literacy: The importance of vocabulary and spelling development.* Retrieved July 10, 2000, from http//www.eduplace.com

Tompkins, G. (2004). *Teaching writing* (4th ed.). Columbus, OH: Merrill Prentice Hall.

Uhry, J. (2002). Finger-point reading in kindergarten: The role of phonemic awareness, one-to-one correspondence, and rapid serial naming. *Scientific Studies of Reading, 6,* 319–341.

Vacca, J., Vacca, R., & Gove, M. (1991). *Reading and learning to read.* New York: HarperCollins.

Veatch, J. (1996). From the vantage of retirement. *The Reading Teacher, 49,* 510–516.

Walsh, K. (2003). Basal readers: The lost opportunity to build the knowledge that propels comprehension. *American Educator, 27,* 24–27.

West, F. (1975). *The way of language: An introduction.* New York: Harcourt Brace Jovanovich.

Wolfe, P., & Nevills, P. (2004. *Building the reading brain, preK–3.* Thousand Oaks, CA: Corwin Press.

Yopp, H., & Yopp, R. (2000). Supporting phonemic awareness development in the classroom. *The Reading Teacher, 54,* 130–143.

Anticipation Statement Answers

1. Disagree

2. Disagree

3. Agree

4. Agree

5. Agree

6. Disagree

7. Disagree

8. Agree

9. Agree: There should be sparing use of picture clues for developing vocabulary in most students in the upper grades. However, their use aids the reading skills of ELLs and at-risk students even in the intermediate grades.

10. Agree: Socioeconomic status is the most important factor affecting vocabulary growth. However, it is not within the capabilities or responsibilities of the average teacher to significantly change students' socioeconomic status.

Reading

Principles, Approaches, Comprehension, and Fluency

CHAPTER 6

Learning to read involves two processes: First, the child must become able to decode or decipher unfamiliar words and gradually develop a sizable vocabulary. Second, the child must be able to comprehend or attach meaning to those words in sentences, paragraphs, pages, and entire books.

The first process has already been discussed in the previous chapter. The second is explored in this chapter because comprehension permeates directly or indirectly all areas of reading, including its principles, emergent reading, and major instructional approaches and models.

Anticipation Statements

Complete this exercise before reading Chapter 6.

Do you agree or disagree with the following statements? Circle your answer. Be prepared to discuss questions in blue.

1.	Learning to read involves two processes: decoding and comprehension.	Agree	Disagree
2.	Reading series books in the intermediate grades does not promote fluency.	Agree	Disagree
3.	Some children are more successful than others at reading because of biological factors.	Agree	Disagree
4.	Two emergent literacy skills that are highly predictive of reading ability are knowledge about books and recognition of the alphabet.	Agree	Disagree
5.	While there is no method guaranteed to teach reading successfully in the elementary school, a classic study found that it was the books selected that were most important in achieving excellence in reading.	Agree	Disagree
6.	The basal reader is the most widely used approach in the United States.	Agree	Disagree
7.	The language experience approach is only recommended for beginning readers in kindergarten and the lower grades.	Agree	Disagree
8.	The balanced approach to reading instruction is the model most teachers use today.	Agree	Disagree
9.	One factor affecting comprehension is the quality of literacy instruction.	Agree	Disagree
10.	If students are consistently asked only literal or recall kinds of questions, they will focus their attention on remembering details and not on analyzing or evaluating the information.	Agree	Disagree

Principles of Teaching Reading

The following generalizations about the teaching of reading, drawn from both research and classroom observation of actual practices, have been compiled in an effort to guide all individuals in planning an effective reading program in the elementary grades (Roe et al., 2005). The first and second principles stress that reading is a complex act involving numerous factors and that reading involves constructing the meaning of a passage represented by printed symbols. All the varied aspects of the reading process should be understood by the teacher, who must also realize that reading does not occur without comprehension of the written passage, no matter how well the child reads orally.

Principles three and four emphasize that there is no one correct way to teach reading and that learning to read is a continuous process. Not only do children learn to read over a period of several years as more sophisticated skills are introduced to them gradually but adolescents and adults also continue to improve their reading ability even after their formal education stops; improvements in reading ability continue to occur primarily because of demands in the workplace. Such continuity serves to illustrate the need for teachers to be acquainted with a variety of reading methods so they may help each classroom learner at assigned reading tasks. The student, whether a native English speaker or an English language learner (ELL), must be given instruction at his or her own level of accomplishment and maturity.

For material related to this concept, go to Video Clip 6.1 on the Student Resource CD bound into the back of your textbook.

The fifth and sixth principles stress that students should be taught word recognition skills that will allow them to independently unlock the meanings and pronunciations of unfamiliar words and that the teacher should diagnose each student's reading ability and use that diagnosis as the basis for planning instruction. No one can memorize all the English words that appear in print. Children must therefore be instructed in skills such as phonic and structural analyses so they can figure out new words for themselves when helpful peers or adults are not available. Still, they acquire these strategies, as well as those related to comprehension, at individual rates so the teacher must be continually aware of each student's performance while preparing lesson plans.

The seventh and eighth principles state that reading and the other five language arts are closely interrelated and that reading is an integral part of all content area instruction. Since there is an exceptionally strong relationship between reading and writing, most educators now advocate teaching reading through a combined reading and writing approach.

The ninth and tenth generalizations emphasize that the student needs to see that reading is an enjoyable pursuit; therefore, the teacher should understand the importance of using complete literature selections in the reading program. Young readers will become convinced of the many

Applicable IRA/NCTE Standards

Standard 1   Students read a wide range of print and nonprint texts to build an understanding of texts, of themselves, and of the cultures of the United States and the world; to acquire new information; to respond to the needs and demands of society and the workplace; and for personal fulfillment. Among these texts are fiction and nonfiction, classic and contemporary works.

Standard 2   Students read a wide range of literature from many periods in many genres to build an understanding of the many dimensions (e.g., philosophical, ethical, aesthetic) of human experience.

Standard 7   Students apply a wide range of strategies to comprehend, interpret, evaluate, and appreciate texts. They draw on their prior experience, their interactions with other readers and writers, their knowledge of word meaning and other texts, their word identification strategies, and their understanding of textual features (e.g., sound-letter correspondence, sentence structure, context, graphics).

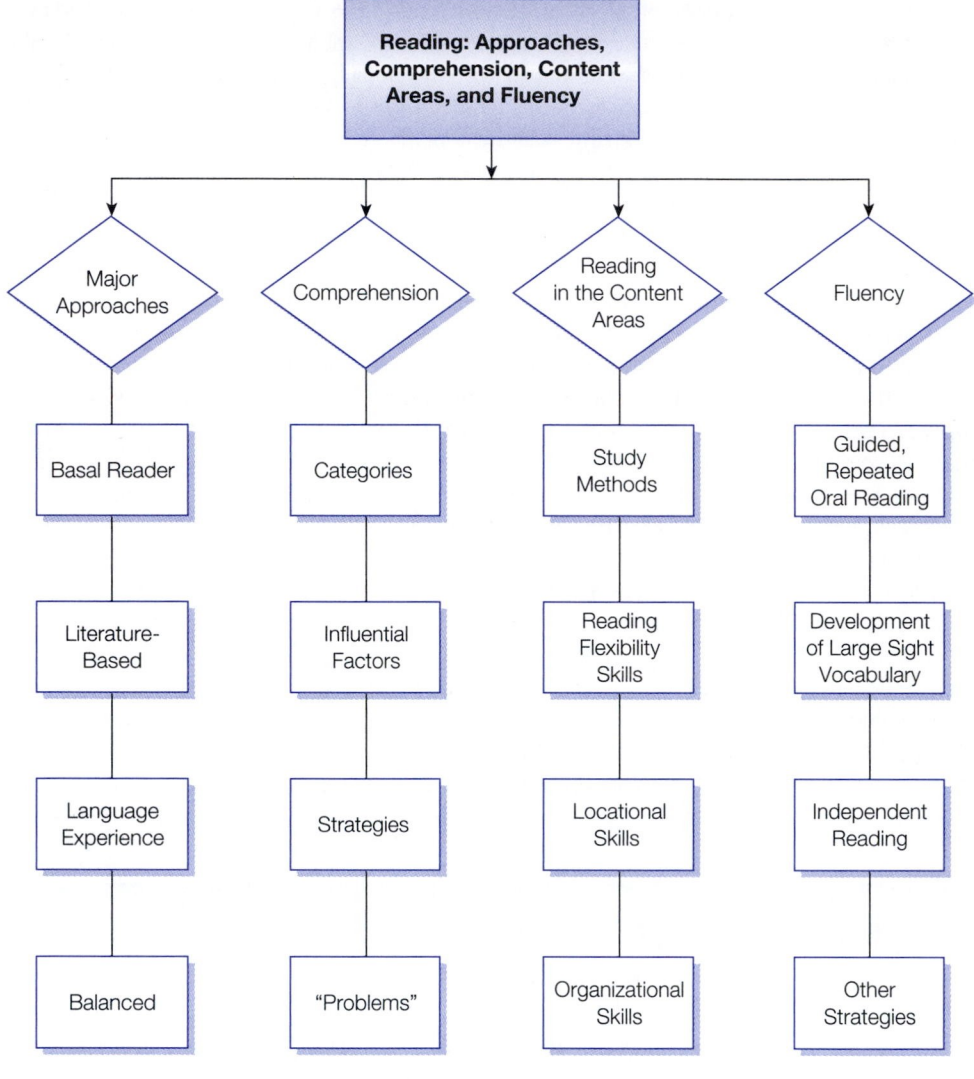

A Graphic Summary of the Contents of This Chapter

benefits of reading by encountering a variety of appropriate materials that meet numerous interest and ability levels; for example, some children like books with repetitive phrases such as Wood's *The Napping House* (2004), whereas others like books with humor such as Dr. Seuss's *The Cat in the Hat Comes Back* (2006). Intermediate grade children discover series books such as Cole's *The Magic School Bus: Lost in The Solar System* (1992) and the other Magic School Bus adventures; their teachers realize that the process of reading books in most series is usually rereading of a sort (because the books only vary slightly one from another in their character or characters) and rereading promotes **fluency**. An essential component of reading instruction, fluency is the ability to read with accuracy and speed in contrast to word-by-word reading. Incidentally, readers as young as second grade are enjoying Rowling's *Harry Potter* series, which not only has reemphasized the importance of motivation but also has proven that reading can indeed be an enjoyable activity for students.

The final two principles point out that reading should be taught in a way that allows every child to become a successful reader and that encouragement of self-monitoring and self-direction of reading is important. Success promotes success and good readers eventually direct their own reading.

Emergent Reading

Some girls and boys who enter school and begin formal reading instruction are considerably more successful than other children who attempt the same task. The difference sometimes lies in biological factors, according to Wolfe and Nevills (2004), but more likely the reasons for the difference are based in the children's literacy development before they ever started kindergarten.

Sometimes termed prereading skills, **emergent literacy** skills are those skills acquired in early childhood that help children benefit the most from formal reading instruction on school entry. These skills have also been proven to have a high correlation with later reading ability (Scarborough, 1989). Furthermore, the National Research Council believes that reading is generally acquired in a relatively predictable manner by students who have normal or above-average language skills and have had experiences during their early childhood years that promote motivation to read and provide exposure to literacy in use (Snow, Burns, & Griffin, 1998).

Two emergent literacy skills appear to be highly predictive of reading ability and cannot be ignored by teachers eager to develop fluent readers. The first is *knowledge about books:* In English, a book is read from left to right and from top to bottom, and it is print that is read and not the pictures, regardless of their color or size. Some school beginners do not always know what a book is or how it must be used (Adams, 1990).

The second critical emergent skill is *recognition of the alphabet.* English is an alphabetic language of 26 letters from which thousands of words can be derived. The skill of naming and recognizing those letters is one of the best predictors of first-grade reading ability (Adams, 1990). Mere recitation of the alphabet, however, is not sufficient. Instead, children must be able to recognize the letters in varied contexts—whether handwritten or typed in different fonts, within words on the chalkboard or book page, or on the television screen or billboard. Students must recognize the letters accurately and quickly because the names of most letters are closely related to their sounds. Consequently as children learn to name the letters, they are starting to learn the sounds they represent. This in turn leads to an understanding of the **alphabetic principle**, which Adams considers to be the single most important concept that students must know when learning to read. That principle is *the understanding that there is generally a predictable relationship between the sounds of spoken language (or phonemes) and the letters and spellings that represent those sounds in written language (or graphemes).* Most students do not make the connection between phonemes and graphemes naturally, but must learn it through careful instruction in phonic analysis, which is discussed in Chapter 5.

Through careful instruction, young children are able to develop an understanding of the alphabetic principle, including the following components of letter knowledge: the name of the letter, the formation of the letter (using both lowercase and uppercase print or manuscript handwriting), the features of the letter (and the direction it must be turned) to distinguish it from other letters (e.g., *b/d, g/q*), the use of the letter in known words (e.g., *book, street, store*), the sound the letter represents in the context of a word (e.g., *string*) and in combination with other letters (e.g., *th, ch*), and the sound the letter represents in isolation (Pinnell & Fountas, 1998). As they read, students use their letter knowledge to decode unfamiliar words.

Almost all children in a literate society develop competencies that are fundamental to their emerging literacy. They learn to read and write early in life; some learn as early as age one. They are aware of environmental print (e.g., on billboards and street signs) and informational print (e.g., on maps and in recipes). They develop concepts of book print and how it differs from other kinds of print. They have a story sense, recognizing the structure of a story and internalizing its elements, especially after numerous read-alouds by parents or preschool teachers. They experience oral language development, which is involved in beginning reading and writing since the language arts are so closely interrelated. They understand how written language works and that anything written down (e.g., scribbles) contains a message. Finally, they learn literacy by experiencing reading and writing as purposeful daily activities (Searfoss, Readence, & Mallette, 2001).

Since children in today's diverse society come to school with a variety of background experiences, teachers may wish to use the following survey questionnaire for emergent reading evaluation soon after the start of the school year; these items represent the essentials of learning to read (adapted from Farris, 2005):

1. Is the child interested in books and can listen attentively to a five-minute story?

2. Can the child tell a story in sequence or remember the main parts of a story?

3. Can the child play independently for short periods of time?

4. Does the child ask for word meanings and recognize that letters make up words?

5. Can the child identify the letters of the alphabet?

6. Does the child attempt to write or draw pictures to illustrate an idea?

7. Does the child enter into a group or class discussion freely?

8. Does the child know the directionality of books?

If the majority of answers to this informal observational survey are positive, it suggests that the child is an emergent reader. However, if the answers are primarily negative, the child should be given many opportunities to develop oral language skills, to listen to literature read-alouds, and to use crayons and pencils for drawing and writing.

Shared Reading

Students in kindergarten and first grade who are emergent readers can participate in **shared reading**, in which they follow along as the teacher reads the selection aloud (Fisher & Medvic, 2000). Considered by some as a natural outgrowth of the lap method or home bedtime story of reading aloud to young children, shared reading re-creates the natural ways that young children learn to speak and that many learn to read (Holdaway, 1979).

While shared reading may involve enlarging the text of favorite rhymes, poems, or songs on chart paper or on sentence strips used in a pocket chart, the most common method is using big books—enlarged versions of the selections chosen by the teacher. These oversized books have pictures and print large enough for students to see and read 12 to 15 feet away as they sit in a semicircle around the teacher. Children become actively engaged in the meaning of the text and the details of the print as the group reads the story together. Teachers should choose texts carefully as emergent readers need stories with rich language, repetitive patterns, a strong storyline, and high-quality illustrations. The teacher and children can reread big books several times over the semester—much like bedtime stories—as emergent readers enjoy familiar stories and increase their control over the reading.

Holdaway (1979) lists three criteria for successful shared reading experiences: The books chosen must be those that students love to hear, the children must be able to see the print themselves, and the teacher must be genuinely enthusiastic while reading the books aloud.

The teacher planning a shared reading lesson should follow these six steps (Tompkins, 2006):

1. Introduce the text by activating prior knowledge (or developing knowledge) on topics discussed in the book and by reading aloud the title of the book and the name of the author.

2. Read the book aloud, using a pointer or ruler to track the text. If the story is repetitive, invite the students to join in the reading.

3. Discuss the book by inviting students to talk about the story and share their reactions.

4. Reread the story, as students take turns turning pages and using the pointer or ruler to track the reading. Invite them to join in reading familiar words and teach them letter–sound relationships and reading strategies during the rereading.

5. Repeat the process and reread the book with the students several more times over a week or more, again having them take turns turning pages and tracking the text. Invite students who can read the text to read along.

6. Have children read independently by distributing individual copies of the book or another text of similar difficulty. Plan follow-up activities.

Shared reading represents a step between reading to children and reading independently by children and can be used with both young children and older readers (Parkes, 2000). Instead of big books, however, intermediate teachers usually distribute copies of chapter books or content area textbooks and then students and teacher (or another fluent reader) read together: One reads aloud and the others read to themselves, following along in the text.

Picture Books That Celebrate Reading

Teachers may wish to share one or more of the following dozen recent picture books that convey to emergent readers the pleasure of reading in the school, the library, or in the home (Crawford, 2007):

Bloom's *Wolf!* (1999)

Browne's *I Like Books* (2004)

Bruss's *Book! Book! Book!* (2001)

Child's *But Excuse Me! That Is My Book* (2006)

Donaldson's *Charlie Cook's Favorite Book* (2006)

Ernst's *Stella Louella's Runaway Book* (1998)

Lehman's *The Red Book* (2004)

McPhail's *Edward and the Pirates* (1997)

McQuinn's *Lola at the Library* (2006)

Pinkney's *Read and Rise* (2006)

Sierra's *Wild About Books* (2004)

Spanyol's *Carlos and the Really Nice Librarian* (2004)

Major Instructional Approaches

While there is as yet no method guaranteed to teach reading successfully in the elementary school, a classic study in reading instruction found that it was the *teacher* who was more important in achieving excellence in reading than any method used (Bond & Dysktra, 1967/1997). Four major approaches are presently employed to guide learners to mature reading. Teachers preferring to borrow a few features from each of them, however, are supported by the International Reading Association (1999), which has stressed that *no single method can teach all children to read*.

Basal Reader Approach

This is the most widely used approach in the United States, with estimates indicating that 75 to 85% of elementary classrooms use it daily (Allington & McGill-Franzen, 2004). While in previous decades as many as 15 publishers offered basal reading series, today the number has been reduced to 4—Harcourt, Houghton, Open Court, and Scott Foresman—because the costs of producing a complete basal reading program range between $20–50 million (Ruddell, 2006). This reduction in the number of publishers' series means that the responsibility for teachers of examining/piloting basals for district acceptance has also been reduced.

Also known as the bottom-up approach or skills-based approach, the **basal reader approach** tends to help students move from the part to the whole by prescribing the acquisition of competencies in a systematic order. The reading process is divided into a series of smaller to larger subskills that must be taught in a rigid order. The major component of this approach is a collection of graded texts for children in Grades K–8 that comprise the chief source for instruction. These texts contain both narrative and expository selections, organized in unit themes (e.g., American Inventors) with a broad variety of genres that include children's literature. The teacher's manual contains lesson plans and developmentally appropriate suggestions and activities involving visual representations. It also often includes reduced-size facsimiles of pages from the student text.

Skills are developed through specific instructional strands (e.g., phonics) that are promoted through assignments in the student practice book or workbook. Sometimes facsimiles of these assignments appear in the teacher's manual in reduced size, with the correct answers. End-of-unit tests assess skills introduced or reviewed in that particular unit.

Reading levels have replaced grade designations in the basal series in an effort to place students at the reading level most appropriate for them, especially for ELLs and at-risk students. The predominant group reading strategy is the directed reading activity (DRA), which is discussed later in this chapter. *In the early grades* word analysis skills and vocabulary items are precisely controlled to present a decodable text. Other aids include big books (enlarged copies of some narrative selections) as well as picture and word cards.

Basal readers have been a tradition in the elementary classroom for several decades and also the subject of considerable controversy. Older series stressed skill development and a controlled vocabulary at the price of comprehension and reading enjoyment. Series published since 2000, however, support language arts instruction in varied ways (e.g., including multiple versions of one story or various excerpts from a full-length book and thus permitting students and teachers to share selections in children's literature). When only a part of the story is included, students are often motivated to read the entire book. Basal readers provide a foundation for reading instruction that is particularly appealing to beginning teachers because their organization is both horizontal (coordination of materials) and vertical (comprehension, word analysis skills, and vocabulary). Obviously, experienced teachers tend to rely on more than the basal series—even with its numerous components—to teach language arts.

The typical procedure for teaching a lesson in the basal reader is the directed reading activity (DRA), which generally follows these steps: (1) preparation *by the teacher* for reading, involving motivation and the introduction of new vocabulary and/or concepts; (2) guided silent reading *by students* as the teacher provides questions and statements to direct them; (3) comprehension development *by the teacher* and discussion *by students* that facilitate increased understanding of the plot, characters, or concepts; (4) oral reading *by students* after they have read the material silently (step 2) and can read the answers to questions asked by the teacher (Ruddell [2006] terms this step "purposeful rereading"); and (5) follow-up practice or activities *by students* in workbooks that review vocabulary and comprehension. Enrichment activities that involve relating the story or selection to art, music, drama, or writing may also occur after certain selections.

A viable alternative to the DRA is the directed reading-thinking activity (DR-TA) approach. Developed by Stauffer (1975) and designed for group comprehension instruction, its primary goal is to develop critical readers. It demands that children become actively involved in the reading process by asking questions about the story, by processing the information as they read the story, and by receiving feedback about their original questions. There are two key phases to the DR-TA approach. The first is directing students' thinking processes throughout the story; the second is promoting skills development based on students' needs (as revealed in the first phase) as well as follow-up or extension activities (Ruddell, 2006). There are four major differences between the DRA and the DR-TA approaches:

1. The DRA approach is "materials oriented" and "teacher-manual oriented" with specific guidelines, questions, and instructional materials. The DR-TA approach has few explicit guidelines, giving the teacher considerable flexibility as well as sole responsibility for lesson development. It can be used in teaching other curricular areas that require reading, unlike the DRA approach, which is primarily concerned with basal reader programs.

2. The teacher's role in the DRA approach is to ask the students to supply answers to questions found in the manual; most of those queries are at the literal level of comprehension, which requires convergent thinking. In the DR-TA approach, however, the teacher asks questions that require a higher level of thinking known as divergent thinking. By so doing, he or she promotes comprehension skills that make reading a dynamic activity that goes far beyond responding to factual questions.

3. In the DRA approach, new vocabulary is introduced before the children open their books. In the DR-TA approach there is no preteaching of vocabulary. Instead, each student must make use of decoding skills to unlock new words as these appear in the story selection, just as she or he would do during similar situations outside the classroom.

4. In the DRA approach, the manual details which comprehension skills will be taught and when they will be presented. In the DR-TA approach, however, there is no such prescription, and therefore, the teacher must develop the art of good questioning as well as the ability to accept alternative answers to certain questions.

Literature-Based Approach

The **literature-based approach** has been defined as instructing children to read by using both fiction and nonfiction literature, written for purposes other than text use for teaching reading (Harp & Brewer, 2005). It is known as the top-down approach, going from the whole to the part.

Its advocates believe that reading materials should be unabridged pieces of literature and that instruction in strategies and skills should be presented in the context of real reading and only on an as-needed basis. There is no prereading vocabulary study. While the focus is on constructing meaning or understanding what is read, there are no comprehension worksheets. Children are offered choices in their literature selections, which cover a wide range of genres, including multicultural books. Finally, students are encouraged to discuss the interpretations of their reading with classmates and adults.

To implement this highly individualistic approach, the teacher must be knowledgeable about children's literature and able to incorporate skills development when it is needed. He or she must also have available class or group sets of core literature books so that several students are reading and responding to the same book at any given time.

Once the program has been introduced, four to five children choose to work in independent reading-response groups, based on their choice of books. These groups are given reading prompts (for use in their discussions) that are designed to evaluate the students' prior knowledge and to generate ideas derived from the text and ideas that go beyond the text to indicate reaction or interpretation. Throughout the reading-response group experience, members maintain journals or individual response logs. When one group has completed its reading and discussion of a book, it may plan and produce a summary activity such as a puppet plan, mural, or readers theater (Ruddell, 2006).

One popular form of the literature-based approach that some teachers use is *individualized reading*. (Although the term is often misunderstood, it does *not* mean that group instruction never takes place or that group activities never occur.) Such an approach is clearly needed for three reasons: First, it involves a variety of materials and can occur even in the absence of the teacher. It therefore simulates closely the type of reading method that literate adults use, and it helps students transfer school learning outside of the classroom. Second, it places a heavy emphasis on the personal enjoyment and satisfaction to be gained through reading, thereby establishing life-long reading habits. Finally, the approach helps the teacher meet the differing reading abilities that exist at every grade level, especially among at-risk students or ELLs. Because such differences actually increase as children grow older, the range of reading abilities among students in the sixth grade has been estimated to be a little more than seven years!

Other advantages of this approach include the development of a healthy rapport between child and teacher as instruction is adjusted to the specific needs of each learner and the equally important reduction of comparison and competition among readers. Small groups can be formed as needed for specific purposes when several students encounter similar and temporary problems in one area, such as contextual analysis. The key concepts underlying this approach are self-motivation, self-selection, and self-pacing.

However, the same concepts also relate to a major requirement of the individualized reading approach: a well-stocked library. In addition to the books in the media center, the classroom library should always have at least 100 carefully selected books that cover a wide range of reading abilities and genres and that are changed monthly. Such a collection is both difficult to house in a convenient corner and costly (in terms of either time or money) to gather. Furthermore, it leads to a second important prerequisite of individualized reading: the time-consuming effort by the teacher to select wisely the broad range of books that can then be promoted to allow for the most beneficial student-teacher conferences. Children can be urged to read a variety of subject matter only if the materials are available on those same subjects and written on reading levels and in styles suitable for elementary students.

Other weaknesses of the individualized reading approach include the substantial recordkeeping required of the teacher (even with computer assistance), the stressful requirement that he or she plan a minireading program for each student, the difficulty of interpreting the program to parents who are more familiar with the basal series and accustomed to their features and procedures, and the problem of insufficient skill development due to insufficient time. Finally, some children may lack the self-discipline needed to benefit from this approach; it becomes increasingly difficult to implement as the range of reading abilities, the size of the class, and the number of remedial readers grow.

Nevertheless, those teachers who wish to use individualized reading in their classrooms should become comfortable with the core of the approach: the student-teacher conference. It is held once a week and is generally centered around the book(s) the child has selected for his or her own reading. Although one may sometimes skip a few steps in the suggested format for such conferences, they usually proceed as follows and run approximately 12–15 minutes:

1. Greet the child and converse briefly about a matter of personal interest, such as soccer (1/2–1 minute).

2. Ask the child what he or she has read since the last conference and what is being presently read, inviting a brief account of the reading material (1–2 minutes).

3. Have the child read a passage aloud from the book he or she is presently reading, noting vocal fluency as well as the difficulty of the material. Offer positive feedback (2 minutes).

4. Check up on a skill reviewed or introduced at the last conference and correct the assignment (see Step 6). Offer praise for any gains made (2 minutes).

5. Review or introduce a new skill (3 minutes).

6. Make a follow-up assignment to be checked at the next conference (1 minute).

7. Help the child set goals for completion by the next conference, telling him or her when that conference will be and which skills will be practiced (1 minute).

8. If a new book must be chosen soon, offer several suggestions, describing each book briefly (1 minute).

9. Compliment the child on progress already made and then dismiss him or her (1/2 minute).

10. Complete record keeping of items covered during the session before motioning the next student to come to the conference table (1 minute).

The individualized conference is also a critical part of the *readers' workshop* used especially in the upper-primary and intermediate grades when students are able to read independently. Much like the writers' workshop (to be discussed in detail in Chapter 10), the readers workshop has the following components: (1) *focus lesson* or minilesson by the teacher on some important aspect of reading (e.g., introducing a new literary genre) as the whole class listens; it may end with the teacher giving a status-of-the-class report to remind students of their individual progress; (2) *independent reading time* as children read quietly and the teacher conducts individualized conferences with some of them during each workshop session to discuss issues that have emerged during their reading; and (3) *sharing time* when the whole class listens as three or four volunteers discuss what they are reading, possibly raising queries about certain characters or events. Readers' workshops are generally held weekly for about 45 minutes.

Language Experience Approach

The **language experience approach** (LEA) is founded on the theory that reading and comprehending written language are extensions of listening to and understanding spoken language. The experiences of the children form the basis of reading materials because it is widely believed that everything that students read in early reading instruction should be as relevant to them as possible and certainly the children's own language is the most meaningful of all to them.

Girls and boys first dictate to the teacher (in groups and then individually) and later themselves write stories about field trips, school activities, and personal experiences outside of school. These stories and other student-produced materials become the texts for learning to read. Many are in the form of charts.

The *rationale* for the approach has been stated as thus:

I can think about what I have experienced and imagined.

I can talk about what I think about.

What I can talk about, I can express in some other form.

Anything I can record, I can recall through speaking or reading.

I can read what I can write by myself and what other people write for me to read.

A typical procedure for introducing the LEA approach involves the following steps (Tompkins, 2006):

1. The teacher selects a purpose and provides an experience that is stimulating for students of this age and background. Ordinary daily activities such as read-alouds and the care of classroom pets can serve to promote LEA. The experience must always be one of interest to the children and one that they have observed/heard or participated in and comprehend.

2. The teacher and children discuss the experience so they can focus on it, review it in greater detail, generate words, organize ideas, and use vocabulary specific to that subject.

3. The teacher records the dictation. Whether it is done originally on the board (and later copied) or on chart paper from the start, the teacher does the printing in front of the children. Furthermore, the language of the students is recorded exactly as it is dictated as much as possible so that they see that their thoughts can be written down and stored for later reading. However, the words of children who speak a dialect should be recorded in conventional spelling. When students take turns dictating sentences, some teachers wisely put the child's initials after his or her contribution to promote pride—and participation.

4. The teacher reads the chart aloud to remind the children what they have written and also to demonstrate how to read with expression. Then the class reads the chart chorally as the teacher moves his or her hand under the words. Next, volunteers are chosen to read parts of the chart aloud. Finally, the class and teacher read the chart chorally.

5. The children examine the text with the teacher's help. They can match word cards to words on the chart or use sequence sentence strips and match them to the line of the chart. They can participate in writing activities related to the content of the chart.

6. The teacher prepares word cards for each child's word bank after becoming convinced that that child has learned to read those words by sight. The word bank is the student's own sight vocabulary collection.

7. The teacher plans skills instruction as needs occur naturally, whether it is as simple as directionality of print or as complicated as punctuation.

Slowly the students begin to write their own experience stories, sometimes in small groups and sometimes individually, choosing at times to illustrate them. They may even decide to read them to their classmates or share them with their family members. Their word banks grow, as the teacher facilitates the development of their sight vocabulary.

The main advantage of the language experience approach is its stress on reading as one part of the language arts process. It also uses the interests and language of the students as the avenue for teaching reading, which makes it both appealing and successful. Still another advantage is its low cost; there is no expensive program to purchase. Finally, skills are presented to the child as they are needed and applied in contextual reading, not in isolation.

On the other hand, the approach has definite limitations. There are no printed content standards of skills to develop, which may lead to a haphazard method of reading instruction. There is a lack of both vocabulary control in general and the systematic repetition of new words in particular. Teachers spend a considerable amount of time preparing charts and worksheets concerned with past experiences as well as on planning activities to motivate future experience stories. Children are apt to become bored rereading the same stories and other passages again and again and may even memorize some of the sentences rather than actually read them.

Briefly, the language experience approach can be used at any elementary grade level by seasoned teachers interested in integrating their writing and reading programs. It has been well received as an appropriate way to present reading to beginning readers in the kindergarten–lower grades and with struggling readers in the intermediate grades, primarily because of the vocabulary and interest levels of the materials. Most important, it has been especially useful with at-risk students and ELLs.

Balanced Approach

A **balanced approach** combines skills development with literature and language arts activities. The program strikes a *balance between* the bottom-up (or skills based) approach and the top-down (or literature-based) view, a *balance between* explicit teacher-directed instruction and student-centered discovery learning, and a *balance between* authentic forms of assessment and standardized norm-referenced assessment (Harp & Brewer, 2005). The core of the program is literature, but students read a variety of materials, including **leveled books**—books that an educator has examined and then determined how difficult it would be for children to read based on features such as font size, number of pages, number of illustrations, text structure, and complexity of vocabulary—and basals as well as trade books; skills are taught both directly and indirectly; and literacy is regarded as reading AND writing, which are tools for learning in the content areas.

Furthermore, reading instruction involves word recognition and identification, fluency, vocabulary, and comprehension; writing instruction involves learning to express meaningful ideas and apply the conventions of spelling, grammar, and punctuation. The goal of the balanced approach is to develop life-long readers and writers (Fitzgerald, 1999; Weaver, 1998).

The balanced approach is supported by the International Reading Association (1999) that believes teachers must know a variety of teaching methods as well as ways of combining them successfully. Furthermore, in 2002 in its concern for diverse classrooms, the IRA stated that teachers must be capable of making decisions about how to provide that balance of reading instruction.

Models of Reading

Five models of reading view reading as an active, constructive process. Three of these, which are older and have been documented by more research, are the bottom-up (or subskills) model, the top-down (or whole-word) model, and the interactive model that includes both of the others (Weaver, 1994). A fourth and newer model is the transactional model, which elaborates on the interactive. Finally, there is the balanced approach, which many teachers have adopted.

The *bottom-up model* is promoted by educators who view reading as a set of subskills that must be mastered by students and integrated to the extent that children use them automatically. Stepwise, they first must learn to recognize letters, then words, and finally words in context. When they combine a high level of accuracy with speed and proceed to read aloud with good expression, children are exhibiting automaticity (Samuels, 1994). Students therefore should not be taught using a method that considers reading as though it were a single process. Instead, for instructional purposes, it is best to think of reading as a set of interrelated subskills that must be practiced in the context of actual reading. Students can build automaticity only by spending considerable time reading, preferably with meaningful material that is easy and interesting.

This part-to-whole model is involved in the basal reader approach, which has been the dominant method to reading instruction for many years. Controversy, however, has developed regarding which set of skills to teach and in what order, and some teachers' overemphasis on learning skills as a goal in itself rather than as a means to an end has been criticized.

The *top-down model* is the whole-to-part model that teaches children to recognize words by sight, without any analysis of letters or sounds. It emphasizes the critical role that the reader's mind plays in comprehending the text. The child uses three cue systems—graphophonic, semantic, and syntactic—and makes educated guesses about the meaning of the reading passage. The advocates of this approach view reading as a holistic experience and believe that what the reader anticipates profoundly affects how she or he actually perceives the text message. Educators, however, have criticized this approach because they believe that children really need to learn word recognition skills (as discussed in Chapter 7) for processing language to become independent readers.

The *interactive model* combines the bottom-up and top-down models and views the reading process as an interaction between the readers and the text. It assumes that students are simultaneously processing information from the materials they are reading (i.e., the bottom-up model) and information from their background knowledge (i.e., top-down model). Gove (1983) states that recognition and comprehension of printed words and ideas result from using both types of information.

The interactive model is based on the *schema theory* (Rumelhart, 1984), which explains how readers receive, store, and use knowledge in the form of *schemata* (the plural of schema—structures for organizing knowledge in the mind). The objective of this approach is to teach students strategies that will help them develop into independent readers who can monitor their own thinking while reading and link prior knowledge to the new material in their text. Consequently, reading becomes a highly individualized process as each reader's schemata and the ability to use them are personal and unique. The more prior knowledge that a reader possesses, the more likely he or she is to construct meaning from the printed text.

The *transactional model* is an elaboration of the interactive model. It takes into consideration the students' intentions when they read and how those can affect understanding (Kirshner & Whitson, 1997). Developed by Rosenblatt (1978), it implies that each child is engaging in a construction of meaning when he or she is reading, and reading is a process in which social, environmental, and cultural factors affect the reader's personal interpretation of the printed page.

When reading is viewed as a transaction or event, the stance that the reader takes must be considered: Is he or she eager to obtain information from the printed page (i.e., the efferent stance), or is the reader reading for entertainment or enjoyment (i.e., the aesthetic stance)? Using the latter stance, students can concentrate on thoughts and feelings that a particular book evokes, for example, Bunting's *Night Tree* (1994). Children adopt an efferent stance when reading Maestro's *The Story of Money* (1995). However, almost every reading experience evokes a balance between aesthetic and efferent reading (Rosenblatt, 1991), and students move back and forth between the two stances, with one exception: Literature should be read primarily for the aesthetic experience.

The *balanced approach* to reading instruction is the model that most teachers use today. One large-scale survey revealed that 89% of elementary teachers believe in this approach because it combines skills development and literature with "language-rich experiences" (Baumann, Hoffman, Moon, & Duffy-Hester, 1998, p. 642).

In a balanced approach literature is the core of the program, and readers develop the ability to take both efferent and aesthetic stances in reading. While word recognition skills are taught both directly and indirectly, reading is seen as more than word identification. Similarly, writing is not merely spelling, grammar, and punctuation, although these remain a part of effective writing as writers must be able to express their meaningful ideas clearly. Together with writing, reading constitutes literacy, and students use both as tools for learning in content areas. While there must be a balance between comprehension and word recognition, the latter is viewed as a means to enable comprehension and never as an end in itself. Finally, the goal of a balanced approach is to develop life-long readers and writers (Baumann & Ivey, 1997; Weaver, 1998).

Guided Reading

Guided reading involves children in small homogeneous groups who read the same text at about the same level of difficulty. Clay (1991) suggests that students should be able to read 91 to 94% of the words in a particular text for a guided lesson to be successful.

Characteristics

The teacher directs guided reading sessions, and skills and strategies are taught in context. Grouping is a critical part of the program, with groups ranging in size from three to eight children who have similar needs in areas such as oral reading skills, vocabulary development, and comprehension. Grouping is flexible, not permanent, and only in response to a specific need so students may work in one group for one reason (e.g., fluency) and in another group for a different reason (e.g., structural analysis). They are grouped and regrouped regularly as their needs change. Sessions run an average of 15 to 25 minutes.

The teacher wisely chooses books that are slightly beyond the students' independent reading level, according to Vygotsky's zone of proximal development, and provides each child with his or her own copy.

Critical to guided reading sessions is direct instructional support, also known as *scaffolding,* whereby the teacher's support is slowly withdrawn and more autonomy is transferred to the children as they gradually demonstrate strategic behaviors in their own learning activities. Also crucial to guided reading is classroom management because the other students must be able to work independently while the teacher works with small groups. Aides or parent volunteers may work with the other children on journal writing or other literacy activities as they help monitor the class.

Finally, the goal of guided reading is for students to be able to read silently and independently (Fawson & Reutzel, 2000; Fountas & Pinnell, 1996, 2001).

Guided reading allows teachers to model reading skills and strategies in context to children reading the same text at about the same level of difficulty.

Steps in Guided Reading

The teacher should follow these steps. First, choose an appropriate book for the small group, collecting a copy for each child. Second, introduce the book to the group to activate prior knowledge, using key vocabulary as the group takes a "picture walk" or "book walk" through the book. Third, have the children read the book independently while providing support to help individuals deal with unfamiliar words, sentences, or ideas. Fourth, provide opportunities for children to respond to the book through questions and discussion. Fifth, involve students in one or two teacher-directed exploring activities such as vocabulary review or word work. Sixth, provide opportunities for independent reading by placing copies of the book under discussion in a book basket or classroom library (Fountas & Pinnell, 1996).

Leveled Books

It is critical that the teacher find books at the proper reading level for each of the guided groups. If children work with a book that is at their *frustration level*—the level at which the material is so difficult that they are unable to comprehend it—they begin to acquire negative attitudes about reading, about their teacher, and even about school in general. Students learn better with a book written at their *independent level* at which they read with comprehension and ease. The best choice is a book written at the students' *instructional level* that they can read with sufficient help from their teacher while simultaneously promoting their reading abilities and love of reading. For some students the material used during guided reading will be at their independent level while others will profit from reading a book at their instructional level. By asking each student to read aloud four or five sentences, the teacher can check the child's fluency level and then place the student in a group using the most appropriate leveled books.

Leveled books are those that an educator has examined and then determined how difficult it would be for a student to read based on features such as font size, number of pages, number of illustrations, text structure, and complexity of the vocabulary. The texts for guided reading may be either fiction or nonfiction (informational). Sometimes teachers work together to level the books in their collections. Fountas and Pinnell (1999) have leveled books specifically for guided reading. Below is listed a sampling of their fiction trade books from A to Z (easiest to most difficult):

Burningham's *Colors* (1985)

Hutchins' *Rosie's Walk* (2005)

Rylant's *Henry and Midge: The First Book* (1996)

Allard's *Miss Nelson Is Missing* (1993)

Cleary's *Ramona's World* (1999)

Paterson's *The Great Gilly Hopkins* (1987)

Myers' *Scorpions* (1995)

Comprehension: Categories and Influential Factors

There are four major categories or levels of comprehension that readers need to achieve. They generally operate together so that students can totally understand the text under scrutiny, as Miss Lucci's first graders learn to do in Vignette 6.1.

VIGNETTE 6.1   Paper Hats and Comprehension

During a communications elective she took in her junior year in college, Miss Lucci studied *Six Thinking Hats*, a short book describing techniques for considering an issue or problem. Different colors represented various approaches, such as brainstorming new ideas, articulating the objective facts, or sharing personal feelings. Although the book was written as a business management tool, its strategy could work in a variety of settings. As she considered how to build reading and listening comprehension among her first-grade students, she wondered if "thinking hats" might hold a clue.

Miss Lucci decided to introduce the new process as she presented a new story. On Wednesday afternoon she gathered the class for a reader's circle and displayed a "big book" copy of *A Bargain for Frances*, a critically acclaimed "I Can Read" book published in 1970 (and one of Miss Lucci's own favorites from childhood). The class had previously enjoyed *Bread and Jam for Frances* and followed along attentively as Miss Lucci read the new adventure.

The class enjoyed the charming story about Frances and her tea set. After finishing the book, Miss Lucci pointed out some new words in the text and complimented the children for their attempts to read portions along with her. She knew Frances's fun rhyming songs made the story enjoyable for her young students.

"You are working so hard on your reading," she said. "I'm proud of you. We will read the book again so you can practice even more. But first we're going to try something new."

Miss Lucci reached into the large basket next to her chair and pulled out a pile of construction paper hats in six colors. While the children watched and wondered, she walked around the semicircle handing a hat to each child. She had intentionally made four or five hats of each color to ensure an approximately equal distribution among her class of 27 students.

"I'm going to ask you some questions about the book," she said as she returned to her seat. "But before I ask the question, I'll say a color. Only the people with that color hat may answer that question. Let's try one. White hats, what color tea set did Frances want?"

"Blue!" Ashley blurted out before remembering her own hat was also blue. She smiled sheepishly.

"It's okay, Ashley," said Miss Lucci. "That was a practice one. Remember to wait for your group. But you're correct, Frances wanted a blue tea set. White hats, let's try another one: What did Frances's mother tell her before Frances went to play with Thelma?"

She waited while the five children sporting white hats pondered the question.

"She said to be careful," Daryl answered after a moment.

"Good job!" Miss Lucci answered. "Okay yellow hats, here's one for you. Why did Frances's mother say to be careful?"

"Because Thelma was mean," Tonya answered.

"Thelma did do some mean things," Miss Lucci agreed. "Yellow hats, give me an example of Thelma behaving badly."

The yellow group successfully identified one of Thelma's tricks, and Miss Lucci proceeded to question the blue, green, red, and purple hats in turn. While the children wearing the white and yellow hats received the easier knowledge and comprehension questions, she asked more sophisticated application and evaluation questions as the lesson continued.

"Red hats, what is another way the story could have ended?" she asked. A moment passed as the children thought.

"Frances and Thelma could get in a big fight and knock each other down," Anna said.

"Well, yes," Miss Lucci replied with a smile. She always enjoyed the answers to this type of synthesis question. "What's another way the author might have ended the book?"

After 15 minutes Miss Lucci asked the students to remove their hats and trade with a neighbor.

"Does everyone have a new color hat?" she asked. "Good. Now we're going to read the story together again, one last time. At the end I'll ask just a few more questions. But remember—now you're in a new group."

The children followed along as Miss Lucci read the book a second time, enjoying the story's humor even more because of their increased comprehension. As she finished the book and began asking another round of questions, the new approach seemed to have real benefit. Although some of the evaluation questions still challenged the young readers, their understanding of the picture book already exceeded the literal questions she'd started with. As an added bonus, the children had demonstrated increased motivation to listen and read actively as she shared the story a second time. She attributed their increased attention to competitiveness—none of the groups wanted to miss a question.

Teachers always tell students to "put on their thinking caps," she thought to herself. *Who knew they were made of construction paper?*

Levels of Comprehension

Literal or text-explicit comprehension: Often described as "reading on the lines," this level requires the reader to process information that is explicitly stated in the text, to understand what the author specifically reported. For example, the reader may be called on to recall or locate precisely stated main ideas, details, directions, or sequences of events. Literal comprehension requires a lower level of thinking skills than the other three levels because the reader must only recall from memory what the book said. Still it is the foundation for content-area courses and remains the most frequently tested comprehension category. It consumes the bulk of instructional time in the classroom and is the level that struggling readers and ELLs strive to attain.

Interpretive or text-implicit comprehension: Described frequently as "reading between the lines," this level demands that the reader process ideas based on what was read but not explicitly stated in the text. It involves understanding what the author meant, and the reader must call on his or her intuition, personal experiences, and imagination as the foundation for making inferences. Children may be asked to predict outcomes, find main ideas, determine word meanings from context, draw conclusions, make generalizations, or infer cause-and-effect relationships. Behaviors commonly associated with critical thinking are involved in text-implicit comprehension, which is said to separate the active reader from the passive reader.

Furthermore, the overall pattern of interpretive processes activated during reading may affect the amount of text actually remembered (van den Brock, Rhoden, Fletcher, & Thurlow, 1996). That is the reason that teachers should pose thought-provoking questions to stimulate classroom discussion and thereby promote interpretive comprehension.

Critical or applied comprehension: Sometimes stated as "reading beyond the lines," this level requires readers to integrate their own thinking with the facts from the text. Consequently, they evaluate and apply information and ideas from the printed page to their own experiences and judgment. It concerns skills such as the abilities to distinguish fact from opinion and fantasy from reality and to detect propaganda techniques, as discussed in Chapter 5.

Creative comprehension: This most advanced level calls for readers to develop original ideas based on the pages read. They must use divergent thinking skills as they ponder new or alternative solutions to problems or crises presented by the writer. They can write new endings to familiar folktales such as Early's *Sleeping Beauty* (1993), Kirsten's *Puss in Boots* (1992), or Galdone's *The Elves and the Shoemaker* (1984) or epilogues to chapter books such as Monjo's *The Drinking Gourd: A Story of the Underground Railroad* (1983), Gardiner's *Stone Fox* (1997), or Paulsen's *Hatchet* (1995).

Factors That Influence Comprehension

Several factors are known to influence the comprehension of all readers, but to varying degrees depending upon the individuals and situations involved.

The first of these factors is *purpose,* which focuses the readers' attention and helps them understand the text. While teachers routinely help students focus in the classroom, self-directed purpose is the better route to promote the feeling of competency that leads students to independent reading both in and out of school. In the classroom, children can make individual predictions about their reading (e.g., Do tsunamis occur in only one part of the world?), and those predictions then become purposes under the careful direction of their teacher. Outside of school, students may wish to assemble a toy for a younger sibling, and thus reading the directions for that task also has a clear purpose. In both instances, comprehension is stronger when the purpose is specific.

The second is *being an active reader* because active readers, according to Blachowitz and Ogle (2001), think as they read. They use their prior knowledge (which stems from previous experiences) and their vocabulary as well as reading strategies to help them comprehend what they are reading presently.

The third factor that affects comprehension is the *type of text* being used. Children who have had experience with story texts may encounter difficulty with expository or informational materials. Therefore, they should be introduced to these materials early and review them often as they usually contain concepts, vocabulary, and format that are markedly different from those found in storybooks. Teachers must keep in mind that the less familiarity students have with expository texts, the harder it is for them to comprehend such books.

The fourth factor affecting comprehension is the *quality of literacy instruction.* The Center for the English Language Arts at the State University of New York, Albany (1998) has identified effective literacy instructors as those who engage the students productively and keep them on task about 90% of the time and use and review/reteach explicit skills instruction in vocabulary, word recognition, writing, and spelling. They schedule daily reading and writing for at least 45 minutes in each skill. They emphasize literature by reading aloud, maintaining a classroom library, and discussing books and author studies; they integrate the curriculum by making direct connections between reading/writing and the content areas. These instructors manage all aspects of classroom learning, including planning, scheduling, and student behavior, and they maintain an environment characterized by fair rules, high expectations, and a learning atmosphere. They offer supportive instructional context by monitoring student accomplishments and establishing realistic but challenging expectations. Finally, they promote self-monitored learning by teaching students how to organize their work habits and use their time productively.

The fifth factor influencing comprehension is *interest*. When children are curious about a subject, sometimes to the point of absorption, they will read to seek information and discover answers to satisfy that curiosity. Some students can even be described as hyperlexic—their interest in reading is strong enough to qualify them as avid readers.

The final factor is *independent practice* preceded by adequate instruction. Life-long readers evolve from students who are allowed to choose their own books, read them independently in class daily, and have the opportunity to discuss and share them with classmates. In Vignette 6.2, Mrs. Baker discovers a new and innovative way to help struggling intermediate readers—by having them practice reading to canine "friends."

VIGNETTE 6.2 A Struggling Reader's Best Friend

As long as she could remember, Mrs. Baker had loved dogs. As a child she enjoyed playing with her border collie named Mac, and since high school she'd volunteered with local animal shelters and cruelty prevention organizations.

During these years of involvement with animals, Mrs. Baker learned of several groups in the community that organized "therapy dog" programs. These nonprofit groups worked with private owners to train dogs for nursing home visits, outings to the children's hospital, and special events. The program provided hours of joy to residents throughout the city.

But Mrs. Baker was most intrigued by another initiative of the therapy dog programs. Last week, while chatting with some friends at her veterinarian's office, she learned that many owners also train their dogs for reading assistance.

"The dogs can't read, of course," her friend Laura laughed. "They sit next to the child while he or she reads aloud. Kids love it and studies show that their reading markedly improves."

Mrs. Baker's fourth-grade class had several struggling readers, including a few ELLs. When she learned that "PAWS," the nearby therapy dog organization, would work with her classroom at no cost, she immediately scheduled an introductory visit.

On Tuesday afternoon, about 15 minutes before the dogs arrived, Mrs. Baker asked Mariana, Ricky, and Darika to follow her to the learning center.

"Don't worry—you're not in trouble!" she said to them quietly as they left the classroom and walked down the hall. "I have a treat for you."

Mrs. Baker knew that inviting the dogs into the large classroom would be distracting (if fun) for the other students and would minimize the chance for these three children to benefit from the special experience. She intentionally scheduled a parent aide to stay with the class for an hour. With Margaret in the classroom supervising independent reading, Mrs. Baker could observe this new activity without interruptions.

When they reached the end of the hall, Mrs. Baker pushed open the door to the learning center and motioned for the three students to sit at a table next to her.

"I know how hard you're working to become better readers," she said. "Today I have some friends who are going to help you."

"More tutors?" Darika asked a little tiredly. Darika's family emigrated to the United States from India just a few years earlier, and she had worked with many private tutors to catch up on her studies.

"No tutors," Mrs. Baker promised. "In fact…"

Just then the door opened, and three smiling adults entered leading three quiet dogs on leashes.

"Dogs?" Ricky asked. "Cool! This is way better than tutors!"

"Right," Mrs. Baker answered. "Each of you can choose a book to read and a reading area here in the learning center. You may sit anywhere you want, but it might be more fun to sit on the floor or on some pillows, because each of you will get to sit with one of these dogs. Go ahead and pick your books and your spots, and then I'll explain what happens next."

The children excitedly scattered to three corners of the room, where brightly colored pillows and cushions invited relaxed study. As the children got settled, Mrs. Baker met briefly with the three adults to determine which dog might be most suitable for each child.

"All the dogs are trained to be reading assistants," said Carla, a petite blond woman with an enormous St. Bernard named Jack. "Each of them should do equally well with any child."

Looking at the well-trained dogs Mrs. Baker had to agree. She dispatched Carla and Jack to Darika's corner, asked Mike and his golden retriever Duke to sit next to Ricky, and pointed Jackie and her adorable schnauzer Mitzi to where Mariana sat waiting.

"Take a few minutes and meet your new friends," Mrs. Baker instructed the students. "After you feel comfortable with your dog, their owners will leave. But first ask any questions you have. When you are ready to sit with the dog by yourself, raise your hand."

After a few moments each of the children sat with one hand raised, delighted at the furry companion curled up next to them.

"That was quick," Mrs. Baker said, smiling at the three dog owners.

"It usually is," Mike said. "We'll be back when the lesson's over. Have fun!"

The three adults left the room and headed to the teacher's lounge where Mrs. Baker had provided coffee and cookies for their hour-long wait. She turned to the students and dogs remaining in the room and announced the next task.

"Each of these dogs is trained to sit next to you and listen while you read to them," she said.

"But they can't understand what we're reading," Ricky said.

"That's true," said Mrs. Baker. Actually, that was one of the best parts of this experiment; the dogs would serve as nonjudgmental listeners that wouldn't be tempted to interrupt or correct pronunciation the way even the best-intentioned human helper might.

"They won't know what you're saying, but they love to sit with kids and listen," she continued. "I want each of you to quietly read your book out loud to your dog. Raise your hand if you get stuck or have trouble with a word. Remember, this is just a way to practice reading, so work at your own pace."

Although the children seemed a little dubious about reading to dogs, this was definitely more fun than their usual reading practice. The three students opened their books and slowly began reading aloud.

Despite the studies proclaiming the success of this approach, Mrs. Baker was prepared for the hour to show few results. At the very least it would be another hour of reading practice and a fun surprise for these hard-working students.

But as the minutes ticked by, Mrs. Baker was amazed at the students' progress. Just a few minutes into the session, little Darika leaned back against the broad expanse of Jack the St. Bernard. She contentedly snuggled with Jack and read him *A Chair for My Mother*, the second-grade-level book she'd chosen.

Meanwhile Mariana sat cross-legged in her corner animatedly sharing an adventure from *Encyclopedia Brown, Boy Detective* with Mitzi, who managed to look interested in the mystery story. In another corner Ricky haltingly read a chapter from *Chocolate Fever*, occasionally looking up to make sure Duke was paying attention. Mrs. Baker smiled to see Duke playfully nudge Ricky each time the boy began daydreaming.

As the hour ended, Mrs. Baker permitted the children to close their books and spend the last few minutes petting the dogs before the owners came back to claim them. She considered the experiment an unqualified success. Each of these children would need further practice in independent and oral reading; one hour could not make struggling readers into experts. But already she noticed improvements in their fluency. The dogs' presence prompted the children to read with more interest, more speed, and less distraction than they'd previously demonstrated. Just as important, the friendly dogs made the entire experience more relaxed and more fun, positioning reading as a skill to enjoy rather than a chore to dread.

Mrs. Baker hoped Margaret could return every Tuesday afternoon; with a scheduled parent assistant, these canine assistants could visit every week.

Comprehension Strategies

Concluding that comprehension can be taught, a report of the National Reading Panel (NRP, 2000) listed several strategies that have proven through research to be highly effective in teaching students to become active readers who understand what they are reading.

- *Self-monitoring:* This strategy assists students in determining when they understand what they have read and when they do not, as well as what strategies they can use to help them understand. It is considered a form of *metacognition* (or thinking about thinking) in which children can ask themselves these questions: "Is what I'm reading making sense?" and "What can I do to be certain that I know what I am reading?" One effective means that teachers can use to present self-monitoring to students is a demonstration of "think-alouds," following specific strategies outlined by Frey and Fisher (2007): (a) choose a short piece of text running from one to four paragraphs, (b) let the text tell you what to do after you have read it several times, (c) keep the think-alouds authentic by using a conversational tone, (d) think like an expert in the subject area under discussion to show students that your understanding of content is affected by prior knowledge, (e) tell students what strategies you are using to help you comprehend the material (e.g., highlighting important phrases or terms), and (f) resist the urge to "over-think" or else the meaning of the passage will be lost.
- *Cooperative learning:* When students work together to discuss comprehension strategies such as "think-alouds," they begin to take more control over their own learning.
- *Story structure:* Once students understand the elements of a story—plot, characterization, setting, theme, style, and point of view—they are better able to comprehend the story and recall it. One means that teachers can use to increase students' understanding of story structure is to introduce them to a plot relations chart that has four headings: "Somebody" (character), "Wanted" (goal), "But" (problem), and "So" (solution) (Schmidt & Buckley, 1991).

- *Summarizing:* This strategy assists the students in identifying critical facts from the text or story. Summarizing demands that readers decide what it is important, how to condense it, and how to rephrase the information. Children must comprehend that summarizing involves the ability to identify and connect main ideas, eliminate unnecessary information, and recall what they have read. An experienced teacher knows that asking students to summarize what they have read is a useful, significant, but difficult assignment, whether verbally or in writing, so he or she may choose to model the strategy (Armbruster, Lehr, & Osborn, 2003). Summarizing is explored further under the Reading in the Content Areas section of this chapter.
- *Graphic organizers:* Visuals that help students organize concepts and ideas, graphic organizers aid in the development of knowledge of text structure. They also aid in the summarization of text, as well as the visual representation of information (Meddey & Jefferies, 2000/2001). Bromley and Irwin-Devine (1999) have identified 50 **graphic organizers**, including flow, tree, and Venn diagrams; concept and compare/contrast maps; and matrices. Three steps are involved in teaching the preparation of graphic organizers: First, the teacher chooses a particular graphic organizer that matches the text under scrutiny and models its outline for the students. Second, student groups complete the modeled example. Third, students individually complete the graphic organizer with teacher assistance, if needed. Hoyt, Mooney, and Parkes (2003) warn, however, that a graphic organizer that does not match the text will actually hinder students' comprehension so teachers must be cautious about their selection.
- *Activating prior knowledge:* This strategy helps readers draw on previous experiences to better understand the new material they are reading. Teachers can assist students in recalling what they already know about the topic, author, or text structure. They can also take the class on a picture walk through a storybook and have readers draw predictions about the plot and characters.
- *Question generating and question answering:* This critical strategy is discussed fully in the next section.

Implementing Strategies for Instruction

It is recommended that only one of the research-based strategies listed above (from the National Reading Panel, 2000) be taught at a time and that children then practice that strategy in a variety of texts before being introduced to another (Barone, Hardman, & Taylor, 2005).

Directed comprehension instruction includes explaining the strategies involved, providing practice in using them, assessing (and if necessary) reteaching them, and finally demonstrating how they can be applied. Such instruction takes place before reading, during reading, and after reading. *Before* the children begin their reading lesson, the teacher can first promote comprehension by making certain the boys and girls are reading materials of an appropriate level of difficulty, with slower readers often needing to spend more time at a particular plateau than one basal series can accommodate and with advanced students doing most of their reading in content texts and other materials because they can read through their basals so quickly. Then the teacher can enhance comprehension by making sure the children have appropriate background concepts by using the introductory activities in the series to activate or build on prior knowledge, whether the topic is river rafting or life in Borneo. Finally, the teacher can promote comprehension by making certain that girls and boys understand that the purpose of reading is to obtain meaning and that what they already know can help them attain that purpose. Children should be made aware of what the teacher is doing and understand why he or she is doing it so they can gradually be taught to accept responsibility for attaining comprehension.

During the reading lesson, the teacher can identify trouble spots such as vocabulary or figurative language and instruct students in how to address those problem areas. (The questions that accompany each guided reading lesson in most basal series may be helpful in this task.) However, the teacher's role is not complete until each child assumes an equal share of the responsibility for comprehension. Students must be taught to monitor their reading and to identify problems and solve them. Skilled readers can use one or more of the following techniques when they come to a problem sentence: Ignore and read on, suspend judgment, form a tentative hypothesis, reread the current sentence, reread the previous context, or go to an expert source.

After the reading, the teacher should focus instruction on summarizing the entire text and on relating it to other information or to other books or stories. All students, and particularly ELLs and slower readers, need this kind of comprehension activity. Other activities include having children write their own stories or participate in discussion comparing the most recently completed story to other stories or contrasting characters found in various assigned selections. One activity that does *not* belong in this segment of the reading lesson is answering a series of detailed, literal questions. Students must not get the impression that reading is just an exercise in factual recall.

Strategies Used by Good Readers

Whether before, during, or after reading, good readers use some strategies in one or more of the stages in the reading process. Not every strategy will be used in every text nor will the order of application be identical in each instance. Consequently, skilled readers choose individually those that work most effectively for them for each text they read. According to Barone and colleagues (2005), *before reading* good readers set a purpose for reading and activate prior knowledge, making connections between real-life experiences and textual content. They predict what the text might be about and then decide which strategies would be useful while reading the text. Finally, they develop mental images and use graphic organizers.

During reading, good readers monitor their own comprehension as they continually make and revise their predictions. They identify the main idea and answer and generate questions. Having determined which strategies would be appropriate for reading this text, they are also able, however, to incorporate remedial strategies when the text does not make sense. Finally, they are able to make inferences, develop mental images, and summarize.

After *reading,* good readers discuss the material, answering and generating questions. They share information after deciding whether or not it is worth remembering. If it is important and should be learned, they use graphic organizers to help them organize the information and identify the main idea. Finally, they develop mental images and summarize the information.

Questioning: A Critical Comprehension Strategy

Among the strategies that the National Reading Panel (2000) concluded have proven to be effective in teaching children how to become active readers (who comprehend what they are reading) is one that is particularly critical: questioning. This strategy covers both question-generating and question-answering skills.

Because they believe that it helps them assess student learning, *teachers traditionally use questioning more than any other strategy for developing comprehension*. Furthermore, the majority of questions at the elementary school level are not only teacher-generated but also explicit and require only one correct answer, thereby qualifying as "lower-order questions." As a result,

Honing questioning skills helps children become active readers, provided that the questions push them to analyze and evaluate information.

numerous studies have concluded that students have little practice in answering implicit or "higher-order" questions and are virtually unprepared for answering those that require critical thinking.

Both lower-order and higher-order questions are included in a classification system commonly referred to as **Bloom's (1956) taxonomy (in the cognitive domain)**: Frey and Fisher (2007) consider this taxonomy to be the cornerstone in the description of questions used in the classroom. The six levels require increasingly more difficult questions, as follows (with examples):

Level One: Knowledge (requiring information)

> Where did...
>
> List the...
>
> What was...
>
> How many...
>
> Name the...

Level Two: Comprehension (understanding meaning)

> Give me an example of...
>
> Describe what...

Tell me in your own words…

Make a map of…

What does it mean when…

Level Three: Application (using learning in new situations)

If you had been there, would you…

How would you solve the problem in your own life?

What would happen to you if…

Would you have done the same as…

On the Internet, find information about…

Level Four: Analysis (using the ability to see parts and relationships)

What kind of person is…

What is the main idea of the story?

What message was the author trying to tell us?

Which part of the story was the most exciting? Funny? Sad?

Which events could not have happened in real life?

Level Five: Synthesis (using parts of the information to create an original whole)

What would it be like to live…

Pretend you are…

Write (or tell) a different ending.

What would have happened if…

Design a…

Level Six: Evaluation (making judgments based on criteria)

Could this story really have happened? Why or why not?

Select the best….Why it is the best?

Which person in the story would you like to meet? Why?

Was…good or bad? Why?

What do you think will happen to….Why do you think so?

Levels One and Two (knowledge and comprehension) are sometimes referred to as literal or explicit questions because the answers to them are found verbatim in the text. They are also the easiest questions to write. Students who have experience with such lower-order questions do well on tests of basic skills because those tests reflect that type of questioning. Knowledge and comprehension questions comprise the bulk of those asked in the typical classroom.

If, however, students are consistently asked only literal or recall kinds of questions, they will focus their attention on remembering details and not on analyzing or evaluating the information and storing it for future use. Instead, they will remember the information only until the questions have been asked (and answered) and then they will promptly forget it. On the other hand, if students are asked to read between or beyond the lines, they will be forced to integrate new input with what they already know about the topic, and therefore, they will retain much of the information. Students will be able to focus attention on significant aspects of the text if they can relate the information from the text to the most appropriate set of background experiences or prior knowledge, develop a coherent framework for remembering or understanding the text material, and practice cognitive skills that they will ultimately be able to use alone (Pearson, 1990).

The following lesson represents an effort to combine those skills:

1. The teacher begins with questions that focus student attention on appropriate background experiences or prior knowledge; for example, *Have you ever been to the municipal zoo? What do you know about that zoo?* Should prior knowledge or experience not be available or developed, the teacher might attempt a longer question; *In our story today about South America, there is a family of jaguars. A jaguar is somewhat like a house cat, somewhat like a wolf, and somewhat like a sports car. Let's see whether we can figure out how a jaguar is like all of those.*

2. The teacher than encourages students to use prior knowledge, whenever possible, to predict what might happen in the story; for example, *If you were lost in the forest as the jaguar family in our story is, and needed food, how would you get it?*

3. The teacher sets up a purpose that lasts as long as possible throughout the story; for example, *What did the jaguar family try to do to solve their problem?*

4. During the guided reading (which occurs during the reading in the primary classroom and immediately after the reading in the intermediate grades), the teacher asks questions that tie together the significant elements in the "story map" (the outline on the board that is a causal chain of events); for example, *What was the first event that caused the family to get lost?*.

5. Immediately after the reading, the teacher returns to the purpose-setting question(s), as suggested in Step 3 above. The teacher can reword or rephrase the question; for example, *Can you tell me in order the three things the jaguar family did to find food?*

6. In discussing the story, the teacher uses this sequence for generating questions: (a) retells the story map at a fairly high level of generality, (b) takes students beyond the literal stage by asking them to compare this story to their own experiences or to another selection or by asking them to speculate about the reactions of the characters when placed in a different situation, and finally (c) returns to the selection in an effort to appreciate the talent of the author. Activities useful for item (a) would include reenactment, discussion, production of a time line of events, or (beginning with students as early as third grade) the development of a flow chart of events. Questions appropriate for item (b) would include, Do you think that the jaguar family acted prudently? Why or why not? and What would you have done if faced with a similar situation? Questions illustrative of item (c) would include, What is your favorite part of the selection? What made you choose that part? and How does the author tell you that the father jaguar feels proud? (Pearson, 1990).

Going beyond the student answering of teacher-generated queries, the true objective of questioning is to move it from the teacher (an external source) to the student (an internal source) (Frey & Fisher, 2007). In that way the student can use the power of questioning as a means for monitoring, extending, or modifying his or her own learning.

An effective means for accomplishing student-generated questioning is the question-answer relationship strategy (QAR; Raphael, 1986). It covers the classifications established by Pearson and Johnson (1978) of text-explicit (Right There), text-implicit (Think and Search), script- and text-implicit (Author and You), and, finally, script-implicit (On Your Own). Teachers can model the QAR framework and typically present it in one lesson.

QAR should not be confused with Bloom's taxonomy of questions because it does not classify questions in isolation as the latter does. Instead, it considers the reader's background knowledge as well as the text because comprehension is influenced by both (McIntosh & Draper, 1996).

Two final but crucial elements to questioning are *wait time* and the *teacher's response to the student's answer*. The first has been defined as the amount of time between the teacher's asking a question about the passage read and allowing a student to respond. Providing sufficient wait time is particularly significant in the area of higher-order questioning because children must have adequate time in which to organize complete, original, and thoughtful answers. The amount of wait time affects both the quantity of the student response (i.e., the actual number of words used in the answer) and the quality of that response (i.e., the level of thinking demonstrated). Furthermore, if teachers respond too quickly after the student begins to answer, those answers are more often apt to be incomplete. Consequently, by increasing the duration of wait time, teachers elicit answers that will probably be clearer and more elaborate, and at the same time, their own replies to the student will be more appropriate.

In addition, teachers should be open to many possible responses to a particular question and not have a preconceived notion of one "correct" answer. They should give the student immediate feedback when he or she gives a correct answer to a comprehension question to reinforce learning.

Teachers' responses to student answers fall into three categories: acceptance, clarification, or rejection—with rejection being defined as a teacher response that could damage the student's self-image and his or her subsequent learning or participation in class discussion. Should the student response be only partially correct, teachers should recognize all its correct aspects while simultaneously directing the student toward the correct response. Even when the child gives an incorrect answer that is irrelevant or incongruent to the teachers' question, it is important that teachers respond in a accepting manner and, at the same time, redirect the child's thinking by clarification measures such as *Let's go back to the story to check that fact* or *Let me ask the question in a different way*.

Teaching Questioning Strategies

Teachers need to pose questions and then show the students how these questions may be answered by modeling aloud the thinking process used to come up with the responses. Such modeling includes sharing with readers what kinds of clues are found in the selection itself as well as how to integrate previously known information (or prior knowledge). By sharing his or her own knowledge as a teacher and by drawing on the background and knowledge of students, the teacher can make the task of presenting comprehension skills much more manageable.

By beginning lessons with questions that focus attention on what students already know about the topic and by encouraging them to use that knowledge to make predictions, teachers are helping the children deal with the questions in a more familiar framework. It is not enough to assign students to read a story and then have students answer questions about it. Instead, each teacher should have children share their thinking processes by going back to the assigned story and inquiring, "How did you know that? Which words gave you the clues that led you to this answer?" Although students who give incorrect responses are often redirected through clarification measures, teachers generally overlook the value of questioning students who give correct responses as well. When such girls and boys respond to questions, they not only reinforce the thinking process of individuals but model that process for their classmates.

Sorting Out Comprehension "Problems"

Many so-called comprehension problems are not really failures to understand the author's meaning (Harris & Sipay, 1990). Instead, the child who fails to respond properly to an assignment involving comprehension may actually be encountering other difficulties that masquerade as comprehension problems. Teachers should therefore consider the following questions before sending the student back for more directed practice in comprehension skills:

- *Was the reader able to decode most of the words in the selection?* If the child seems generally confused about an entire selection, the teacher should ask him or her to choose a particularly difficult passage and read it aloud. Then, if the problem seems to involve decoding, the teacher should try to ensure that the student's next assignment involves material at a more acceptable level of difficulty.

- *Did the reader understand the specialized vocabulary of the selection?* When the code is too complex, decoding cannot occur. So the teacher must give careful attention to technical vocabulary and introduce such words prior to their appearing in a reading assignment. Students will then be able to recognize those words in print quickly and be alert to important points in the assignment before reading begins.

- *Did the reader follow directions?* Teachers must be certain that children understand directions before starting a task. One way to demonstrate that understanding is to have the directions rephrased by a student or aide or to have the class do one sample question together as a written guide for everyone to follow.

- *Did the reader's experiential background interfere with comprehension?* When the reader's background is substantially different from that of the author's or teacher's, a "wrong" interpretation of a paragraph or passage is possible even though that interpretation is completely understandable in terms of the reader's own experience. Consequently, the teacher should evaluate readers' background through informal discussion before making reading assignments and then either change the assignment or introduce the necessary background or concepts. (This question is one of special importance when working with ELLs.)

- *Was the reader interested in the selection?* Comprehension is likely to be enhanced when students have questions that they are seeking to answer or when the teacher introduces the assignment in a way that piques their curiosity or arouses their enthusiasm.

- *Was the reader able to write the answer correctly?* Teachers must be able to distinguish between a child's spelling, handwriting, or grammatical problems and his or her comprehension problems. One way to handle the situation is to ask for oral answers if written responses are not decipherable. Student dictation, especially with ELLs or primary grade children, may help too.

- *Did the reader understand the question?* Sometimes misunderstandings arise from the form in which the question is asked, not from a student's lack of knowledge. When a student can repeat a question but still does not understand it, the teacher should either rephrase the question or have another student explain what was asked.

- *Could both the teacher's and the student's answers be correct?* Or could the child's answer be right and the teacher's wrong? As mentioned earlier in this chapter, teachers must be open to the possibility of several correct replies and not restrict themselves to answers suggested in the manuals or those based on personal interpretations of the author's message or viewpoint. Although a teacher cannot accept every answer a child offers, he or she should examine each reply on its own merits.

Reading in the Content Areas

Reading in the content areas demands the acquisition of **study skills** so that the learner can obtain, organize, and present information. And although the acquisition process may not appear to be especially exciting, the skills themselves are critical if the reader is going to be able to do anything with what he or she has decoded and comprehended. Study skills enable children to find and interpret information from numerous sources and to synthesize it to achieve a resolution of a question or the solution of a problem. In other words, study skills are valuable *learning tools,* and many students do poorly in school because they have never learned to use them.

Study skills should be taught in both the primary and the intermediate grades. Although the need is more obvious at the intermediate level, primary teachers can help students become aware of the need for such skills (e.g., learning to read simple maps and picture or circle graphs). Teachers at both levels can introduce study skills or techniques during a content class when the need arises or during a reading class. However, students will sense the need for such skills and retain the techniques longer if they are given a chance to apply them, preferably in the context in which they will use them. Consequently, the wise teacher periodically sets aside time during a content class to present a study skill that the children will need to use immediately in that lesson. She or he knows that *teaching study skills in isolation is unproductive and artificial.*

Reading in the content areas should include lessons in study methods, reading flexibility skills, locational skills, and organizational skills.

Study Methods

Best taught through teacher modeling followed by a whole class walk-through, SQ3R is the classic and most widely used study technique (Anderson & Armbruster, 1984). It consists of five steps:

1. *Survey:* Children read the table of contents, the introductory and concluding paragraphs, and the headings and marginal notes; then they inspect any visual aids such as maps, graphs, or illustrations. The purpose is to obtain an overview of the author's intent and the format of the section, article, or chapter. Sometimes unfamiliar vocabulary poses a problem for some students and should therefore be defined promptly. This step enhances prior knowledge.

2. *Question:* Children change each heading and subheading into a question before that section is read. The purpose is to focus reader attention, to offer a means for self-checking comprehension, and to provide a goal for reading. This step requires the most explanation from the teacher.

3. *Read:* Children read in order to answer the questions formulated in Step 2. The objective is to notice how the paragraphs are organized (to help readers recall the answers they uncover). Students should also be warned not to overlook any important information not included in the questions already developed and should be cautioned to make brief notes during the purposeful reading time.

4. *Recite:* Many consider this step to be the most critical of the five. Children give the answers to each of the questions formulated earlier and do so without looking back at the material. Recitation may be done subvocally or in some more permanent written form such as note taking or informal outlining. The primary purpose is to self-check how well the material has been understood and recalled. The check is really accomplished by the student's expressing the author's language in his or her own words. A secondary purpose is to help memorize the information.

5. *Review.* Children reread to correct or verify the answers given during the recitation just completed. The purpose is to recall the main points of the selection, article, or chapter and to understand the relationships among the various points. This step involves spending considerable time to go over the material promptly (both after reading and at varying intervals) to ascertain how well the material is still understood.

A second study method, especially appropriate for children in Grades 4 through 6, is the RESPONSE approach (Jacobson, 1989). While it asks students to generate questions, much like SQ3R, it adds the additional step of listing important points as well as new terms and concepts. It demands interaction between the student and the teacher as the student completes a form and the teacher "responds" either in class discussion or in writing. The areas to be completed are Important Points, Questions, and New Terms/Concepts/Vocabulary/Names—all with page numbers. By including page numbers, this study method is efficient for both teachers and students.

A third study method was developed expressly for use in mathematics, especially with word or story problems, and is titled SQRQCQ (Fay, 1965). It consists of six steps:

1. *Survey:* Children read through the problem quickly to obtain an idea of its general nature.

2. *Question:* Children must determine what is being asked in the problem.

3. *Read:* Children read the problem slowly, paying close attention to specific details.

4. *Question:* Children decide which mathematical operations must be carried out and, in some instances, in which order are these operations to be completed.

5. *Compute:* Children must perform the computations decided upon in Step 4.

6. *Question:* Children must examine the results of the computation performed in Step 5 and determine whether they have reached a correct and reasonable answer.

Reading Flexibility Skills

Reading flexibility has been defined as adjusting one's rate of reading to one's purpose for reading, to one's prior knowledge, and to the nature of the reading matter (Harris & Sipay, 1990). It therefore becomes one aspect of monitoring one's reading comprehension and is a concern during silent reading only. Children in the *intermediate* grades should be introduced to four skills: skimming, scanning, study reading, and surveying.

Skimming: Skimming is a quick type of superficial reading that is completed in an effort to get the overall gist of the material. Girls and boys generally skim at about twice the normal reading rate, selectively eliminating nearly one-half of the material because they are in a hurry and therefore willing to accept lowered comprehension. They may read only the topic sentence and then let their eyes drift down through the paragraph, picking up a date or name. Their intention is to get the main idea from each paragraph with only a few specific facts.

Instances when skimming is useful include sampling a few pages to determine whether the material is worth reading, looking through reading matter to judge whether it contains the kind of information the reader is researching, and previewing a text chapter before settling down to serious study in an effort to get a general idea of its scope. In this kind of skimming, the student must have a particular purpose in mind.

Scanning: One special type of skimming is called scanning and involves rapid reading to locate answers to very specific questions concerned with matters such as names, dates, or telephone numbers:

Which state produces the most corn?

What are the leading industries of Chicago?

Who was Hannibal?

Who accompanied Armstrong on the first trip to the moon?

When was the first television broadcast?

What is the telephone number of this school?

Two common occasions that call for scanning are using a dictionary and using an index or television schedule. Children quickly identify with such practical needs and sense the obvious importance of scanning.

Study reading: Study reading differs from scanning because it demands a deliberate pace that allows reflection and rereading. Readers must contrast text concepts with their own prior knowledge. The emphasis is not on simple recall but on comparing and evaluating information. Students preparing to write a thoughtful essay are not concerned with reading rate because the quality of their reflection is more important than the speed with which it can be completed.

Surveying: The purpose of surveying is to preview a large piece of text to get an overall sense of its contents. A long chapter or entire book should be surveyed before it is read. A survey might include an examination of the table of contents and the index, but not detailed reading. Chapter books of fiction as well as novels would be surveyed differently from nonfiction materials. Therefore, the rate for reading surveys depends upon the type of texts and the purpose for reading them.

Locational Skills

Students need to be able to access necessary materials quickly to be able to engage in such activities as inquiry learning. Exemplary elementary classrooms are those in which students are encouraged to regard themselves as researchers (Allington, 2002). They therefore approach learning through inquiry, which promotes independent learning and the discovery of knowledge. It is critical, however, that students have experience with nonfiction writing and reading before attempting the inquiry process for gathering information. The teacher must also instruct the students in how to use locational aids in books and how to access databases (Tower, 2000).

Book Utilization Skills

Children should gradually learn the parts of a book that are useful in locating needed information, whether it is a basal reader or a trade book or even a content area textbook. Such a skill is especially valuable for ELLs or struggling readers.

In the upper primary grades children are usually introduced to three printed parts of a book (e.g., title page, table of contents, and the glossary) and to two items in the physical makeup of a book (e.g., the spine that helps readers locate books on the shelves and the text or body of the book). Older students can learn about the preface/introduction, the appendices, the footnotes, and bibliographies. All students should become aware of the importance of graphic media and know how to interpret charts, tales, diagrams, and other aids. Some textbooks even contain marginal notes that further serve children as guides to reading.

Because of the nature of reference tools in the content areas, the one part of a book that demands special attention is the *index*. Children must acquire the ability to locate and use indexes. They can begin by comparing the tables of contents to the indexes in several books to learn that, while the table of contents lists the broad areas of a book's coverage, it is the index that offers a more detailed and alphabetical listing of the names and items mentioned in that book, along with the page numbers where they can be found. If a desired entry cannot be located, a synonym for the original word must be determined, thereby promoting thinking skills on the part of the students.

Learning to use such reference books as a dictionary (which can be introduced as early as the primary grades) has already been discussed in Chapter 5. Another common reference book is an encyclopedia, now often offered electronically in a CD-ROM or DVD-ROM format accessed by a computer. Learning how to use an encyclopedia is considered a skill for older students since its articles, according to Roe, Smith, and Burns (2005), are "very difficult for many intermediate grade readers to comprehend" (p. 358). Classes that use other reference sources (such as newspapers, periodicals, brochures, and pamphlets) to obtain information for an inquiry report will require special instruction by the teacher.

Accessing Computer Databases

Students in most elementary schools today need to be able to access information from a computer database, defined as an electronic file cabinet in which large amounts of data or information are stored in an organized fashion in separate file folders on a computer. The data are categorized and indexed for easy retrieval. Many databases can be accessed through the Internet.

Organizational Skills

As students prepare reports in content areas, they need to organize the facts and ideas they encounter in their reading of reference books, periodicals, and content-area texts together with material retrieved from the Internet. Sometimes teachers at the elementary level overlook the importance of presenting the three organizational skills of outlining, note taking, and summarizing because they mistakenly believe that such skills are more appropriately presented to students in middle school.

Outlining

Organizing factual material that has been collected and assimilated requires a high level of classification ability. Although the purpose of an outline is the more significant point for students at the elementary level to learn, some attention should still be paid to promoting an understanding of the structure of an outline. Such a structure or form usually reflects a hierarchy of ideas or a sequence of events much like the following example:

I. A main topic demands a Roman numeral.

    A. A subtopic requires indentation and a capital letter.

        1. A detail needs indentation and an Arabic numeral.

        2. Another detail on the same subtopic needs indentation and an Arabic numeral too.

    B. Another subtopic requires indentation and a capital letter as well.

II. Another main topic demands another Roman numeral.

    A. Subtopic

        1. Detail.

        2. Detail.

    B. Subtopic

        1. Detail.

Two types of outlines important for students to understand and develop are the *sentence outline* (in which each point is a complete sentence) and the *topic outline* (which is composed solely of key words and phrases). Teachers should present the sentence outline first because the task of choosing key words and phrases is a difficult one for most children.

While students need to begin learning to outline in the intermediate grades, the prerequisite skill to outlining is identification of the main idea and supporting information, which should be taught beginning in the last half of the first grade. Children can be told that the first step in forming the framework or outline is to extract the main ideas or topics from the material they have heard or read and then list them with Roman numerals in sequential order. Next, they list subtopics beside capital letters, which are placed below the main topics they support. Details subordinate to the subtopics are indented still further and preceded by Arabic numerals.

It is recommended that the use of a *formal* outline be presented before teaching children to prepare *informal* outlines, which of course do not contain the various numerals and letters.

Note Taking

Once students understand outlining, it is easier for teachers to present the note-taking process in which children actually learn to make meaningful notes in their own words about information from a textbook or speaker. They can be helped to develop some class standards for note taking: read or listen first before writing down only the important facts in your own words, rechecking for accuracy whenever possible; and use underlining or highlighting to indicate emphatic ideas or key words and phrases, but never record every word, excepts for laws, rules, and direct quotations.

In the early grades, note taking is generally a group activity, culminating in an experience chart. In the middle and upper grades, however, students can be encouraged to keep individual notes (sometimes written on index cards) during a field trip or as they listen to a resource speaker, watch a video, or work in cooperative learning groups. Both Laase (1997) and Seitz (1997) suggest using sample paragraphs and the overhead projector to model note taking for the class.

Summarizing

Summarizing occurs as part of the reading program starting in the first grade. Each experience story, for example, is a small summary, and during social studies lessons, the conclusions reached after class discussions are often summarized on the board. This skill demands the ability to choose the most significant points in a report, article, story, or chapter and to relate these points in a sequential order.

Rules essential to summarization have been identified as follows (Brown & Day, 1983):

1. Delete trivial or unnecessary information.

2. Delete material that is important but redundant.

3. Substitute a superordinate term for a list of items (e.g., *pets* for *dogs, cats, hamsters*).

4. Substitute a superordinate term for the components of an action (e.g., write "Scott went to Chicago" instead of "Scott left the apartment. He took a shuttle that went to the airport. Finally, he boarded the plane for Chicago.").

5. Select a topic sentence.

6. Invent a topic sentence if one is not given.

Children can use the two deletion rules (1 and 2) at an early age but fifth (and even seventh) graders have difficulty with the generalization and integration rules (3 and 4) and with the topic sentence rule (5). The invention rule (6) is the last to develop (Brown & Day, 1983).

During think-aloud sessions, the teacher should model the deletion of nonessential material, the selection of superordinate terms, and the construction of topic sentences. Then the class must practice each of these rules, beginning with many easy materials before advancing to longer passages. Understanding and using the rules of summarization have proved to have a positive effect on reading comprehension.

Fluency

Listed as one of the five essential components of reading instruction by the National Reading Panel (2000), **fluency** has been defined by the NRP as "the ability to read with speed, accuracy, and proper expression" in contrast to word-by-word reading. While attention to fluency is appropriate for all grade levels, it is regarded as one of the most neglected areas of reading instruction (Samuels, 2002).

Fluency plays a critical role in overall reading development because, according to Wolfe and Nevills (2004), the final step in reading is decoding automacity so that the brain's conscious processing functions are completely available for understanding print. In addition to identifying words with sufficient *speed,* fluency is related to reading comprehension in two other ways: Readers must have the ability to *group words into phrases* that can be understood and to read *accurately* so they understand the text message (Barone et al., 2005). Nevertheless, fluency and comprehension are separate processes, and it has been noted again and again that some children are fluent readers who do not understand what they are reading.

Numerous factors affect reading fluency, including the following: (a) the student's level of automacity and accuracy in decoding, which means that the reading brain can access phonological, morphological, orthographical, and perceptual processing at the letter and word level (Wolfe & Nevills, 2004); (b) the student's level of orthographic knowledge, which means that students are able to recognize high-frequency words and also process less familiar words; (c) the brain's rate of processing words as children read, with some students being fast processors (and therefore fluent readers) and others, not; (d) the student's background or interest in reading the text; and (e) the student's familiarity with the text, which is directly linked to the number of times he or she has read it.

Strategies That Promote Fluency

A critical element in the development of fluency is feedback, which occurs when the teacher, aide, or more capable student offers a helpful reaction to the efforts of an ELL or other at-risk reader.

The most highly rated approach for developing fluency is *guided, modeled, repeated oral reading* (National Reading Panel, 2000). The teacher should choose to model fluent reading only from passages that are within the word recognition and comprehension ability of the struggling reader, and then have him or her imitate that model. This process should be repeated several times from the same passage until the struggler comes closer and closer to the model provided. The experienced teacher does not interrupt any read-aloud efforts but supplies any word over which the struggling reader is hesitating.

Others who can help students with repeated oral reading are aides, cross-age tutors, community volunteers, as well as parents who have been given passages in take-home book bags. Basically, when girls and boys read and reread the same material three or four times with assistance and support, it helps them improve in their ability to phrase text confidently, read difficult words, and comprehend the material.

Another well-recognized strategy for fluency is the *development of a large sight vocabulary.* Basic sight words that comprise more than 60% of the words in beginning reading materials and more than 50% of words used in materials for the upper grades are the most common words used in the English language. Flashcards have been deemed useful for practice in reading single words (Levy, Abello, & Lysysnchuk, 1997) when those same words are later found in the text.

For material related to this concept, go to Video Clip 6.2 on the Student Resource CD bound into the back of your textbook.

A third recommended strategy for fluency is *independent reading*. This helps students increase their reading rate through silent reading at an appropriate reading level. Children who read more do better in school, and therefore school is where many books of different levels and interests are or should be available. Surprisingly, the National Reading Panel (2000) concluded, after examining only a few studies and most of those lasting less than a year, that there was no evidence to support more independent reading in school! Most teachers would definitely disagree with the NRP's conclusion as they continue to stock classroom libraries of different genres to meet the needs of all their students and especially those who are ELLs or struggling readers.

Other strategies that are also useful in improving fluency are the following:

- *Readers theater,* which allows the children to practice oral reading by dramatizing a story (or part of a story) they have read. Though this reading does not require memorization, costumes, or sets, it is usually planned and practiced. Students develop fluency in reading through rereading of text in preparation for a performance (Martinez, Roser, & Strecker, 1998/1999). Readers theater is discussed at length in Chapter 11.
- *Choral reading* (also known as choral speaking), whereby students read along in a group led by the teacher. The teacher first models reading the selected material and then has a small group practice with her or him several times. There are various formats for choral reading, depending upon the experience and age of the children. Patterned or predictable books and poetry are read with attention to using voices to orchestrate the reading. As with readers theater, choral speaking is discussed at length in Chapter 11.
- *Paired or partner reading,* in which a more capable reader is paired with a less fluent reader as they take turns reading aloud to one another. Materials chosen are generally more difficult than those read independently. Another possibility is to pair two students of equal reading ability to practice rereading a text after listening to the teacher, aide, or another adult read it initially. A further option is to pair children from different grade levels, (e.g., a second grader and a third grader) both of whom have fluency problems and allow them to work on second-grade-level passages (Wolfe & Nevills, 2004).
- *Tape-reading,* in which an audiotape of a book read by a fluent reader is played to a non-fluent reader. The latter first follows along, pointing to each word, and then reads along with the tape. Eventually that reader will read the book independently without the tape.
- *Neurological impress method,* which involves the teacher and the nonfluent student reading aloud from the same material simultaneously. However, the teacher reads slightly faster than the child to keep the reading fluent. Usually the teacher is seated next to the student, focusing his or her ear near the ear of the child and pointing to the words as they are read (Johns & Berglund, 2002).
- *Echo reading,* in which a less fluent reader immediately imitates or echoes the performance of a more fluent reader. Student A reads a sentence and then Student B reads the same sentence. This "first-and-follow" routine continues throughout the passage until both students can reread the passage individually at an increased rate. Another version of echo reading begins with the teacher distributing copies of the selection he or she will read aloud; after the teacher read-aloud, the children echo the selection that introduces new words and concepts.
- *Language experience approach,* which involves the teacher writing down on a chart what the children say and then reading and rereading it with them to promote knowledge about letter-sound relationships and sight words. Later the students individually may wish to walk over to the chart rack and read *and reread it for themselves, particularly if their names or initials complete each sentence.*

A sample lesson plan incorporating the concepts introduced in this chapter appears on p. 194.

Assessment

Regardless of the approach used to teach reading, a comprehensive assessment should be done to ensure success for the learner. Along with standardized testing, classroom assessments are critical in guiding and planning reading instruction. Each student's phonemic awareness, phonics, fluency, and comprehension skills should be assessed. These assessments will determine the student's independent and instructional reading levels. Along with these formal assessments, informal information gathered through interviews, work samples, demonstrations, and anecdotal records complete the student's reading portfolio. With this information the teacher can determine each student's needs and plan accordingly.

Working With English Language Learners

Beginning ELLs: Beginning ELLs need social, emotional, and academic support when learning to read. Using chanting, discussions, realia, and word cards for labeling, prior to reading the text, helps the students acquire enough vocabulary orally and in print that they can be successful when reading from the book. The teacher and the other students can provide the assistance necessary for the student to practice.

Early intermediate and intermediate ELLs: Along with all of the beginning-level support, early intermediate and intermediate ELL students may benefit from audiotapes of the text. Following along in the text as they listen to the words read in the listening center will help them hear the sound of the language and also reinforce vocabulary. For additional support and practice the students may take small tape recorders and tapes home to listen to books and lessons.

Early advanced and advanced ELLs: Early advanced and advanced ELLs continue to be successful when visuals and concrete experiences are used to enhance verbal lessons and instructions. In reading this translates to readers theater, plays, and videos of the text.

Practical Instructional Activities and Ideas

- *Daily read-alouds:* The teacher should read aloud quality literature daily. This not only models the reading process but demonstrates the joy of reading for pleasure.
- *Dictated stories:* The teacher can have the students dictate stories as a class. The teacher charts the stories. The students then read the story back as the teacher points to the words.
- *Alphabet books:* The teacher can read aloud alphabet books, which are available for all ages. This will help the students make the connection between the letters and the sounds and develop some concepts necessary for reading success.
- *Oral presentations:* In science and social studies, the students may work in small groups to develop and present an oral presentation to the class on the current area of study. This activity offers a low-stress environment and provides plenty of opportunity for concept and vocabulary development.
- *Learning centers:* The teacher sets up literacy learning centers, such as make-a-book and poetry play, to encourage language development through interaction and play.
- *Predictable books:* The teacher reads predictable books with a repetitive pattern to establish and reinforce the relationship between letters and sounds.

LESSON PLAN 6.1 Daily Fluency Practice

Objective

- Students improve their fluency skills.

Materials

- Fluency passages marked with word counts
- File folders
- Colored pencils
- Graph paper to record results
- Overheads of a passage and the graph paper

Content Standards

Language Arts: Word Fluency

- Students understand the basic features of reading.
- Students apply this knowledge to achieve fluent oral and silent reading.

Day 1

- Teacher talks to students about improving reading fluency by comparing it to riding a bike. What was it like when you first learned to ride a bike? What happened? How did it feel? How did you get better? How did you improve your skills and confidence? Fluency is the same. It takes time and practice.
- Teacher models stapling graph paper in the folder for charting word count, writing a name on the tab, and decorating the folder to personalize it.
- Students complete their folders.

Day 2

- Teacher reviews the discussion of fluency and chooses a student to help model the process.
- With the passage on the overhead, Teacher reads it and the student helper watches the clock to tell Teacher when to stop reading (one minute).
- The student helper puts a slash after the last word Teacher read.
- Teacher shows the class how to count the number of words that were read in the one minute.

- Teacher shows the student how to record on the graph the number of words read.
- Teacher chooses reading partners to ensure compatible reading levels and personalities and informs students.
- Using a practice passage and a practice graph (not the one in their folders) the partners each take a turn reading, timing, and graphing.

Day 3

- Teacher passes out the reading folders and passage for the rest of the week.
- Students read and record their fluency counts.
- The class discusses the process, and the students take the passage home to practice for homework each day.
- Reading begins with a partner fluency session each day. Progress is shared with the parents. Teacher provides new passages based on improvement and need.

Integration Across the Curriculum

Science, Social Studies, and Health

- Students complete K-W-L charts to access prior knowledge of a new topic in social studies, health, and science.
- For each unit of study, students create word banks of new vocabulary words along with illustrations to remind them what the words mean.

Literature

- The teacher uses pieces of children's literature as mentor text to model decoding and comprehension strategies.
- Students use stories in basal readers and big books as shared reading.
- Students read and discuss literature in book clubs or literature circles.
- The teacher uses exemplary children's literature as read-alouds.

Visual and Performing Arts

- The students create a word wall as they come across new words in their reading.

Physical Education

- Students play "Reading Relay." Divide the class into teams for a relay race. Each student takes a turn running across the field to the team bucket. Each pulls a strip from the bucket, reads and follows the directions on the strip, and then runs back to the line to tap the next person. The first team that is finished wins.

Music

- Students read the lyrics of songs to notice their similarity to poetry.
- Students learn and perform songs that reinforce language concepts ("The Synonym Song").
- Students sing songs to reinforce phonemic awareness ("Apples and Bananas").

Parents as Partners

- *Reading at home:* Parents should model good reading practices by reading books for personal pleasure as well as manuals for different kinds of information.
- *Shared print.* Parents should share magazines and newspapers and encourage the child to find familiar words in advertisements.
- *Visiting the library:* Parents should visit the children's room at the local public library, help the child obtain a library card and book(s), and then make going to the library a weekly trip.
- *Environmental print at home:* Parents should read with the child cereal boxes, menus, place mats, coupons, and other forms of print.
- *Traveling vocabulary:* Parents should take the child on visits and trips, using specific terms when discussing the experience, such as *gate, flight attendant, pilot,* and *luggage.*
- *Environmental print outside:* Parents should point out and read familiar signs, such as "Burger King," "Wal-Mart," and "Stop," and encourage the child to read them too.
- *Books on tape:* Parents can listen with the child to stories or books recorded on audiotapes, which are readily available at the local library; this is especially helpful for ELLs of any age.
- *Promoting pride:* Parents can encourage a positive school attitude by posting notes from school, "refrigerator art," and "papers to be proud of."
- *Study space:* Parents can provide a quiet place for the child to read without distractions.

Student Study Site

The Companion Web site for *Language Arts: Integrating Skills for Classroom Teaching* www.sagepub.com/donoghuestudy
Visit the Web-based study site to enhance your understanding of the chapter content. The study materials include chapter summaries, practice tests, flashcards, and Web resources.

Additional Professional Readings

Boushey, G., & Moser, J. (2006). *The daily five alive: Fostering literacy independence in the elementary grades.* Portland, ME: Stenhouse.

Fink, R. (2006). *Why Jane and John couldn't read—and how they learned: A new look at striving readers.* Newark, DE: International Reading Association.

Jalongo, M. (2005). "What are all these dogs doing at school?": Using therapy dogs to promote children's reading practice. *Childhood Education, 81,* 152–158.

Keene, E. (2008). *To understand: New horizons in reading comprehension.* Portsmouth, NH: Heinemann.

Kelley, M., & Clausen-Grace, N (2007). *Comprehension shouldn't be silent: From strategy instruction to student independence.* Newark, DE: International Reading Association.

McVicker, C. (2007). Young readers respond: The importance of child participation in emerging literacy. *Young Children, 62,* 18–22.

Serafini, F., & Youngs, S. (2008). *More (advanced) lessons in comprehension: Expanding students' understanding of all types of texts.* Portsmouth, NH: Heinemann.

Sibberson, F., & Szymusiak, K. (2003). *Still learning to read: Teaching students in grades 3–6.* Portland, ME: Stenhouse.

Stead, T. (2005). *Reality checks: Teaching reading comprehension with nonfiction K–5.* Portland, ME: Stenhouse.

Wirt, B., Bryan, C., & Wesley, K. (2005). *Discovering what works for struggling readers: Journeys of exploration with primary grade students.* Newark, DE: International Reading Association.

Children's Literature Cited in the Text

Allard, H. G. (1995). *Miss Nelson is missing!* Boston: Houghton.

Bloom, B. (1999). *Wolf!* New York: Orchard Books.

Browne, A. (2004). *I like books.* Cambridge, MA: Candlewick.

Bruss, D. (2004). *Book! Book! Book!* New York: Arthur A. Levine.

Bunting, E. (1991). *Night tree.* San Diego, CA: Harcourt.

Burningham, J. (1985). *Colors.* New York: Random House.

Child, L. (2006). *But excuse me! That is my book.* New York: Dial Books.

Cleary, B. (1999). *Ramona's world.* New York: HarperCollins.

Cole, J. (1992). *The magic school bus: Lost in the solar system.* New York: Scholastic.

Donaldson, J. (2006). *Charlie Cook's favorite book.* New York: Dial Books.

Early, M. (1993). *Sleeping Beauty.* New York: Harry Abrams.

Ernst, L. (1998). *Stella Louella's runaway book.* New York: Simon & Schuster

Galdone, P. (1984). *The elves and the shoemaker.* Boston: Houghton.

Gardiner, J. R. (1997). *Stone Fox.* New York: HarperCollins.

Hutchins, P. (2005). *Rosie's walk.* New York: Simon & Schuster.

Kirstein, L. (1992). *Puss in boots.* Boston: Little, Brown.

Lehman, B. (2004). *The red book.* Boston: Houghton.

Maestro, B. (1993). *The story of money.* New York: Clarion.

McPhail, D. (1997). *Edward and the pirates.* Boston: Little, Brown.

McQuinn, A. (2006). *Lola at the library.* Boston: Charlesbridge.

Monjo, F. N. (1983). *The drinking gourd: A story of the underground railroad.* New York: HarperCollins.

Myers, W. D. (1995). *Scorpions.* New York: Amistad.

Paterson, K. (1997). *The great Gilly Hopkins.* New York: HarperCollins.

Paulsen, G. (1995). *Hatchet.* Boston: Houghton.

Pinkney, S. (2006). *Read and rise.* New York: Cartwheel.

Rylant, C. (1996). *Henry and Mudge: The first book.* New York: Atheneum.

Seuss, Dr. (2006). *The cat in the hat comes back.* New York: Random House.

Sierra, J. (2004). *Wild about books.* New York: Knopf.

Spanyol, J. (2004). *Carlos and the really nice librarian.* Cambridge, MA: Candlewick.

Wood, A. (2004). *The napping house.* San Diego: Harcourt.

References

Adams, M. (1990). *Beginning to read: Thinking and learning about print.* Cambridge: MIT Press.

Allington, R. (2002). What I've learned about effective reading instruction from a decade of studying exemplary elementary classroom teachers. *Phi Delta Kappan, 83,* 740–747.

Allington, R., & McGill-Franzen, A. (2004). Looking back, looking forward: A conversation about teaching reading in the 21st century. In R. Ruddell & N. Unrau (Eds.), *Theoretical models and practices of reading* (8th ed.). Newark, DE: International Reading Association.

Anderson, T., & Armbruster, B. (1984). Studying. In P. Pearson, R. Barr, M. Kamil, & P. Mosenthal (Eds.), *Handbook of reading research.* New York: Longman.

Armbruster, B., Lehr, F., & Osborn, J. (2003). *Put reading first: The research building blocks for teaching children to read* (2nd ed.). Washington, DC: Partnership for Reading.

Barone, D., Hardman, D., & Taylor, J. (2005). *Reading First in the classroom.* Boston: Allyn & Bacon.

Baumann, J., Hoffman, J., Moon, J., & Duffy-Hester, A. (1998). Where are teachers' voices in the phonics/whole language debate: Results of a survey of U.S. elementary teachers. *The Reading Teacher, 51,* 636–650.

Baumann, J., & Ivey, G. (1997). Deliberate balance: Striving for curricular and instructional equilibrium in a second-grade literature/strategy-based classroom. *Reading Research Quarterly, 23,* 244–276.

Blachowitz, C., & Ogle, D. (2001). *Reading comprehension: Strategies for independent learners.* New York: Guilford.

Block, C., & Pressley, M. (Eds.). (2002). *Comprehension instruction: Research-based best practices.* New York: Guilford.

Bloom, B. (1956). *Taxonomy of educational objectives. The classification of educational goals: Handbook I: Cognitive domain.* New York: Longman.

Bond, G., & Dykstra, R. (1997). The cooperative research program in first-grade reading instruction. *Reading Research Quarterly, 32,* 348–427. (Original work published in 1967)

Bromley, K., & Irwin-Devine, L. (1999). *50 graphic organizers.* New York: Scholastic.

Brown, A., & Day, J. (1983). *Microrules for summarizing text: The development of expertise.* Champaign: Center for the Study of Reading, University of Illinois.

Center for the English Language Arts. (1998). *Newsletter.* Albany: State University of New York.

Clay, M. (1991). Introducing a new storybook to young readers. *The Reading Teacher, 45,* 264–273.

Farris, P. (2005). *Language arts: Process, product, and assessment* (4th ed.). Long Grove, IL: Waveland.

Fawson, P., & Reutzel, D. (2000). But I only have a basal: Implementing guided reading in the early grades. *The Reading Teacher, 54,* 84–97.

Fay, L. (1965). Reading study skills: Math and science. In J. Figurel (Ed.), *Reading and inquiry.* Newark, DE: International Reading Association.

Fisher, B., & Medvic, E. (2000). *Perspectives on shared reading: Planning and practice.* Portsmouth, NH: Heinemann.

Fitzgerald, J. (1999). What is this thing called "balance"? *The Reading Teacher, 53,* 100–107.

Fountas, I., & Pinnell, G. (1996). *Guided reading: Good first teaching for all children.* Portsmouth, NH: Heinemann.

Fountas, I., & Pinnell, G. (1999). *Matching books to readers: Using leveled books in guided reading.* Portsmouth, NH: Heinemann.

Fountas, I., & Pinnell, G. (2001). *Guiding readers and writers in grades 3–5: Teaching comprehension, genre, and content literacy.* Portsmouth, NH: Heinemann.

Frey, N., & Fisher, D. (2007). *The Reading for information in the elementary school.* Columbus, OH: Merrill/Prentice Hall.

Gove, M. (1983). Clarifying teachers' beliefs about reading. *The Reading Teacher, 37,* 261–267.

Harp, B., & Brewer, J. (2005). *The informed reading teacher: Research-based practice.* Columbus, OH: Merrill/Prentice Hall.

Harris, A., & Sipay, E. (1990). *How to increase reading ability* (9th ed.). New York: Longman.

Holdaway, D. (1979). *Foundations of literacy.* Auckland, New Zealand: Ashton Scholastic.

Hoyt, L., Mooney, M., & Parkes, B. (2003). *Exploring informational texts: From theory to practice.* Portsmouth, NH: Heinemann.

International Reading Association. (1999). High-stakes assessments in reading: A position statement of the International Reading Association. *The Reading Teacher, 53,* 257–263.

International Reading Association. (2002). *What is evidence-based reading instruction?* Newark, DE: Author.

Jacobson, M. (1989). RESPONSE: An interactive study technique. *Reading Horizons, 29,* 86–92.

Johns, J., & Berglund, R. (2002). *Questions, answers, and evidence-based strategies.* Dubuque, IA: Kendall-Hunt.

Kirshner, D., & Whitson, J. (1997). *Situated cognition: Social, semiotic, and psychological perspectives.* Mahwah, NJ: Lawrence Erlbaum.

Laase, L. (1997). Study skills: Note-taking strategies that work. *Instructor, 58.*

Levy, B., Abello, B., & Lysysnchuk, L. (1997). Transfer from word training to reading in context: Gain in reading fluency and comprehension. *Learning Disability Quarterly, 20,* 173–188.

Martinez, M., Roser, N., & Strecker, S. (1998/1999). I never thought I could be a star: A readers theatre ticket to fluency. *The Reading Teacher, 52,* 326–334.

McIntosh, M., & Draper, R. (1996). Using the question-answer relationship strategy to improve students' reading of mathematics texts. *Clearing House, 69,* 154–162.

Meddey, D., & Jefferies, D. (2000/2001). Guidelines for implementing a graphic organizer. *The Reading Teacher, 54,* 350–357.

National Reading Panel. (2000). *Teaching children to read: An evidence-based assessment of the scientific research literature on reading and its implications for reading instruction.* Washington, DC: National Institute of Child Health and Human Development.

Parkes, B. (2000). *Read it again! Revisiting shared reading.* York, ME: Stenhouse.

Pearson, D. (1990). Asking questions about stories. In A. Harris & E. Sipay (Eds.), *How to increase reading ability* (9th ed.). New York: Longman.

Pearson, D., & Johnson, D. (1978) *Teaching reading comprehension.* New York: Holt, Rinehart and Winston.

Pinnell, G., & Fountas, I. (1998). *Word matters.* Portsmouth, NH: Heinemann.

Raphael, T. (1986). Teaching children question-answering relationships, revisited. *The Reading Teacher, 39,* 516–522.

Roe, B., Smith, S., & Burns, P. (2005). *Teaching reading in today's elementary school* (9th ed). Boston: Houghton Mifflin

Rosenblatt, L. (1978). *The reader, the text, and the poem: The transactional theory of the literary work.* Carbondale, IL: Southern Illinois University Press.

Rosenblatt, L. (1991). Literature: S. O. S.! *Language Arts, 68,* 444–448.

Ruddell, R. (2006). *Teaching children to read and write* (4th ed.). Boston: Allyn & Bacon.

Rumelhart, D. (1984). Understanding understanding. In. J. Hood (Ed.), *Understanding reading comprehension.* Newark, DE: International Reading Association.

Samuels, S. (1994). Toward a theory of automatic information processing in reading: Revisited. In R. Ruddell, M. Ruddell, & H. Singer (Eds.), *Theoretical models and processes of reading.* Newark, DE: International Reading Association.

Samuels, S. (2002). Reading fluency: Its development and assessment. In A. Farstrup & S. Samuels (Eds.), *What research has to say about reading instruction.* Newark, DE: International Reading Association.

Scarborough, H. (1989). Prediction of reading disability from familial and individual differences. *Journal of Educational Psychology, 81,* 101–108.

Schmidt, B., & Buckley, M. (1991). Plot relationships chart. In J. Macon, D. Bewell, & M. Vogt (Eds.), *Responses to literature: Grades K–8.* Newark, DE: International Reading Association.

Searfoss, L., Readence, J., & Mallette, M. (2001). *Helping children learn to read* (4th ed.). Boston: Allyn & Bacon.

Seitz, E. (1997). Using media presentations to teach notetaking, main idea, and summarization skills. *Journal of Adolescent and Adult Literacy, 40,* 562–563.

Snow, C. , Burns, M., & Griffin, P. (1998). *Preventing reading difficulties in young children.* Washington, DC: National Academy Press.

Stauffer, R. (1975). *Directing the reading-thinking process.* New York: Harper & Row.

Tompkins, G. (2006). *Literacy for the 21st century* (4th ed.). Columbus, OH: Merrill/Prentice Hall.

Tower, C. (2000). Questions that matter: Preparing elementary students for the inquiry process. *The Reading Teacher, 53,* 550–557.

van den Brock, P., Rhoden, K., Fletcher, C., & Thurlow, R. (1996). A "landscape" view of reading: Fluctuating patterns of activation and the construction of a stable memory representation. In R. Britton & A. Graeser (Eds.), *Models of understanding text*. Mahwah, NJ: Lawrence Erlbaum.

Weaver, C. (1994). *Reading practice and process: From sociopsycholinguistics to whole language*. Portsmouth, NH: Heinemann.

Weaver, C. (Ed.). (1998). *Reconsidering a balanced approach to reading*. Urbana, IL: National Council of Teachers of English.

Wolfe, P., & Nevills, P. (2004). *Building the reading brain preK–3*. Thousand Oaks, CA: Corwin Press.

Anticipation Statement Answers

1. Agree

2. Disagree

3. Agree

4. Agree

5. Disagree

6. Agree

7. Disagree

8. Agree

9. Agree: As long as the students have interesting books, spend time reading, and discuss the reading with their peers, they will learn to comprehend regardless of the quality of instruction. However, knowing the comprehension strategies and watching demonstrations of those strategies in use improve comprehension.

10. Agree: Students do not need to be asked questions to be actively engaged with a text. However, consistent attention to minute facts from the reading trains the reader to shift his or her attention from the big idea or story to focusing on details.

Reading and Children's Literature

CHAPTER 7

The main objective of reading programs in the elementary school is to develop readers who are not only able to read but who will also continue to do so throughout their lives. To help attain this goal, reading programs must offer students many opportunities to read literature. Skills instruction must unfailingly be presented in a context that motivates children to read and enjoy good books.

Although the basal reader approach is the most widely used instructional approach for literacy development in the United States, it was never intended to be a self-contained approach. Teachers must always supplement the basals with other printed resources, including literary works, so that students can use the skills they have acquired and thereby maintain proficiency in reading. Both enjoyment and appreciation grow as children read widely among the many genres of books available to them.

Children's literature is the collection of quality trade books read to and by children and covering topics of interest and relevance to boys and girls through fiction and nonfiction, through prose and poetry. This collection includes more than 350,000 children's titles currently in print (Children's Books in Print, 2007) and the more than 8,000 new children's titles published annually in the United States (Bogart, 2004), plus thousands more published in English worldwide each year.

Anticipation Statements

Complete this exercise before reading Chapter 4.

Do you agree or disagree with the following statements? Circle your answer. Be prepared to discuss questions in blue.

1.	Response to literature can serve as a means to help children deal with difficult personal issues.	Agree	Disagree
2.	Literature programs can and should include a balance of literary genres.	Agree	Disagree
3.	After finishing books for independent reading, students should always complete follow-up activities to check for understanding.	Agree	Disagree
4.	Multicultural and international literature can help children from diverse backgrounds make connections to the literature.	Agree	Disagree
5.	Stories for children should have a clear sequence of events: a beginning, middle, and end.	Agree	Disagree
6.	Poetry has no universally agreed-on definition.	Agree	Disagree
7.	Nonfiction works for children should be within the comprehension level of the readers, but also inspire further inquiry.	Agree	Disagree
8.	Reading preferences of boys and girls reflect similar interests throughout the grades.	Agree	Disagree
9.	Children's literature that deals with concepts such as death or divorce is not appropriate for use in the classroom.	Agree	Disagree
10.	When evaluating children's literature, the format of the book is more important than the content.	Agree	Disagree

Literature in Elementary Education: Values and Functions

Today more than ever, literature plays a critical role in elementary education. Even though children's initial exposure to literature is through Mother Goose and other traditional rhymes and stories, students should gradually experience every form of literature in a comprehensive school program that is sequentially plotted throughout the elementary grades. Such a program not only strengthens the developmental reading curriculum but also contributes in a significant way to the attainment of several other objectives of elementary education:

- The school aims to meet the needs of individual students—and literature is widely diversified.
- The school aims to provide a learning program that will utilize the natural interests of its students—and literature in its many forms appeals to all age groups.
- The school aims to provide socially satisfying experiences for its children and to develop in them a wider social understanding—and good stories and pleasing verse are enjoyed more when they are shared with others.
- The school aims to give each child self-insight—and books introduced in childhood can sometimes bring about a profound change in one's outlook on life.
- The school aims to give each student a knowledge and appreciation of his or her cultural heritage—and literature is the means whereby much of that heritage is preserved and perpetuated.
- The school aims to stimulate and foster creative expression—and book experiences are an exciting springboard to art, drama, and other expressionistic activities.

A properly structured literature program provides a balance among the various genres relevant to this segment of the language arts—*genre* refers to content (what is said and how it is said) and represents one of the systems for categorizing books. In this way students have at least minimal encounters with each genre at every age level, and their teachers remain aware of the need to explore the many and diverse offerings included within each genre. A balance can then be attained between prose and poetry and between fiction and nonfiction with all their varied divisions. Such a balanced offering actively strengthens and expands student skills in oral and written language as well as in literature.

The value of teaching literature is multifaceted. First, it promotes aesthetic and intellectual growth in several different ways: It entertains and enchants, motivates reading and leads to improved reading skills, and expands vocabulary. Second, it builds a sense of rootedness, refines students' feelings, and develops mature personalities. Third, it promotes ethical responsibility and shows the reader what good and evil look like. Finally, it develops a sense of citizenship and fosters an awareness of society (California Department of Education, 1987).

Applicable IRA/NCTE Standards

Standard 1   Students read a wide range of print and nonprint texts to build an understanding of texts, of themselves, and of the cultures of the United States and the world; to acquire new information; to respond to the needs and demands of society and the workplace; and for personal fulfillment. Among these texts are fiction and nonfiction, classic, and contemporary works.

Standard 2   Students read a wide range of literature from many periods in many genres to build an understanding of the many dimensions (e.g., philosophical, ethical, aesthetic) of human experience.

Standard 9   Students develop an understanding of and respect for diversity in language use, patterns, and dialects across cultures, ethnic groups, geographic regions, and social roles.

Source: *Standards for the English Language Arts*, by the International Reading Association and the National Council of Teachers of English, Copyright 1996 by the International Reading Association and the National Council of Teachers of English. Reprinted with permission. http://www.ncte.org/about/over/standards/110846.htm

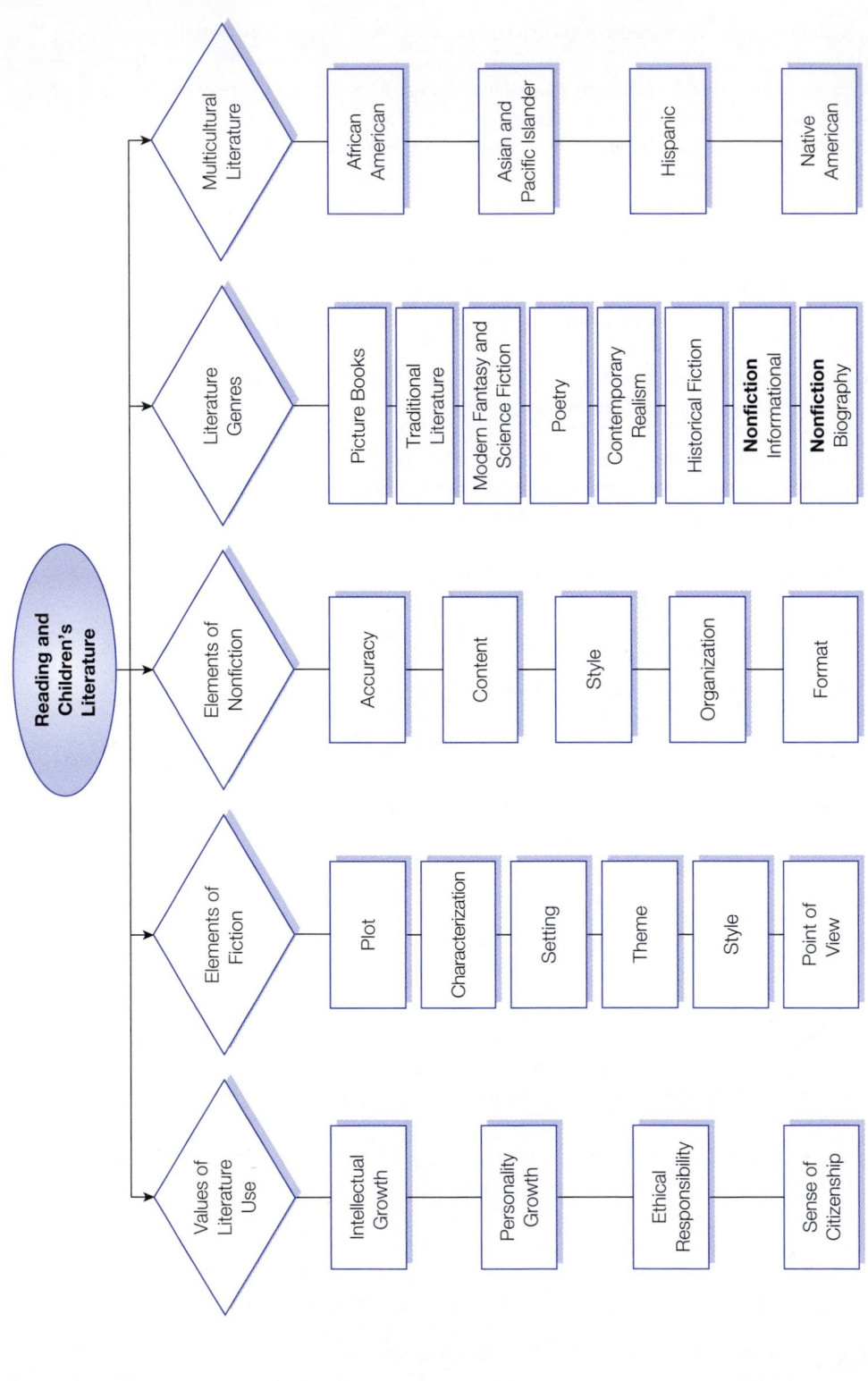

A Graphic Summary of the Contents of This Chapter

Reading and Children's Literature

- Multicultural Literature
  - African American
  - Asian and Pacific Islander
  - Hispanic
  - Native American
- Literature Genres
  - Picture Books
  - Traditional Literature
  - Modern Fantasy and Science Fiction
  - Poetry
  - Contemporary Realism
  - Historical Fiction
  - **Nonfiction** Informational
  - **Nonfiction** Biography
- Elements of Nonfiction
  - Accuracy
  - Content
  - Style
  - Organization
  - Format
- Elements of Fiction
  - Plot
  - Characterization
  - Setting
  - Theme
  - Style
  - Point of View
- Values of Literature Use
  - Intellectual Growth
  - Personality Growth
  - Ethical Responsibility
  - Sense of Citizenship

The school literature program should be structured to attain certain objectives, according to Lukens (1999), because literature itself performs particular functions. It provides both pleasure and understanding. It shows human motives for what they are, inviting the readers or listeners to identify with or react to fictional characters. Literature provides a framework for experience, placing relevant episodes into coherent sequence, thereby showing life's unity or meaning.

Furthermore, continues Lukens (1999), literature reveals life's fragmentation as well, sorting the world into segments that can be identified and examined. It facilitates a focus on essentials, permitting listeners to experience with varied intensity, but with new understanding, the parts of life they have known. Literature reveals how both institutions of society and nature itself affect human life. Last, literature leads or entices readers and hearers into meeting a writer-creator whose medium (words) they know, whose subject (human nature) they live with, and whose vision (life's meaning) they hope to understand.

What Literature Does for Readers and Writers

In addition to these lofty goals enunciated by elementary school administrators and program planners, literature has some concrete benefits for student readers and writers.

Children read for enjoyment and wish to share that with others.

Children read fiction, nonfiction, or poetry for a variety of reasons, according to Stewig (1988):

- They read for sheer enjoyment (e.g., Dahl's *Charlie and the Chocolate Factory* [2007]).
- They wish to escape from present situations (e.g., Cleary's *Ralph S. Mouse* [1993]).

For material related to this concept, go to Video Clip 7.1 on the Student Resource CD bound into the back of your textbook.

- They wonder about the nature of a character or an unspecified outcome and thereby their imagination is stimulated (e.g., Munthe's *Meet Matisse* [1983] and Gans' *When Birds Change Their Feathers* [1980]).
- They are able to gain an understanding of themselves, particularly if they seem to differ from their peers in personality (e.g., Lowry's *Anastasia Krupnik* [1987], which spawned a series) or physical appearance (e.g., Miner's *New Beginning: An Athlete Is Paralyzed* [1982]).
- They are able to gain an understanding of others (e.g., Fox's *A Likely Place* [1987]).
- They learn to understand the nature of language, especially the dialects of persons from different parts of the United States as well as those from other countries (e.g., Lenski's *Strawberry Girl* [1987] and Graham's *Every Man Heart Lay Down* [1993]).
- They travel to other times and places (e.g., Turkle's *Thy Friend, Obadiah* [1982] and Avi's *The True Confessions of Charlotte Doyle* [1990]).
- They gain information in all subject matter areas including science, social studies, and mathematics (e.g., Aliki's *Fossils Tell of Long Ago* [1990], Adler's *A Picture Book of Benjamin Franklin* [1990], and Hulme's *Sea Squares* [1991]).

Literature also benefits children's writing in several ways (Cramer, 2001). It offers models for writing as children learn about the craft of writing through broad exposure to literature. It enlightens the mind and entertains, allowing children to value differences and explore options for themselves. Reading literature expands students' vocabulary, broadens their knowledge of language generally, and increases and enriches the cultural knowledge so necessary for children in today's multicultural society. It explores the major themes of life, helping students see more clearly the world as well as each other. It also develops a love for reading, which in turn promotes writing. Finally, reading literature helps children develop a sense of story, so critical to narrative and poetic writing as discussed in Chapter 8.

Children's Needs and Reading Interests

For material related to this concept, go to Video Clip 7.2 on the Student Resource CD bound into the back of your textbook.

Developmentally, certain basic needs of children remain the same today, despite the rapid pace of social change. Directly or indirectly, books written by thoughtful and sensitive authors can help girls and boys better understand themselves and others (Sutherland, 2004) by addressing these needs:

- *The need for security:* Both physical and material security are addressed in books ranging from **folktales**—traditional literature that begins quickly with a problem, continues with simple characters and a fast-paced plot, and ends with a satisfying solution—to contemporary realistic fiction to biographies of heroes. Book examples include Brown's *Dick Whittington and His Cat* (1988) and Turner's *Grasshopper Summer* (2000).
- *The need to love and be loved:* This need involves family affection, warm friendships, and devotion to pets as well as impersonal romance. Book examples include Jukes' *Like Jake and Me* (2005), Byars' *The Summer of the Swans* (2005), and Apy's *Beauty and the Beast* (1991).
- *The need to belong:* Every child wants to be an accepted member of a group. Book examples include Tunis's *Keystone Kids* (1990) and Cohen's *Molly's Pilgrim* (1983).
- *The need to achieve:* A strong motivating force is the need for competence, which is sometimes accompanied by frustration. Book examples include Lawlor's *How to Survive Third Grade* (1991), Estes' *The Hundred Dresses* (2004), and Collins' *Farmworker's Friend: The Story of Cesar Chavez* (1996).

- *The need for change:* Books of varied sorts may be used to help children meet their need for healthy change from the pressure of routines, adult tensions, and the need to conform. Book examples include Dr. Seuss's *Horton Hatches the Egg* (2004), Merrill's *The Pushcart War* (1985), and Sobol's *Encyclopedia Brown and the Case of the Sleeping Dog* (1998). Tall tales, mystery stories, and science fiction all help meet readers' need for change.
- *The need to know:* The need to investigate and to learn is a critical one that books can satisfy. Book examples include Kostyal's *Trial by Ice* (1999), Severance's *Einstein: Visionary Scientist* (1999), Murphy's *Blizzard!* (2000), and Blumberg's *Shipwrecked! The True Adventures of a Japanese Boy* (2001).
- *The need for beauty and order:* In addition to their needs for knowledge and security, children also have an aesthetic need to grow in their ability to appreciate poetry and the visual and performing arts. Book examples include Grimes' *A Pocketful of Poems* (2001), Yolen's *Color Me a Rhyme: Nature Poems for Young People* (2000), Greenberg and Jordan's *Vincent van Gogh: Portrait of an Artist* (2001), and Ganeri's *The Young Person's Guide to Shakespeare* (1999).

Children's needs are readily reflected in their reading interests, and hundreds of well-documented studies reveal that before age nine, there are few differences in those interests between girls and boys (Glazer, 1997). However, between ages 10 and 13, the interests begin to diverge. Studies regarding children's literary preferences have revealed that sex-related preferences are now apparent at a younger age than they were before. Such studies also show that gifted children prefer books liked by a slightly older age group and have a wider range of interests compared to average readers; in contrast, students of average ability like mysteries, realistic fiction, humor, and adventure. Fiction rates high, especially humorous fiction for most children. Children's reading tastes have largely crystallized by the fifth grade. Social and environmental influences affect children's book choices, although peer recommendations are particularly important to intermediate students. Finally, the overwhelming majority of both younger and older readers are initially attracted to a book by its subject matter.

Since 1975 the Children's Book Council and the International Reading Association have conducted an annual survey in which 10,000 students read and vote on recently published books. Publishers send multiple copies of some 500 books to review teams in five regions of the United States where the books are then read to or by the students. Children's votes are tabulated in March, and the results are published in the October issue of *The Reading Teacher* as "Children's Choices." The annotated lists provide classroom teachers with the *most current reading interests* of beginning readers (ages 5–7), young readers (ages 8–10), and advanced readers (ages 11–13).

Criteria and Resources for Selecting Quality Books

More than 350,000 English-language children's books are in print and the number is still growing. Each year eight thousand new titles are published in this country alone. Despite this deluge, the discriminating selection of a quality book for a specific class or student cannot yet be computerized. It still requires a knowledge of the interests, reading ability, and maturity level of that class or child, coupled with a knowledge of the best books to meet those interests and abilities.

Qualities that make children's books outstanding and therefore qualified as literature include the following *general characteristics,* argue Temple and his colleagues (2002): Good books expand awareness, giving children a broader understanding of other people and the world. They provide enjoyment but are not directly didactic. They tell the truth about the human experience with characters who are life-like and with insights that are accurate. Good books have both original-ity and integrity. They embody quality in their choice of words, convincing plot, and believable characters.

Specific characteristics of good books that elevate them to literature standing are numerous. They have **style**—language in which carefully chosen words are properly arranged. Their illustra-tions extend the content beyond those words, and their **theme** or underlying idea unifies the text. Fiction demands a well-defined **plot** (or what happens in the story), memorable and believable characters, a detailed **setting** (or where and when the story takes place), a precise **point of view** (or who is telling the story), tension or suspense to sustain interest, mood or atmosphere evoked by the writing, and pacing that will vary according to the author's plan. Nonfiction is concerned with accuracy, organization, and content in addition to style and illustrations/format (Jacobs & Tunnell, 2004). A book's design and layout (which include all the visual elements) will be the final determinant of whether or not readers select it.

Teachers who personally enjoy juvenile books can speak convincingly when introducing such literature to their classes. Children want to know briefly what each story is about, and a short preview—or sales pitch—concerning a particular book helps them acquire this information. Since most students commonly use a variety of readily accessible media at home, the satisfaction they can receive by reading well-written books must be explored in the classroom. This means that the teachers need to keep current in their knowledge of new books as well as remain familiar with older books that are sometimes issued in new editions.

To meet that need, teachers can consult such professional periodicals as *The Reading Teacher* (published eight times a year by the International Reading Association), *Language Arts* (published eight times a year by the National Council of Teachers of English), *Childhood Education* (pub-lished six times a year by the Association for the Education of Young Children), *Booklist* (published biweekly except in July and August by the American Library Association), *Book Links* (published bimonthly by the American Library Association), *School Library Journal* (published monthly), and *The Horn Book Magazine* (published bimonthly). Newspapers, notably the *New York Times,* also publish monthly columns devoted to reviews of new children's literature. There are also numerous bibliographies that are updated regularly and include the following:

A to Zoo: Subject Access to Children's Picture Books (Bowker-Greenwood)
Best Books for Children (Bowker-Greenwood)
The Children's Catalog (Wilson)
The Elementary School Library Collection: A Guide to Books and Other Media (Bro-Dart)
Subject Guide to Children's Books in Print (Bowker)

Use of such book selection aids will help keep teachers informed of titles worthy of being termed **children's literature.** They should also keep in mind the many award-winning books, notably the Caldecott Medal and Honor Books and the Newbery Medal and Honor Books, as well as books that have earned such recognition as the Coretta Scott King Award or the Boston Globe/Horn Book Award. Book awards are announced annually, generally in January or February.

With the ever-increasing number of juvenile books from which to choose, teachers must rely on certain criteria to help them identify quality books for children. A major criterion for both fiction and nonfiction is **format** (or the physical appearance of the book). Although no book should ever be selected on the basis of format alone, matters of illustration, typography, binding, spacing, and paper quality cannot be ignored when books are chosen for classroom use. Such books must represent the combined efforts of the best editors, illustrators, book designers, printers, and authors.

Other criteria are discussed in the next section.

Elements of Literature

While children read both fiction and nonfiction books, each category requires different elements to qualify as literature.

Elements of Fiction

Students' reading will not be limited to stories, but these will remain the first and enduring favorite with girls and boys. Good stories possess six strong elements:

1. *Plot:* Children are most interested in the action or what happens in the story. In a well-written book, the action is plausible and credible, developing naturally from the behavior and decisions of the characters. It does not depend on coincidence or contrivance. A story must have a beginning, middle, and end. Students prefer a *chronological plot* with an orderly sequence of events such as in Curtis's *Bud, Not Buddy* (1999). *Flashbacks* are another type of plot device found mostly in chapter books for older readers such as George's *My Side of the Mountain* (1988) since students generally lack the maturity to understand flashbacks until about age 10. Briefly, the story plot has been described by Sawyer (2000) as "a kind of road map" to that story.

   Teachers should avoid books with stories that have no conflict and no suspense, predictable stories, stories that are overly sentimental or full of events that appear to occur merely by chance, and stories with endings that do not solve all the problems presented (Sharp, 1997).

2. *Characterization:* The personalities (animal or human) portrayed in children's books must be convincing and lifelike, must display realistic strengths and weaknesses, and must be consistent in their representation. Though not every character in a well-constructed story will change, there is frequent personality development as happenings occur and problems are solved. Also, characters should speak and behave in accordance with their culture, age, and educational experience. Books with sound **characterizations** for the primary ages include Brown's *Arthur's Teacher Moves In* (2000), one of more than 25 titles about the popular aardvark and his family. Readers in the intermediate grades enjoy Cleary's *Ramona's World* (1999), which is one of a series about an elementary school student and her family.

   Teachers should avoid books with characters that are one-dimensional and never changing, those that are unbelievable and unconvincing, or those that are stereotypes (Sharp, 1997).

3. *Setting:* The setting is the time and place of the action. It may be in the past, the present, or the future. The story may take place in a specific locale, or the setting may be deliberately vague to convey the feeling of all large cities or rural communities. It should in all cases be clear, believable, and, in historical fiction, authentic.

   Both the time and the place should affect the action, the characters, and the theme. Younger readers can quickly grasp the setting of McCloskey's *Make Way for Ducklings* (2004), and older students can understand the setting for Paterson's *Bridge to Terabithia* (2004). Common settings for children's books are nature, schools, and the home.

   Teachers should avoid books with settings that are inconsistent or incompletely described or stories in which activities occur that are in conflict with the setting (Sharp, 1997).

4. *Theme:* A good book demands a worthy theme or underlying idea that provides a dimension of the story beyond the action of the plot. It may be the acceptance of self or others, the overcoming of fear or prejudice, or simply the process of growing up. Though often based on high ethical or moral standards, the theme should not overwhelm the plot or characters of the story. It always reveals the author's purpose in writing the story. In a well-written book, the theme avoids moralizing and yet effectively evolves from the events of the story and unifies them. Such a book, for example, is Steptoe's *Mufaro's Beautiful Daughters* (1987).

   Teachers should avoid books that are didactic or have adult-oriented themes that are beyond the readers' developmental levels and understanding (Sharp, 1997).

5. *Style:* The style of writing in a book is the manner in which the author has selected and arranged words in presenting the story. A quality book possesses a style that respects students as intelligent individuals with rights and interests of their own. Children resent a style that is patronizing, that is overly sentimental, or that contains too much description or material for reflection. Some readers prefer books not written in first person. Primary-grade children like to listen to Goble's *The Girl Who Loved Wild Horses* (1982). Intermediate-grade students appreciate the contemporary dialogue in several of the books by Claudia Mills, Johanna Hurwitz, Lois Lowry, Andrew Clements, and Gary Paulsen.

   Teachers should avoid books that contain adult-sounding language by characters who are children or language that is too mature for the intended readers (Sharp, 1997).

6. *Point of view:* A single incident may often be described differently by each individual witnessing or experiencing it, much as it is in real life. Consequently, point of view refers to the teller of the story and his or her values, feelings, or background. Contemporary fiction for intermediate grade students is often told from the perspective of only one character in the story (e.g., the viewpoint of a child) although written in the third person, whether he or she is the main character or only a bystander, as in Taylor's *Roll of Thunder, Hear My Cry* (2001). That novel is related by Cassie, an astute nine-year-old. Sometimes authors prefer to tell the story through a first-person narrator, generally the main character of the story (the use of "I"), as in Veciana-Suarez's *Flight to Freedom* (2002).

   Teachers should avoid books with a changing point of view or those with an unclear point of view (Sharp, 1997).

Elements of Nonfiction

When teachers understand the elements of nonfiction literature and how they work together, they become more analytical about it, according to Lynch-Brown and Tomlinson (2005). That knowledge helps improve their judgment of informational books and of biographies, which more closely resemble fiction than nonfiction because they are more narrative than expository. Quality nonfiction possesses five strong elements:

1. *Accuracy:* The author is qualified and knowledgeable, the information current and authentic, the distinction made clearly between fact and theory, and the opinions identified. Bias and stereotyping are avoided, and diversity is revealed. Finally, references and additional readings are provided. Book examples include Onyefulu's *Saying Goodbye: A Special Farewell to Mama Nkwelle* (2001) and Lauber's *Painters of the Caves* (1998).

2. *Content:* The topic must be covered adequately, present different viewpoints, and be within the interest and comprehension levels of the intended readers. The book should foster a spirit of inquiry, demonstrate the scientific method, and show interrelationships. Book

examples include Waters' *Samuel Eaton's Day: A Day in the Life of a Pilgrim Boy* (1996) and Giblin's *The Riddle of the Rosetta Stone: A Key to Ancient Egypt* (1991).

3. *Style:* The information should be presented directly and clearly in interesting language appropriate for the intended readers. The text should involve students in the topic and, together with graphic elements and technical vocabulary, help them understand the concepts. Book examples include Dorros's *Follow the Water From Brook to Ocean* (1991) and Arnosky's *All About Frogs* (2002).

4. *Organization:* An organized structure of the content is critical if children are to find it useful. The arrangement of the information will help readers, as will reference aids such as maps, glossaries, tables of contents, indices, and bibliographies. Book examples include Guiberson's *Cactus Hotel* (1991) and Colman's *Corpses, Coffins, and Crypts: A History of Burial* (1997).

5. *Format:* The format is the total look of a book, which should be responsive both to its content and its purpose. In a nonfiction book the format can make the book more appealing to its readers and contribute to its clarity. The illustrations should extend the text and include captions when needed. Book examples include Sattler's *Our Patchwork Planet: The Story of Plate Tectonics* (1995) and Facklam's *The Big Bug Book* (1994).

Literature Genres

There are various categories or genres of children's literature, each of which possesses a particular set of traits. Teachers' knowledge of the characteristics of each genre helps in the development of student understanding of a book. Admittedly, there are variations that exist within each genre classification, according to Lukens (1999), and sometimes a book will fit into more than one genre. Nevertheless, children should become familiar with and read books from eight different genres as they move through the grades.

Picture Books

Picture books are those books in which the illustrations are as important as the text (Glazer, 1997). Types of picture books include the following:

- *Picture storybooks* that have narratives with recognizable plot structures such as Cooney's *Miss Rumphius* (1982) and Bunting's *Smoky Night* (1994)
- *Wordless books* that have no text and rely on illustrations only such as Turkle's *Deep in the Forest* (1999) and Collington's *The Midnight Circus* (1993)—these are popular with English Language Learners (ELLs) who can understand the story on their own
- *Picture books of poetry and song* that include poems, such as Siebert's *Heartland* (1989), and songs, such as Zelinsky's *The Wheels on the Bus* (1990); they have a relatively brief text useful in a book format that generally runs 32 pages
- *Picture books for older readers* that have a content or style beyond the understanding of primary students, such as Innocenti's *Rose Blanche* (1996) and the Provensens' *Shaker Lane* (1987)
- *Concept books* that introduce as well as clarify concepts such as Konigsburg's *Samuel Todd's Book of Great Colors* (1990) and Koch's *Hoot Howl Hiss* (1991); concept books include alphabet books and counting books

Traditional Literature

Traditional literature is described by Temple and colleagues (2002) as the collection of stories and poems whose authors are unknown and that have been passed down from generation to generation without ever having been written down. There are several types of traditional literature.

Folktales begin quickly with a presentation of the problem and continue with uncomplicated characters, fast-paced plots, and satisfying solutions. They often reflect cultural beliefs and attributes as in Martin's *The Rough-Faced Girl* (1992) and Lawson's *The Dragon's Pearl* (1993). Common varieties include cumulative tales, trickster tales, numbskull tales, beast tales, realistic tales, fairy tales, and pourquoi tales.

Myths are similar to pourquoi tales and answer "why?" questions arising out of early people's desire to understand and explain natural phenomena and the world around them; two examples are Belting's *Moon Was Tired of Walking on Air* (1992) and Hamilton's *In the Beginning: Creation Stories From Around the World* (1988).

Fables are brief stories that teach a lesson and usually conclude with a moral such as Pinkney's *Aesop's Fables* (2000) and Ross's *Foxy Fables* (1986).

Legends and tall tales are labeled legends when based on stories of real or supposedly real heroes or heroines but are termed tall tales when those legends are exaggerated, especially with a humorous intent: San Souci's *Young Guinevere* (1993) is a legend, whereas Kellogg's *Mike Fink* (1992) is a tall tale.

Epics are extended tales of powerful heroes or even a series of tales focused on those heroes, such as Sutcliff's *The Wanderings of Odysseus: The Story of the Odyssey* (2005) and Gerez's *Louhi, Witch of North Farm* (1986).

Modern Fantasy and Science Fiction

Considered by many to be the most difficult genre to write, *modern fantasy* is fiction containing an element of unreality that may include talking animals, fanciful characters, and magic beings. When it deals primarily with the future and is set in other worlds, it is labeled *science fiction* since it is based on scientific fact and explores technology. Glazer (1997) observes that modern writers sometimes fall back on traditional fantasy—legends, myths, fables, and folktales—for content or the form of their stories of fantasy and science fiction. Categories of modern fantasy are numerous, according to Jacobs and Tunnell (2004), and include the following:

- *Toys and objects that come to life* in books like Conrad's *The Tub Grandfather* (1993) and Waugh's *The Mennyms* (1994)
- *Tiny humans* in books like Norton's *The Borrowers Avenged* (1982) and Dahl's *The Minpins* (1991)
- *Peculiar characters and situations* in books like Mayne's *Hob and the Goblins* (1994) and Travers' *Mary Poppins* (2006)
- *Imaginary worlds* in books like Pullman's *The Golden Compass* (1996) and Carroll's *Alice in Wonderland* (1994)
- *Magical powers* in books like Rowling's *Harry Potter and the Goblet of Fire* (2000) and Catling's *The Chocolate Touch* (2006)
- *Supernatural tales* in books like Conrad's *Stonewords* (1990) and Hahn's *Wait Till Helen Comes: A Ghost Story* (1986)
- *Time-warp fantasies* in books like Hahn's *A Time for Andrew* (1994) and Pearce's *Tom's Midnight Garden* (1992)

- *High fantasy* in books like Lewis's *The Lion, the Witch, and the Wardrobe* (1994) and Alexander's *The High King* (1999)

Categories of science fiction are more limited than those of modern fantasy and are intended almost exclusively for older students. They include primarily the following, according to Temple and his colleagues (2002):

- *Projecting scientific principles* in books like Ames's *Anna to the Infinite Power* (1981) and Sleator's *The Duplicate* (1988)
- *Utopian and dystopian societies* in books like Auer's *The Blue Boy* (1992) and Christopher's *Wild Jack* (1991)
- *Surviving environmental catastrophes* in books like Karl's *Strange Tomorrow* (1985) and Walsh's *The Green Book* (1982)
- *Science fantasies* in books like Spinner and Etra's *Aliens for Lunch* (1991) and Bechard's *Star Hatchling* (1995); the only category that does include a few books for younger children

A final word on science fiction comes from Lukens (1999), who states that no other genre or subgenre has caused such a sharp distinction between readers who are strong devotees and those who are not.

Poetry

There is no one definition of poetry that has been universally accepted. There are those who vow that poetry is simply a feeling, and others who contend that poetry is words performed and compare the work of a poet to that of a musician. Still others believe that poetry, especially that for children, is writing that transcends literal meaning. It must be stressed, however, that *most writing that has rhythm, rhyme, or short lines is verse and not poetry*. There are several types of poetry.

Narrative poetry tells a story, such as Moore's *The Night Before Christmas* (2005) and Lear's *The Owl and the Pussycat* (1991).

Ballads are long narrative poems that can be adapted for singing and are usually concerned with a single episode but also sometimes involve dialogue and repeated refrains, such as Thayer's *Casey at the Bat: A Ballad of the Republic Sung in the Year 1888* (2000) and "Robin Hood and Allan-a-Dale" in Manning–Sanders' *A Bundle of Ballads* (1959).

Lyric poetry is usually short and emotional, often descriptive or personal, with no prescribed length or structure except that it is melodic and could be set to music. Many of the poems of Robert Louis Stevenson, Christina Rossetti, Eve Merriam, and Henry Behn can be termed lyrical as they have a singing quality.

Haiku poetry is unrhymed lyric poetry with three lines and a total of 17 syllables (5 in the first and third lines and 7 in the second line). It is a Japanese name for a poem that comes from ancient China. Many **haiku** poems may be divided into two parts: first, a simple description that refers to a season, and second, a statement of feeling or mood. Books of haiku poetry include Lewis's *Black Swan/White Crow* (1995) and Shannon's *Spring: A Haiku Story* (1996).

Limerick poetry consists of five lines of carefully organized nonsense poetry, with the first two lines rhyming, the third and fourth lines rhyming, and a surprising fifth line, as in Ciardi's *The Hopeful Trout and Other Limericks* (1989) and Kennedy's *Uncle Switch: Loony Limericks* (1997). Contrary to popular belief, Edward Lear did not originate the limerick, but did do much to popularize it.

Free verse is in direct contrast to limericks and haiku since it is unstructured with no required rhyme or rhythm and can be about a broad range of possible topics from daily experiences to philosophical thoughts. Although it sounds much like other poetry when read aloud, it often looks different on the printed page, as in Giovanni's *Spin a Soft Black Song* (1987) and Jones's *The Trees Stand Shining* (1993).

Concrete poetry illustrates itself as it uses the shapes of lines or words to comprise the poem and so is meant to be seen more than heard, as in Froman's *Seeing Things* (1974) and Lewis's *Doodles, Dandies: Poems That Take Shape* (1998).

Contemporary Realism

Stories in contemporary realistic fiction are set in the present with characters who encounter everyday experiences, problems, and relationships. Of all the genres in children's literature, this is the most popular because it is all about the reader. There are four major types, according to Huck and colleagues (2004). Two of these include becoming one's own person and coping with problems of the human condition; both are discussed in a section of this chapter titled Bibliotherapy. The third major type—living in a diverse world—is also discussed later in this chapter. The fourth major type—popular realistic fiction—includes the following subtypes:

- *Animal stories* in which the animal protagonist behaves like an animal and is not personified; this is a favorite genre with children who especially like horse and dog stories as in Haas's *Beware the Mare* (1993), which is followed by three sequels, and Hesse's *Sable* (1994)
- *Sport stories* that often present a hero or heroine who struggles to become accepted as a member of a team and eventually succeeds through hard work and determination, as in Christopher's *Penalty Shot* (1997) and Spinelli's *There's a Girl in My Hammerlock* (1991)
- *School stories* that concern students from kindergarten through the intermediate grades, as in Poydar's *First Day, Hooray!* (1999) and Hill's *The Year of Miss Agnes* (2000)
- *Mystery stories* that have won more children's choice awards than any other type of story and range from simple "whodunits" to complex character studies, as in Van Draanen's *Sammy Keyes and the Hotel Thief* (1998) and Byars' *The Dark Stairs* (2006)

Historical Fiction

Another form of realistic fiction is labeled historical fiction since it is set in a period remote enough from modern times to be considered history (Lynch-Brown & Tomlinson, 2005). Special concerns that are of unique importance to this genre are that historical accuracy is mandated and dealt with honestly, that the story not only brings the historical era to life but also portrays it through the eyes of the young protagonist, and that the writing style avoids giving undue emphasis to historical detail (Jacobs & Tunnell, 2004). Types (according to Blos, 1993) include the following:

- *Fictionalized memoirs* that are written by authors who have lived through a bygone era and include numerous details about daily life that interest readers, as in Wilder's *Little House in the Big Woods* (2007), which was the first of a series about the Ingalls/Wilder family, and Lee's *Earthquake* (2001)
- *Fictionalized family history* stories that carry on a tradition of passing family stories from one generation to another, as in Taylor's *Song of the Trees* (1975), which was the first of a series about the Logan family, and Holms's *Our Own May Amelia* (1999)
- *Fiction based on research*, such as Mazer's *Good Night, Maman* (1999) and Park's *A Single Shard* (2001); this subgenre constitutes the bulk of historical fiction for children and ranges

from books about the beginnings of civilization and civilizations of the ancient and medieval worlds to the post–World War II era from 1945 to the 1980s

Nonfiction: Informational Books

Used to supplement texts and other curricular resources, informational books are books that present concepts, generalizations, and facts about one particular topic. Informational books cover mathematics, social studies, science, music, and other curricular areas.

Teachers need to be familiar with the varied criteria used to evaluate informational books. The first of these is author *qualification,* covering competence in the chosen field and the ability to communicate knowledge to children and to distinguish among opinions, theories, and facts. The second criterion is *accuracy and currency* because students cannot be supplied with facts that are out of date or superficial or that rely on anthropomorphism (i.e., giving human traits to things that are not human) or on teleology (i.e., believing that there is an overall design in nature); *in many informational books the copyright date is crucial.* A third criterion is *interesting and accurate illustrations,* which help children comprehend technical principles and terms. A fourth criterion is the *scope and organization* of the text, requiring logical sequencing and both a simplification and limitation of material. A fifth criterion is *elimination of stereotyping and the presentation of differing views on controversial subjects. Self-containment* is the sixth criterion so that students need not consult other books or sources in an effort to understand the material presented because their enthusiasm for a particular subject may be quite brief. The final criterion is *style,* which should be lively and use vocabulary geared to the reading ability of the students.

A varied selection of informational books includes Ancona's *Powwow* (1993); Bryan's *All Night, All Day: A Child's First Book of African American Spirituals* (1991); Burleigh's *Flight: The Journey of Charles Lindbergh* (1991); French's *Caterpillar, Caterpillar* (1993); Fritz's *Shh! We're Writing the Constitution* (1987); Lankford's *Hopscotch Around the World* (1992); Simon's *Snakes* (1992); and Zaslavsky's *Number Sense and Nonsense* (2001).

Nonfiction: Biography

While biographies for adults must be completely documented, biographers for children have more latitude when describing and discussing the lives of real individuals. Still, the information presented must be based on known facts about both the subject and his or her time period. In that respect, biography differs from historical fiction.

Biographies belong in a literature program, according to Temple and colleagues (2002), because they help children learn from the lives of others and they encourage students to recognize links between a person's life and the historical and social times in which he or she lived.

Criteria for selecting biographies for children include two of those already cited when evaluating informational books (*accuracy* and *style*) as well as two others: *choice of subject* (a person of interest to children who has had an impact on society, whether positively or negatively) and *characterization* (the author's balanced approach when selecting actions, feelings and thoughts of the subject).

Types of biographies for children include *authentic biography* or true nonfiction, which represents the growing trend for young readers today and includes Fritz's *You Want Women to Vote, Lizzie Stanton?* (1995) and Stanley's *Michelangelo* (2000). A second type is *fictionalized biography,* which is the most common kind of biography for young readers because it allows the author more freedom to dramatize certain events and to personalize the subject even though the book is grounded in thorough research, as in Lasky's *The Librarian Who Measured the Earth* (1994) and

Latham's *Carry on, Mr. Bowditch* (2003). A subgenre of fictionalized biography is *biographical fiction,* which is more fiction than fact and consists entirely of imagined conversations and reconstructed action. Relatively rare today, it takes a historical character and uses him or her as the core of a story that is only semi-historical, as in Ringgold's *If a Bus Could Talk: The Story of Rosa Parks* (1999).

Children may also become interested in series biographies, a current trend that follows a format approach and includes the same kinds of information about each subject. Publishers include, for primary grades, Random House with its *Step-Up Biographies* and Holiday House with its *Picture Book Biographies,* and, for intermediate grades, Carolrhoda Books with its *Creative Minds,* and *Trailblazers, Achievers, and Sports Achievers,* and Little, Brown and Company with *Sports Illustrated for Kids.*

Bibliotherapy: Books That Help Children Cope

Simply stated, **bibliotherapy** is using books to help students cope better with adjustment issues and emotional problems. As children grow and develop, they encounter a multitude of concerns stemming from sibling relationships, family mobility, hospital confinement, parental separation, physical handicaps, or other issues. Some of their concerns arise chiefly within themselves, whereas others evolve from outside events or conditions that affect the children: for example, Jim and his divorced mother live alone, Jaime is obese and friendless, Jennifer's grandfather died last week, and seven-year-old Luis has already lived in several different states. Much like Luis, the children in Mrs. Lyons' room in Vignette 7.1 will soon be moving to other parts of the country and saying goodbye to their friends, due to the relocation of their parents' employer.

VIGNETTE 7.1   Using Bibliotherapy

Like the rest of the town, Mrs. Lyons feared that the big local automaker might relocate to another part of the country. She knew the decision would leave hundreds of people without work and force almost as many families to relocate. She decided to prepare her first graders for the possibility by introducing several books about moving and saying goodbye to friends.

Mrs. Lyons consulted several journals and online sources to find picture books that dealt with the subject in a way her six- and seven-year-olds could understand. The class already enjoyed a daily story time, and she decided to read one of these books to the class every few days and test the response.

She began with *The Berenstain Bears' Moving Day,* which not only described a young character's move to a new home but the parents' problems that necessitated it. The students sympathized with Brother Bear's fears and smiled when his parents promised he could take all his toys and books to the new house.

After reading the story, Mrs. Lyons led the class in a short discussion. "Why did Brother Bear have to move away?" she asked.

"Because there weren't trees," Ian said, referring to Papa Bear's dilemma as a carpenter who runs out of lumber.

"Because of the dirt," added Anna.

"You're both right," Mrs. Lyons responded. "Papa Bear didn't have enough trees, and Mama Bear's garden wouldn't grow. They had to move to find more trees and a better place to grow vegetables." With the story as a springboard, Mrs. Lyons led the children in a discussion about "grown-up" jobs. Several members of the class, including a few children whose parents worked at the auto plant, participated in the discussion.

"So if my dad got a different job, I might have to go away," said Victor. Victor's father didn't work at the auto plant, but Mrs. Lyons still carefully considered her response. Before beginning this reading emphasis, she had decided she would encourage helpful conversations in the classroom, but would not cause unnecessary alarm or overstep her boundaries into conversations that parents should lead.

"That might happen someday," she answered after a moment. "Or it might not. If it happened, you might feel sad like Brother Bear at the beginning of the story."

"And then when I made friends at my new house, I'd be happy like Brother Bear at the end!" Victor interrupted.

"Right," she said, and inwardly sighed with relief.

Over the next few weeks, Mrs. Lyons read a few more stories about moving, interspersing them among the story time favorites and facilitating discussions about the characters' actions and feelings.

At the end of the month, her fears were realized and the automaker announced a shutdown of the plant in just a few weeks' time. Within days, several families informed her they would be moving at the winter break. News of the upcoming moves spread through the classroom.

Mrs. Lyons had saved one last book about moving, Viorst's charming *Alexander, Who's Not (Do You Hear Me? I Mean It) Going to Move* (1995). As she read it to the class, the children remembered the character from other *Alexander* books and thoroughly enjoyed this latest tale of rebellion against adults. They laughed as he suggests alternatives to moving and sat quietly as he talks about the "special people" and "special places" dear to his heart.

After finishing the book, Mrs. Lyons said, "We have some people in our class who are moving, don't we?" The students nodded solemnly. "They will say goodbye to their special places and special people, too. They will make friends in their new school, but it will be sad to say goodbye."

"I don't want to go!" said Erin, one of the children leaving in December.

"You sound like Alexander," her friend Andrea said with a smile, and the class laughed and relaxed.

"It's normal to feel that way," said Mrs. Lyons. "So here's what I'd like us to do. If you are moving, I want you to draw a picture of a special place or special person that you're leaving here. If you're not moving, I want you to draw a picture or write a message for the students who are. Work quietly and later this afternoon you can each share your work with the class."

Mrs. Lyons watched the students find crayons and sheets of paper. She knew the moves would be difficult for the children and it would take more than a few picture books to ease that transition. But the students were talking about their feelings and finding a context for them in works of literature. It was a positive step.

Books can help these students attain some degree of understanding of their personal difficulties and learn to accept problems in a wholesome manner. Books that provide a source of insight and relief from the varied pressures that young readers face during the ups and downs of normal development comprise bibliotherapy.

Sawyer (2000) has identified five benefits of using bibliotherapy. First, it provides accurate information, allowing each child to see problems in a proper perspective. Second, it offers mutuality and reduces the sense of isolation that a child may feel when confronted with a problem that seems insurmountable. Third, it develops empathy for persons who appear to the child as being different. Fourth, it offers options for resolving difficult problems as book characters provide alternative ways to solve critical situations. Finally, it gives a reaffirmation of life that may not eliminate the child's problem but does help put it in perspective after all of the negative coverage offered daily by the media.

Once defined as the interaction between the content of a particular piece of literature and the personality of the reader, bibliotherapy may generally be used by the teacher in two ways. Teachers use *preventive bibliotherapy* because they believe that students will be better able to make satisfying adjustments to some trying situations in the future, provided they have met similar problems in the stories they read or hear. In this sense, preventive bibliotherapy is analogous to an inoculation: It contributes to understanding and compassion as it offers children attitudes and standards of behavior that will help them adjust to some or most of the personal difficulties they may encounter. On the other hand, with *therapeutic bibliotherapy* teachers may attempt to solve students' actual problems vicariously through books. By recognizing their concerns and possible solutions in literature, the children will presumably gain new insight and become more able to take steps toward resolving personal difficulties. They need reassurance as well as the knowledge that they are not the only ones facing particular problems.

Books designed to help change social and emotional behavior in a *nonclinical* context—for children without severe mental health conditions—can be part of bibliotherapy. Their content must be worthwhile and accurate, and their style must be respectful to children and not trivialize problems or resolve them in an overly simplified manner. Even fiction books must be realistic so that early in each story the child must be able to identify with the characters and the solution. Racial, religious, or ethnic groups must be pictured with accuracy and dignity. In short, any book selected for bibliotherapy should be a captivating book that children today want to hear or read.

A Sample of Selected Books Useful in Bibliotherapy

Those books marked with an *E* are picture books or easy-to-read books planned especially for the kindergarten–primary grades; those marked with a *J* are intended for intermediate grade students. In either case the teacher should examine each book to determine its appropriateness and use for his or her particular class.

A. FAMILY RELATIONSHIPS

1. Adoption
   (E) Gordon's *The Boy Who Wanted a Family* (1980)
   (J) Rosenberg's *Being Adopted* (1984)

2. Grandparents
   (E) Dexter's *Grandma* (1993)
   (J) Naylor's *Alice the Brave* (1995)

3. Stepparents

  (E) Keats' *Louie's Search* (1984)

  (J) Wright's *My New Mom and Me* (1981)

4. Siblings

  (E) Grant's *Will I Ever Be Older?* (1981)

  (E) LeRoy's *Billy's Shoes* (1984)

5. Divorce

  (E) Paris's *Mom Is Single* (1980)

  (J) Hogan's *Will Dad Ever Move Back Home?* (1980)

B. PERSONAL TRAITS

1. Courage

  (J) Calhoun's *The Night the Monster Came* (1982)

  (J) Crofford's *A Matter of Pride* (1981)

2. Honesty/Dishonesty

  (E) Blue's *Wishful Lying* (1980)

  (J) Hughes's *Honestly, Myron* (1982)

3. Loneliness

  (E) Skurznski's *Martin by Himself* (1979)

  (E) Teibl's *Davey Come Home* (1979)

4. Obesity

  (E) Philips' *Don't Call Me Fatso* (1980)

  (J) Smith's *Jelly Belly* (1981)

5. Perseverance

  (E) Simon's *Nobody's Perfect, Not Even My Mother* (1981)

  (J) Watanabe's *Get Set! Go!* (1984)

6. Shyness

  (E) Sharmat's *Say Hello, Vanessa* (1979)

  (J) Oppenheimer's *Working on It* (1980)

7. Being Bullied

  (E) Smith-Mansell's *Stop Bullying Bobby! Helping Children Cope With Teasing and Bullying* (2004)

  (J) DePino's *Blue Cheese Breath and Stinky Feet: How to Deal With Bullies* (2004)

C. ADJUSTMENT TO CHANGE IN ENVIRONMENT

1. Going to Camp

  (J) Danziger's *There's a Bat in Bunk Five* (1980)

  (J) O'Connor's *Yours Till Niagara Falls, Abby* (2008)

Bibliotherapy uses books to help children cope with emotional problems and adjustment issues, including those related to family relationships, personal traits, and changes in environment and physical ability.

2. Moving to a New Home

   (E) Viorst's *Alexander, Who's Not (Do You Hear Me? I Mean It!) Going to Move* (1995)

   (J) Paterson's *Flip-Flop Girl* (1994)

3. Going to the Hospital

   (E/J) Cilotta, Livingston, & Wilson's *Why Am I Going to the Hospital?* (1983)

   (E/J) Marino's *Eric Needs Stitches* (1979)

4. Going to a New School

   (E) Hamilton-Merritt's *My First Days of School* (1982)

   (E) Delton & Hoban's *The New Girl at School* (1979)

D. ADJUSTMENT TO PHYSICAL DISABILITY

1. Visual Impairment

   (E) Condra's *See the Ocean* (1994)

   (J) Lantz's *Mom, There's a Pig in My Bed!* (1992)

2. Hearing Impairment

   (E) Millman's *Moses Goes to School* (2000)

   (J) Blatchford's *Going With the Flow* (1998)

3. Speech Problem

   (E) Lears' *Ben Has Something to Say* (2000)

   (J) Kelley's *The Trouble With Explosives* (1976)

4. Cerebral Palsy

   (E/J) Fassler's *Howie Helps Himself* (1982)

   (J) Tuitel & Lamson's *The Barn at Gun Lake* (1998).

E. DEATH

1. Of a Parent

   (E) Dokas's *Remembering Mama* (2002)

   (J) Adler's *Daddy's Climbing Tree* (1993)

2. Of a Grandparent

   (E) Aliki's *The Two of Them* (1987)

   (E) Yolen's *Grandad Bill's Song* (1994)

3. Of a Pet

   (E/J) Graeber's *Mustard* (1982)

   (J) Fairless's *Hambone* (1980)

Selected Activities

When developing either a preventive or a therapeutic bibliotherapy lesson, teachers should plan activities to make certain that the problem or concern has been understood. Sometimes, ELLs and at-risk students may not readily comprehend the underlying theme of the book just presented. For this latter group especially, a useful strategy is creative problem solving *during* the reading whereby the teachers read almost the entire book aloud before stopping to collect predictions:

They ask students to ponder the clues from the book and attempt to determine how the main character's problem will be solved. Then when the read-aloud is completed, the children compare their predictions with the author's solution.

Teachers who wait to implement activities *after* they have shared the book have several choices. Young children can be challenged through such projective devices as drawing or puppetry. Older students may wish to retell what happened in the story itself and explore the results of certain behaviors or feelings; they then reach a generalization about the consequences of certain conditions or traumas. Sometimes, both primary and intermediate students prefer to respond by personal journal writing, which allows greater privacy than discussion or art.

Living in a Diverse World: Multicultural Literature and International Literature

Multicultural literature comprises books that are published in the United States and involve cultural interests within this country. Books comprising *international literature,* on the other hand, are divided into two categories: (1) those written and published in the United States but set in another country and (2) those written and published in countries outside the United States and translated into English (if originally written in another language). Both multicultural and international literature can have important effects on the elementary school student because they promote an understanding and appreciation of persons who at first appear to differ from the reader while simultaneously offering a reassuring and positive picture of that reader's own culture; they also introduce students to literary traditions of varied world cultures or cultural groups in this country (Jacobs & Tunnell, 2004).

Multicultural Literature

Teachers who wish to evaluate a book of multicultural literature before choosing to read or share it with students should consider, according to Temple and his colleagues (2002), whether the author or illustrator is an insider (i.e., one who writes or illustrates based on a personal heritage) as in Polacco's *The Keeping Quilt* (1998); whether cultural details are accurate and integrated naturally, as in Yep's *Dragon's Gate* (1993); whether the culture is presented multidimensionally to reveal its range and depth of experiences, as in Walter's *Justin and the Best Biscuits in the World* (1986); and whether the language is used authentically, as in Soto's *Pacific Crossing* (1992).

There are four major microcultures listed under multicultural literature: African American, Asian and Pacific Islander, Hispanic American, and Native American. Lynch-Brown and Tomlinson (2005) caution, however, that teachers should be aware that each microculture contains subgroups that differ from one another in language, present location, race, country of origin, and traditions. Teachers must therefore not present these microcultures as completely uniform because such overgeneralization is both false and a form of stereotyping.

Listed below are a sampling of multicultural titles from the final (2002) edition of *Adventuring With Books* (McClure & Kristo). These represent books that meet specific criteria for excellence, *appeal to all age levels,* and include both prose and poetry, fiction and nonfiction:

African American Literature

Cline-Ransome's *Satchel Paige* (2000)

Dunbar's *Jump Back, Honey: The Poems of Paul Laurence Dunbar* (1999)

Hopkinson's *Under the Quilt of Night* (2002)

Johnson's *Lift Every Voice and Sing: A Pictorial Tribute to the Negro National Anthem* (2000)

Nobisso's *John Blair and the Great Hinkley Fire* (2000)

Smith's *Just the Two of Us* (2001)

Williams' *Girls Together* (1999)

Woodson's *The Other Side* (2001)

Asian and Pacific Islander Literature

Arcellana's *The Mats* (1999)

Bercaw's *Halmoni's Day* (2000)

Compestine's *The Runaway Rice Cake* (2001)

Compestine's *The Story of Chopsticks* (2001)

English's *Nadia's Hands* (1999)

Gilles' *Willie Wins* (2001)

Lewis's *I Love You Like Crazy Cakes* (2000)

San-Souci's *In the Moonlight Mist: A Korean Tale* (1999)

Yin's *Coolies* (2001)

Hispanic American Literature

Amado's *Barrilete: A Kite for the Day of the Dead* (1999)

Ancona's *Charro: The Mexican Cowboy* (1999)

Gerson's *Fiesta Feminina: Celebrating Women in Mexican Folktales* (2001)

Kimmel's *The Two Mountains: An Aztec Legend* (2000)

Laufer's *Made in Mexico* (2000)

Pitcher's *Mariana and the Merchild: A Folktale From Chile* (2000)

Rockwell's *The Boy Who Wouldn't Obey: A Mayan Legend* (2000)

Sierra's *The Beautiful Butterfly: A Folktale From Spain* (2000)

Native American (Indigenous Peoples) Literature

Ahenakew's *Wisahkecahk Flies to the Moon* (1999)

Bruchac's *Pushing Up the Sky: Seven Native American Plays for Children* (2000)

Francis's *When the Rain Sings: Poems by Young Native Americans* (1999)

Goble's *Storm Maker's Tipi* (2001)

Kusugak's *Who Wants Rocks?* (1999)

Nelson's *Gift Horse: A Lakota Tale* (1999)

Schick's *Navajo Wedding Day: A Dine Marriage Ceremony* (1999)

Waboose's *SkySisters* (2000)

International Literature

While multicultural literature helps children understand American society, international literature promotes an appreciation for a global society. These books were originally published in a country other than the United States in the language of that country but later were published again in this country. The most common international books come from English-speaking countries such as Canada, Australia, New Zealand, and the United Kingdom because they need no translation (e.g., the *Harry Potter* series by Rowling and the Narnia series by Lewis, all of which were first published in England). Those from non-English-speaking countries must be translated carefully with a fluent and readable narrative that still retains some flavor of the country of origin and even includes a few foreign words and phrases. Above all, critics agree, they should not be too "Americanized."

Listed below are examples of books from the final (2002) edition of *Adventuring With Books* (McClure & Kristo) that meet specific criteria for excellence, including concepts and themes appropriate for children in Grades K–6:

For Primary Grades (K–2)

Godard's *Mama, Across the Sea* (2000); first published in France

Highet's *The Yellow Train* (2000); first published in France

Lester's *Ernie Dances to the Didgeridoo: For the Children of Gunbalanya* (2001); first published in Australia

Lindenbaum's *Bridget and the Gray Wolves* (2001); first published in Sweden

Stark's *Can You Whistle, Johanna? A Boy's Search for a Grandfather* (1999); first published in Sweden

Tibo's *Naomi and Mrs. Lumbago* (2001); translated from the French

Wheatley's *Luke's Way of Looking* (2001); first published in Australia

For Intermediate Grades (3–6)

Bjork's *Vendela in Venice* (1999); first published in Sweden

Buchholz' *The Collector of Moments* (1999); first published in Germany

Carmi's *Samir and Yonatan* (2000); first published in Israel

Dumas' *A Farm: Reflections From Yesteryear* (1999); first published in France

Le Rochais's Desert Trek: An Eye-Opening Journey Through the World's Driest Places (2001); first published in France

Rodda's *Rowan of Rin* (2001); first published in Australia

Skarmeta's *The Composition* (2000); first published in Venezuela

Vos's *The Key Is Lost* (2000); first published in Germany

For All Grades (K–6)

Sortland's *Anna's Art Adventure* (1999); first published in Norway

Vincent's *A Day, a Dog* (1995); first published in France

Wild's *Fox* (2001); first published in Australia

Instructional Activities

Literature can be shared in a variety of meaningful ways in which children enjoy participating and that grow naturally from the love of books. Such learning experiences furnish an opportunity for students to develop their creative potential and relate their personal feelings. Those experiences also provide exposure to new media and new ways of thinking about books so they can indeed become lifelong readers.

The activities that teachers can plan with or for their students should meet varying ability levels. Some are primarily *motivational* experiences, and others are especially *interpretive* activities although the division between the two types is not always distinct. *Often an interpretive or culminating activity for one child will serve as a motivating literary experience for another.* Teachers serve as the primary force, bringing literature into the classroom to promote or motivate children to read. However, they also guide or assist them when children wish to share their books with one another. Teachers should be aware that it is not necessary to follow each book that is read with some kind of report or interpretive exercise; they should not be distressed when some students (notably the higher achievers) prefer to continue reading rather than to take time out to participate in creative expression.

Motivational Activities

Storytelling: The most developmentally appropriate means of first exposing children to narrative literature is through the medium of the storyteller. Once introduced to storytelling, students can begin to appreciate the oral tradition of literature and may even be encouraged to tell their own stories one day. Telling stories is not difficult once the tale has been carefully chosen and a relaxed atmosphere established. The teacher–storyteller should perform dramatically—with gestures, body movements, facial expressions, and voice changes. When the story is finished, no follow-up is necessary—unless the tale prompted insight into cultural similarities or social values. A sampling of recently published collections of appropriate tales for storytelling includes Bini's *A World Treasury of Myths, Legends, and Folktales: Stories From Six Continents* (2000); Doherty's *Fairy Tales* (2000); Hausman and Hausman's *Cats of Myths: Tales From Around the World* (2000); Schwartz and Bush's *A Coat for the Moon and Other Jewish Tales* (1999); and Yolen's *Not One Damsel in Distress: World Folktales for Strong Girls* (2000).

Story reading: While many stories can be either told or read to the class, there are two broad categories of stories that can never be told effectively and must always be read. The first category covers picture books because their illustrations are an integral part of the plot, as shown in Chall's *Sugarbush Spring* (2000). The second category includes stories whose charm lies in their language due to either (a) the marked use of dialect, as exemplified in Look's *Henry's First-Moon Birthday* (2001) or (b) the strong individualistic style of the author, as in Kipling's *Just So Stories* (1996).

For reading aloud to children, teachers should look for books that they genuinely like themselves and that the students are not apt to read personally. Some of the older Newberry Medal books, for example, are considered dull by the standards of today's children, at least until their teacher reads them aloud to the group.

Both primary and intermediate students enjoy hearing their teacher read aloud, sometimes immediately after lunch recess or as the final activity of the day. Bunting's *The Memory String* (2000) is a favorite with younger children, whereas older students like Gantos's *Joey Pigza Swallowed the Key* (1998). Intermediate students may sometimes volunteer to read aloud to primary children during weekly visits with their "Buddies" whenever the teachers can arrange it.

Writing blogs: Teachers in the intermediate grades can have their children join a classroom online book club, much like Mrs. Hendershot does with her fourth graders, in which each student writes blog entries about the books he or she has read and also reads about what classmates have read and enjoyed, such as Alexander's *The Golden Dream of Carlo Chuchio* (2007), Ellis's *Jakeman* (2007), Gifford's *Moxy Maxwell Does Not Love Stuart Little* (2007), and Holt's *Piper Reed, Navy Brat* (2007).

VIGNETTE 7.2   Book Clubs and Blogs

After several years teaching second grade, Mrs. Hendershot had transitioned to fourth. The school district needed more teachers for older students, and she was ready for some new challenges.

At first, the semester unfolded as Mrs. Hendershot expected. After all, she had been certified K–6 and her student teaching experiences had included several classes of older students. It was a lot of work, but she enjoyed preparing new lesson plans that involved higher-level math, science, and language arts skills.

However, after several weeks Mrs. Hendershot noticed significant developmental differences between her previous classes of younger children and her new 9- and 10-year-old students. For one, they enjoyed expressing personal tastes in music, style of dress, and hobbies. At the same time, they also exhibited a more intense need to belong. To this end, the children gravitated to clubs, teams, and other structured opportunities for play and work in groups—and they talked during class much more.

In addition to these behaviors, Mrs. Hendershot noticed that her new class talked less about their schoolwork. While the little ones gave and received opinions quite easily, her fourth graders often "clammed up" or refused to contribute.

She especially noticed this tendency during reading and writing activities. First graders enjoyed reading aloud, hearing others read, and reacting to the material; the older students only reluctantly participated in class discussions. And while young children enjoyed reading and talking about a variety of books, the emerging individuality of the older students resulted in less interaction.

As she identified these differences, Mrs. Hendershot decided to rework her plans and build on the natural tendencies of her fourth graders. Her curriculum would not change, but she would initiate several activities to accomplish a new goal—dialogue about literature.

As the children entered the classroom a few days later, they noticed several large posterboard signs around the room sporting large blue letters naming different literary genres. Mrs. Hendershot instructed the students to grab a notebook and a pencil, choose their favorite type of writing, and move to that area of the room. "Rearrange the chairs so that your group is sitting in a circle," she added. After several seconds of considering their options, the children began relocating to "Mystery," "Biography and History," "Poetry," "Science Fiction," and "Real-Life Stories."

As Mrs. Hendershot expected, even this first step prompted a few questions. "I don't like any of these," Jeremy grumbled. "Well, pick the one you dislike the least," Mrs. Hendershot said cheerfully. Jeremy reluctantly joined the mystery fans.

When every student was sitting quietly in a group, Mrs. Hendershot explained that they had just joined their first book club. "In the middle of each group is a pile of brand-new books," she said. "The poetry club has collections of poetry, the history group has biographies, and so on. Today and tomorrow you will have time to read the book. If you don't finish the book at school, take it home for homework. The day after tomorrow each group will re-form and talk about the reading. Everybody grab a book!"

In addition to providing time to read during class, Mrs. Hendershot took a few minutes again the next day to discuss the clubs and the scheduled discussion time. By the third day, each of the children had completed their assigned book and seemed interested in sharing ideas with other like-minded readers.

That morning, Mrs. Hendershot briefly explained the process and ground rules for each group. The ideas of taking turns to talk and journaling about what they learned were familiar ones for the students, and they seemed energized by the challenge of identifying a club director, illustrator, and wordsmith by the end of the session. After concluding the introduction, Mrs. Hendershot asked the children to form their groups and begin by sharing their favorite part of their club's book.

She enjoyed observing the groups as she strolled around the classroom. The poetry group spent the first ten minutes deciding which poem to talk about first. The biography group got down to business after a short tangential discussion about Jack the Ripper. "We should read about him next time," Emily offered helpfully as Mrs. Hendershot walked by. "He's much more interesting than Charles Lindbergh."

Each group eventually settled into a rhythm of asking questions, thinking about ideas, and sharing answers. Mrs. Hendershot was proud of the children's willingness to try the new activity and surprised by their enthusiasm. A few students even seemed disappointed when the group time ended.

The students needed less "getting-started" time the next day; within a few minutes of circling their desks the club members had launched into discussion. Several children shared thoughts about the literature from their journals, and two illustrators contributed drawings of major scenes.

As the group time ended for the day, Mrs. Hendershot praised the students for their progress so far and introduced another new activity to create dialogue about the literature—a class blog.

"On our computer," she said, gesturing to the PC in one corner of the room, "I've created a simple blog page. Who knows what a blog is?" Not surprisingly, almost every student was familiar with the journal-style Web sites and their common features.

"We will continue to meet in our current book clubs for one more week," she continued. "I will assign some activities for your club to work on in addition to your discussion time. For instance, I may have the poetry group write a poem or ask the science fiction group to draw pictures of the planet in their story. But on our blog, everyone from every group can talk about the literature. Think of it as one online book club—it is a way for each of you to share what you're learning by writing blog entries, reading what your classmates write, and leaving comments. I want each of you to spend time contributing to the blog."

As the students left for the day, Mrs. Hendershot reviewed the week and her plans for the days ahead. By capitalizing on their needs for belonging by creating "affinity" groups, Mrs. Hendershot had made it easier for her students to explore literature. The blog would create an additional opportunity for dialogue—this time, across genres and across groups. Each step moved the classroom closer to becoming a more diverse community of readers.

After another week I'll ask them each to choose a new genre and a new group, she decided as she gathered her papers together and headed home. *By the end of the semester these students will be more eager to talk about books than their first-grade brothers and sisters!*

Attending children's theatre productions: Local papers may occasionally carry announcements concerning a local production for child audiences by a professional or college theatre group. Classroom discussions of the book to be dramatized, such as Galdone's *The Elves and the Shoemaker* (1984), can then be planned. Happily, admission prices for children for such productions are generally reduced.

Attending book fairs: During the annual Public Schools Week in the spring or the national Children's Book Week in November, some schools schedule book fairs to which all the grades are invited to display their creative reactions to particular works of children's literature. The fairs are held in the library media center and may involve commercial exhibits.

Keeping an author's birthday calendar: Primary teachers can post a large monthly birthday calendar and mark it with pictures of authors whose prose or poetry the class has enjoyed hearing and reading. In the intermediate grades the calendar can include a list of each author's books as well. Such calendars are particularly motivating if the names of students are listed together with those of the authors.

Joining a book club: Children can become interested in literature through membership in a publisher-owned book club such as Arrow, Scholastic, Troll, Trumpet, or Weekly Reader. Each publisher has separate clubs according to grade level.

By joining such a club, students focus on book reading and ownership. Teachers who distribute book club materials and organize the ordering of paperbacks for students also benefit as they earn bonus points that allow them to order free books for their classrooms. Paperbacks include a full range of quality literature from award-winning books to joke books.

Meeting book characters in person: Children can dress up as their favorite book characters and tell about themselves and their experiences. Some schools even have a characters parade on Halloween in lieu of traditional celebrations, which have been banned in some districts. Popular characters include Arthur (from the series by Marc Brown), Aldo (from the series by Johanna Hurwitz), Amber Brown (from the series by Phyllis Reynolds Naylor), and Ramona (from the series by Beverly Cleary).

Reading and writing newspaper headlines: A startling headline such as "Brave Dentist Threatened by Patient" may be tacked on the bulletin board, and primary children would then be encouraged to investigate further and discover Steig's *Doctor De Soto* (1982). Older students would be intrigued with "Stray Dog Runs Wild in Local Market" and discover DiCamillo's *Because of Winn-Dixie* (2000).

Participating in field or walking trips: Primary classes that visit the harbor during a study trip may wish to read Gibbons' *Boat Book* (1983) upon their return to the classroom. Schools that have limited funds for bus trips may encourage walking trips to the local fire station and thereby have young students eager to examine Flanagan's *Ms. Murphy Fights Fires* (1997). Older students can visit historical sites in their area, usually by bus but occasionally on foot, and then read books (sometimes printed privately and sold in the gift shop) about those places, such as Behrens' *Missions of the Central Coast* (1996) for California students.

Listening to community speakers: Resource speakers may be recruited from the community through the local Chamber of Commerce. These persons visit schools to make presentations to students, often as a public service, and thereby elicit interest in topics such as energy. After the visit older children may become interested in books like Chandler and Graham's *Alternative Energy Sources* (1996).

Making and reading monthly bulletin board displays: Students in the intermediate grades and teachers/students in the primary grades can arrange bulletin boards that announce new books (e.g., this year's Caldecott or Newbery Medal and Honor books) or book events (e.g., sale of used books at the local public library sponsored by its Friends organization). Some boards may feature authors such as David Wiesner, Russell Freedman, Sharon Creech, or Molly Bang who are prolific and award-winning writers. Other boards may stress literary categories such as sports stories or tall tales.

Teachers who join the Children's Book Council (12 W. 37th Street, New York 10018) for a one-time fee can receive a variety of materials ranging from posters to bookmarks to author brochures for the price of self-addressed stamped envelopes. These materials are useful for bulletin boards.

Interpretive Activities

Using story dramatization: Young children who have heard or read Howe's *Jack and the Beanstalk* (1989) can be quickly prompted to participate in story dramatization. Any props that are needed can be easily improvised by the players.

Making puppets and holding puppet shows: Children at every grade level can construct puppets of their favorite book characters, using a variety of materials ranging from paper bags to soda straws. Some groups may even prefer to present puppet shows based on such stories as Mayer's *Beauty and the Beast* (2000) or Kellogg's *The Three Little Pigs* (1997).

Constructing mobiles: Although the framework of the three-dimensional design is made of wire or wood, the pendants or suspended objects on the mobile can be made from a wide collection of materials that students can bring from home. The class may prefer to restrict the pendants to representing characters or events from a single story such as Speare's *The Sign of the Beaver* (1983) or to confine them to the stories of a single author like Virginia Hamilton.

Sometimes it is the teacher who supplies the materials for the mobile-making project. First, the students each list important quotations, incidents, vocabulary, or characters from a book they recently heard or read. Then they are given index cards, glue, thread, and scissors. Next, they cut the cards into different shapes (e.g., squares for quotations). The students copy each item on their list on a different card. Finally, they hang the card shapes one below the other in proper vertical sequence.

Making transparencies: Children can make transparencies of drawings of selected characters or scenes from a book that they have enjoyed reading. Once the drawings are completed, the book, such as Strand's *Grandfather's Christmas Tree* (1999), can be read aloud, wholly or in part, as the transparencies are projected on the overhead.

Making collages: Students, in groups or individually, can prepare a collage depicting a favorite scene from a book like Bunting's *Night Tree* (1991). On the background of a large piece of brown wrapping paper or burlap (to represent the setting) are attached an assortment of materials to represent the characters and objects.

Creating rhythms or dances: When a group or an entire class has completed a book like England's *3 Kids Dreamin'* (1997), the students may like to create a rhythmical interpretation of the story. More than one series of basic movements may be possible, and the audience may choose the dance interpretation that it prefers.

Painting murals: Brightly illustrated murals made of tempera paint, construction paper, and colored chalk may develop from the reading of a single book such as Lynch's *Gold Dust* (2000). A mural may also represent the composite of many books on a single topic such as The Zoo.

Presenting pantomime skits: Some young readers, especially those who are shy or have speech handicaps, enjoy sharing with their peers scenes from a book such as Child's *I Will Never NOT EVER Eat a Tomato* (2000). The pantomimes they present are short, lasting five minutes or less.

Drawing cartoons: Intermediate students familiar with newspaper and magazine cartoons can draw their own cartoons to depict important situations, problems, and events from a favorite book like Corey's *You Forgot Your Skirt, Amelia Bloomer! A Very Improper Story* (2000).

Filing instant replays: Children can be encouraged to dictate or write on index cards their brief accounts of the most exciting or critical incident in a book they have read such as Hearne's *Who's in the Hall? A Mystery in Four Chapters* (2000) for primary children or Stanley's *The Mysterious Matter of I. M. Fine* (2001) for older students. The 3 × 5 cards are then placed in a small box on the library table and shared by both teacher and the class.

Literature Circles: A Popular Interpretive Activity

Literature circles are simply small (temporary) groups of three to eight children who have all read the same book and wish to talk about it. They use written or drawn notes to guide both their reading and discussion. They may also develop their own questions about that book and then assist one another in answering those questions. A literature circle may last for one day on a picture book or two to three weeks on a novel. Nevertheless, when one book is finished and its discussion ends, the circle disbands and the students form new groups with new books.

Sometimes known as literature groups, literature study groups, or book clubs, literature circles promote both independent reading and writing as well as collaborative learning (Kroll & Paziotopoulos, 1991). It must be stressed that *the teacher's role is strictly that of facilitator,* not instructor or group member. While in Grades K–3, the teacher is generally present throughout the discussion; he or she supports it but does not dominate. In Grades 4–6 the teacher roams among the groups, resolving problems or lending support. Obviously, during literature circle time, some groups are choosing or reading their books while others are sharing their reactions and feelings, both oral and written, about a particular piece of literature, whether it is a picture book, novel, or biography.

Both fiction and nonfiction books are appropriate for literature circles. In either case, what is key to the success of such circles is that *there must be a variety and a sufficient number of book sets available* so children can choose. Once the teachers have collected the sets, they should then give book talks as they display one book from each set on the library table or chalk tray and finally ask the students to make their first and second choices.

Teachers should be aware of some of the benefits of using literature circles (Scott, 1994). First, such sharing of personal reactions to good books is necessary for students to improve their reading comprehension and develop their strategies and proficiency in responding to books. Second, since there is no ability grouping in literature circles, its members are concerned solely with the ideas and responses of their peers to particular books. Third, literature circles use the social atmosphere in the classroom to promote reading and involvement with books. Fourth, they support children's personal growth and confidence in future participation both at school and in the community. Fifth, the long-term goal of literature circles is to aid their members in becoming lifelong readers who enjoy sharing their reading interests with family and friends.

Regardless of grade level, literature circles share several common characteristics: Students each select personally the book they wish to read and then form temporary groups around that choice. They write in journals or reading logs and share their notes with the group. The discussions in the group are open and natural conversations centered about the students' reactions, connections, or questions about the core book; such in-depth discussions are sometimes termed *grand conversations* (Peterson & Eeds, 1990) as they attempt to promote genuine comprehension of the narrative. The circles meet on a regularly scheduled basis, with constant monitoring of the discussion process by the teacher. Finally, according to Samway and Whang (1996) and Martinez-Roldan and Lopez-Robertson (2000), ELLs and students in multicultural classrooms both benefit from participating in literature circles.

Classes that are new to literature circles might benefit from an introductory minilesson developed by Darigan, Tunnell, and Jacobs (2002):

1. An Inner Circle is set up in the middle of the room, comprised of five to six children (previously chosen and prepared) and the teacher.

2. An Outer Circle is set up behind the Inner Circle comprised of the rest of the students in the class.

3. The Inner Circle talks while the Outer Circle observes, knowing that its members will have an opportunity to talk later when they represent the Inner Circle.

4. Inner Circle members must stay on the topic at hand, be able to document their reactions to the book, and be respectful of each other's contributions.

To initiate stimulating discussion in a literature circle, each member of that group needs to play a specific role (Daniels, 2002). In a circle of six students, for example, the *director* would keep the discussion going, the *connector* would connect the story to the experiences of the group, the *illustrator* would share his or her drawing of a critical event in the book, a *passage master or literary luminary* would read aloud a passage that is especially appealing or dramatic and explain why it was chosen, the *word wizard* or *wordsmith* would remark on the author's unique word choices, and the *summarizer* would review both the book and the group's discussion of it. The teacher wisely demonstrates each role first before the initial discussion starts, since the students will rotate their roles after each session.

A sample lesson plan incorporating the concepts introduced in this chapter appears on p. 233.

Assessment

Due to the highly affective nature of individual responses to literature, the task of assessing student understanding of literary works calls for careful and authentic measures. Interaction with literature often involves all of the six language processes of reading, writing, listening, speaking, viewing, and visual representation. Teachers need to address each of these areas when gauging student progress. Regular and informal observations of students engaged in activities such as literature circles are essential in determining whether students are successfully communicating their ideas and reactions to reading. Do students use vocabulary terms appropriate for their grade level to converse knowledgeably about literary elements (e.g., character, plot, setting) and genres? Do students make predictions and ask "what if" questions? Written and creative interpretations such as book reviews, illustrations, and story dramatizations offer additional opportunities to check for student understanding. Do students make personal connections to reading, consider viewpoints other than their own, and show an appreciation for aesthetics?

Determining student engagement and progress when reading for pleasure requires a little detective work. Teachers can check reading logs and other written records to gather information about time spent reading and types of books students select for independent reading. Do students choose a variety of genres? Do they have a favorite author or exclusively read science fiction or nonfiction books? Again, teacher observations of student reading habits yield important clues to student preferences. Enthusiasm for reading, spontaneous book talks with peers, and engagement during silent reading periods offer insights to students' interaction with literature and attitudes about reading in general.

Working With English Language Learners

Children's literature is a key component to assisting ELLs in developing their reading skills. Interesting books from a variety of genres engage all learners and provide motivation for students to read new words and participate in literacy activities.

Multicultural and international literature works are very important for ELLs because they help diverse learners connect with what they are reading through their own knowledge of the culture depicted in the story and by seeing faces that look like theirs in the illustrations. Diverse learners can "relate" to the characters and situations in multicultural/international books.

Beginning ELLs: Beginning ELL students need exposure to short, high-quality, interesting stories, biographies, and informational books that connect to units of study in science and social studies. Stories that contain rhyme and repetition and are predictable provide extra support for the ELL student. Picture books, including storybooks, **wordless books** such as Briggs' *The Snowman* (1988), picture books of poetry and song, and concept books such as Ehlert's *Eating the Alphabet: Fruits and Vegetables From A to Z* (1994) provide a scaffold for students as they are learning to read in English.

Early intermediate and intermediate ELLs: As ELL children progress through the intermediate levels of English fluency they will be able to begin to read and comprehend more difficult books, including traditional literature such as folktales, myths, and fables. Interestingly, folktales, myths, and fables often also fall under the category of multicultural or international literature and so can be used by the classroom teacher to connect to students' cultures and languages. Examples include many multicultural versions of Cinderella from countries around the world: from Korea, Louie's *Yeh Shen* (1996), from India, Mehta's *The Enchanted Anklet* (1985), and from the Middle East, Climo's *The Persian Cinderella* (1999). Numerous retellings of the Gingerbread Man are also available including Kimmel's *The Runaway Tortilla* (2000) and Compestine's *The Runaway Rice Cake* (2001). Additional multicultural book titles that represent different cultural perspectives are McDermott's *Anansi the Spider: A Tale From the Ashanti* (1987), Palacco's *Rechenka's Eggs* (1988), and Oughton's *How the Stars Fell Into the Sky: A Navajo Legend* (1992).

Early advanced and advanced ELLs: Advanced ELLs can venture into more difficult traditional literature, such as legends and epics. They can also begin to try modern fantasy and science fiction, a very popular genre among older children now. Rowling's *Harry Potter and the Sorcerer's Stone* (1998) is generally considered to be appropriate for children ages 9 to 12; however, for advanced ELLs it may be more suitable for Grade 6 and up. Osborne's *The Magic Treehouse* (1998) is a fantasy series involving time warps and time travel. The books in this series are shorter chapter books and can be used for younger ELL students (Grades 3–5).

Practical Instructional Activities and Ideas

- *Listening centers:* Students can listen and read along with stories on audio cassette tapes and CDs that can be purchased inexpensively or checked out from the library. Often popular and classic stories are available in languages other than English. Fluent readers can record their own story reading for classmates to enjoy. Older students who have "reading buddies" can record favorite stories for younger students.
- *Sketch-to-stretch:* Students respond to a reading by sketching an image that connects them with the text. Teachers can have students draw after a read-aloud or after a period of independent silent reading. Students are encouraged to discuss the sketches with their peers. Although this technique is often used to aid comprehension, it is also an effective strategy in promoting student engagement and connecting students to literature on a more meaningful level.

- *Character masks:* Students can create masks using heavy-weight cardstock or, for the more adventurous, papier maché to represent characters from books. Students can then work in small groups to pantomime scenes from the story. Stories for this activity should include many characters. Animals are a favorite role for children to portray. Carle's *The Very Busy Spider* (1984) and the familiar fables of Aesop are possible titles to perform. Students can also propose and act out alternate endings.

- *Cooking:* Teachers can plan cooking activities with works of children's literature. After reading Muth's *Stone Soup* (2003) or Sendak's *Chicken Soup With Rice* (1991), teachers can send notes home to parents requesting that each child contribute one food item for their own collaborative crockpot of stew or soup. (Invite parents to help and share the meal.) If a school has restrictions about cooking activities, an alternative could be to prepare trail mix or a fruit salad based on the same concept of each individual making a small contribution for the common good. Concrete experiences are valuable in building understanding for all learners, and ELLs reap additional benefits from hands-on learning. Literature with themes on food, nutrition, and celebrations also offer opportunities to incorporate math, science, health, and social studies.

- *Opening lines:* Teachers discuss with students the importance of the first few lines of a book in grabbing the reader's attention. As students begin to read chapter books that contain fewer illustrations and graphic features, the first impression provided by the lead-in sentences is crucial. Teachers can provide examples from books with strong openings such as White's *Charlotte's Web* (2001) and Curtis's *The Watsons Go to Birmingham* (1995) as well as stories with weaker leads. Student opinions will undoubtedly vary about what is "strong" or "weak" and thus will stir up lively conversations about language and literature. As students become experts at spotting quality lead-ins, they can begin to discover attention-getting openers on their own to share with the class.

- *Bilingual books:* Many works of children's literature are written in two languages within the same book such as Ramirez's *Quinito's Neighborhood* (2005). Teachers can provide students access to bilingual books for independent reading times and include them in class read-alouds. Invite parents or other volunteers who speak another language to read these books with the class. Students who are ELLs will enjoy hearing the familiar sounds of their language, and all learners will delight in the experience of listening to the cadence of a different language.

- *Poem of the day:* A special time each day can be set aside for a poetry reading. Teachers can share many different types of poems including a variety of styles and topics while making sure to provide nonrhyming or free verse examples. Students can be encouraged to bring in favorite poems to read/share with class (with teacher approval). Finally, budding poets can recite their own works.

- *Mock trials:* After reading classic fairy tales, students can bring the characters to court. Is Goldilocks guilty? Should the Big Bad Wolf be sentenced to a term of community service? Not only does story reenactment encourage students to examine the stories more closely but it also leads them to consider alternate viewpoints.

- *Travel brochure:* To emphasize the story element of setting, teachers can have students create travel brochures advertising where the story takes place. The requirements for the brochure can be modified to accommodate a range of ability levels by increasing or decreasing the amount of written text, illustrations, or pages. Technology can easily be integrated into this activity by requiring students to search Internet resources for information and images or by using a desktop publishing program.

- *Story mapping:* Students can reconstruct the important elements of a story by drawing a story map. Graphic organizers can be photocopied for this purpose, but teachers who prefer a more creative, less-structured approach can permit students to sketch out their own interpretations of character, plot, setting, conflict, and resolution depending on ability level and purpose of assignment.

Figure 7.1 One Student's Sketch of the Story of Lionni's *Swimmy* (2007)

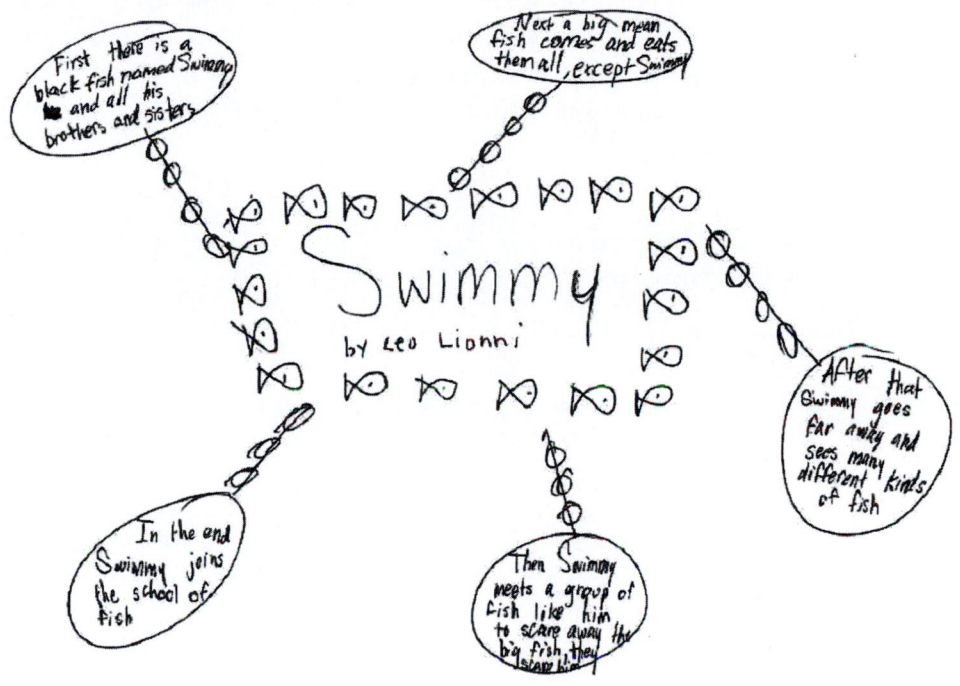

LESSON PLAN 7.1 Estimation and Rounding

Linking Literature to Content Areas

Language Arts Components: Reading and Writing

Subject Area: Mathematics

Grade: 5

Topic: Large Numbers

Time Frame: 1 week

Objective

- Students work in small groups to estimate, round, and manipulate very large numbers.

Materials

Per Class

- *How Much Is a Million?* (1985) by David M. Schwartz
- Pre-made charts with the headings "one million," "one billion," and "one trillion"

Per Group

- Blank chart paper
- Colored markers

Per Student

- Practice pages for estimating and rounding very large numbers
- Assessment pages for estimating and rounding very large numbers

one million	*one billion*	*one trillion*

Content Standards

Mathematics: Number Sense

- Students understand the relative magnitude of numbers.

Vocabulary

- Million
- Billion
- Trillion

Open

Engage

- Teacher explains that today we are going to learn about very large numbers.
- Teacher reads the book *How Much Is a Million?* to the class.
- Teacher shows the class the charts with the heading "one million," "one billion," and "one trillion." He or she leads the class in a discussion of what examples were given in the book for each and records student responses on the charts.

one million	one billion	one trillion
– tower of kids up to an airplane	– tower of kids past the moon	– tower of kids to Saturn
– 23 days to count	– 95 years to count	– 200,000 years to count
– whale-sized goldfish bowl	– goldfish bowl as big as a stadium	– goldfish bowl as big as a harbor
– 70 pages of 100 stars	– 10 miles of 100 stars pages	– roll of paper with stars from New York to New Zealand

Body

Explore

- Students work in small heterogeneous groups of four at their tables (one leader, one head recorder, one materials manager, one reporter).
- Groups explore the concept of very large numbers (one million). Each group is assigned one example from the book (e.g., tower of kids to the moon, 70 pages of 100 stars, etc.) to check to see if the author was correct in his calculations. The group must show their calculations on chart paper using words, numbers, and drawings.
- Teacher circulates throughout the room to facilitate group work and answer questions.

Expand

- Teacher gathers the whole class together.
- Each group shares its findings with the whole class via the reporter.
- Teacher and class discuss each group's findings.
- Teacher then demonstrates to the students how to estimate very large numbers (e.g., one million) using the information they learned from the book and their calculations. Students practice estimating very large numbers in their small groups.
- Teacher shows the students how to round numbers to one million, one billion, and one trillion. Students practice rounding very large numbers in their small groups.

Close

Apply

- Students think of their own examples to show one million. An example could be with popcorn. How big would the bag have to be? If time permits, the groups could convert their examples to one billion and one trillion.
- Students record their ideas on chart paper using words, numbers, and pictures. Students must show their calculations and the calculations must be correct.
- Teacher circulates to answer questions.

Assessment

- Individual: Each student completes a worksheet demonstrating that he/she can round very large numbers (millions, billions, and trillions).
- Individual: Each student completes a worksheet demonstrating that he/she can estimate very large numbers (million, billions, and trillions).
- Group: The teacher can assess the charts from "EXPLORE" and "APPLY" for accuracy, neatness, teamwork, etc.

Integration Across the Curriculum

Science

- Teacher can read a children's literature book, such as Dr. Seuss's *Fox in Socks* (2005), that ties into a science unit. In this example, at one point the fox plays in "gooey goo," a material that is similar to a substance that children can make by mixing white glue with a solution of water and Borax detergent. Concocting this "goo" works well in a unit on matter in first grade.

Social Studies

- Children's literature can be integrated with social studies units on topics such as The Community, State History, United States History, and Native Americans. The teacher can use grade-level appropriate literature pieces that support the state standards. Books that focus on family and community include Rylant's *When I Was Young in the Mountains* (1982), Flournoy's *The Patchwork Quilt* (1985), and William's *A Chair for My Mother* (1982). Historical fiction such as Hesse's *Out of the Dust* (1997) and autobiographies and biographies such as Uchida's *The Invisible Thread* (1995) offer students additional opportunities to connect with people and periods in history.
- Teachers can integrate geography concepts with both fiction and nonfiction books. Leedy's *Mapping Penny's World* (2000) introduces young children to map skills and spatial relationships. Teachers can enrich readings about time and place with globes, maps, timelines, and atlases. Nonfiction books that represent world cultures in an authentic manner such as Kindersley's *Children Just Like Me* (1995) can help develop children's awareness of a worldwide, global community.

Math

- Many children's books emphasize mathematics skills and concepts such as counting, number, and operations. Teachers can introduce new math concepts by reading books about shapes, ordinal numbers, and measurement. For example, Pallota's book *Hershey's Fractions* (1999) shows how a chocolate bar can be divided into equal parts and represented by simple fractions. Children can practice the concept by dividing up a real chocolate bar and writing the corresponding fractions.
- Teachers can also have grade-appropriate children's books that emphasize math in their classroom libraries. Children can choose to read these books during independent reading time. Carefully selected books can reinforce math concepts and skills previously taught. Axelrod's *Pigs in the Pantry* (1997) teaches about cooking and measurement, and Murphy's *The Best Bug Parade* (1996) introduces size comparisons. Geometry concept books include Hoban's *Shadows and Reflections* (1990) and Feldman's *Shapes in Nature* (1991).

Visual and Performing Arts

- Several good nonfiction books describe the lives and works of famous artists. Often these books are part of a series. *Smart About Art* (Grosset & Dunlap, 2001) is one series that spotlights artists like van Gogh, Matisse, Kahlo, and Cassatt, among others.

- Teachers can also encourage children to appreciate children's books as works of art in their own right. Illustrations use a wide variety of media, color palettes, and styles to evoke a mood and help convey the writer's intent. Rich photographs also enhance the beauty of the text. Books written with an awe and appreciation of nature but that still maintain high standards of content join science and art together in an amiable relationship. Ehlert's *Leaf Man* (2005) incorporates rich color copies of autumn leaves to heighten a sense of wonder about nature for any age group.

- Younger children can enjoy using puppets to act out Aesop's fables such as "The Fox and the Grapes" and "The Tortoise and the Hare."

Health

- Teachers can integrate books on health into health units. Teachers should choose fiction and nonfiction books that can serve as an entry point into a lesson or unit or can be used as reinforcement at midpoints. For example, a unit on the skeletal system can include Barner's *Dem Bones* (1996). This book teaches content information (e.g., lay and scientific names for the bones) through the visual (pictures) and auditory (song) modalities. Because this book is based on a traditional African American spiritual, it can be linked to the social studies curriculum as well.

- With current public concerns about childhood obesity and diabetes, teachers can stress good nutrition and the importance of exercise with children's literature that focuses on good lifestyle choices. Leedy's *The Edible Food Pyramid* (2007) has been updated to reflect the new food pyramid and nutrition guidelines.

Music

- Many traditional songs have been made into children's books. Zelinsky's *The Wheels on the Bus* (1990) and Trapani's *Itsy Bitsy Spider* (1993) are familiar examples that children will enjoy singing along with the teacher. Other books tell stories of characters who become directly involved in music in some way. Falconer's *Olivia Forms a Band* (2006) is one such example and is part of the popular *Olivia* series. Nonfiction children's books that address concepts in music or the lives of musicians offer additional depth. Nonfiction books that would interest children include Rubin's *The Orchestra* (1992) and Brunning's *Rock 'n' Roll* (1999). Still other books emphasize rhyme and rhythm and come with audiotape or CD versions so books can be "sung" in the classroom. Martin and Archambault's book *Chicka Chicka Boom Boom* (2000) serves double-duty as a fun and engaging song and a way for children to learn the alphabet.

Parents as Partners

These six suggestions encourage children to read children's literature at home:

1. *School literacy programs:* School-wide programs that encourage students to read children's literature at home can be very helpful to students' literacy development. Examples include summer library programs, Read Across America, and celebrations of Dr. Seuss's birthday (March 2, 1904).

2. *Homework reading log:* Teachers can encourage reading at home by making reading a required part of homework and including a reading log in the homework packet.

3. *Reading chair:* Teachers can have a comfortable chair in the classroom, such as a rocking chair, from which children can read books to the class that they have selected from the school or classroom library and wish to share. Parents can emulate this by setting aside a corner in the home for reading quietly.

4. *Book bags:* Teachers can provide weekly take-home book bags with three to four books selected for each student, based on his or her reading level and interests. If students are ELLs, teachers should also include books in their primary language whenever possible and encourage parents to read and enjoy these books with their children at home in a relaxed atmosphere.

5. *Library ambassador:* If the class is unable to visit a local library, teachers can invite a library representative to preview new books and discuss special programs that many libraries offer, such as hands-on demonstrations and guest speakers. Teachers should welcome parents to attend so they can be informed about the wide variety of resources the library has to offer, such as computer and Internet access, recommended reading lists, and bookmobile services. Teachers can later send home an informational newsletter for parents who were unable to attend the classroom event.

6. *Guest reader day:* Teachers can invite parents, grandparents, other family members, and even the principal to read aloud and share favorite books for an afternoon of reading on The Day of the Reader. Students can also participate by taking turns reading parts of their favorite books to visitors.

Student Study Site

The Companion Web site for *Language Arts: Integrating Skills for Classroom Teaching*
www.sagepub.com/donoghuestudy
Visit the Web-based study site to enhance your understanding of the chapter content. The study materials include chapter summaries, practice tests, flashcards, and Web resources.

Additional Professional Readings

Anderson, N. (2007). *What should I read about? A guide to 200 best-selling picture books.* Newark, DE: International Reading Association.

Glazer, J., & Giorgis, C. (2005). *Literature for young children* (5th ed.). Columbus, OH: Merrill/Prentice Hall.

Johnson, D. (2008). *The joy of children's literature.* Boston: Houghton Mifflin.

Kanten, W., Kristo, J., McClure, A., & Garthwaite, A. (2005). *Living literature: Using children's literature to support reading and language arts.* Columbus, OH: Merrill/Prentice Hall.

Lehman, B. (2007). *Children's literature and learning: Literary study across the curriculum.* New York: Teachers College Press.

Norton, D. (2005). *Multicultural children's literature: Through the eyes of many children* (2nd ed.). Columbus, OH: Merrill/Prentice Hall.

Raphael, T., Pardo, L., & Highfield, K. (2002). *Book club: A literature-based community.* Newark, DE: International Reading Association.

Sandmann, A., & Ahern, J. (2002). *Linking literature and the learner.* Silver Spring, MD: National Council for the Social Studies.

Wolf, S. (2004). *Interpreting literature with children.* Mahwah, NJ: Lawrence Erlbaum.

Yopp, H., & Yopp, H. (2006). *Literature-based reading activities* (4th ed.). New York: Pearson Education.

Children's Literature Cited in the Text

Adler, C. S. (1993). *Daddy's climbing tree*. New York: Clarion.

Adler, D. A. (1990). *A picture book of Benjamin Franklin*. New York: Holiday House.

Ahenakew, F. (1999). *Wisahkecahk flies to the moon*. Winnipeg, Manitoba, Canada: Pemmican.

Alexander, L. (1999). *The high king*. New York: Henry Holt.

Alexander, L. (2007). *The golden dream of Carlo Chuchio*. New York: Holt.

Aliki. (1987). *The two of them*. New York: Morrow.

Aliki. (1990). *Fossils tell of long ago*. New York: HarperTrophy.

Amado, E. (1999). *Barrilete: A kite for the day of the dead*. Toronto: Groundwood.

Ames, M. (1981). *Anna to the infinite power*. New York: Atheneum.

Ancona, G. (1993). *Powwow*. San Diego: Harcourt.

Ancona, G. (1999). *Charro: The Mexican cowboy*. San Diego: Harcourt.

Apy, D. (1991). *Beauty and the beast*. New York: Henry Holt.

Arcellana, F. (1999). *The mats*. La Jolla, CA: Kane/Miller.

Arnosky, J. (2002). *All about frogs*. New York: Scholastic.

Auer, M. (1992). *The blue boy*. Hightstown, NJ: Macmillan.

Avi, A. (1990). *The true confessions of Charlotte Doyle*. New York: Scholastic.

Axelrod, A. (1997). *Pigs in the pantry*. New York: Simon & Schuster.

Barner, B. (1996). *Dem bones*. San Francisco: Chronicle.

Bechard, M. (1995). *Star hatchling*. New York: Viking.

Behrens, J. (1996). *Missions of the central coast*. Minneapolis: Lerner.

Belting, N. M. (1992). *Moon was tired of walking on air*. New York: Houghton.

Bercaw, E. C. (2000). *Halmoni's day*. New York: Dial.

Bini, R. (2000). *A world treasury of myths, legends, and folktales: Stories from six continents*. New York: Harry N. Abrams.

Bjork, C. (1999). *Vendela in Venice* (P. Crampton, Trans.). Stockholm: R&S Books.

Blatchford, C. H. (1998). *Going with the flow*. Minneapolis: Carolrhoda.

Blue, R. (1980). *Wishful lying*. New York: Human Sciences Press.

Blumberg, R. (2001). *Shipwrecked! The true adventures of a Japanese boy*. New York: HarperCollins.

Briggs, R. (1988). *The snowman*. New York: Random House.

Brown, M. (1988). *Dick Whittington and his cat*. New York: Atheneum.

Brown, M. (2000). *Arthur's teacher moves in*. New York: Little, Brown.

Bruchac, J. (2000). *Pushing up the sky: Seven Native American plays for children*. New York: Dial.

Brunning, B. (1999). *Rock 'n' roll*. New York: Peter Bedrick.

Bryan, A. (1991). *All night, all day: A child's first book of African American spirituals*. New York: Atheneum.

Buchholz, Q. (1999). *The collector of moments* (P. Neumeyer, Trans.). New York: Farrar, Straus and Giroux. (Original work published 1997)

Bunting, E. (1991). *Night tree*. San Diego: Harcourt.

Bunting, E. (1994). *Smoky night*. San Diego: Harcourt.

Bunting, E. (2000). *The memory string*. New York: Clarion.

Burleigh, R. (1991). *Flight: The journey of Charles Lindbergh*. New York: Philomel.

Byars, B. (2005). *The summer of the swans*. New York: Viking.

Calhoun, M. (1982). *The night the monster came*. New York: Morrow.

Carle, E. (1984). *The very busy spider*. New York: Philomel.

Carmi, D. (2000). *Samir and Yonatan* (Y. Lotan, Trans.). New York: Scholastic.

Carroll, L. (1994). *Alice in wonderland*. New York: Putnam.

Catling, P. S. (2006). *The chocolate touch*. New York: HarperCollins.

Chall, M. W. (2000). *Sugarbush spring*. New York: HarperCollins.

Chandler, G., & Graham, K. (1996). *Alternative energy sources*. Minneapolis: Lerner.

Child, L. (2000). *I will never NOT EVER eat a tomato*. Cambridge, MA: Candlewick.

Christopher, J. (1991). *Wild Jack*. Hightstown, NJ: Macmillan.

Christopher, M. (1997). *Penalty shot*. New York: Little, Brown.

Ciardi, J. (1989). *The hopeful trout and other limericks*. New York: Houghton Mifflin.

Cilotta, C., Livingston, C., & Wilson, D. (1983). *Why am I going to the hospital?* New York: HarperCollins.

Cleary, B. (1993). *Ralph S. Mouse*. New York: HarperCollins.

Cleary, B. (1999). *Ramona's world*. New York: HarperCollins.

Climo, S. (1999). *The Persian Cinderella*. New York: HarperCollins.

Cline-Ransome, L. (2000). *Satchel Paige*. New York: Simon & Schuster.

Cohen, B. (1983). *Molly's pilgrim*. New York: Morrow.

Collington, P. (1993). *The midnight circus*. New York: Knopf.

Collins, D. R. (1996). *Farmworker's friend: The story of Cesar Chavez*. Minneapolis, MN: Carolrhoda.

Colman, P. (1997). *Corpses, coffins and crypts: A history of burial*. New York: Henry Holt.

Compestine, Y. C. (2001). *The runaway rice cake*. New York: Simon & Schuster.

Compestine, Y. C. (2001). *The story of chopsticks*. New York: Holiday House.

Condra, E. (1994). *See the ocean*. Nashville: Ideals.

Conrad, P. (1990). *Stonewords: A ghost story*. New York: HarperCollins.

Conrad, P. (1993). *The tub grandfather*. New York: Joanna Cotler.

Cooney, B. (1985). *Miss Rumphius*. New York: Viking.

Corey, S. (2000). *You forgot your skirt, Amelia Bloomer!* New York: Scholastic.

Crofford, E. (1981). *A matter of pride*. Minneapolis: Carolrhoda.

Curtis, C. P. (1999). *Bud, not Buddy*. New York: Delacorte Press.

Curtis, P. (1995). *The Watsons go to Birmingham*. New York: Scholastic.

Dahl, R. (1991). *The minipins.* London: Jonathan Cape.

Dahl, R. (2007). *Charlie and the chocolate factory.* New York: Knopf.

Danziger, P. (1980). *There's a bat in bunk five.* New York: Delacorte Press.

Delton, J., & Hoban, L. (1979). *The new girl at school.* New York: Dutton.

DePino, C. (2004). *Blue cheese breath and stinky feet: How to deal with bullies.* Washington, DC: Magination Press.

Dexter, A. (1993). *Grandma.* New York: HarperCollins.

DiCamillo, K. (2000). *Because of Winn-Dixie.* Cambridge, MA: Candlewick.

Doherty, B. (2000). *Fairy tales.* Cambridge, MA: Candlewick.

Dokas, D. (2002). *Remembering Mama.* Minneapolis, MN: Augsburg Fortress.

Dorros, A. (1991). *Follow the water from brook to ocean.* New York: HarperCollins.

Dumas, P. (1999). *A farm* (M. Logue, Trans.). Mankato, MN: Creative Editions. (Original work published 1997)

Dunbar, P.L. (1999). *Jump back, Honey: The poems of Paul Laurence Dunbar.* New York: Hyperion.

Ehlert, L. (1994). *Eating the alphabet: Fruits and vegetables from A to Z.* New York: Red Wagon Books.

Ehlert, L. (2005). *Leaf man.* Orlando: Harcourt.

Ellis, D. (2007). *Jakeman.* Markham, Ontario, Canada: Fitzhenry and Whiteside.

England, L. (1997). *3 kids dreamin'.* New York: Simon & Schuster.

English, K. (1999). *Nadia's hands.* Honesdale, PA: Boyds Mills.

Estes, E. (2004). *The hundred dresses.* San Diego: Harcourt.

Facklam, M. (1994). *The big bug book.* New York: Little, Brown.

Fairless, C. (1980). *Hambone.* Plattsburgh, NY: Tundra.

Falconer, I. (2006). *Olivia forms a band.* New York: Atheneum.

Fassler, J. (1982). *Howie helps himself.* Morton Grove, IL: Albert Whitman.

Feldman, J. (1991). *Shapes in nature.* New York: Children's Press.

Fitzgerald, J. D. (1995). *The great brain is back.* New York: Dial.

Flanagan, A. K. (1997). *Ms. Murphy fights fires.* New York: Children's Press.

Flournoy, V. (1985). *The patchwork quilt.* New York: Dial.

Fox, P. (1982). *A likely place.* Highstown, NJ: Macmillan.

Francis, L. (1999). *When the rain sings: Poems by young Native Americans.* New York: Simon & Schuster.

French, V. (1993). *Caterpillar, caterpillar.* Cambridge, MA: Candlewick.

Fritz, J. (1987). *Shh! We're writing the Constitution.* New York: Putnam.

Fritz, J. (1995). *You want women to vote, Lizzie Stanton?* New York: Putnam.

Froman, R. (1974). *Seeing things: A book of poems.* New York: Crowell.

Galdone, P. (1984). *The elves and the shoemaker.* New York: Clarion.

Gallaz, C., & McEwan, I. (1985). *Rose Blanche.* Mankato, MN: Creative Company.

Ganeri, A. (1999). *The young person's guide to Shakespeare.* San Diego: Harcourt.

Gans, R. (1980). *When birds change their feathers.* New York: HarperCollins.

Gantos, J. (1998). *Joey Pigza swallowed the key.* New York: Farrar, Straus and Giroux.

George, J. C. (1988). *My side of the mountain.* New York: Dutton.

Gerez, T. de. (1986). *Louhi, witch of North Farm.* New York: Viking.

Gerson, M. (2001). *Fiesta femenina: Celebrating women in Mexican folktales.* Cambridge, MA: Barefoot Books.

Gibbons, G. (1983). *Boat book.* New York: Holiday House.

Giblin, J. C. (1993). *The riddle of the Rosetta Stone: Key to ancient Egypt.* New York: HarperTrophy.

Gifford, P. (2007). *Moxy Maxwell does not love Stuart Little.* New York: Random.

Gilles, A. A. (2001). *Willie wins.* New York: Lee & Low.

Giovanni, N. (1987). *Spin a soft black song.* New York: Hill and Wang.

Goble, P. (1982). *The girl who loved wild horses.* New York: Athenum.

Goble, P. (2001). *Storm Maker's tipi.* New York: Athenum.

Godard, A. (2000). *Mama, across the sea* (G. Wen, Trans.). New York: Henry Holt. (Original work published 1998)

Gordon, S. (1980). *The boy who wanted a family.* New York: HarperCollins.

Graeber, C. (1982). *Mustard.* New York: Simon & Schuster.

Graham, L. (1993). *Every man heart lay down.* Honesdale, PA: Boyds Mills Press.

Grant, E. H. (1981). *Will I ever be older?* Portsmouth, NH: Heinemann.

Greenberg, J., & Jordan, S. (2001). *Vincent Van Gogh: Portrait of an artist.* New York: Delacorte Press.

Grimes, N. (2001). *A pocketful of poems.* New York: Clarion.

Guiberson, B. Z. (1991). *Cactus hotel.* New York: Henry Holt.

Haas, J. (1993). *Beware the mare.* New York: Greenwillow.

Hahn, M. D. (1986). *Wait till Helen comes: A ghost story.* New York: Clarion.

Hahn, M. D. (1994). *A time for Andrew.* New York: Clarion.

Hamilton, V. (1988). *In the beginning: Creation stories from around the world.* San Diego, CA: Harcourt.

Hamilton-Merritt, J. (1982). *My first days of school.* New York: Simon & Schuster.

Hausman, G., & Hausman, L. (2000). *Cats of myth: Tales from around the world.* New York: Simon & Schuster.

Hearne, B. (2000). *Who's in the hall? A mystery in four chapters.* New York: Greenwillow.

Hesse, K. (1994). *Sable.* New York: Henry Holt.

Hesse, K. (1997). *Out of the dust.* New York: Scholastic.

Highet, A. (2000). *The yellow train.* Mankato, MN: Creative Editions.

Hill, K. (2000). *The year of Miss Agnes.* New York: Margaret K. McElderry.

Hoban, T. (1990). *Shadows and reflections.* New York: Greenwillow.

Hogan, P. Z. (1980). *Will Dad ever move back home?* Orlando, FL: Steck-Vaughn.

Holms, J. L. (1999). *Our only May Amelia*. New York: HarperCollins.

Holt, K. (2007). *Piper Reed, Navy brat*. New York: Henry Holt.

Hopkinson, D. (2002). *Under the quilt of night*. New York: Atheneum.

Howe, J. (1989). *Jack and the beanstalk*. New York: Little, Brown.

Hughes, D. (1982). *Honestly, Myron*. New York: Atheneum.

Hulme, J. N. (1991). *Sea squares*. New York: Hyperion.

Innocenti, R. (1996). *Rose Blanche*. New York: Creative Paperbacks.

Johnson, J. (2000). *Lift every voice and sing: A pictorial tribute to the Negro national anthem*. New York: Jump at the Sun.

Jones, H. (1993). *The trees stand shining*. New York: Dial.

Jukes, M. (2005). *Like Jake and me*. New York: Yearling.

Karl, J. (1985). *Strange tomorrow*. New York: Dutton.

Keats, E. J. (1984). *Louie's search*. New York: Simon & Schuster.

Kelley, S. (1976). *The trouble with explosives*. New York: Simon & Schuster.

Kellogg, S. (1992). *Mike Fink*. New York: HarperCollins.

Kellogg, S. (1997). *The three little pigs*. New York: HarperCollins.

Kennedy, X. J. (1997). *Uncle Switch: Loony limericks*. New York: Margaret K. McElderry.

Kimmel, E. A. (2000). *The runaway tortilla*. New York: Winslow.

Kimmel, E. A. (2000). *The two mountains: An Aztec legend*. Fremont, CA: Shen's Books.

Kindersley, A. (1995). *Children just like me*. New York: Kindersley.

Kipling, R. (1996). *Just so stories*. New York: HarperCollins.

Koch, M. (1991). *Hoot howl hiss*. New York: Greenwillow.

Konigsburg, E.L. (1990). *Samuel Todd's book of great colors*. New York: Atheneum.

Kostyal, K. M. (1999). *Trial by ice*. Washington, DC: National Geographic Society.

Kusugak, M. (1999). *Who wants rocks?* Minneapolis: Tandem Library.

Lankford, M. D. (1992). *Hopscotch around the world*. New York: HarperCollins.

Lantz, F. L. (1992). *Mom, there's a pig in my bed!* New York: Avon.

Lasky, K. (1994). *The librarian who measured the earth*. New York: Little, Brown.

Latham, J. L. (2003). *Carry on, Mr. Bowditch*. New York: Houghton.

Lauber, P. (1998). *Painters of the caves*. Washington, DC: National Geographic Society.

Laufer, P. (2000). *Made in Mexico*. Washington, DC: National Geographic Society.

Lawlor, L. (1991). *How to survive third grade*. New York: Aladdin.

Lawson, J. (1993). *The dragon's pearl*. New York: Clarion.

Lear, E. (1991). *The owl and the pussycat*. New York: Putnam.

Lears, L. (2000). *Ben has something to say*. Fremont, CA: Shen's Books.

Lee, M. (2001). *Earthquake*. New York: Farrar, Straus and Giroux.

Leedy, L. (2000). *Mapping Penny's world*. New York: Holt.

Leedy, L. (2007). *The edible food pyramid*. New York: Holiday House.

Lenski, L. (1987). *Strawberry girl*. New York: Yearling.

Le Rochais, M.-A. (2001). *Desert trek: An eye-opening journey through the world's driest places* (G.L. Newman, Trans.). New York: Walker.

Leroy, G. (1984). *Billy's shoes*. Columbus, OH: McGraw-Hill.

Lester, A. (2001). *Ernie dances to the didgeridoo*. New York: Houghton.

Lewis, C. S. (1994). *The lion, the witch, and the wardrobe*. New York: HarperCollins.

Lewis, J. P. (1995). *Black swan/white crow*. New York: Atheneum.

Lewis, J. P. (1998). *Doodle dandies: Poems that take shape*. New York: Atheneum.

Lewis, R. A. (2000). *I love you like crazy cakes*. New York: Little, Brown.

Lindenbaum, P. (2001). *Bridget and the gray wolves* (K. Board, Trans.). Stockholm: R&S Books. (Original work published 2000)

Lionni, L. (2007). *Swimmy*. New York: Knopf.

Look, L. (2001). *Henry's first-moon birthday*. New York: Atheneum.

Louie, A.-L. (1996). *Yeh Shen*. New York: Putnam.

Lowry, L. (1984). *Anastasia Krupnik*. New York: Yearling.

Lynch, C. (2000). *Gold dust*. New York: HarperCollins.

Manning-Sanders, R. (1959). *A bundle of ballads*. London: Oxford University Press.

Marino, B. P. (1979). *Eric needs stitches*. New York: HarperCollins.

Martin, B., & Archambault, J. (2000). *Chicka chicka boom boom*. New York: Simon & Schuster.

Martin, R. (1992). *The rough-faced girl*. New York: Putnam.

Mayer, M. (2000). *Beauty and the beast*. San Francisco: SeaStar.

Mayne, W. (1994). *Hob and the goblins*. New York: DK Children.

Mazer, N. F. (1999). *Good night, Maman*. San Diego: Harcourt.

McCloskey, R. (1941). *Make way for ducklings*. New York: Viking.

McDermott, G. (1987). *Anansi the spider: A tale from the Ashanti*. New York: Holt, Rinehart and Winston.

Mehta, L. (1985). *The enchanted anklet*. Toronto: Lilmur.

Merrill, J. (1985). *The pushcart war*. New York: Harper & Row.

Millman, I. (2000). *Moses goes to school*. New York: Farrar, Straus and Giroux.

Miner, J. C. (1982). *New beginning: An athlete is paralyzed*. Minneapolis: Tandem Library.

Moore, C. C. (2005). *The night before Christmas*. San Francisco: Chronicle.

Munthe, N. (1983). *Meet Matisse*. New York: Little, Brown.

Murphy, J. (2000). *Blizzard*. New York: Scholastic.

Murphy, S. (1996). *The best bug parade*. New York: HarperCollins.

Muth, J. (2003). *Stone soup*. New York: Scholastic.

Naylor, P. R. (1995). *Alice the brave*. New York: Athenum.

Nelson, S. D. (1999). *Gift horse: A Lakota story*. New York: Harry N. Abrams.

Nobisso, J. (2000). *John Blair and the great Hinkley Fire*. New York: Houghton.

Norton, M. (1982). *The borrowers avenged*. San Diego: Harcourt.

O'Connor, J. (2008). *Yours till Niagara Falls, Abby*. Winter Park, FL: Hastings House.

Onyefulu, I. (2001). *Saying goodbye: A special farewell to Mama Nkwelle*. Brookfield, CT: Millbrook.

Oppenheimer, J. L. (1980). *Working on it*. San Diego: Harcourt.

Osborne, M. P. (1998). *The magic treehouse*. New York: Random House.

Oughton, J. (1992). *How the stars fell into the sky: A Navajo legend*. Boston: Houghton Mifflin.

Pallota, J. (1999). *Hershey's fractions*. New York: Corporate Board Books.

Paris, L. (1980). *Mom is single*. New York: Children's Press.

Park, L. S. (2004). *A single shard*. New York: Clarion.

Paterson, K. (1977). *Bridge to Terabithia*. New York: HarperCollins.

Paterson, K. (1994). *Flip-flop girl*. New York: Dutton.

Pearce, P. (1992). *Tom's midnight garden*. New York: HarperCollins.

Phillips, B. (1980). *Don't call me fatso*. Orlando, FL: Steck-Vaughn.

Pinkney, J. (2000). *Aesop's fables*. San Francisco: SeaStar.

Pitcher, C. (2000). *Mariana and the merchild: A folktale from Chile*. Grand Rapids, MI: Eerdmans.

Polacco, P. (1988). *Rechenka's eggs*. New York: Philomel.

Polacco, P. (1998). *The keeping quilt*. New York: Simon & Schuster.

Poydar, N. (1999). *First day, hooray!* New York: Holiday House.

Provensen, A., & Provensen, M. (1987). *Shaker lane*. New York: Viking.

Pullman, P. (1996). *The golden compass*. New York: Knopf.

Ramirez, J. (2005). *Quinito's neighborhood*. New York: Children's Press.

Ringgold, F. (1999). *If a bus could talk: The story of Rosa Parks*. New York: Simon & Schuster.

Rockwell, A. (2000). *The boy who wouldn't obey: A Mayan legend*. New York: Greenwillow.

Rodda, E. (2001). *Rowan of Rin*. New York: Greenwillow. (Original work published 1993)

Rosenberg, M. B. (1984). *Being adopted*. New York: HarperCollins.

Ross, T. (1986). *Foxy fables*. New York: Dial.

Rowling, J. K. (2000). *Harry Potter and the goblet of fire*. New York: Scholastic.

Rubin, M. (1992). *The orchestra*. Richmond Hill, Ontario, Canada: Firefly Books.

Rylant, C. (1982). *When I was young in the mountains*. New York: Dutton.

San Souci, D. (1999). *In the moonlight mist: A Korean tale*. Honesdale, PA: Boyds Mills Press.

San Souci, R. D. (1993). *Young Guinevere*. New York: Doubleday.

Sattler, H. R. (1995). *Our patchwork planet*. New York: HarperCollins.

Schick, E. (1999). *Navajo wedding day: A Dine marriage ceremony*. Tarrytown, NY: Cavendish.

Schwartz, D. M. (1985). *How much is a million?* New York: Harper Trophy.

Schwartz, H., & Rush, B. (1999). *A coat for the moon and other Jewish tales*. Philadelphia: Jewish Publication Society.

Sendak, M. (1991). *Chicken soup with rice*. New York: Harper Trophy.

Seuss, Dr. (2004). *Horton hatches the egg*. New York: Random House.

Seuss, Dr. (2005). *Fox in socks*. New York: Beginner Books.

Severance, J. B. (1999). *Einstein: Visionary scientist*. New York: Clarion.

Shannon, G. (1996). *Spring: A haiku story*. New York: Greenwillow.

Sharmat, M. W. (1979). *Say hello, Vanessa*. New York: Holiday House.

Siebert, D. (1989). *Heartland*. New York: HarperCollins.

Sierra, J. (2000). *The beautiful butterfly: A folktale from Spain*. New York: Clarion.

Simon, N. (1981). *Nobody's perfect, not even my mother*. Morton Grove, IL: Albert Whitman.

Simon, S. (1992). *Snakes*. New York: HarperCollins.

Skarmeta, A. (2000). *The composition* (E. Amado, Trans.). Toronto: Groundwood.

Skurzynski, G. (1979). *Martin by himself*. New York: Houghton.

Sleator, W. (1988). *The duplicate*. New York: Dutton.

Smith, R. K. (1981). *Jelly belly*. New York: Delacorte Press.

Smith, W. (2001). *Just the two of us*. New York: Scholastic.

Smith-Mansell, D. (2004). *Stop bullying Bobby! Helping children cope with teasing and bullying*. Far Hills, NJ: New Horizon Press.

Sobol, D. J. (1998). *Encyclopedia Brown and the case of the sleeping dog*. New York: Delacorte.

Sortland, B. (1999). *Anna's art adventure*. Minneapolis: Carolrhoda.

Soto, G. (1992). *Pacific crossing*. San Diego: Harcourt.

Speare, E. G. (1983). *The sign of the beaver*. New York: Houghton.

Spinelli, J. (1991). *There's a girl in my hammerlock*. New York: Simon & Schuster.

Spinner, S., & Etra, J. (1991). *Aliens for lunch*. New York: Random House.

Stanley, D. (2000). *Michelangelo*. New York: HarperCollins.

Stanley, D. (2001). *The mysterious matter of I.M. Fine*. New York: HarperCollins.

Stark, U. (1999). *Can you whistle, Johanna? A boy's search for a grandfather* (E. Segerberg, Trans.). Oakland, CA: Wetlands Press. (Original work published 1997)

Steig, W. (1982). *Doctor De Soto*. New York: Farrar, Straus and Giroux.

Steptoe, J. (1987). *Mufaro's beautiful daughters*. New York: Amistad.

Strand, K. (1999). *Grandfather's Christmas tree*. San Diego: Silver Whistle.

Sutcliff, R. (2005). *The wanderings of Odysseus: The story of the Odyssey*. London: Frances Lincoln.

Taylor, M. D. (1975). *Song of the trees*. New York: Dial.

Taylor, M. D. (2001). *Roll of thunder, hear my cry*. New York: Dial.

Teibl, M. (1979). *Davey come home*. New York: Harper & Row.

Thayer, E. L. (2000). *Casey at the bat: A ballad of the Republic sung in the year 1888*. New York: Handprint.

Tibo, G. (2001). *Naomi and Mrs. Lumbago* (S. Ouriou, Trans.). Plattsburgh, NY: Tundra.

Trapani, I. (1993). *Itsy bitsy spider.* Watertown, MA: Whispering Coyote.

Travers, P. L. (2006). *Mary Poppins.* San Diego: Harcourt.

Tuitel, J., & Lamson, S. (1998). *The barn at Gun Lake.* Minneapolis: Tandem Library.

Tunis, J. R. (1990). *Keystone kids.* San Diego: Harcourt.

Turkle, B. (1982). *Thy friend, Obadiah.* New York: Viking.

Turkle, B. (1999). *Deep in the forest.* Minneapolis: Tandem Library.

Turner, A. (2000). *Grasshopper summer.* New York: Aladdin.

Uchida, Y. (1995). *The invisible thread.* New York: Beech Tree.

Van Draanen, W. (1998). *Sammy Keyes and the hotel thief.* New York: Knopf.

Veciana-Suarez, A. (2002). *Flight to freedom.* New York: Scholastic.

Vincent, G. (1995). *A day, a dog.* New York: Handprint.

Viorst, J. (1995). *Alexander, who's not (Do you hear me? I mean it!) going to move.* New York: Atheneum.

Vos, I. (2000). *The key is lost* (T. Edelstein, Trans.). New York: HarperCollins.

Waboose, J. B. (2000). *SkySisters.* Tonawanda, NY: Kids Can Press.

Walsh, J. P. (1982). *The green book.* New York: Farrar, Straus and Giroux.

Walter, M. P. (1986). *Justin and the best biscuits in the world.* New York: HarperCollins.

Watanabe, S. (1984). *Get set! Go!* New York: Philomel.

Waters, K. (1996). *Samuel Eaton's day: A day in the life of a pilgrim boy.* New York: Scholastic.

Waugh, S. (1994). *The mennyms.* New York: Greenwillow.

Wheatley, N. (2001). *Luke's way of looking.* La Jolla, CA: Kane/Miller.

White, E. B. (2001). *Charlotte's web.* New York: HarperCollins.

Wild, M. (2001). *Fox.* La Jolla, CA: Kane/Miller.

Wilder, L. I. (2007). *Little house in the big woods.* New York: HarperCollins.

Williams, S. A. (1999). *Girls together.* San Diego, CA: Harcourt.

William, V. (1982). *A chair for my Mother.* New York: Greenwillow.

Woodson, J. (2001). *The other side.* New York: Putnam.

Wright, B. R. (1981). *My new mom and me.* Portsmouth, NH: Heinemann.

Yep, L. (1993). *Dragon's gate.* New York: HarperCollins.

Yin. (2001). *Coolies.* New York: Philomel.

Yolen, J. (1994). *Grandad Bill's song.* New York: Philomel.

Yolen, J. (2000a). *Color me a rhyme: Nature poems for young people.* Honesdale, PA: Boyds Mills.

Yolen, J. (2000b). *Not one damsel in distress: World folktales for strong girls.* San Diego: Silver Whistle.

Zaslavsky, C. (2001). *Number sense and nonsense.* Chicago: Chicago Review.

Zelinsky, P. (1990). *The wheels on the bus.* New York: Dutton.

References

Blos, J. (1993). Perspectives on historical fiction. In M. Dunnell & R. Ammon (Eds.), *The story of ourselves: Teaching history through children's literature.* Portsmouth, NH: Heineman.

Bogart, D. (Ed.). (2007). *Bowker annual: Library and book trade almanac.* New Providence, NJ: B. R. Bowker.

California Department of Education. (1987). *Handbook for planning an effective literature program.* Sacramento: Author.

Children's books in print. (2007). New Providence, NJ: R. R. Bowker.

Cramer, R. (2001). *Creative power: The nature and nurture of children's writing.* New York: Addison Wesley Longman.

Daniels, H. (2002). *Literature circles: Voice and choice in the student-centered classroom.* York, ME: Stenhouse.

Darigan, D., Tunnell, M., & Jacobs, J. (2002). *Children's literature: Engaging teachers and children in good books.* Columbus, OH: Merrill/Prentice Hall.

Glazer, J. (1997). *Introduction to children's literature* (2nd ed.). Columbus, OH: Merrill/Prentice Hall.

Huck, C., Hepler, S., Hickman, J., & Kiefer, B. (2004). *Children's literature in the elementary school* (8th ed.) Boston: McGraw Hill.

Jacobs, J., & Tunnell, M. (2004). *Children's literature, briefly* (3rd ed.). Columbus, OH: Merrill/Prentice Hall.

Kroll, M., & Paziotopoulos, A. (1991). *Literature circles: Practical ideas and strategies for responding to literature.* Darien, IL: Kroll.

Lukens, R. (1999). *A critical handbook of children's literature* (6th ed.). New York: Addison Wesley Longman.

Lynch-Brown, C., & Tomlinson, C. (2005). *Essentials of children's literature* (5th ed.). Boston: Allyn & Bacon.

Martinez-Roldan, C., & Lopez-Robertson, J. (2000). Initiating literature circles in a first-grade bilingual classroom. *The Reading Teacher, 52,* 270–281.

McClure, A., & Kristo, J. (Eds.). (2002). *Adventuring with books* (13th ed.). Urbana, IL: National Council of Teachers of English.

Peterson, R., & Eeds, M. (1990). *Grand conversations: Literature groups in action.* New York: Scholastic.

Samway, K., & Whang, G. (1996). *Literature study circles in a multicultural classroom.* York, ME: Stenhouse.

Sawyer, W. (2000). *Growing up with literature* (3rd ed.). Albany: Delmar/Thomson.

Scott, J. (1994). Literature circles in the middle school. *Middle School Journal, 26,* 37–41.

Sharp, P. (1997). *Only the best: A checklist to guide the selection of children's and young adult literature.* Portland, OR: Designs for Learning.

Stewig, J. (1988). *Children and literature* (2nd ed.). Boston: Houghton.

Sutherland, Z. (2004). *Children and books* (10th ed.). New York: Longman.

Temple, C., Martinez, M., Yokota, J., & Naylor, A. (2002). *Children's books in children's hands* (2nd ed.). Boston: Allyn & Bacon.

Anticipation Statement Answers

1. Agree

2. Agree

3. Disagree

4. Agree

5. Agree

6. Agree

7. Agree

8. Disagree

9. Disagree: Books with these types of themes can be beneficial by offering support and understanding to students with troubling issues. However, teachers must preview and evaluate texts for appropriateness and quality.

10. Disagree: Although the format (physical appearance) of a book is a very important criterion, teachers need to critique text on a variety of points such as content, theme, plot, and character believability (free from stereotypes) to adequately appraise children's literature.

PART III
Writing as a Language Art

Writing

Process, Genres, and Motivational Strategies

CHAPTER 8

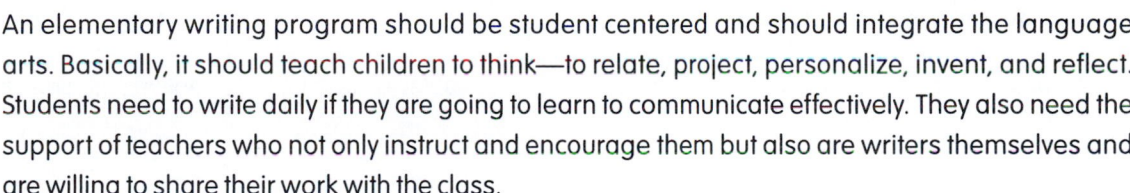

An elementary writing program should be student centered and should integrate the language arts. Basically, it should teach children to think—to relate, project, personalize, invent, and reflect. Students need to write daily if they are going to learn to communicate effectively. They also need the support of teachers who not only instruct and encourage them but also are writers themselves and are willing to share their work with the class.

Anticipation Statements

Complete this exercise before reading Chapter 8.

Do you agree or disagree with the following statements? Circle your answer. Be prepared to discuss questions in blue.

1.	To be successful at independent writing activities, children first need to be able to accurately recognize and form all letters of the alphabet.	Agree	Disagree
2.	Experiences with children's literature foster student interest in writing and stimulate good writing practices.	Agree	Disagree
3.	The five major stages of the writing process follow a straightforward and linear sequence.	Agree	Disagree
4.	Oral language proficiency correlates positively with writing ability.	Agree	Disagree
5.	Young children are able to make connections between punctuation and oral speech patterns.	Agree	Disagree
6.	Publishing of student writing encourages students to edit and revise their work while promoting a sense of self-worth.	Agree	Disagree
7.	Students should self-select writing topics.	Agree	Disagree
8.	Persuasive writing comes easily to most students.	Agree	Disagree
9.	Motivational writing strategies used for younger elementary students are generally not as effective for older students.	Agree	Disagree
10.	The main influences on children's writing performance are the classroom environment and teacher instruction/support.	Agree	Disagree

Guidelines for the Teaching of Writing

The curriculum for written composition in the elementary grades is concerned both with **writing genres** or the varied forms of promoting content that students wish to relate and the **writing process** needed for the most effective communication of that content. Both areas are addressed most effectively when teachers plan curriculum according to the following guidelines:

- *The child must recognize the significance of writing in his or her own life and in the lives of others.* Through daily contact with items such as labels, posters, maps, menus, coupons, charts, bulletin boards, and magazines, students can be taught to recognize the importance of writing—in the home, school, and community. Older children can study historical documents to help them accept the critical role of writing in both the present and the past.

- *The child must have a variety of experiences and interests about which to write.* Firsthand happenings at home or at school, on a field trip, or at a club meeting are all useful means of input. So are vicarious experiences through selected print or electronic media. Finally, hobbies and sports from camping to softball furnish material for writing. Input, however, can and must be supplied during the entire year through ongoing classroom activities and school events.

Applicable IRA/NCTE Standards

Standard 4   Students adjust their use of spoken, written, and visual language (e.g., conventions, style, vocabulary) to communicate effectively with a variety of audiences and for different purposes.

Standard 5   Students employ a wide range of strategies as they write and use different writing process elements appropriately to communicate with different audiences for a variety of purposes.

Standard 6   Students apply knowledge of language structure, language conventions (e.g., spelling and punctuation), media techniques, figurative language, and genre to create, critique, and discuss print and nonprint texts.

Standard 7   Students conduct research on issues and interests by generating ideas and questions, and by posing problems. They gather, evaluate, and synthesize data from a variety of sources (e.g., print and nonprint texts, artifacts, people) to communicate their discoveries in ways that suit their purpose and audience.

Standard 8   Students use a variety of technological and information resources (e.g., libraries, databases, computer networks, video) to gather and synthesize information and to create and communicate knowledge.

Standard 10   Students whose first language is not English make use of their first language to develop competency in the English language arts and to develop understanding of content across the curriculum.

Standard 11   Students participate as knowledgeable, reflective, creative, and critical members of a variety of literacy communities.

Standard 12   Students use spoken, written, and visual language to accomplish their own purposes (e.g., for learning, enjoyment, persuasion, and the exchange of information).

SOURCE: *Standards for the English Language Arts*, by the International Reading Association and the National Council of Teachers of English, Copyright 1996 by the International Reading Association and the National Council of Teachers of English. Reprinted with permission. http://www.ncte.org/about/over/standards/110846.htm

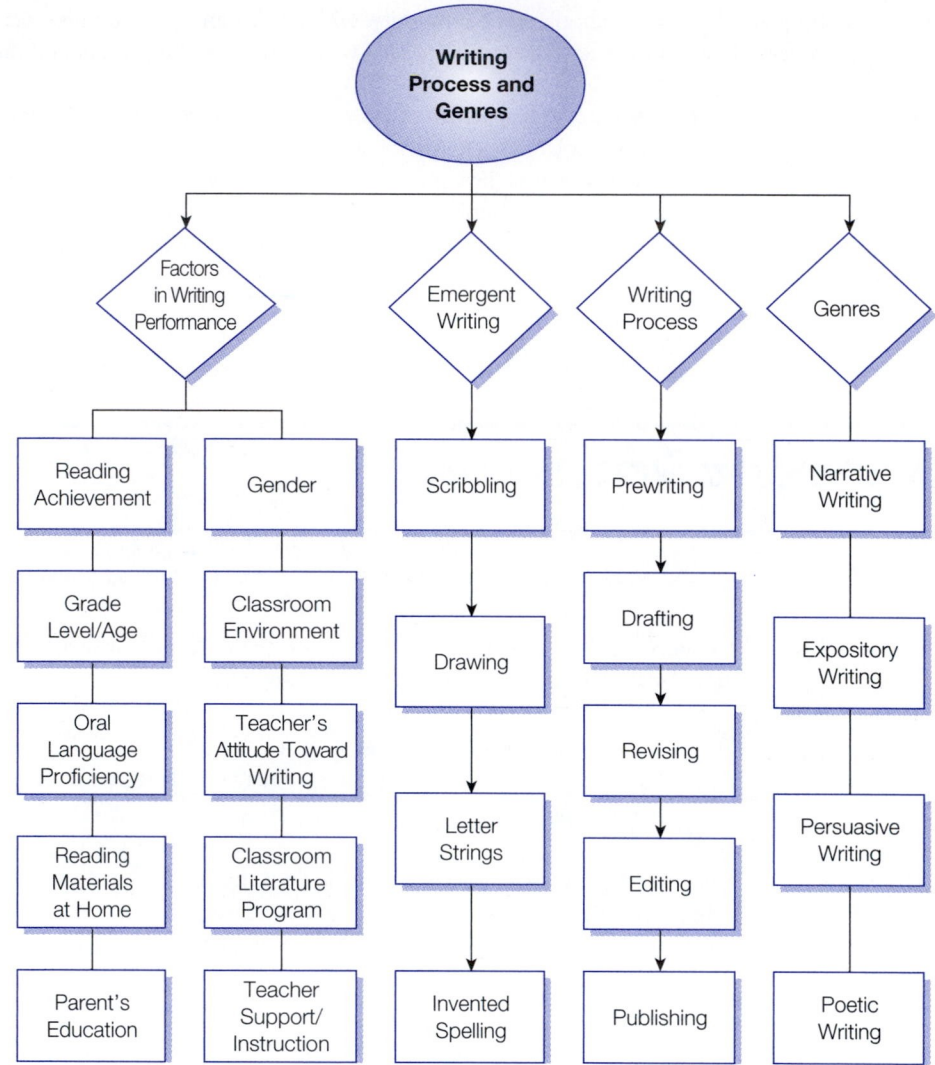

A Graphic Summary of the Contents of This Chapter

- *The child must enjoy a satisfying and supportive classroom environment in which he or she can communicate orally.* Speaking and listening habits profoundly influence children's ability to write, so until they can express themselves clearly through oral means, they generally are not ready to write. However, in a pressure-free atmosphere where students believe that their values, encounters, and feelings matter and can be shared freely with others, they are more apt to be able to use their oral contributions as a basis for their writing.
- *The child must hear and read literature to write well.* Next to direct experience, the reading children do is usually their most important source of new words and ideas. Because carefully chosen literature that is presented effectively can do much to stimulate good writing, a teacher should plan many types of literary experiences, including story dramatization discussed in Chapter 12.

- *The child must have a teacher who enjoys and practices writing.* Boys and girls taught by teachers who see writing only as a tedious chore with minimal application will adopt exactly the same attitude. In contrast, teachers who are writers themselves and willing to share their work with the class will promote student writing efforts.
- *The child must have broad-based experiences in which writing is integrated across the curriculum.* Students need frequent opportunities to write in content areas, such as math, social studies, and science. Often, these writing opportunities require separate journals for each subject.
- *The child must realize that a writer always communicates with someone when he or she writes.* The subject or subjects being addressed comprise "the audience." Writing style and language are both dependent on the nature of that audience. Elementary school boys and girls usually move from inner-person or self-as-audience to an unknown audience.
- *The child must appreciate that vocabulary is a major element contributing to effective writing.* Students can be taught to use a variety of sources for locating the words they need, including appropriately graded dictionaries, word boxes, glossaries in basal readers, spelling/vocabulary books, and special chalkboard or chart lists. To further improve their written communication, children must also learn to select expressive words, use synonyms and antonyms, and become acquainted with a beginning thesaurus.
- *The child must be aware that writing occurs in various genres/domains/purposes/forms.* Although these genres are not totally separate, each has a place in writing and thinking development. They include narrative (or expressive), expository (or informational), poetic, and persuasive.
- The child must understand that the writing process actually consists of five major stages: prewriting, drafting, revising, editing, and publishing. These stages are not necessarily linear or sequential in nature, and the amount of attention given to each stage will vary from student to student and from assignment to assignment. Beginning writers will generally spend more time in the prewriting stage than experienced writers.

Factors Affecting Children's Writing Performance

A variety of factors affects children's written efforts. In recent years studies have established the positive correlation of the following factors with the development of *most* student writers:

Reading achievement: Students who read well also write well, whereas those who read below grade level also write below the level of their peers. Furthermore, as students' level of comprehension increases, so does the number of compound and compound-complex sentences that appear in their writing.

Grade level and chronological age: Advances in grade and age correlate positively with the increasing length of written sentences. However, the difference between the low-achieving groups and their peers also widens at each successive grade level.

Oral language proficiency: Children who are rated above average in their use of oral language are also rated above average in writing, producing more words per assignment. Those below average in verbal ability also rate the same in written language.

Availability/use of reading materials in the home: Students from homes where families read and there are books, magazines, newspapers, and reference materials have substantially higher average levels of writing achievement than do students from homes where families do not read and reading materials are limited.

Parents' level of education: Students whose parents have a post–high school education have substantially higher average levels of writing achievement than do those whose parents have only graduated from high school. In turn, children of high school graduates are better writers than children whose parents have not completed high school.

Gender: On measures of complexity, boys and girls score generally at the same levels. On most measures of quantity, however, girls score significantly higher than boys. Girls also tend to write compositions that are judged to be of higher quality for that grade level.

Classroom environment: In informal environments children demonstrate that they do not need supervision in order to write. Such settings seem to favor boys, who write more than girls do in such environments, whether the writing is assigned or unassigned. Formal environments, on the other hand, seem to be more favorable to girls because they write more and also more often than boys do in these kinds of settings, whether the writing is assigned or not.

Teacher's positive attitude toward writing: If teachers dislike writing, their attitude will be adopted by the students. However, if teachers routinely compose with the class, the children will see that their teachers value writing. Briefly, if teachers want students to write, then they themselves must write and even share their work with the class.

Strong literature program in the classroom: The ability of children to write often depends on their access to hearing and reading good books. A balance between fiction and nonfiction, between prose and poetry, and between modern fantasy and modern realism will aid the writing program. Teachers should set aside time every day to share literary books with the students.

Teacher support and instruction: Teachers must introduce and guide children's efforts in the various genres of writing. In turn, students must acquire strategies to increase the quality and quantity of their written work. They need to be motivated by their teachers.

Emergent Writing

Although it was once believed that children could not learn to write until after they were able to read—and preferably had a minimal spelling vocabulary—teachers today realize that boys and girls can and do learn to write at an early age, provided that they are given encouragement—and writing tools—and see writing modeled. Each child passes through a series of stages in writing development, although not in a linear fashion and always at an individual rate.

Early Writing Stages

Scribbling: While young children make wavy lines or loops on paper as soon as they can hold a pencil or crayon, it is not until some time between ages two and five that they discover that their marks have meaning. They then may turn to a nearby adult (parent or teacher) to ask, "What does it say?" If that response is supportive, children will eventually, though gradually, emerge into alphabetic writing. Some features of that conventional type of writing, however, such as left-to-right and top-to-bottom directionality, do appear as early as the scribbling stage.

Drawing: Young children consider writing and drawing to be synonymous ways of communicating meaning and so will frequently "read" their drawings to interested adults. Moreover, drawing plays a supporting role in writing even after students have acquired the conventional forms of writing (Cramer, 2001). Children write with drawings for several reasons, primarily because drawing does not demand the same type of fine motor skill as alphabetic writing and because they have not acquired the alphabetic system for expressing meaning and see no special need to do so. Again, some features of conventional writing are apparent as early as the drawing stage.

Letter strings: Once girls and boys have learned to form letters and numbers, they begin to combine and recombine random strings of them in an effort to convey messages. (While there is no systematic connection between letters and sounds, some features of conventional writing do appear in these strings just as they did in earlier stages.) Of course, children need reassurance that they have "said" something important that a supportive adult can understand, so they may ask, "What did I write?" (Clay, 1975).

Invented spelling: This is considered a boon to **emergent writing** because it teaches children much of what they need to know about written language and therefore contributes to their learning to read and write (Fresch, 2001). Students become aware of letter–sound relationships and can use these in their writing, which now becomes alphabetic. Although at first a single letter will represent an entire word, such as "D" for *dog,* children gradually acquire more knowledge about letter–sound correspondence and consequently insert more speech sounds in their spelling.

Principles of Emergent Writing

There are several principles of emergent writing that were first identified by Clay (1975). These provide clues for teachers who wish to nurture children's early writing.

- *Meaning principle*: Written language is meaningful, and girls and boys see it on television, in books and magazines, and throughout the marketplace. Therefore, they too wish to communicate meaning through their written work.
- *Exploration principle*: Risk taking and discovery are crucial to learning to write, just as they are to learning to speak. Consequently, early writers investigate the use of letters and words in an effort to understand how they may affect their work. Their initial efforts may not always be decipherable, but should still be encouraged.
- *Sign principle*: The writing marks that children place on a paper stand for something in addition to the symbols themselves; indeed, those symbols convey meanings. Children must learn a daunting number of forms in which the symbols appear, including uppercase and lowercase letters, numbers, manuscript and cursive writing, punctuation marks, and other conventions of written language. Students learn the sign principle comfortably, according to Cramer (2001), if the environment provides meaningful exposure to print.
- *Generative principle*: Realizing that a few letter-like forms, used in a variety of combinations, can generate many "words" is an important principle for emergent writers. While these young children cannot spell or make traditional letters, they are convinced that the letters they do make carry messages. This is an important step toward writing.
- *Directional principle*: English is written from left to right and from top to bottom, and emergent writers may experience periods of confusion as they try to understand directional orientation. Such confusion is generally normal, developmental, and temporary and rarely a sign of dyslexia (Cramer, 2001).
- *Inventory principle*: Recalling what one knows is a metacognitive activity, and young children like to determine their letter and word knowledge. Consequently, they make "inventories" of uppercase and lowercase letters and various groups of words (e.g., those in a certain category such as family members, words beginning with a certain letter, or known words). What matters is that children take stock of what they know and then set new goals while teachers gain more information about student progress.
- *Spacing principle*: Emergent writers must learn to leave space between words. Those who initially ignore word boundaries or have difficulty indicating them should be allowed to use a temporary crutch of leaving a space between words the width of their finger or pencil.

Prerequisites for Beginning Writing

As young students slowly acquire the principles of emergent writing, the teacher is also introducing them to three skills that they must have to become independent writers.

1. *Writing the alphabet*: While beginners can copy words without ever knowing letters and sounds, this is not the same as making deliberate connections between them. Knowledge of the alphabet, together with **phonemic awareness** (as defined below), allows children to connect letters to sounds. They can then start to invent the spelling of many words and thus, with adult support, begin writing independently shortly after entering first grade or even kindergarten. They need not be able to form all the letters of the alphabet, but merely a few vowels and half of the consonants.

2. *Phonemic awareness*: The abilities to recognize that words are made up of a particular set of sounds and to manipulate those sounds are helpful for beginning writers. Once they can isolate one sound from another within words, they become able to associate speech sounds with the letters that represent them (Adams, 1990).

3. *Associating letters with sounds*: Girls and boys who can talk have learned the phonetics of their language. Long before starting school, they can recognize even slight differences in the sounds of the voices that surround them. This knowledge of phonology assists children in their writing earlier than has been previously recognized.

Abilities Needed for Effective Writing

Although good writing demands numerous skills, children need four major skills or abilities to achieve success in their writing efforts. Generally, these skills should not be taught in isolation but rather as opportunities arise. Nevertheless, in classes with English Language Learners (ELLs) or at-risk students, teachers should plan direct instruction in these areas, either with small groups or even an entire class, when they perceive that the children are not skilled in writing sentences or paragraphs or do not understand punctuation and capitalization rules.

Ability to Write a Sentence

This ability to write sentences begins to be developed in the primary grades with considerable practice in oral language as children use sentences that are clearly spoken and make sense. They can learn to write simple declarative sentences (e.g., Mrs. Licona is tall.) and simple interrogative sentences (e.g., Do you like peanut butter?), but always in the active voice. Intermediate students can learn to write compound declarative statements that may be either in the active voice (e.g., Josh and Sam are brothers.) or passive voice (e.g., Luis and Yuki are well liked.), as well as imperative sentences in which the subject (*you*) is understood but not stated (e.g., Look out!) and exclamatory sentences (e.g., Fire!).

Children at both grade levels learn that a sentence is a vital unit of language that expresses a complete thought. Older students also learn that each sentence has a subject (usually a noun or pronoun) and a predicate (verb) that must agree in number. It also ends with a period (.), a question mark (?), or an exclamation point (!).

Two common results occur when children begin to write sentences: Primary students often string several sentences together by overusing the conjunction *and,* whereas intermediate grade students write run-on sentences by overusing the comma.

Ability to Write Paragraphs

A paragraph contains one major idea and consists of a topic sentence, followed by several related sentences, and ending in a concluding sentence. Generally the first sentence in the paragraph is the topic sentence that states the subject of the paragraph and provides clues about its main idea. The start of each paragraph is indented, which helps remind writers that (another) new main idea will immediately follow. In a longer piece of writing, every paragraph is a separate subsection.

The sentences in a single paragraph must have a sequential order and some sort of coherence, whether the paragraph involves an explanation or describes a series of events. Teachers sometimes introduce children to the importance of this rule by placing on the overhead several paragraphs that contain sentences that are out of order. Students are then asked to organize each paragraph in a logical sequence.

Ability to Use Capitalization

During the preschool years children use only capital letters, but then in kindergarten and first grade they learn how to write both uppercase (or capital) letters and lowercase letters. Throughout the primary grades students learn many uses for capital letters, ranging from capitalizing their own first and last names, as well as the names of other people, to the use of capitals in letter writing, beginning with the inside address.

Children in the intermediate grades build on their earlier experiences, expanding and refining their ability to capitalize. However, they also have a tendency to overcapitalize by capitalizing too many words in a sentence under the mistaken assumption that all "important" words must be capitalized (Tompkins, 2004).

The most common uses of capitalization, according to Cramer (2001), are the following: first word in a sentence, first word in a quotation, proper nouns, proper adjectives, names of the days and months, initials, abbreviations, titles, and in the greeting and closing of a friendly letter.

Ability to Use Punctuation

Learning capitalization rules and how to use punctuation are both developmental processes. Children learn punctuation marks because these marks replace in writing the various intonation patterns students use commonly in oral expression; that is, the simple purpose of punctuation is clarity.

Starting in preschool, children notice punctuation marks and begin to distinguish them from alphabet letters (Clay, 1991). Then in kindergarten and first grade, students are introduced to end-of-sentence punctuation marks and learn to use them properly about half the time (Cordeiro, Giacobbe, & Cazden, 1983). One study of first- through third-grade bilingual writers found similar developmental patterns among second-language writers (Edelsky, 1983).

As children move through the grades, their punctuation skills improve naturally the more they read and write. They acquire "the mental image of sound" needed to convey meaning through punctuation (Chafe, 1988). Occasionally, however, a teacher may wish to present a short lesson to help convince the class how critical it is to use punctuation marks correctly. That lesson has four steps for the teacher to follow:

a. Read a brief paragraph carefully chosen from a piece of children's literature.

b. Place a transparency of the same paragraph on the overhead with the punctuation mark or marks omitted.

c. Hold a class discussion about how to punctuate the paragraph to aid comprehension.

d. Display the original paragraph.

A follow-up lesson would involve distributing unpunctuated paragraphs to small groups to correct using the punctuation marks.

The most common punctuation marks are the period (.), the question mark (?), the exclamation mark (!), the colon (:), the semicolon (;), the comma (,), quotation marks (","), the apostrophe ('), the dash (—), and the parenthesis ( ).

The Writing Process

In the past, in the traditional approach to writing, students depended on teachers to supply the topic for any assignment, thereby promoting what Graves (1976) terms "writing welfare." Today, however, children learn to assume responsibility for selecting their own topics for writing. This daunting task is accomplished through the *writing process* during which teachers guide students through five distinct stages of writing, sequentially labeled prewriting, *drafting, revising, editing,* and *publishing*.

The amount of attention and time spent on any given stage will vary from child to child depending on several factors, including the writing's *purpose, audience,* and *form.* The first factor is concerned with whether the student is writing to inform, entertain, or persuade; this purpose affects both the audience and the form of the product. Intended audiences vary from teachers, classmates, or family members to businesses or newspapers; however, children may also choose to write for themselves. The form of that writing may be a story, poem, or report, although students should gradually become familiar with many genres, including, chiefly, journal writing, narrative or story writing, poetry writing, expository or informational writing, descriptive writing, and persuasive writing. Since some ELLs are not familiar with writing genres, according to Gibbons (2002), they require special instruction in this area to succeed in school.

Prewriting

Said to be the main ingredient of the writing process, **prewriting** has been defined as "anything that is done prior to composing and that creates motivation, increases conceptual knowledge…stimulates the imagination or spurs new thinking" (Bergquist, 1996, p. 16). Its goal is simply to move the writer from merely thinking about a topic to the physical activity of writing about it. No wonder Murray (1990) believes that 70% or more of writing time should be spent in prewriting, as Mrs. Cartwright does with her sixth-grade students in Vignette 8.1.

VIGNETTE 8.1   **Ad Writing in Sixth Grade**

Mrs. Cartwright enjoyed teaching economics to her sixth-grade students, but wondered how much of the information they really understood. Like many preteens, they had mastered the art of buying (and asking Mom or Dad to buy). They were savvy consumers, but how could she help them grasp the fundamentals of supply, demand, and competition? Creating a real-life experience seemed the perfect strategy—and an excellent opportunity to teach prewriting and persuasive writing skills.

The next Wednesday Mrs. Cartwright led the class in a review as they ended the unit on capitalism. She knew they expected a test on the material the next day and wasn't surprised to see grins of relief when she announced she would postpone the exam.

"You will still be tested," she said. "But first, we're going to apply some of the ideas we've learned." She organized the students into groups of four and explained that each group was now an incorporated business. "Together you will decide what type of company you want to be—what you will provide or sell in our classroom 'marketplace.' And you will work together to create a promotional strategy to share your product with others."

After explaining more details about the project, Mrs. Cartwright allowed the newly formed business teams 45 minutes of group time for decision making. The students quickly began sharing thoughts; with amusement Mrs. Cartwright noticed one group huddling close together and speaking in whispers. Although the students thought only of making money, Mrs. Cartwright knew the talking was also a form of prewriting for the ad copy each group would later produce.

She continued the prewriting exercise by meeting with the groups one at a time to discuss their progress and answer questions. As expected, several of the groups planned to sell favorite products like homemade cookies and brownies before recess. Another group, which included several good students, wanted to offer tutoring and homework assistance. A third group pooled their video game collections and set a price for renting the titles to their classmates.

Other teams surprised Mrs. Cartwright with their creativity. "We don't have anything special to sell," Ryan said during his group's conference. "But every business gets part of the classroom for their store, right? So we're going to be cleaners—everyone else can hire us to make their part of the room look better for their customers."

After the small group meetings, Mrs. Cartwright pulled the class back together to continue preparing the students for persuasive writing. "I liked your business ideas," she told the students. "But it's not enough to have a good idea—you must let others know about the product you're offering. How do companies usually do this?"

"Advertising!" the class responded. "Exactly," she replied. "You'll need to consider the best ways to market your product, and your team will work together to write those advertisements."

With this introduction, Mrs. Cartwright launched a brainstorming session, prompting the students to consider how "real" businesses promote their products. After listing the children's ideas on the board, she gave each student an advertisement she had clipped from a newspaper or magazine or printed from the Internet.

"What is the message in your ad? What is the company trying to say, and does it do a good job?" she asked. "Take a few moments to write down your answers to those questions, and then I'll ask you to share your thoughts with the class."

After a few minutes of silent work, Carrie raised her hand with a question. "I don't understand my ad," Carrie said. "The company wants to sell toothpaste, but doesn't show anyone brushing their teeth."

Rick craned his neck over her shoulder and glanced at her ad. "It's full of facts about cavities and stuff."

"Why would a company create an ad that doesn't show anyone using the product?" Mrs. Cartwright asked. "What group could they be targeting with this strategy?"

"Dentists," said Rick. The class laughed and continued a lively discussion. By the end of the exercise, the students had analyzed a variety of print and digital advertising methods; in addition, they suggested several classroom-specific ideas, including daily and weekly rental of bulletin board space and ad space in the class's weekly newsletter.

Mrs. Cartwright dismissed the students for lunch and was pleased to hear several children still discussing the project. The class had worked hard in small groups, teacher conferences, brainstorming, and individual writing, and in just one morning the economics unit had taken on new life. The children even seemed eager to start developing marketing plans to share their business ideas with the rest of the class. The persuasive writing assignment would still be a challenge, but prewriting work had made all the difference.

Strategies for promoting prewriting vary with the age and writing experience of each student. Younger or less experienced writers are in greater need of them than older, more mature writers. Strategies that are both possible and useful and can readily be adapted to students with varied writing backgrounds include the following:

For material related to this concept, go to Video Clip 8.1 on the Student Resource CD bound into the back of your textbook.

- *Drawing*: Using art makes ideas come alive for both primary and older students. Teachers can encourage children to talk about their crayon or tempera drawings or even record their thoughts on the drawings themselves if children are not yet ready to write independently.
- *Talking*: Three kinds of talk can be useful for writing and so should be encouraged by the teacher (Cramer, 2001). The first is self-talk by the students as they plan and as they write; this is said to monitor thinking. The second is peer talk, which is generally informal and can occur in small groups as children discuss their writing plans. The third kind is teacher–student talk as children prepare to write, and it can take the form of prewriting conferences conducted individually, in small groups, or with the whole class.
- *Reading*: Both reading aloud and reading independently, depending on student ability and background, help prepare writers. Reading aloud informational books, for example, develops interest in a subject while it also provides the facts needed to substantiate the written product. In turn, such reading aloud frequently leads to independent reading because students are usually eager to read books that have been read aloud to the class. Published authors can offer children models of such challenging writing components as story beginnings or the concluding lines of free verse.
- *Mapping*: Done successfully as early as kindergarten, a map is an outline in graphic form, showing how topics are related to subtopics that in turn are related to supporting details. The type of writing to be done determines the form of the map; for example, a story map in the lower grades may consist of the topic and three subtopics (i.e., the beginning, the middle, and the end). Older students can benefit from a more complex map, especially if it is done as a group activity.
- *Questioning and researching*: Children jot down a few questions about real or imaginary situations (e.g., What would our town do during an extended power outage? What would happen if people could become invisible whenever they wanted to?). Students could research real topics on the Internet, in books or magazines, or in other resources. However, if the question were purely hypothetical, a creative writer could fantasize happily about the solution.

- *Brainstorming*: The teacher suggests one general topic (e.g., winter), and the children respond orally with as many related ideas as possible (e.g., building a snowman, sore throats, hockey). All ideas—whether appropriate or unrelated—are respected and must be called out quickly, as there is generally a time limit involved. Responses are recorded on the board. Although **brainstorming** is used often in other areas of the curriculum, it is particularly effective for prewriting because it enables children to become familiar with the range of ideas available in a specific category, such as poetry writing or biographical writing.
- *Factstorming*: While conducted much like brainstorming, factstorming, as described by Hennings (2002), concerns the student responses that offer factual—*not creative*—information about a topic. It can be held either as a pre- or post-information-gathering exercise or both. The teacher asks subject-centered questions, about elephants for example, and the facts elicited are written on the board. These data are then grouped and analyzed for shared relationships. Factstorming is especially valuable for expository writing when the reader is seeking data about a topic.

Drafting

Facing a blank sheet of paper and writing that first rough draft are never easy. However, students who have spent time doing one or more of the prewriting activities described above find drafting less intimidating. Students can write independently or in pairs, small groups, or at times even large groups, depending on the assignment or the teacher's instructions. Furthermore, at this stage, they need not worry about spelling, grammar, punctuation, or other mechanical constraints. Some find, according to Tompkins (2004), that as they prepare their drafts they may need to alter their earlier conclusions about the writing assignment's purpose, audience, and form; an anticipated story, for instance, may evolve into a report or poem.

An important element in **drafting** is the opening sentence or writing lead, which should attract the attention of the audience. Intermediate students especially should consider this matter carefully and develop such techniques as dialogue, questions, problems, brief stories, or facts in their effort to provoke the interest of the intended readers.

The teacher's principal responsibilities during the drafting stage are to be certain that the classroom atmosphere is conducive to writing and that he or she is available for reassurance, assistance, or occasional prodding. The children should see their own teacher modeling writing tasks from time to time, thereby directly displaying empathy for writers and indirectly validating his or her ability to teach writing.

Revising

During the third or **revising** stage, children rework their drafts, but the changes deal only with the *content* of the written text. To make their communication more precise, they insert and/or delete words and phrases and often rearrange their writing. According to Heard (2002), students must understand that revision is not a punishment. Instead, since the word means "seeing again," students should first reread their rough drafts and make some changes. Next, they can share that rough draft with their teacher and a small writing group of classmates, both of whom supply compliments and feedback, but only after listening to the composition. Finally, the students each commit to a plan for revision, which includes some or many of the suggestions offered.

At this point, the use of the computer is helpful, whether it is in a centralized school lab or in the individual classroom, because it simplifies the manipulation of the written text. Nevertheless, the final draft is still the creative effort—and responsibility—of the original writer.

For material related to this concept, go to Video Clip 8.2 on the Student Resource CD bound into the back of your textbook.

Editing

It is in the fourth or **editing** stage that students become concerned with the mechanical aspects of their writing or what Cramer (2001) terms "surface changes." These aspects include principally spelling, punctuation, paragraph indentation, capitalization, sentence structure, grammar, and format. Teachers should realize that the most effective way to teach mechanical skills occurs during the editing stage, rather than through workbook pages or practice exercises (Fearn & Farnan, 1998; Weaver, 1996), since children want to communicate with a genuine audience and sense the importance of correcting their mechanical errors.

In the early grades most editing is done in conference with the teacher since many beginning compositions are relatively brief and so require less editing time. By the third grade, however, students are more self-reliant and can be slowly introduced to editing techniques that they will eventually apply on their own. By the intermediate grades, many children can edit independently, provided that they have been oriented to correct proofreading procedures. Students in those grades often are pleased to use professional proofreaders' marks, such as shown in Figure 8.1.

A teacher can demonstrate proofreading by placing an unedited composition (written by an anonymous student) on the overhead projector. He or she reads it slowly, touching each word with a pen or pencil and marking or correcting possible errors with proofreaders' marks. Children can then proofread their own work, at first searching for only one type of error (e.g., capitalization), but gradually becoming able to proof an entire paper by themselves. Sometimes they may prefer to trade papers and peer-edit with a neighbor. Some classrooms even have "editorial boards" comprised of students especially adept at helping others locate mechanical errors.

Publishing

Publishing or sharing written work with an appropriate audience is the single best way to encourage children to revise and edit their writing (Elbow, 2002). It is an essential component of the writing process because it helps students become aware of the significance of their work. Otherwise, they may believe that what they write only fulfills a teacher-made assignment and has no importance of its own. In reality, however, there are four benefits of sharing written work, according to Cramer (2001). First, published pieces integrate writing with listening, speaking, reading, and content subjects and so they meet broader curricular goals. Second, they foster acknowledgment and acceptance of children's writing, promoting children's self-worth as writers. Third, students are motivated to improve their written products because publishing is a form of review by

Figure 8.1 Common Proofreading Marks

∧	Insert a word, punctuation mark, or sentence.	Christmas is here∧
≡	Capitalize.	He is mr. Mason.
/	Don't capitalize.	She moved to the State of Washington.
ℐ	Delete a word, punctuation mark, or sentence.	I can can go home.
¶	Start a new paragraph.	. . . my aunt. The horse ran away . . .

peers and others. Finally, an interested audience advances and strengthens the child writers' understanding of their own capabilities.

Sharing and publishing writing can be done in a variety of ways, including some that are done strictly within the classroom or school and others that involve outside sources.

Teachers *can prepare books or booklets* to be placed on the classroom library table where other students can read them. They may be individual efforts (e.g., "Family Pets") or collected works of small groups, all writing on a single subject (e.g., "The Importance of the Gettysburg Address"). Forms of such books range from simple *cardboard books* (whose covers are the same size as the stapled written pages) to the more elaborate *canned books* (in which an adding machine tape of written stories is rolled up and inserted into a juice can). Such "cans" can be decorated and placed on a shelf of Canned Books. Intermediate students can learn bookbinding under adult supervision and so prepare hardcover books.

Writing can be shared *with partners or small groups of classmates*. This sharing not only improves writing but also fosters pride and a belief that the writers have something worthy to express.

An "Author's Chair" arrangement can be set up whereby children share their work *with the entire class*. The teacher and students set rules jointly to encourage girls and boys to read aloud their work. Students take turns sitting on a high stool or "Chair" while the audience listens attentively and offers thoughtful but positive comments. Experienced teachers offer to set an example for this strategy by being the first to volunteer to sit in the "Author's Chair."

Writing can also be shared with audiences outside the classroom, as in the following activities:

- Reading the work aloud to parents, siblings, and other family members; grandparents are generally among the most enthusiastic supporters of young writers
- Participating in an Authors' Luncheon held monthly at the school site, with each classroom represented
- Participating in a Young Authors' Conference held yearly at a designated school district site or at a nearby college
- Submitting work to the PTA newsletter, school newspaper, or student page in a local newspaper
- Submitting work to national magazines and organizations that publish children's work; their names are available in Henderson's *Market Guide for Young Writers* (1996)

When students share their writing, teachers must consider the social interactions within the classroom context, according to Dyson (1993). These include the teacher's behavior, the children's behavior, and the interaction between the teacher and the children. Students must be taught how to respond to their classmates' work, and teachers themselves must model proper reactions without dominating the sharing period.

Finally, not all writing needs to be published or shared. Occasionally, writers may wish to put away or even discard some pieces for personal reasons. Still, they need reassurance that whatever they write is appreciated and useful.

Writing Genres

As mentioned earlier, a critical consideration in writing is the form or *genre* that any piece will take. This form in turn relates to its purpose (e.g., Does it inform or does it persuade?). There are four major genres of writing that students in the elementary grades encounter: *narrative, expository, persuasive,* and *poetic.*

Narrative Writing

Narrative writing concerns personal experience and imaginative writing. The first efforts a young child makes on paper indicate the beginning of narrative writing. Initially there is scribbling, then drawing of circles and lines to portray objects and persons, and finally the forming of letters. All this time, the "writing" remains both personal and important as children have a strong desire to share their ideas and thoughts with others through writing. Elementary students can complete various types of narrative writing.

Journal Writing

In every kind of journal or diary, the focus is always on the writer's thoughts and therefore not on the correctness of English mechanics. Britton and his associates (1975) describe this type of writing as a written conversation either with oneself or with trusted readers who are more concerned with the writer than with any mechanical errors. Journals are used for different purposes and kept for various reasons. Primarily, however, they encourage metacognition. Tompkins (2004) has identified six types of journals.

Personal Journals: In personal journals, children write about the events in their lives (e.g., a movie they went to see last Sunday), as well as about topics they want to discuss (e.g., their wish to own a motorcycle someday). Many classes commonly start each day with children writing informally for a few minutes in their notebooks or tablets. While younger students are eager to share their journal entries with the class, older children become concerned with issues of privacy and may wish only to share their thoughts with a trusted teacher. Personal journals are often collected and kept on a shelf near the teacher's desk after the entries have been made; they are then

Journals encourage metacognition, and younger students are eager to share their personal journals with others.

distributed the following day. Even beginning students can write or draw/write in their personal or dialogue journals (McGee & Richgels, 1996).

Dialogue Journals: In contrast to personal journals, dialogue journals resemble a written conversation with the teacher or a classmate. The student writes a short message of one or two sentences and leaves space on the same page for the correspondent to prepare a reply. Second-language learners especially benefit from writing dialogue journal entries and are more successful in this endeavor than in writing reading logs (Reyes, 1991).

Double-Entry Journals: Students divide each journal page into two parts, writing different kinds of information in each part (Barone, 1990). They can use these for either reading logs or learning logs. For reading logs, they can write questions or predictions on the left side, and then in the right column, they write the answers after reading the assigned literature or text. For learning logs they write major facts in the left column and their reactions to those facts on the right side. Younger students can just draw the predictions on the left side and then draw what actually occurred in the right column.

Simulated Journals: Intermediate students can assume the identity of another person and write from that individual's point of view. They can become a historical figure like Neil Armstrong or Marie Curie, or a character in a story like Ramona or Harry Potter. They must, however, include details from that historical period or from the story in their journal entries.

Reading Logs: Sometimes known as reading journals, literature journals, or literature response journals, reading logs record a list of books the writer has read during the school year plus his or her comments about each book. Students' responses to the poems, stories, and informational books they have read can be in the form of drawings as well as words or essays and include new vocabulary. Reading logs, according to Hancock (1993), may include character assessment and interaction, story involvement, the making of inferences and predictions, the expression of wonder or confusion, and literary criticism. Teachers can read the logs, tally the responses, and plan minilessons about responses that children are not using. Primary and older students alike can prepare reading logs although at different levels of maturity.

Learning Logs: Learning logs are records or reactions to what students are learning in content areas. In science, for example, they would include notes, diagrams, new vocabulary, observations, and directions for experiments, just as Mrs. Wong and Miss Pike do with their second graders in Vignette 8.2.

VIGNETTE 8.2   Science Learning Logs in Second Grade

Mrs. Wong and Miss Pike attended college together, often taking the same classes and helping each other with coursework as they pursued their teaching credentials. Now the good friends each taught a second-grade class at the same elementary school.

While Mrs. Wong had a natural aptitude for writing, Miss Pike loved to teach scientific principles and ideas. With the blessing of the administration, the teachers designed a project involving both subjects and both classrooms.

The idea was simple: conduct two experiments to correlate with the science curriculum, teach each class one of the two lessons, partner each child with a peer from the other class, supervise as the partners taught each other the experiments they just learned, and coach the children in writing about the experience. Miss Pike looked forward to the students mastering an experiment, and Mrs. Wong knew their notes, directions, and journal entries would be an important step in developing expository writing skills.

The teachers created two experiments for the project. In the first, Mrs. Wong's students would learn about carbon dioxide by filling a 1-liter bottle with water and vinegar, carefully spooning baking soda into an uninflated balloon, and then wrapping the mouth of the balloon around the top of the bottle. When they lifted the balloon and allowed the baking soda to fall into the vinegar and water, the mixture would create carbon dioxide and quickly inflate the balloon.

The second experiment also featured a bottle and balloon, but with very different results. In this project, Miss Pike's students would learn that hot air expands and cool air contracts. After pouring hot water into a bottle and placing a balloon on top, students would observe the balloon inflating from the expanding air (although less dramatically than in the first experiment!). Next the students would place the bottle-and-balloon combo into a bowl of ice water and watch as the bottle's change in temperature sucked the hot air out of the deflating balloon.

The teachers practiced the experiments over the weekend and kicked off Monday morning with an intro to the new science unit. Mrs. Wong demonstrated the carbon dioxide project for her class; they enjoyed the rapid expansion of the bright yellow balloon and Mrs. Wong's rush to keep the balloon from inflating too quickly and spraying the front row with vinegar.

As Mrs. Wong taught one experiment, Miss Pike demonstrated the other in her own classroom next door. Her students also enjoyed watching each step of the process and especially liked watching the bottle pull the balloon inside with the last bit of contracting air.

After completing the demonstrations, each teacher shared the scientific explanation and instructed the children to break into groups of three. "I'm going to do the experiment one more time, but I will do each step more slowly so you can follow along," they said. "Two of you will do the experiment. The third person will write down each step in a learning log." The teachers distributed materials as the students rearranged into groups and prepared to re-create the exciting effects.

Despite a little spilled water and a popped balloon or two, each group in both classrooms successfully completed the assigned experiment. One task remained before ending the day's lesson; the teachers knew the writing portion of the unit—and the students' ability to effectively teach another child the experiment—depended on the children writing and following clear directions.

Each teacher asked the students who logged the directions to come to the front of the room and stand in a line. "One at a time, I want you to share the steps in the experiment," each teacher told her journalers. "I'll write down the steps in order on the board. Using your notes we will compose a final version of the directions."

With input from the students up front and several eager children in their seats, both teachers led their classes in identifying and correctly ordering the steps in the completed experiments.

As they finished, the teachers reinforced the importance of the joint writing exercise. "Tomorrow you will use these directions to teach a student from the class next door how to do the experiment you just learned," the teachers said. "Be sure to copy our final version into your learning logs."

On Tuesday morning the students looked forward to meeting their partner and sharing a new experiment. They arrived to find both classrooms rearranged, with the desks grouped around the perimeter of the room and a large supply area occupying the center. The teachers assigned the pairs and allowed each duo to choose a workspace in one of the rooms. "First the student from my class should teach the baking soda experiment," said Mrs. Wong. "Then the student from Miss Pike's class will teach the hot air experiment. Remember to follow the directions in your learning log. All your supplies are available on the table in the middle of the rooms. Have fun!"

The teachers walked through the rooms as the students busily started to work. A hum of activity and conversation soon filled the room, and the teachers observed more than one student "teacher" double-checking the log for the correct procedure. Although the groups worked at different speeds, within 20 minutes each group successfully completed the first experiment and began the second.

"Miss Pike, I think this would be easier to explain if we could draw pictures to go with our directions," said Chad. "Great idea!" she responded. "Write a note so you don't forget. When we're done here you can share it with the class."

As the groups finished the second experiment, the teachers coached each pair in cleaning up and returning extra materials to the center table. "When you've finished both projects, return to your workspace and write in your learning log," the teachers said. "Record what happened with the experiment you taught and the experiment you learned. Write down any questions you have. Work quietly and we'll talk about the experiments when everyone is finished."

When every group had completed both projects (and wiped up the spilled water), the students returned to their regular classrooms and, after quickly pushing desks back into place, debriefed the morning's work. Like Chad, a few students suggested enhancements to make the directions easier to follow or to teach. Several more asked questions about the new experiment they just learned; the students seemed to comprehend the concepts more readily after the fun of applying them.

Mrs. Wong and Miss Pike were pleased with the science experiments and even more delighted with the larger experiment in team teaching across subjects. By working as a class to write the steps to an experiment, the young students gained a positive first experience with one type of expository writing. By using those directions to teach another student, they also developed an appreciation of writing for an audience. And by alternately functioning as both teacher and student, the children developed a deeper understanding of some key scientific principles. The two friends looked forward to working together again soon—although perhaps on something less messy.

Letter Writing

One of the ways to develop children's writing ability is to encourage letter writing, even among young students learning to read. Such early letter writing reinforces reading skills, according to Clay (1991). Again, as in journal writing the focus is on content and purpose, but gradually more attention is paid to correct form for either friendly or business letters. The former are described as letters written to someone the child knows personally (a friend or relative) or would like to know personally (such as a pen pal). They include invitations, thank-you letters, and letters to favorite authors or illustrators. Business letters, on the other hand, are written to companies, stores, nonprofit organizations, government offices, or even civic or political leaders.

An appropriate introduction to letter writing is modeled by the teacher on the overhead while the class observes. Then there is discussion regarding the recipient or audience, the topics to be covered, and the organization of the contents. Finally the writing starts.

Pen pals are popular with elementary students. Some attend another school in the same district (which saves postal expense), whereas others have submitted their names to organizations such as World Pen Pals, PO Box 337, Saugerties, NY 12477 (www.world-pen-pals .com); Student Letter Exchange, 211 Broadway, Suite 201, Lynbrook, NY 11563 (www.pen-pal .com); or International Friendship League, founded in Britain, 3 Creswick Road, Acton, LONDON W3 9HE (www.ifl.org.uk). *Stone Soup* magazine, headquartered in Santa Cruz, California, maintains its own list of pen pal Web sites at www.stonesoup.com/links/penpal. In letters to pen pals, students generally write about their hobbies, school activities, families, and friends.

If school facilities include access to the Internet, children can learn to send messages electronically to pen pals or friends anywhere in this country or even around the world who have similar access to e-mail. Such letter writing is fast and the messages are short—one or two screens in length—so they can be easily read on the computer screen. They begin and end just as other friendly letters do. E-mailing has proved to be an incentive for students who usually do not care to write very much.

Story Writing

Dealing with personal and imaginative experiences, story writing encourages creativity. In addition to experiences, other sources for stories are the children's feelings and beliefs (Graves, 1989).

Young children learn the concept of story writing by hearing stories read and told frequently, first at home or preschool, and then by elementary teachers who read to them daily. Then gradually they begin to consider themselves as authors when their teachers, according to Lamme (1989), explain that books are written by persons called authors, not by mysterious machines, and then read aloud several books by the same author.

Children can next be introduced to the five elements of story structure—plot, setting, characters, theme, and point of view—previously discussed in Chapter 7. To help them get started on a story, *beginning* writers can each complete a worksheet related to most of these elements before starting to write. Such a worksheet should include the following items: Title of Story, Setting—Place, Setting—Time, Main Character(s), Other Characters, Problem (plot), and Resolution (plot).

Elementary children, even those in the middle and upper grades, have only a limited sense of *theme,* thinking differently about that story element than adults do (Au, 1992; Lehr, 1991). They may confuse it with plot, which is the action of the story, whereas the theme is the underlying message and is rarely stated directly (e.g., death is the theme in Rawlings' *The Yearling*, 1985).

The element of *viewpoint* also presents some challenges to students as each writer must decide in advance who will tell the story and then follow that viewpoint completely, for example, a first-person viewpoint as in Fox's *The Slave Dancer* (1982) or an objective or third-person viewpoint as in Zemach's *The Little Red Hen: An Old Story* (1983).

Some teachers, especially those in the primary grades, begin story writing by having the students collaborate on class stories until they feel comfortable writing stories on their own. A useful in-between step for third or fourth graders is writing stories to accompany a wordless picture book, such as dePaola's *Pancakes for Breakfast* (1978). Struggling fifth- and sixth-grade writers respond to the more sophisticated *The Mysteries of Harris Burdick* (1984) by Van Allsburg.

Expository Writing

Also known as informational or nonfiction writing, **expository writing** uses composition to satisfy a practical need. Its focus is on putting information across in a style that will give the reader new knowledge. Kindergartners and first graders write many informational compositions, although it has been widely believed that their first writing is narrative (Bonin, 1988). Actually, some teachers of these

Although expository writing is more difficult than narrative writing, a teacher can guide a student by posing the right questions.

young children prefer to introduce expository writing to the class before narrative writing because it is based on facts and is therefore easier to structure (e.g., how to take care of the class aquarium).

Elementary students generally, however, find informational writing difficult because, while narrative writing sounds similar to spoken language, expository writing does not. Consequently, teachers interested in introducing nonfiction writing successfully to children should follow the four-step model developed by Wray and Lewis (1997):

1. *Demonstration*: The teacher models for the whole class the steps involved in researching and preparing informational writing.
2. *Joint activity*: Student groups each compose a single collaborative piece of informational writing.
3. *Supported writing*: The teacher assists individual students by providing an outline or guiding questions.
4. *Independent writing*: Students each research and write on their own, following the process approach. The teacher provides assistance as needed.

There are numerous types of expository writing, the most common being reports, both collaborative and individual. Some reports are based on research that can be done in the library or on the Internet. A first step in teaching young children how to write research reports is the *All About . . .* books, which are not truly research books but lists of facts that students have discovered about one subject (Sowers, 1985). The students write entire booklets on a single topic (such as grasshoppers) with one piece of information and one illustration on each page. The emphasis is on the sharing of information, which is the gist of nonfiction writing.

Other types of expository writing include alphabet books, autobiographies, biographies, dictionaries or glossaries, and directions. Again, although they can be written individually, most can also be written collaboratively, especially in classes with second-language learners or struggling writers.

Persuasive Writing

Elementary students have considerable difficulty with **persuasive writing**, which has proved to be the most challenging genre for many of them. They are less able to compose written arguments than they are to write in the expository or narrative form. Although most are capable of persuasive speaking or orally winning over someone to their cause or viewpoint, they cannot write persuasively very well.

Studies conducted among sixth graders by McCann (1989) and Crowhurst (1991) concluded that persuasive writing receives little attention in elementary schools partly because teachers believe that it is too difficult for children to master. Yet, both researchers found that persuasive writing does improve with direct instruction: Students' work becomes longer and better organized with more conclusions and greater elaboration of supporting reasons.

The format for beginning persuasive writing is a five-sentence paragraph: one sentence for a statement of topic and opinion, three sentences for reasons for that opinion, and a one-sentence conclusion. Each of these elements is modeled and taught separately before students can assemble them into a paragraph.

Student writers should realize that there are three basic ways to persuade the reader to agree with them. The first is an appeal to *reason* that is supported by factual information of concern to the reader's intellect. The second is an appeal to *character*, which involves trusting the reputation of the persuader. The third is an appeal to *emotions* that attempts to arouse the reader's anger, fear, or other strong feeling.

Forms of persuasive writing include (but are not limited to) letters, advertisements/commercials, posters, and essays. Topics come from home and school activities, study units in social studies and science, and literature. Books with persuasive appeals can be shared with both primary and intermediate grade students and include the following: for younger children, Brown's *The Important Book* (1997), Ness's *Sam, Bangs, and Moonshine* (1966), and Zolotow's *William's Doll* (1972); and for older students, Cohen's *Molly's Pilgrim* (1983), Cowcher's *Antarctica* (1990), and Van Allsburg's *Jumanji* (1991).

Poetic Writing

While there is no one general definition of poetry as there is for other forms of writing, it has been recently described as "the expression of ideas and feelings through a rhythmical composition of imaginative and beautiful words selected for their pleasant sounds" (Lynch-Brown & Tomlinson, 2005, p. 44). For elementary children to learn to write poetry, they must first have it read to them and read it themselves. Gradually, with a supportive teacher, they can learn to write five types of poems: formula poems, free-form poems, syllable-and-word-count poems, rhymed verse poems, and model poems (Tompkins, 2004).

Although lessons involving the writing of poetry do not always follow neatly the stages of the writing process described earlier, most of these poetic types can be introduced through a four-step presentation:

1. The teacher presents a short introduction or conceptual overview.

2. The teacher reads examples of poems written in that style by peers (to boost the confidence of young would-be poets).

3. Children write either individually or in groups in a work session. The teacher provides as much personal assistance as needed since even a small amount of such interest is sufficient to promote creativity. Dictation may be useful with children who have an especially difficult time expressing themselves poetically.

4. The teacher shares student poetry promptly after a work session of 20 to 30 minutes. An audience reinforces poetic efforts and encourages beginners. The teacher (not the child writer) should read aloud the new poetry because students sometimes have difficulty reading their own handwriting. Furthermore, the teacher can edit the poems as he or she reads them, eliminating possible obscenities and focusing on particularly appealing portions. Should some students prefer not to have their work read aloud, the teacher should of course honor their wishes.

Simple *formula poems* as developed by Koch (2000) involve repetition and include I wish . . . poems (where each line begins with the same two words); color poems (where each line generally starts with the same color); five-senses poems (where each of the five lines concerns one sense); and if I were... poems (where each line tells how the poets would feel and what they would do if they were something else).

Free-form poems ignore rhyme, repetition, or proper use of punctuation marks to weave together words and phrases that tell a story or express a thought. Forms include concrete poems (where words are arranged pictorially on a page, sometimes in the shape of an object); found poems (where words are cut out of newspapers or other printed material and arranged poetically); and poems for two voices (where poems are written in two columns, side by side, and read together by two readers or two groups of readers, sometimes separately, sometimes as a duet).

Syllable-and-word-count poems include haiku, cinquains, and diamantes, previously discussed in Chapter 7. The first two types consist of five lines each, whereas diamantes have seven lines. All are carefully structured.

Teachers interested in introducing the writing of cinquains can follow a five-step approach:

1. The teacher chooses a *general topic* that allows flexibility and is one with which everyone is familiar (e.g., Foods I Love to Eat). Cinquain poems may tell a story, but usually they describe something.

2. There is individual *brainstorming* as students list words or phrases about the chosen topic. The teacher moves about the class, encouraging and reassuring. After three to five minutes, words may be shared with the class.

3. Students *select one of the words or phrases* elicited during the previous step.

4. There is additional student *brainstorming,* again with considerable teacher encouragement and again for a short time.

5. A cinquain *poem is written.* A simple five-line form is imposed on all the words that have been brainstormed, generally with two syllables in the first line, four in the second, six in the third, eight in the fourth, and two in the fifth. The poem need not rhyme. Nor do all of the brainstormed words have to be used, although some may be repeated, added, or reordered. However, this formula must be followed: The first line contains a one-word title or subject, the second line describes the title or subject, the third line expresses action, the fourth line expresses feelings or observations, and the fifth line describes or renames the subject.

Older students prefer working in groups of three or four, having discovered quickly that cinquains almost write themselves. Younger children, on the contrary, respond more positively when allowed two or three sessions in which to complete their cinquains.

Rhymed verse poems can be written by intermediate students and include five-lined limericks and four-lined clerihews. The first is light verse, often with a surprise or humorous ending, such as that contained in O'Brien's *Daffy Down Dillies: Silly Limericks by Edward Lear* (1992). The second follows a formula: The first line is a person's name (e.g., a character in a story or a historical figure), the second line rhymes with the first, and the third and fourth lines rhyme with one another (e.g., Taylor's *Brief Candles: 101 Clerihews,* 2000).

Model poems as suggested by Koch (1990) allow students to read a poem composed by an adult poet and then write their own poem using the same theme expressed in the model. A favorite is Viorst's *If I Were in Charge of the World* (1981).

Motivational Strategies That Promote Writing

Teachers soon realize that children often do not leap at the opportunity to write, regardless of the genre of the writing task or whether that assignment has been self-selected or prescribed by the teacher. So the problem of motivating writers remains acute, partly because students are more accustomed to electronic devices that stress the spoken word over the written word. Consequently, special efforts must be made to kindle student excitement about writing and to make it a daily project involving the major genres. Most of the motivating situations or topics described in this section can be adapted easily to other grade levels.

Kindergarten–Third Grade

As Parent-Conference Week approached, the kindergarten students painted pictures about springtime. They then *dictated labels* for their paintings that were displayed both in the corridor and in the classroom.

When the kindergarten class learned that an unnamed nine-year-old kangaroo had hopped away from the local children's zoo, each child wished to draw the kangaroo and then *dictate a name and one sentence* telling why the animal had decided to escape.

The kindergarten class planned to make fudge to serve during the Open House festivities. After each child had participated in purchasing, measuring, or mixing the ingredients, the group *dictated the recipe* for the teacher to post on a chart near the serving table. The classroom microwave worked well, and the parents were appreciative.

After the school response to the first fire drill of the year had not been successful, the kindergartners discussed the experience and then cooperatively *dictated all the steps for responding* properly to the next fire drill.

After the kindergarten class had listened to their teacher read and share Sendak's *Where the Wild Things Are* (1988), children made animals from discarded gift boxes and scrap materials, including yarn, velvet, colored cord, egg cartons, and feathers. The following day each student was asked to *write a name* for his or her "wild thing." Some even asked to *write an original definition* of their creations.

After school one day, the teacher pasted large paper footprints on the floor and the walls of the classroom. The next morning the first graders were delighted to *dictate an experience chart story* about their strange visitors.

Tasha, whose family had recently arrived in the community, invited all the girls in her first-grade class to a Halloween party. However, none of them was familiar with the area in which Tasha lived, so the teacher worked with the girls to help them *write down the directions* to Tasha's house.

When six-year-old Liu Pei got the mumps, her classmates told their teacher that they wished to *write get-well messages* to their friend. These messages were placed in a large brown envelope together with some humorous drawings the children had made to cheer up Liu Pei.

The first-grade class planned to sell popcorn during their economics unit to raise money for the class library. The children chose to cooperatively *write an announcement* about Friday's popcorn sale that they could read to other primary classes.

In a school located close to a lake, the first-grade teacher suggested one morning that the children put on their coats and walk over to see the waves on the lake. The lake was especially choppy that day, and the students commented excitedly about the waves. Back in the classroom, the teacher asked each child to write one sentence describing how the waves made him or her feel. The papers were collected and assembled into group *free verse*.

When two second graders reported during the same week that their pet cats had had litters, they and their classmates decided to *write a classified ad* of 15 words or less that would help them find good homes for the new kittens. The ad was later posted—in excellent manuscript printing—on the news board at the local market.

The teacher placed on the chalk tray large flashcards with nonsense titles, such as "How to Catch a Snapperdinck" and "The Day I Met a Rhinorafloose." Each second grader selected one flashcard to illustrate. Later the children were able to *write original fanciful stories* about their drawings. Students who preferred to create their own titles rather than use the teacher's stock titles were encouraged to do so.

Second graders discussed the significance of numbers in everyday life. They noted that four, for example, is the number of seasons in one year and the number of directions on the compass. Then each student chose one number (under 100) and prepared to *write a quatrain* about that number.

The second graders had visited the municipal zoo on Monday. On Tuesday several children asked questions about some of the less familiar animals they had seen, such as the llama. Other students wondered how the lions and elephants had been captured and brought to the zoo. So the teacher arranged for a class visit to the media center. There each child or small group of students used the Internet or other resources to gather data and *write an expository report* about the animals in which there was special interest.

Each month the PTA program chairperson selected a different grade to supply the entertainment for the evening meeting. When it came time for the second graders to perform, their teachers suggested that they *write invitations* to each of their families to attend the Thanksgiving songfest they had been rehearsing.

During National Safety Week the boys and girls in the third grade decided as a class to *write a list* of rules titled "How to Be a Safe Pedestrian." The list was then carefully copied on chart paper and posted in the office for a week.

The third graders first constructed hand puppets based on Finch's version of *The Three Billy Goats Gruff* (2001). Next, they built a puppet theatre out of a bicycle carton. Then they *wrote scripts* and decided to tape the dialogue. In that way, the puppeteers could concentrate on manipulating the puppets while the tape supplied the voices.

The third-grade teacher placed a silver gravy boat on his desk one morning as he shared with the class Pullman's *Aladdin and the Enchanted Lamp* (2005). Each student was then allowed to rub the "magic lamp" three times before starting to *write a description* of his or her three wishes.

A professional music instructor visited the school where several of his students were enrolled and presented two violin concerts in the auditorium. The third-grade teacher whose class had attended the first performance encouraged her students to *write notes of appreciation* to the school visitor to let him know how much they had enjoyed the concert.

The third graders had been invited to perform at the school science fair some of the classroom experiments they had done with magnets. To assure a successful learning experience, the teacher urged any student or group of students who had volunteered to do an experiment at the fair to *write down the steps of the procedure*.

Fourth Grade–Sixth Grade

Fourth graders became concerned with consumer education. After each student brought in one colorful label from a grocery item, they *wrote short television commercials* describing the product honestly. Later the class voted for the best 30-second commercials.

In the midst of their unit on Japan the fourth-grade class became interested in *writing haiku and tanka*. After the initial drafts were approved, large sheets of wrapping paper were spread around the room. Then the nine-year-olds copied their poems with vigorous strokes of their paint brushes or thick-tipped felt pens.

During the early part of October, the children in the fourth grade each chose to *keep a personal journal* (as might have been written by Columbus in the final days of his first voyage to the New World) or to *keep a logbook* of the Niña, the Pinta, or the Santa Maria (as might have been written by the first mate of each vessel) during the fall of 1492. The final entry in either the journal or the logbook was dated October 12.

The fourth graders listened intently to their principal after she stopped by one morning to discuss and review appropriate behavior on the school bus. She encouraged them to *take notes* during her visit so the whole class could later implement the important points of the discussion.

Some of the boys and girls in the fourth- and fifth-grade combination class had brothers on the high school football team. The class was invited to see the game one Friday evening. The following Monday, the children decided to *write new cheers* for the team.

Early in December when the newspapers were filled with advertisements of gift items for the upcoming Christmas or Hanukkah holidays, the fifth-grade teacher collected many pages of such ads and brought them to school. Each student chose one or two pages and *wrote a math story problem* involving some of the games, clothes, toys, or other gift items. The following day the problems were exchanged and solved.

Fifth graders decided to *write original realistic stories* for their first-grade "buddies." Working individually or in pairs, they chose subjects of interest to six-year-olds with beginning vocabulary skills. After the stories had been carefully edited, illustrated, and printed, the pages were stapled and the books delivered to the first-grade students.

For enrolling the largest number of new PTA members, the fifth-grade class earned a new wall map of the United States. Each child chose one state for an in-depth study and *wrote business letters of inquiry* to the major chambers of commerce in that state. The replies, accompanied by some free materials, arrived within two months.

When the district nurse visited the fifth grade, she reviewed the importance of good nutrition and the daily need for the basic food groups. Then she suggested that each student *complete a table,* listing the kinds of food he or she should eat for balanced breakfasts, lunches, and dinners for one week.

To launch a unit on myth writing, the teacher read aloud to his fifth-grade class from the d'Aulaires' *Ingri and Edgar Parin d'Aulaire's Book of Greek Myths* (1962). The adventures of Prometheus and other gods were used to motivate each student to *write an original myth* that offered a convincing explanation of cosmic phenomena to a primitive group of people.

The fifth- and sixth-grade students were eligible to join the Safety Patrol whose members helped as crossing guards for the children coming to or leaving school. The Patrol meetings were held weekly and their advisor selected a different secretary each month to *write up the minutes of the meetings*.

On January 17 (Benjamin Franklin's birthday), the sixth graders decided to *write proverbs* much like those contained in *Poor Richard's Almanac*. Some even chose to paint or otherwise illustrate their maxims. One student drew a boy and his dog clinging frantically to a rope as they recalled, "When you come to the end of your rope, make a knot and hang on."

The sixth-grade teacher cut out intriguing newspaper headlines and pasted each on a sheet of lined writing paper. Then the papers were turned face down on the front table, and each student selected one sheet on which to *write a news story* that fit the headline. The next day the teacher provided the original newspaper articles so that the children could compare their stories with the published accounts.

The sixth-grade class was responsible for writing, duplicating, assembling, and distributing the *Commonwealth School Register*, a student-produced newsletter, each month. Some of the students especially enjoyed *writing editorials* on such diverse topics as longer lunch breaks, after-school programs, and dress codes.

The winter that their state was experiencing record snowstorms, the sixth graders became interested in meteorology. They studied about the weather and *kept weather logs* for two weeks. Each daily log consisted of two sections, one for observations and one for actual weather measurements (temperature, humidity, barometric pressure, wind, and precipitation) as listed in the daily newspaper.

Attending the local high school one year was an exchange student from Scotland. The sixth-grade teacher invited him to her classroom, and the young man enjoyed talking to the children. He arranged to get names of girls and boys in Scotland who wished to correspond with their peers in the United States. The sixth graders soon started *writing friendly letters or e-mailing* their foreign pen pals and exchanging inexpensive souvenirs.

Writing Development Through the Grades

Teachers should be aware of what they can expect of students in the area of writing as the children move through the grades. Although wide variations exist among child writers in any grade level, still there are some similarities among students in each grade that may guide teachers as they plan their writing lessons.

Kindergarten

Beginning kindergarten children display a broad range of writing abilities. A few can already write due to encouragement at home or preschool, others have only a limited knowledge of alphabet letters, while still others are completely unaware that an alphabet even exists. Most kindergarten students, according to Sulzby (1992), do enter school in the scribbling and drawing stage. By the second semester, however, those drawings may relate a message that is actually legible in some instances, with real letters and invented spelling.

Once children acquire a rudimentary knowledge of print, they consider themselves to be writers, states Calkins (1994), and they quickly learn the conventions of written language. Teachers can promote this interest by providing paper and envelopes for letter writing or index cards for labeling objects around the room.

First Grade

First graders begin narrative or story writing, with pattern stories a special favorite. Patterned writing often evolves from literary picture books that have repetition, for example, Martin's *Brown Bear, Brown Bear, What Do You See?* (1983). Beginning writers find such patterns appealing because they can use them as a crutch and need only to fill in the blanks in their own stories. Expository or informational writing can also be done in a fill-in-the-blank style (e.g., A field trip to the zoo could be written up as "We visited the zoo. We saw big animals like…We saw small animals like…The noisiest animal was…").

After patterned writing children may next choose to follow the example of writing unpatterned stories as read aloud to them by their teacher (e.g., Cronin's *Click, Clack, Moo: Cows That Type,* 2000). Such books furnish new ideas that students need in order to write effectively.

Some first graders who write every day complete many different forms of writing, including keeping daily personal journals and science journals of concluded experiments, compiling word lists related to math, and preparing follow-up stories or reports related to literature read to them (Morrow, Tracey, Woo, & Pressley, 1999).

Finally, primary teachers should remember that, although first graders like to write, they do not like to revise. In fact, if asked to rework a piece without being able to incorporate any new ideas themselves, many become inhibited and fail to progress in their writing abilities (Salinger, 1992).

Second Grade

As children enter the stage of concrete operations, they begin to realize that while some topics are acceptable for writing, others are not. Although earlier in the first grade, students wrote mostly for their own enjoyment, now they desire approval and acceptance of their work by an audience. This concern, coupled with their limited writing experience, results in the destruction of several drafts before they are satisfied with their work.

A favorite type of writing at this age is a "bed-to-bed" story, which is a narrative of the happenings that occur from the time the child awakes in the morning until he or she falls asleep at night (Calkins, 1994). It does not matter whether the purpose of the story is to relate a child's birthday, for example; the same ritual persists, and eating breakfast or preparing for bed earns the same amount of attention as the actual opening of the gifts. In other words, when second graders write about an episode, they wish to include everything so that the finished piece is more like a detailed report with little or no personal reactions.

Second graders have been described as "authors of opposites" (Calkins, 1994; Skolnick & Frazier, 1998) because at times they write with complete confidence and in other instances their efforts are plainly laborious. For this reason, their writing on the whole is less creative than that of first graders.

Teachers of second graders should continue to model a writing strategy (e.g., adding more and different descriptive words) before assigning the class to use that strategy. They also should spend time daily on reading and sharing children's literature that can serve as new models for the students' work (e.g., Chinn's *Sam and the Lucky Money,* 1995, and Bunting's *The Wednesday Surprise,* 1989). They know that some second graders prefer to imitate the plots of familiar tales such as Galdone's *The Little Red Hen* (1979).

Third Grade

Third graders continue to be concerned with the mechanics of writing just as they were in the second grade. They wish to be certain that their spelling, punctuation, capitalization, and grammar are correct, as is their new responsibility for cursive writing.

Bed-to-bed stories continue, and these children tend to include every detail in their description of an event. They therefore need the teacher's help in learning to summarize because they do not know which details to omit as they revise their work. Editing is also difficult for many third graders.

Third graders prefer writing narratives with simple sentences and paragraphs. Nevertheless, some do become interested in writing informational reports about topics in social studies and science. Others enjoy experimenting with poetic forms or developing story problems involving math concepts.

Fourth Grade

While third graders generally write in a straightforward predictable style, fourth graders are creative and individualistic in their writing. Their growth in background experiences is reflected in their written work, and they enjoy preparing more factual reports than they did earlier. These students are eager to share their work with others so they accept revision and editing more readily than children in the lower grades.

It has been found that, although fourth graders enjoy writing, they do not spend much time writing outside the classroom. This places additional importance on planning writing activities that challenge nine-year-olds at school.

Fifth and Sixth Grades

This age group has diverse skills, interests, and abilities, but that variability is an asset and can be reflected in their writing (Hansen, 1986). Students discover that everyone has his or her own strengths and weaknesses, and they should write in areas that emphasize personal uniqueness. They can then "celebrate, challenge, and defend" their own writing as well as that of their classmates and even well-known authors of children's literature. Upper grade students are growing in their confidence as writers and are able to discuss writing problems with their peers. They aim for perfection and persist in improving each piece through several drafts. Happily, they handle mechanical skills comfortably, although they still have some difficulty in developing new ideas and organizing their writing.

One study found that fifth and sixth graders regard good writers as those who listen to others, read a lot, have an adequate vocabulary, are familiar with their topics, and write in a style that interests others (Bright, 1995). Furthermore, good writers are determined workers who write often.

A sample lesson plan incorporating the concepts introduced in this chapter appears on p. 285.

Samples of Children's Writing

Each of the compositions on the following pages has been written by students (ages 5 to 11) and represents a child's approach to life. Whether in poetry or prose, illustrated or not, each piece is straightforward, inquisitive, and observant. Essentially each composition displays each student's awareness and thinking skills—which have been nurtured by a supportive teacher.

Sally

Sally was picking flowers. It started to rain, She started going into the tent. Then it started getting sunny again so she took a nap. Then she ran and skipped and walked.

Renee

Why the Platypus Is So Mixed Up

When God was done creating the world, he had some leftover parts. He had a giant chimney, the skin of a beaver, the bill of a duck, and two pairs of geese feet.

Well, he thought and planned and pondered and finally thought of something to do with the giant chimney. He would stick it down in the United States and call it Chimney Rock!

Now he had gotten rid of the chimney, but what about the other things? Well, God thought and thought and at last came up with something. He would make it into an animal! It would be a little bit strange but so what?

So he mixed them together and came up with the duck-billed platypus. Poor creature!

Carol

Written in Grade 5

The Cat and the Mouse

It was a stormy day. It was lightning outside. It was raining outside. The cat and the mouse were outside. The cat saw the mouse. The mouse was drowning. The mouse said, "Help! Help!" The cat picked the mouse up. He took him onto some dry land. The cat was getting ready to eat the mouse. The mouse got away. He looked at the cat and said, "Thank you but I don't like you chasing me or eating me."

Daren

Dictated in Grade 1

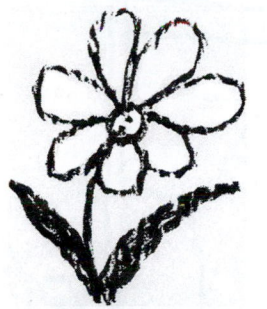

Round is the center of a flower
so the petals will stay on.

Carol
Written in Grade 1

City

Fast, busy

Rushing, moving, hurrying

Streets, buildings, trees, fields

Yielding, rolling, harvesting

Quiet, free

Country

Martin
Written in Grade 6

Turtle

Below the shell and
Above the plastron,
A little creature lurks.

Ben
Written in Grade 4

My Lost Tooth

By Cheryl's Class

I was happy when I came to school this morning. Nothing was wrong. My tooth was loose. I went to the cafeteria to eat my lunch. I was happy. Nothing was wrong. I hoped my tooth would come out. I took one bite of a potato chip, and my tooth went clear up into my mouth. It was just hanging there. It was just hanging by one little edge. I pulled it clear out. I was happy! I could take it home so I could put it under my pillow. I hoped I would get some money from the fairy. Susie told me to hold it in my hand real tight. My tooth was in a paper napkin. Then I accidentally dropped it into the big trash can with my milk carton. It dropped so fast I couldn't catch it! I went to Mr. Hunt, our principal. I was almost starting to cry. Mr. Hunt tried to look for it. He looked in a napkin, but it wasn't there. He looked in everything. My tooth wasn't there. I came to the room to tell my teacher. I was crying! I told her that I lost my tooth. We wrote this letter to the fairy.

Dear Fairy,

I lost my tooth. I accidentally dropped it in the trash can with my milk carton. It was a big trash can in the Orangethorpe School cafeteria. Please forgive me, and please give me some money!

Love,

Cheryl

P.S. The children in Room 25 helped me write this letter. Mr. Hunt, our principal, helped me look for the tooth. We couldn't find it.

Skidder

This is a John Deere 540-A skidder. It weighs about thirty tons and is about ten or eleven feet tall. It lifts with a hydraulic blade. This skidder has a winch line on it. It winches about four-foot logs. There are 440, 540, 640, and 740 John Deere skidders. Sometimes they fill the tires of a skidder with water for extra weight.

Jim
Written in Grade 4

Who Am I?

I have many things I want to say
But
No one will listen.

I have many things I want to do
But
No one will let me.

I have many places I want to go
But
No one will take me.

And the things I write are corrected
But
No one reads them.

Jody
Age 8

The Sad Worm

The sad worm is trying to climb up the tree to get the apple, but he couldn't climb up the tree.

It is a sunny day and the sad worm is trying to get in his hole, but he can't find it.

The sad worm climbs up the tree and finds his hole in the tree, then he changes into being happy.

John Wilde

There was a young Frenchman
    of Cault
Who had but one little fault;
    He liked to rob banks
    To steal all their francs,
Until one day he got locked in
    a vault.

Paul
Written in Grade 6

Cat

Quiet, gentle

Rolling, playing, climbing

Yarn, mice, shoes, bones

Running, digging, jumping

Noisy, rough

Dog

Lori
Written in Grade 6

There was a young man from
    Orum
Who bought some new pants
    and he wore 'em.
He stooped and he sneezed;
He wiggled his knees;
And he knew right where he
    had tore 'em.

Jeff
Written in Grade 6

Family Farm

My name is Don M. I live on a small dairy farm. It's a lot of work.

We milk the cows twice a day and have to make sure they have hay and water all the time. A cow drinks about 35 gallons of water a day. That's a lot. It's my responsibility to make sure their water tub stays filled. They drink out of an old bathtub. I fill it twice a day or three times when it's hot.

There should always be hay in the feeder, so the cows can eat it whenever they want. A cow has to spend a lot of time eating and chewing. First, she eats very fast, getting as much hay down her as she can. That hay goes into her first stomach or rumen. Then she lays down and just like a burp, a wad of food comes back up to her mouth so she can chew it. This is called chewing the cud or ruminating. A cow spends about eight hours a day just chewing her cud. A cow has four stomachs in all. She needs her complex stomach system in order to digest grass and hay and get food value out of them. Her fourth stomach is like ours, the other three are extra, just for digesting this roughage.

Don

Age 11

Someday when I retire I would like to be a kind lady.

Brenda
Written in Grade 1

"A Thought"

To all the people in the world,

Remember this thought,

That everyone serves a purpose.

So find your own,

And be happy.

Blake
Age 12

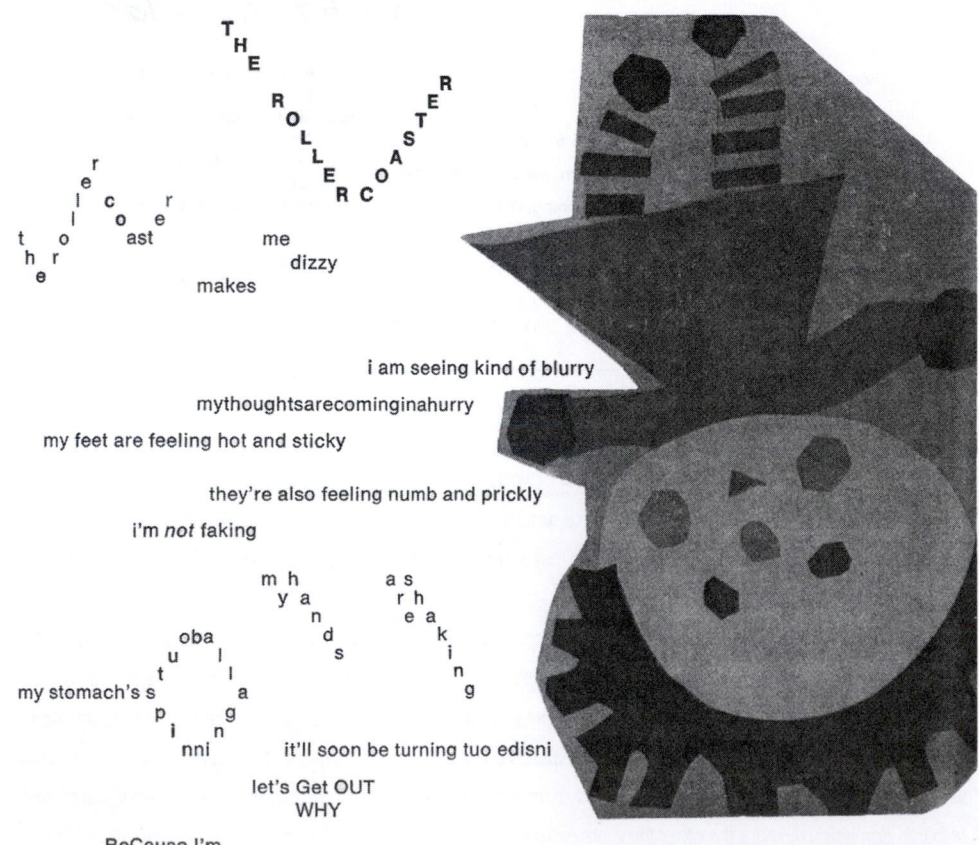

i am seeing kind of blurry

mythoughtsarecominginahurry

my feet are feeling hot and sticky

they're also feeling numb and prickly

i'm *not* faking

it'll soon be turning tuo edisni

let's Get OUT
WHY

BeCause I'm

ScArEd!

Janine
Written in Grade 6

Fish

Fish	swim	and
bob	and	eat
food	and	swim
so	gracefully	and
have	a	stroke
like	a	butterfly
when	I	
watch	them	in my
fish	tank.	

Greg

Written in Grade 4

Diamanté

Predator

Strategic, unpredictable

Hunting, stalking, attacking

Lions, Serengeti dogs, gazelles, zebra

Fleeing, warning, eating

Careful, alert

Prey

Paul

Written in Grade 4

Where the Witches Sleep

If I knew where the witches slept, I'd go there every day

I'd have to be in a place very far away

I'd hide behind a big black pot and there I'd quietly lie

I'd wait for the witches to arrive from their nightly fly

I'd tiptoe down the dark dank cave and then I'd secretly pry

into their magic book of spells, of spider's legs and flies

Lizard's gizzards and all that gook, just waiting to be boiled and cooked

Imaginary, yet it's true but you really must construe

When I get very angry and am feeling very rotten, I stir up
a pot of frog leg

stew, and my troubles are forgotten.

Kim

Written in Grade 6

Bam, Bam, Bam

Bam, bam, bam

Goes the steel wrecking ball;

Slam, slam, slam

Against a concrete wall.

It's raining bricks and wood

In my neighborhood;

Zam goes a chimney,

Zowie goes a door.

Bam, bam, bam

Goes the steel wrecking ball,

Changing it all,

Changing it all.

Eugene
Written in Grade 4

Assessment

Spelling tests, benchmark writing assessments, and vocabulary and grammar quizzes are traditional measures used to assess students' writing progress. However, methods that authentically chart student growth, such as student portfolios, give a more comprehensive picture of student progress over time. Jointly, students and teachers can discuss and select student samples that include a range of genres and applications. Self-evaluations allow students to reflect on their writing. By recognizing strengths and defining areas of weakness, students and teachers can set goals for writing improvement. Teachers can provide rubrics in advance of writing assignments so students are clear about criteria and expectations. Teacher observations of students engaged in individual and group tasks also offer an informal means of assessment about how students work collaboratively, problem solve, and use time effectively. Student-teacher conferences and classroom conversations, especially for beginning writers, provide additional information and insight about the content of student writing that the student may not be able to effectively express with written words.

Working With English Language Learners

The writing process for English Language Learners (ELLs) follows the same steps as those for students who speak English as their first language. Because the writing process is already divided into manageable "chunks" of prewriting, drafting, revising, editing, and publishing, providing additional support where needed is easily modified for ability levels for all learners. However, greater cognitive demands are placed on ELLs because students are simultaneously immersed in learning speech, reading, and writing—and the challenge is even greater for older students. When planning instruction and activities, teachers need to be aware of the extra support that ELLs require so they can develop essential skills to become successful and enthusiastic writers.

Beginning ELLs: Beginning ELL writers, like most beginning writers, require a great amount of teacher modeling and support. All students need to be provided with frequent opportunities to write to make progress toward achieving writing goals. All writers should be encouraged to pursue topics of personal interest. Shared writing, a print-rich environment, and sight word practice will help build vocabulary skills, although the primary focus at the beginning ELL level is on content rather than language conventions. Teachers should accept invented spelling and inconsistent punctuation. Drawing activities also help students communicate who do not yet have the ability to express complex ideas in written form. Teachers can provide additional scaffolding by continuing to expose students to quality children's literature including culturally relevant books. Teachers should present beginning ELLs with many opportunities to participate in oral language activities; hearing the language in a variety of contexts assists students in developing an ear for the sound, flow, and structure of English. Teachers should provide consistent and immediate feedback and create an environment conducive to stimulating literary discourse. ELLs benefit from social interaction and cooperative learning activities with peers and should be included in lessons when appropriate, constructive, and meaningful.

Early intermediate and intermediate ELLs: Intermediate ELL students continue to develop their "voice" and explore self-selected topics, but teachers now can begin to place greater emphasis on organization, vocabulary, and experimentation with different styles and sentence structures. Students can begin to consider audience and purpose when writing. As all students progress through the grade levels, academic language becomes more challenging, and it is especially demanding for ELLs. Project- or theme-based units that integrate subject areas assist students in more thoroughly developing key concepts and related vocabulary terms. Teachers can provide extra support by including charts, pictures, realia, books, educational Web sites, videos, and concrete experiences to facilitate comprehension. Teachers should continue to provide group activities, such as peer response groups, to encourage social interaction. Word webs, cluster maps, and graphic organizers can help provide structure and a secure starting point to the blank page that overwhelms even facile writers on occasion.

Early advanced and advanced ELLs: At this stage, students still continue to work on style and structure, but now have the skills and experience to move on to more complex tasks. Word choice, descriptive language, and complex sentence structures become more important in developing personal voice and style. Students are ready, with teacher and peer support, to tackle more demanding genres, such as persuasive essays and detailed research reports. Students are more adept at revising and editing work and are aware of the purpose and intended audience. Teachers should continue to provide comprehensible input and opportunities for students to peer-evaluate and self-evaluate. Teachers should plan instruction to give ELLs opportunities to develop and practice grammar and spelling skills in context; it is important that teachers give students frequent practice in using written conventions in authentic applications and not only in isolated exercises such as spelling tests or vocabulary quizzes. Advanced ELLs are able to publish writing individually and collaboratively and continue to develop critical thinking skills in response to literature, thus emphasizing that writing is not only a highly personal endeavor but also a visual and social process that interconnects with arts, sciences, and all other subject areas.

Practical Instructional Activities and Ideas

- *Read-alouds:* Previously recommended in Chapter 7, reading quality children's literature also supports progress in the domain of writing. Through daily read-alouds, teachers create opportunities for students to listen to and interact with informational, narrative, and multicultural texts, thus familiarizing learners with the syntax, rhythm, and conventions of English. By posing questions such as "what do you think the author was trying to communicate to the reader?" (purpose), teachers can emphasize specific strategies that authors (and illustrators) implement to persuade, inform, and affect the reader.

- *Sensory writing:* Teachers can plan concrete experiences to help students write descriptive paragraphs or poems using the five senses. Simple food items such as strawberries, popcorn, or apples can evoke touch, smell, sight, sound, and taste while conjuring up personal connections and memories that add richness to the writing experience. Other examples taken from nature are seashells, rocks, seed pods, and leaves.

- *Personal artifacts:* In a variation of the previous activity, teachers can ask students to bring in an object with personal significance or interest to prompt a personal narrative. For example, if a student brought in a piece of weathered driftwood found at the beach, the student can write about the physical features of the object as well as the circumstances and memories of that day.

- *Classroom newspaper:* Collaborative efforts at class bookmaking have already been described in this chapter, and a classroom newspaper serves as a variation on this activity. Depending on ability level, the teacher provides support as needed. Students can peruse newspapers to brainstorm elements to include, such as headline stories, interviews, book reviews, cartoons, weather reports, class activities, and photographs. The final publication can be entirely handmade, computer generated, or be a combination of media.

- *Language treasure hunt:* Teachers can direct students to "hunt" for powerful words, interesting phrases, metaphors, and other examples of language that grab the reader's attention or have a unique or affective quality. As an extension activity, students can write down their own "golden" sentences and share their discoveries with the class.

- *Alternate endings:* Students reinterpret fairy tales, fables, and other favorite stories by writing alternate endings and/or changing characters. One of many books to introduce students to this concept is Scieszka's *Squids Will Be Squids* (1998). Teachers can add another level to this activity by having students write scripts and then perform their interpretations.

- *Star of the week:* Every week a different student is featured as the "star." Students complete a sheet with interview-type questions about favorite subjects, pets, family, and special personal interests to share with the class. Teachers encourage students to bring in photographs to share and display in a place of honor in the classroom. Classmates can write letters to the "star" at the end of the week.

- *Shared student writing samples:* Teachers can copy student writing samples (anonymous) onto transparencies to evaluate with the class. Using an overhead projector, the teacher models constructive feedback by making positive comments such as pointing out good word choices, the correct use of commas, and powerful figurative language. Conversely, teacher offers useful, but sensitive, suggestions on how to improve writing such as substituting a better word for "fun" or pointing out the lack of periods. At the end of the critique, the teacher gives students the opportunity to claim authorship if they wish to be recognized for their writing efforts.

- *How to . . . make a peanut butter sandwich:* A popular instructional strategy that emphasizes the importance of sequence and attention to detail when writing directions is the construction of a peanut butter sandwich (or jam or baloney if peanut allergies are an issue). Teachers then challenge students to write out the "how to" steps and based on student directions, teachers build the sandwich. (For beginning writers, this can take the form of shared writing.) Invariably, an important detail, such as the need for a knife, is omitted and the sandwich making comes to a laughable end. The teacher then gives students a second chance to revise their original directions. Students then work with a partner to create their own sandwich and enjoy a delicious snack.

- *"I am" poems:* Teachers have students brainstorm ideas about "self" by giving examples and asking questions about their accomplishments, fears, family, food likes and dislikes, friends, and favorite things. When students have created a diverse list of words and phrases from which to choose, they are ready to compose a unique, free-verse poem that begins with "I am" and repeats the phrase. Students can illustrate or incorporate a design into the final published piece that complements the feeling or mood of the poem.

LESSON PLAN 8.1   Comic Strip Story

Linking Words and Images

Language Arts Components: Writing and Visual Representation

Grade: 2–5

Topic: Comic Strip Stories

Time Frame: 1 week

Objective

- Students create an original comic strip.

Materials

- Writing paper
- Comic strip template
- Pencils
- Fine-point black ink pens
- Colored pencils, crayons, and markers
- An assortment of age-appropriate comic books and newspaper comics pages
- Optional—computer/scanner for final comic book publication

Content Standards

Writing Applications: Write Narratives

- Establish a plot, point of view, setting, and conflict.
- Show rather than tell the events of a story.

Vocabulary

- Characters
- Setting
- Plot
- Conflict
- Genre

Open

Engage

- In whole-group arrangement, teacher asks students to brainstorm genres of literature they have learned about (historical fiction, biography, poetry, etc.).
- If students list "comic books" as a genre, teacher asks if students think that comics could be considered a genre and discuss student responses.
- Teacher passes out selection of comic books, newspaper comics pages, and examples from other sources.

Body

Explore

- Students work in small groups to discuss and analyze story elements: plot, character, setting, and conflict. Teacher also instructs students to consider visual elements: dialogue boxes or bubbles, color, frames, and style.
- Teacher circulates room to ensure that students are on task and to mediate any group discussions.

Expand

- After groups have sufficiently discussed questions, teacher gathers whole group back together to discuss small group findings.
- Teacher tells class that each student will be creating his or her own comic strip using basic story elements of character, plot, conflict, and setting. (Its complexity will depend on the age group. A simple, beginning/middle/end, three frame can be used for younger students, and a multipanel series can be used for advanced or older students. Many storyboard templates can be downloaded from the Internet.)
- Teacher shows template to students.

First . . .   Next . . .   At last . . .

- Teacher explains that stories must follow the format of first, next, last or a logical sequence of events, but encourages students who want to write more or be creative to make their own storyboards. Teacher reviews the elements that need to be included: character, plot, setting, and conflict (event).
- Teacher passes out rubric for assignment and discusses/clarifies any questions or misunderstandings.
- Teacher assures students that plenty of paper and templates are available for rough drafts and that students will most likely need to revise and edit to make their story comic more interesting and visually attractive. Illustrations need to be inked in with pen, but it is the illustrator's decision whether to use color.
- Students and teacher brainstorm story ideas, helping students who do not already have a topic.

Close

Apply

- Teacher passes out blank paper and templates while permitting students to freely discuss ideas for storylines.
- Students continue to write, sketch, revise, and edit during several class sessions of approximately 45 minutes each.
- Teacher provides support and input as needed.
- As students finish, Teacher can assist students in scanning finished comics into the computer to compile as a class publication.
- Originals can be displayed on a bulletin board or other place of prominence.

Assessment

- Teacher gathers whole class for an art show and critique. Group discusses successes and makes suggestions on how particular elements could be improved on next time. Teacher can use self-evaluation or peer-evaluation forms for this portion or keep the session informal.
- Rubric: Teacher provides children with a rubric in advance that describes expectations for neatness, creativity, completeness, logical sequence, spelling, and other criteria pertinent to assignment.
- Student and Teacher may elect to include finished comic in writing portfolio.
- Teacher observations: Did student use time wisely? Did student participate in class discussions and end-of-project critique? Did student offer assistance to other students and ask for help if needed?

Integration Across the Curriculum

Science

- Science journals offer a natural partnership for writing, illustration, and observation. Students record what they have learned in a science inquiry lesson or experiment, jot down questions, draw diagrams, and sketch what they have observed.

- Students and teachers can create charts together that categorize and classify. Animals can be put into categories according to size, habitat, color, diet, and body covering. Rocks can be tested for color, hardness, and density and listed on a chart based on physical characteristics.
- When studying a unit on weather, teachers can read books such as Barrett's *Cloudy With a Chance of Meatballs* (1978). Students can write their own descriptive and preposterous stories about storms and food falling from the sky.

Social Studies

- Books with a geographical theme are a great opportunity to write letters and postcards and to create maps. In Brown's *Flat Stanley* (1964), the main character is flattened and travels around the country via the mail. Students can send their own "Flat Stanley" out in the world with letters asking questions and information about his adventures. Many online projects also exist for the *Flat Stanley* activity. Eventually, Stanley returns, and students can discuss, compare experiences, and write about his travels.
- Students can create family trees when studying genealogy or family histories. Leedy's *Who's Who in My Family?* (1995), designed for younger readers, deals with complex family relationships like adoption and second families in a sensitive and accepting manner.

Math

- Cookbooks blend reading, writing, science, and math conveniently in one location. Students can select a simple recipe and rewrite it for a different number of portions or add/delete ingredients to improve on the original. They can write their own recipes for the "perfect sandwich" or a new flavor of ice cream. Students can submit original recipes to one of the many cooking contests sponsored for young chefs.
- Students can write their own math story problems and trade with a classmate to solve.
- Teachers can set up a pretend restaurant. Students can create menus and daily specials; take orders; and write up receipts for diners. Teachers can provide either play or real food. Extension: Students can write and perform a play or provide another form of entertainment for a "dinner theatre" atmosphere.

Literature

- After reading a book such as E. B. White's *Stuart Little* (2005) or Dahl's *James and the Giant Peach* (1961), students can view the movie version. (Teachers should obtain parental permission for movies not rated G.) Using a Venn diagram, students can compare and contrast the versions. Students can vote if they preferred the book or the movie and discuss the reasons for their decision.

Visual and Performing Arts

- Using the book *Just Like Me: Stories and Self-Portraits by Fourteen Artists* (1997), edited by Harriet Rohmer, students can create self-portraits and artists' statements to hang side by side in the classroom art gallery. *Just Like Me* features a two-page format: self-portraits on one side by notable children's book illustrators and, on the facing page, an artist's personal statement in child-friendly text. The student–artist statement can take the form of an "I am" poem. Teachers can discuss how a self-portrait is similar to an autobiography.
- Teachers can have students write and recite poems or narratives about famous paintings or artworks. Possibilities can range from the abstract works of Jackson Pollock to the more

representational paintings and murals of Diego Rivera to a work of public sculpture at the local park. Students can create their own artist sketchbooks to take with them on these excursions.

Health

- Teachers can pass out school lunch menus and have students analyze the food choices according to the current food pyramid guidelines. Students can rewrite the menu reflecting healthier food choices and personal tastes and preferences.
- Students can write letters to district or state officials making recommendations for alternative school menu choices, such as salad bars, a greater variety of fresh produce, or healthier main entrees.

Physical Education

- Teachers can have students write directions for the game *Simon Says* on slips of paper to put into a bag or box. For example, a student can write "hop on your left foot while singing Happy Birthday" or "walk like a duck and say your name backward." The sillier, the better! Students take turns being "Simon" and reading directions.
- Students can write out plans and a materials list for an obstacle course. Teachers review student plans for practical applications and physical education value and make suggestions for revisions. Students can help set up activity and invite other classes to participate.

Music

- While listening to an instrumental piece of music such as classical or jazz, teachers prompt students to sketch how the music made them feel or what the music made them think about. Students discuss images in small groups and then add a written response to enhance the visual image. The written interpretation can be a single word, poem, or paragraph.
- Teachers can provide an assortment of musical instruments that students can experiment with through sound and touch. Students then write a paragraph or poem describing the instrument. Maracas, bells, drums, kazoos, rainsticks, and harmonicas are a few examples of inexpensive or easily obtained instruments. Extension: Students can create own instruments with recycled or "found" materials and write directions about how to make and/or play the instrument.

Parents as Partners

The following suggestions are designed to promote home–school connections with writing:

- *Interviews:* Teachers can send home a list of questions for students to use when interviewing a friend or family member. The questions can focus on a social studies theme such as How Things Change Over Time, in which students interview parents or grandparents about when they were young. A math activity can include a graphing project in which data are collected about a favorite holiday or ice cream flavor.
- *Interactive homework:* Teachers can create homework assignments that students can share with a family member. Students can help cook a meal, go on a bike ride or walk, or play a game together. Students then write and illustrate the experience in a style of their choice.

- *Family meet-the-authors night:* An extension of the Author's Chair activity described earlier: Teachers can work together to plan a school-wide or grade-level event for young authors to share and read their creative works. Often parents are unable to attend school events during work hours, and special nights give families an opportunity to interact with teachers, parents, and school staff in a friendly atmosphere. The event can also center around a theme such as Earth Day or Career Day.

- *Watch television together:* Teachers can include a homework assignment that asks parents to watch a television program together with their children. The teacher provides a "report card" for students and parents to complete about different program elements. Were the characters believable? Did the plot have suspense? Would you recommend this to a friend? Is the program appropriate for a younger sibling?

Student Study Site

The Companion Web site for *Language Arts: Integrating Skills for Classroom Teaching*
www.sagepub.com/donoghuestudy
Visit the Web-based study site to enhance your understanding of the chapter content. The study materials include chapter summaries, practice tests, flashcards, and Web resources.

Additional Professional Readings

Angelillo, J. (2005). *Writing to the prompt: When students don't have a choice.* Portsmouth, NH: Heinemann.

Baghban, M. (2007). Scribbles, labels, and stories: The role of drawing in the development of writing. *Young Children 62*(1), 20–26.

Heard, G., & Laminack, L. (2008). *Climb inside a poem: Reading and writing poetry across the year.* Portsmouth, NH: Heinemann.

Lassonde, C. (2006). Listening for students' voices through positional writing practices. *Language Arts, 83,* 404–412.

Olness, R. (2005). *Using literature to enhance writing instruction.* Newark, DE: International Reading Association.

Parsons, S. (2005). *First grade writers.* Portsmouth, NH: Heinemann.

Prescott-Griffin, M. (2007). *Writer to writer: Fluency and craft in the multilingual classroom.* Portsmouth, NH: Heinemann.

Ray, K. (2008). *Already ready: Nurturing writers in preschool and kindergarten.* Portsmouth, NH: Heinemann.

Solley, B. (2005). *When poverty's children write.* Portsmouth, NH: Heinemann.

Wilson, L. (2006). *Writing to live: How to teach writing for today's world.* Portsmouth, NH: Heinemann.

Children's Literature Cited in the Text

Barrett, J. (1978). *Cloudy with a chance of meatballs.* New York: Aladdin.

Brown, J. (1964). *Flat Stanley.* New York: Harper Trophy.

Brown, M. (1997). *The important book.* New York: HarperCollins.

Bunting, E. (1989). *The Wednesday surprise.* New York: Clarion.

Chinn, K. (1995). *Sam and the lucky money.* New York: Lee & Low.

Cohen, B. (1983). *Molly's Pilgrim.* New York: Morrow.

Cowcher, H. (1990). *Antarctica.* New York: Farrar.

Cronin, D. (2000). *Click, clack, moo: Cows that type.* New York: Simon and Schuster.

Dahl, R. (1961). *James and the giant peach.* New York: Puffin.

D'Aulaire, I., & D'Aulaire, E. (1962). *Ingri and Edgar Parin d'Aulaire's book of Greek myths.* New York: Doubleday.

DePaola, T. (1978). *Pancakes for breakfast.* San Diego: Harcourt.

Finch, M. (2001). *The three billy goats Gruff.* Cambridge, MA: Barefoot.

Fox, P. (1982). *The slave dancer.* New York: Macmillan.

Galdone, P. (1979). *The little red hen.* New York: Houghton Mifflin.

Leedy, L. (1995). *Who's who in my family?* New York: Holiday House.

Martin, B. (1983). *Brown bear, brown bear, what do you see?* New York: Holt.

Ness, E. (1966). *Sam, Bangs and moonshine.* New York: Holt.

O'Brien, J. (1992). *Daffy down dillies: Silly limericks by Edward Lear.* Honesdale, PA: Boyds Mills.

Pullman, P. (2005). *Aladdin and the enchanted lamp.* New York: Scholastic.

Rawlings, M. (1985). *The yearling*. New York: Macmillan.

Rohmer, H. (Ed.). (1997). *Just like me: Stories and self-portraits by fourteen artists*. New York: Children's Press.

Scieszka, J. (1998). *Squids will be squids: Fresh morals, beastly tales*. New York: Viking.

Sendak, M. (1988). *Where the wild things are*. New York: HarperCollins.

Taylor, H. (2000). *Brief candles: 101 clerihews*. Baton Rouge, LA: Louisiana State University Press.

Van Allsburg, C. (1984). *The mysteries of Harris Burdick*. Boston: Houghton Mifflin.

Van Allsburg, C. (1991). *Jumanji*. New York: Houghton.

Viorst, J. (1981). *If I were in charge of the world and other worries*. New York: Atheneum.

White, E. B. (2005). *Stuart Little*. New York: Harper Trophy.

Zemach, M. (1983). *The little red hen: An old story*. New York: Farrar, Straus, and Giroux.

Zolotow, C. (1972). *William's doll*. New York: HarperCollins.

References

Adams, M. (1990). *Beginning to read: Thinking and learning about print*. Cambridge: MIT Press.

Au, K. (1992). Constructing the theme of a story. *Language Arts, 69,* 106–111.

Barone, D. (1990). The written responses of young children: Beyond comprehension to story understanding. *New Advocate, 3,* 49–56.

Bergquist, V. (1996). A potpourri of prewriting ideas for the elementary teacher. In C. Olson (Ed.), *Practical ideas for teaching writing as a process at the elementary school and middle school level*. Sacramento: California Department of Education.

Bonin, S. (1988). Beyond storyland: Young writers can tell it other ways. In T. Newkirk & N. Atwell (Eds.), *Understanding writing* (2nd ed.). Portsmouth, NH: Heinemann.

Bright, R. (1995). *Writing instruction in the intermediate grades*. Newark, DE: International Reading Association.

Britton, J., Burgess, T., Martin, N., McLeod, A., & Rosen, H. (1975). *The development of writing abilities*. London: Macmillan.

Calkins, L. (1994). *The art of teaching writing* (2nd ed.). Portsmouth, NH: Heinemann.

Chafe, W. (1988). What good is punctuation? *Quarterly of the National Writing Project, 10,* 8–11.

Clay, M. (1975). *What did I write?* Portsmouth, NH: Heinemann.

Clay, M. (1991). *Becoming literate: The construction of inner control*. Portsmouth, NH: Heinemann.

Cordeiro, P., Giacobbe, M., & Cazden, C. (1983). Apostrophes, quotation marks, and periods: Learning punctuation in the first grade. *Language Arts, 60,* 323–332.

Cramer, R. (2001). *Creative power: The nature and nurture of children's writing*. New York: Addison Wesley Longman.

Crowhurst, M. (1991). Interrelationships between reading and writing persuasive discourse. *Research in the Teaching of English, 25,* 314–338.

Dyson, A. (1993). *Social worlds of children learning to write in an urban primary school*. New York: Teachers College Press.

Edelsky, C. (1983). Segmentation and punctuation: Developmental data from young writers in a bilingual program. *Research in the Teaching of English, 17,* 135–136.

Elbow, P. (2002). Writing to publish is for every student. In C. Weber (Ed.), *Publishing with students: A comprehensive guide*. Portsmouth, NH: Heinemann.

Fearn, L., & Farnan, M. (1998). *Writing effectively: Helping children master the conventions of writing*. Boston: Allyn & Bacon.

Fresch, M. (2001). Journal entries as a window on spelling knowledge. *The Reading Teacher, 54* (5), 500–513.

Gibbons, P. (2002). *Scaffolding language, scaffolding learning*. Portsmouth, NH: Heinemann.

Graves, D. (1976). Let's get rid of the welfare mess in the teaching of writing. *Language Arts, 53,* 645–651.

Graves, D. (1989). *Experiment with fiction*. Portsmouth, NH: Heinemann.

Hancock, M. (1993). Exploring and extending personal response through literature journals. *The Reading Teacher, 46,* 466–474.

Hansen, J. (1986). *When writers read*. Portsmouth, NH: Heinemann.

Heard, G. (2002). *The revision toolbox: Teaching techniques that work*. Portsmouth, NH: Heinemann.

Henderson, K. (1996). *Market guide for young writers*. New York: Writer's Digest.

Hennings, D. (2002). *Communication in action* (8th ed.).Boston: Houghton Mifflin.

Koch, K. (1990). *Rose, where did you get that red?* New York: Vintage.

Lamme, L. (1989). Authorship: A key facet of whole language. *The Reading Teacher, 42,* 704–710.

Lehr, S. (1991). *The child's developing sense of theme: Responses to literature*. New York: Teachers College Press.

Lynch-Brown, C., & Tomlinson, C. (2005). *Essentials of children's literature* (4th ed). Boston: Allyn & Bacon.

McCann, A. (1989). Student argumentative writing knowledge and ability at three grade levels. *Research in the Teaching of English, 23,* 62–76.

McGee, L., & Richgels, D. (1996). *Literacy's beginnings: Supporting young readers and writers*. Boston: Allyn & Bacon.

Morrow, L, Tracey, D., Woo, D., & Pressley, M. (1999). Characteristics of exemplary first-grade literacy instruction. *The Reading Teacher, 52,* 462–476.

Murray, D. (1990). *Shoptalk: Learning to write with writers*. Portsmouth, NH: Heinemann.

Reyes, M. de la Luz. (1991). A process approach to literacy using dialogue journals and literature logs with second language learners. *Research in the Teaching of English, 25,* 291–313.

Salinger, T. (1992). Critical thinking and young literacy learners. In C. Collins & J. Mangieri (Eds.), *Teaching thinking*. Hillsdale, NJ: Lawrence Erlbaum.

Skolnick, J., & Frazier, J. (1998, April). *A new view of composing.* Paper presented at the annual meeting of the American Educational Research Association, New York.

Sowers, S. (1985). The story and the "all about" book. In J. Hansen, T. Newkirk, & D. Graves (Eds.), *Breaking ground: Teachers relate reading and writing in the elementary school.* Portsmouth, NH: Heinemann.

Sulzby, E. (1992). Research directions: Transitions from emergent to conventional writing. *Language Arts, 69,* 290–297.

Tompkins, G. (2004). *Teaching writing* (4th ed.). Columbus, OH: Merrill/Prentice Hall.

Weaver, C. (1996). *Teaching grammar in context.* Portsmouth, NH: Heinemann.

Wray, D., & Lewis, M. (1997). *Extending literacy: Children reading and writing nonfiction.* New York: Routledge.

Anticipation Statement Answers

1. Disagree
2. Agree
3. Disagree
4. Agree
5. Agree
6. Agree
7. Agree
8. Disagree
9. Agree: Generally, some motivational strategies are more age appropriate than others. However, teachers need to consider ability levels, language proficiency, and student interests when planning activities. Drawing and drama activities are easily modified to accommodate a wide range of abilities and interests.
10. Disagree: Other factors that affect writing efforts are reading level, availability of reading materials, gender, and parent education levels. However, environment and teacher instruction/support are instrumental in student growth as successful writers.

Writing Tools

Handwriting, Keyboarding, Spelling, and Grammar

CHAPTER

9

Teachers carefully nurture students into becoming writers who are able to express their thoughts in written form. With this objective, however, comes the responsibility to help children develop the ability to present those thoughts in an increasingly correct style through legible handwriting, accurate keyboarding, standard spelling, and correct grammatical constructions.

Anticipation Statements

Complete this exercise before reading Chapter 9.

Do you agree or disagree with the following statements? Circle your answer. Be prepared to discuss questions in blue.

1.	There are prerequisite skill areas for handwriting, two of which are hand-eye coordination and letter perception.	Agree	Disagree
2.	There are two forms of handwriting taught in the elementary schools.	Agree	Disagree
3.	Keyboarding improves language arts skills.	Agree	Disagree
4.	Teachers should wait until students are in the intermediate grades to introduce keyboarding.	Agree	Disagree
5.	Parents continue to rank spelling as a significant subject area in the elementary curriculum.	Agree	Disagree
6.	Research shows that English spelling is 80–85% regular.	Agree	Disagree
7.	Students develop spelling skills in systematic stages.	Agree	Disagree
8.	There is a reciprocal relationship between spelling and reading.	Agree	Disagree
9.	A knowledge of basic grammatical terms is important to students in Grades 1–6.	Agree	Disagree
10.	The most prevalent grammar today is transformation-generative grammar.	Agree	Disagree

Handwriting and Keyboarding

A surge of interest in handwriting has occurred since the College Board in 2005 added a handwritten essay to the SAT. That addition was made in an effort to reverse the de-emphasis in recent decades on handwriting and composition that may be negatively affecting children's learning all the way through high school and college (Kelley, 2007). Evidence is growing that handwriting fluency is a basic building block of learning. From kindergarten through fourth grade students think and write at the same time. Consequently, when children struggle with handwriting, their spelling and math skills are affected as well. Both of these subjects are easier for students to learn when handwriting becomes an automatic process and children do not have to remember how to form each and every letter and numeral.

Handwriting can be defined as the production of symbols that, when placed together, represent words. However, there is no widespread acceptance of what constitutes legible handwriting. Furthermore, modern society prefers electronically processed print to penned script. It is this preference that has been influencing handwriting instruction during recent decades. While still emphasized in kindergarten and primary grades, such instruction has generally been overlooked by intermediate teachers and students.

Nevertheless, handwriting merits attention throughout the school day, with instruction sessions and practice involving elementary school children in practical writing situations related to reading, spelling, social studies, and science assignments.

Fundamental Facts About Teaching Handwriting

Educators agree on the need to teach handwriting, although many admit that it is the most poorly taught segment of the elementary curriculum, especially in the intermediate grades. Nevertheless, handwriting continues to play an important role both in and out of school in the integrated program of language arts. Handwriting is linked with writing at all grade levels, even kindergarten. It is primarily a tool of communication, and students who write for a valid reason accept the significance of handwriting. It therefore must receive direct and systematic instruction by teachers who are aware of the numerous facts concerned with the teaching of handwriting.

Because handwriting is an individual production influenced by physical, mental, and emotional factors, a child's progress in mastering handwriting skills is closely related to his or her total growth and development. Therefore, some children who do not achieve academic success may still become highly skilled in handwriting because its major prerequisite—motor control—is not highly correlated with intelligence or scholastic achievement.

The primary goal in teaching handwriting is legibility, which differs from neatness. It has been defined as the ease with which something can be read. A child's paper may be legible but not neat. The secondary goal in teaching handwriting is fluency (without loss of legibility). While not a factor in the early grades, fluency or speed of writing gradually increases beginning in Grade 3 and helps with note taking and drafting original material. Correct posture, correct hand movement, and proper positioning of the writing paper and writing tools must be developed for each child to ensure handwriting success.

Most children are taught two forms of handwriting: manuscript (or printing) and cursive (or connected). Printing is introduced first in kindergarten or first grade followed by a transition to

Applicable IRA/NCTE Standards

Standard 6   Students apply knowledge of language structure, language conventions (e.g., spelling and punctuation), media techniques, figurative language, and genre to create, critique, and discuss print and non-print texts.

Standard 10   Students whose first language is not English make use of their first language to develop competency in the English language arts and to develop understanding of content across the curriculum.

Source: *Standards for the English Language Arts*, by the International Reading Association and the National Council of Teachers of English, Copyright 1996 by the International Reading Association and the National Council of Teachers of English. Reprinted with permission. http://www.ncte.org/about/over/standards/110846.htm

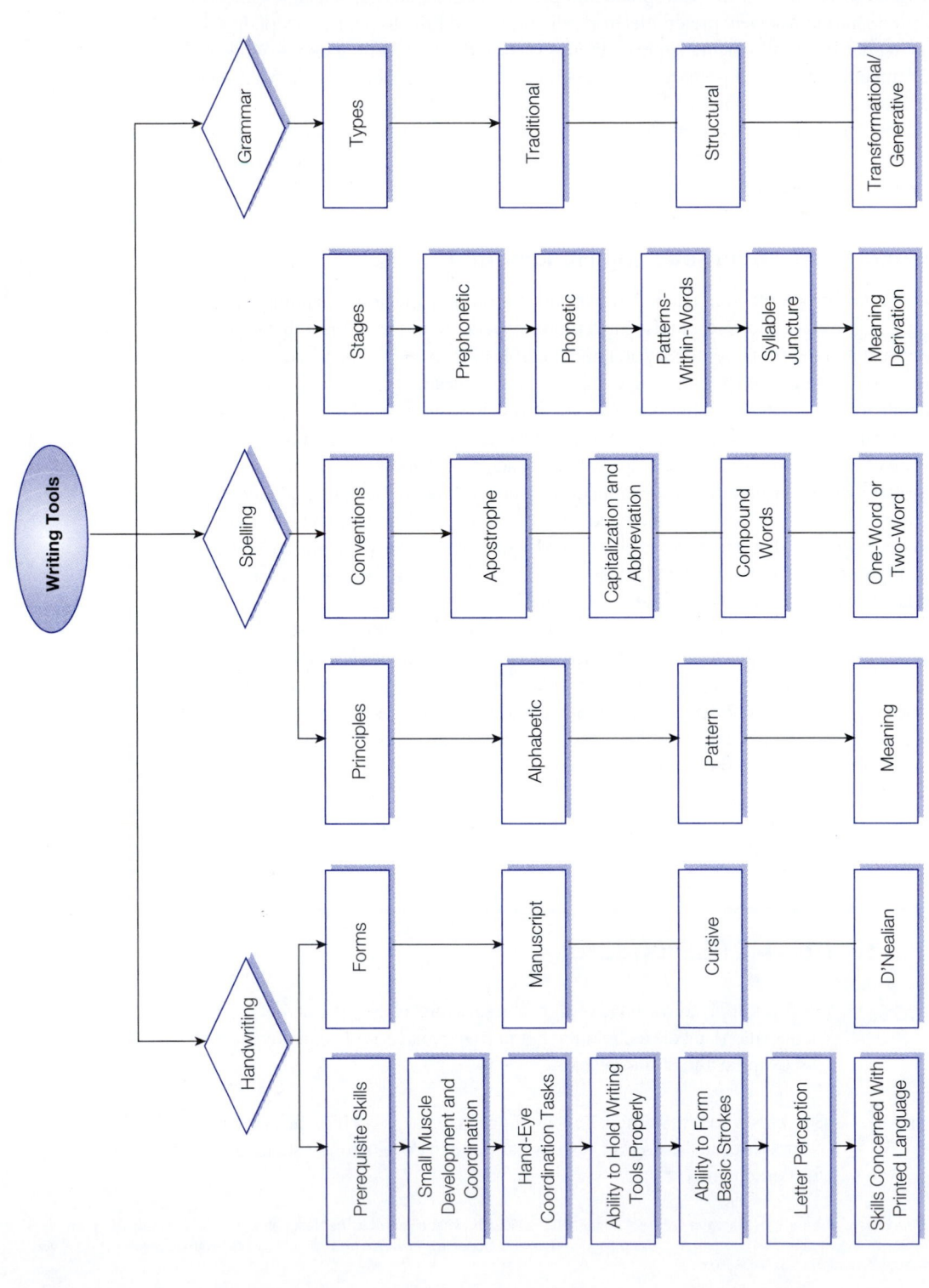

A Graphic Summary of the Contents of This Chapter

cursive in late second grade or early third grade. To teach handwriting most effectively, teachers should use the following strategies:

- With young children, demonstrate the strokes of the letters on the chalkboard or on an overhead projector.
- Model handwriting with wall charts of manuscript printing for first and second graders and of cursive writing for third graders and up. To enable ready reference by children, these charts frequently come in long horizontal strips that can be mounted above the chalkboard.
- Teach handwriting in mini-lessons since short lessons and practice sessions presented several times a week are more effective than a single, lengthy period weekly.
- Do not teach children to write letters in rote fashion, according to the alphabet, but preferably in relation to spelling or phonics lessons in progress so they can write words that begin with the letter under scrutiny.
- Whether in manuscript or in cursive, introduce letters based on similarity of the strokes involved in their production (e.g., in lowercase manuscript print, counterclockwise circles are *a, c, e,* and *o*).
- After children have learned both manuscript and cursive, review both forms periodically with them throughout the intermediate grades.

Prerequisite Skills for Beginning Writing

Many years ago, after conducting extensive experimental work with young children, Maria Montessori stated that learning to write demands both intelligence and an efficient motor

Eye-hand coordination enables beginning writers to use the lines on the chalkboard to carefully place their manuscript letters.

mechanism. Children can acquire the mental readiness through experiences that value handwriting and promote their interest in learning to write. They attain motor readiness through activities that teach them how to hold the writing tools and to perform the simple movements required.

Educational researchers have identified six prerequisite skill areas for handwriting (Lamme, 1979). The first is *small muscle development and coordination.* When children start school, they use their arm and leg muscles fairly well, but skill in the use of the wrist and finger muscles comes more slowly. Before they can develop skill in writing, they must be able to hold the chalk, crayon, or pencil without noticeable strain and be able to make their finger muscles respond so that they can copy simple geometric or letter-like characters. Forcing students to write before they are physically ready may cause long-term or even permanent problems with their handwriting.

The second handwriting skill area is *hand-eye coordination,* which is clearly related to the development of small muscle skills. Therefore, activities used to promote small muscle development, such as working with jigsaw puzzles, using scissors, or playing with blocks, also promote hand-eye coordination. Even large-muscle activities, such as jumping rope or climbing a ladder, are helpful for enhancing hand-eye precision.

The *ability to hold writing tools properly* is the third prerequisite skill area. Young children can learn to manipulate tools during such experiences as cooking (with spatulas and spoons), gardening (with rakes and hoes), and painting (sponges and brushes). Then as beginning writers they can use standard (adult) pencils from the start. Their teacher may quickly determine if they are holding those pencils properly (with the correct amount of pressure) by checking writing papers for dents or for strokes that are too faint. Children who grip their pencils too tightly may be unable to write comfortably for a reasonable period of time.

A fourth prerequisite skill area is the *ability to form basic strokes.* Circles and straight lines should be made smoothly in the appropriate direction and with clean intersections. Such strokes should evolve through activities such as drawing, stirring, and painting. Until circles and straight lines occur naturally in a child's drawings of houses, trucks, flowers, and the like, the girl or boy may not be ready for formal handwriting instruction because the transition from drawing to handwriting is a slow process for some students.

Letter perception is the fifth prerequisite skill area. Since handwriting is more than a physical activity, attention to perception in a handwriting program develops better writers. In the initial stages of handwriting, letter reversals may often occur, but generally disappear as children mature. The importance of adult modeling of correct letter formation is critical. Students must perceive the way that the alphabet letters are formed. The more often they see their teacher write on paper (and not merely on the chalkboard or a transparency) the better. Equally important is self-correction of initial attempts at handwriting as an aid in letter perception because incorrect habits are difficult to break later.

The sixth and final prehandwriting skill is actually *an entire set of skills concerned with the orientation to printed language.* One such skill is an interest in writing and a desire to write. As the children observe their teacher writing in a meaningful way, their desire to write themselves should begin to grow. They soon sense a personal need to communicate in writing and enjoy learning to write their names. As the students watch, the teacher writes their dictated captions for pictures and experience charts as well as dictated messages to absent classmates.

Another skill is an understanding of the left-to-right progression. Before starting to write, children need to know the meaning of the terms *left* and *right.* While some begin school with an understanding of the difference between the terms, other students must gradually begin to comprehend them through teacher-planned psychomotor activities.

Still another skill is language maturity. When children verbalize satisfactorily, their conversations provide meaningful vocabularies for the first writing experiences. They enjoy listening to stories as well as composing and sending written messages. They should have many opportunities to dictate stories, reports, and funny or scary incidents. When writing for the students, the teacher is introducing them to writing and reading as well as helping them bridge the gap between oral and written language.

Handwriting Forms

Currently three forms of handwriting are taught and used in the elementary school: manuscript (or printing), cursive (or connected), and D'Nealian handwriting. Students learn and use manuscript writing in the primary grades, switching to cursive writing in the late second or early third grade. In the intermediate grades both forms are used, depending on the assigned task. The third form is an alternative form that combines the cursive and manuscript styles.

Manuscript writing arrived in the United States from England nearly a century ago and is today part of the curriculum in many primary grades throughout the country. It has two major advantages: It requires lower levels of perceptual and motor readiness than other forms of writing, and it is very similar to the print found in books and in the children's world outside the classroom, thereby providing a motivation for learning to read (Duvall, 1985; Farris, 1982; Graham, 1992). Manuscript writing requires only two basic strokes that are similar to those used by children when drawing and that parallel their perceptual and motor development. It can be written with little physical strain and so allows children to rest between strokes if necessary; because letters are separated, even students with poor muscular control can produce readable results. Manuscript writing demands few eye movements, making it easier on the eyes of all young children and especially those with visual difficulties. Finally, it can be written rapidly without loss of legibility and so helps children express themselves in writing.

Manuscript writing is very similar to the print used in books, with only two lowercase letters (*a* and *g*) that are different in type than in handwriting, and it resembles the print in the children's world outside the classroom (e.g., SCHOOL BUS, STOP). Because manuscript writing resembles the print found in many primary reading materials, only one alphabet needs to be mastered, and Piaget's work suggests that the preoperational child (usually from two to seven years of age) will learn to write and read better and faster when a single alphabet is used. Manuscript writing therefore increases the quantity and quality of written composition and promotes spelling because many spelling errors are really handwriting illegibilities (see Figure 9.1).

Despite these advantages, manuscript writing is often abandoned in the intermediate grades, once the children have learned a new form, cursive writing. However, teachers in those grades should remain familiar with manuscript writing to ensure that students will continue to use it for some assignments (e.g., the preparation of maps or posters).

Cursive writing is usually introduced in late second grade or early third grade, with third grade being by far the more popular time for learning it. Cursive (or connected) writing is not faster, easier, or more legible than manuscript writing, but society—and parents—demand the transition from printing to cursive handwriting (see Figure 9.2).

Students also want to become cursive writers because they consider the form to be the way that adults write. They are ready for such instruction when they (a) have shown an interest in learning cursive writing; (b) can write well all the manuscript letters from memory; (c) have begun to join those letters; and (d) can read writing, since a definite relationship exists between the ability to read print and to read cursive writing. Children who have developed adequate skill in reading manuscript-style print will need little instructional help in reading cursive style.

The cursive style involves four performance tasks (see Figures 9.3 and 9.4 for the most difficult letters and combinations). First, children must learn to habitually turn the paper in front of them. Second, they must keep their nonwriting hand out of the way, at the top of the sheet, for easy

Figure 9.1 Manuscript Handwriting Alphabet

(a)

(b)

Figure 9.2 Cursive Handwriting Alphabet

(a)

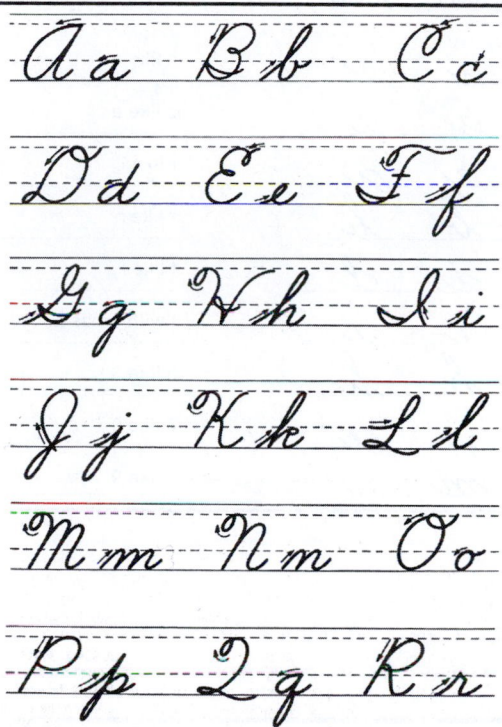

(b)

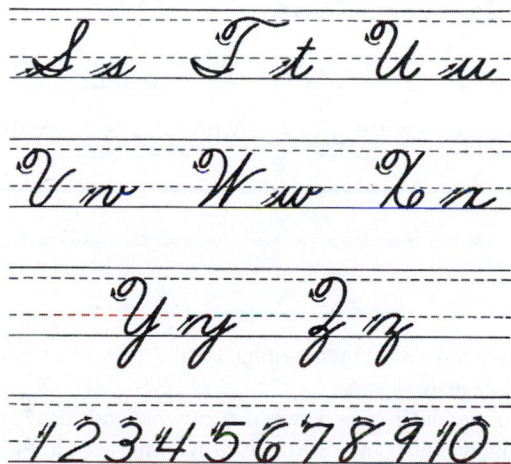

Figure 9.3 The Most Difficult Numerals and Cursive Letters Constitute Half of All Handwriting Illegibilities

	Right	Wrong		Right	Wrong
a like o	*a*	*a*	n like u	*n*	*u*
a like u	*a*	*u*	o like a	*o*	*a*
a like ci	*a*	*a*	r like i	*r*	*r*
b like li	*b*	*b*	r like n	*r*	*u*
d like cl	*d*	*d*	t like l	*t*	*t*
e closed	*e*	*e*	t with cross above	*t*	*t*
h like li	*h*	*h*	5 like 3	*5*	*5*
i like e with no dot	*i*	*e*	6 like 0	*6*	*0*
m like w	*m*	*w*	7 like 9	*7*	*7*

Figure 9.4 The Most Difficult Cursive Combinations

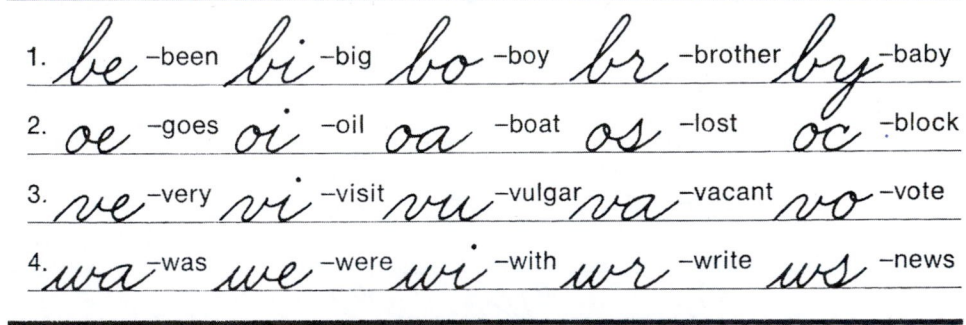

1. *be* –been *bi* –big *bo* –boy *br* –brother *by* –baby
2. *oe* –goes *oi* –oil *oa* –boat *os* –lost *oc* –block
3. *ve* –very *vi* –visit *vu* –vulgar *va* –vacant *vo* –vote
4. *wa* –was *we* –were *wi* –with *wr* –write *ws* –news

paper shifting. Third, they must slant their writing. Finally, they must learn to slide their pens or pencils laterally to join the cursive letters.

Table 9.1 summarizes the differences between manuscript and cursive writing.

D'Nealian handwriting was first developed in 1978 in Michigan by a teacher/principal, Donald N. Thurber, and combines cursive and manuscript writing (see Figures 9.5a and 9.5b).

Children begin learning D'Nealian handwriting by printing in slanted script that resembles cursive writing. They learn to make 21 of the lowercase manuscript letters with a continuous stroke, retracing at times as they work in traditional cursive. Since students slant the manuscript forms from the very start, no new alignment procedures are needed for the transition to cursive, which

Table 9.1 Differences Between Manuscript and Cursive Writing

Characteristics	Manuscript Writing	Cursive Writing
Basic strokes	Circles and straight lines	Slant strokes, connecting strokes, and ovals
When pencil is lifted from the paper	After each letter	On completion of each word
Spacing	Determined by shape of letters	Controlled by the slant and manner of making connective strokes
Similarity between upper- and lowercase letters	Nearly one-third are very similar	Every letter differs considerably
Similarity to book print	Very similar	Not similar

can occur as early as late first grade or early second grade. However, teachers planning to use the D'Nealian style should be aware that researchers have concluded that there is insufficient evidence of benefits of using a special, slanted alphabet like D'Nealian (Graham, 1992; Ourada, 1993).

Criteria for Determining Handwriting Quality

The aims of the handwriting program are legibility and fluency, and the only form of rating for any young writer occurs when he or she and the teacher set up goals for the improvement of personal writing skills. Studies have shown that students have difficulty judging the quality of their own work, especially if they are poor handwriters. Thus, class or group discussion of legibility and fluency should precede the student-teacher conference.

Since a legible paper has best been described as one that can be read with ease, *legibility* is said to be the most important quality of handwriting (Farris, 1991; Hodges, 1991). While this is true of both manuscript and cursive writing, legibility plays an even more important role in the cursive method since proper connections between various letters and letter formations promote to a larger degree the overall clarity of the writing compared to one written in manuscript. Six letters—*h, l, k, p, r,* and *z*—account for 30% of all illegibilities in cursive handwriting, with *r* alone responsible for 12% of the total (Horton, 1970).

Legibility for manuscript and cursive writing has six components (Hackney, 1993):

1. *Alignment:* All letters in both manuscript and cursive writing should be uniform in size and consistently touch the baseline.

2. *Letter formation:* Manuscript writing consists of horizontal, vertical, and slanted lines and circles or parts of circles. Cursive writing consists of slanted lines, curved lines, and loops, as well as connecting strokes to join letters.

3. *Line quality:* This quality has been described as the evenness, smoothness, and thickness of the pen or pencil line. Varying line quality results from inconsistent pressure, which in turn is due to fatigue or overly rapid writing.

Figure 9.5a One Alternative Form of Handwriting: D'Nealian Manuscript Alphabet

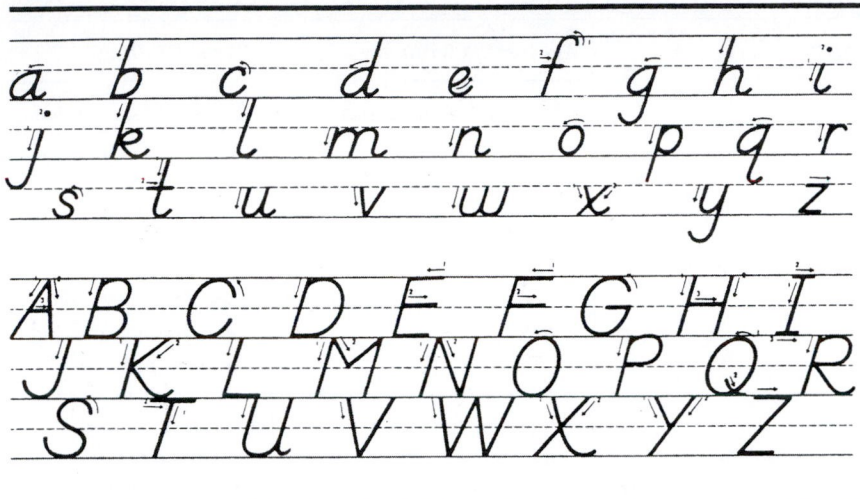

Figure 9.5b D'Nealian Cursive Alphabet

4. *Size and proportion.* Proportion refers to the height of the letters in relation to each other and to the writing space. During the elementary grades, children's handwriting gradually becomes smaller, and the proportional size of uppercase to lowercase letters increases. For beginners in cursive handwriting, for example, the proportional size of the letters is two to one, but in the intermediate grades, it is three to one.

5. *Slant.* There should be no slant in manuscript writing because letters are vertical. All cursive letters slant slightly to the right. Letters should be consistently parallel. Left-handed students should tilt their papers to the right, and right-handed students should tilt theirs to the left.

6. *Spacing.* Spacing between letters in words and between words in sentences should be consistent. If a child uses inconsistent spacing between letters and words, the writing becomes more difficult to read and possibly illegible.

Although all six elements are important in elementary school handwriting, the major emphasis is on letter formation and spacing.

In addition to legibility, the other goal of handwriting instruction is *fluency.* Also described as the other half of the handwriting equation (as it is concerned with the *rate* of writing), fluency means an uninterrupted flow of handwriting without special attention to the actual production of the letters and the words. It is attained only after students have had considerable practice and have finally mastered letter formation. When handwriting becomes automatic, composing fluency grows and writers gradually develop more speed. Consequently, fluent writers are those children who can focus on the content that comprises meaningful writing and then compose their message readily.

Left-Handed Children

About 10% of children in any elementary classroom are left-handed so most teachers will work with approximately three such children a year. Fortunately, instruction for them is only slightly different from that provided for right-handed students. More important, left-handed students should not be treated as children with special needs.

Hand dominance is generally established by the time the students start school, as most children develop a preference for their right or left hand some time during the first four years of life (Bloodsworth, 1993). If unsure of any child's choice, the teacher should observe that boy or girl as he or she throws a ball, reaches for a book, or paints a picture. Though not infallible, these actions provide clues concerning the child's hand preference.

It must be stressed that handwriting demands fine motor control. Consequently, for those students who enter kindergarten using both hands interchangeably, instruction should be postponed until they develop a dominant hand.

Left-handed students require special instruction in three areas:

1. *Pencil grip:* Left-handed writers should hold their writing tools an inch or more farther from the tip than do right-handed writers. This allows them to avoid dragging their hand across the page and also to see better what they have just written. They must keep their elbows close to their bodies and their wrists straight. Their writing instrument should point over their left shoulder.

2. *Paper position:* Left-handed students should tilt their papers slightly to the right. It is recommended that each writer find the best location for the paper because the height of the individual student as well as the slant of the desk may necessitate some adjustment in paper position. Left-handed children in Grades 3 and higher should investigate "left-handed notebooks" that have the spiral on the right side rather than the traditional left.

3. *Handwriting slant:* Left-handed students often write their cursive letters vertically or even slant their letters slightly backward. They should use pushing strokes rather than pulling strokes.

Left-handed students should be grouped together for instructional purposes. This will prevent the confusion that often results when the teacher attempts to instruct both right- and left-handed writers at the same time. When grouped together for instruction, left-handed children can help one another with paper position and letter formation. Furthermore, when first learning to write, left-handed students write more slowly than right-handed children. Consequently, they should be allowed additional time to complete in-class assignments.

Keyboarding or Word-Processing Skills

A common alternative to handwriting, **keyboarding** can be simply defined as typing on the computer. While debate continues about when to introduce keyboarding instruction in the elementary school, some experts believe that it should begin as soon as students demonstrate manual dexterity and an interest in working on the keyboard, even as early as kindergarten (Lockard, Abrams, & Many, 1997). Ideally by the third grade, children are able to type as fast as they can handwrite.

Keyboarding has been shown to improve language arts skills (Crews, North, & Erthal, 2006). It aids reading comprehension, vocabulary, word study skills, spelling, and writing and editing skills. Furthermore, keyboarding also improves handwriting since both are psychomotor skills that demand eye-hand coordination.

Teachers planning keyboarding lessons should realize that practice sessions in the elementary school should be *short* (averaging 10–20 minutes in most grades), *frequent and regular* (since keyboarding is a psychomotor skill), and *focused* (since the correct order in which to teach keyboarding is proper technique, appropriate speed, and accuracy). Immediate feedback is critical for learning efficiency.

The most important goal in keyboarding is to move the students from an emphasis on finger movements to a stress on meaningful language use.

Practice should also be *incremental*. The major goal at K–2 levels is keyboard awareness. Rogers' (1997) program stresses the multisensory approach to teach key location and allows students to keep their eyes on a textbook while typing. In Grades 3 through 5, approximately two new alphabetic keys should be introduced per session together with a review of prior keys. Students should have ample time to learn new keys and regularly practice the keys previously learned.

Keyboarding skills should be introduced early before students develop the bad habits of hunt-and-peck typing (Ubelacker, 1992). Such habits are hard to replace with more efficient ones. Children can learn keyboarding through Internet resources, teacher-directed lessons, or software packages.

Typing, like any psychomotor skill involving the repetition of identical movements, eventually becomes automatic, which results in an increase in typing speed. Nevertheless, any focus on speed and typing accuracy should be developmentally appropriate for the students.

Teachers must realize that the most important goal in keyboarding is to move the students from an emphasis on finger movements to a stress on meaningful language use during class assignments, as Mr. Kim does with his fifth graders when he asks them to write to businesses as young consumers in Vignette 9.1.

VIGNETTE 9.1 Keyboarding for Practical Purposes

Two years ago, the elementary schools across the district began teaching keyboarding in third grade and also made significant investments in desktop computers for each classroom. Mr. Kim, a fifth-grade teacher, was pleased with this early introduction to typing since it meant his students would begin the school year with a mastery of the basics.

Because students of all ages learn keyboarding skills best through short periods of repetition and practice, the curriculum called for him to regularly review posture, finger position, and the home row keys. However, Mr. Kim wanted the children to discover the why—not just the how—of keyboarding. He knew their enthusiasm for practice and correct technique would increase if he could also help them discover the practical value of a well-typed document. Because the students would continue to work on typing speed in the intermediate grades, he also felt comfortable with an approach focusing on accuracy rather than words per minute.

So after several weeks of keyboarding review, Mr. Kim led the class in a fun, far-ranging brainstorming session about products they enjoyed; popular brands of gym shoes, snack foods, video games, and even cell phones topped the list. During journal time he asked each student to pick a favorite product and draft a handwritten letter to the company that produced that food, item of clothing, or electronic device. "It doesn't have to be a long letter," he said, "but it's important to tell businesses when we think they're doing a good job. Please finish your letter by Monday."

The next day he asked the class to share stories about products that could be improved. "My little brother has shoes that light up red when he walks, only they stopped lighting up and my mom was mad," offered one child. This reminded several other students of similar experiences or annoyances, and the class quickly generated another list of products, services, and companies. Mr. Kim smiled to himself at the young consumers and asked the children to write a letter to one of these businesses as well. "Not a mean letter," he reminded them, "but a letter telling them what you didn't like so they can fix the problem. This one's due on Monday too!"

Because Mr. Kim knew his students already felt extremely comfortable using the Internet to find information, he also asked the children to use the school computers or their computers at home to search for the mailing addresses of their selected companies.

When the students arrived Monday morning they found an example of a professional letter on each desk and a copy of the same letter projected onto the screen at the front of the room. Mr. Kim presented a quick lesson covering the fundamentals of typing and spacing the date, address, and paragraphs, and then asked each student to practice keyboarding one of the letters from his journal in this new format.

Mr. Kim walked around the room during the exercise, stopping frequently to encourage individual students and answer questions. After each child had completed and printed a first draft, he asked them to swap letters and check each other's work. He led them through the proofreading session by revisiting the main points of the morning's lesson on correct formatting, and also asked the students to mark any spelling or grammar mistakes.

For several days the students typed and edited their two letters, practicing both the new concept of business writing and the more familiar keyboarding skills. By the end of the week every child had produced clean, correct copies of both a "compliment" and "complaint" letter. Mr. Kim helped them sign and mail each one.

After a few weeks, one student received a response from his letter to an airline that had bumped him from a flight the summer before. As the days passed, more students received return letters from both the companies they had praised and those they had not. Several students received coupons, special discount offers, or free product samples. The children enjoyed not only the freebies but also the recognition and fun of receiving a "grown-up" letter in the mail.

A few students received no responses to either letter, which Mr. Kim expected. He reminded the entire class that, even if a company does not acknowledge the letter, the goal of the assignment was to communicate professionally. "Each of you can feel proud that you shared your thoughts with a business leader," he said.

As the semester progressed, Mr. Kim continued regular keyboard practice and also began requiring the students to type book reports, group work, and other assignments. However, he occasionally revived the letter project and created opportunities for the children to repeat the cycle of brainstorming, writing, research, typing, and peer-editing. Mr. Kim knew the combination of tasks helped the students connect their typing practice to a world of work outside their own school assignments. He expected the feedback they received to reinforce his own teaching about the importance of keyboarding, and he enjoyed the added surprise of seeing his young students become more thoughtful writers and more critical customers.

Spelling

Our society places a high premium on correct **spelling**, a writing tool that focuses on correct letter selection and sequencing, thereby making writing easier to read correctly. Often educated persons are identified as such solely on their ability to spell words accurately as revealed in their written communication. Parents who are aware of this identification are concerned that their children learn to spell correctly, and therefore continue to rank spelling as a significant subject area in the elementary curriculum.

Principles and Conventions of Spelling

Understanding the principles and conventions of English spelling is basic to efficient teaching of the subject. Briefly, a *spelling principle* is a fundamental truth about the spelling system itself. It is stable and inherent in the structure of the English language, such as the meaning principle (explained later in this section). On the other hand, a *spelling convention* is a common practice in English spelling that results from common usage and may change over time as custom dictates, such as the apostrophe connection (described below). Principles and conventions, according to Cramer (1998), are most likely to become part of the child's spelling knowledge base through direct instruction that is supplemented when needed by reading (to increase the language knowledge base) and by writing (to supply the application).

There are three principles of English orthography that students master as they move through the stages of spelling development:

For material related to this concept, go to Video Clip 9.1 on the Student Resource CD bound into the back of your textbook.

1. *The alphabetic principle* (i.e., letters represent sounds): Since English has 44 sounds but only 26 letters, one sound can be represented by more than one letter. Such irregularities in letter-sound relationships do cause some spelling problems and thereby also promote the false assumption the English language is incredibly irregular. Actually, research concluded decades ago (Hanna, Hanna, Hodges, & Rudorf, 1966) found that American English spelling is 80–85% regular when the other principles governing spelling are taken into consideration.

2. *The pattern principle* (i.e., letters are combined in predictable ways to spell sounds): Students master this principle during phonics lessons as they learn, for example, how to spell vowel and consonant patterns. They also learn that the spelling of a sound may be constrained by the letters that surround it and by its position in a word; for example, *gh* never has an */f/* sound at the beginning of a word (as in *ghost*), but does so in the medial or ending position (as in *rough*).

3. *The meaning principle* (i.e., words related in spelling and meaning may have different pronunciations): Students should be taught this principle early because it is one of the most efficient and useful means of helping them become aware of spelling concepts that share a common base (Fowler & Liberman, 1995). Once children understand the relationship between, for example, *sign or signal* and *legal or legality,* they will know how to write words whose spellings they could only guess at earlier. They will also be less confused by irregular spellings. Since there are thousands of meaning-connection words, this principle becomes increasingly effective with each succeeding grade level.

Four conventions improve spelling ability as students become aware of them, learn to understand them, and finally incorporate them in their writing:

1. *The apostrophe convention:* Spelling errors due to an omitted or misplaced apostrophe are routine. Teachers should therefore explain that this punctuation mark (') can be used in contractions to indicate the omission of one or more letters (e.g., *aren't* for *are not*). It can also be used to show possessive forms of singular or plural nouns or indefinite pronouns: *Jim's house, students' reports, nobody's business.* Lastly, it can be used to form plurals of numbers and letters (e.g., *two 9s in .995*). Among the most frequently misspelled contractions are *didn't, don't, we're, there's, you're, they're, let's,* and *it's* (Cramer & Cipielewski, 1995).

2. *Capitalization and abbreviation conventions:* Proper nouns name specific persons, places, or things and must start with capital letters. Failure to do so ranks among the most prevalent capitalization errors although there are other capitalization conventions as well. Like capitals, abbreviations are another convention of spelling. Periods follow abbreviated words

and are considered part of the spelling of those words, for example, *Sept.* for *September.* Students must be taught that periods and capitals are an essential part of the correct spelling of certain words.

3. *Compound word conventions:* Combinations of two or more words that function as a single unit of meaning are defined as compound words. They can be written as closed compounds or single words (e.g., *baseball*), as open compounds or separate words (e.g., *ice cream*), or as hyphenated words (e.g., *sixty-two*). Misspelled compounds include the same types of errors that other words exhibit plus one additional error: spacing. A spacing error occurs when closed compounds are written as two words or open compounds are spelled as one word.

4. *One-word or two-word conventions:* Confusion arises over such words as *all ways/always, tonight/to night, forever/for ever,* and *because/be cause* as well as many others. Some of this confusion arises when words start with an *a* (which is both an article and an alphabetic letter) or with *to* or *be* (which are single words as well as the first two letters in longer words). Confusion is often linked to usage and meaning (e.g., *gonna* for *going to*), but is still rated as a spelling error.

Fundamental Facts About Spelling

Before an instructional agenda for spelling can be established for any elementary grade level, teachers must recall certain basic facts about the subject of spelling:

- *Spelling is a developmental process.* As children grow older, they gradually move toward a better comprehension of English orthography. The several stages of spelling development evolve systematically, and students do not fluctuate between them nor do they regress in their progress. Research shows that spelling accuracy improves with age (Jongsma, 1990).
- *Learning to spell is more an active conceptual process than it is a memorization process.* As students advance through school, their ability to spell becomes more and more related to their understanding of the structural and semantic relationships of words. As they interact with language both in and out of school, they develop a more mature insight about spelling.
- *Learning to spell has certain unique aspects.* Spelling has the special function of representing language graphically through handwriting or word processing. It forms a link between verbal and written forms of expression. It is a multisensory process involving visual, auditory, oral, and haptical abilities. Most children are able to use all these sensory modes in learning to spell, but they hardly use them all to the same degree or in the same way. Slower learners, for example, admit that the most effective way for them to learn to spell involves pronunciation of the words by classmates or the teacher.
- *Learning to spell should occur simultaneously with children's learning to assign letters to sounds for decoding purposes* (Wolfe & Nevills, 2004). This helps students acquire the same new language patterns across varied language arts domains and so strengthen the networks of neural connections formed in the brain.
- *There is a reciprocal relationship between spelling and reading.* Spelling knowledge enables students to read unknown words, and reading knowledge enables them to spell unknown words (Garcia, 1997). Reading gives children the opportunity to see standard spelling in print, and consequently to develop visual memories for words. The reciprocal connection between learning to spell and learning to read is most evident in the primary grades (Stanovich, 1988). Many of the abilities required for reading are also required for spelling (e.g., phonemic awareness, recognition of letter names and letter sounds, and visual discrimination among words). Generalizations regarding vocabulary development, phonic analysis, and structural analysis are the same in reading as they are in spelling.

Finally, for some students, seeing words in print may be a more effective means of learning to spell than hearing them (Ehri & Wilce, 1987). Nevertheless, note that the act of spelling involves encoding (going from sounds to letters) while the act of reading involves decoding (going from letters to sounds).

- While spelling instruction can be organized in many different ways, it is most compatible with the reading brain when spelling words are arranged into groups with common word patterns and is sequenced grade by grade. Moats (2001) suggests the following forms of spelling instruction for the early grades: kindergarten programs linked to phoneme awareness; first-grade programs stressing consonant and vowel correspondence; second-grade programs linked to more complex spelling patterns; and third-grade programs emphasizing syllabication, compounds, and word endings.

- *Spelling is a writing tool.* The chief reason for learning how to spell is to make writing easier to read correctly, thereby promoting accurate communication between the recipient and the writer. Numerous opportunities occur in daily life where correct spelling can become a critical issue; one example is accessing information on the Internet. (As for using a spell-checker, it is helpful when computers are available, although some persons argue that the device has definite limitations that affect its general use.)

- *Writing supports the spelling program.* It gives children a reason to learn how to spell. This ability in turn enhances their writing because they do not have to concentrate on the mechanics of words, but can instead be totally involved in the creative process. Spelling comes into focus especially during the editing-proofreading stage of writing since that is the best time for stressing the detailed knowledge needed to check for spelling mechanics. Writing and spelling, by approximation, give children basic concepts about print and its meaning function, as well as the spelling patterns inherent in the alphabetic system (Cramer, 1998). Briefly, writing makes practical use of spelling.

Stages of Spelling Development

Long before boys and girls start school, they acquire the fundamentals of their native language and even learn to use a grammar to put words together to form sentences. Language development therefore proceeds from the simple to the complex. So too does spelling development; maturing children gradually progress toward a greater understanding of English orthography.

However, students do not proceed as spellers randomly or by rote. Nor do they all learn spelling in exactly the same way. Still, researchers, beginning with Henderson (1990), have found that the stages of spelling form a systematic developmental sequence and that children only occasionally fluctuate radically between stages or regress. While the names of the stages differ from one researcher to another, the major features and substantive content of each of the five stages remain essentially the same. Cramer (1998) chose the following names:

1. *Prephonetic stage* (typically for ages 3–5): In this stage, children in preschool or kindergarten try to imitate writing by the random use of scribbles, letter-like forms, and those alphabetic symbols that they are able to produce from recall. Examples include IMMPMPT and BDRNMPM, both of which can only be "read back" by the spellers themselves. Students usually lack knowledge of the entire alphabet, the distinction between lowercase and uppercase letters, and the left-to-right direction of English spelling. Most use uppercase letters only. Yet children implicitly understand that speech can be recorded by graphic symbols.

   Teachers (and parents) can help children through this emergent or preliterate stage by implementing, in a consistent manner, developmentally appropriate activities such as the following: reading aloud alphabet books and books with rhymes, writing students' names on drawings and work papers while focusing on the letters, and calling attention to environmental print on labels and posters in the classroom as well as to signs and logos in the neighborhood.

2. *Phonetic stage* (typically for ages 5–7): Also known as the *letter name stage,* it occurs when children represent the essential phonetic elements of words by alphabetic letters, even though the letters used may be wrong. Although phonetic spelling does not resemble standard spelling, it is readable to most first-grade teachers and to the writers themselves. Examples of early phonetic spellings are PPL for *people* and PRD for *purred.* Although phonetic spellers are more likely to use consonant letters than vowel letters, their spelling gradually becomes more conventional with beginning, middle, and ending sounds. Examples of later phonetic spellings are CLEN for *clean* and KLOZ for *close.*

   Young spellers during this stage believe that (a) every sound feature of a word can be represented by one letter or by a combination of letters and (b) the graphic form of a word contains every speech sound in the same order as that sound is heard. While students do match letter names to sounds, this strategy does not always result in correct spelling of a sound in a given word (due to inconsistencies in English spelling patterns). Common errors are caused by consonant digraphs in which two letters represent one sound.

   Teachers can help children through this phonetic stage by implementing, in a consistent manner, developmentally appropriate activities such as the following: initiating dialogue journal writing between student and teacher; establishing and maintaining individual word banks; and locating audiences—perhaps peers, upper-grade "buddies," or parents—for the writers who volunteer to share their work.

3. *Patterns-within-words stage* (typically for ages 7–9): Students in this stage, which is also called the transitional stage, go beyond simple one-to-one letter-sound correspondence and begin to realize that English spelling is more complicated. There are four important clues in this stage that children are moving past phonetic spelling: (1) the appearance of the silent vowel marker or signal (e.g., *cake, time*); (2) the growth of short vowel patterns in single-syllable words (e.g., *red, hot*); (3) the appearance of correctly spelled consonant digraphs and blends (e.g., *ship, stop*); and (4) the emphasis on teaching-learning of single-syllable long vowel patterns.

   Teachers can help students through this patterns-within-words stage by implementing developmentally appropriate activities such as the following: studying word patterns (because a large number of words can be formed by adding an initial consonant to a small number of such patterns, e.g., vowel pattern *est*); completing teacher-directed or student-directed word sorts on the chalkboard where words are separated by categories; and recording and organizing those word sorts under various headings in word study journals.

4. *Syllable-juncture stage* (typically for ages 9–11): Since the juncture of syllables within words is the place where syllables come together, letters may be dropped (e.g., *bake + ing = baking*), doubled (e.g., *sit +ing =sitting*), or changed (e.g., *cry =cried*). Word study during this spelling stage focuses on prefixes, suffixes, base words, and syllables. It begins with common two-syllable words and then moves to common polysyllabic words.

   Teachers can help students through this challenging stage by implementing developmentally appropriate activities such as the following: promoting the continued use of word study journals, with additional categories including base words, for example; working (on the chalkboard or overhead) with compound words to show how each word in a compound word assists in its new meaning; and sorting word cards by proper plural endings (i.e., *s* or *es*).

5. *Meaning-derivation stage* (typically for ages 11–14): At this final level of spelling development, students learn that even though the pronunciation of words related in meaning may differ, their spellings remain constant (e.g., *act, action; major, majority*).

Consequently, spellers who have progressed through the earlier stages can now confidently examine meaning-related words, many of which have been derived from Greek, Latin, and French. Admittedly, according to Chomsky (1970), most of this new polysyllabic vocabulary will occur more often in print than in spoken language.

Teachers can assist student growth in the meaning-derivation stage by implementing developmentally appropriate activities such as the following: helping children learn the meanings of common prefixes and suffixes and variations in the ways that these can be correctly joined to base words; assisting beginners with the study of homophones (words that have a different spelling and meaning but are pronounced the same—e.g., *their, there*) as these represent the second most common spelling errors in Grades 4 through 6 (Cramer & Cipielewski, 1995); and planning numerous writing activities for meaningful practice of spelling words.

Invented Spelling

Often defined to anxious parents as temporary spelling, **invented spelling** is better described as students' first efforts to spell words that they have not yet mastered.

While generally confined to the first stage of spelling development—the prephonectic stage—and the early phase of the second or phonetic stage, invented spelling actually permeates every stage. Intermediate students sometimes create invented spelling for those words that they do not know how to spell conventionally. Although their teacher may regard such efforts as misspellings, older students who are in the final three stages of spelling development still use invented spellings occasionally.

Preschool children who have had experiences with print by watching adults read and having adults read to them develop their own knowledge of written language. (This knowledge is promoted especially by access to writing tools.) However, to invent spelling, they need four interconnected skills: (1) the ability to write all the letters of the alphabet that they individually require; (2) phonemic awareness, especially of the segmenting of sounds they individually require; (3) knowledge of some letter-sound relationships; and (4) the understanding that letter-sound relationships are written in a left-to-right sequence (Cramer, 1998).

Read (1971, 1975) studied invented spelling among preschoolers, beginning at ages three and a half, and found that different children invented the same system of spelling. Their inventions were not only uniform and systematic from child to child but also consistent with the underlying phonemic system of English.

Linguistic knowledge about early invented spelling, as determined by researchers since 1970, should become familiar to teachers in the early elementary grades. It will help them understand basic concepts of how young students connect letters with sounds:

- Sounds made by doubled letters *t* and *d* are spelled with one letter (e.g., *padl* for *paddle*).
- Two nasal sounds, *m* and *n,* are omitted when they occur just before another consonant (e.g., *plat* for *plant*)
- Long vowels are spelled by the name of the letter that matches the sound (e.g., *rak* for *rake*)
- Short vowels are spelled by the letter-name that has the sound closest to the one being replaced (e.g., *git* for *got*)
- R-controlled vowels are omitted (e.g., *hrd* for *heard*)
- Past-tense marker *–ed* is spelled with a *t* or a *d* (e.g., *stpt* for *stopped*)

- Syllable sonorants (*l, m,* and *n*) carry the vowel sound in a syllable (e.g., *opn* for *open*)
- Affricative sounds such as *dr, tr,* and *ch* are spelled *jr, gr, chr,* and *h* (e.g., *griv* for *drive*)
- One or more letters may stand for an entire word (e.g., *r* for *are*)

These generalizations regarding invented spelling and young children apply to most students but not all of them. Obviously, children progress through the stages of spelling growth at individual rates. Still, teachers in the kindergarten and early primary grades must be aware of linguistic features of invented spelling so they can better understand the writing efforts of beginning students.

Indeed, invented spelling has important instructional benefits, according to researchers: Students in an invented spelling program *read better* and *produce more and better writing* than their counterparts in traditional language arts programs. They also *spell better* conventionally than their counterparts in traditional spelling programs. These facts must be stressed with anxious parents who should also be reminded that invented spelling is temporary and will be replaced by standard spelling during the course of carefully developed spelling programs.

Approaches to Teaching Spelling

Although there are a variety of approaches to teaching spelling in the elementary school, most fall within one of the following three categories: commercial or basal spelling textbooks, modified basal spelling textbooks, and individualized or personalized programs. These are not mutually exclusive and features of each can be blended together by the experienced teacher intent on implementing the strengths of each to meet the needs of a particular grade level or class.

Commercial spelling textbooks are used in most American schools daily. They are generally chosen by teacher committees and/or the district administration. Classroom teachers like them because such series are convenient to use and are a familiar entity to parents.

Most modern spelling textbooks series have three features in common: (1) a grade-level student textbook with 30 weekly lessons or units and 6 review lessons across the school year; lessons typically run four to six pages and include a word list, a spelling principle, and practice exercises concerned with writing, editing, and general word study; (2) a teacher's manual (with directions for each week's work), which may include a scope and sequence chart, enrichment suggestions, and testing materials; and (3) ancillary materials coordinated with the basic text including but not limited to bilingual materials, computer software, diagnostic and placement tests, and writing activities.

A well-written commercial spelling program can help facilitate the teaching of spelling by providing the following (Templeton,1991):

- Appropriate lists of words that students know from their reading and need to use in their writing; in the intermediate grades, these lists include some words related in spelling and meaning to these familiar words
- A scope and sequence of spelling patterns to guide word-study programs over the elementary grades
- Instructionally sound activities that demand that students examine words from different perspectives, thereby de-emphasizing rote memorization

In these ways, well-designed commercial spelling programs reinforce the principle that spelling is logical and rarely haphazard. In the intermediate grades, they emphasize the linkage of spelling to vocabulary through the "spelling-meaning connection."

Teachers choosing to use a *modified basal spelling textbook series* adjust the commercial basal programs in ways that better meet the needs of their students. They may choose to use more than one grade level book from the series. They may ask students to add to their weekly lessons words that they misspell in their writing or words they have a special interest in learning. Teachers also may present words in thematic units so that words emphasized during the reading and oral language instruction become part of the spelling instruction that week. Finally, they may group students with similar problems who then work together on specific objectives using sample words from all grade-level texts. On the fifth day these groups split up into pairs to examine all the writing samples the partners did that week to see if the words and rules studied that week transferred to their writing.

A third approach to elementary school spelling is the *individualized or personalized approach*, in which words are drawn from the children's writing and from reading and cross-curricular sources. Most teachers introducing this approach initially teach spelling to several instructional groups according to ability levels. When both the teacher and the students are accustomed to working comfortably without the familiar spelling book, the teacher gives each child a placement test and then, based on the results, develops with the student an individualized list of words to learn. Students proceed at their own rate, using partners or a tape recorder for completing the pre- and posttests. Words are usually kept in spelling journals, but some teachers prepare special forms for that purpose.

Implementing an individualized spelling program demands that the teachers have good organizational and time management skills. They must be able to help compile appropriate word lists for each child. They must incorporate sufficient follow-up activity sessions to ensure that the child does indeed study the words regularly. Finally, they must teach spelling principles and phonics generalizations as individual needs arise.

A popular variation of the individualized approach is the cooperative spelling approach in which the teacher and students work together. It is the teacher who assigns all children a certain number of the same words to assure that they acquire a basic spelling vocabulary. It is the children, however, who must assume responsibility for their own learning by adding words individually misspelled in their writing or found in their reading.

Selecting Spelling Words

There are an estimated one million American English words. Fortunately, there is no need to learn to spell anywhere near that number as words have different levels of usefulness. Beck, McKeown, and Kucan (2002) propose one such classification system that divides words into three tiers based on their usefulness:

Tier 1: Basic, everyday words that generally do not have to be taught in elementary school

Tier 2: Useful words that need to be taught in elementary school

Tier 3: Specialized, less common words that not all students need to learn before high school

Tier 2 words are part of language used in school and should therefore comprise the core of spelling words taught to children.

Yet spelling words should be chosen according to more criteria than just their usefulness. When compiling spelling lists, first consider their frequency of use. Numerous lists of *high-frequency words* have been developed by competent researchers over many years, but these need to be checked against each other to make sure that the 1,000 most frequently used words are taught early. This formidable task becomes easier when one takes into account the other five criteria for selecting spelling words.

1. *Frequently misspelled words in written language:* Spelling error analysis research has shown that certain words cannot be mastered in one or two learning sessions. Instead, these troublesome words or "demons" need to be retaught across several grade levels and therefore included in spelling lists again and again.

2. *Linguistically patterned words in written language:* Linguistic features include sound, structure, meaning, and etymology, and well-organized spelling lists should consider all of them. Some features of English spelling are more complicated than others; for example, vowel spellings are more variable than consonant spellings and so prove more challenging to beginning spellers.

3. *Developmentally appropriate words in oral and written language:* Students should learn to spell words that correspond to their level of development in speaking, writing, and reading, as well as the stages of spelling development discussed earlier. For instance, young children should not be asked to learn to spell words that are not in their speaking vocabulary.

4. *Content-related words in oral and written language:* As students move through the grades, they encounter specialized vocabularies in content subjects like math, social studies, and science. Their teachers can then add such words to weekly lists as "bonus words," choosing them from content area texts (where they are often labeled as Key Vocabulary) or from content lists in spelling textbooks.

5. *Personally chosen words from written language:* Personal words are selected, with teacher assistance, by children who have misspelled them in writing or mispronounced them in reading. They should be words that are in the students' word recognition and meaning vocabularies. In most cases, such personal words only supplement the established spelling list, usually to the extent of three to five words per week. However, teachers using a totally personalized spelling approach must determine the balance between (teacher) assigned words and (student) personal words.

Guidelines to Spelling Instruction

While reading and writing are crucial for spelling development, more systematic instruction in the spelling of words is necessary for most students (Invernizzi, Abouzeid, & Gill, 1994), as Ms. Potter realizes when working with her second graders in Vignette 9.2.

VIGNETTE 9.2 Spelling Centers in the Second Grade

Lori Potter, a second-grade teacher at a suburban elementary school, remembered her own early spelling instruction as a monotonous cycle of word lists and memorization. Although these methods worked to some extent, after taking a graduate class on learning styles Ms. Potter became convinced she could develop more effective activities to teach her young students to spell.

She appreciated the school's chosen curriculum, which introduced vowel patterns and spelling rules throughout the semester, so she based her weekly word lists on its suggestions. However, as she distributed the first list on a Monday in early September, she also gave each child four brightly colored, laminated slips of paper: one red, one blue, one yellow, and one green. She then directed their attention to three learning centers around the room, each marked in one of the primary colors.

"At the red center you will practice hearing your words and then spelling them," Ms. Potter explained. "At the yellow center you will practice seeing and reading your new words. And at the blue center you will practice writing the words."

Of course, Ms. Potter knew that by its very nature the study of spelling often required using two or more of these skills at one time. Therefore no one center could effectively incorporate only one style of learning. However, she hoped the different emphasis in each station would engage the students while also providing an integrated experience.

She continued the explanation by saying, "Each day you will have time to visit one spelling center. You have one ticket for each center, so you may visit each area one time during the week. When you choose the one you want to visit, drop your ticket in the box at that center."

Noticing the students looking for a green area, she said, "Your green ticket allows you to enter any of the centers, so you can pick your favorite and do it again. That means we will do spelling four days—red, blue, yellow, and green. On Friday we will have a quiz where you can show me what you've learned."

After helping the students create construction paper "wallets" to hold their stashes of colored tickets, Ms. Potter announced that the children could select their first center. They delighted in dropping the colored papers into the ticket boxes outside each area and exploring the activities inside.

In the red center, the children discovered tables with portable CD players and headphones. Each CD played a recording of Ms. Potter first saying that week's words and then slowly spelling each one. The recording played through the entire ten-word list two times. By the end of the second time through, several of the students softly repeated, "Lake. L-A-K-E," along with the recording. A few other students used paper and markers to write the words as they listened to the correct spelling.

In the yellow center, the children sat down to a table next to a large whiteboard. At the table were ten small magnet boards and letters. This week, the list introduced the long *a* sound and words ending with a silent *e*, so on each child's board Ms. Potter had spelled "cake" with the letter magnets. After the students correctly read the word, she asked if they could replace a letter to form another word. After a minute of trial and error, one student successfully spelled "bake" with his magnets. Ms. Potter reinforced the learning by writing "cake" on the white board, crossing out the *c*, and writing "bake" underneath. Next to the two words she drew a sketch of an oven with a freshly baked cake inside.

Together Ms. Potter and the students repeated the exercise, with the students spelling "lake," "take," "tame," "game," and "same." By the end of the lesson, silly pictures incorporating the pairs of words covered the whiteboard.

At times, the children created words not on the spelling list (or suggested nonsense words); because Ms. Potter guided the lesson to ensure the children eventually spelled all ten of the required words, she encouraged their experimentation and considered it extra practice with the new skill.

In the blue center, the students gathered around the room's second large whiteboard on the other side of the room. There, Ms. Potter's student teacher, Ben, stood ready to provide leadership. Ms. Potter felt comfortable that after several weeks in this area, the students would require little supervision; by the time Ben left at the end of the semester, the children would be able to work in the blue center independently.

Ms. Potter had written the ten words along the bottom of the board with plenty of space above and between each one. Ben asked each child to select a word and a blue marker and write that word on the board above Ms. Potter's guide word. He gave each child a minute or two to finish and then asked the students to pair up and look at their partner's work.

"Did your friend write his word correctly?" asked Ben. Several of the students nodded or said "Yes!" A few studied the words more closely to make sure before offering an opinion. One boy declared "No".

"Tell us what mistake you see," Ben asked the boy nervously. He had been hesitant about Ms. Potter's recommendation that students evaluate each other's work in this center, but she assured him that with a little guidance the children would quickly learn to offer suggestions to each other in helpful ways.

"She spelled cake with a *k* at the beginning," said the boy. "It should be a *c*. There is only one *k*, at the end."

To Ben's relief, the girl who had written "kake" nodded and quickly moved to erase and rewrite the word correctly. After confirming the correct spelling of the other nine words, Ben asked the children to pick a new word next to a new partner. He repeated the exercise until every child had practiced writing each word. By the end of the lesson, he began to enjoy the give-and-take among the children.

"You wrote that good," said one little girl to another. "She wrote it well," corrected Ben. "And yes, she did. Good job!"

After only twenty minutes, each student had completed the first spelling center. Although several children wanted to spend another ticket and try another area, Ms. Potter gathered the group back together. She knew the value of building anticipation for the new activity and felt pleased by the project's initial success. Although each child would not enjoy each center equally, the variety of activities—and the opportunity to choose a favorite to experience twice—ensured that each child would find at least one way to learn in his or her preferred style. She looked forward to verifying the success of the new approach in coming weeks—and for the first time, she looked forward to grading Friday's spelling quizzes!

Systematic spelling instruction uses several tried-and-true methods. Research has shown that children learn spelling words more readily when they are presented in *list form,* rather than in sentences or paragraphs (Gentry & Gillet, 1993). *The periodic review of spelling words,* usually every six weeks, is required for reinforcing the nearly 5,000 words used most often in writing. Spelling instruction should also incorporate phonics since phonics generalizations are an *aid* to correct spelling (Gentry, 1996). Phonics must not, however, comprise the entire program.

The use of the *test-study-test method* requires considerable individual responsibility, but has been proven to produce good results (DiStefano & Hagerty, 1985). On Monday, students take a self-corrected pretest of the new spelling words; on Friday, they take a final test of them. During the intervening four days, children identify those words that they cannot spell readily and must therefore focus on learning that week.

A systematic spelling program also incorporates *activities that promote instruction* such as (a) completing word sorts, in which students separate word cards into two or more categories that focus on a particular spelling pattern; (b) establishing and expanding word walls as shown earlier in Figure 5.4— large sheets of paper hanging in the classroom on which is written the vocabulary from word sorts plus related words of interest from content areas; (c) maintaining individual spelling logs or word study notebooks that must be kept current and consulted often since they not only include misspelled or confusing words but they also promote understanding of word structure and link reading to spelling; and (d) making words from sets of small (one- to two-inch) letter cards that can be arranged to spell words that are increasingly longer or more complex or that fit a particular pattern (Cunningham, 2005).

Spelling Strategies That Must Be Taught

A strategy is a plan designed to elicit a certain purpose. In spelling that purpose is to learn unknown words and add them into the long-term memory bank of the speller. The major strategy in the beginning stages of spelling is sound cues. As children move through the grades, it has been noted that good spellers acquire a broader collection of strategies than do poor spellers. They are also more likely to use those that they personally find to be most effective. Since teaching spelling strategies is generally overlooked in the elementary program, it must be assumed that good spellers learn efficient strategies on their own. However, it is important for teachers to introduce and/or emphasize the following strategies for both good and weak spellers:

- *Visualization strategy:* This is a strategy used much more often by good spellers than by poor ones (Radebaugh, 1985). Defined as the creation of a mental picture, **visualization** is also used in other learning situations. In spelling, children can be taught to visualize the new word (or a related word) in its written form (e.g., *reductions* on a sales banner) or to visualize a setting in which images are portrayed to help spell the new word (e.g., *hurricane* during a news telecast). Visualization can be taught as a spelling strategy by teachers who ask questions (e.g., Have you seen this word in print before? and If so, where?) and make suggestions (e.g., Imagine a silly picture of this word).

- *Pronunciation strategy:* According to an analysis of spelling errors by Cramer and Cipielewski (1995), there is a class of words that are misspelled because they are mispronounced or not completely articulated (e.g., *middle, February, little)*. Clear enunciation of the underarticulated or unarticulated demon part of the word can help students spell correctly more words to which this strategy applies.

- *Mnemonic strategy:* **Mnemonics** are helpful for a few special words that are troubling to a particular individual. Defined as a memory strategy, it is designed to aid recall of a particularly difficult word or word part (e.g., *you* in *young* could be recalled by *you are young;* and *hide* in *hideous* could be recalled by *hide from the hideous monster)*. Children should be encouraged to create their own mnemonics for perennially difficult spellings.

- *Divide–and–conquer strategy:* Since long words are misspelled more often than short ones, students should be taught to *divide* long words into structurally proper parts and *conquer* the parts separately. For example, *truck/er, humming/bird, hu/man/oid*.

- *Analogous word strategy:* Words that share a linguistic feature that is comparable or similar are termed analogous words. Some share a common phonogram (usually a vowel-consonant combination) and are referred to as rhyming words (e.g., *cake, lake, rake, take)* or family words. Others share the same consonant digraph, the same base word, or the same suffix. There are numerous similarities among words, and some children have figured them out by themselves through reading and writing experiences. Nevertheless, this strategy should be introduced to all students because it increases awareness of spelling patterns and therefore also promotes the spelling growth of elementary children.

- *Spelling consciousness strategy:* This is a difficult strategy to present because it involves teaching students to monitor their own ability to recognize whether a word is spelled correctly or not. Aspects of this strategy involve (a) *sensory awareness,* which results only as a byproduct of the other five strategies and takes months, if not years, of promoting those strategies; (b) *editing and proofreading,* which are said to be the best avenues for developing spelling consciousness and cannot be compromised; (c) *looking for misspelled words on public signs* as homework or bonus assignments; some of these occur through carelessness, but others are misspelled deliberately to evoke attention; and (d) *word awareness* as promoted by the teacher who is personally interested in and curious about words and may share, for example, some of the books by Fred Gwynne, who memorably and humorously taught children about homophones in books like *The King Who Rained* (Aladdin, 1988).

Grammar

Grammar is an established part of the elementary language arts curriculum, and parents who were taught grammar expect their children to have the same opportunity. It is also a highly controversial and problematic area, controversial since there are several definitions of the term **grammar** and problematic because research has repeatedly shown that teaching formal grammar makes no difference in verbal behavior or in writing improvement (Braddock, Lloyd-Jones, & Schoer, 1963; Cazden, 1972; Hillocks, 1987). Therefore, when grammar is taught, it should be done less formally and in the context of speaking and writing as these two language skills prevail daily in the classroom. (In this text, grammar is defined as a set of abstract rules of communication and the underlying structure of language that humans use intuitively.)

Reasons for Teaching Grammar

Despite continuing controversy about teaching grammar to elementary children, it remains part of the language arts curriculum. Grammar is a basic skill, providing a foundation for learning language that is crucial to success both in and out of school. It also enriches language by which human knowledge is transmitted through the generations. Learning English grammar makes it less troublesome to learn another language since some concepts about English nouns and verbs, for example, may transfer to a foreign language. Standardized tests of language, often mandated by state boards of education, determine students' knowledge of the rules of grammar through objective means that are easy to grade. For these reasons, teachers and other community members continue to advocate the teaching of grammar to elementary children.

Fundamental Facts About Grammar

Before establishing an agenda for teaching the subject of grammar in the elementary school, teachers must review basic facts about grammar. Grammar constitutes the rules of a language and how that language works. It has also been defined as a description of the syntax or structure of a language and prescriptions for its use (Weaver, 1996). While every language has its own grammar, knowing the grammar of one language makes it easier to learn the grammar and structure of another.

Yet grammar differs from **usage**, which represents the conventions of language appropriate in particular circumstances. It has been noted that grammar is the rationale of language but usage is its etiquette (Newkirk, 1978). Both the audience and the circumstances determine the grammar and usage that people employ in speaking. By the age of five or six, children already have a considerable understanding of English grammar. Furthermore, by age eight or nine, they know the system as well as they will ever know it (Devine, 1989). Students in Grades 2 through 6 need to know grammatical terms because they use them when revising and editing their writing. Specifically, students should know the names of the parts of speech (and how these are used in sentences) by the end of fourth grade, with *nouns* and *adjectives* introduced in Grades 1 and 2; *verbs, pronouns,* and *adverbs* in Grade 3; and *prepositions* and *conjunctions* in Grade 4. *Interjections* are relatively uncommon in children's writing. Beginning in Grade 3, students should also learn the parts of a sentence (subject and predicate) and noun-verb agreement.

English grammar has four types of sentences, depending on their structure: *simple* (My mother is a tall woman.); *compound* (Dad went fishing but I stayed home.); *complex* (When he was sick, he went to see the doctor.); and *compound-complex* (If it wasn't raining, he could have played soccer with his friends, and they would have had a great time.). It also has four types of sentences, depending on their intent or purpose: *declarative* (those that make a statement such as "The bus is here."), *interrogative* (those that ask a question such as "Where is the dog?"), *imperative* (those that make a demand such as "Sit down!"), and *exclamatory* (those that evoke surprise or strong emotion such as "Hurrah!").

Major Types of Grammar and Their Language Elements

The three types of grammar presently used to categorize the workings of the English language are traditional grammar, structural grammar, and transformation-generative grammar. All of them share the same three basic elements of language: phonology, morphology, and syntax. (These were discussed earlier in the book and are only reviewed briefly here.)

Phonology or the science of speech sounds is the first element because sound is essential to language. Its basic unit is the **phoneme**, which is the smallest, most distinctive speech sound. **Morphology**, the second grammar element, is the study of word formation patterns. Its smallest meaning-bearing units are **morphemes**, which represent the building segments of words (i.e., prefixes, suffixes, roots). Some of these are free and can stand independently (e.g., *teach*), whereas others are bound and cannot stand alone (e.g., *-er*) although they still have meaning. The third element of grammar is **syntax**, which is the study of the relationships among words in a sentence because word order is crucial to meaning. It should be emphasized that all three elements work together and cannot be readily separated.

All of them are included in the three types of grammar that have affected language teaching in the American classroom during the past century. What the majority of children study today is actually an eclectic combination of components from all three and is often referred to as school grammar or simply grammar.

The first and oldest grammar is *traditional grammar,* which is Latin-based and originated in England during the 18th century. It is basically a prescriptive grammar that teaches how language should be written. From traditional grammar come the eight parts of speech and their functions: nouns, pronouns, verbs, adverbs, adjectives, conjunctions, prepositions, and interjections. Nouns and verbs are the building blocks of sentences, representing the subject and the predicate. Pronouns may replace nouns in sentences; and adjectives, adverbs, and prepositions modify nouns and verbs. Sentences are labeled simple, compound, complex, and compound/complex. Sentence types are defined as declarative, interrogative, imperative, and exclamatory. These terms are still used in English grammar texts today.

The second type of grammar is *structural grammar,* which was developed in the United States during the 1930s by Leonard Bloomfield and other linguists. Unlike traditional grammar, which is prescriptive and mainly concerned with written language, this grammar is descriptive and stresses the importance of studying spoken language. It analyzes the structure and features of a language and classifies words according to their functions (or "slots") in particular sentences. Finally, it considers how language is really used in both standard and nonstandard approaches, taking into account language differences among social classes and geographical regions, and dialects of different groups.

Developed in the United States in the 1950s by linguist Noam Chomsky, the third major kind of grammar is *transformational-generative grammar.* Its proponents assert that if preschool children with limited experience can generate thousands of new sentences based on the early sentence structure that they have acquired, there must be an underlying process that can be explained and taught. The basic theory behind this kind of grammar is that kernel sentences (simple declarative sentences) can generate new sentences through expansion or combination. This grammar is concerned with both the surface structure (human speech) and the deep structure (ideas, thoughts, meaning) underlying actual speech performance. Teachers who promote the use of sentence combining and sentence expansion as means for improving student writing should realize that such use is the result of research based on transformational-generative grammar.

For material related to this concept, go to Video Clip 9.2 on the Student Resource CD bound into the back of your textbook.

Fundamental Facts About Grammar Instruction

In addition to reviewing the basic facts about English grammar, elementary teachers should also reexamine the preferred strategies for presenting grammar to children:

- Memorizing grammar rules is both unproductive and inefficient. Instead, young children's oral grammatical knowledge gained before entering school should be extended in school through authentic reading and writing activities. Teaching grammar in isolated units is less than effective, according to Weaver (1996) who believes that grammar is best presented in the context of writing conferences.
- Mini-lessons are one effective way to teach grammar. These are sometimes offered on the chalkboard as short daily lessons (often called Daily Oral Language or DOL) that examine sentences with errors. Such whole-class lessons help students focus their attention on the importance of standard grammar for genuine communication with an audience. At other times, these mini-lessons take the form of carefully chosen worksheets that aid small groups in need of reinforcement or practice on specific skills.
- Whole-class mini-lessons using transparencies can introduce students to grammar in passages from the teacher's own writings, passages written by an anonymous child or a self-assured classmate, or passages from all the students in the class on a rotating basis. Such sharing ensures that children do not lose confidence in their own abilities to use grammar properly.
- Sharing children's literature, including carefully chosen picture books and chapter books, can also promote understanding of such grammatical concepts as various types of sentences. The teacher can discuss these concepts after the children finish reading the book or chapter.
- Providing girls and boys with numerous opportunities to attempt a wide range of writing assignments—writing reports, poetry, letters, and plays—helps them use different syntactic structures (Wray & Medwell, 1994). Interactions among student writers promotes the use of model language and the growth of standard grammar, especially among those still struggling with nonstandard grammar.
- Knowledge of grammar enriches the reading experience as well as the writing session. Students who know the basic grammar rules have a tool that enables them to relate to an author's use of language. For example, in William Steig's *Sylvester and the Magic Pebble* (Aladdin, 1987), when Sylvester finds "a remarkable pebble," the primary teacher can discuss "remarkable," explaining its meaning; describe it as an *adjective;* and ask the class to listen for other adjectives in the story. Children will quickly—and often proudly—begin to incorporate adjectives into their own stories.

These books help clarify grammar for elementary school children in a pleasant, often rhyming manner, with illustrations:

Bailey's *Miss Myrtle Frag, the Grammar Nag* (Absey, 2000)

Cleary's series *Words Are Categorical* (Carolrhoda, 1999–2004), including these titles:

- *Dearly, Nearly, Insincerely: What Is an Adverb?*
- *Hairy, Scary, Ordinary: What Is an Adjective?*
- *I and You and Don't Forget Who: What Is a Pronoun?*
- *A Mink, a Fink, a Skating Rink: What Is a Noun?*
- *To Root, to Toot, to Parachute: What Is a Verb?*
- *Under, Over, by the Clover: What Is a Preposition?*

Heller's *Behind the Mask: A Book About Prepositions* (Penguin Putnam, 1995)

Heller's *Many Luscious Lollipops: A Book About Adjectives* (Penguin Putnam, 1989)

Heller's *Up, Up, and Away: A Book About Adverbs* (Penguin Putnam, 1991)

A sample lesson plan incorporating the concepts introduced in this chapter appears on p. 326.

Assessment

In the elementary years children are increasingly using written language to put their ideas and experiences into words. For students to participate successfully within this writing context, they need to develop the ability to set their words on paper with ease. This demands their use of four major writing tools: spelling, grammar, handwriting, and word processing.

Growth in the proper use of all three continues in a sequential development throughout the elementary grades as these tools represent an integrated component of the language arts. Teachers and students alike must recognize that the ultimate goal of acquiring skills in spelling, grammar, handwriting, and word processing is the ability to express oneself well in written language. Consequently, children's individual progress in these areas can best be evaluated on the basis of dated examples of written products carefully appraised on a monthly or quarterly basis.

Working With English Language Learners

Of all the language arts skills, the writing tools may be at once the easiest and most difficult to master for English learners. Handwriting can be taught as easily to most English learners as to native speakers of English. For students whose native language carries roughly the same alphabet as English, how to form the letters in manuscript or cursive would be taught the same way to both groups. When they teach handwriting, teachers need to be aware of students whose native language has no written alphabet or in which the alphabet is significantly different from English. The skills of spelling and grammar are much more difficult for ELLs to master. ELLs should be allowed to use invented spelling, and teachers must be aware of the sequential stages of spelling development.

Beginning ELLs: *Handwriting:* At first, beginners should be able to copy the English alphabet from a paper or the board. Later they should be able to write the alphabet from memory. They can also copy common words that have been displayed in the classroom, from teacher-made class charts or from labeled objects in the room. Beginning ELLs can also copy words from word banks to label diagrams, for example, for science or social studies content. An example would be labeling the parts of a flower in science. *Spelling:* Beginning ELLs can use invented spelling to write words they already have in their vocabulary. These children will pick out the sounds they hear and can write those letters. ELLs have special needs with regard to spelling in that they may have difficulty hearing certain sounds or sound combinations. For example, native Spanish speakers have difficulty distinguishing between "sh" and "ch." Mini-lessons to small groups of ELLs can help target these areas of need. It is not a good idea to impose spelling tests on ELLs at this level.

Early intermediate and intermediate ELLs: *Handwriting:* Intermediate ELLs can copy sentences from objects labeled in the classroom or from classroom charts and diagrams. *Spelling:* Intermediate ELLs increasingly use standard spelling; as children approach more standard spelling, they can be expected to take class spelling tests.

Early advanced and advanced ELLs: *Grammar:* Advanced ELLs should be able to write independently using correct grammar. Older ELLs can be expected to write multi-paragraph pieces using correct grammar.

Practical Instructional Activities and Ideas

- *Tracing spelling words:* Students can write spelling words on index or blank word cards and then trace over the words with glue and sprinkle glitter on top. An alternative is to use glitter glue pens to trace over the spelling words.
- *Penmanship homework:* Students in kindergarten through Grade 3 should practice penmanship with their families through homework. Beginning in kindergarten, students should each practice writing their name each night. This practice can begin with the first name and later the last name can be added. Students in first and second grade can practice writing familiar words. In third grade, students learn cursive handwriting and will need follow-up practice at home. Teachers must introduce proper letter-writing techniques in class first. Fourth graders must continue to practice cursive writing so that it becomes fluid and legible.
- *Journal writing:* Students in kindergarten through Grade 2 can benefit from daily writing in a journal. Teachers can introduce topics or allow children to self-select topics. Students can use invented spelling as they write. Entries in the journals document over time students' progression through the stages of spelling development.
- *Copying:* Students can practice their penmanship when they copy stories or letters from the board or chart paper. Teachers and students generate the material together as a group, the teacher writes the sample on chart paper or on the board, and then the students copy it.
- *Spelling cards:* Teachers can easily and inexpensively create spelling cards from index cards. Students can combine letter cards to make words in a language arts center. For example, *c*, *a*, and *t* make "cat." Older students can combine cards with parts of words or whole words to make compound words; for example, "pop" and "corn" to make "popcorn" or "re" and "visit" to make "revisit."
- *Purposeful writing:* Beginning in second and third grade, students can write thank-you notes, invitations, and letters. Because these activities have a purpose—to communicate information to others—students should be encouraged to use legible handwriting and conventional spelling.
- *Grammar charts:* Students can learn and review the parts of speech through class-generated charts, which can be tied to literature (see Table 9. 2) or to a content area such as science (see Table 9.3). The teacher writes the words on the chart as students generate them. Students can then make sentences or songs using the parts of speech.

Table 9.2 *The Very Hungry Caterpillar* Grammar Chart (Grades 1–3)

Adjective	Noun	Verb
beautiful	butterfly	crawls
brown	caterpillar	flies
tiny	egg	eats
furry	chrysalis	lays

Table 9.3 Volcanoes Grammar Chart (Grades 4–6)

Adjective	Noun	Verb	Adverb	Prepositional Phrase
huge	volcano	explode	violently	above the mountain
massive	volcanoes	run	slowly	
beautiful	crater	rumble	quickly	in the mountain
dormant	lava	move	quietly	on top of the mountain
extinct	shield volcano	shake		
active	stratovolcano	lies		
red hot	cinder cone			
thick				
runny				

- *Keyboarding games:* There are interesting and educational software games available for children that help them practice keyboarding skills. Students can play these games during whole-class computer lab or independently at computers in the classroom when they finish their work or during language arts centers.

- *Spelling games:* To make spelling practice fun, teachers can lead whole-class spelling games. In one such game, the class is divided into two groups. Students on each team take turns spelling words. If they spell a word correctly, their team earns a point. In sixth grade, for example, the game can include frequently misspelled words, such as "they're," "their," and "there." The spelling bee is a classic activity that adds an element of fun and competition to studying spelling words. Students take turns being given a word by the teacher. If they spell the word correctly, they stay in the game. If they miss a word, they are out. The last one standing wins. Care should be taken that spelling words match students' ability levels and that there is not too much emphasis on winning. Students should root for their classmates, rather than criticizing each other.

- *Educational videos:* Videos such as "Schoolhouse Rock" help students review or learn grammar in a fun way, through songs and cartoons. Examples from this particular video include "Conjunction Junction" and "Lolly, Lolly, Lolly, Get Your Adverbs Here."

LESSON PLAN 9.1   A Week of Spelling

Language Arts Component: Writing

Grade: 2

Topic: Spelling

Time Frame: 1 week

Objective

- Students write spelling words with 80% accuracy as evidenced by a spelling test on Friday.

Materials

- List of the weekly spelling words taken from new vocabulary in the reading lesson

Content Standards

Language Arts: Written Conventions, Spelling

- Students spell frequently used irregular words correctly.
- Students spell basic words correctly.

Day 1

- *Whole Class:* Teacher gives students a pretest in spelling, and those who spell all 10 words correctly do not have to study the words for the week (they can be assigned an alternate "challenge" list or be given an alternate assignment for the week).
- Students take the spelling words home to study. Homework packet includes the list of spelling words and appropriate activities at home, such as writing the words and tracing over with a crayon.

Day 2

- *Whole Class:* Students write each spelling word in a sentence (optional: students who have time illustrate each sentence).

Day 3

- *Whole Class:* Students alphabetize each spelling word.

Day 4

- *Whole Class:* Students take a second pretest; those who spell all the words correctly do not have to take the test on Friday.
- Students write missed spelling words on index cards with pencil and trace over with glitter glue. Students who earned 100% on the test get to do a special activity planned by the teacher.

Day 5

- *Whole Class:* Students take the final test.

Assessment

- Pretests and final tests serve as the final assessments.

Integration Across the Curriculum

Science

- Students and teacher create grammar charts (see Table 9.3) together for virtually any area of science. Example chart topics include insects (life science), volcanoes (earth science), and matter (physical science).
- Students copy words from the board or a word bank in order to label scientific diagrams or posters.
- Students have spelling word lists from science units. An example list could be *leaf, stem, flower, roots,* etc. Students will learn meaningful spelling lists that are tied to instructional units more easily.

Social Studies

- Students and teacher create grammar charts (see Table 9.3) together for virtually any area of social studies. Sample chart topics include *Native Americans, Mesopotamia, Egypt,* and *My Family.*
- Students have spelling word lists from social studies units. A sample list could be *mother, father, brother, sister, aunt, uncle, grandpa, grandma,* etc. Students will learn meaningful spelling lists that are tied to instructional units more easily.

Math

- Students use their spelling words to create math problems. They can count the number of letters in each spelling word and add or subtract the values of the word from each other.

Literature

- The teacher reads books aloud to the class that highlight various parts of speech, as in Cleary's *Words Are Categorical* series.

Visual and Performing Arts

- Students use their spelling words to create mini works of art. Older children (fourth to sixth grade) can write the words with block lettering, create a pattern for the inside of each letter (e.g., stripes, polka dots, etc.), and color the background using colored pencils or markers. They could compare their word art to examples of modern or pop art.
- Younger children can act out some words in their spelling lists, such as sad or push.

Health

- Students have spelling word lists from health topics. A sample list could include *lung, heart, bones,* and *stomach.* Students will learn meaningful spelling lists that are tied to instructional units more easily.

Physical Education

- Spelling baseball, an outdoor game played on a baseball field: The teacher forms two teams; teacher has a list of words to spell, divided into groups for "single," "double," "triple," and "home run" depending on difficulty. Students who are "at bat" are given a choice of difficulty of spelling word by the teacher, who is the pitcher. If they spell the word correctly, they go to the appropriate base, and if they miss the word, they are out. Students continue until they have three outs, then the teams switch sides. The teacher keeps track of runs scored.

Music

- Students sing their spelling words to familiar melodies.
- Students create "raps" using their spelling words.
- Students use the grammar chart to create songs to the tune of "The Farmer in the Dell."

Parents as Partners

Parents can impress on their children the importance of good homework habits. By showing interest, they are showing their children they care about how well they do in school. Parents can *help with homework* in the following ways:

- Help children study for spelling tests by having the child create word cards at home on index cards. The child can use these cards throughout the week to study for the test. The day before the spelling test, parents can give the child a pretest. The child should be praised for correct words and told to write the missed words three times for practice. Parents can display the child's successful spelling tests from school on the refrigerator.
- Make sure that their children hold a pencil correctly and that they are forming the letters correctly. Playing with play dough at home helps children strengthen their hands and develop the fine motor skills needed for handwriting.
- *Read books aloud* to or with their children. Students will catch onto correct spelling and grammar as they repeatedly hear correct language usage from books or speech.
- *Sing songs* to children from the time they are infants. This is another enjoyable way for children to learn language conventions naturally.

- *Make up games* to play in the car or during a free moment (in line at the grocery store or waiting at a restaurant). In one such game the parent prononouces words and has the children take turns spelling them. Word difficulty should be tailored to the age and developmental level of each child.
- Children who are fortunate enough to have a computer to use at home can *practice keyboarding skills* through educational games or word-processing programs. If a child does not have a computer at home, the parent can take him or her to a local library. Libraries generally have computers in the children's section that can be used for about an hour at a time.

Student Study Site

The Companion Web site for *Language Arts: Integrating Skills for Classroom Teaching*
www.sagepub.com/donoghuestudy
   Visit the Web-based study site to enhance your understanding of the chapter content. The study materials include chapter summaries, practice tests, flashcards, and Web resources.

Additional Professional Readings

Berger J. (2001). A systematic approach to grammar instruction. *Voices From the Middle, 8,* 43–49.

Berninger, V. (1997). Treatment of handwriting problems in beginning writers: Transfer from handwriting to composition. *Journal of Educational Psychology, 89,* 652–666.

Fresch, M., & Wheaton, A. (2002). *Teaching and assessing spelling.* New York: Scholastic.

Haussamen, B., et al. (2003). *Grammar alive!* Urbana, IL: National Council of Teachers of English.

Laminack, L., & Wood, K. (1996). *Spelling in use.* Urbana, IL: National Council of Teachers of English.

Miller, S., Smith, M., Fidanque, A., & Sullivan, G. (2000). *Keyboarding success* (2nd ed.). Eugene, OR: International Society for Technology in Education.

Olinzock, A. (1998). Computer skill building—the answer to keyboarding instruction? *Business Education Forum, 52,* 24–26.

Snowball, D., & Bolton, F. (1999). *Spelling K–8.* York, ME: Stenhouse.

Weaver, C., McNally, C., & Moerman, S. (2001). To grammar or not to grammar: That is *not* the question. *Voices From the Middle, 8,*17–33.

Wenze, G., & Wenze N. (2004). Helping left-handed children adapt to school expectations. *The Reading Teacher, 81,* 25–30.

Children's Literature Cited in the Text

Bailey, L. (2000). *Miss Myrtle Frag, the grammar nag.* Spring, TX: Absey Press.

Cleary, B. (1999). *A mink, a fink, a skating rink: What is a noun?* Minneapolis: Carolrhoda.

Cleary, B. (2000). *Dearly, nearly, insincerely: What is an adverb?* Minneapolis: Carolrhoda.

Cleary, B. (2000). *Hairy, scary, ordinary: What is an adjective?* Minneapolis: Carolrhoda.

Cleary, B. (2001). *To root, to toot, to parachute: What is a verb?* Minneapolis: Carolrhoda.

Cleary, B. (2002). *Under, over, by the clover: What is a preposition?* Minneapolis: Carolrhoda.

Cleary, B. (2004). *I and you and don't forget who: What is a pronoun?* Minneapolis: Carolrhoda.

Gwynne, F. (1998). *The king who rained.* New York: Aladdin.

Heller, R. (1989). *Many luscious lollipops: A book about adjectives.* New York: Penguin Putnam.

Heller, R. (1991). *Up, up, and away: A book about adverbs.* New York: Penguin Putnam.

Heller, R. (1995). *Behind the mask: A book about prepositions.* New York: Penguin Putnam.

Steig, W. (1987). *Sylvester and the magic pebble.* New York: Aladdin.

References

Beck., I., McKeown, M., & Kucan, I. (2002). *Bringing words to life.* New York: Guilford Press.

Bloodsworth, J. (1993). *The left handed writer.* Arlington, VA: ERIC Document Reproduction Service ED 356494.

Braddock, R., Lloyd-Jones, R., & Schoer, I. (1963).*Research in writing composition.* Urbana, IL: National Council of Teachers of English.

Cazden, C. (1972). *Child language and education.* New York: Holt.

Chomsky, C. (1970). Reading, writing and phonology. *Harvard Educational Review, 40,* 287–309.

Cramer, R. (1998). *The spelling connection.* New York: Guilford.

Cramer, R., & Cipielewski, J. (1995). Research in action: A study of spelling errors in 18,599 written compositions of children in grades 1–8. In *Spelling: An overview of research and current research information and practice* (pp. 11–40). Glenview, IL: Scott, Foresman.

Crews, T., North, A., & Erthal, M. (2006). *Elementary/middle school keyboarding strategies guide* (3rd ed.). Reston, VA: National Business Education Association.

Cunningham, P. (2005). *Phonics they use* (4th ed.). Boston: Allyn & Bacon.

Devine, T. (1989). *Teaching reading in the elementary school: From theory to practice.* Boston: Allyn & Bacon.

DiStefano, P., & Hagerty, P. (1985). Teaching spelling at the elementary level: A realistic perspective. *The Reading Teacher, 38,* 373–377.

Duvall, B. (1985). Evaluating the difficulty of four handwriting styles used for instruction. *ERS Spectrum, 3,* 13–20.

Ehri, I., & Wilce, L. (1987). Cipher versus cue reading: An experiment in reading acquisition. *Journal of Educational Psychology, 79,* 3–13.

Farris, P. (1982). *A comparison of handwriting strategies for primary grade students.* Arlington, VA: ERIC Document Reproduction Service.

Farris, P. (1991). Handwriting instruction should *not* become extinct. *Language Arts, 68,* 312–314.

Fowler, A., & Liberman, I. (1995). The role of phonology and orthography in morphological awareness. In L. B. Feldman (Ed.), *Morphological aspects of language processing* (pp. 157–188). Hillsdale, NJ: Erlbaum.

Garcia, C. (1997). *The effect of two types of spelling instruction on first grade reading, writing, and spelling achievement.* Unpublished doctoral dissertation, Oakland University, Rochester, MI.

Gentry, J. (1996). *My kid can't spell: Understanding and assisting your child's literacy development.* Portsmouth, NH: Heinemann

Gentry, J., & Gillet, J. (1993) *Teaching kids to spell.* Portsmouth, NH: Heinemann.

Graham, S. (1992). Issues in handwriting instruction. *Focus on Exceptional Children, 25,* 1–14.

Hackney, C. (2003). *Zaner-Bloser handwriting.* Columbus, OH: Zaner-Bloser.

Hanna, P., Hanna, J., Hodges, R., & Rudorf, E. (1966). *Phoneme-grapheme correspondences as cues to spelling improvement.* Washington, DC: U.S. Department of Health, Education and Welfare, Office of Education.

Henderson, E. (1990). *Teaching spelling* (2nd ed.). Boston: Houghton Mifflin.

Hillocks, G., Jr. (1987). *Research on written composition: New directions for teaching.* Urbana, IL: National Conference on Research in English.

Hodges, R. (1991). The conventions of writing. In J. Flood, J. Jensen, D. Lapp, & J. Squire (Eds.), *Handbook of research on teaching the English language arts* (pp. 1052–1064). New York: Macmillan.

Horton, L. (1970). Illegibilities in the cursive handwriting of ninth graders. *Elementary School Journal, 70,* 446–450.

Invernizzi, M., Abouzeid, M., & Gill, J. (1994). Using students' invented spelling as a guide for spelling instruction that emphasizes word study. *Elementary School Journal, 95,* 155–167.

Jongsma, K. (1990). Spelling-reading links. *The Reading Teacher, 43,* 608–609.

Kelley, B. (2007, November 12). The writing on the wall. *Newsweek, 150,* 69.

Lamme, L. (1979). Handwriting in an early childhood classroom. *Young Children, 35,* 18–23.

Lockard, J., Abrams, P., & Masny, W. (1997). *Microcomputers for twenty-first century educators.* New York: Longman.

Moats, L. (2001). *Speech to print: Language essentials for teachers.* Baltimore: Brookes.

Newkirk, T. (1978). Grammar instruction and writing: What we don't know. *English Journal, 67,* 46–54.

Ourada, E. (1993). Legibility of third grade handwriting: D'Nealian versus traditional Zaner-Bloser. In G. Coon & G. Palmer (Eds.), *Handwriting research and information: An administrator's handbook.* Glenview, IL: Scott-Foresman.

Radebaugh, M. (1985). Good spellers use more visual imagery than poor spellers. *The Reading Teacher, 38,* 532–536.

Read, C. (1971). Pre-school knowledge of English phonology. *Harvard Educational Review, 41,* 1–34.

Read, C. (1975). *Children's categorization of speech sounds in English.* NCTE Research Report No. 17. Urbana, IL: National Council of Teachers of English.

Rogers, H. (1997). A longitudinal study of elementary keyboarding computer skills. *Academy of Educational Leadership Journal, 1,* 55–57.

Stanovich, K. (1988). *Children's reading and the development of phonological awareness.* Detroit, MI: Wayne State University Press.

Templeton, S. (1991). Teaching and learning the English spelling system: Reconceptualizing method and purpose. *Elementary School Journal, 92,* 185–201.

Ubelacker, S. (1992). Keyboarding, the universal curriculum tool for children. *Proceedings of the 9th International Conference on Technology and* Education, 809–810. Austin, TX

Weaver, C. (1996). *Teaching grammar in context.* Portsmouth, NH: Heinemann.

Wolfe, P., & Nevills, P. (2004). *Building the reading brain.* Thousand Oaks, CA: Corwin Press.

Wray, D., & Medwell, J. (1994). *Teaching primary English: The state of the art.* New York: Routledge.

Anticipation Statement Answers

1. Agree

2. Disagree

3. Agree

4. Disagree

5. Agree

6. Agree

7. Agree

8. Agree

9. Agree: Knowledge of grammar improves writing ability. However, learning grammatical rules in isolation is useless.

10. Disagree: The most popular grammar is a combination of traditional, structural, and transformational-generative grammar. However, school grammar does include sentence combining and sentence expansion, and those improve student writing.

The Writers' Workshop

One way of implementing the writing process—prewriting, drafting, revising, editing, and publishing—is through the writers' workshop. Students read, research, talk with peers, think, and scribble, amid a community of writers. They learn in a safe environment to develop their writing skills under the guidance of a supportive teacher during a large block of time.

The writers' workshop is a regular period set aside for writing several times each week, daily if possible. Ideally, according to Ray (2001), the workshop schedule should be as dependable as lunchtime is in the school, beginning at the same time each day, so children learn to regard it as an accepted routine.

The workshop sets the stage for writing as an ongoing lifetime skill used for a variety of purposes and for multiple audiences (Hughey & Slack, 2001). Its hallmarks include ownership, self-monitoring, feedback, and individualized instruction (Atwell, 1998). Hence, the term "writers' workshop" seems more appropriate than "writing workshop," which is the earlier and more popular designation.

Anticipation Statements

Complete this exercise before reading Chapter 10.

Do you agree or disagree with the following statements? Circle your answer. Be prepared to discuss questions in blue.

1.	Writers' workshop should be part of a consistent daily schedule.	Agree	Disagree
2.	A minimum of three workshops per week is necessary for providing young writers the experience they need.	Agree	Disagree
3.	Mechanical skills lessons are not part of a writers' workshop.	Agree	Disagree
4.	The first five minutes of a writers' workshop should be silent, followed by time for writing, sharing with peers, and holding conferences with the teacher.	Agree	Disagree
5.	A writers' workshop is simple to implement and requires only a few basic materials.	Agree	Disagree
6.	Each grade level should have the same set of rules for a writers' workshop.	Agree	Disagree
7.	One major component of a writers' workshop is focus lessons.	Agree	Disagree
8.	When students do not revise their writing, it is because they are not capable of doing so.	Agree	Disagree
9.	Writing is a social act.	Agree	Disagree
10.	The genre unit and the author unit can both be used in the upper and lower grades.	Agree	Disagree

Essentials of the Workshop

Before introducing newcomers to the structure of the **writers' workshop,** the classroom teacher must make certain preparations to ensure that students will be productively engaged in quality writing.

Finding Time for the Whole Class to Write

Students need a block of time in which to write. Both Graves (1994) and Calkins (1994) agree that a minimum of three workshops weekly is needed, with each workshop lasting 45 to 60 minutes. Frequent and regular times for writing are required for children to develop writing skills. Ray (2001) adds that it takes a considerable amount of time for writers to acquire the experience to become good writers, so they need to write, write, and write some more, even when some of their pieces are not very good. It is the *quantity* of time that matters if good writers are to develop.

Today's teachers, faced with the daunting pressure of standardized testing, may wonder how to meet that time requirement. One way to justify the needed allocation of time for writing is to stress that separate periods of instruction for spelling, handwriting, and grammar are incorporated into the workshop period. Since the skills of listening, speaking, and reading are also necessarily involved in the classroom writers' workshop, the time segment can be simply earmarked as language arts. In this way, that segment becomes a more purposeful and meaningful activity, in which varied skills are applied.

One time management suggestion is to divide the daily writing time allotment into shorter periods, although with predictable starting and ending times. In this way, young writers learn what mature writers already know: Writing benefits, probably more than other subjects, from rest (Hughey & Slack, 2001). Children need to learn to put their piece away, reflect on it, and then return to it to evaluate and revise it. Even as they plead "for a little more time" to complete the piece on their first attempt, it is better for the teacher to stop the writing on an enthusiastic note so the children will willingly return to work on that piece at a later time.

No matter how the time is structured, teachers must remember that *the time allotments suggested in this section assume that the students are familiar with the five stages of the writing process* and need only to have them reviewed by the teacher from time to time.

Applicable IRA/NCTE Standards

Standard 4 Students adjust their use of spoken, written, and visual language (e.g., conventions, style, vocabulary) to communicate effectively with a variety of audiences and for different purposes.

Standard 5 Students employ a wide range of strategies as they write and use different writing process elements appropriately to communicate with different audiences for a variety of purposes.

Standard 9 Students develop an understanding of and respect for diversity in language use, patterns, and dialects across cultures, ethnic groups, geographic regions, and social roles.

Standard 10 Students whose first language is not English make use of their first language to develop competency in the English language arts and to develop understanding of content across the curriculum.

Standard 11 Students participate as knowledgeable, reflective, creative, and critical members of a variety of literacy communities.

Standard 12 Students use spoken, written, and visual language to accomplish their own purposes (e.g., for learning, enjoyment, persuasion, and the exchange of information).

SOURCE: *Standards for the English Language Arts*, by the International Reading Association and the National Council of Teachers of English, Copyright 1996 by the International Reading Association and the National Council of Teachers of English. Reprinted with permission. http://www.ncte.org/about/over/standards/110846.htm

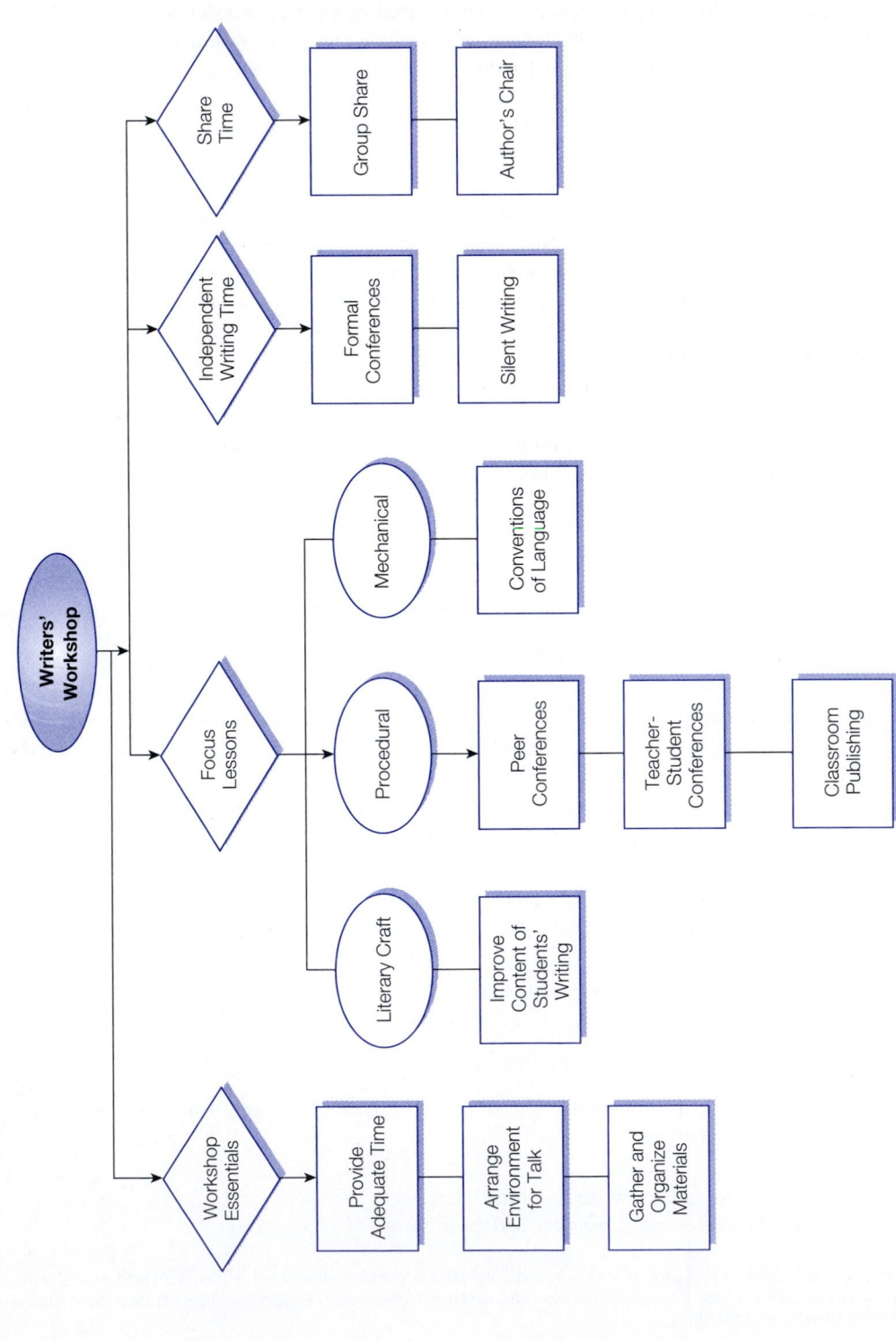

A Graphic Summary of the Contents of This Chapter

Arranging the Environment for Talk

Since writing can be a social act, children often wish to share their own writing with peers and to hear or read what classmates are writing as well. Therefore, teachers should arrange to cluster students during the workshop period at desks or tables that can be easily moved to promote discourse about the written pieces—talk, of course, that is limited to praise or concerns about those pieces. (This rule must be explained each time and strictly enforced to make the workshop a useful adjunct to the writing program.) Peers can offer empathy as well as practical suggestions.

Occasionally, when some writers want more privacy, the teacher can set aside one area in the room where those students may write in a quieter atmosphere with a "Do Not Disturb" sign prominently displayed. In spacious classrooms children may even be able to sit on the floor and write on their whiteboards, somewhat away from the table/desk section.

A conference table is always needed in the workshop so the teacher can confer with individuals on a scheduled basis and also meet occasionally with small groups of students who need additional support or reassurance. Finally, there must be a Writers' Workshop Center, a designated area where the whole class gathers at the start and conclusion of the workshop period to emphasize that this classroom is a writing community.

Gathering and Organizing Materials

Preplanning involves gathering needed resources to support the workshop effort and organizing them to maximize the effective use of class time by promoting student responsibility. The following materials are needed.

Paper: Younger children should get lined paper from assigned helpers at the start of the workshop. Older students can obtain their own paper at a central location or even maintain a fresh supply in their writing portfolio.

Pencils: Children need two sharp pencils every morning. A container for "dull" pencils should be available together with one container with a few fresh pencils for "emergencies." There should be no pencil sharpening during workshop time to distract or interrupt.

Bookmaking supplies: These include but are not limited to cardboard, contact paper, cloth, and wallpaper for book covers, as well as scissors, staplers, art supplies, and other equipment for binding books.

Writer's notebooks: Boys and girls should each have a notebook in which to record new vocabulary they have heard and wish to use in their writing, as well as ideas they pondered when they were not writing and that they may want to explore. A spiral-bound 6" × 9" notebook is a handy size.

Daily writing folders: Students need plain manila or pocketed folders in which to store their ongoing daily writing papers. These folders are to be kept in designated boxes in the classroom or in the children's desks.

Portfolios: Final or published copies of writing are to be kept apart from daily folders. Colored manila folders or other special folders work well to hold those final copies. Hughey and Slack (2001) recommend that photocopies be made of the final work and sent home while the originals remain in the portfolio. At the end of the year, complete portfolios may be sent home or forwarded to the next grade, depending on school policy.

Reference materials: As they write, children need ready access to dictionaries, thesauri, encyclopedias, and the Internet. Editing and revising are vastly improved when all such references are available. Some schools even provide each child with a dictionary, which further enhances initial drafts.

Bulletin board space: Teachers should have a special display, possibly titled "Good Workshop Writing," for samples of student work (since publication is the last step in the writing process). Two cautions: First, each child must have the opportunity to submit his or her best work regularly while retaining the final privilege of refusal. Second, the display should be changed monthly to maintain currency and interest.

For material related to this concept, go to Video Clip 10.1 on the Student Resource CD bound into the back of your textbook.

Implementing the Writers' Workshop

For teachers in the primary grades or for those in the intermediate grades whose students have never been involved in a writers' workshop, one successful way to lay its foundation is through *the read-aloud*. The teacher reads several selections from quality books to the children, paying special attention to the names of the author and/or author–illustrator, discussing how the author began the book, and eliciting an understanding of the message presented in the book. Then the teacher tells the children that they too can and will become authors! Next, he or she describes the writers' workshop and the materials they will be using to write their pieces. Finally, each child receives a writing folder, and the teacher reviews some *workshop rules appropriate for that grade level and class*. For example, in second grade the rules could include the following:

Write on only one side of the paper.

Put a date on everything you write.

Don't worry about spelling.

Don't erase.

Do not talk during the first five minutes of writing.

Confer quietly about your piece with your neighbors.

Share ideas politely.

Other rules that may be placed on charts in the Writers' Workshop Center cover such topics as Proofreading Reminders, Great Beginnings, The Best Endings, and Examples of Editing Rules. On the inside covers of each child's writing folder can be pasted information regarding "The Writing Process," "Skills I Can Use," and "Things I Might Write About."

On the opening day of writers' workshop in classes where it is being introduced to newcomers, the teacher again takes the lead by assembling the group and showing the children how to select a writing topic. He or she lists three interesting possibilities (e.g., rescuing a lost kitten, traveling through the Mojave Desert, flying a kite) and discusses each one at some length. After the teacher decides which topic he or she will write about today, the students are asked to share which topics they each choose to write about. Then the teacher notes each topic title on the board by the child's name. Students next collect their own writing folders and materials to begin working at their tables. The teacher writes too—for at least five minutes—to model the importance of writing time. The room is quiet.

On the second day the children are told about other components in addition to writing that will be included in the workshop. They are also introduced to these *possible* time allotments for that workshop: 10 to 15 minutes for instruction or focus lessons, 20 to 30 minutes for independent writing time, and 10 to 15 minutes for share time. The first and last are whole class experiences that promote the concept of a community of writers as they open and close the workshop period.

Finally, teachers must realize that, while implementing writers' workshop, they must also create a therapeutic writing environment (Cramer, 2001). This means that they must trust and respect children, receive writing graciously, practice empathetic teaching, replenish their own and students' creative energy, uncover and enlarge talent, and include everybody. The last concept is particularly important for at-risk students and English Language Learners (ELLs).

First Major Component of the Workshop Session: Focus Lessons

Focus lessons, sometimes called mini-lessons, consist of direct instruction that provides children with information about writing. These open each workshop session, bringing the teacher and children together for approximately 10 to 15 minutes. This physical coming together, according to

Ray (2001), serves to promote an important "intellectual gathering" of a writers' community. The most effective writing workshops are those that have routines and structures for grouping students for the focus lessons.

At one time these lessons were mostly organized on a hopscotch approach, with varied topics presented on different days with little or no continuity. Teachers found, however, that such an approach was not nearly as efficient as organizing the topics into units of study (Anderson, 2005). Therefore, teachers now prepare and "focus" the lessons on a single topic or unit for a period of two weeks or more, depending on the grade level of the class. These lessons are teacher-centered, many with no student input at all (Ray, 2001). Teacher talk dominates the lessons, which may have a procedural, literary craft, or mechanical skills focus.

Procedural lessons are held most often at the beginning of the school year and involve such topics as the following:

- *Peer conferences*: The children must learn where and how to best confer with classmates about their pieces. Sometimes the most appropriate place is at the same table with a neighbor; at other times, it may be in a corner away from the rest of the class. However, it is always critical that only quiet voices are used in peer conferences. Furthermore, the efforts of the author must be respected in all instances; therefore, he or she must make any revision decisions, for example.
- *Teacher-student (content) conferences*: Since these conferences occur while the class is writing, the students should know how they will be chosen for the conference and what their roles and that of the teacher will be during the meeting. (Generally a schedule is posted to save time.) The usual format is as follows: The child reads; the teacher listens, questions, and makes suggestions. Some experienced teachers prefer to come to the student (rather than have the student come to the conference table) because then they can better control the length (2–4 minutes) of the session; they do this by kneeling at the child's desk or using a chair with wheels to move about the room. Incidentally, these conferences do not concern editing problems as students are generally encouraged to solve mechanical errors in spelling, grammar, punctuation, or capitalization by themselves or with the aid of a classmate or reference tool (e.g., dictionary).
- *Classroom publishing*: Since most writing is intended to be read by an audience, publishing includes preparing the best student pieces for publication. Whether these eventually appear in class books or student newspapers, on hallway or classroom bulletin boards, or as thank-you notes mailed to resource visitors, the teacher must first provide a focus lesson describing the new publishing procedure so everyone understands what is expected.

Literary craft lessons comprise the majority of focus lessons presented during the year. Briefly, they concern improvement of the content of the students' writing, including using descriptions to develop solid characters, writing strong beginnings and endings, and using dialogue. These lessons address genres, authors, illustrators, techniques, styles, and literary works. Matters such as plot, characters, setting, theme, point of view, onomatopoeia, metaphors, and similes are all involved in literary craft focus lessons, *depending on the grade level and maturity of the children*.

For Grades K through 6, literary craft lessons may include study of one writer's body of work, study of how to read texts like writers, and poetry genre study (Ray, 2001). Units in the early grades also study different kinds of writing, writing for audiences, the label book genre, the alphabet book genre, where writers get ideas, and why writers write. Units of study for older students include the literary nonfiction genre, writing in professional lives, what writers need to gather from the world to maintain a published writing life, and a *historical fiction genre study,* which could include authors and titles such as the following:

Genre Unit: Historical Fiction

Bunting's *Dandelion* (1995)

Curtis' *Bud, Not Buddy* (1995)

Cushman's *The Ballad of Lucy Whipple* (1996)

Taylor's *Mississippi Bridge* (1990)

Yep's *Hiroshima* (1995)

Genre studies and author studies are usually interspersed throughout the year and follow a specific pattern: *immersion* in one genre or in one author's work followed by *whole class study* of that genre or author and culminating in *student writing* as influenced by that same genre or author.

Genre studies help student writers understand the general pattern of organization underlying stories in any one literary category, even though their formats may vary widely in style and complexity. Children develop an appreciation for the many ways that they can create their own stories by reading or listening to books representing many different genres. A successful and satisfying way to promote writing among primary students and hesitant intermediate writers, for example, is preparing predictable pattern books. These books involve considerable repetition of text and numerous illustrations.

Author studies are valuable because they can introduce children to the craft of writing stories by using the basic strategy of *elaboration techniques* (Hughey & Slack, 2001). This strategy helps the writers learn to employ language effectively. It has two dimensions: (1) expanding ideas with description by using similes, metaphors, onomatopoeia, lively verbs, carefully chosen adverbs, and sensory adjectives and (2) adding detailed information to increase content by using sentence expansion and paragraph expansion, both of which answer the journalistic questions of Who, What, Why, Where, When, and How. Additional elaboration evolves from inquiry into the plots, settings, and characters that the writers are developing. For example, an author study could revolve around the popular Jon Scieszka and his books:

The Stinky Cheese Man and Other Fairly Stupid Tales (1992)

The Frog Prince Continued (1994)

Math Curse (1995)

The True Story of the 3 Little Pigs (1996)

Squids Will Be Squids (1998)

From in-depth studies of favorite authors, children can also learn the importance of *revision* and how it must occur *throughout* the writing process. In contrast to editing, which concerns only cosmetic changes to the text by repairing such areas as spelling and grammar, revision involves changes to the actual structure, content, style, or meaning of the text. It allows students to discover more about what they know, change what they feel, change what they think, make connections between facts or experiences, and alter their point of view (Murray, 1990). Revision has been termed a fluid process that tries to promote the most effective communication of ideas; therefore, there are no definitive "right" or "wrong" ways to revise (Hughey & Slack, 2001). Nevertheless, for elementary school writers, revision is probably the most difficult part of the writing process.

There are four revision operations—adding, deleting, substituting, and rearranging—with each requiring different considerations. For young writers, according to Cramer (2001), adding is the easiest and rearranging the most difficult operation, with substituting and deleting falling somewhere in between:

1. *Adding* information is probably the simplest way to introduce content revision to children; even first graders can quickly understand the idea of adding to their composition. Yet good writing is not wordy or too repetitive.

2. *Deleting* information removes content that is irrelevant and redundant. Good writing is concise.

3. *Substituting* one piece of information for another or one sentence or word for a different sentence or word is the simultaneous act of adding and deleting.

4. *Rearranging* words and ideas enables them to be put into their most effective sequence. Good writing is orderly and can be facilitated by using the computer, when one is available, to rearrange sentences, paragraphs, and bigger pieces of information within a composition.

Atwell (1998) believes that, generally, students do not revise their writing because they do not have the "methods for manipulating the page." They do not know how to add, delete, or change information nor can they move it around. Consequently, she introduces children to such basic revision tools as *carets* {^} (for inserting new material), *arrows* (for extending writing, for example, into the margins), and *cut and paste* or *cut and tape* (for inserting new paragraphs and reordering existing ones).

A sample focus lesson on revision for students above the second-grade level can proceed as follows:

1. The teacher has available an overhead projector, a chalkboard, and a marker. The children each have on their desk a draft of their own writing that has been completed recently.

2. The teacher projects a draft of her or his own writing *or* a draft of student writing volunteered by an unnamed child. He or she has the class read the piece silently and then *offer positive comments* about it. These are listed on the board. Next the students reread the draft silently and then *recommend improvements*. These suggestions too are listed on the board.

3. The teacher comments on the list of improvements, instructing the students to focus on other than minor writing faults (e.g., a misspelled word).

4. The teacher chooses *one* item from the student list of improvements (e.g., more descriptive words are needed) and then has the children apply that item to their own piece of writing.

5. The teacher circulates about the classroom, offering assistance.

6. The teacher periodically repeats the lesson, gradually increasing the number of items from the student list of improvements, to promote writing growth.

Finally, some of the students in both primary and intermediate grades may recall and employ revision strategies that Heard (2002) has developed because these are labeled with ear-catching phrases, such as Give a Yard Sale for Extra Words (to eliminate unnecessary vocabulary), Opening the Front Door (to write appropriate introductory sentences), Looking Through a Magnifying Glass (to expand descriptions), Rearranging the Furniture (to move parts of the writing to other places), and Leaving the House (to be creative with the ending of a piece of writing).

Mechanical skills lessons focus on the conventions of language: spelling, grammar, capitalization, punctuation, and handwriting. Teachers should plan focus lessons that deal directly with elements of those conventions that a classroom of students needs to study or review. The key to that planning is an examination of the writing actually done in that one class to determine which conventions are not being using correctly. For instance, if students are writing dialogue but are unable to punctuate and capitalize it properly, at least one focus lesson is needed to remedy that problem. *When children see a specific and immediate reason to learn a particular skill and that skill is taught to them in a meaningful context, they learn it more quickly and retain it longer.* Of course, the content of some mechanical skills lessons may need to be repeated, depending on the grade level and maturity of the students.

Ray (2001) has found that student writers need help from time to time with issues of capitalization, punctuation, and spelling, as well as grammar issues of agreement (subject-verb, pronoun-antecedent), and of structure (sentences and paragraphs).

Whether the focus lesson involves mechanical skills, literacy craft, or procedure, it should conclude with a preview of what each student will do during the independent writing time segment of the workshop. Teachers often base independent writing time on *a status-of-the-class report* and use a checklist (and sometimes choose to provide each child with his or her own version) to determine at which stage every student is in the writing process (e.g., prewriting or editing stage). This report also gives classmates an opportunity to learn from their peers some appropriate workshop behaviors (e.g., clustering ideas for a story or decorating a book cover) and to acquire the vocabulary to describe their own writing activities.

Second Major Component of the Workshop Session: Independent Writing Time

The bulk of the workshop session is spent on writing, with children working independently on varied projects as they move through all five stages of the writing process. The session generally opens, however, with five minutes of silent writing before peer and teacher-student conferences begin and student writing starts. This brief period of silence serves as a transition *from* the whole class teacher-directed focus lesson (sometimes involving discussion) and status-of-the-class report *to* the serious core of the writing workshop. Since writing is more than putting pencil to paper or fingers to computer keys (Hughey & Slack, 2002), children need time to reread their last piece or else to mentally review the day's topic before writing or possibly consider ideas for a new area of interest. To emphasize the importance of the writing task, however, teachers also use this time to model proper behavior and ponder quietly.

During this component of the workshop session, the teacher should notice the wide variety of behaviors in which the young writers are engaged. Some who are choosing new topics are reflecting, talking quietly (after the initial five minutes of silence), observing, or writing. Some are writing, pausing occasionally to reread what they have written or to confer with a classmate about the topic. Others are editing pieces as they prepare them for publication, and some classmates are in the final stages of publication.

While the student writers are occupied with working independently (except for an infrequent peer conference about their work), the teacher is equally busy since "the writing conference lies at the heart of the writing workshop" (Fletcher & Portalupi, 2001). Some teachers hold a conference with each student weekly by moving about the classroom in a regular pattern, thereby meeting about one fifth of the group each day. Other teachers divide their independent writing time into two segments: First, they spend the initial 10 to 20 minutes checking briefly (for 1 or 2 minutes each) on 10 or more students each day; second, they spend the rest of this time on more formal conferences, usually with children who are revising their pieces (Tompkins, 2004).

Formal conferences are scheduled on the bulletin board so that each child knows in advance when he or she will meet individually with the teacher, much like Miss Ortiz does in Vignette 10.1, as she has planned today's writing conferences with students with last initials L through P.

The second major component of the writers' workshop is independent writing time, which affords students the opportunity to reread earlier writing or explore a new area of interest.

VIGNETTE 10.1 Poetry Writing and Teacher Conferences

"And Jason Walter, my checklist shows you are working on final revisions of your poetry collection," said Miss Ortiz, finishing the day's status-of-the-class report. "Does that reflect your progress?"

Jason nodded enthusiastically and rushed to say, "But I need help with one of my poems before I print it out. I keep working on it, but . . ." He shrugged, indicating frustration with his work.

"Today's writing conferences are for students with last names L through P," Miss Ortiz said, "but I will try to make time to meet with you after I've worked with those students. In the meantime, I'm sure your classmates could give you good advice. Will you ask some others for help during independent writing?"

Jason nodded and looked relieved at his teacher's suggestions. He caught the eye of two students seated in his group and motioned at his paper, silently recruiting them to be peer editors. As Miss Ortiz helped the class make the transition to silent writing, he looked forward to receiving feedback on his tricky haiku.

Miss Ortiz used the silent writing time to review the list of students participating in today's teacher-student conferences. In focus lessons and in other portions of language arts time, she had been leading the class in a comprehensive study of poetry, including a variety of genres, types of rhyme, and examples of figurative language. As a final project, she asked each student to choose five different poetic forms and write original poems incorporating their new knowledge. The projects were due in two weeks, and she knew today's conferences would include other students like Jason who were struggling with one or two parts of the work.

"End of silent writing," she announced after five minutes. "Please continue your work and remember to talk quietly if you conference with a partner." With a smile she beckoned Abby Lawrence to her desk.

Abby excelled in writing basics like spelling and grammar. She enjoyed writing reports and reading for pleasure, but she had struggled with the less structured aspects of the poetry unit. Miss Ortiz wasn't surprised to see Abby arrive with a slight frown and a folder full of revisions.

"I'm working on the free-verse poem about a personal experience," Abby said.

"What experience did you choose?" asked Miss Ortiz.

"Riding a roller coaster," Abby replied.

"That's interesting. I've never read a poem about that before. See, you're already being creative!" Miss Ortiz said with a smile.

Abby grinned shyly before answering, "Well, yeah, but I don't know what to say."

Miss Ortiz knew the intimidation a blank sheet of paper could cause. "What is one thing you remember about riding the roller coaster?" she asked Abby.

"It was so high off the ground. It was pretty scary."

"How high?" she pressed a little. "What can you compare it to?"

"Well . . . when I looked down from the top, all the trees on the ground looked like little pieces of broccoli," Abby said.

"What a great simile!" exclaimed Miss Ortiz. "Do you remember what a simile is?"

"Sure," said Abby, and she rattled off the familiar definition.

"You just created an original simile without even trying to," Miss Ortiz said. "You created a picture with your words, instead of just saying the roller coaster was high and scary."

As Abby processed the new thought, Miss Ortiz continued. "You probably don't want to write a whole poem of just similes, although you could try. But if you think about how you felt and what you thought about riding the coaster, I'm sure you will find lots of things to say." She closed the conference by suggesting Abby use the remainder of independent writing time to brainstorm a list of memories and feelings about the roller coaster ride. Abby agreed to present a draft of the completed poem at next week's conference and returned to her desk eager to start the list.

Miss Ortiz scanned the room before beginning the next conference. As usual, most students were working quietly, reviewing their poems or assembling printed copies in portfolios. A few students were passing papers back and forth, editing and commenting on each other's drafts. The students usually excelled at group work, but once or twice a week they needed a reminder of the workshop rules. A group of girls in the back began to giggle and Miss Ortiz silenced them with a look.

Even as the girls returned to writing, Miss Ortiz braced herself and nodded at Patrick. As expected, he arrived at her desk with an attitude.

"I'm done with my poems," he said.

"Completely done?" she asked. "Are you satisfied with them?"

"Yeah," Patrick replied. "They're good enough. I want to be a lawyer like my dad, and lawyers don't write poetry."

"No, but they do have to communicate with each other and help other people understand ideas," Miss Ortiz said. "Would you agree that sharing your thoughts is a big part of being a lawyer?"

Patrick grudgingly nodded.

"If you want to talk more about how poetry could help you be a better lawyer, I would like to have that conversation," she said. "But we'll need to do it outside of writer's conference because we just have a few minutes. Okay?"

Again Patrick offered a nod, this one less reluctant.

"Why don't you show me one poem you'd like to talk about for the rest of our time?" she asked. He selected the cinquain and they reviewed it together.

After several more five- and six-minute conferences, Miss Ortiz had finished meeting with all the assigned students for the day and looked for Jason. He sat deep in thought, eyes to the ceiling, absent-mindedly tapping his cheek with the eraser of his pencil. She hated to disturb his concentration, but wanted to keep her promise.

She approached his desk quietly. "Jason, you may keep working on your own or we can talk about your poem now. What would you like to do?"

"Work on my poem!" he said, and grabbed a few papers before following her.

"Okay," Miss Ortiz said. "Now what do you want to talk about first?"

Scheduling formal conferences enables both parties to prepare for them, thereby making the conference a valuable part of the workshop. It is advisable to create a record-keeping system to keep track of the conference schedule, thus ensuring that the teacher confers with all students routinely and weekly. The conferences, which should last between four to seven minutes, should build on each writer's strengths, with the teacher giving specific praise wherever writing is well done. The teacher may follow these steps in the conference:

1. First, talk to the children about what they are doing as writers. Listen carefully. Discover their intentions for a particular piece.

2. Second, talk to the students about how to be better writers. Assess their needs and then decide what to teach them.

3. Third, teach *one* needed skill or strategy.

4. Fourth, develop an individual plan with each writer so that he or she knows what to do next. Record that plan for the next conference.

Although formal conferences follow a general pattern throughout the elementary grades, the *content* changes depending on the ability and age of the students. Fletcher and Portalupi (2001) have outlined that content and the suggestions for writing improvement that teachers may offer at each level:

Grades K Through 1

- Add more details to their drawing, because many students "write" stories using only pictures but can "read" them aloud. They can be encouraged to add more details to their drawings.
- Add words to their drawing by labeling parts of the picture or writing a sentence or two on a precut strip of paper taped to the bottom of the drawing.
- Add more details to their writing. When a child is able to verbally describe more about the subject, he or she can add more information to the writing.
- Add one or more pages so that young writers are not confined to one sheet of paper, but can continue with their writing on a stapled second page.
- Use the "two finger rule" for spacing between words to make it easier for the reader to understand what has been written.
- Include a beginning, middle, and end so the child can expand on what has already been written.
- Sound out words (without the teacher's help). This area of invented spelling aids emergent spellers as they write about their pictures.

Grades 2 Through 4

- Sharpen the lead (i.e., the opening sentence or paragraph) to help seize the reader's attention.
- Break a large topic like "Our Home" into manageable segments or chapters. Sometimes a simple table of contents is needed.
- Cut and tape to add information. Show the student how to reread and then determine where the new writing needs to be inserted. With permission, literally cut open the story at that point and use tape to add a blank sheet of paper. This gives the student a "window" where he or she can introduce additional information.
- Target the most important part of the story, omitting some of the less relevant details.
- Focus on one subject in a single piece of writing rather than on two or more ideas, each of which could be a separate piece of work.
- Anticipate readers' questions. Consider information that has been omitted from the piece but is needed by listeners or readers to clarify the meaning of the writing or the intent of the writer.

Grades 5 Through 6

- Develop a simple timeline to mark the critical events in the story. Then determine a suitable beginning and ending as well as areas that can be left out.
- Decide on the Most Important Thing (MIT) and then write another draft with this new focus.
- Slow down the climax and expand it with additional details or feelings so the reader will not rush through it.
- After talking about the topic, choose authentic details to make the writing more vivid.
- Develop the characters and reduce the number of details about the plot.

A successful formal conference ends on a positive note as teachers show that they care about each child both as a writer and as a person. They do so by smiling and nodding and by listening intently to everything the girl or boy says, thereby indicating that the writing being done truly matters. Anderson (2005) believes that the way teachers listen can actually "change students' writing lives," inspiring students to "stretch themselves as writers."

Third Major Component of the Workshop Session: Share Time

Although some teacher-student conferences and peer conferences occur in every workshop session, it is still critical to set aside time at the end of each session when the entire class meets together for a group session called **share time**. It is an established routine as teacher and class meet in the same designated area at the conclusion of each writers' workshop for approximately 5 to 10 minutes. It offers students the opportunity to share their writing with the whole class and allows the teacher to model how to give and receive responses to written work. Ray (2001) stresses that students should be responsible for most of the talk during share time, just as the teacher was responsible for most of the talk during focus lessons.

For material related to this concept, go to Video Clip 10.2 on the Student Resource CD bound into the back of your textbook.

Nevertheless, if share time is to be a productive segment of the workshop, it is the teacher who must gradually develop group cohesion within the classroom so that the young writers' initial reluctance to share their writing is overcome (Cramer, 2001). Sharing pieces of writing with classmates gives the children a sense of how an audience understands and reacts to their writing. It also fosters pride, convincing students that they have worthy ideas to share with the rest of the world; finally, it helps them prepare their pieces for a public appearance outside the classroom.

The writing conference, a regular meeting between student and teacher to discuss their writing, is the heart of the writers' workshop.

The major type of share time is a *group share* session, during which two or three students sit, one at a time, in the Author's Chair and share their work with their classmates. Mrs. Lee in Vignette 10.2 introduces her second graders to sharing their writing by first sharing her own work and then asking for suggestions on how to improve it. She does this by posing questions that promote discussion.

VIGNETTE 10.2   Novice Writers in the Author's Chair

Mrs. Lee had enjoyed teaching a recent series of focus lessons to her second-grade class; the unit included an overview of fairy tales as a genre, read-alouds of both well-known and less familiar stories, and even a lesson on the Brothers Grimm and their compilation of old folktales during the early 19th century.

At the end of the unit, Mrs. Lee shared the familiar story of Little Red Riding Hood and then read "The Wolf's Story," a contemporary retelling from the wolf's point of view. The two versions provided just the example she needed to introduce this element of characterization to the young students, and they enthusiastically spent several sessions of independent writing time rewriting their favorite fairy tales from new perspectives.

Today the children would begin sharing their first drafts. Mrs. Lee looked forward to hearing and seeing the illustrated stories. First, however, she would share her own work. Share time was still a relatively new experience for the children, and she had discovered that they responded more thoughtfully to each other's writing when they could first practice commenting on hers.

After the class gathered on the reading rug, Mrs. Lee settled into the Author's Chair and read "Finding Snow," her retelling of "Snow White and the Seven Dwarfs" from the prince's point of view. The boys especially enjoyed hearing about the strong hero riding through a forest looking for adventure, and all the children liked Mrs. Lee's simple drawings and the new twist on a beloved story.

Mrs. Lee finished reading and asked for suggestions to improve her work. Understandably, the children sat silently at first, reluctant to critique a teacher's work. To encourage discussion, she asked a few questions. "Did the prince seem different from the way you pictured him in the original story?" she asked. Several students said yes, and she asked follow-up questions to elicit their thoughts. For several minutes the students considered their impressions of the prince from both versions. "How did I use words to tell you about the prince?" Mrs. Lee asked. "How could I make it better?"

As the children continued discussing the differences in characterization, Mrs. Lee felt confident the students were ready to provide good feedback to each other. She asked a volunteer to share. Randy quickly raised his hand and, after wiggling into a comfortable position in the Author's Chair, animatedly read his story. The children listened intently as he told the tale of the lonely—and hungry—witch in the forest who waited for Hansel and Gretel to arrive. Mrs. Lee was delighted to see the children's enjoyment of the story.

After Randy finished, Mrs. Lee opened the discussion by praising Randy's willingness to read first and his use of good adjectives in describing the witch's house of treats. "Who else would like to share their thoughts about Randy's work?" she asked the class.

After a brief moment, Maria raised her hand and said, "I liked the story but I thought the witch was supposed to be scary. In your story she was kind of funny."

"Randy, how did you want readers to see the witch in your story?" Mrs. Lee asked him.

"What she planned to do to Hansel and Gretel was scary, but I think the witch was silly," Randy answered. "She thought a stick was Hansel's finger because she couldn't see very well, and she let Gretel trick her into looking in the oven. She didn't seem very smart."

"How did Randy use words to describe the witch?" Mrs. Lee asked. "Randy, do you want to change anything in your story based on the class's feedback?"

After Randy shared there was time for one more reader, and Mrs. Lee again directed the class in active listening as Hannah read her version of Cinderella from the perspective of a stepsister. As before, Mrs. Lee was careful in coaching the students to critique the stories and in helping the young authors evaluate possibilities for improvement.

At the end of share time, several more students clamored to read their stories. Mrs. Lee picked two to read during the next day's share time and considered making a sign-up list for the following days. Apparently I don't need to read first anymore, she thought to herself with satisfaction. Share time had become an anticipated experience.

In share time, listeners in the primary grades generally gather on the reading rug, but in the intermediate grades, they stay at their desks or tables. As the author reads his or her piece or portion of it, the members of the audience prepare to ask meaningful questions aloud in an effort to improve their classmate's writing. In some instances, and especially, at the beginning of the year when many students may be hesitant to share and thus receive oral critiques of their work, the teacher may propose a "quiet share." In this way, the Author's Chair still remains occupied by one student at a time; however, the listeners write their questions or suggestions for improvement on a clipboard or tablet. Signed or unsigned, these praises or concerns are then given to the authors for their consideration.

A special—and occasional—type of group share is a *celebration share* during which writers read the pieces they have published. Since they have already completed the work on them, their classmates offer only oral praises for the finished pieces and the efforts involved in their production.

Finally, some teachers find it useful from time to time to use a portion of the share time for a *read-aloud* that helps students better understand the elements of writing, such as the lead, the setting, the climax, and the ending. Picture books are an ideal genre for the writers' workshop (Fletcher & Portalupi, 2001) since they can be read in a single session and display the writing elements clearly. Furthermore, they also stimulate ideas for children who may claim from time to time that they have "nothing to write about."

A sample lesson plan incorporating the concepts introduced in this chapter appears on p. 352.

Assessment

As the months go by in a writers' workshop, it is hoped that the teacher will observe students developing skills in these six areas, depending on their maturity (adapted from Ray, 2001, pp. 215–217):

1. A sense of self as writers (e.g., ask, "What would you say you do best as a writer right now?")

2. Acquiring ways of reading the world like writers, and collecting different ideas thoughtfully (e.g., ask, "How much are you writing and how often?")

3. A sense of deliberate purpose about their writing (e.g., ask, "What are your plans for working on this piece over the next few days [or weeks]?")

4. Becoming members of a literate, responsive community (e.g., ask, "What kinds of help have you been giving other writers in our room?")

5. A sense of craft, form, and genre in writing by reading texts like writers (e.g., ask, "Who are the published writers you are learning from?")

6. A sense of audience and an understanding of how to prepare work for publication (e.g., ask, "What was your process for proofreading this? What corrections did you make?")

Working With English Language Learners

Writing can be laborious for English learners because the sounds that they hear may be very different from conventional spelling. For example, a child may hear "tabo" when someone says the word "table." As a second-language learner, it can be difficult to distinguish sounds, and children at the beginning stages of writing try to write what they hear.

A writers' workshop works well for ELLs because it has a consistent structure, provides plenty of writing experience over time, includes mini-lessons on mechanics, occurs in a friendly low-anxiety environment, and encourages children to write without worrying about making mistakes.

Beginning ELLs: Beginning ELL students should be encouraged to copy words and write simple words, phrases, and sentences. One way to support these children is to have them write about characters or events from familiar stories, ones that the teacher has read several times to the class.

Early intermediate and intermediate ELLs: Intermediate ELLs continue to write simple sentences, but are becoming more independent in their writing. They can begin to write short paragraphs. One way to support them at this level is to provide students with a pattern to use. For example, students can write a friendly letter after the teacher has taught them the basic format and components of such a letter, and has provided the "skeleton" of the letter to copy from the board or chart paper. Students can insert their own words to personalize the letter.

Early advanced and advanced ELLs: Advanced ELLs can begin to fully participate in the writing process through the writers' workshop. At this time, they can write short paragraphs and short narratives. They are beginning to use more complex vocabulary and conventional spelling and grammar. However, these students will still need extra support from the teacher until their writing skills are equivalent to their native English-speaking peers.

Practical Instructional Activities and Ideas

- *Penmanship:* Students must be taught the correct way to write manuscript (kindergarten through second grade) and cursive (Grades 3 to 6) handwriting. They should have many opportunities to practice handwriting. This can be accomplished during the writers' workshop through focus lessons on handwriting, as well as during the final stage of the writing process (publishing), when stories must be recopied in the students' best writing.

- *Hamburger writing:* An interesting way to visualize the parts of a paragraph is to use "hamburger writing." The teacher uses a chart with a line drawing of a hamburger: top bun, three layers (e.g., cheese, meat, lettuce), and bottom bun. The top bun is the introduction, the three layers provide the supporting details, and the bottom bun is the conclusion. Students can refer to the hamburger chart to help them remember the parts of a paragraph. Some teachers call this exercise the "juicy hamburger" when children add numerous details to the three layers.

- *Author of the week:* Children's literature can serve as a starting point for writing activities during the writers' workshop. Teachers can read books each week written by a featured creator, such as Patricia Polacco. This creates a theme and naturally focuses the children's attention on the concept of "author" and "illustrator."

- *Writing a friendly letter:* The friendly letter format, including the date, salutation, body, closing, and signature, is taught in the primary grades, usually Grade 2. Teachers can introduce the friendly letter format using a chart. Children can write letters to friends, family members, or pen pals. They can write friendly letters to invite parents to attend Back to School Night, Parent Conferences, Science Night, and Open House. Another opportunity is to have children write "get well" letters when a classmate has been absent for a period of time due to illness or injury.

- *Story writing:* Children should be encouraged to write narratives or stories during the writers' workshop. The teacher can provide many ideas for stories by sharing children's literature with the class. The more that children become familiar with story elements, such as characters and plot, the better able students will be to write their own stories.

- *Thank-you notes:* Children should be encouraged to write in meaningful situations. An example is having them each write a thank-you note to a guest speaker who came to their class. Another example is to have them write a thank-you note after they have taken a field trip to a local site, such as the post office, a restaurant, grocery store, or the police department.

- *Birthday stories:* This is a meaningful writing activity for children that serves as a remembrance of a particular grade. On each child's birthday, the students in the class write a personalized story or letter to that child. The teacher compiles these stories into a book for the birthday child who can then take it home.

- *Writing prompts:* Sometimes it is difficult for children to think of subjects to write about. One strategy is to provide them with a "prompt." A good example is to cut out interesting pictures from discarded magazines and glue them to the top of a sheet of writing paper. Children choose a writing prompt they like and write about it on the lines below the picture. Examples of "prompting" pictures include those of a dog or cat from a pet food ad or those of a faraway place such as an island, city skyline, or park.

- *Research tools:* Children can begin to use research tools, such as dictionaries and thesauri, during writers' workshop. They can use the Internet to look up information for reports and use library resources to find out more information. Nonfiction books with information on science and social studies topics can be available in the classroom as well. An excellent example is the "Eyewitness" series of books published by Dorling Kindersley (DK), which range in topic from plants to the solar system to World War II to U.S. presidents.

- *Research reports:* Children in Grades 3 to 6 can write research reports about topics, issues, or events. An example in a third-grade class studying the solar system is to have each student write a report on a particular planet.

- *Persuasive essay:* Children in Grades 5 or 6 can write compositions that state and support a position. An example in a sixth-grade class would be an essay about an issue that is important to the community, such as installing a stoplight at a busy intersection.

LESSON PLAN 10.1 Self-Publishing

Language Art Component: Writing

Grade: 3

ELL Level: Advanced

Time Frame: 1–2 weeks

Objective

- Students write, illustrate, and publish their own story.

Materials

- Writing paper
- Pencils
- Colored pencils, crayons, or markers
- Construction paper for book covers
- Rubric that lists expectations for the assignment

Content Standards

English Language Development (ELD): Writing

- Students edit writing for standard spelling, punctuation, and capitalization.
- Students use simple patterns to organize written work.
- Students write a story that describes the setting, characters, and events.

Language Arts: Writing

- Students write a story that develops a plot and is interesting to read.
- Students write legibly in cursive.

Vocabulary

- Plot
- Main character
- Setting

Open

- Teacher reminds students of rules for writers' workshop.
- Focus Lesson: Story Elements
  - o Teacher gathers children for a whole-class lesson.
  - o Students help teacher complete a sample story elements chart.

Sample Story Elements Chart

Characters	Setting
Little girl	Backyard
Father	Present time

  - o Students work independently to brainstorm an interesting character or characters and setting. They record on their own story elements chart.
- Focus Lesson: Plot Analysis Chart
  - o Teacher gathers children for a whole-class lesson.
  - o Students help teacher complete a sample plot analysis chart.

Sample Plot Analysis Chart

Beginning	Middle	End
The little girl and her dad were playing soccer in the backyard.	The little girl tried to kick the ball into the goal, but instead she kicked it over the wall! The neighbors weren't home, so what they could do? (problem)	Dad climbed over the wall and got the ball! (resolution)

  - o Students work independently to brainstorm a plot for their story. They record on their own plot analysis chart.

Body

- First Draft
  - o Student writes rough draft of story with a clear beginning, middle, and end; at least one main character; and an appropriate setting. Teacher reminds the class that there needs to be a problem and a resolution in the story to make it exciting.
- Student-Teacher Conferences
  - o Teacher meets with student to offer suggestions for plot, characters, and setting.

- Revising
  - o Student adds and changes details of the story based on feedback from teacher.
- Editing
  - o Student circles words she or he thinks are incorrect, looks for missing punctuation, and checks for appropriate capitalization and grammar.
  - o Student shares work with a peer. Peer circles and/or corrects errors in punctuation, spelling, and grammar.
- Final Draft
  - o Student corrects remaining circled items with the aid of a dictionary.

Close

- Publishing: Students recopy their stories in their best writing, illustrate pages of the stories, and create illustrations for the covers. Teacher staples each child's work together to make a book. Covers can be laminated for durability.
- Students each read the final version of their story to a partner in class.
- Stories are displayed in the library corner of the classroom so that children can read them at their leisure.

Assessment

- Writing portfolio: Published story is placed in the student's writing portfolio after being displayed in the classroom.

Integration Across the Curriculum

Science

- Students write a story that has a science theme. Teachers can read a sample book for inspiration. An example is *Planting a Rainbow* (1992) by Lois Ehlert. This is a story about growing a garden each year from seeds, cuttings, or small plants and then using the flowers to make a bouquet. Students can each write their own story about plants they have planted or would like to grow, such as pumpkins.

Social Studies

- Students each write a story that has a social studies theme. Teachers can read a motivating story such as *Grandfather's Journey* (1993) by Allen Say. This book is about immigration. Students can then each write their own fictional or nonfictional story about how they or their family members came to the United States.

Math

- Students each write a story that includes a math concept. First graders, for example, could write and illustrate a counting book.

Literature

- Students can write their own versions of stories based on familiar children's tales, such as Cinderella, Hansel and Gretel, and Snow White and the Seven Dwarfs. They can be innovative and create their own twist in the plot.

Visual and Performing Arts

- Students can illustrate their stories, copying the work of familiar artists. For example, the illustrations in *Stellaluna* (1993) by Janell Cannon are a combination of colored pencil and watercolors.
- Students can dramatize and perform their stories, taking on the roles of their altered characters.

Health

- Students can each write a story about Healthy Habits, such as eating right, exercising, or brushing teeth. The story could be nonfiction and factual or whimsical and fictional. For example, a student could write a story about a child who forgot to use a toothbrush, fell asleep, and the "plaque monsters" came!

Physical Education

- Students can work in groups to write the directions for a new PE game.

Music

- Students can write their own rap about spelling "demons."

Parents as Partners

- *Homework help:* Children could complete a story elements chart. Parents can help students brainstorm interesting characters and settings.
- *Editing help:* Students can take pieces of writing home that need to be edited and ask parents to help them correct spelling, punctuation, and grammar.
- *Reading to and with children:* Parents can help their children with writing by reading exciting stories to them and discussing the characters, setting, and plot.
- *Oral stories:* Parents and children can make up stories together and tell them aloud. "Ghost stories" are a classic and enjoyable version of oral stories.

Student Study Site

The Companion Web site for *Language Arts: Integrating Skills for Classroom Teaching* www.sagepub.com/donoghuestudy

Visit the Web-based study site to enhance your understanding of the chapter content. The study materials include chapter summaries, practice tests, flashcards, and Web resources.

Additional Professional Readings

Buckner, A. (2005). *Notebook know-how: Strategies for a writer's notebook*. Portland, ME: Stenhouse.

Calkin, L. (2005). *One on one: The art of conferring with young writers*. Portsmouth, NH: Heinemann.

Cappello, M. (2006). Under construction: Voice and identity development in writing workshop. *Language Arts, 83*(6), 482–491.

Culham, R. (2003). *6 +1 Traits of writing: The complete guide—Grades 3 and up*. New York: Scholastic.

Fletcher, R. (2000). *How writers work*. New York: HarperCollins.

Harwayne, S. (2001). *Writing through childhood*. Portsmouth, NH: Heinemann.

Horn, M., & Giacobbe, M. (2007). *Talking, drawing, writing: Lessons for our youngest writers*. Portland, ME: Stenhouse.

Lesure, D., & Richardson, K. (2002). *Help me learn to write: Strategies for teaching struggling writers (Grades 3-6)*. Peterborough, NH: Crystal Springs Books.

Orehovec, B., & Alley, M. (2007). *Revisiting the writing workshop: Management, assessment, and mini-lessons*. New York: Scholastic.

Overmeyer, M. (2005). *When writing workshop isn't working*. Portland, ME: Stenhouse.

Ray, K. (2006). *Study driven: A framework for planning units of study in the writing workshop*. Portsmouth, NH: Heinemann.

Children's Literature Cited in the Text

Bunting, E. (1995). *Dandelion*. San Diego: Harcourt.

Cannon, J. (1993). *Stellaluna*. New York: Harcourt.

Curtis, C. (1995). *Bud, not Buddy*. New York: Delacorte.

Cushman, K. (1996). *The ballad of Lucy Whipple*. New York: Clarion.

Ehlert, L. (1992). *Planting a rainbow*. New York: Voyager.

Say, A. (1993). *Grandfather's journey*. Boston: Houghton Mifflin.

Scieszka, J. (1992). *The stinky cheese man and other fairly stupid tales*. New York: Viking

Scieszka, J. (1994). *The frog prince continued*. New York: Puffin.

Scieszka, J. (1995). *Math curse*. New York: Viking.

Scieszka, J. (1996). *The true story of the 3 little pigs*. New York: Puffin.

Scieszka, J. (1998). *Squids will be squids*. New York: Puffin.

Taylor, M. (1990). *Mississippi bridge*. New York: Dial.

Yep, L. (1995). *Hiroshima*. New York: Scholastic.

References

Anderson, C. (2005). *Assessing writers*. Portsmouth, NH: Heinemann.

Atwell, N. (1998). *In the middle* (2nd ed.). Portsmouth, NH: Heinemann.

Calkins, L. (1994). *The art of teaching writing* (2nd ed.). Portsmouth, NH: Heinemann.

Cramer, R. (2001). *Creative power: The nature and nurture of children's writing*. New York: Addison Wesley Longman.

Fletcher, R., & Portalupi, J. (2001) *Writing workshop: The essential guide*. Portsmouth, NH: Heinemann.

Graves, D. (1994). *A fresh look at writing*. Portsmouth, NH: Heinemann.

Heard, G. (2002). *The revision toolbox: Teaching techniques that work*. Portsmouth, NH: Heinemann.

Hughey, J., & Slack, C. (2001). *Teaching children to write*. Columbus, OH: Merrill Prentice Hall.

Murray, D. (1990). *Shoptalk: Learning to write with writers*. Portsmouth, NH: Boynton/Cook.

Ray, K. (2001). *The writing workshop*. Urbana, IL: National Council of Teachers of English.

Tompkins, G. (2004). *Teaching writing* (4th ed.). Columbus, OH: Merrill Prentice Hall.

Anticipation Statement Answers

1. Agree

2. Agree

3. Disagree

4. Agree

5. Agree

6. Disagree

7. Agree

8. Disagree

9. Agree: Writing involves communication with others. However, it is a silent communication unless shared with fellow students.

10. Agree: Both author units and genre units can be adapted to the reading and writing abilities of all students. However, the range of both abilities among younger children is considerably narrower than among intermediate students.

PART IV
Oral Language Arts

Listening and Speaking

CHAPTER

11

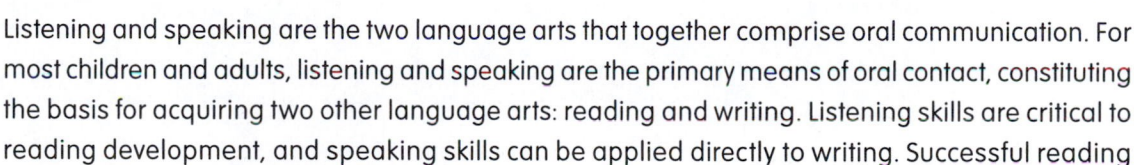

Listening and speaking are the two language arts that together comprise oral communication. For most children and adults, listening and speaking are the primary means of oral contact, constituting the basis for acquiring two other language arts: reading and writing. Listening skills are critical to reading development, and speaking skills can be applied directly to writing. Successful reading and writing conferences in the elementary school, for example, rely on valid and dynamic oral communication among the students.

Oddly enough, although reading and writing are the more recently developed communication skills in American society, they have been more readily accepted as part of the school curriculum than have the older skills of listening and speaking.

Anticipation Statements

Complete this exercise before reading Chapter 11.

Do you agree or disagree with the following statements? Circle your answer. Be prepared to discuss questions in blue.

1. Listening is fundamental to success in all other areas of the language arts.	Agree	Disagree
2. There are two components of listening—conversational and presentational.	Agree	Disagree
3. Listening is a complex process.	Agree	Disagree
4. There are only a few ways teachers can assist children in listening and understanding.	Agree	Disagree
5. Several factors influence classroom listening, including hearing, age, home environment, and student involvement.	Agree	Disagree
6. A supportive classroom environment can help children with communication skills.	Agree	Disagree
7. Storytelling has several sequential stages.	Agree	Disagree
8. Research shows that teacher talk tends to dominate classrooms.	Agree	Disagree
9. Listening skills must be taught.	Agree	Disagree
10. Readers theater provides an excellent opportunity for speaking practice.	Agree	Disagree

Listening

Listening is important for several reasons. First, it is generally fundamental to success in all other areas of the language arts. Second, quantitatively, it is the most critical of the six modes because nearly half of the adult's working day and more than half of the child's classroom activity time are spent in listening. Third, the explosion of knowledge and of technology during the past few decades has demanded the processing of greater amounts of information through listening by larger numbers of adults and children. Finally, it was added to the list of basic skills by the U.S. Office of Education under Public Law 95-561 (Elementary and Secondary Education Act), giving it official recognition. Consequently, despite today's emphasis on literacy instruction, most elementary teachers agree that students need to know how to listen.

Realistically, the skill of listening is more effective when it is part of a two-part communication process. *Conversational listening* occurs during face-to-face encounters in which listeners and speakers take turns. A classroom example would be literature circles (or small group literary discussions). There is also *presentational listening* during which one or more persons are speakers and the listeners are the audience. This occurs in the classroom, for instance, when the teacher reads aloud to the students from a chapter book.

Relationship of Listening to Other Language Arts

Language in all its facets is an integrated phenomenon. Because effects in one of language's subsystems will later show up in the others, improving listening is likely to lead to improved performance in the other language arts.

Research has established a positive correlation between *listening and speaking*. Not only are speech patterns learned largely through listening to other persons speak; in turn, the growth of the listener function in an individual probably plays an important role in the ultimate development of his or her skill as a speaker. An interesting dimension in the listening–speaking relationship is distortion, which can create differences between messages sent and messages delivered due to such matters as preoccupation by listeners, attention span failure, environmental interference, and poor organization.

Both *listening and reading* are phases of language that serve as major means of acquiring information. Both are a complex of related skill components based on similar higher mental processes. Both are more easily practiced in a relaxed environment in which the ideas and vocabulary are at least partially familiar to the listeners or readers. Finally, both use signals, such as intonation and pauses in oral language and their corresponding punctuation marks in written language.

There are also differences between these two language arts. In listening, the rate is determined by the speaker, the ideas are usually presented only once, the listener loses a portion of the content whenever his or her attention lapses, and the listener's appraisal of that content is often influenced by the speaker's use of body language or voice inflections. In contrast, communication through reading is less personal and may include visual aids. The reader proceeds at his or her own rate

Applicable IRA/NCTE Standards

Standard 4 — Students adjust their use of spoken, written, and visual language (e.g., conventions, style, vocabulary) to communicate effectively with a variety of audiences and for different purposes.

Standard 6 — Students apply knowledge of language structure, language conventions (e.g., spelling and punctuation), media techniques, figurative language, and genre to create, critique, and discuss print and nonprint texts.

Standard 9 — Students develop an understanding of and respect for diversity in language use, patterns, and dialects across cultures, ethnic groups, geographic regions, and social roles.

Standard 10 — Students whose first language is not English make use of their first language to develop competency in the English language arts and to develop understanding of content across the curriculum.

Standard 11 — Students participate as knowledgeable, reflective, creative, and critical members of a variety of literacy communities.

Standard 12 — Students use spoken, written, and visual language to accomplish their own purposes (e.g., for learning, enjoyment, persuasion, and the exchange of information).

SOURCE: *Standards for the English Language Arts*, by the International Reading Association and the National Council of Teachers of English, Copyright 1996 by the International Reading Association and the National Council of Teachers of English. Reprinted with permission. http://www.ncte.org/about/over/standards/110846.htm

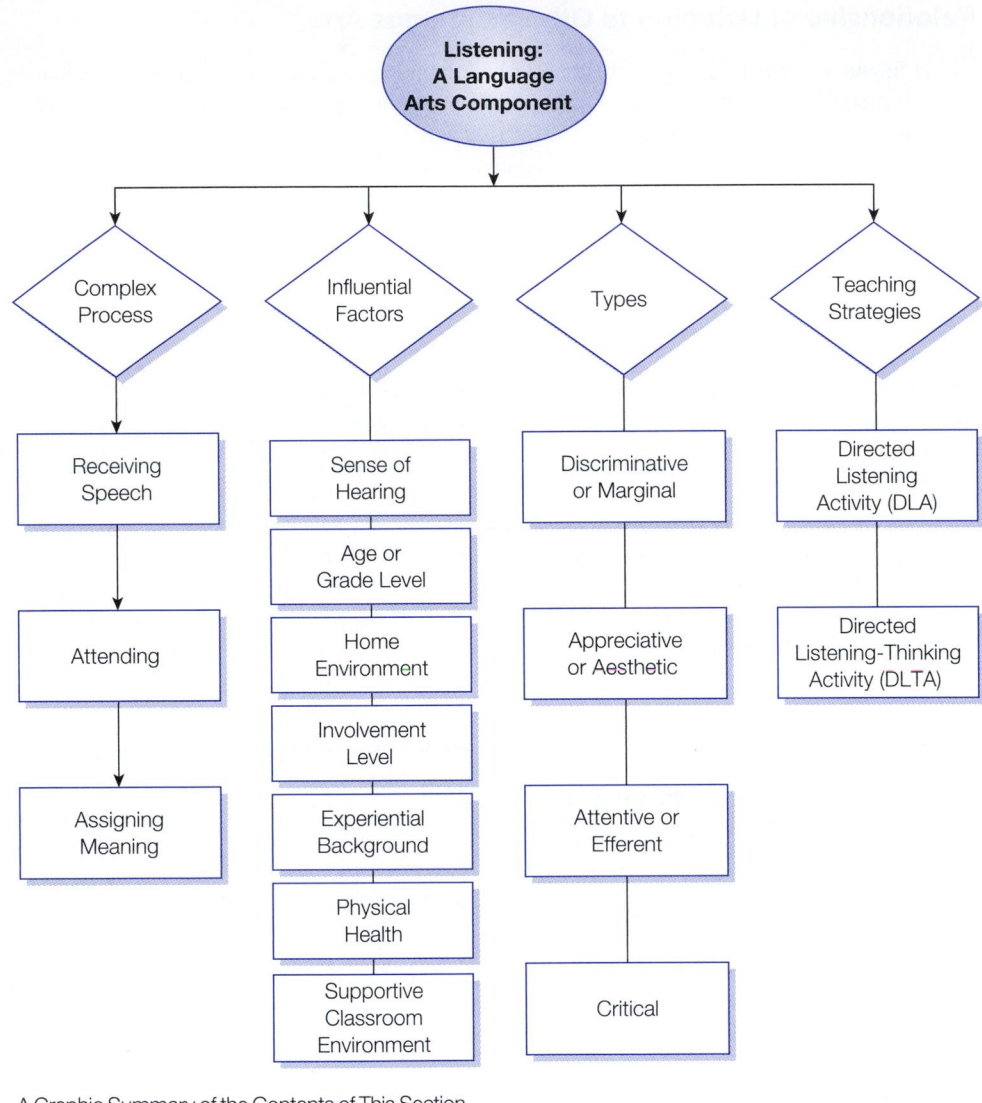

A Graphic Summary of the Contents of This Section

and may reread the material as often as necessary to gain the information. In addition, printed ideas are more apt to be expressed in a well-organized fashion.

The relationship between *listening and writing* revolves around comprehension. While composing ideas in written form, some students speak and listen internally as they record; so-called inner listening occurs especially during revising and is important to comprehension. Listening is essential to the writing process as children share their writing during conferences and receive feedback.

The relationships between *listening and viewing* and *listening and visually representing* are obvious since children learn through visual and auditory media long before they acquire literacy; the language arts are used simultaneously as well.

The Complex Process of Listening

Listening is an intricate process and not merely a synonym for hearing. While hearing is a critical aspect of listening, it must be followed by the construction of meaning from what is heard in order to become listening. The process whereby the mind converts spoken language to meaning actually has three steps, according to Wolvin and Coakley (1995).

The first is *receiving* speech whereby listeners hear or take in the aural stimuli (or combined aural and visual stimuli) presented by the speaker. In the case of sign language, the "listener" must interpret the visual stimuli provided by the signer.

The second step concerns *attending* or paying attention to the important information in the speech while ignoring distracting or irrelevant stimuli. This step depends on the listener's motivation or interest in the message as well as on the absence or presence of strong distractions in the environment. It is the most crucial part of the listening process and teachers can help the class with attending by doing the following:

- Discussing the signals for being "ready to listen" (e.g., making eye contact with the speaker)
- Anticipating and minimizing possible distractions (e.g., clearing the desk)
- Waiting for full attention (e.g., using a signal)
- Explaining the purpose for the listening in which they are about to engage (e.g., knowing the kind of response or activity that will be expected)
- Using cues to let listeners know what is most important for them to attend to (e.g., jotting notes on the chalkboard)

The third step is *assigning meaning* or understanding the message. The listener must incorporate the information in the message into his or her existing conceptual framework. The extent to which this occurs is largely dependent on the clarity of the message and on the listener's prior knowledge. Teachers can assist the class in assigning meaning in the following ways:

- Helping students listen purposefully by having them predict what the message will contain so they can later check their predictions against what they hear
- Checking the listeners' prior knowledge through discussion and questioning to ensure that they can make sense out of the speaker's presentation
- Using direct or vicarious experiences to develop new vocabulary or concepts mentioned in the message
- Providing visual aids to clarify the message if necessary; some students are able to use imagery and form pictures in their mind based on what they hear
- Having children briefly explain or summarize the message to determine to what extent they were able to comprehend it

Factors That Influence Classroom Listening

There are numerous factors that affect the learning process generally and classroom listening particularly.

The first and most obvious is *hearing sense*. The human ear is able to detect sounds in the range of 125 to 8,000 hertz (Hz—cycles per second) according to the international scientific standardized unit for measuring frequency. During the hearing process the ear receives and modifies speech sounds in the range of 250–3,000 Hz. Approximately 5% to 10% of the school population is deemed to be hearing-impaired. Furthermore, some students who have a hearing problem have been incorrectly diagnosed as learning disabled or having an attention deficit disorder.

A second factor is *grade level or chronological age*. Younger children pay more attention to their teachers than do intermediate students. For K–2 children with their limited reading ability, listening is their major means of obtaining information. On the contrary, intermediate students with their increased number of outside activities sometimes appear to be distracted in the classroom and to be paying less attention to the teacher's directions or discussion.

Another factor is the *home environment*. Students from smaller families or spacious homes generally obtain higher listening scores than those from larger families or crowded homes. It has been speculated that heightened noise and confusion in a large group or a smaller space lead to the development of protective insulation or a nonlistening attitude that children transfer to the classroom.

A fourth factor is the *involvement level* required of the listeners. It has generally been described as an enhancing factor because child listeners must concentrate and actively process the information heard. Still, it may become an inhibiting factor if the speaker's voice is monotonous or if the message conveyed relates to topics beyond the listeners' interest or understanding.

The extent to which meaning is associated with speech depends initially on the listeners' *experiential background*. Words are more easily comprehended when they form a part of predictable and meaningful talk. Children who come to school with a broad background of experiences can understand more of the words that they hear and therefore listen more intently to their teachers and peers.

A sixth factor concerns the *physical condition of the listeners*. Students who are hungry or tired are not physiologically able to attend effectively to the listening tasks.

The final factor is a *supportive classroom environment* that is relatively quiet. Children learn to communicate best when they have the chance to practice in small groups first and later in increasingly larger groups. Such an environment has opportunities for interaction, and when listeners are active in the communication process, their level of involvement increases. This interaction often depends on the group structure so children should be encouraged to work with partners or in table/interest groups on special assignments.

Types of Listening

For material related to this concept, go to Video Clip 11.1 on the Student Resource CD bound into the back of your textbook.

There are four types of listening designated by their purposes, according to Wolvin and Coakley (1995). They differ primarily in the amount of concentration demanded.

The first is *discriminative* or **marginal listening** whose purpose is to distinguish sounds. It is the least demanding and yet the most frequent type of listening, and has been described as background listening. It occurs when one is able, for example, to distinguish between street noises and someone's voice. Teachers are said to use discriminative listening to determine during a group lesson if the rest of the class is on task. Most children as young as five or six can discriminate among sounds and use this type of listening as they develop phonemic awareness. Older students apply discriminative listening during spelling and syllabication lessons. Both elementary groups learn to "listen" to nonverbal messages that parents, teachers, and others communicate.

The second type is *aesthetic* or **appreciative listening** whose purpose is enjoyment. Students listen to a singer, reader, speaker, or music for pleasure. They may also simply listen to agreeable sounds, indoors or outdoors, such as a cricket's chirp. Teachers can encourage children's appreciative listening by reading aloud narratives or poems with figurative language or by viewing videotapes of stories introduced earlier during a thematic unit.

Storytelling is another opportunity for children to learn to listen appreciatively to their teacher, media center specialist, or their peers. In most grades students enjoy telling their own round-robin chain stories in which each participant carries on from where the preceding speaker stopped. Finally, watching performances of a children's theater group involves appreciative listening. The theater provides enjoyment and expression, allowing the young audience to identify with the onstage characters and actions.

When students listen to learn information, they are using their *efferent or* **attentive listening** skills. This type of listening demands that the attention of the listener be focused on one person or one electronic medium so that he or she can purposefully respond either orally or in a written fashion. In the primary grades children can be sent on errands throughout the building after they have received exact directions about how to get to the principal's office or how to locate the media center. They should have opportunities to recall the directions given for their safety regarding standards for fire drills and playground behavior. They can explain to newcomers how to handle a particular classroom routine that requires three or four steps in sequence (e.g., how to take care of paint brushes after an art lesson). In the intermediate grades one group of students can explain the steps in a science experiment while a second group follows the directions and a third group evaluates both procedures.

This type of listening, which occupies a large part of the school day, also includes the ability to understand a message and recall vital information. As teachers read aloud books related to social studies topics, for example, whether these are fiction or nonfiction, elementary children can answer specific questions about the material presented. Gradually, they can learn how to take notes, particularly after listening to informational books, and begin to recognize main ideas and supporting facts. They must always try to determine the writer's or speaker's purpose and then organize the facts provided.

The fourth type of listening is **critical listening**, which students use to evaluate information. It is the most complex kind of listening to teach or to learn because it is an analytical process. Since children are being asked to make judgments, critical listening requires higher-level thinking skills, such as those Mr. Merritt wishes to promote among his sixth graders in Vignette 11.1.

Attentive or efferent listening, which occupies a large part of the school day, demands that a listener focus on one person or electronic medium in order to respond and recall vital information.

VIGNETTE 11.1 **Oral Language in the Sixth Grade**

As Mr. Merritt finished reviewing the semester and his own development as a sixth-grade teacher, he realized the majority of his lessons primarily involved lecturing to the class. Although he knew the children would continue to encounter this teaching style, he wanted them to interact more with the material—and with each other—the rest of the school year. He decided to begin with the next history unit and outlined a class project that included practice with several types of listening and speaking.

When the students returned from winter break, they found the desks rearranged into groups throughout the classroom. As the students took their seats, he explained the project.

"Each group will research a decade of United States history, from the 1940s to the 1990s," he began. "Look at the poster hanging on the wall by your group—this is your decade." The students craned their necks to identify each group's assigned time period.

"Each member of your group will become an 'expert' on one aspect of that decade," he said. He turned to the blackboard where he had listed politics and government, arts and entertainment, business and finance, science and medicine, and international events.

"I will meet with the groups one at a time this afternoon and tell you which person will study each topic," he continued. Mr. Merritt had considered a variety of ways to determine the individual assignments, finally making the decision based on his knowledge of the personality, work style, and strengths of each student.

"You will work individually to research your subject," he said. "We will have computer time and library time, but I also expect you to work on this as homework. As a group, you will prepare a presentation that includes everyone's work. At the end of the project, each group will teach the class about one whole decade!"

Mr. Merritt had designed a few other requirements for the individual research portion and planned to explain the details as he met with each small group to assign subjects and answer questions. He didn't want to overwhelm them with too much information upfront; just as important, he planned to use these smaller team meetings to continue introducing the themes of active listening and group dynamics.

Mr. Merritt used the rest of the session to lead the students in a brainstorming exercise focusing on the five areas of study. He listed ideas on the board as the children suggested a variety of subtopics for each major subject. He refrained from commenting other than to affirm the students who contributed and to prompt further areas for discussion. By the end, the class had a fuller understanding of what each subject included.

The children also asked good questions that clarified the boundaries between subjects. "Computers should be part of business," said Amy. "No, they're entertainment," Ethan replied. Together the class decided some topics legitimately fit into multiple categories and that individual groups would decide how to present those subjects.

After lunch, Mr. Merritt met one at a time with each group of children. "I have a few more details to share with you," he said. "If you have questions, write them in your notebook; at the end of our meeting everyone can ask questions."

He knew the children couldn't wait to find out their assigned subject, so he quickly passed each student a folder with his or her topic printed on the front. "You may use this folder to organize your work," he said. "I will leave our brainstorming list from this morning on the board, and you can write the list for your subject in your folder to remind you of areas to research."

He outlined the specific expectations—presentation length, due dates, number of sources, and visual aid guidelines—that accompany a new project. To reinforce comprehension he also distributed hand-outs with the information.

"Before I answer questions, I have one more thing to explain," Mr. Merritt said. "In each group, at least two members will do an interview. The interview can be with a family member, or a friend, or you can go with an adult and interview someone you don't know. Each group will decide as a team which two members will do the interviews. You will need to determine if any group members know someone who experienced a historical event or can share something special about one of the subjects. I will work with the students doing interviews to help them prepare."

As Mr. Merritt met with each group, explaining the requirements and answering the children's many questions, he felt optimistic about the new approach. The interviewing skill would reinforce listening and speaking for a portion of the class, and the combination of individual research and group presentations would require every student to discuss, share ideas, listen to feedback, make decisions, and delegate work in new ways. As an unexpected bonus, he found himself practicing his own listening and speaking skills as he clarified the assignment and responded to questions. Mr. Merritt realized he would continue to learn right along with the class.

Students as early as the primary grades are capable of critical listening. For example, a day after telling the class the story of Galdone's *The Gingerbread Boy* (2006), the teacher can read Schaefer's *The Wright Brothers* (2000) and ask the children to prove why yesterday's tale was fantasy and today's story was real. Another day, the teacher can pose a series of questions, some of which are meaningful and some are not. The child responding must decide whether the question is nonsense (e.g., Why is the grass red?) or whether the question is reasonable (e.g., If chickens are birds, why can't they fly?).

Intermediate students can listen to recordings of talks or conversations by unidentified persons and then determine whether the speakers showed prejudice or used inflammatory words. On another day they can listen to a selection containing directions (e.g., for making an origami zebra figure) that contains some extraneous information; after omitting all irrelevant facts, the class must then make the figure.

Lessons in critical listening in the elementary school should teach children to do the following:

- Distinguish fact from fantasy
- Select relevant statements from unimportant ones and defend the choices
- Detect and evaluate the bias or lack of objectivity on the part of the speaker/writer
- Distinguish well-supported statements from opinions and evaluate them
- Assess the qualifications of the speaker/writer
- Recognize and appraise the effects of devices the speaker may use to sway the listener, such as music, voice intonation, or propaganda strategies

Eight propaganda devices that elementary students can learn to identify in television commercials or other kinds of advertisements are (1) *name calling* or placing a label on something/

someone to create an unpleasant association; (2) *bandwagon* or claiming that everyone is using the product; (3) *card stacking* or presenting only one side of the issue; (4) *snob appeal* or using flattery to attract people to buy what only the "elite" purchase; (5) *glittering generality* or making broad but unsubstantiated claims about an individual's character or a product's quality; (6) *testimonial* or having well-known personalities serve as the product's spokespersons; (7) *transfer* or having the listeners identify directly with the celebrities and their attributes; and (8) *rewards* or offering token gifts or rebates to entice people to purchase large ticket items.

It is important to introduce propaganda devices to children a few at a time, with specific examples. They can listen to commercials using each device and discuss the effect the ads have on them. They should be aware that propaganda strategies are used to sell both products and ideas and that they vary in presentation depending on the audience; for example, Saturday morning television shows strongly aimed at young children offer commercials that differ from those for teenagers.

Strategies for Teaching Listening

Two structured teaching lessons are the directed listening activity (DLA) and the directed listening–thinking activity (DLTA). Both are used in the presentation of listening materials, but the DLA is better suited for teaching individuals, small groups, or an entire class. Larger groups of six to eight students benefit more from DLTA lessons. Underlying both listening activities is teacher direction, which relieves tension and promotes sharper attending.

The directed listening activity uses the familiar format of a basal reader lesson except that the student must listen to the story as it is being read without seeing the printed copy. The teacher should (a) choose a story with a clear plot and a logical sequence of events (e.g., Monjo's *The Drinking Gourd,* 1970); (b) tell the children *why* they should listen; (c) provide suggestions that will help listeners organize and comprehend the material (e.g., the meaning and significance of the title); (d) read the material without any interruptions; and (e) encourage students to follow up their listening by discussing and summarizing the material heard. The DLA is particularly useful for English Language Learners (ELLs) and for special-needs students with learning disabilities because it can focus on the development of a specific skill such as sequencing.

The directed listening–thinking activity is a lesson that teaches children to use details they hear to predict what will happen next (Stauffer, 1975). The teacher should (a) divide the class into groups of 6 to 10 students to ensure good discussion and ensuing predictions; (b) select a story with a simple plot and easily delineated events (e.g., Bartone's *Peppe the Lamplighter,* 1993); (c) plan to stop two to five times during the reading, each before a critical point in the plot; (d) at each stop, have students summarize what has taken place and then make predictions; (e) accept all predictions without comment but encourage children to defend their stance based on their prior experience and knowledge; (f) read the next part of the story and review the predictions made earlier, having students deny or confirm previous predictions before they anticipate future happenings; and (g) encourage all children to become involved in the discussion, which must always center on the story.

Both the DLA and the DLTA demand read-alouds, and these stories should be chosen prudently. To help achieve their goal of teaching listening, the stories must be brand new to all or most of the students. The plot and characters should also be of strong interest to the age group involved.

Helping Special-Needs Students With Impaired Hearing

The average elementary classroom has two or three students with mild to serious, undiagnosed hearing loss. Their teachers should be sure to follow these guidelines:

- Seat them carefully. Place the children 6 to 10 feet from the area where most teaching occurs. Allow them to move their seats if the teaching center moves to another part of the room. Make sure that each student's better ear is positioned toward the source of significant sounds and not toward the windows or hallway.
- Speak naturally. Avoid using loud tones or too many gestures. Avoid talking when walking about the room or when facing the chalkboard. Avoid placing hands or books in front of the face when speaking. Use clear enunciation. Check often and informally to make sure that the special-needs children comprehend the discussion.
- Assist them casually. Write new words on the chalkboard because names of people and places are difficult for them to understand. Ask other students to help them get the correct assignment. Give special help during language activities such as spelling and reading in which sounds have unusual importance. Repeat instructions as often as needed.
- Watch their physical condition. Prevent further hearing loss by noting respiratory infections and other ailments. Prevent undue fatigue from the stress of seeing and listening intently by providing alternating periods of physical activity and inactivity in the day's planning.
- Encourage their participation in hobbies/activities.

Speaking

Since effective oral communication is not inherent, most of what children know of language when they enter kindergarten has been learned by accident. Boys and girls have used their listening skills to develop their **speaking** abilities, by hearing and innately mastering the sounds of their first language.

Whether children are academically advantaged or not, their language patterns are largely established by the time they reach school age. Since speech habits formed in the preschool years vary greatly with the individual child, elementary teachers who recognize those variations must modify their programs to meet student needs. They realize that oral language is important because it is the mode in which their students feel most secure and it is the one that is the most commonly used among adults and children alike. Incidentally, it is the one form of language that all global groups develop: Of the nearly 3,000 languages in the world today, fewer than 10% have developed a written form. Students fortunate enough to travel outside the United States should find that fact significant.

Although oral language is a crucial component of the elementary school day, research shows that it is the teacher, and not the students, who is doing the talking. An estimated two thirds of classroom talk is teacher talk (Wells & Chang-Wells, 1992), and children spend more time listening to their teachers than being actively engaged in language interaction with other students and adults.

Yet, both talking and listening are critical components of the language arts curriculum. Children's experience with, and knowledge of, the linguistic organization of spoken language is fundamental to their learning to read (Pinnell & Jaggar, 2003). Talking also affects students' ability to write. This is particularly true among young, emergent composers to whom writing is said to be as much an oral language activity as a written one (Dyson & Genishi, 1982).

Fortunately, teachers cognizant of the importance of oral language for all children in every grade can choose among several speech arts that promote language as a communication tool: discussion, interviewing, storytelling, choral speaking, readers theater, and reporting.

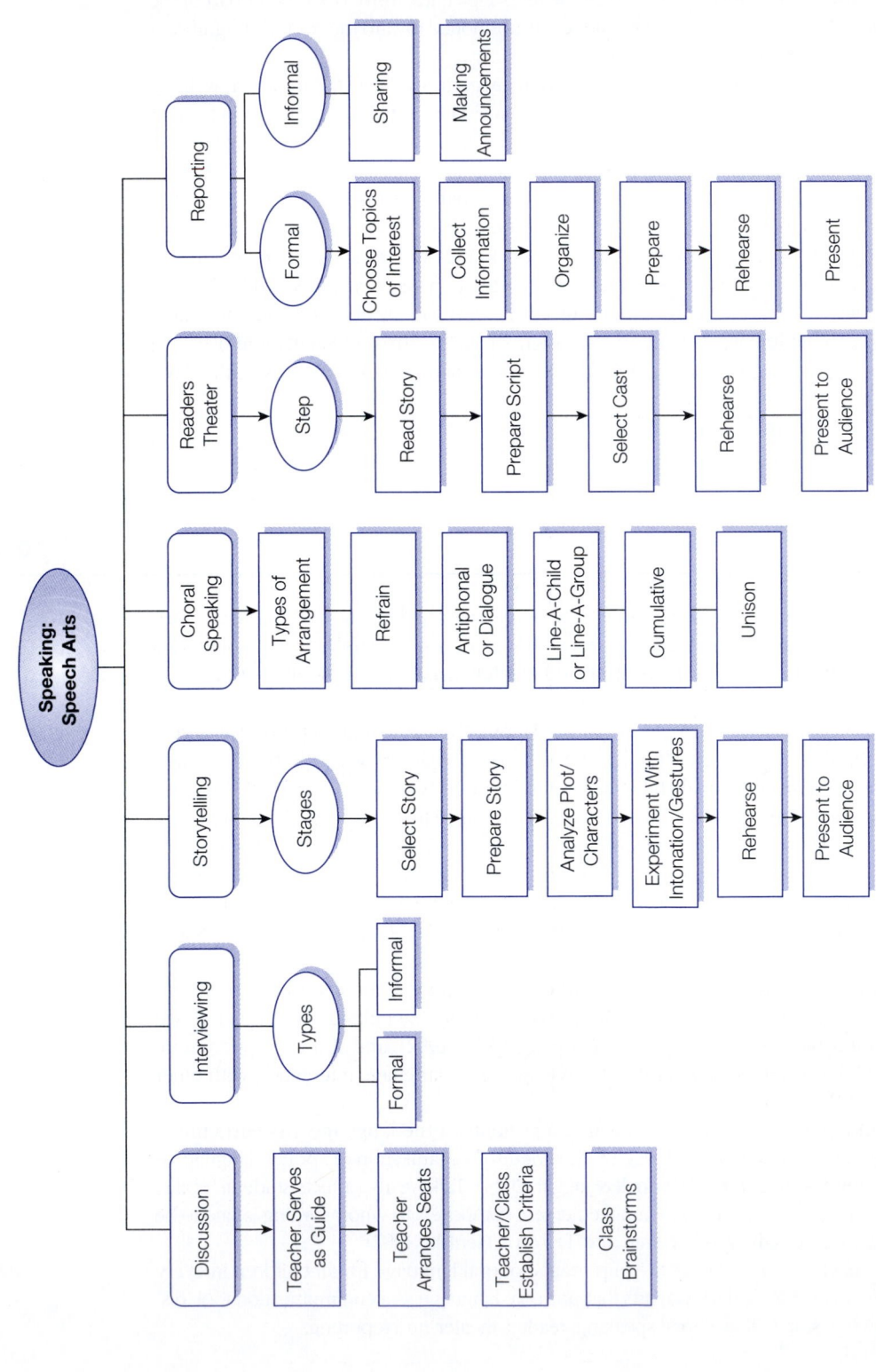

A Graphic Summary of the Contents of This Section

Discussion

Described as using oral language in a group setting, discussion can begin as early as kindergarten and the primary grades. The teacher serves as the discussion guide and demonstrates how the class must adhere to the topic, raise related questions, hypothesize, and draw conclusions. Gradually elementary students incorporate these skills into their own discussions although this is usually not until the third or fourth grade.

The kinds of topics most appropriate for beginning discussion call for listing or enumeration ("How many ways can an animal get food?" or "How can you tell what will cost a dollar and what will cost a dime?"), which in turn leads to comparison topics by making the category either one of similarities or one of differences ("In what ways are cars and airplanes alike?" or "What are the differences between birds and bears?"). A third kind of topic calls for chronology—planning an action or telling how something is made ("How can Andy get his bike back?" or "How shall we go about building a miniature village?").

Teachers must be careful not to confuse recitation with discussion. The distinction between the two is based on the purpose of the activity (Welton, 2002). A *recitation* only determines orally how well students understand and retain prior information. Discussion, on the other hand, serves several purposes, including sharing different viewpoints on an issue, developing student interest in a topic, generating and/or synthesizing ideas, or providing closure to an activity.

Teachers, especially in the intermediate grades, must keep in mind these other important characteristics of a discussion (Dillon, 1984): The discussion is open to all students and to all arguments; it is open-ended and the discussants are open-minded; the time limit is flexible; and the learning outcomes are also not predictable. Vignette 11.2 highlights the importance of these characteristics, as Mr. Merritt's sixth graders begin to recognize the close relationship between speaking and listening.

VIGNETTE 11.2 Listening and Speaking in the Sixth Grade

Over the next few weeks, Mr. Merritt provided opportunities for students to visit the school library, search for images and information on the Internet, and use CD-ROMs and DVDs to learn more about their assigned subjects.

In addition to providing this time for individual work, he also set aside 15 minutes every afternoon for the children to "regroup" and discuss their upcoming presentation as a team. Mr. Merritt knew the students' initial attempts to report their progress and make group decisions could be difficult, so he created a short checklist as a reference tool. The list included questions for each student to answer at the daily meetings ("What subtopics from our blackboard list are you researching? Have you learned anything that might help someone else on your team?"), as well as discussion prompts for the entire group ("How will you organize the final presentation? In what order will you present the information?"). The reference sheet ended with a weekly checklist to keep the groups on pace with their work; a quick glance at the list would remind the groups to choose interviewers by the end of week one, determine visual aids by week two, and reach other goals at later times.

As he expected, many students initially shared just a sentence or two with their teams. In other groups, one or two overly talkative children monopolized the discussions. Mr. Merritt circled through the room, gently steering the discussions back on track when necessary.

By the end of the first week, he found the new strategy producing results; on Friday he observed the children not only listening politely to each other's daily updates but also asking questions to move the work forward.

"Why do you think we should all dress like hippies?" asked one boy in the 1960s group. "We don't have to study fashion."

"Because the hippies dressed that way to make a statement about their beliefs," said his female teammate researching politics and government. "I think. I'll check."

"So we would be teaching the class about a clothing style connected to how people felt about the government, right?" asked the group member responsible for researching arts and entertainment. "But what about my subject? Musicians like the Beatles also made a difference in how people dressed."

Mr. Merritt smiled and moved on to the next group. *Listening, summarizing each other's thoughts, and expressing different viewpoints*, he thought. *This is working!*

At the end of the second week, Mr. Merritt met with the children who were conducting interviews. He enjoyed seeing the enthusiasm of the dozen students—it was obvious most of them volunteered for the extra work because they had a parent, grandparent, or family friend with a connection to the time period. They eagerly shared ideas about questions and discussion topics. Mr. Merritt coached the students in refining those thoughts into solid interview questions, and found the 1:12 ratio extremely helpful in teaching this new skill.

Finally the week of presentations arrived. Mr. Merritt planned one presentation each day, with two on Friday. A few days before the 1940s group kicked off the reports, he reviewed the grading requirements with the class—and threw in a surprise.

"As I explained when we began working on this project, I will grade individual work and also the group presentations," he said. "Those grades will include the content of your presentation, making eye contact with the audience, visual aids, the organization of the whole project, and the other requirements we've discussed." The students nodded; Mr. Merritt had included all the expectations in his instructions at the beginning.

"However, your work is not done when you've completed your presentation," he continued. "When the other groups teach about the other decades, I want you to take good notes. Don't try to write everything—write the main ideas and write questions to ask at the end. Also, write at least one thing you learn about each decade that you'd like to study more and why you find it interesting. We'll discuss some of these ideas after the presentation."

Mr. Merritt finished the instructions by saying, "One more reason to take good notes and listen well—we will finish the reports on Friday and on Monday we will have a test on all six decades based on the presentations. I will ask you questions from each team's work, so you will want good notes to study over the weekend!"

As expected, the children groaned about the Monday test, but their good-natured complaining did little to lessen Mr. Merritt's excitement about the students' progress.

He knew many of the children felt nervous about speaking in front of their peers, and he knew this project was just one step toward creating a class of better listeners. But he realized his willingness to explore these teaching methods had enabled the students to learn in new ways and to be ready for even more challenges in speaking and listening. He couldn't wait to experience the finished presentations, and lead the discussions—instead of lectures!—that would follow.

Two practical aspects of promoting good discussion are seating arrangements and group membership. Greater and more effective interaction is fostered by face-to-face grouping patterns. When initially arranging small discussion groups of five to seven children, the teacher wisely considers the abilities and personalities of individual students. The very first time such discussion groups are created, the shyer children should not be placed with classmates who like to dominate conversation. Too, disruptive students or others with attitude problems, especially in the intermediate grades, need to be assigned carefully. The most successful heterogeneous groups involve children with similar interpretive, social, and reading abilities.

In the primary grades group discussion can be initiated in a variety of ways, such as by a read-aloud that elicits excitement or controversy, a stimulating television program, or a national news event that needs further clarification for young students. To make the discussion meaningful for all participants, the class with the assistance of the teacher should establish certain ground rules, which may include the following:

When anyone is speaking, everyone should listen and be polite.

Speakers must talk clearly and stick to the point.

Everyone must respect the rights of other persons to state their opinions.

All persons should try to contribute to the discussion, but no one should dominate it.

In the intermediate grades, additional ground rules should be set by the children to foster advanced communication skills:

Everyone can participate in meetings conducted according to simplified parliamentary procedure.

Everyone can become a discussion leader by keeping speakers on the topic, helping all students to contribute, not allowing anyone to dominate or letting arguments start, and summarizing the main points of discussion.

Both in the intermediate and primary grades, a meaningful process used in discussion groups is **brainstorming**. This occurs when all students have the opportunity to contribute, without inhibition, suggestions or possible solutions to real or proposed problems. The emphasis is on quantity. All ideas are accepted and recorded, usually on the chalkboard or overhead projector. Generally the time allowed for such interaction is limited, ordinarily to five minutes, in order to motivate responses and stretch imaginations. Real-life dilemmas to which the children can directly relate are especially effective for brainstorming sessions.

After some experience in brainstorming, students in the intermediate grades are ready for more formal discussion including *panel discussions* and *debates*. The first involves three to seven students under the direction of a leader or moderator who discuss a specific topic or problem before an audience. Each panel member, including the moderator, must prepare an individual oral report on some aspect of the assigned topic; he or she becomes an "expert" on that subject (e.g., Nominating and Electing the Vice President of the United States). A question-and-answer period from the audience often follows.

A *debate* is the presentation of arguments between two teams (often consisting of two members each) that represent different sides of the same issue. That proposition or issue can be stated briefly and affirmatively (e.g., Only sixth graders can be officers on the Student Council.). The affirmative team supports the proposition and the negative team attacks it. Debaters must be well informed.

Debates rarely take place in the elementary school before the fifth grade due to the extensive researching of facts required before the debate and the level of verbal interaction between the teams during the debate. There is a chairperson chosen to introduce the topic and the team members, a timekeeper (since elementary debates average 30 minutes), and judges to determine which side debated better and so becomes the winner. Often the judges include all the members of the class who are not debating.

Interviewing

A special type of discussion demands a question-and-answer format and is known simply as an **interview**. Since children routinely watch interviews on television news programs, they are familiar with the procedure. Therefore, the ability to conduct interviews has become a speech activity comfortably practiced by students from kindergarten through sixth grade.

Interviewing can be divided into *informal* and *formal* styles, with the latter involving more preplanning and formulation of questions in advance by the group or individual students. The presentation, for example, of a shy five-year-old who brought miniature wooden animals to show the class during a sharing period could become more focused if her classmates *informally* interviewed her. They could ask spontaneously, one at a time, about where the animals came from, whether or not they have names, and where she keeps them. Since some children are more extroverted than others, teachers may prefer to assign a certain day of the week to a table or row for sharing. In that way, everyone has an opportunity to be interviewed and also realizes that he or she should choose each week a topic or event to relate. (Parents also appreciate knowing when their young children will be interviewed so they can help them with their choices.) The fact that the questioning during informal interviewing is brief and casual is reassuring to beginning presenters.

On the other hand, the anticipated visit of a room mother familiar with the Chinese New Year celebration would prompt a different and more *formal* type of questioning. In the lower grades children could work as a whole class, developing a list of questions on the chalkboard with the help of their teacher. In the intermediate grades, students could divide up into groups and write their own questions to ask the resource visitor. The formal interview usually involves 10 to 12 questions and answers and is conducted less casually. The information collected can often be discussed after the visitor leaves.

Younger children gain experience in formal interviewing by first preparing a few questions and then interviewing each other in the classroom setting; later they can go home to interview a parent, brother or sister, or even a grandparent who lives nearby. After that experience, the students can walk in small teams around the school grounds to interview the principal, media specialist, custodian, cafeteria manager, and resource teacher.

Students in the intermediate grades can set up interviewing criteria and techniques and list these on charts. They can interview teachers (or parents) who have recently visited other countries as well as foreign exchange students who live in the school area. A few more outgoing children may even elect to work in small groups or individually to conduct interviews with residents in retirement homes or others familiar with the history of the town, area, or county. Information gathered through such *oral history* projects, whether by audio tape or written report, may later be published in the school or community newspaper.

Teachers experienced in preparing students for interviewing always remind them to do the following:

Brainstorm possible questions and then narrow the list to those that will most likely provide useful and interesting information.

Avoid questions that require only "yes" or "no" answers.

Write the questions on note cards and place them in sequential order.

Keep the interview on the subject.

Be courteous and a careful listener.

Ask some open-ended questions that allow the interviewee to reply with enough information.

Take notes or electronically record answers.

Keep the interview within the preset time limits.

Thank the person at the end of the interview.

Interviewers should also remember *not* to do the following:

Criticize the interviewee.

Argue with the interviewee.

Wander from the topic.

Ask closed questions that require only a single "no" or "yes" answer.

Show nervousness or a lack of courtesy.

Elementary teachers hesitant about implementing interviewing programs should be aware of four benefits of such a course (Haley-James & Hobson, 1980). First, bringing outside guests (such as motorcycle officers and traffic engineers) into the classroom increases interest in listening, writing, speaking, and reading. It releases a drive to communicate as children assume language roles allowed too often only to adults. Second, students enjoy being in control as active participants, and in some instances, they are able to abandon earlier images of themselves as school failures. Third, interviewing unifies the communicative process because listening and speaking lead naturally to writing and then to reading. Finally, when children become interested in their topics, they write more and use more vocabulary.

Storytelling by Teachers and Students

Storytelling has existed for many years in many cultures, and despite the advent of mass media, most elementary school children today still prefer to listen to stories rather than hearing them read. In fact, more than one five-year-old, when faced with a teacher who was about to read a picture book, has reportedly been heard to say, "Tell it with your face." And older students also benefit as they learn to tell stories by having listened to their teacher relate stories aloud.

Storytelling stimulates the imagination of children in general and benefits the development of their communication skills in particular. It also broadens their language abilities and motivates students to read, even those who are reluctant readers. It provides special rapport with the audience as no book separates the tellers from the listeners. Finally, it introduces students to the literary traditions and values of different cultures.

Storytelling is not difficult and child audiences are highly appreciative of teachers who are not reluctant to attempt it. Those new to storytelling will find it enjoyable by following six sequential stages.

The first is *selection of a story,* which must be both appropriate for the intended audience and be appealing to the storyteller. Important characteristics include a quick beginning, considerable action, natural dialogue, a definite climax, and a satisfying conclusion. Speaking characters should

For material related to this concept, go to Video Clip 11.2 on the Student Resource CD bound into the back of your textbook.

be limited to three or four so as not to confuse the listeners. Fables, folktales, and modern fantasies such as those written by Aesop, the Brothers Grimm, and Laura Numeroff, respectively, appeal to children in the primary grades. Older students like to listen to selections from books by Louis Sachar, Lois Lowry, and Avi.

The second stage in storytelling is *preparation of the story,* which is broken down into three steps: (a) dividing it into action units (which can be summarized on index cards), (b) using some words exactly as written by memorizing certain segments verbatim (which may include repeated phrases or certain words); and (c) learning the essence of the story (which concerns the sequence in particular).

The third stage is *analyzing the plot and the story characters.* The fourth is *experimenting with intonation and gestures.* The fifth stage is *rehearsing the story without an audience.*

The sixth and final stage is *presentation to a live audience.* Here the pace of the story can be adapted to the interest and age levels of the students. It can also be personalized and children's names substituted for those of some of the characters. Sometimes the story can even be modified to meet the special needs of the class at the time.

After the teacher–storyteller has finished, there is often no follow-up planned. However, questions prompting insight into cultural similarities or into social values may seem to be in order after certain types of stories.

As students listen to stories told by their teacher, one or more may wish to become storytellers too. They can learn to do so through *interactive storytelling,* which is a strategy that encourages children to supply dialogue or sound effects during the teacher's presentation (Trousdale, 1990). It works effectively with students from kindergarten through the intermediate grades and promotes their ability to tell stories on their own.

With the support of their teacher, child storytellers succeed as they follow the steps suggested to them by Hamilton and Weiss (1990): (a) select a story you personally enjoy; (b) read it aloud several times; (c) prepare a diagram or story map to help you visualize the sequence of events and then practice using the map; (d) tell the story using your own vocabulary (except for unique phrases or expressions) and your own gestures; (e) audio tape your version and listen to it to help your pacing; (f) think about your characters and how you imagine them to talk; and (g) practice telling the story to a mirror, to an imaginary audience, or to anyone who will listen (including the family dog).

Children can use props such as picture cards, flannel boards, stuffed animals, or other objects to tell some stories. These props help audiences focus their attention and give novice storytellers additional confidence. Other suggestions for those students who are still hesitant are (a) using wordless picture books to relate what is happening and (b) participating in chain stories whereby the teacher or a classmate starts an exciting story and then others in the class take turns adding sentences to it.

Choral Speaking

Choral speaking (also known as choral reading) is a technique of group recitation (or reading) of poetry or poetic prose without music and under the direction of a leader or teacher. It can be introduced to children as early as kindergarten.

There are several benefits of choral speaking (McCaslin, 2006). First, it can be successfully performed regardless of class size, student age, or space. It promotes good habits of speech through enjoyable exercise rather than drill, eliciting proper pitch, rate, volume, and tone quality. Clear diction and vocal expression are also acquired during the exercise. Third, it provides an opportunity for social cooperation because it emphasizes group rather than individual effort. Additionally, it gives the shy child or the child with a speech impairment an opportunity to speak. Fifth, it provides a pleasant introduction to poetry. And finally, choral speaking is a satis-fying activity in itself.

Fortunately, there are various types of choral speaking in which elementary students can take part. To make these experiences successful, teachers must first understand the rhythm and the tempo of a particular poetry selection, as well as the quality of the children's voices. Then, with that background in mind, they can choose among the five major types of arrangements.

The *refrain arrangement* is easiest for beginners. It involves poems with a refrain or chorus. The teacher recites most of the narrative and the class responds with words that constitute the refrain or repeated line(s). One example of this arrangement is the following anonymous poem:

Little Brown Rabbit

Teacher: Little brown rabbit went hoppity-hop,

Group: Hoppity-hop, hoppity-hop!

Teacher: Into a garden without any stop,

Group: Hoppity-hop, hoppity-hop!

Teacher: He ate for his supper a fresh carrot top,

Group: Hoppity-hop, hoppity-hop!

Teacher: Then home went the rabbit without any stop,

Group: Hoppity-hop, hoppity-hop!

At first, this "group" would consist of the entire class. Then eventually it could be performed with four different groups of children, each having one line.

The *antiphonal or dialogue arrangement* suits poems that demand alternate speaking between two groups. These may alternate between high or light voices and low or loud voices; sometimes they can alternate between girls' and boys' voices. Often it is simply a question-and-answer session or dialogue between two voices. One example is the following anonymous poem:

To London Town

Group A: Which is the way to London Town

To see the king in his golden crown?

Group B: One foot up and one foot down,

That's the way to London Town.

Group A: Which is the way to London Town

To see the queen in her silken gown?

Group B: Left! Right! Left! Right! Up and down,

Soon you'll be in London Town

Differing only slightly from the antiphonal variety, the *line-a-child or line-a-group arrangement* involves not two but three or more individual children or groups. This arrangement is popular with students because it possesses variety and offers the challenge of picking up lines quickly in exact tempo. Because children must come in on cue, beginning efforts should have them standing in the order in which they present their lines. One anonymous example is the following:

Five Little Squirrels

All:	Five little squirrels sat in a tree.
Group A.:	The first one said, "What do I see?"
Group B:	The second one said, "A man with a gun."
Group C:	The third one said, "We'd better run."
Group D:	The fourth one said, "Let's hide in the shade."
Group E:	The fifth one said, "I'm not afraid."
All:	Then bang went the gun, and how they did run.

The *cumulative arrangement* differs from the line-a-group arrangement in that the addition of each group to the presentation is permanent, not temporary, in order to attain a crescendo effect and a satisfying climax. While it is one of the more difficult forms of choral speaking, an entire class can take part at once. An example from Mother Goose is the following:

I Saw a Ship a-Sailing

Group 1:	I saw a ship a-sailing,
	A-sailing on the sea;
Groups 1–2:	And, oh, it was all laden
	With pretty things for thee!
Groups 1–3:	There were comfits in the cabin,
	And apples in the hold;
Groups 1–4:	The sails were made of silk,
Groups 1–5:	And the masts were all of gold.
Group 1:	The four-and-twenty sailors
	That stood upon the decks
Groups 1–2:	Were four-and-twenty white mice
	With chains about their necks.
Groups 1–3:	The captain was a duck,
	With a packet on his back;
Groups 1–4:	And when the ship began to move,
	The captain cried,
Groups 1–5:	"QUACK, QUACK!"

Even more difficult than the cumulative variety is the fifth and final *unison arrangement*. In one sense, it is the simplest of all arrangements because an entire class or group speaks every line together. However, only a teacher experienced in choral speaking can skillfully direct a large number of voices speaking simultaneously. Still, when the class and the teacher have considerable background in choral speaking, unison arrangements become dramatically effective. Obviously, they are better suited to intermediate grade students. An example of a poem for unison recital is the following, whose author is unknown:

Weather

Whether the weather is fine,

Or whether the weather is not,

Whether the weather is cold,

Or whether the weather is hot,

We'll weather the weather,

Whatever the weather,

Whether we like it or not.

In addition to poetry, there is also some poetic prose that is dramatic, simple, and understood quickly by an audience hearing it for the first time. It possesses a marked rhythm and expresses a universal sentiment. Prose suitable for choral speaking includes—for older students—portions of Carson's *The Sea Around Us* (2003) and selections from O'Dell's *Island of the Blue Dolphins* (1960). For younger readers there are the texts from Potter's *The Complete Adventures of Peter Rabbit* (2003) as well as some portions of McCloskey's *Time of Wonder* (1989).

Whether the choice is prose or poetry, it must elicit student interest and involvement. Children prefer selections that contain humor, repetition, surprise, action—and brevity.

Finally, the teacher must be aware of some guidelines involved in choral speaking. First and foremost, the material chosen must be literature. Then the attention of the class must focus on the meaning of the selection and not on its delivery. Furthermore, the teacher must listen continually to the tone quality of the group and stress good diction and articulation. The children cannot be allowed to singsong their lines or lapse into being overdramatic. Last, all participants must have the same understanding of the selection and a sensitivity to words.

Readers Theater

Unlike choral speaking, which involves group voices, a **readers theater** presentation concerns individual students. It is an oral reading and dramatic interpretation of a prepared script based on a literary work. Usually 2 to 12 students perform before an audience. They may either sit (often on high stools) or stand. There is no memorization and only minimal use of backdrops, costumes, or props. Physical movement is merely suggested.

There are several benefits to adding readers theater to the language arts program. First, it gives the children the feeling that they are part of the story itself, and that reaction motivates them to read more (Wolf, 1998). Second, it builds on students' love of series books and books on the same topic; this in turn helps them improve their overall reading ability and eventually gives them confidence to develop their own readers theater presentations. Third, readers theater has been shown to improve reading fluency in particular, especially for those children who need to practice eliminating hesitancies in their speech (Martinez, Roser, & Strecker, 1999). Fourth, it lets all students participate and gain self-assurance in speaking before an audience. Fifth, the listening ability of children increases together with their vocal phrasing, expression, and rate. Finally, readers theater promotes writing as students become motivated to prepare their own scripts from books they have heard or read with enjoyment.

Once the teacher has explained to newcomers what is involved in readers theater and how they can each participate, the steps involved in a readers theater presentation are, briefly, choosing and introducing the story, preparing the script, selecting the cast, rehearsing, and presenting before an audience. These steps are described in more detail below:

1. The teacher may tell or read the story aloud to young children or have older students take turns reading aloud to the class a chapter or episode from a novel. (Appropriate choices are those with sufficient action, numerous characters, and considerable dialogue; lengthy descriptions are *not* helpful.) The teacher should plan on an extended response to improve understanding and promote discussion.

2. The teacher prepares the script of the story (just heard or told) with the assistance of the children; later as they become more experienced with the idea, it is the teacher who assists them with the writing. Then, the next-to-last draft is displayed on the overhead, and the entire class offers suggestions for improvement. Finally, the revised script is distributed to everyone in the class. (Some teachers prefer to use commercial scripts from sources such as Readers Theatre Script Service, P.O. Box 178333, San Diego, CA 92117, which produces kits with parts written for different reading difficulty levels from early to upper elementary grades; see also the Appendix for Web sites from which teachers can obtain scripts.)

3. The teacher selects the cast by encouraging children to volunteer to participate. During the first few sessions interested children should become familiar with all the parts before choosing their characters. An important role in some performances is that of narrator or storyteller who speaks directly to the audience and describes the situation, theme, and characters. Sometimes the narrator is given dialogue that includes the story's descriptive passages so there is a smooth transition from beginning to end and the audience understands the plot.

4. The teacher oversees the rehearsals. Children can first practice individually and then as a group. They must learn to focus, the narrator looking toward the audience and the other players toward the other characters with whom they are talking, according to the story.

5. The teacher directs the final production, which is staged in front of an audience and may be videotaped. The readers may stand or sit; however, for anxious students, sitting is more relaxing and stools more useful than chairs for indicating a platform stage. Rather than entering or exiting as in plays, children can simply step forward if standing, or lean slightly forward if seated, when entering and then reverse the action when exiting. At the end of the presentation, the performers should become quiet so that a pause comes over the room; then they all close their scripts, stand, and bow.

For elementary school students, 10 to 30 minutes of playing time are most effective, with presentations made in the classroom, media center, or multipurpose room, depending on the confidence of the readers.

When choosing material for readers theater, it is critical to remember that basically this is a *reading* exercise and students must be able to read the material independently. Although it is often considered to be an activity for intermediate students, children as early as second grade can participate in readers theater provided that they can read the story and write the script (Forsythe, 1995).

No matter what the elementary grade level, the teacher must choose material that will not only excite the class but will also lend itself readily for dramatic interpretation and so hold the attention of the potential audience. All literary genres can be used successfully, depending on the interest and ability levels of the readers/writers. Sample selections for younger students include the following:

Huck's *Princess Furball* (1989)

Kellogg's *Jack and the Beanstalk* (1997)

Williams's *A Chair for My Mother* (Morrow, 1984)

Intermediate students can write scripts from portions of books such as the following:

Avi's *The True Confessions of Charlotte Doyle* (1990)

Freedman's *Lincoln: A Photobiography* (1987)

Lowry's *Number the Stars* (1989)

Reporting

In the lower grades there is *informal reporting*. The teacher begins by sharing with the class some anecdotes or incidents from his or her own life in order to extend the children's background and experiences. The teacher then encourages the students to report on news that they think is important by helping them understand which incidents are appropriate for sharing with the class and which are better suited to telling the teacher alone. After listening attentively to the reports the students share with their classmates, the teacher asks the class for constructive comments. He or she also compliments each speaker on some aspect of the report. Sometimes the cues of Who? What? Where? When? Why? and How? may be explained and listed on a chart.

In turn, the children begin to develop sensitivity to suitable topics for informal reporting and to gain confidence in their ability to share ideas with others. In their role as listeners, they pay close attention and ask questions related to the reports presented. In their role as reporters, they try to remember to speak clearly, to make eye contact with their audience, to use an opening sentence that provokes attention, and to keep to the topic.

Informal reporting, sometimes known as sharing time in the primary grades, is important for several reasons. It is the only official classroom time when out-of-school experiences are acceptable subjects for discussion in school. Second, it allows each child legitimately to be the center of attention, at least for a few minutes. Third, speakers learn to elaborate on their chosen topics. Fourth, such reporting develops body control. Fifth and last, it helps promote a sense of audience both on the part of speakers and classmates.

Because some students are less self-conscious when they do show-and-tell holding an object, especially one that is personally significant to them, their oral reports are likely to be longer, livelier, and less rambling. Young children find it easier to share facts and experience while they are showing objects that can be held in the hand and admired by the class—an arrowhead, a stuffed animal, or a seashell, for example.

In the intermediate grades that same sense of audience can result from a voluntary, sharing activity called In the News. Individual students or groups can report on major school news such as the upcoming Jog-A-Thon; community affairs such as next weekend's Friends of the Library Used Book Sale; and national and world events involving sports, elections, or catastrophic weather. Listeners may wish to inquire for additional details.

A form of reporting in which such audience feedback is not generally involved is *making announcements.* All elementary school students can learn to make short but complete announcements to their classmates about the arrival of a new puppy at their house or the upcoming visit from Japan of their grandmother. Those in the intermediate grades can use the public address system to announce the monthly winners for the Best Writers competition by grade level. What matters most in this area of reporting is that the announcements must concern actual events and thereby offer an opportunity for the practical use of language.

Students in the intermediate grades can also be taught *formal reporting,* which involves organized accounts by individuals or groups who have been shown how to outline and research reference materials. In addition to being a good listening session for the audience, such reporting provides an opportunity to build on skills in the selection and collection of material and the coordination and presentation of the report. Children can learn how to limit the scope of their talks and how to choose pertinent material quickly by skimming and scanning. They can learn to take notes relevant to their major ideas and to organize that material logically by making an outline and preparing a summary. Some students may wish to prepare transparencies or use other visual aids to enhance their presentation.

The teacher must help the children take the following six steps involved in formal reporting:

1. *Choose topics of genuine interest* to them, such as sports or personal hobbies. Subject reports in categories of special interest in science (e.g., The Human Body) or social studies (e.g., The American Revolution) can also stimulate student enthusiasm. Prior knowledge and experience may affect the topic selection as well and so make the final presentation more effective.

Intermediate students can outline and research reference materials in order to present a formal report to the class.

2. *Collect information.* Sources include the Internet, reference books, encyclopedias, magazines, interviews with persons with special backgrounds in the selected topic, and videotapes. Information must be recorded in the form of brief notes on index cards in the student's own words.

3. *Organize the information for presentation.* Students must review their notes and decide what to include and how to sequence their material. Three to five main ideas should be incorporated (with pertinent supporting details) on data charts designed by hand or on a computer.

4. *Prepare the report, including any visuals.* Information from the data chart must be transferred onto note cards to make the final report both well organized and interesting. Cards should contain only key words, no sentences. In addition, visuals such as maps, charts, diagrams, pictures, or photographs should be collected to motivate the audience and reduce speaker anxiety. Electronic media may be incorporated at this stage.

5. *Rehearse the presentation.* Students should rehearse in class with a partner or at home in front of a mirror or a sympathetic family member. The note cards they prepared in Step Four will help them recall the main points of the subject matter and enable them to speak more extemporaneously and comfortably.

6. *Present the report.* Students must remember to speak loudly so all can hear, maintain eye contact with the audience, stress their key points with the aid of the note cards, and incorporate their visuals at appropriate times. They should also plan to use an interesting opening remark—such as a question or a brief anecdote relevant to the subject of the report.

In addition to helping the student speakers with their reports, the teacher must also prepare the audience for its role. Each member should listen carefully and look at the speaker during the presentation. Later, questions should be addressed, and comments and compliments made to the student who spoke.

A sample lesson plan incorporating the concepts introduced in this chapter appears on p. 388.

Assessment

Listening

Following directions: Teachers can do "following directions" activities with the children to assess their listening skills. An example would be a paper-folding activity, such as origami, in which the children must pay close attention in order to correctly create a bird or other design out of paper. Teachers can easily see if the children have listened carefully and followed directions. Younger children can do worksheets that require following directions (e.g., "color the apple red").

Teacher observation: Teachers can play "Simon Says" or other direction-following games with the children and then observe how well they are listening

Speaking

SOLOM: The SOLOM (Student Oral Language Observation Matrix) was developed to assist teachers in assessing ELLs' oral language level in English. Teachers evaluate students' language skills in comprehension, fluency, vocabulary, pronunciation, and grammar on a 5-point scale. The total scores determine the ELL level (beginning, intermediate, advanced).

Anecdotal records: Teachers can take informal notes when students are making oral presentations or in other classroom situations that call for oral language use.

Audio tapes: Teachers can record each student as she or he reads aloud from a book or speaks in front of the class, for example. The student and teacher can then listen to the tape and discuss areas of strength and areas to improve in speaking.

Rubrics: Teachers can evaluate students when making oral presentations to the class by using a rubric.

Working With English Language Learners

Listening and speaking are critical components of instruction for English Language Learners. Teachers must address these two areas so that children can have success in the language skills of reading and writing. Modifications for listening and speaking lessons should be tailored to the language needs of each level of English learner.

Beginning ELLs: Several teaching strategies can be used to promote listening and speaking at the beginning level. Total Physical Response (TPR) is a strategy that involves the learner in kinesthetic, visual, and auditory learning. During lessons using TPR, children follow the teacher's directions with physical responses, such as pointing or doing actions. Another excellent strategy for ELLs is the Natural Approach. In this strategy teachers make use of real objects to teach vocabulary and get children speaking one or two words at a time or in short phrases. A low-anxiety classroom environment is critical to the success of both methods.

Early intermediate and intermediate ELLs: The use of games is an excellent strategy to help middle-level English learners practice their listening and speaking skills. Simple math or language arts games, such as Bingo! or Sorry!, allow children to practice their listening and speaking skills in a pleasant, low-anxiety environment. Games provide a highly motivating vehicle for communication because one needs to be understood to play the game. Another excellent strategy for middle-level ELLs is the use of visuals. Pictures, drawings, and diagrams all help student comprehension and support listening activities. These same visuals can serve as a support to students as they speak to the teacher or peers. Picture books serve as a springboard to retelling of stories and discussion of story setting and characters at this ELL level.

Early advanced and advanced ELLs: Advanced and near-fluent ELLs benefit from more complex listening and speaking activities. As with all levels of ELLs, repetition is extremely valuable. These children can listen to and give short presentations. They can summarize points and retell grade-level stories. Visuals, realia, and hands-on activities all support comprehension at this ELL level.

Practical Instructional Activities and Ideas

- *Poems, rhymes, and songs:* Teaching poems, rhymes, and songs helps children in Grades K–2 develop their listening and speaking skills. Poems and songs also help ELLs learn new vocabulary and learn about sentence structure while getting a "feel" for correct language use. Repetition in reciting poems and rhymes or singing songs provides needed practice in language for all learners, including ELLs.

- *Oral directions:* Children of all ages can develop listening and speaking skills by understanding and following oral directions. Young children (K–2) can be given one- or two-step directions, older children (Grades 3–4) three- or four-step directions, and still older children (Grades 5–6) can be given multiple-step directions. The game format, such as "Simon Says" or a scavenger hunt, is an enjoyable way to teach how to follow directions.
- *Show and tell:* Sharing has been a popular teaching technique for 30 to 40 years at least. What child doesn't love to bring in a favorite item for "show and tell"? Children of all ages can also share life events or personal experiences with the class. These types of sharing activities make an excellent bridge to writing activities. For example, children could share what they did during spring break and then write about it.
- *The five Ws and an H:* Teachers can read stories to younger children and then ask them to verbally recall the "who, what, when, where, why, and how" of the story. Literary genres that work well for retelling include fairy tales, fables, and sequential and predictable stories. An excellent example is *The Very Hungry Caterpillar* by Eric Carle (1994). This story has a memorable sequence, and the text can be supported with visuals, such as picture cards or flannel board pieces.
- *Story elements:* Younger children can recall story elements, such as plot, setting, and characters of literature selections. When the teacher writes down student responses in chart format, it helps all learners, including those with special needs, visual learners, and ELLs.
- *Oral reports:* Younger children (Grades 1–3) can do short oral reports based on information they have gathered about a topic. For example, a first-grade class might do animal reports. Older children (Grades 4–6) can give longer oral reports and can use volume, pitch, phrasing, pace, modulation, and gestures appropriately to enhance meaning. Older children can also use props or charts they have created when they are making an oral presentation.
- *Musical elements:* Older children can identify the musical elements of literary language, such as rhymes, repeated sounds, and onomatopoeia. Younger children can listen for rhyming words in a story that is read to them or provide their own rhyming words. Even silly rhymes, such as those found in Dr. Seuss books, help children develop important elements of literacy, such as phonemic awareness.
- *Appreciating and learning:* As children pass from the primary grades into the upper elementary grades, they move from learning to read to enjoying and appreciating literature and reading to acquire information. They can begin to read aloud fiction, poetry, and biographical texts for those purposes.
- *Family trees:* Students can interview family members, peers, school site administrators, or teachers and then report their findings to the class. As an extension, the information they gather can be compiled into a report. An example is a family tree interview in which children interview their parents, grandparents, and extended family members to find out where their ancestors came from. This information can be shared with the whole class, as children place push pins on various countries on a world map. The children can then each research a country to find out more about their own heritage.
- *Presentations:* Older children (Grades 4–6) can make narrative presentations in which they describe an event and its importance, informative presentations in which they present information on a particular topic, or persuasive presentations in which they present a point of view and evidence to support it.
- *Recitation:* Children in fourth or fifth grade can memorize and recite short (two to three stanza) poems, soliloquies, or dramatic dialogues. The teacher can look for correct use of tempo, diction, volume, and phrasing.
- *Literary criticism:* Older children can identify, analyze, and critique persuasive techniques such as "glittering generalities", promises, dares, and flattery that are present in the media.
- *Oral response:* Older children can provide more sophisticated oral responses to literature, summarizing important details of a story, explaining the imagery in the story, and providing examples.

LESSON PLAN 11.1   Fruit and Colors

Language Arts Components: Reading and Writing

Grade: 1

Topic: English Language Learning: The Natural Approach

Time Frame: 1 week

Objective

- Students demonstrate knowledge of the names of various fruits and colors by following simple directions.

Materials

- *Eating Your Way Through the Alphabet: Fruits and Vegetables From A to Z* by Lois Ehlert (1994)
- Real or artificial fruits of all kinds
- Index cards
- Metal rings for index cards

Content Standards

English Language Development (ELD): Reading Comprehension

- Students speak in words, phrases, or sentences.
- Students answer questions with one- to two-word responses.
- Students respond to questions using nonverbal communication.

Language Arts: Listening, Speaking, Comprehension

- Students listen attentively.
- Students ask questions to aid their understanding.
- Students follow simple one- and two-step directions.

Vocabulary

- Apple
- Banana
- Orange
- Pineapple
- Pomegranate
- Tangerine

- Lemon
- Mango

Open

Day 1

Whole Class

Teacher: "Today we will read a story about different kinds of fruits and vegetables. Then we will do centers about fruit and color names."

Teacher does a picture walk, then reads book to the class.

Teacher explains what the students are to do at each center.

Body

Days 2–4

Small Groups With Teacher

Teacher shows the children the basket of fruit and takes out each type of fruit one by one and asks if anyone knows the name of the fruit. Teacher asks them to name each color. If the students do not know it teacher provides the fruit and color name. Teacher also shows the students a word card with the fruit name and the color word for each one. Teacher has children point to fruit as she or he names them. Teacher has children name fruit and colors. If time, teacher and children can reread the story book.

Small Groups at Centers

Center 1: Students use watercolor paints to paint line drawings of fruit in the appropriate colors. Teacher can create a blackline master of the outline of each kind of fruit with the name written below. The pages can be assembled into a book for each student.

Center 2: Students listen to the story at the listening center.

Center 3: Students write fruit names and color words on index cards to be added to their ring of word cards. Students practice reading the cards with a friend after they have finished writing them.

Close

Day 5

Whole Class

Teacher reads the book to the class again. Students name the various fruit and colors on each page.

Assessment

Teacher assessment of individual students to determine which students can read the word cards on their rings.

Integration Across the Curriculum

Science

- Students listen to fictional stories that relate to science content, such as different kinds of insects in *The Very Quiet Cricket* by Eric Carle (1997).

Social Studies

- Students who come from other states take turns telling the class about their own personal history, such as what state or region their family comes from or about the people in their family (brothers, sisters, parents, grandparents). Students may use a map of the United States in their presentations. Presenters learn how to speak with proper phrasing, pitch, and modulation. The audience members learn and practice good audience skills, such as listening attentively and applauding appropriately.

Math

- Students in Grades 4 through 6 can discuss how to solve math-related riddles such as "The Mongolian Postal Service" in Sloane and Miller's (1992) *Lateral Thinking Puzzlers*.

Literature

- Students verbally analyze assigned fiction and nonfiction books, including genre, story elements, and literary devices.

Visual and Performing Arts

- Guided drawing: Students listen as teacher gives them step-by-step directions for how to do a simple line drawing. Teacher draws a sample at the same time as the students do.
- Older students (Grades 5 and 6) can tell stories to their "buddies" in Grades 1 and 2.

Health

- Students research and prepare oral informative presentations on ways children can enhance and maintain health, for example, by daily teeth brushing and flossing, eating fruits and vegetables, and exercising regularly.

Physical Education

- Students work in a small group to plan and teach a PE game such as *Steal the Bacon* to their peers.

Music

- Students learn and sing a variety of songs that connect to other curricular areas such as science or social studies; for example, they learn "The Ants Go Marching" to tie into a science unit on insects.

Parents as Partners

- *Talking to children:* One of the best ways parents can help their children develop listening and speaking skills is to talk and listen to them. Parents can ask their children daily about what they learned or did at school. Breakfast or dinnertime is a good time for family members to share their day with each other.
- *Reading to children:* Parents can read aloud to their children to help them develop listening comprehension skills. Parents can ask children questions about what they read, so that they can recall story sequence or details about the story.
- *Playing games with children:* Parents can play board or card games, such as Go Fish, Monopoly, Old Maid, and Scrabble, with their children. As they play, they provide children the opportunity to practice their listening and speaking skills.

Student Study Site

The Companion Web site for *Language Arts: Integrating Skills for Classroom Teaching*
www.sagepub.com/donoghuestudy
Visit the Web-based study site to enhance your understanding of the chapter content. The study materials include chapter summaries, practice tests, flashcards, and Web resources.

Additional Professional Readings

Abbott, C., & Godinho, S. (2004). *Speak, listen, and learn.* Portland, ME: Stenhouse.

Boyce, J., Alber-Morgan, S., & Riley, J. (2007). Fearless public speaking: Oral presentation activities for the elementary classroom. *Childhood Education 83,* 142–150.

Fredericks, A. (2007). *Nonfiction readers theatre for beginning readers.* Portsmouth, NH: Teacher Ideas Press.

Haven, K. (2000). *Super simple storytelling: A can-do guide for every classroom, every day.* Portsmouth, NH: Teacher Ideas Press.

Kendall J., & Khoun, O. (2005). *Making sense: Small group conversation lessons for English language learners.* Portland, ME: Stenhouse.

Opitz, M., & Zbaracki, M. (2004). *Listen hear! 25 effective comprehension strategies.* Portsmouth, NH: Heinemann.

Trostle, S., & Donato, J. (2001). *Storytelling in emergent literacy: Fostering multiple intelligences.* Clifton Park, NY: Delmar/Thomson.

Williams, J. (2001). Classroom conversations: Opportunities to learn for ESL students in mainstream classrooms. *The Reading Teacher, 54,* 750–757.

Woodard, C., Haskins, G., Schaefer, G., & Smolen, L. (2004). Let's talk. *Young Children, 59,* 92–95.

Worthy, J. (2005). *Readers theater for building fluency.* New York: Scholastic.

Children's Literature Cited in the Text

Avi. (1990). *The true confessions of Charlotte Doyle.* New York: Orchard.

Bartone, E. (1993). *Peppe the lamplighter.* New York: HarperTrophy.

Carle, E. (1994). *The very hungry caterpillar.* New York: Philomel.

Carle, E. (1997). *The very quiet cricket.* New York: Philomel.

Carson, R. (2003). *The sea around us.* New York: Oxford University Press.

Ehlert, L. (1994). *Eating your way through the alphabet: Fruits and vegetables from A to Z.* San Diego: Harcourt.

Freedman, R. (1987). *Lincoln: A photobiography.* Boston: Houghton Mifflin.

Galdone, P. (2006). *The gingerbread boy.* New York: Clarion.

Huck, C. (1989). *Princess Furball.* New York: Greenwillow.

Kellogg, S. (1997). *Jack and the beanstalk.* New York: Morrow.

Lowry, L. (1989). *Number the stars.* Boston: Houghton Mifflin.

McCloskey, R. (1989). *Time of wonder.* New York: Viking.

Monjo, F. (1970). *The drinking gourd.* New York: HarperCollins.

O'Dell, S. (1960). *Island of the blue dolphins.* Boston: Houghton.

Potter, B. (2003). *The complete adventures of Peter Rabbit.* London: Warne.

Schaefer, P. (2000). *The Wright brothers.* Mankato, MN: Capstone.

Sloane, P., & Miller, M. (1992). *Lateral thinking puzzlers.* New York: Sterling.

Williams, V. (1984). *A chair for my mother.* New York: Morrow.

References

Dillon, J. (1984). Research on questioning and discussion. *Educational Leadership, 42*(3), 50–56.

Dyson, A., & Genishi, C. (1982). Whatta ya tryin' to write? Writing as an interactive process. *Language Arts, 59,* 126–132.

Forsythe, S. (1995). It worked! Readers theatre in second grade. *The Reading Teacher, 49,* 3, 264–265.

Haley-James, S., & Hobson, C. (1980). Interviewing: A means of encouraging the drive to communicate. *Language Arts, 57,* 497–502.

Hamilton, M., & Weiss, M. (1990. *Children tell stories: A teaching guide.* Katonah, NY: Richard C. Owen

Martinez, M., Roser, N., & Strecker, S. (1998). I never thought I could be a star: A readers theatre ticket to fluency. *The Reading Teacher, 52,* 326.

McCaslin, N. (2006) *Creative drama in the classroom and beyond.* New York: Pearson.

Pinnell, G., & Jagger, A. (2003). Oral language: Speaking and listening in the elementary classroom. In J. Flood, D. Lapp, M. R. Squire, & J. M. Jensen (Eds.), *Handbook of research on teaching the English language arts* (3rd ed.). Mahwah, NJ: Lawrence Erlbaum.

Stauffer, R. (1975). *Directing the reading-thinking process.* New York: Harper & Row.

Trousdale, A. (1990). Interactive storytelling: Scaffolding children's early narratives. *Language Arts, 67,* 164–173.

Wells, G., & Chang-Wells, G. (1992). *Constructing knowledge together: Classrooms as centers of inquiry.* Portsmouth, NH: Heinemann.

Welton, D. (2002). *Children and their world.* Boston: Houghton Mifflin.

Wolf, S. (1998). The flight of reading: Shifts in instruction, orchestration, and attitudes through classroom theatre. *Reading Research Quarterly, 33,* (4) 409.

Wolvin, A., & Coakley, C. (1995). *Listening* (3rd ed.). New York: McGraw-Hill.

Anticipation Statement Answers

1. Agree

2. Agree

3. Agree

4. Disagree

5. Agree

6. Agree

7. Agree

8. Agree

9. Agree: There is a distinction between hearing and listening. However, it could be argued that everyone listens because it is a naturally occurring behavior.

10. Agree: Readers theater offers many benefits, including motivation to read more and creating a love of series books and books on the same topic. However, it is a reading exercise and children must be able to read the material independently.

Creative Drama

CHAPTER 12

It was Piaget (1962) who first concluded that language development goes through three stages: an actual experience with an object or action, a dramatic reenactment of that experience, and vocabulary that verbally represents the entire generalized idea. Based on his constructivist theory, drama is a natural part of the development of human language and thought. Long before children can even speak, they are able to communicate effectively through dramatic means, and play becomes their primary learning activity. Vygotsky (1986) with his social interactionist perspective agreed that activity is the chief force behind the development of human language and thought. Consequently, the use of drama in the elementary classroom underlies a social constructivist approach to language learning while simultaneously providing an effective way to teach oral language as well as literacy (Wagner, 2003).

Creative drama is an umbrella term covering a broad range of informal classroom activities ranging from puppetry to story dramatization (by interpretation) and later to story dramatization (by improvisation). It is a fairly direct extension of play, with very little of it being rehearsed. Nevertheless, because creative drama involves so many different modes of expression, it reflects all of the multiple intelligences that Gardner (1999) proposed and therefore possesses numerous benefits.

Anticipation Statements

Complete this exercise before reading Chapter 12.

Do you agree or disagree with the following statements? Circle your answer. Be prepared to discuss questions in blue.

1.	The use of drama in the elementary classroom underlies a social constructivist approach to language learning based on Piaget and Vygotsky.	Agree	Disagree
2.	Creative drama includes pantomime, puppetry, story interpretation, and story improvisation.	Agree	Disagree
3.	Creative drama allows children to develop imagination.	Agree	Disagree
4.	Creative drama promotes social awareness.	Agree	Disagree
5.	Creative drama can help children develop better habits of speech.	Agree	Disagree
6.	The use of drama in the elementary classroom does not provide an opportunity to release emotion in a healthy way.	Agree	Disagree
7.	Creative drama provides a good introduction to the theater arts.	Agree	Disagree
8.	Drama offers an opportunity for experience with literature.	Agree	Disagree
9.	Drama is not appropriate for children with special needs.	Agree	Disagree
10.	Creative drama can be adapted for a classroom that includes English Language Learners.	Agree	Disagree

Benefits of Creative Drama

According to the Children's Theater Association of America (CTAA, 1981), participation in **creative drama** has the potential to *promote* a positive self-image, social awareness, a clarification of values and attitudes, empathy, and an understanding of the art of theater; and to *develop* problem-solving skills, language and communication abilities, and creativity.

The benefits of drama may depend on the age of the children, the experience of the teacher or leader, and the particular situation involved. Nevertheless, according to McCaslin (2006), drama makes possible the following opportunities to some extent for all elementary students:

- An opportunity to develop the imagination (which comes more easily to young children but must also be nurtured in older students)
- An opportunity to build social awareness in a diverse society (since drama can help children understand the customs and traditions of ethnicities other than their own)
- An opportunity to develop better habits of speech (because students are strongly motivated to be heard—except in pantomime, of course—and properly understood)
- An opportunity for the healthy release of emotion (because all children sometimes experience a variety of negative feelings, and drama allows them to express those emotions through acceptable means)
- An opportunity for independent thinking (since drama is often a group act in which everyone's contributions matter)
- An opportunity for experience with literature (because many genres, properly dramatized, stimulate interest in good fiction and biography and even set a model for original writing)
- An opportunity for recreation (since drama is fun and exists for the enjoyment of the students, whether at the school site or other setting, such as a community center, summer camp, or neighborhood club)
- An opportunity to be introduced to the theater arts (which include listening, viewing, and becoming involved in an essentially universal experience)

Applicable IRA/NCTE Standards

Standard 4	Students adjust their use of spoken, written, and visual language (e.g., conventions, style, vocabulary) to communicate effectively with a variety of audiences and for different purposes.
Standard 9	Students develop an understanding of and respect for diversity in language use, patterns, and dialects across cultures, ethnic groups, geographic regions, and social roles.
Standard 10	Students whose first language is not English make use of their first language to develop competency in the English language arts and to develop understanding of content across the curriculum.
Standard 11	Students participate as knowledgeable, reflective, creative, and critical members of a variety of literacy communities.
Standard 12	Students use spoken, written, and visual language to accomplish their own purposes (e.g., for learning, enjoyment, persuasion, and the exchange of information).

SOURCE: *Standards for the English Language Arts*, by the International Reading Association and the National Council of Teachers of English, Copyright 1996 by the International Reading Association and the National Council of Teachers of English. Reprinted with permission. http://www.ncte.org/about/over/standards/110846.htm

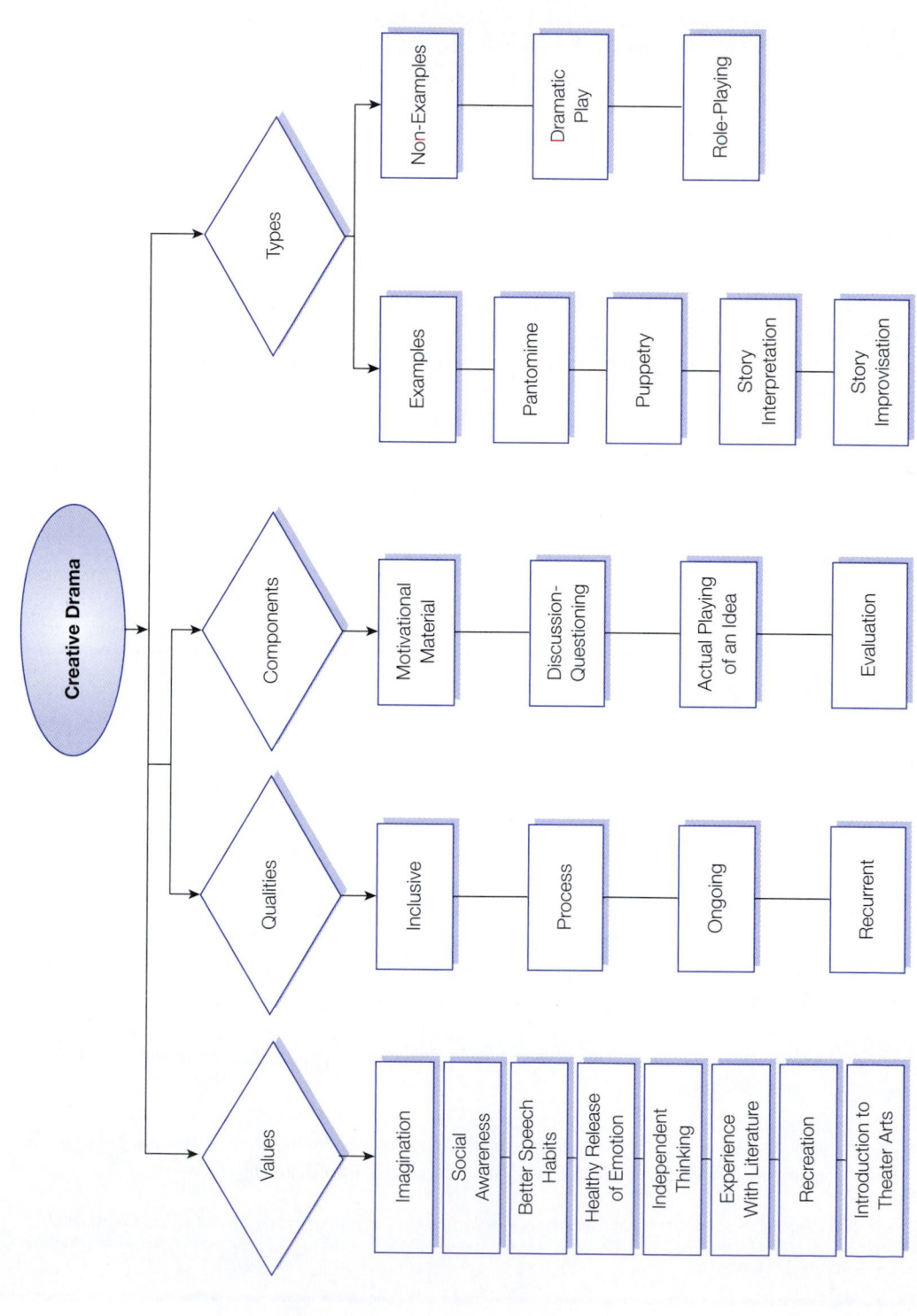

A Graphic Summary of the Contents of This Chapter

Qualities and Components of Creative Drama

Certain qualities and components are unique to creative drama and thereby make it a valuable language art, according to past president of the National Council of Teachers of English. John Warren Stewig (1983; Stewig & Buege, 1994). Among the significant qualities are the following:

The first is an *inclusive quality*. All children can participate and should be encouraged to do so, regardless of talent (or lack of talent) that they have shown in dramatic actions.

The second is a *process quality*. Creative drama emphasizes the involvement of children in expressing their feelings toward a stimulus material, rather than their presenting a polished performance for a large audience.

The third characteristic is its *ongoing quality*. If the original goal of the teacher is not reached in one session, it can be accomplished in later sessions because the emphasis in creative drama remains on the process, and never on the product.

The fourth is a *recurrent quality*. During all drama experiences, several elements prevail, including conflict, characterization, movement, and plot. At varying times all elementary children work with these elements because they are of concern to players from kindergarten through the intermediate grades.

In addition to these four qualities, there are also four components of creative drama:

1. *Motivational material that appeals to the children's senses*: Carefully chosen literature is the standard example of motivational material. Still there are also visual stimuli (such as art reproductions, photographs, and artifacts), tactile stimuli (such as the surface features of wood, glass, or corrugated cardboard that the children can touch), olfactory stimuli (such as unfamiliar spices like savory that the students can smell), and gustatory stimuli (such as a lemon the children taste).

2. *Discussion–questioning segment that occurs during or after the motivational material*: While the discussion appears to be spontaneous, it is nevertheless directed by the teacher through questioning. He or she can lead off with queries such as the following (which are keyed directly to the motivational material above):
   - Literature: Do you have any clues as to the identity of the mysterious speaker in the poem?
   - Visual stimuli: Look at the expression on the girl's face. What are some words we could use to describe that expression?
   - Tactile stimuli: Feel the surface of the cardboard. Is it regular or irregular?
   - Olfactory stimuli: What does the spice smell like? Where might you encounter such a smell?
   - Gustatory stimuli: Who might be tasting this? Where would they be?

   These are only examples of queries to which there is more than one right answer. The teacher should elicit several responses so as to promote critical thinking and participation in the drama itself.

3. *Actual dramatization of an idea that varies in complexity depending on such variables as the age of the children, their dramatic experience and creativity, and the expertise of the teacher*: It may sometimes be just a simple pantomime like brushing one's teeth. Other times it may be a lengthy improvisation of a familiar folk tale such as "The Little Red Hen" that the children have written themselves.

4. *Evaluation*: In creative drama, evaluation takes three different forms. First and foremost is self-evaluation by every player as he or she gains in confidence and ability to participate. A second form is concurrent evaluation in which both the teacher and the group discuss during each session some ways of improving certain actions or impressions. A third form is terminal evaluation that occurs at the end of each session as teacher and children determine together what went well and what skills and feelings need to be addressed at the next session.

Major Types of Creative Drama

In the elementary classroom there are several types of creative drama, including pantomime (which requires no dialogue but only bodily movement by the players), puppetry (which involves dialogue but only limited physical movement by the players), **story interpretation,** and **story improvisation,** the last two of which are obviously rooted in literature.

What Is Not Included in Creative Drama

For material related to this concept, go to Video Clip 12.1 on the Student Resource CD bound into the back of your textbook.

Two areas that are sometimes and erroneously considered creative drama are dramatic play (which is wholly unstructured play by very young children) and role-playing (which was once described as dramatic play for students in Grades 1–6).

Dramatic play is spontaneous play by girls and boys in preschool or kindergarten; it has neither plot nor sequence, just conversation and action. Children reenact their own experiences; imitate the activities of adults, animals, and inanimate objects; and live in an imaginary world. They are the parent, teacher, bus driver, nurse, firefighter, and scores of other characters they have met in the home, school, and community.

During the play period, girls and boys can move about freely, choosing their own activities, equipment, materials, and companions, as long as their selection does not interfere with the well-being of nonplayers. What they do is completely exploratory and experimental. *Dramatic play concerns being rather than playing.* A child can be a barking dog, a galloping pony, or a soaring airplane. In dramatic play there is no definite beginning, middle, or end because it may start anywhere and conclude abruptly, especially in the early stages, when a child says, "I'm done."

Role-playing involves the children assuming the role of characters in a conflict or disagreement and acting out the plot to find a resolution to the situation. While it is not structured by teachers, it is always supervised by them. Role-playing is said to help children see their own private world and how it overlaps with the private worlds of others. It is informal and spontaneous.

Pantomime

The art of acting without words, **pantomime**, is often considered one of the most satisfying ways of starting work in creative drama. It is by nature kinesthetic and uses both sides of the brain simultaneously. Most children are natural mimes and easily become comfortable using this art form when given a little direction and structure. Teachers like it because the length of any activity is highly flexible (from a few seconds to an hour), few if any resources are needed, and any space may be used creatively.

Pantomime is important in language programs for three reasons, according to Hennings (2002). First, children can release, through pantomime, certain inhibitions about expressing themselves nonverbally. Second, they assume control over those nonverbal expressions, which are as important in face-to-face encounters and in story dramatization as they are in pantomime. Finally, children begin to understand the significance of body language in communication and also become aware of the nonverbal expressions that others send to them.

Pantomime is an excellent starting point for creative drama, as it allows performers to convey information and emotions to the audience without words.

Pantomime can help students prepare for story dramatization by letting them become accustomed to transmitting ideas, emotions, and actions to the audience through the medium of body movement, facial expression, and posture. Confidence gained through success in pantomime quietly prepares the way for subsequent success in handling dialogue.

Because mime is done silently, all the students in the class can participate differently, and simultaneously at times, without disturbing anyone. Perhaps this is why children enjoy it, even those who are introverted and generally find oral activities distressing. It offers each child an opportunity to develop physical freedom and a feeling of self-worth without the additional problem of dialogue.

Pantomime stimulates the imagination and sharpens observations and perceptions because participants must recall how actions are performed (e.g., planting seeds in a window box) and what objects are truly like (e.g., a large container needed to hold a birthday gift). If the performers are to pantomime holding imaginary objects, they should practice with the actual objects first. To express a single action, children must learn to use all parts of the body. To indicate drowsiness, for example, they can rub their eyes, stretch their arms, droop their shoulders, cover a yawn, or sit down wearily.

Students must realize that during a pantomime *every action is done in total silence*. Although it is permissible to move one's lips as if talking, the lips must not form actual words. This basic tenet of pantomime is a challenging one for most boys and girls to follow.

The goal of an effective pantomime is that it be clearly presented so that the action pantomimed becomes easy to identify. Sometimes children get the mistaken impression that a pantomime has been well performed if no one is able to decipher the activity. However, the contrary is true. The *most successful pantomimes are those that are readily understood*.

Performance: Introduction

Pantomime must start as a whole-class activity, with every student interpreting a feeling or action. When everyone is involved (including the teacher), children respond more freely. The ideas can be suggested by a student or by the teacher. One way to introduce pantomime to children in Grades K–2 is to have them walk in a circle and pretend to be walking barefoot on the hot sand, or leaves blowing in the wind, or airplanes coming in on the landing strip.

In working with children, the activities used for introductory pantomime must be those in their own environment. Making one's bed is more familiar to most students than fishing in a lake and can therefore be readily imagined and performed.

In introducing pantomime to older boys and girls who have never engaged in such dramatic activities before, the teacher must always assume the lead and give an informal demonstration. Dropping a heavy book on one's foot is an action that will elicit other pantomimes by students who have seen comics perform humorous pantomimes on television. Their exaggerated actions in turn will probably stimulate pantomimes by groups of shyer children.

Performance: Individual Pantomimes

Once elementary students are accustomed to performing in unison, whether as an entire class or a group, they can enact individual pantomimes. Some of these are labeled "*pretend to be*" and others "*pretend to do*." Younger children can pretend to be animals, for example, while older students can pretend to be storybook characters. Pretending-to-do pantomimes involve both familiar and not-so-familiar actions such as brushing one's hair and riding a roller coaster.

While individual pantomimes are initially large-movement actions and therefore relatively brief, children gradually become experienced enough to select topics for more lengthy actions. At this stage they can either develop their own themes or choose to mime situations such as these:

Seeing a young child mistreating a kitten, becoming angry, running between the girl and the pet, rescuing the frightened animal, and finally scolding the foolish child

Receiving a letter from Aunt Jennifer with an invitation to visit Disney World with her, thinking about how much fun this will be, and hurrying to share the news with a friend

Walking down the street on the way home from school, noticing one's dog dart into the street for a greeting just as a truck comes rapidly around the corner, and reacting promptly

A variation of the above type of pantomime is the *double pantomime* in which children choose partners and perform such actions as the following:

A parent cutting the hair of a wiggling boy

A Boy Scout escorting an elderly person across the road

A beginning driver backing out of the garage with a nervous friend

Performance: Group Pantomimes

After some practice with double pantomimes, the students can attempt team or group pantomimes that involve feelings, character analysis, and finer movements. Demanding the cooperation of four or five children, group pantomimes are especially suited for those students who are still hesitant about giving individual performances but nevertheless enjoy pantomime. Groups in the primary (or even intermediate) grades may decide to perform a *narrative pantomime* in sequence from a complete picture book such as the following:

Arthur's New Puppy by Marc Brown (1993)

Sam and the Lucky Money by Karen Chinn (1995)

The Snowy Day by Ezra Keats (1963)

The Paper Bag Princess by Robert Munsch (1980)

A Chair for My Mother by Vera Williams (1984)

Crow Boy by Taro Yashima (1976)

Material suitable for group pantomime in the intermediate grades includes many of the folktales, legends, and modern fantasy to which the students have been introduced during their literature periods. Narrative pantomimes may also be developed from such complete books as these:

And Then What Happened, Paul Revere? by Jean Fritz (1996)

Stone Fox by John Gardiner (1980)

Sarah, Plain and Tall by Patricia MacLachlan (1985)

Shiloh by Phyllis Naylor (1991)

Hatchet by Gary Paulsen (1987)

In summary, pantomime is generally considered a very satisfying way to begin work in creative drama. Without the additional burden of dialogue, players learn to express themselves through body movement. Pantomime is a skill that stimulates the imagination. Young children accept it as a natural way of expression, while older students find it easier to begin with pantomime before attempting story dramatization.

Puppetry

Puppetry, an effective way to introduce classroom drama, serves several purposes in the language arts program. It helps develop student imagination and speaking skills. It enables shy or introverted children to express through their puppets what they cannot say or do as themselves. It demands attentive listening on the part of the audience since whatever actions occur are limited to the puppets. Last, as students begin to prepare their own scripts, puppetry also offers a meaningful and exciting motivation for writing.

Because young children watch familiar puppets routinely on television shows such as *Sesame Street* or *Between the Lions,* teachers can initiate creative drama successfully through puppetry by presenting several puppets for the children to handle and then showing a puppet play, much like Miss Rizkallah does in Vignette 12.1. Teachers know that students often react to puppets as though they were real animals or people and do not consider puppets as dolls (although they often resemble them). Instead, puppets are "actors" who come to life through the aid of puppeteers and create an engaged and responsive audience. Best of all, children of all ages can create their own.

VIGNETTE 12.1   Folktales and Puppetry

Miss Rizkallah's success with puppetry was more by serendipity than by design. Her kindergarten play area had always been stocked with hand puppets that she had bought herself. There was no budget for them at her school, and her personal budget was limited too, but she assembled a random collection of puppet animals and characters that she found at yard sales and bargain tables.

Realizing that she could easily and inexpensively copy the pricy puppet theater she had noticed in a catalog, and relieved to see that it required only sewing skills, no carpentry, she gathered some simple materials. Miss Rizkallah mounted a spring curtain rod in an inner doorway, sewed a casing into a three-foot length of sturdy, bright blue fabric, and hung it from the rod. In the middle section, she attached tie-back curtains to the top piece. Finally, using right and left side panels the same length as the curtains, she hung another plain length of fabric as a sort of skirt at the bottom. Her young learners played imaginatively there with the various puppets from time to time.

However, the day she found a furry, not-too-scary wolf and one well-padded pig, she knew the puppet theater's scope would expand to make an important connection to literature. Now the children could act out *The Three Little Pigs*, and Miss Rizkallah planned to focus on the textual elements of this one story to introduce or reinforce several reading concepts.

The children had always enjoyed hearing *The Three Little Pigs*, replete with satisfying wolf speech and the excitement of escape. The new puppets allowed her students to experience these features more thoroughly, not to mention the aspects of, for example, cause and effect, as the wolf puppet blew down the hastily constructed, lightweight twig and straw houses. Miss Rizkallah had decided to turn the needed props into a craft project, with the children gluing pieces of straw or tiny broken twigs onto houses they drew, then standing them up by pasting them to a simple, folded tagboard "L." To simulate the brick house, they glued their paper buildings onto cement bricks. In the story's reenactment, by the time the wolf arrived at the diligent pig brother's sturdy brick house and could not huff and puff it down, the students had acquired the vocabulary of *twig*, *straw*, and *brick*, as well as their properties, such as *light*, *flimsy*, and *solid*. Additionally, they had observed the quality of cooperation among the pig brothers, all ideas they were developmentally ready to absorb.

After another reading of *The Three Little Pigs*, Miss Rizkallah and a classroom aide donned the new puppets and modeled a puppet version of the tale, with the one pig puppet taking all the porcine roles. Then, taking turns, pairs of children acted out their interpretation of what they remembered, adhering more and less to the actual plot and taking particular delight in the wolf's HUFF-PUFF dialogue, both of which improved with time and repetition. Not unexpectedly, after adding puppetry, *The Three Little Pigs* became the children's most-requested story, and more important, they clearly had developed expertise in and ownership of the folktale, one of the basic literary genres of our culture.

In the conceptual-symbolic mode of Piaget's preoperational period, occurring from two to seven years of age, egocentric speech becomes intercommunicative, and although not ensuring the development of logical thought, language growth certainly facilitates such thought progression. Miss Rizkallah's kindergartners still find their way to the puppet theater every day for spontaneous, imaginative play, but their activities now include the ordered re-creation of a favorite folktale; she feels pleased to see the literature and the puppetry running parallel to and in support of the conceptual-symbolic component of her students' intellectual development.

In fact, Miss Rizkallah has decided that the worth of adding puppetry to literature supersedes her budgetary restraint, and she is now eagerly acquiring additional animals for a repertoire of "three" stories/poems: *The Three Billy Goats Gruff*, *The Three Bears*, and *The Three Little Kittens*.

Making Puppets

While commercially manufactured puppets are available, students in the elementary grades can make and decorate a wide variety of their own puppets. All that is needed—besides imagination—is a supply of scrap materials together with items such as paper bags, Styrofoam cups, cardboard tubes or cylinders, tongue depressors or popsicle sticks, paper plates, socks, or rectangular boxes. Children can make both hand puppets (said to be the most satisfactory for any age level) and finger puppets, which are the smallest kind of puppets. The latter can be slipped on the fingers and used with larger hand puppets.

Directions for making a few of the more popular puppets are as follows:

- *Paper bag puppet*: Draw a face at the bottom of the bag where it folds flat, being sure that the mouth is in the center of the crease. Next, put your hand into the bag and open and shut the crease so the "mouth" speaks. Decorate with crayons, paint, and yarn.
- *Stick puppet*: Take a piece of cloth (8" to 9" square) and holding the popsicle or tongue depressor erect, drape the cloth over it. Next, push the covered end of the stick into a Styrofoam or ping-pong ball. Decorate with glitter, yarn, and buttons.
- *Sock puppet:* Take an old sock and put your hand inside it. Next, put your thumb in the heel and your fingers in the toe. You now have the lower and upper jaws of a mouth. Decorate by adding eyes and other markings to create a bird, a crocodile, and the like.
- *Paper plate puppet*: Use crayons or paint to draw a face on a 10–inch plate. Decorate to show expression. Then, attach a stick or ruler to the back of the plate as a handle.
- *Cylinder puppet*: Use a cardboard tube from a household item, realizing that the length and diameter of the tube will determine the size of the puppet. Decorate with paint, yarn, and clothing. Manipulate puppet by inserting fingers in the bottom of the tube.
- *Finger puppet*: Cut the "fingers" off an old light-colored or white glove. Draw faces on them. Then slip the glove fingers over your own and you have five little puppets.
- *Cup puppet*: Glue facial features and other decorations on a Styrofoam cup. Then attach a stick or (heavy-duty) straw to the inside as a handle.
- *Cloth puppet*: With adult assistance, sew together two pieces of cloth on all sides except the bottom. Decorate with fabric, yarn, and other materials.

Performing With Puppets

Puppet stages are generally simple in the elementary classroom. Some possibilities are as follows:

- *A large appliance box or packing crate:* Cut out one section in the upper front from which the puppets can be seen. Remove the back so the puppeteers can enter.
- *A rectangular table:* Turn the table on its side. Drape a sheet across the front so only the puppets are displayed.
- *A door:* Drape a sheet across the bottom half and display the puppets in the upper half.
- *A blanket:* Have two children hold it in place (while the puppeteers crouch behind it) and adjust it to suit the height of the players.

Elementary teachers can help beginning puppeteers have successful experiences by following simple rules. First, keep the production short. Second, use only puppets that can be manipulated easily. Third, have each child manipulate only one puppet at a time. Fourth, show students how to hold the puppets and how to portray their basic actions (such as head movements, hand waving, etc.) and what each means. Fifth, have children practice with their voices to express feelings vocally before attempting to perform as puppeteers. Sixth, encourage students to improvise their lines. Finally, limit the number of puppets in a show to three or four, as the best stories for motivating elementary puppeteers have no more than two or three characters on stage at the same time (e.g., the folktale of *The Fisherman and His Wife*, which includes two adults and a flounder).

Story Dramatization: Interpretation

The most popular and readily accessible means for students to "act out" a literary experience, *story dramatization* helps elementary children develop a new dimension in understanding literature.

Boys and girls who are younger or less experienced in creative drama generally want to do stories already familiar to them and only gradually abandon stereotypes and conventions for more original creations. Briefly, this process illustrates the sequence of *interpretation* and *improvisation*. In planning story dramatization with students, the teacher begins with an accurate interpretation of a story. Later as the children mature and become more knowledgeable and comfortable with dramatization, the teacher can proceed to improvisation, which demands going beyond the basic story in an attempt to extend or expand on the thematic material.

Elementary students develop a new understanding of literature through dramatization or improvisation.

Developmental Steps

When the class appears ready for story dramatization, *the teacher tells or reads a well-structured story* that possesses most or all of the following traits:

Brevity—as in one of Kipling's *Just So Stories* (1996)

One setting—as in Slobodkina's *Caps for Sale* (1996)

Natural, interesting characters—as in Brown's *Stone Soup* (2005)

Strong, simple, dramatic conflict—as in Dr. Seuss's *The 500 Hats of Bartholomew Cubbins* (1989)

Simple plot that hinges on action—as in the Grimm Brothers' *The Shoemaker and the Elves* (1979)

Dialogue that furthers the action—as in Blegvad's *The Three Little Pigs* (1982)

Strong climax and a quick, definite ending—as in Zemach's *The Three Wishes: An Old Story* (1986)

Before reading or telling the intended story, the teacher becomes so familiar with it that he or she can reflect on the thoughts, movements, appearances, and feelings of the characters in order to make them real. The teacher attempts to establish one version to which the students can repeatedly return in the dramatization, just as Mrs. Benson does in Vignette 12.2.

VIGNETTE 12.2 Story Interpretation

Mrs. Benson loved every book in the *Little House* series by Laura Ingalls Wilder. She planned to read each one aloud, chapter by chapter, to her children so they, too, could grow up loving the descriptions of pioneer life in America's early days and the little girl named Laura who faced that life with such spirit.

Mrs. Benson didn't have children of her own, yet—but she taught two dozen energetic fourth graders at school. As she considered incorporating story dramatization into her course plans, a chapter from the *Little House* books seemed the perfect choice. She assumed many of the students watched reruns of the popular TV show based on the books and knew the children might approach the stories with preconceived ideas about the familiar characters. Mrs. Benson also wanted the project to interest the boys in her classroom; although she knew they would enjoy the excitement and fun of Laura's adventures, she also knew they might initially balk at reading and dramatizing "stories about girls." For both reasons she selected a chapter from *Farmer Boy* (1994), a book in the series that described the childhood of Laura's husband, Almanzo Wilder. She was sure her nine- and ten-year-old students would enjoy reading the story of nine-year-old Almanzo.

Mrs. Benson assigned selected chapters from several of the other books, as well as many from *Farmer Boy*, to comprise a language arts unit. In addition to reading the excerpts, the students researched the geography, population distribution, and political issues of the United States in the late 19th century as part of their social studies work. Mrs. Benson even included an afternoon of butter churning and dipping candles (two activities detailed in *Farmer Boy*) so the children could better understand the lifestyle of the book's characters.

After two weeks of study, she felt sure the students were ready to experiment with story interpretation. Mrs. Benson selected Chapter 18, "Keeping House," in which the Wilder parents visit relatives and leave Almanzo and his older siblings to take care of the homestead. While their parents are gone, the four children use up all the white sugar making ice cream and cake, bicker with each other over household chores, and feed candy to the pig. At the end of the week, Almanzo argues with his especially bossy sister Eliza Jane and, in his anger, throws a brush full of black stove polish at her head. She ducks, the brush hits the white parlor wallpaper, and Almanzo dreads the punishment he'll receive when his parents return. At the end of the chapter, however, he discovers Eliza Jane has patched and cleaned the stained wallpaper before their parents could notice. When Almanzo asks why, Eliza Jane replies, "You're the only little brother I've got."

Mrs. Benson felt sure the students would easily relate to struggling with brothers and sisters, and she appreciated the chapter's positive portrayal of those relationships among the Wilder children. She also knew the students would like the idea of a week with no parents and would enjoy interpreting the various ways the children got into trouble.

During the reading or telling, the teacher watches for external clues from the children that may indicate their interest and involvement. It is vital that all or most of them like the narrative that will be dramatized. The teacher may be certain that they will enjoy the story if it appeals to their emotions.

The teacher's own viewpoint is also important. She or he can hardly guide children to create successful dialogue and action from literary selections with values or characterizations that the teacher does not personally accept.

Once a story has been heard, *the teacher poses questions to stimulate discussion of sequence, characters, and setting.* The children must be able to bring out in their dramatization the essential elements of the story just heard. So the teacher asks the students carefully framed questions to target the key actions and lines that will move the play along. In some cases, more than one discussion period may be necessary to stimulate thought about the story, plot, and people; it is preferable not to pose more than five specific questions during a single discussion.

After they have successfully analyzed the story, the children determine the characterization and the scenes. Whether the story requires one scene or several, the students will find that the playing proceeds more smoothly if they decide in advance the number of scenes and the characters who appear in each scene and if they plot all of these details on the board.

Characterization being principally a matter of imagination, the teacher should always stress developing a character from within. Girls and boys should try first to understand how the other person thinks and feels before they attempt to act like the person.

As they follow the general outline of the story, *the children create the dialogue and the dramatization.* Due mainly to the discussion periods held earlier, they can generally speak all or nearly all of the key lines. They can also create other phrases to make the play their own and to round out the characterizations. For the first performance, the teacher designates a space within the room as a stage or playing area and chooses five or six confident volunteers. That group is then permitted a brief planning conference away from the rest of the class so that each member will know exactly what to do and say.

Now the play is ready to begin and must move along without interruption because, to the children, this step is the most important of all. The teacher should try to limit performance in the lower grades to 5 minutes and in the intermediate grades to 15 minutes.

As soon as the performance is finished, *the class promptly evaluates the presentation.* Such appraisal under the positive guidance of the teacher is critical training for all age levels, beginning in the second grade. It starts with an acknowledgment of the performance's strengths: What did you see that you liked? Once accustomed to looking for what is good or what they liked, the children can soon reach the second level of discussion: How can we make that scene more real (or more powerful, more exciting)? What shall we change or add the next time we play it?

Throughout the discussion, the students should examine the actions and consider the voices and diction of the actors. They can study the characterizations carefully, using the character names (and not the player names) in order to be more objective in their criticism. They can ask each other such questions as the following:

- Was the play just like the story we heard?
- Were the characters the way we imagined them to be?
- What did we like about the opening scene?
- What did we like best about the performance?
- How could we improve the play the next time we act it out?

Slowly the class can be led through creative drama appraisal to realize that first dramatic efforts may appear to be uneven, but the quality of the story dramatization should slowly improve. Therefore, every sincere effort on the part of each child is acceptable and praiseworthy, and every child has the right to reject or modify proposed changes in the roles attempted.

Finally, *the children reenact the* dramatization, incorporating the constructive criticisms just discussed. Props are still kept simple and at a minimum. Eventually, several casts are drawn up, with every child playing at least one part. Variations in action and dialogue are anticipated (and appreciated) during each performance.

Suggested Stories

Many traditional folktales have proved suitable for story interpretation and can be adapted to various age groups. Found readily in most standard anthologies of children's literature, they include *The Three Billy Goats Gruff*, *Hansel and Gretel*, *Jack and the Beanstalk*, *Little Red Riding Hood*, *Puss in Boots*, *The Gingerbread Boy*, and *The Three Bears*.

Short complete books that invite dramatization by elementary students, some as early as second grade, cover a wide range of fiction and biography and include the following:

Corduroy by Don Freeman (2008)

What's the Big Idea, Ben Franklin? by Jean Fritz (1988)

Hill of Fire by Thomas Lewis (1971)

The Little Engine That Could by Watty Piper (2005)

Ahyoka and the Talking Leaves by Peter and Connie Roop (1992)

The Year of the Panda by Miriam Schlein (1990)

In addition to complete books, single chapters from some series books (such as those about Henry Huggins or Ramona Quimby by Beverly Cleary) can also be dramatized. Certain chapters from books appealing especially to intermediate students and written by Katherine Parerson or Linda Sue Park, for example, have proved popular for story interpretation by older students.

Story Dramatization: Improvisation

Improvisation involves going beyond the basic literary material. Students are compelled to extrapolate and enrich the material by drawing from within themselves. Their thoughts, emotions, and conclusions are based on, but not really found in, the story or biography in question.

For example, as a prelude to beginning improvisation, the teacher tells or reads the familiar myth of King Midas to the class that has been interpreting stories for some time. Then he or she might ask some of the following questions (according to Stewig, 1983):

For material related to this concept, go to Video Clip 12.2 on the Student Resource CD bound into the back of your textbook.

- Why do you feel that the king was so greedy? What might have caused him to be that way?
- Why was his daughter so sweet despite the fact that she had been raised by him alone in the castle, with only her father as an example?
- How did the king react to other people? (Remember that the story did not show him interacting with other people.) How did he treat his servants and the townspeople?
- In what other ways might he have resolved his problem?

Other more general questions could be asked regarding the physical, social, and psychological facets of additional characters in the story.

The teacher must emphasize to the students that there is no one right answer to an inferential question and that all responses are valuable. Children will then be encouraged to offer a variety of opinions and insights before any improvisation session begins.

Only after the students have had enough time to reflect on both the questions and possible answers can they proceed to the final developmental steps previously explored in the earlier section, "Story Dramatization: Interpretation." The *players create the dramatization complete with dialogue and action.* That in turn is followed by an evaluation session and subsequent reenactment of the improvisation.

Shy children or those who are English Language Learners (ELLs) may be reluctant to become involved in improvisation. Teachers must be especially patient with them while still encouraging their participation. One effective means of including ELL students is to have them share folktales from their own culture during improvisational activities related to a study of folktales.

A sample lesson plan incorporating the concepts introduced in this chapter appears on p. 411.

Suggested Stories

For the Primary Grades

Miss Nelson Is Missing by Harry Allard (1985)

Don't Forget the Bacon by Pat Hutchins (1978)

Nothing Ever Happens on My Block by Ellen Raskin (1989)

The Three Little Wolves and the Big Bad Pig by Eugene Trivizas (1993)

The Napping House by Audrey Wood (1984)

For the Intermediate Grades

Strider by Beverly Cleary (1991)

The Case of the Baker Street Irregulars by Robert Newman (1978)

Soup by Robert Newton Peck (1974)

Missing May by Cynthia Rylant (1992)

Maniac Magee by Jerry Spinelli (1990)

Assessment

Appraising the growth of the child in creative drama can be made on an informal and individual basis through observation. It is important to determine to what extent he or she does the following:

- Participates freely and wholeheartedly in imaginative or informal drama
- Finds enjoyment and satisfaction as a member of the audience at informal drama activities
- Controls situations by words rather than by physical force
- Is developing the nonverbal elements of communication such as body language
- Is able to interact comfortably with others
- Can recall a series of episodes in sequence and distinguish between central ideas and supporting details
- Is able to organize stories for dramatic expression
- Has developed physical coordination
- Has improved voice quality and projection
- Has increased in self-confidence and self-direction, whether working alone or before an audience
- Is broadening his or her vocabulary
- Is forming the habit of original, flexible thinking

- Is expanding his or her problem-solving ability
- Has developed respect for the creative activities that she or he has experienced and for the creative efforts of classmates

Working With English Language Learners

Creative drama provides an engaging way for teachers to adapt instruction to meet the needs of English Language Learners. Drama is fun and helps children personally connect to the stories they are reading. Creative drama is a "hands-on" language arts activity, and concrete activities are helpful to ELLs. Visuals, such as props made for use with drama, provide another way to modify instruction for ELL students. Modifications should be tailored to the language needs of each level of English learner.

Beginning ELLs: Pantomime works well with beginning ELLs because children do not have to speak to participate.

Early intermediate and intermediate ELLs: Dramatizing stories is a good way for early intermediate and intermediate ELLs to participate in story retelling because it allows children to respond in short phrases or sentences.

Early advanced and advanced ELLs: As students approach fluency in speaking, reading, and writing English they can participate in creative drama in more sophisticated ways. For example, they can begin to write short improvisational scripts or dramatize teacher-written scripts based on familiar stories.

Practical Instructional Activities and Ideas

- *Engaging in fantasy play*: Very young children can begin to create, perform, and participate in theater by engaging in fantasy play and re-creating situations in familiar settings. Teachers can provide "settings" for such play in the classroom, such as a kitchen area, dress-up area, and puppet theater. A kitchen area can be elaborate, with a child-sized oven, sink, and refrigerator, or simple—containing a box of toy dishes, play food, and plastic utensils. Similarly, a dress-up area can be elaborate or simple. A corner of the classroom can include chairs, bean bags, and a trunk of adult-sized clothing, shoes, and hats. If space is limited, a simple plastic storage box with a lid containing dress-up clothes and shoes can be stored in a closet and brought out during dramatic play. A puppet theater or just a box of hand puppets can serve as another theater center. In all of the spaces mentioned above, children will use their imaginations and creativity to re-create familiar situations and "play pretend," all the while developing oral language and social skills.
- *Acting out group pantomimes*: The teacher can read a story to the whole class and have the children join in by acting out parts of the story in pantomime. This is especially good for kindergartners, who need plenty of movement during the day. An example is *Where the Wild Things Are* by Maurice Sendak (1988). At times during that book, the wild things "roll their terrible eyes," "gnash their terrible teeth," and "show their terrible claws"—easy gestures for four- and five-year-olds to pantomime. That book also calls for roaring, and although pantomime is silent, children would enjoy doing this as well!
- *Retelling familiar stories*: The teacher can read a familiar story to the children and have them retell it with improvisation or without rehearsal. Short, simple stories work best. Here are some examples of familiar stories from specific genres.

- Folktales: *Cinderella, Snow White, The Little Mermaid, The Princess and the Pea*, and *Beauty and the Beast*
- Nursery rhymes: *Jack Sprat, The Old Woman Who Lived in a Shoe*
- Myths: *King Midas, Theseus and the Minotaur*
- Fables: *The Tortoise and the Hare, Once a Mouse*

Teachers can read any of the above-mentioned stories, brainstorm a story element chart together as a whole class, and have children retell the story using the story elements identified.

Story Elements Chart

Characters	Setting	Plot

- *Dramatizing familiar stories:* The teacher can read a familiar story to the class and then have a few children act out the main parts of the story. Short, simple stories with just a few characters work best, such as fairy tales, myths, and fables. Older children can organize their dramatization of the story to include a beginning, middle, and an end.
- *Creating innovations on a story:* The teacher can read a familiar story to the children and ask them to create an alternate ending. This can be done individually or in small groups. Examples of stories that would be ideal for brainstorming alternate endings include *The Three Little Pigs, The Little Red Hen, The Gingerbread Boy, Jack and the Beanstalk*. Students can act out scenes from any of the above-mentioned books.
- *Writing scripts and improvisation*: Schools often have annual shows that include singing, dancing, and short plays. Students can work together to create a short play for such occasions. Parents and other family members enjoy attending these events. In addition, individual classes sometimes present plays for parents or for other groups of students. Small groups of students can work together to create short skits for a class program. For example, a fifth- or sixth-grade class might perform a play for a first-grade class. The topic of the skits could be related to literature or to practical issues, such as safety.
- *Acting out character parts*: Students can dramatize characters within a given story, either through improvisation or by retelling. Personality differences in characters serve as a springboard for this dramatization. For example, characters can be friendly, angry, sorrowful, mean, or frightened. Students learn to recognize emotions in others by watching these brief performances.
- *Improvising characters*: Students can dramatize characters in a literary piece, contrasting very different characters based on their actions and motives. For example, they can play characters who are selfish/giving, generous/greedy, or hard-working/lazy.

- *Creating props and masks*: Students can create simple props and character masks to use during dramatization.
- *Creating a play*: Students can collaborate as actors, directors, script writers, or technical artists to create formal or informal theater performances. This can be done as a whole class or in small groups. Some students can serve as set decorators or costume makers, thus connecting to the visual arts.
- *Putting on cooperative one-act plays*: Students work together in small groups of about four to write and perform one-act plays. The teacher assigns specific tasks to each student, such as researcher, writer, director, materials manager, actor, or set decorator. This assignment of responsibility ensures that students each have something to do and helps them stay focused. The tasks can be tailored to the needs and strengths of the children; for example, some are artistic, and some are outgoing. Creating a safe, low-anxiety environment facilitates children's success.

LESSON PLAN 12.1   Where the Wild Things Are

Language Arts Components: Viewing and Visual Representation

Grade: Kindergarten

Topic: Pantomime and Puppetry

Time Frame: 1 week

Objective

- Students retell a familiar story using puppets and pantomime.

Materials

- *Where the Wild Things Are* by Maurice Sendak
- Scissors
- Glue
- Tempera paint
- Paint brushes
- Sample created by teacher
- Paper plate
- Popsicle stick
- Listening center with taped version of the story and six to eight individual books

Content Standards

English Language Development (ELD): Reading Comprehension

- Students speak in words, phrases, or sentences.

Language Arts: Reading

- Students retell familiar stories.

Visual and Performing Arts: Theater

- Students use props in role-playing.

Vocabulary

- Roar
- Gnash
- Claws
- Wild
- Animals
- Max

Open

Day 1

Whole Class
    Teacher: "Today we will read a story about a boy who visits a faraway place and meets WILD THINGS."
    Teacher does a picture walk and then reads book to the class.
    Teacher explains what the students are to do at each center.

Body

Days 2–4

Small Groups With Teacher
    Teacher reads the story, stopping at points to show children how to pantomime the different characters' actions.

Small Groups at Centers
    Center 1: Students create a character stick puppet. Parent helper or teacher's aide helps children.
    Center 2: Students listen to the story at the listening center.
    Center 3: Students create "I can read" books. They cut out pictures of wild animals out of magazines such as *National Geographic* and paste them onto pages in their book. Parent helper, teacher, or aide can write the names of the animals on the pages for the children.

Close

Day 5

Whole Class

Teacher reads the book to the class again. Students hold their stick puppets up at the correct point in the story. Students roar, speak, and pantomime at the correct point in the story, using gestures and their stick puppets.

Assessment

Teacher observation during body and close of lesson

Integration Across the Curriculum

Science

- Students apply the theatrical concepts of beginning, middle, and end to other content areas, such as science. For example, they act out the life cycle of the butterfly.
- Students use problem-solving and cooperative skills to dramatize a story or a current event from science.

Social Studies

- Students dramatize different cultural versions of similar stories from around the world. For example, the fairy tale *Cinderella* has several versions.
- Students select or create appropriate props, sets, and costumes for a cultural celebration or pageant.
- Students create scripts that reflect particular historical periods or cultures.

Math

- Students dramatize a familiar story that involves mathematics concepts, for example, *The Doorbell Rang* by Pat Hutchins (1989) or *Anno's Counting House* by Mitsumasa Anno (1982).

Literature

- Students use movement and voice to reinforce vocabulary.
- Students dramatize a familiar story that involves a piece of children's literature, such as *If You Give a Cat a Cupcake* by Laura Joffe Numeroff (2008).

Visual and Performing Arts

- Students create props and masks for use in pantomimes, retellings, and improvisations.

Health

- Students dramatize the various body systems they are reading about, such as the circulatory system.
- Students produce a play about the food groups and healthy food choices.

Physical Education

- Students understand the interrelationships between history and culture, including games/sports/play/dance.

Music

- Students dramatize musical selections, for example, arm and hand movements to coordinate with wind, rain, snow, and sun for *The Four Seasons* by Vivaldi.

Parents as Partners

- *Sock puppets at home:* It's easy to extend creative drama into the home by providing directions to make sock puppets at home. Parents just need a few old socks, white glue, and decorations, such as wiggly eyes, pom-poms, and feathers. Teachers can also have the children make the puppets at school and then send the puppets home with a suggested activities sheet. Parents can donate old, clean socks for the project. Another idea is to send home an assortment of decorations and a directions sheet. Children can improvise characters and engage in dialogues with friends and family members. They can even portray two characters at a time, with one puppet on each hand! When parents join in the fun, the experience is even more enjoyable and promotes more learning.
- *Dramatic reading:* Parents can add a twist to reading at home with their children by choosing a story that has several characters to act out. A good example is the Paddington series by Michael Bond. These beloved children's books have several main characters, such as Paddington Bear, Mr. and Mrs. Brown, daughter Judy, and son Jonathan, as well as many other minor characters, such as taxi cab driver, nanny, and store manager. Parents and children take turns reading their parts of the story, using appropriate voices. Children can read the parts of animals or children, and parents can read the parts of adults and the narrator. It's important to choose stories that are appropriate to the child's reading level and keep in mind that humorous stories help engage children. Paddington gets into many difficult and funny situations, such as inadvertently getting covered in tea and marmalade during teatime. Paddington is a bear who speaks, carries a suitcase, and wears clothes, and once again, this element of charm and fancy draws children into the stories.
- *Oral storytelling interviews:* Children can interview their parents or grandparents at home and ask about their culture's oral traditions. For example, oral storytelling is a tradition that is prevalent in many cultures and has been handed down for generations. Children can also interview a parent or grandparent to ask them to tell a story from long ago, when they were the child's age. It is fun to hear adventures one's parents had. Sometimes stories about immigrating to this country will be told. Teachers can provide students a questionnaire sheet to fill out during the interview.

Student Study Site

The Companion Web site for *Language Arts: Integrating Skills for Classroom Teaching* www.sagepub.com/donoghuestudy

Visit the Web-based study site to enhance your understanding of the chapter content. The study materials include chapter summaries, practice tests, flashcards, and Web resources.

Additional Professional Readings

Akcan, S. (2005). Puppet theater time in a first grade French-immersion class. *Young Children, 60* (2), 38–41.

Booth, D. (1998). *Story drama.* York, ME: Stenhouse.

Brown, V., & Pleydell, S. (1999). *The dramatic difference: Drama in the preschool and kindergarten classroom.* Portsmouth, NH: Heinemann.

Creech N., & Bhavnagri, N. (2002). Teaching elements of story through drama to 1st graders: Child development frameworks. *The Reading Teacher, 78,* 219–224.

Engler, L., & Fijon, C. (1996). *Making puppets come alive.* Mineola, NY: Dover.

Heller, P. (1996). *Drama as a way of knowing.* Portland, ME: Stenhouse.

Kornfield, J., & Leyden, G. (2005). Acting out: Literature, drama, and connecting with history. *The Reading Teacher, 59,* 230–238.

Peck, S., & Virkler, A. (2006). Reading in the shadows: Extending literacy skills through shadow-puppet theater. *The Reading Teacher, 59,* 774–785.

Podlozny, A. (2000). Strengthening verbal skills through the use of classroom drama: A clear link. *Journal of Aesthetic Education, 34,* 239–275.

Schneider, J., Crumpler, T., & Rogers, T. (2006). *Process drama and multiple literacies: Addressing social, cultural, and ethical issues.* Portsmouth, NH: Heinemann.

Children's Literature Cited in the Text

Allard, H. (1985). *Miss Nelson is missing.* New York: Houghton.

Anno, M. (1982). *Anno's counting house.* New York: Philomel.

Blegvad, E. (1982). *The three little pigs.* New York: Macmillan.

Brown, M. (1960). *Stone soup.* New York: Macmillan.

Brown, M. (1993). *Arthur's new puppy.* New York: Little, Brown.

Chinn, K. (1995). *Sam and the lucky money.* New York: Lee & Low.

Cleary, B. (1991). *Strider.* New York: Morrow.

Freeman, D. (2008). *Corduroy.* New York: Viking Press.

Fritz, J. (1988). *What's the big idea, Ben Franklin?* New York: Coward.

Fritz, J. (1996). *And then what happened, Paul Revere?* New York: Putnam.

Gardiner, J. (1980). *Stone fox.* New York: HarperCollins.

Grimm, Brothers. (1979). *The shoemaker and the elves.* New York: Price Stern Sloan.

Hutchins, P. (1978). *Don't forget the bacon!* New York: Farrar, Straus & Giroux.

Hutchins, P. (1989). *The doorbell rang.* New York: Harper Trophy.

Keats, E. (1963). *The snowy day.* New York: Viking Press.

Kipling, R. (1996). *Just so stories.* New York: Morrow.

Lewis, T. (1971). *Hill of fire.* New York: HarperCollins.

MacLachlan, P. (1985). *Sarah, plain and tall.* New York: HarperCollins.

Munsch, R. (1980). *The paper bag princess.* Toronto: Annick Press.

Naylor, P. (1991). *Shiloh.* New York: Macmillan.

Newman, R. (1978). *The case of the Baker Street Irregulars.* New York: Atheneum.

Numeroff, L. J. (2008). *If you give a pig a party.* New York: Laura Geringer.

Paulsen, G. (1987). *Hatchet.* New York: Simon and Schuster.

Peck, R. (1974). *Soup.* New York: Knopf.

Piper, W. (2005). *The little engine that could.* New York: Penguin.

Raskin, E. (1989). *Nothing ever happens on my block.* New York: Aladdin.

Roop, P., & Roop, C. (1992). *Ahyoka and the talking leaves.* New York: Lathrop, Lee.

Rylant, C. (1992). *Missing May.* New York: Orchard.

Schlein, M. (1990) *The year of the panda.* New York: HarperCollins.

Sendak, M. (1988). *Where the wild things are.* New York: Harper Trophy.

Seuss, Dr. (1989). *The 500 hats of Bartholomew Cubbins.* New York: Random House.

Slobodkina, E. (1996). *Caps for sale.* New York: HarperCollins.

Spinelli, J. (1990). *Maniac Magee.* Little, Brown.

Trivizas, E. (1993). *The three little wolves and the big bad pig.* New York: Scholastic.

Wilder, L. A. (1994). *Farmer boy.* New York: Harper Trophy.

Williams, V. (1984). *A chair for my mother.* New York: Greenwillow.

Wood, A. (1984). *The napping house.* San Diego: Harcourt.

Yashima, T. (1976). *Crow boy.* New York: Viking Press.

Zemach, M. (1986). *The three wishes: An old story.* New York: Farrar, Straus & Giroux.

References

Children's Theater Association of America. (1981). *Children's Theatre Review, 30*(2), 2.

Gardner, H. (1999). *Intelligence reframed.* New York: Basic Books.

Hennings, D. (2002). *Communication in action* (8th ed.). Boston: Houghton Mifflin.

McCaslin, N. (2006). *Creative drama in the classroom and beyond* (8th ed.). Boston: Allyn & Bacon.

Piaget, J. (1962). *Play, dreams, and initiation into childhood.* New York: Norton.

Stewig, J. W. (1983). *Informal drama in the elementary language arts program.* New York: Teachers College Press.

Stewig, J. W., & Buege, C. (1994). *Dramatizing literature in the whole language classroom*. New York: Teachers College Press.

Vygotsky, I. S. (1986). *Thought and language*. Cambridge: MIT Press.

Wagner, B. I. (2003). Imaginative expression. In J. Flood, D. Lapp, R. Squire, & J. M. Jensen (Eds.), *Handbook of research on teaching the English language arts* (3rd ed.). Mahwah NJ: Erlbaum.

Anticipation Statement Answers

1. Agree

2. Agree

3. Agree

4. Agree

5. Agree

6. Disagree

7. Agree

8. Agree

9. Disagree: Depending on the special needs of individual children, drama can be an excellent teaching tool. However, drama may not be appropriate to every kind of special need.

10. Agree: Drama promotes feelings of inclusion among ELL students. However, some forms, such as story improvisation, present additional obstacles to them.

Appendix

Technology Connections for the Language Arts

Part I. Foundations of the Language Arts

Chapter 1. Language and the English Language Arts

California State Department of Education

http://www.cde.ca.gov/be/st

Information regarding standards and frameworks designed to encourage the highest achievement of every student by defining the knowledge, concepts, and skills that students should acquire at each grade level.

Center for Applied Linguistics (CAL)

http://www.cal.org/index.html

CAL was the first organization of its kind to focus on the identification of qualified personnel for language-focused professions, professional development for language teachers, and the development of linguistically sound materials for English as a second language and foreign language instruction. Site includes research, resources, and professional development.

FunBrain.com

http://www.funbrain.com/teachers/index.html

Site is full of games and activities for K–8 language arts students and teachers.

Language and Cognition

http://www.sparknotes.com/psychology/psych101/languageandcognition/section1.html

Site provides a study guide for the structure of language and cognition.

The Origins of Language and Thought in Early Childhood

http://www.massey.ac.nz/~alock/hbook/george.htm

Site discusses Piaget and Vygotsky.

ReadWriteThink

http://www.readwritethink.org/literacy/index.html

NCTE and IRA are working together to provide educators and students with access to the highest-quality practices and resources in reading and language arts instruction through free, Internet-based content.

Chapter 2. Children as Language Learners and Thinkers

Bilingual Research Journal

http://brj.asu.edu/

Site offers current research, abstracts, and book reviews.

English Language Learning

http://www.colorincolorado.org/educators/reachingout/welcoming

A bilingual site for families and educators of English Language Learners.

Language Acquisition

http://en.wikipedia.org/wiki/Language_acquisition

Site discusses language acquisition, the process by which the language capability develops in a human.

Literacy Needs of Emergent and Early Readers

http://www.ncrel.org/sdrs/areas/issues/content/cntareas/reading/li100.htm

Site offers research and strategies to address the literacy needs of emergent and early readers.

Second-Language Acquisition

http://en.wikipedia.org/wiki/Second_language_acquisition

Site discusses second-language acquisition, the process by which people learn languages in addition to their native language(s).

Second-Language Acquisition

http://www.sk.com.br/sk-krash.html

Site discusses Stephen Krashen's theory of second-language acquisition.

Chapter 3. Formal and Authentic Assessment

Assessment Web Sites in Education

http://www.csulb.edu/divisions/students2/CSULB_Student_Assessment_Findings/Assessment_Websites_in_Education/index.htm

Site sponsored by California State University, Long Beach, offers links to assessment-related professional articles, research, and tools including many government resources (CDE, U.S. Department of Education).

Dr. Helen Barrett on Electronic Portfolio Development

http://newali.apple.com/ali_sites/ali/exhibits/1000156/

Site from the University of Alaska features an education expert explaining the benefits of creating a portfolio for assessment, as well as tips on using portfolios in the classroom.

Phonemic Awareness Assessment Tools

http://teams.lacoe.edu/documentation/classrooms/patti/k-1/teacher/assessment/tools/tools.html

Site provides teachers with phonemic awareness assessments, such as rhyming and sound isolation. Includes links to obtain forms for Yopp-Singer Test of Phonemic Segmentation and also QuickTime movies showing how to correctly administer phonemic awareness tests.

Rubistar

http://rubistar.4teachers.org/index.php

Free site allows teachers to create their own rubrics or select from a variety of templates. Additional features include ideas for projects across the curriculum and an interactive rubric tool.

Rubrics 4 Teachers

http://www.rubrics4teachers.com

This site contains a large selection of rubrics. In addition to weekly featured rubrics, teachers can select from many archived rubrics on topics from podcasting to science experiments.

ThinkWave

http://www.thinkwave.com/index.asp

Teachers can download free grade book software to create reports, maintain attendance records, and record grades. However, to receive the full capabilities of this software and online service, teachers must purchase product for a fee and/or a subscription.

Chapter 4. Integrating Language Arts Across the Curriculum

Art Education Links

http://www.princetonol.com/groups/iad/lessons/middle/arted.htm

Site offers a plethora of ideas, lesson plans, rubrics, and links to integrate dance, theatre, music, and the visual arts into a comprehensive curriculum.

Kiddyhouse

http://www.kiddyhouse.com

Information and activities on thematic units for teachers ranging from clip art to literature-based lesson plans for the early primary grades. A variety of resource links is also available, and there are separate pages for children and parents.

The Literacy Web

http://www.literacy.uconn.edu/index.htm

Sponsored by the University of Connecticut, this site contains ideas and links for integrating literacy, including multicultural literature, throughout the curriculum such as technology and thematic units by grade level. Site also provides information on current research, articles, books, and professional development resources relating to literacy.

NSTA Outstanding Science Trade Books for Students K–12

http://www.nsta.org/publications/ostb/

Lists and summaries of quality science trade books that can assist teachers in connecting the language arts and science in areas of life science, environment, health, earth, and physical sciences. Books also include biographies of notable scientists.

Outreach World

http://www.outreachworld.org/index.asp

A comprehensive site for locating resources to integrate social studies concepts and global thinking with the language arts and other subject areas. Teachers can access educational materials, lesson plans, articles, and recommended books by searching the site according to grade level, disciplines, and geographic location.

PBS Teachers

http://www.pbs.org/teachers/

Web site provides standards-based lesson plans and resources according to subject matter and grade level. The site also offers an early childhood themed archive covering topics in math, visual and performing arts, science, and health.

Part II. Reading as a Language Art

Chapter 5. Word Recognition Skills and Vocabulary Development

Education Place

http://www.eduplace.com/activity/

Houghton Mifflin presents this Web site full of creative activities in content areas ranging from citizenship to ecosystems.

Game Goo

http://www.earobics.com/gamegoo/gooey.html

Phonics games for children that develop concepts such as the alphabetic principle, letter–sound correspondence, rhyme, sentence, and word order. Games are organized by ability level, and the site provides corresponding standards.

Get Ready to Read

http://www.getreadytoread.org/frontpage/Itemid,1/

A program of the National Center for Learning Disabilities, this site seeks to provide educators and parents with tools to promote early childhood literacy. Screening tools, games, and activity cards are available in both English and Spanish.

Reading Rockets

http://www.readingrockets.org/

Funded by a grant by the U.S. Department of Education, this Web site provides multimedia information for teachers, parents, and others who want to help children succeed in reading. It has many articles, suggestions, and book recommendations to assist beginning and struggling readers.

Sadlier Oxford

http://www.sadlier-oxford.com/index.cfm
Site has many vocabulary, phonics, and word study activities for emergent and early readers, as well as Learning Links for a range of ability levels and interests.

Starfall

http://www.starfall.com
Targeted for first-grade students, this site engages all beginning readers with its progressive levels moving from alphabet letters and sounds to simple text that they can read alone or with the help of audio. The site also teaches reading strategies such as "chunking" and the "silent e."

Chapter 6. Reading: Principles, Approaches, Comprehension, and Fluency

Center for Creative Learning

www.creativelearning.com
Nonprofit organization promotes critical thinking skills in children.

Developing Reading Fluency

http://www.auburn.edu/rdggenie/fluency.html
Site offers the definition and approaches to teaching reading fluency.

Dynamic Indicators of Basic Early Literacy Skills

http://dibels.uoregon.edu/measures/orf.php
Site includes data systems, testing materials, and resources to measure reading fluency.

Reading Comprehension

http://www.readingquest.org/strat/
Site offers strategies to improve comprehension. Some strategies are accompanied by hand-outs or blackline masters.

Reading Fluency

http://www.nifl.gov/partnershipforreading/publications/reading_first1fluency.html
Site provides the definition, research, and questions concerning reading fluency.

Reading Workshop

www.manatee.k12.fl.us/sites/elementary/samoset/resources/rcompindex.htm
Site offers strategies to improve reading comprehension, along with online tutorials, a kids' reading lab, and reading comprehension practice sheets.

Chapter 7. Reading and Children's Literature

ALA Great Websites for Kids

http://www.ala.org/gwstemplate.cfm?section=greatwebsites&template=/cfapps/gws/default.cfm
Web site sponsored by the American Library Association and screened especially for children. The literature section connects students to reputable authors' Web sites and award-winning books.

Children's Book Press

http://www.childrensbookpress.org
This nonprofit publishing company site provides links to authors' Web sites, teaching guides, and lessons to accompany the multicultural literature it publishes.

Colorín Colorado

http://www.colorincolorado.org
Web site focuses on assisting educators and Spanish-speaking families in locating reading resources. A small amount of information and materials is available in other languages.

Moonlit Road

http://www.themoonlitroad.com/welcome001.html
Web site for older students that features ghost stories and folktales from the American South. Some stories have audio.

Multicultural Children's Literature

http://www.lib.msu.edu/corby/education/multicultural.htm#web
Page provides links to Web sites and journal articles that deal specifically with the use and selection of children's literature in the classroom. Book resources are also listed.

Part III. Writing as a Language Art

Chapter 8. Writing: Process, Genres, and Motivational Strategies

Cheryl Sigmon's Web Site

http://www.cherylsigmon.com/handouts.asp
Web site provides handouts (graphic organizers, templates) to assist children in organizing writing and analyzing features of text and elements of fiction. Free downloads in PDF file form.

Expository Writing @ Web English Teacher

http://www.webenglishteacher.com/expwriting.html
Site links to lesson plans to teach and practice expository writing skills.

Make Beliefs Comix!

http://www.makebeliefscomix.com
Students can create comic strips with characters and dialogue online.

Narrative Web Sites

http://www.kent.k12.wa.us/curriculum/writing/sec_writing/Bib/Narrative.htm
Web page provides links to narrative writing lessons, prewriting activities, and story-starting writing prompts.

Sincerely Yours Pen Pals

http://www.sincerelyyourspenpals.com

Web site that allows teachers to set up "buddy" classroom pen pals using traditional "snail mail" to promote safety and give students the excitement of receiving a real letter. Additionally, it is a worldwide effort, and not all children have access to computer-based mail.

Writing With Writers Jack Prelutsky

http://teacher.scholastic.com/writewit/poetry/jack_home.htm

This page from Scholastic.com takes students through the steps to write and publish their own silly poems. The site also contains lesson plans and activities on a wide variety of literary genres and topics including descriptive writing and brainstorming.

Chapter 9. Writing Tools: Handwriting, Keyboarding, Spelling, and Grammar

Amazing Incredible Handwriting Worksheet Maker

http://www.handwritingworksheets.com

Site allows teachers and parents to create custom handwriting worksheets.

BrainPop

http://www.brainpop.com

Web site with colorful graphics and movies starring Tim and Moby who educate and entertain children about English topics such as grammar and punctuation. The site also covers the other main subject areas of social studies, art, science, health, math, and technology. For younger children, there is BrainPop Jr. Although many of the movies and activities can be viewed for free, a subscription is required to obtain full access.

FunBrain: Spelling

http://www.funbrain.com/spell/index.html

Site with free educational games, including Spell Check, a game that gives children correctly spelled and misspelled words to check. Grammar games such as Grammar Gorilla help children identify parts of speech in an engaging and interactive way.

Handwriting for Kids

http://www.handwritingforkids.com/handwrite/index.htm

Site with printable manuscript and cursive tracing guides, customized "My name is" sheets, various sizes of handwriting paper, and sheets for tracing commonly used words.

Stufun

http://www.stufun.com

Stufun = students + fun. Site for children that has grammar exercises, online picture dictionary, and more.

SuperKids Spelling Builder – Hangman

http://www.superkids.com/aweb/tools/words/hangman/
Site offers a wide selection of hangman puzzles in many subject areas to improve students' spelling.

Chapter 10. The Writers' Workshop

Kathy Schrock's Guide for Educators

http://school.discoveryeducation.com/schrockguide/
Web site contains categorized lists to locate lesson plans and teacher tools. It has many links to literature and ELA Web sites that include ideas and activities for developing writing techniques.

Making Books With Children

http://www.makingbooks.com
Web site provides ideas for creative formats to showcase student writing and art in book form.

The Story Kitchen

http://www.brucevanpatter.com/storykitchen.html
Site generates creative prompts and encourages children to write their own endings to engaging stories.

Stone Soup

http://www.stonesoup.com/main2/printmagazines.html
Web page from children's magazine, which publishes creative works written exclusively by children, lists alternate print sources for young authors to submit work for publication.

Teaching Ideas: Creative Writing

http://www.teachingideas.co.uk/english/creative.htm
Site offers creative prompts for young writers and their teachers.

WritingFix

http://writingfix.com/writingfix_for_kids.htm
Site offers writing and spelling games for students.

Young Writers' Workshop

http://www.meddybemps.com/9.700.html
Site offers free workshop starters for young writers and an online writing contest for kindergarten and primary students.

Part IV. Oral Language Arts

Chapter 11. Listening and Speaking

BookPALS Storyline Online

http://www.storylineonline.net
The Screen Actors Guild Foundation presents actors reading, via video streaming, quality children's books.

Kids' Storytelling Club

http://www.storycraft.com/files/welcome.htm
Site offers storytelling tips and activities for teachers and students.

Listening Games and Activities

http://www.articlesforeducators.com/dir/language_arts/listening_skills/listening_games.asp
Site offers games to improve listening skills.

Readers Theater Scripts and Plays

http://www.teachingheart.net/readerstheater.htm
Site offers quick and easy readers theater scripts for educators.

Scripts for Schools

http://scriptsforschools.com
Site offers a selection of readers theater scripts for elementary through high school students.

Top English Teaching–Listening Activities

http://www.topenglishteaching.com/directory/activities/listening/listening.htm
Site offers more activities for young listeners.

Chapter 12. Creative Drama

Creative Drama & Theatre Education Resource Site

http://www.creativedrama.com
This Web site provides information on the definition of creative drama, resources, classroom ideas, theater games, and book list.

The EFL Playhouse

http://www.esl4kids.net/fingerplays.html
Web site offers a selection of finger plays and action rhyme activities to promote active engagement through movement and oral language with young children and English Language Learners.

The Kennedy Center ArtsEdge

http://artsedge.kennedy-center.org
A useful Web site with links for arts lesson plans, standards, and articles. Teachers can narrow search parameters by dance, music, theater, or visual arts and also search by other subjects linked to lessons, such as language arts, math, physical education, and technology.

Kids 4 Broadway

http://www.pacificsites.net/~kidsplay/free.htm
Site provides theater games and activities for kids.

The Puppetry Home Page

http://www.sagecraft.com/puppetry/
Web site with links and information on puppetry: definitions, traditions around the world, puppet making, festivals, and museums.

Telling Stories: ESL Strategies Drama Page

http://www.prel.org/eslstrategies/drama.html#

Web site gives strategies and video samples to retell or re-create a folktale through a series of dramatization activities such as pantomime, tableau, and narration. The lessons can be modified to accommodate different ability and grade levels.

Glossary

Alphabetic principle: The understanding that there is generally a predictable relationship between the sounds of spoken language (or phonemes) and the letters and spellings that represent those sounds in written language (or graphemes).

Analytic phonics: The whole-to-part-to-whole approach to teaching phonics that begins with whole words.

Anecdotal record: A description or reporting of observed behavioral incidents, useful for authentic assessment.

Appreciative listening: Listening whose purpose is enjoyment.

Attentive listening: Listening that requires that the attention of the listener be focused on one person or one electronic medium.

Authentic assessment: The direct examination of student performance on useful intellectual tasks.

Balanced approach: A reading program that combines skills development with literature and language arts activities. It is a balance between the skills-based approach and the literature-based approach.

Basal reader approach: A reading program that consists of a collection of graded texts for children in grades K–8, student workbooks, teachers manuals, and ancillary materials. Also known as the skills-based approach since it prescribes the acquisition of competencies in a systematic order.

Bibliotherapy: The use of books to help students cope better with adjustment issues and emotional problems.

Bloom's taxonomy (in the cognitive domain): A classification system that is considered the cornerstone in the description of questions used in the classroom. There are six levels that require increasingly more difficult questions.

Brainstorming: A meaningful process used in discussion groups wherein all students have the opportunity to contribute without inhibition.

Characterization: The personalities (animal or human) portrayed in children's books that must be convincing and lifelike.

Checklist: List of specific behaviors or skills to be marked off as a student performs them; useful for authentic assessment.

Children's literature: Collection of quality trade books read to and by children and covering topics of interest and relevance to boys and girls; both fiction and nonfiction.

Choral speaking: A technique of group recitation or reading of poetry or poetic prose without music and under the direction of a leader or teacher.

Closed syllables: Syllables that end in consonants with the vowels typically representing short sounds.

Compound words: Words made up of two (or sometimes three) words that have been joined together to form a new word (e.g., *snowman*).

Consonant blend: Two or more adjacent consonant sounds that are combined although each retains its separate identity (e.g., *twig*).

Consonant digraph: Two adjacent consonant letters that are combined into a single speech sound (e.g., *ship*).

Contextual analysis: Using the surrounding linguistic environment to determine the meaning of an unknown word.

Creative drama: Spontaneous drama generated under the direction of the teacher and typically organized around literature.

Criterion-referenced tests: Standardized tests whose goal is for all students to demonstrate mastery of specific skills and information taught according to district and state standards.

Critical listening: The most complex kind of listening and one that students use to evaluate information.

Cursive writing: Connected writing in which students slant their writing and slide their pens or pencils laterally to join the cursive letters. Written with slanted strokes, connecting strokes, and ovals.

Decodable books: Texts that are written with a high percentage of words that use letter–sound relationships that the students already know.

Diphthong: Two vowel sounds combined, beginning with the first and gliding smoothly into the second (e.g., *oy* as in *toy*).

Diversity: Differences in the elementary classroom that receive recognition: academic, cultural, and linguistic.

Drafting: Second stage of writing process, which consists of putting ideas on paper as clearly and quickly as possible without regard to the mechanics of English.

Dramatic play: Spontaneous play by children in preschool or kindergarten that is unplanned by the teacher, unstructured, and therefore not creative drama.

Editing: Fourth stage of the writing process, which focuses on improving the mechanical aspects of a piece, such as punctuation, capitalization, and spelling.

Emergent literacy: Skills acquired in early childhood that help children benefit the most from formal reading instruction on school entry.

Emergent writing: Behaviors prior to conventional writing and observable in young children, such as scribbling, drawing, letter strings, and invented spelling.

Expansion: Corrective feedback that restates (partly or wholly) the student's incomplete statement and thereby makes it a logical and complete thought.

Expository writing: Informational or nonfiction writing that meets a practical need.

Fluency: An essential component of reading instruction, it is the ability to read with accuracy and speed in contrast to word-by-word reading.

Focus lessons: Direct instruction during a writers' workshop that usually opens each session and consists of minilessons that provide children with information about writing.

Folktales: Type of traditional literature that begins quickly with a problem, continues with simple characters and a fast-paced plot, and ends with a satisfying solution.

Formal or traditional assessment: A collection of data using standardized tests or procedures under controlled conditions.

Format: The total look of a book, which should be responsive both to its content and its purpose.

Grammar: A set of abstract rules of communication and the underlying structure of language that humans use intuitively, once defined as the "rationale of language."

Graphemes: The sounds of language represented by visual symbols.

Graphic organizers: Visuals that assist students to organize concepts and ideas, thereby helping in the development of knowledge of text structure.

Guided reading: An instructional strategy that is teacher-directed for a specific purpose and involves children reading the same text at about the same level of difficulty and doing so in small homogeneous groups.

Haiku: Unrhymed lyric poetry with three lines and 17 syllables.

Hand dominance: Also called handedness; consistent or dominant preference for using either the left or the right hand. Generally established by the time the student starts school.

Handwriting: Production of symbols that, when placed together, represent words; primarily a tool of communication.

High-stakes testing: Using standardized tests to determine whether schools have met local, state, or federal standards; failure to do so may result in sanctions against teachers, schools, or school districts.

Improvisation: Creative drama in which students go beyond the basic literary material and enrich it by drawing from within themselves.

Integrated unit: A thematic unit that integrates the language arts but includes most or all of the curricular areas centered about a unifying theme (e.g., The Ocean).

Integration of language arts: Teaching listening, speaking, writing, reading, viewing, and visual representation while teaching in the content areas.

Interviewing: A special type of discussion that demands a question-and-answer format.

Intonation: Pitch or highness or lowness of the voice; it is an aspect of English phonology.

Invented spelling: Also known as temporary spelling; occurs when children attempt to spell words they do not know how to spell conventionally and so use phonemic cues.

Juncture: Pauses or interruptions or suspensions in the flow of sound.

Keyboarding: Typing on the computer.

Language arts: That part of the elementary school curriculum that concerns reading, writing, speaking, listening, viewing, and visual representation.

Language experience approach: A reading program that emphasizes the teaching of the language arts and is founded on the theory that reading and comprehending written language are extensions of listening to and understanding spoken language.

Learning log: Record of or reaction to what students are learning in content areas, which may include diagrams, directions for experiments, notes, observations, and vocabulary.

Leveled books: Books that an educator has examined and then determined how difficult it would be for children to read those books based on features such as font size, number of pages, number of illustrations, text structure, and complexity of vocabulary.

Listening: The act of receiving speech, attending to the important information in the speech, and understanding the message; considered one of the six language arts components.

Literary craft lessons: The majority of focus lessons given during writers' workshop sessions and that concern improvement of the content of student writing.

Literature circles: An approach to reading instruction in which small groups of students all read the same book and respond to it, with the teacher's help.

Literature-based approach: A reading program that instructs children to read by using both fiction and nonfiction literature written for purposes other than text use for teaching language arts.

Literature-based unit: A thematic unit that integrates the language arts during the study of one author or one literary genre.

Manuscript writing: A form of handwriting taught and used in the elementary school, it is more commonly called printing. Written with only circles and straight lines.

Marginal listening: Listening whose purpose is to distinguish sounds. The most frequent type of listening.

Metacognition: Conscious knowledge that individuals have about how they learn. It occurs before, during, and after each language art.

Mnemonics: A memory strategy designed to aid recall of a word or word part.

Morpheme: The smallest unit of meaning of a language that cannot be broken down into any smaller part. It is not necessarily identical with words or syllables.

Morphology: The forms or structure of a language.

Multiple intelligences: The broad category of intelligence includes (according to Howard Gardner, 1999) linguistic, musical, logical-mathematical, spatial, bodily-kinesthetic, intrapersonal, interpersonal, naturalist, and existential intelligence.

Narrative: A real or make-believe story expressed orally or in writing.

Norm-referenced tests: Tests that compare the accomplishments of one grade-level classroom to all of the same grade-level classrooms in the district, state, or nation to determine if that school curriculum reflects the goals of what students should know at a specific grade level.

Open syllables: Syllables that end in vowel sounds that are usually long.

Pantomime: Acting without words; useful in beginning creative drama.

Persuasive writing: Writing presents desire, want, or belief and then provides reasons why that desire or want should be fulfilled or that belief is acceptable.

Phoneme: The smallest, distinctive speech sound.

Phonemic awareness: The ability to orally segment and manipulate phonemes (speech sounds) within words.

Phonic analysis: The relationships between letters or graphemes and sounds or phonemes and of approaches for teaching those relationships. It is popularly known as phonics.

Phonological awareness: An umbrella term that includes not only phonemic awareness but also an awareness of the words, rhymes, syllables, and sounds in language together with the ability to blend individual phonemes into meaningful spoken words.

Phonology: The sounds of language that are called phonemes and are represented by symbols called graphemes.

Plot: The action in a story or what happens at the beginning, middle, and end.

Point of view: The feelings, background, and values of the teller of a story.

Portfolio: Selected collection of student work arranged chronologically and useful for evaluating student progress.

Pragmatics: The study of language choices that people make in social settings and the effects that such choices have on others.

Prewriting: Initial stage and main ingredient of the writing process, it includes reading, brainstorming, and searching the Internet.

Print-rich environment: Surroundings, including classroom, that have numerous materials of varying difficulties that promote basic concepts and affect both written and spoken language development.

Publishing: Final stage of the writing process, which involves sharing written work with an appropriate audience. Also known as publication.

Readers theater: An oral reading and dramatic interpretation of a prepared script, based on a literary work.

Revising: Third stage of the writing process, which concerns changing the content of the written piece.

Rime: The vowel and the following consonants in a syllable (e.g., *ake* in *cake*).

Role-playing: Spontaneous drama that involves children assuming the role of characters in a conflict or disagreement and acting out the plot to find a resolution to the situation. Supervised by the teacher but not structured and therefore not creative drama.

Rubric: Explicit grading criteria of student performance in different content areas and at different levels of proficiency, useful for authentic assessment.

Semantics: The study of word meanings, which is the most important aspect of language.

Setting: The time and place of the action in a story.

Share time: The final component of the writers' workshop session during which students volunteer to share their work with the whole class.

Shared reading: An instructional strategy involving a teacher reading aloud to students while they follow along in the text. Often a big book (an enlarged version of a picture book) is used so the students can see the print easily.

Sight words: Words that are instantly recognized on seeing them either in isolation or in context.

Speaking: The act of communicating through talking, considered one of the six language arts components.

Spelling: A writing tool that makes writing easier to read correctly. Focuses on correct letter selection and sequencing.

Standards: Exact definitions of what students should demonstrate or know. Includes content standards (knowledge to be taught in various subjects) and performance standards (demonstration by students of their mastery of specific subjects).

Story improvisation: Dramatization of a piece of children's literature that extends or expands the thematic material and is planned by the teacher and students.

Story interpretation: Accurate dramatization of a piece of children's literature, as planned by the teacher and students.

Stress: Amount of vocal emphasis given to a syllable or word; an aspect of English phonology.

Structural analysis: A word recognition skill that uses word parts to determine the meaning and pronunciation of unfamiliar words.

Study skills: Skills that enable children to find and interpret information from many sources and to synthesize it into the resolution of a question or the solution of a problem.

Style: The manner in which the author has selected and arranged words in presenting a story.

Syntax: Word order of a language and how words or groups of words are arranged to convey meaning.

Synthetic phonics: The part-to-whole approach to teaching phonics that starts with letter sounds.

Theme: An underlying idea that provides a dimension of the story beyond the action of the plot.

Usage: The conventions of language appropriate in particular circumstances, once defined as the "etiquette of language."

Viewing: The receptive language art that is a communication process allowing students to receive information from a broad variety of visual materials and to learn to interpret and evaluate them.

Visual representation: The productive language art that allows students to convey information or express themselves to others through such means as artwork, photography, or physical performance.

Visualization: Creation of a mental picture.

Vowel digraph: Two adjacent vowel letters that are combined into a single speech sound (e.g., *each*).

Wordless book: A picture with no text that relies strictly on illustrations.

Writers' workshop: An instructional approach to writing that is based on the stages of the writing process and stresses self-selection of topics, independent work time, conferencing, and sharing of products. It is sometimes called writing workshop or writer's workshop.

Writing genres: Classifications of writing based on form, technique, or content.

Writing process: Method of writing that includes five stages, beginning with prewriting and concluding with publication.

Index

About the Author

Mildred R. Donoghue (EdD, UCLA; and JD, Western State University, College of Law, Fullerton) is a Professor of Education and Reading at California State University, Fullerton. She teaches courses in the elementary credential program and in the graduate program in elementary curriculum and instruction (emphasis: early childhood education). She is a member of Alpha Upsilon Alpha (Honor Society of the International Reading Association; IRA) and has published nine books to date in the language/literacy field, the latest being *Using Literature Activities to Teach Content Areas to Emergent Readers* (2001). She serves on the editorial review boards of *Journal of Children's Literature* (National Council of Teachers of English) and *The Dragon Lode* (IRA) and has established the Donoghue Children's Literature Center at the Pollak Library at Cal State Fullerton.